COMPREHENSIVE CURRICULUM
OF BASIC SKILLS
GRADE 5

Deep Sea
SPORTS

Editors:
Patricia Opaskar & Mary Ann Trost
Project Editor:
Dawn Downs Purney

AMERICAN EDUCATION PUBLISHING®

W9-BXX-708

TABLE OF CONTENTS

Grade 5 - Comprehensive Curriculum

TABLE OF CONTENTS

READING

Name: Fri. July 4/08

Spelling: Digraphs

A **digraph** is two consonants pronounced as one sound.

Examples: sh as in **shell**, **ch** as in **chew**, **th** as in **thin**

Directions: Write **sh**, **ch** or **th** to complete each word below.

1. _th_ reaten

2. _ch_ ill

3. _sh_ ock

4. _sh_ iver

5. _th_ aw

6. _ch_ allenge

7. peri _sh_

8. _sh_ ield

9. _ch_ art

10. _th_ rive

Directions: Complete these sentences with a word, or form of the word, from the list above.

1. A trip to the South Pole would really be a (**ch**) _challenge_ .

2. The ice there never (**th**) _thaw_ because the temperature averages –50°C.

3. How can any living thing (**th**) _thrive_ or even live when it's so cold?

4. With 6 months of total darkness and those icy temperatures, any plants would soon

   (**sh**) _perish_ .

5. Even the thought of that numbing cold makes me (**sh**) _shiver_ .

6. The cold and darkness (**th**) _threaten_ the lives of explorers.

7. The explorers take along maps and (**ch**) _chart_ to help them find their way.

8. Special clothing helps protect and (**sh**) _shield_ them from the cold.

9. Still, the weather must be a (**sh**) _shock_ at first.

10. Did someone leave a door open? Suddenly I feel a (**ch**) _chill_ .

Spelling: Listening for Sounds

Not every word spelled with **ow** is pronounced **ou** as in **powder** and **however**. In the same way, not every word spelled with **ou** is pronounced **ou** as in **amount** and **announce**. The letters **ou** can be pronounced a number of ways.

Directions: Write the word from the box that rhymes with each of the words or phrases below. Some words are used twice.

doubt ✓✓	amount ✓	avoid ✓✓	annoy ✓✓	announce ✓
choice ✓	poison ✓	powder ✓✓✓	soil ✓✓	however ✓

joys in ___poison___

shout ___doubt___

a boy ___annoy___

employed ___avoid___

now never ___however___

voice ___choice___

a bounce ___announce___

enjoyed ___avoid___

two counts ___annouce___

loyal ___soil___

crowd her ___powder___

Joyce ___choice___

a count ___amount___

employ ___annoy___

louder ___powder___

trout ___doubt___

Name: _Fri. July 4/08_

Spelling: The j and ch Sounds

The **j** sound can be spelled with a **j** as in **jump**, with a **g** before **e** or **i** as in **agent** and **giant**, or with **ge** at the end of a word as in **page**.

The **ch** sound is often spelled with the letters **ch** but can also be spelled with a **t** before **u**, as in **nature**.

Directions: Use words from the box to complete the exercises below.

| statue ✓ | imagination ✓ | jealous ✓ | future ✓ | arrangements ✓ |
| furniture ✓ | stranger ✓ | project ✓ | justice ✓ | capture ✓ |

1. Say each word and then write it in the correct row, depending on whether it has the **j** or **ch** sound.

   j _imagination_   _Jealous_   _arrangements_
   Stranger   _project_   _Justice_   _J / ch_

   ch _statue_   _future_   _furniture_   _cature_

2. Write a word from the box that belongs to the same word family as each word below.

   imagine _imagination_   arranging _arrangements_

   strangely _stranger_   furnish _furniture_

   just _justice_   jealousy _jealous_

Directions: Complete each sentence with a word containing the given sound.

1. What is your group's (**j**) _project_ this week?

2. There is a (**ch**) _statue_ of George Washington in front of our school.

3. She used her (**j**) _imagination_ to solve the problem.

4. My sister keeps rearranging the (**ch**) _furniture_ in our room.

Name: _Sat. July 5/08_

Spelling: Words With Silent Letters

Some letters in words are not pronounced, such as the **s** in **island**, the **t** in **listen**, the **k** in **knee**, the **h** in **hour** and the **w** in **write**.

Directions: Use words from the box to complete the exercises below.

wrinkled ✓	honest ✓	aisle ✓	knife ✓	wrist ✓
rhyme ✓	exhaust ✓	glisten ✓	knowledge ✓	wrestle ✓

1. Write each word beside its silent letter. Two words have two silent letters—write them twice.

s _aisle_

t _glisten_ _wrestle_

h _honest_ _rhyme_ _exhaust_

w _wrinkled_ _wrist_ _knowledge_ _wrestle_

k _knife_ _knowledge_ _____

2. Write in the missing letter or letters for each word.

_w_ res _t_ le   ex _h_ aust   _k_ nife   glis _t_ en   ai _s_ le

_k_ nowledge   _w_ rinkle   r _h_ yme   _h_ onest   _w_ rist

Directions: Complete each sentence with a word that has the given silent letter. Use each word only once.

1. He always tells the truth. He's very (**h**) _honest_.

2. I like (**s**) _aisle_ seats in airplanes.

3. I need a sharper (**k**) _knife_ to cut this bread.

4. I think a long hike might (**h**) _exhaust_ me.

5. Did you sleep in that shirt? It is so (**w**) _wrinkled_!

6. The snow seemed to (**t**) _glisten_ in the sunlight.

7. To play tennis, you need a strong (**w**) _wrist_.

Name: _sat. July 5/08_

Adelina

Spelling: Syllables

A **syllable** is a part of a word with only one vowel sound. Some words have only one syllable, like **cat**, **leaf** and **ship**. Some words have two or more syllables. **Be-lief** and **trac-tor** have two syllables, **to-ge-ther** and **ex-cel-lent** have three syllables and **con-ver-sa-tion** has four syllables. Some words can have six or more syllables! The word **ex-tra-ter-res-tri-al**, for example, has six syllables.

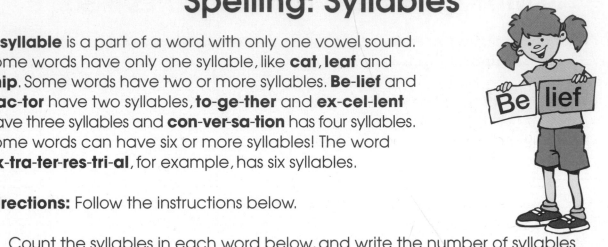

Directions: Follow the instructions below.

1. Count the syllables in each word below, and write the number of syllables on the line.

    a. badger   _2_   f. grease   _1_

    b. location   _3_   g. relationship _4_

    c. award   _2_   h. communication _5_

    d. national   _3_   i. government   _3_

    e. necessary _4_   j. Braille   _1_

2. Write four words with four syllables each in the blanks.

    a. _Conversation_   c. _Comprehensive_

    b. _Adelina_   d. _Water bottle_

3. Write one word with five syllables and one with six syllables. If you need help, use a dictionary.

    Five syllables: _participating_

    Six syllables: _extraterrestrial_

Name: _Sat. July 5/08_

Sun, July 20/08

Writing: Sounding Out Syllables

Directions: Use words from the box to complete the exercises below.

decision ✓	division ✓✓	pressure ✓✓	addition ✓	ancient ✓
subtraction ✓✓	confusion ✓✓	multiplication ✓	social ✓	correction ✓

1. Write each word in the row showing the correct number of syllables.

Two: _pressure_   _Social_   _ancient_

Three: _addition_   _desision_   _correction_

Confusion   _division_   _Subtraction_

Five: _Multipaction_

2. Write in the missing syllables for each word.

_So_ cial   sub _t r a c_ tion   mul _t i_ pli _c a_ tion   pres _s u r e_

di _v i_ sion   an _c i e n t_   deci _s i o n_   ad _d i_ tion

_C o n_ fusion   cor _r e c_ tion

3. Beside each word below, write a word with the same number of syllables. Use each word from the box only once.

daily	_Social_	challenging	_Subtraction_
syllable	_Confusion_	election	_correction_
decreasing	_addition_	threaten	_ancient_
advantage	_division_	shivering	_decision_
title	_pressure_	experimenting	_Multiplication_

Name: _Sun. July 20/08_

Writing: Word Families

A **word family** is a group of words based on the same word. For example, **playful**, **playground** and **playing** are all based on the word **play**.

Directions: Use words from the box to complete the exercises below.

decision	division ✓	pressure ✓	addition ✓	create ✓
subtraction ✓	confusion ✓	multiplication ✓	social ✓	correction ✓

1. Write the word that belongs to the same word family as each word below.

   correctly _Correction_   confused _Confusion_

   divide _division_   subtracting _Subtraction_

   pressing _pressure_   society _Social_

   multiply _Multiplication_   decide _decision_

   added _addition_   creativity _create_

2. Complete each sentence by writing the correct form of the given word.

   Example: Have you (decide) <u>decided</u> what to do? Did you make a (decide) <u>decision</u> yet?

   I am (add) _____adding_____ the numbers right now. Would you check my

   (add) _addition._ ?

   This problem has me (confuse) _confused_ . Can you clear up my

   (confuse) _Confusion_ ?

   This is a (press) _pressure_ problem. We feel (press) _pressured_

   to solve it right away.

   Is he (divide) _dividing_ by the right number? Will you help him with his

   (divide) _division_ ?

   Try to answer (correct) _corectly_ . Then you won't have to make any

   (correct) _correction_ on your paper later on.

Writing: Word Families

Directions: Write the word that belongs to the same word family as each word below.

doubt	amount	avoid	annoy	announce
choice	poison	powder	soil	however

avoidance _____avoid_____   annoyance _____annoy_____

doubtful _____doubt_____   soiled _____soil_____

announcement ___announce___   poisonous _____poison_____

choose _____choice_____   amounted _____amount_____

powdery _____powder_____   whenever ____however____

Directions: Complete each sentence by writing the correct form of the given word.

Example: Are you (doubt) <u>doubting</u> my word? You never (doubt) <u>doubted</u> it before.

1. The teacher is (announce) ___announcing___ the next test. Did you hear what he (announce) ___announced___ ?

2. This stream was (poison) ___posined___ by a chemical from a factory nearby.

3. Is the chemical (poison) ___posined___ any other water supply? How many (poison)___posins___ does the factory produce?

4. My cat always (annoy) ___annoys___ our dog.

5. Last night, Camie (annoy) ___annoyed___ Lucas for hours.

6. I think Carrie is (avoid) ___avoiding___ me. Yesterday, she (avoid) ___avoided___ walking home with me.

Name: _____

Spelling: Double Consonants

When adding endings such as **ing** and **ed** to verbs, use the following rule: Double the final consonant of verbs that have short vowel sounds and end with only one consonant. For example, **rip** becomes **ripped** and **beg** becomes **begging**. However, do not double the final consonant in words that end in double consonants. For example, **rock** ends with two consonants, **ck**. So even though it has a short vowel sound, **rock** becomes **rocked**.

Directions: Add **ed** to the verbs below. Remember, when a verb ends with **e**, drop the **e** before adding an ending (**taste**, **tasting**). The first one has been done for you.

top	_topped_	rip	_____
pet	_____	punch	_____
sob	_____	rinse	_____
brag	_____	stock	_____
scrub	_____	lack	_____
flip	_____	dent	_____

Directions: Add **ing** to the verbs below. The first one has been done for you.

flap	_flapping_	snack	_____
scrub	_____	flip	_____
stock	_____	rinse	_____
dent	_____	brag	_____
pet	_____	lack	_____
sob	_____	punch	_____

Name: _____

Writing: Verb Forms

Directions: In the following story, some of the verbs are missing. Write the proper form of the verbs shown, adding **ed** or **ing** when necessary.

What's Your Verb Form?

Yesterday, I was (brag) _____ to my brother about how much I (help) _____ our mother around the house. I had (scrub) _____ the kitchen floor, (wipe) _____ off all the counters and (rinse) _____ out the sink. I was (pour) _____ the dirty water out of the bucket when our mother came in. She looked around the kitchen and (smile) _____ . "Who did all this work?" she (ask) _____ .

I was (get) _____ ready to tell her what I had done when my brother (interrupt) _____ me. "We both did! We've been (work) _____ very hard!" he said. "He's not (tell) _____ the truth!" I said to Mom. "I did everything!" My brother (glare) _____ at me.

"Is that true?" asked Mom. My brother (look) _____ at the floor and (nod) _____ . He was (think) _____ about all the trouble he would get into. Instead, Mom smiled again. "Well, that's okay," she said. "The rest of the house needs to be (clean) _____ , too. You can get (start) _____ right away!"

Grade 5 - Comprehensive Curriculum

Name: _____

Spelling: Math Plurals

To make most nouns plural, add **s**. When a noun ends with **s**, **ss**, **sh**, **ch** or **x**, add **es**: bus—bus**es**, cross—cross**es**, brush—brush**es**, church—church**es**, box—box**es**. When a noun ends with a consonant and **y**, change the **y** to **i** and add **es**: berry—berr**ies**. For some words, insteading of adding **s** or **es**, the spelling of the word changes: man—men, mouse—mice.

Directions: Write the correct plural or singular form of the words in these math problems. Write whether the problem requires addition (**A**), subtraction (**S**), multiplication (**M**) or division (**D**). The first one has been done for you.

1. 3 (box)   <u>boxes</u>   – 2 (box)   <u>boxes</u>   =   <u>1 box</u>   <u>S</u>

2. 2 (supply) _____ + 5 (supply) _____ = _____ ___

3. 4 (copy) _____ x 2 (copy) _____ = _____ ___

4. 6 (class) _____ ÷ 2 (class) _____ = _____ ___

5. 5 (factory) _____ – 3 (factory) _____ = _____ ___

6. 3 (daisy) _____ x 3 (daisy) _____ = _____ ___

7. 8 (sandwich) _____ + 4 (sandwich) _____ = _____ ___

8. 3 (child) _____ – 1 (child) _____ = _____ ___

9. 10 (brush) _____ ÷ 5 (brush) _____ = _____ ___

10. 4 (goose) _____ + 1 (goose) _____ = _____ ___

11. 3 (mouse) _____ + 1 (mouse) _____ = _____ ___

Name: _____

Spelling: More Plurals

Remember, in some words, an **f** changes to a **v** to make the plural form.

Examples: life — li**v**es   wife — wi**v**es   knife — kni**v**es   leaf — lea**v**es

Directions: Complete these sentences by writing the correct plural form of the given word. Also, circle the spelling errors and write the words correctly on the lines to the right.

1. The (leaf) _____ are dry and rinkled.   _____

2. The (knife) _____ glisened in the sun.   _____

3. I think the (child) _____ in this school are honist.   _____

4. The (supply) _____ were stacked in the isle.   _____

5. (mouse) _____ rimes with twice.   _____

6. Some people feel exausted all their (life) _____.   _____

7. The (class) _____ were trying to gain more
   knowlege about Olympic athletes.   _____

8. The kittens were wresling in the (bush) _____.   _____

9. Jamie nearly broke his rist trying to carry all those

   (box) _____.   _____

10. Some kings had several (wife) _____ who new
    about each other.   _____

11. (Daisy) _____ are knot expensive.   _____

12. Right your name on both (copy) _____.   _____

13. We watched the (monkey) _____ play on the
    swings for ours.   _____

14. Do you like (strawberry) _____ hole or sliced? _____

Name: _____

Spelling: Finding Mistakes

Directions: Circle the four spelling mistakes in each paragraph. Then write the words correctly on the lines below.

Last nite, our family went to a nice restaurant. As we were lookking at the menus, a waiter walked in from the kichen carrying a large tray of food. As he walked by us, he triped, and the tray went flying! The food flew all over our table and all over us, too!

_____   _____

_____   _____

Last week, while my dad was washing the car, our dog Jack dicided to help. He stuck his nose in the pale of soapy water, and it tiped over and soaked him! As he shook himself off, the water from his fur went all over the car. "Look!" Dad laffed. "Jack is doing his part!"

_____   _____

_____   _____

For our next feild trip, my class is going to the zoo. We have been studying about animals in sceince class. I'm very eksited to see the elephants, but my freind Karen really wants to see the monkeys. She has been to the zoo before, and she says the monkeys are the most fun to watch.

_____   _____

_____   _____

It seems the rain will never stop! It has been rainning for seven days now, and the sky is always dark and clowdy. Everyone at school is in a bad mood, because we have to stay inside during resess. Will we ever see the son again?

_____   _____

_____   _____

Name: _____

Spelling: Finding Mistakes

Directions: Circle the four spelling mistakes in each paragraph. Then write the misspelled words correctly on the lines below.

According to the newspaper, a man came into the store and stood near a clerk. The clerk was stockking the shelves with watches. Then the man suddenly grabed several watches and raced out of the store. The clerk shouted, "Stop him! He's robing us!" The police searched for the man, but they still lak a suspect.

_____   _____

_____   _____

Tony always braged about the tricks he could do with his skateboard. One day, he tried to skate up a ramp and jump over three bikes. Well, he landed on the last bike and dentted it. The last I saw Tony, he was runing down the street. The owner of the bike was chassing him.

_____   _____

_____   _____

One day, I was peting my dog when I felt something sticky in his fur. It was time for a bath! I put hIm In a tub of water and scrubed as best I could. Then I rinced the soap out of his fur. He jumped out of the tub, soaking wet, and rolled in some dirt. I sighed and draged him back into the tub. This dog makes me tired sometimes!

_____   _____

_____   _____

Last night, my little sister started braging about how fast she could wash the dishes. I told her to prove it. (It was my turn to do the dishes.) She started fliping the dishes around in the sink, washing them as fast as she could. I noticed she was rinseing only about half of them. Finally, it happened. She droped a cup on the floor. Dad made me finish the dishes, but at least she did some of them.

_____   _____

_____   _____

Name: _____

Spelling: Finding Mistakes

Spelling
Mistake

Directions: Circle the spelling mistakes in each paragraph. Write the words correctly on the lines below.

Some poisions that kill insects can also threten people. Often these pouders and sprays are used on corn, beans and other plants we eat. Unless these plants are well scrubed, we may eat a small amount of the poison.

_____ _____ _____ _____

Sometimes the poison is put into the soyl and moves into the plant through its roots. Then it stays in the plant in spyte of all our rinseing. All we can do is avoyd eating food that has been grown this way. Howver, that also means we have to expect more insects in our food. Its a hard chioce! Some people dout that a little bit of poision will hurt them, while others have made a dicision to grow their own food.

_____ _____ _____

_____ _____ _____ _____

_____ _____

Yesterday, the teacher anownced a new projict. She chalenged us to think of a new arangement for the furnichure in the room. We voated to put the chairs in groups. Then Brian said it would be easier to cheet that way. I was annoyd. I told him we had more pryde than that!

_____ _____ _____

_____ _____ _____

_____ _____ _____

Name: _____

Spelling: Proofreading Practice

Directions: Circle the six spelling and pronoun mistakes in each paragraph. Write the words correctly on the lines below.

Jenna always braged about being ready to meet any chalenge or reach any gole. When it was time for our class to elekt it's new officers, Jenna said we should voat for her to be president.

_____ _____ _____

_____ _____ _____

Simon wanted to be ours president, too. He tried to coaks everyone to vote for his. He even lowned kids money to get their votes! Well, Jenna may have too much pryde in herself, but I like her in spit of that. At least she didn't try to buy our votes!

_____ _____ _____

_____ _____ _____

Its true that Jenna tried other ways to get us to vote for hers. She scrubed the chalkboards even though it was my dayly job for that week. One day, I saw her rinseing out the paintbrushes when it was Peter's turn to do it. Then she made sure we knew about her good deeds so we would praize her.

_____ _____ _____

_____ _____ _____

We held the election, but I was shalked when the teacher releesed the results. Simon won! I wondered if he cheeted somehow. I feel like our class was robed! Now Simon is the one who's braging about how great he is. I wish he knew the titel of president doesn't mean anything if no one wants to be around you!

_____ _____ _____

_____ _____ _____

Adding Suffixes

A **suffix** is a syllable at the end of a word that changes its meaning.
The suffixes **ant** and **ent** mean a person or thing that does something.

Examples:

A person who occupies a place is an **occupant**.
A person who obeys is **obedient**.

A **root word** is the common stem that gives related words their basic meanings.

When a word ends in silent **e**, keep the **e** before adding a suffix beginning with a consonant.
Drop the **e** before adding a suffix beginning with a vowel.

Examples:

announce + ment = **announcement**
announce + ing = **announcing**

Announce is the root word in this example.

Directions: Combine each root word and suffix to make a new word. The first one has
been done for you.

Root word	Suffix	New word
observe	ant	observant
contest	ant	_____
please	ant	_____
preside	ent	_____
differ	ent	_____

Directions: Use the meanings in parentheses to complete the sentences with one of the
above new words. The first one has been done for you.

1. To be a good scientist, you must be very ___observant___. (pay careful attention)

2. Her perfume had a strong but very _____ smell. (nice)

3. Because the bridge was out, we had to find a _____ route home.
    (not the same)

4. The game show _____ jumped up and down when she won the
    grand prize. (person who competes)

5. Next week we will elect a new student council _____ . (highest officer)

Adding Suffixes

The suffix **less** means without; **ative** means having the nature of or relating to; **ive** means having or tending to be.

Examples:
Faultless means without fault or blame.
Formative means something that can be formed or molded.
Corrective means something that fixes a problem.

Directions: Combine each root word and suffix to form a new word. The first one has been done for you.

Root word	Suffix	New word
sleep	less	sleepless
imagine	ative	_____
talk	ative	_____
impress	ive	_____
attract	ive	_____

Directions: Use the meanings in parentheses to complete the sentences with one of the above new words.

1. The night before his birthday, Michael spent a _____ night. (wide awake)

2. Our history teacher is a rather _____ man who likes to tell jokes and stories. (fond of speaking)

3. That book has such an _____ plot! (showing creativity)

4. Monica thought the dress in the store window was very _____ . (pleasing)

5. The high school basketball team was _____ in its Friday night game, beating their rivals by 30 points. (making an impact on the mind or emotions)

Grade 5 - Comprehensive Curriculum

Name: _____

Adding Prefixes

A **prefix** is a syllable at the beginning of a word that changes its meaning. The prefixes **il**, **im**, **in** and **ir** all mean not.

Examples:
Illogical means not logical or practical.
Impossible means not possible.
Invisible means not visible.
Irrelevant means not relevant or practical.

Directions: Divide each word into its prefix and root word. The first one has been done for you.

	Prefix	Root Word
illogical	il	logical
impatient		
immature		
incomplete		
insincere		
irresponsible		
irregular		

Directions: Use the meanings in parentheses to complete the sentences with one of the above words.

1. I had to turn in my assignment _____ because I was sick last night. (not finished)

2. It was _____ for Jimmy to give me his keys because he can't get into his house without them. (not practical)

3. Sue and Joel were _____ to leave their bikes out in the rain. (not doing the right thing)

4. I sometimes get _____ waiting for my ride to school. (restless)

5. The boys sounded _____ when they said they were sorry. (not honest)

6. These towels didn't cost much because they are _____. (not straight or even)

Adding Prefixes

The prefix **pre** means before. The prefix **re** means again.

Examples:
  Preview means to see in advance.
  Redo means to do again.

Directions: Write sentences using these words with prefixes.

1. prefix _____

_____

2. redirect _____

_____

3. regain _____

_____

4. predetermine _____

_____

5. reorganize _____

_____

6. prepackage _____

_____

7. redistribute _____

_____

8. precook _____

_____

Synonyms

A **synonym** is a word with the same or similar meaning as another word.

Examples: bucket — pail   happy — cheerful   dirty — messy

Directions: Match the words on the left with their synonyms on the right. The first one has been done for you.

tired	beverage
start	notice
get	boring
fire	busy
dull	sleepy
big	couch
noisy	receive
crowded	begin
sofa	loud
drink	halt
sign	large
stop	flames

Directions: Rewrite the sentences below using synonyms for the bold words.

1. Because the road was **rough**, we had a **hard** time riding our bikes on it.

   _____

2. After the accident, the driver appeared to be **hurt**, so someone **ran** to call an ambulance.

   _____

3. Yesterday everyone stayed after school to pick up litter, and now the school yard is **nice** and **clean**.

   _____

Name: _____

Synonyms

Directions: Circle a word or a phrase in each sentence that is a synonym for a word in the box. Write the synonym on the line.

challenged	shocked	thaw	chart	frighten
perish	chill	shivering	thrive	shield

Example: The writing was in an (old) code.　　　___ancient___

1. A fish out of water will quickly die.　　_____

2. The ice carving is beginning to melt.　　_____

3. I was amazed when I saw how he looked.　　_____

4. The puppy was trembling with excitement.　　_____

5. Ferns need moisture to grow well.　　_____

6. Are you trying to scare me?　　_____

7. Let the salad get cold in the refrigerator.　　_____

8. She tried to protect him from the truth.　　_____

9. He made a list of different kinds of birds.　　_____

10. They dared us to enter the contest.　　_____

Directions: Write your own sentences using five words from the box. If you're not sure what a word means, look it up in a dictionary.

_____

_____

_____

_____

_____

Name: _____

Finding Synonyms

Directions: Circle a word, or group of words, in each sentence that is a synonym for a word in the box. Write the synonym on the line.

statue	imagination	jealous	future	arrangements
furniture	stranger	project	justice	capture

Example: She will (lend) me her book.   _loan_

1. He tried to catch the butterfly.   _____

2. No one knows what will happen in the time to come.   _____

3. They are loading the chairs and tables and beds into the moving van.   _____

4. We almost finished our team assignment.   _____

5. They made plans to have a class party.   _____

6. Penny made a model of a horse.   _____

7. The accused man asked the judge for fairness.   _____

Directions: Write your own sentences for these words: **stranger, imagination, jealous**. Then choose one other word from the box and use it in a sentence. Make each sentence at least ten words long. The sentences should show that you know what the word means.

1. _____

_____

2. _____

_____

3. _____

_____

4. _____

_____

Name: _____

Synonyms

Synonyms are words that mean the same or nearly the same.

Examples:
small and **little**
big and **large**
bright and **shiny**
unhappy and **sad**

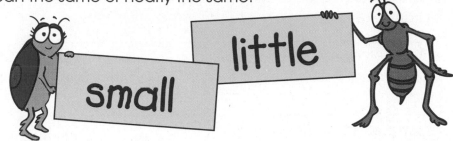

Directions: Write a synonym for each word. Then use it in a sentence. Use a dictionary if you are unsure of the meaning of a word.

1. cup _____

_____

2. book _____

_____

3. looking glass _____

_____

4. hop _____

_____

5. discover _____

_____

6. plan _____

_____

7. lamp _____

_____

8. friend _____

_____

9. discuss _____

_____

10. rotate _____

_____

Antonyms

An **antonym** is a word with the opposite meaning of another word.

Examples: hot — cold
up — down
start — stop

Directions: Match the words on the left with their antonyms on the right. The first one has been done for you.

asleep	sloppy
sit	shut
excited	full
north	awake
wild	tame
hairy	stand
open	bored
quick	bald
neat	south
hungry	slow

Directions: In the sentences below, replace each bold word with a synonym or an antonym so that the sentence makes sense. Write the word on the line. Then, write either **synonym** or **antonym** to show its relationship to the given word. The first one has been done for you.

1. If the weather stays warm, all the plants will **perish**.   <u>live — antonym</u>

2. Last night, mom made my favorite meal, and it was **delicious**. _____

3. The test was **difficult**, and everyone in the class passed it. _____

4. The music from the concert was so **loud** we could hear it in the parking lot! _____

5. The bunks at camp were **comfortable**, and I didn't sleep very well. _____

Name: _____

Finding Antonyms

Directions: Write a word that is an antonym for each bold word in the sentences below.

1. Jared made his way **quickly** through the crowd. _____

2. My friends and I arrived **late** to the party. _____

3. My sister loves to watch airplanes **take off**. _____

4. The teacher seems especially **cheerful** this morning. _____

5. When are you going to **begin** your project? _____

Directions: Write antonyms for the following words on the lines. Then write a short paragraph using all the words you wrote.

dirty _____   whisper _____

old _____   carefully _____

down _____   night _____

sit _____   happy _____

_____

_____

_____

_____

_____

_____

_____

_____

Antonyms

Antonyms are words that mean the opposite.

Examples:
 tall and **short**
 high and **low**
 top and **bottom**

Directions: Write an antonym for each word. Then use it in a sentence. Use a dictionary if you are unsure of the meaning of a word.

1. tired _____

_____

2. bright _____

_____

3. sparkling _____

_____

4. tame _____

_____

5. fresh _____

_____

6. elegant _____

_____

7. real _____

_____

8. odd _____

_____

9. unruly _____

_____

10. valor _____

_____

Homophones

Homophones are words that sound alike but have different spellings and meanings. The words **no** and **know** are homophones. They sound alike, but their spellings and meanings are very different.

Directions: Use words from the box to complete the exercises below.

hour	wring	knot	whole	knew
wrap	knight	piece	write	

1. Write each word beside its homophone.

    peace _____   new _____   ring _____

    hole _____   rap _____   night _____

    not _____   right _____   our _____

2. Write three words that have a silent **k**. _____ _____ _____

3. Write one word that has a silent **h**. _____

Directions: Circle the misused homophones in each sentence. Then rewrite the sentences, using the correct homophones.

1. By the time knight fell, I new she was knot coming.

    _____

2. I would never have any piece until I new the hole story.

    _____

3. He spent an our righting down what had happened.

    _____

4. I could see write through the whole in the night's armor.

    _____

Name: _____

Homophones

Homophones are words that are pronounced the same but are spelled differently and have different meanings.

Example: to, two, too

Directions: Use these homophones in sentences of your own.

1. forth _____

    _____

2. fourth _____

    _____

3. shown _____

    _____

4. shone _____

    _____

5. they're _____

    _____

6. their _____

    _____

7. there _____

    _____

8. not _____

    _____

9. knot _____

    _____

Name: _____

Homophones

Directions: Complete the story below by writing the correct homophones for the words in parentheses.

Last Saturday, I went to (meat)

_____ my friend, Andrea, at

the mall.

When I got there, I noticed she looked a

little (pail) _____ .

"What's wrong?" I asked her.

She (side) _____ . "I'm

(knot) _____ feeling so

(grate) _____ ," she said. "I don't (no) _____ what's

wrong with me."

"Maybe you (knead) _____ to take some aspirin," I said. "Let's go to

the drugstore. It's this (welgh) _____ ."

As we were walking, we passed a (flour) _____ shop, and I bought

(sum) _____ roses for my mother. Then we found the drugstore, and

Andrea bought some aspirin and took (too) _____ of them. An (our)

_____ later, she felt much better.

That (knight) _____ , I gave the roses to my mother. "You shouldn't

(waist) _____ your money on (presence) _____ for me!"

she said, but she was smiling. I (new) _____ she was pleased.

"That's okay, Mom, I wanted to buy them for you," I said. "But now I'm broke. How

about a (lone) _____ ?"

Grade 5 - Comprehensive Curriculum

Homographs

Homographs are words that have the same spelling but different meanings and pronunciations.

pres´ent	n.	a gift
pre sent´	v.	to introduce or offer to view
rec´ord	n.	written or official evidence
re cord´	v.	to keep an account of
wind	n.	air in motion
wind	v.	to tighten the spring by turning a key
wound	n.	an injury in which the skin is broken
wound	v.	past tense of wind

Directions: Write the definition for the bold word in each sentence.

1. I would like to **present** our new student council president, Mindy Hall.

   _____

2. The store made a **record** of all my payments.

   _____

3. **Wind** the music box to hear the song.

   _____

4. His **wound** was healing quickly.

   _____

5. The **wind** knocked over my bicycle.

   _____

6. I bought her a birthday **present** with my allowance.

   _____

Similes

A **simile** uses the words **like** or **as** to compare two things.

Examples:
  The snow glittered **like** diamonds.
  He was **as** slow **as** a turtle.

Directions: Circle the two objects being compared in each sentence.

1. The kittens were like gymnasts performing tricks.

2. My old computer is as slow as molasses.

3. When the lights went out in the basement, it was as dark as night.

4. The sun was like a fire, heating up the earth.

5. The young girl was as graceful as a ballerina.

6. The puppy cried like a baby all night.

7. He flies that airplane like a daredevil.

8. The girl was as pretty as a picture.

9. The snow on the mountain tops was like whipped cream.

10. The tiger's eyes were like emeralds.

Directions: Complete the simile in each sentence.

11. My cat is as _____ as _____ .

12. He was as _____ as _____ .

13. Melissa's eyes shone like _____ .

14. The paints were like _____ .

15. The opera singer's voice was as _____ as _____ .

16. My friend is as _____ as _____ .

Name: _____

Metaphors

A **metaphor** is a direct comparison between two things. The words **like** or **as** are not used in a metaphor.

Example: The **sun** is a **yellow ball** in the sky.

Directions: Underline the metaphor in each sentence. Write the two objects being compared on the line.

1. As it bounded toward me, the dog was a quivering furball of excitement.

   _____

2. The snow we skied on was mashed potatoes.

   _____

3. John is a mountain goat when it comes to rock climbing.

   _____

4. The light is a beacon shining into the dark basement.

   _____

5. The famished child was a wolf, eating for the first time in days.

   _____

6. The man's arm was a tireless lever as he fought to win the wrestling contest.

   _____

7. The flowers were colorful circles against the green of the yard.

   _____

Name: _____

Idioms

An **idiom** is a phrase that says one thing but actually means something quite different.

Example: A **horse of a different color** means something quite unusual.

Directions: Write the letter of the correct meaning for each bold phrase. The first one has been done for you.

a.   refusal to see or listen
b.   misbehaving, acting in a wild way
c.   made a thoughtless remark
d.   lost an opportunity
e.   got angry
f.   pay for
g.   unknowing
h.   feeling very sad
i.   get married
j.   excited and happy

__f__   1.   My parents will **foot the bill** for my birthday party.

_____   2.   Tony and Lisa will finally **tie the knot** in June.

_____   3.   Sam was **down in the dumps** after he wrecked his bicycle.

_____   4.   Sarah **put her foot in her mouth** when she was talking to our teacher.

_____   5.   I really **missed the boat** when I turned down the chance to work after school.

_____   6.   I got the **brush-off** from Susan when I tried to ask her where she was last night.

_____   7.   Mickey is **in the dark** about our plans to throw a surprise birthday party for him.

_____   8.   The children were **bouncing off the walls** when the baby-sitter tried to put them to bed.

_____   9.   The students were **flying high** on the last day of school.

_____   10.   My sister **lost her cool** when she discovered I had spilled chocolate milk on her new sweater.

Name: _____

Idioms

An **idiom** is a figure of speech that has a meaning different from the literal one.

Example:

Dad is **in the doghouse** because he was late for dinner.

Meaning: Dad is in trouble because he was late for dinner.

Directions: Write the meanings of the idioms in bold.

1. He was a **bundle of nerves** waiting for his test scores.

_____

2. It was **raining cats and dogs**.

_____

3. My friend and I decided to **bury the hatchet** after our argument.

_____

4. He gave me the **cold shoulder** when I spoke to him.

_____

5. My mom **blew up** when she saw my poor report card.

_____

6. I was **on pins and needles** before my skating performance.

_____

7. When the student didn't answer, the teacher asked, "**Did the cat get your tongue**?"

_____

8. The city **rolled out the red carpet** for the returning Olympic champion.

_____

9. They hired a clown for the young boy's birthday party to help **break the ice**.

_____

Review

Directions: Circle the word or phrase that best defines the bold words.

1. The woman has a very **pleasant** voice.

   loud   nice   strange

2. He had a very **imaginative** excuse for not turning in his homework.

   creative   difficult to believe   acceptable

3. I didn't get credit for my answer on the test because it was **incomplete**.

   not correct   too short   not finished

4. Will you **wind** the music box for the baby?

   air in motion   injury in which the skin is broken

   tighten the spring by turning a key

5. To enroll in the school, you must bring your birth certificate or some other legal
   record for identification.

   to keep an account   a flat disk that plays music

   written or official evidence

6. We use the crystal **pitcher** when we have company.

   printed likeness of a person or object

   baseball team member   container for pouring

7. This block is as **light as a feather**!

   very heavy   not heavy at all   bright

8. The whole family was there when Bill and Lynn **tied the knot** last weekend.

   were caught in a trap   bought a house   got married

9. I will have to **foot the bill** for the damage you caused.

   kick   pay for   seek payment

10. Carol **lost her cool** when the party was called off.

    got angry   had a fever   went home

11. The kite **soared like an eagle**.

    flapped and fluttered   glided along high in the air

    crashed to the ground

Review

Directions: Write a synonym for each word.

1. amusing _____
2. prison _____
3. terrifying _____
4. flee _____

Directions: Write an antonym for each word.

5. insult _____
6. famine _____
7. discourage _____
8. generous _____

Directions: Write a homophone pair.

9. _____   _____

Directions: Write a sentence containing a simile.

10. _____

Directions: Write a sentence containing a metaphor.

11. _____

Directions: Write the letter of the correct meaning for the idiom in each sentence.

a. made a thoughtless remark
b. lost an opportunity
c. pay for
d. feeling very sad
e. excited and happy

_____ 12. My uncle promised to foot the bill for a new computer if I got terrific grades this year.

_____ 13. Tony was down in the dumps when his team lost the game.

_____ 14. The opposing team was flying high after the win.

_____ 15. Jonah put his foot in his mouth when he told his mother what he really thought of her new hairdo.

_____ 16. Sean really missed the boat when he turned down the chance to travel to England.

Name: _____

Using a Dictionary

Directions: Read about dictionaries. Then answer the questions.

Dictionaries are books that give definitions of words. Dictionaries list words in alphabetical order. **Guide words** at the top of each page show the first and last words listed on the page. All other words on the page are listed in alphabetical order between the guide words. This helps you locate the word you want quickly and easily.

In addition to definitions, dictionaries also show the following: how to pronounce, or say, each word; the individual syllables found in each word; the part of speech for each word; and the plural form or verb forms if the base word changes.

Some dictionaries provide considerably more information. For example, *The Tormont Webster's Illustrated Encyclopedic Dictionary* includes many color illustrations of terms, a pronunciation key on every other page and two pages of introductory information on how to use the dictionary effectively.

Other highlights of the *Tormont Webster* are **historic labels** that tell the history of words no longer in common use; **geographic labels** that tell in what part of the world uncommon words are used; **stylistic labels** that tell whether a word is formal, informal, humorous or a slang term; and **field labels** that tell what field of knowledge—such as medicine—the word is used in.

1. Where are guide words found? _____

_____

2. What is the purpose of guide words? _____

_____

3. Which label tells if a word is a slang term? _____

4. Which label tells the history of a word? _____

5. Which type of information is not provided for each word in the dictionary?

☐ definition

☐ part of speech

☐ picture

Using a Dictionary

Directions: Use the dictionary entry below to answer the questions.

ad-he-sive (ad-he'-siv) *adj.* 1. Tending to adhere; sticky.
2. Gummed so as to adhere. *n.* 3. An adhesive substance
such as paste or glue. **ad-he-sive-ly** *adv.* **ad-he-sive-ness** *n.*

1. Based on the first definition of **adhesive**, what do
   you think **adhere** means?

   _____

   _____

2. Which definition of **adhesive** is used in this sentence?
   The tape was so adhesive that we couldn't peel it loose. _____

   _____

3. Which part of speech is **adhesive** used as in this sentence?
   We put a strong adhesive on the package to keep is sealed. _____

4. How many syllables does **adhesive** have? _____

5. Is **adhesive** used as a noun or an adjective in this sentence?
   The adhesive we chose to use was not very gummy. _____

6. **Adhesive** and variations of the word can be used as what parts of speech? _____

   _____

Directions: Write sentences using these words.

7. adhesiveness _____

   _____

8. adhesively _____

   _____

9. adhere _____

   _____

Name: _____

Using the Dictionary

Guide words are the words that appear at the top of dictionary pages. They show the first and last words on each page.

Directions: Read the guide words on each dictionary page below. Then look around for objects whose names come between the guide words. Write the names of the objects, and then number them in alphabetical order.

babble	buzz
___ ___	___
___ ___	___
	___

magic	myself
___ ___	___
___ ___	___
	___

cabin	cycle
___ ___	___
___ ___	___
	___

pea	puzzle
___ ___	___
___ ___	___
	___

dairy	dwarf
___ ___	___
___ ___	___
	___

scar	sword
___ ___	___
___ ___	___
	___

feast	future
___ ___	___
___ ___	___

tack	truth
___ ___	___
___ ___	___

Grade 5 - Comprehensive Curriculum

Name: _____

Using a Dictionary: Guide Words

Directions: Use the guide words and page numbers shown on the top of the dictionary pages below. Write the page number where each word would be found.

156 blur — boatmanship

boat neck — body 157

158 body check — boisterous

1. boast _____

2. bodkin _____

3. body language _____

4. board _____

5. bodice _____

6. bobbin _____

7. boar fish _____

8. boatload _____

9. boilermaker _____

10. body clock _____

11. bogie _____

12. bode _____

13. bodily _____

14. blurt _____

15. blusher _____

16. bodiless _____

17. boardroom _____

18. blurb _____

19. boggle _____

20. boccie _____

Name: _____

Using a Dictionary: Multiple Meanings

If a word has more than one meaning, you will find that information in a dictionary.

Directions: Use the dictionary entry below to answer the questions about the word **record**.

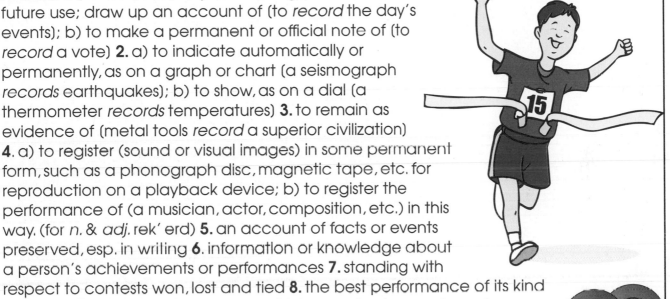

re-cord *v.* (ri kord´) **1.** a) to put in writing, print, etc. for future use; draw up an account of (to *record* the day's events); b) to make a permanent or official note of (to *record* a vote) **2.** a) to indicate automatically or permanently, as on a graph or chart (a seismograph *records* earthquakes); b) to show, as on a dial (a thermometer *records* temperatures) **3.** to remain as evidence of (metal tools *record* a superior civilization) **4.** a) to register (sound or visual images) in some permanent form, such as a phonograph disc, magnetic tape, etc. for reproduction on a playback device; b) to register the performance of (a musician, actor, composition, etc.) in this way. (for *n.* & *adj.* rek´ erd) **5.** an account of facts or events preserved, esp. in writing **6.** information or knowledge about a person's achievements or performances **7.** standing with respect to contests won, lost and tied **8.** the best performance of its kind to date **9.** something, as a disk, on which sound or images have been recorded **10.** *adj.* surpassing all others.

1. How many and which parts of speech are listed for all definitions of **record**? _____

    _____

2. Including all the subheadings, how many definitions are listed? _____

3. Which definition uses the example of a thermometer recording a temperature? _____

4. Which definition describes a record you might play to listen to music? _____

5. Is **record** used as a noun or a verb in this sentence?
    She held the all-time record for most wins.   _____

6. Is **record** used as a noun or a verb in this sentence?
    I will record our conversation.   _____

Name: _____

Multiple Meanings

Directions: Circle the correct definition of the bold word in each sentence. The first one has been done for you.

1. Try to **flag** down a car to get us some help!

   (to signal to stop)
   cloth used as symbol

2. We listened to the **band** play the National Anthem.

   group of musicians
   a binding or tie

3. He was the **sole** survivor of the plane crash.

   bottom of the foot
   one and only

4. I am going to **pound** the nail with this hammer.

   to hit hard
   a unit of weight

5. He lived on what little **game** he could find in the woods.

   animals for hunting
   form of entertainment

6. We are going to **book** the midnight flight from Miami.

   to reserve in advance
   a written work

7. The **pitcher** looked toward first base before throwing the ball.

   baseball team member
   container for pouring

8. My grandfather and I played a **game** of checkers last night.

   animals for hunting
   form of entertainment

9. They raise the **flag** over City Hall every morning.

   to signal to stop
   cloth used as symbol

Name: _____

Using a Dictionary: Choosing the Correct Word

Directions: Use a dictionary to look up the words in parenthesis. Then write the correct words in the blanks.

_____ 1. Our class visited an art (galley/gallery) last week to learn about paintings and sculptures.

_____ 2. He didn't (scrutinize/scruple) his essay very carefully before handing it in.

_____ 3. She squeezed the clay in her hands until it became (plentiful/pliable).

_____ 4. The quarterback's (laudable/laughable) performance helped his team win the game.

_____ 5. The science that deals with the universe beyond Earth's atmosphere is known as (astronomy/astrology).

_____ 6. My mother was (grateful/graphic) that I helped her with the dishes.

_____ 7. The police did not have any (tantamount/tangible) evidence that the man was guilty.

_____ 8. It was very (unfortunate/unfamiliar) that she broke her arm right before the big game.

_____ 9. The gardener was using a (trough/trowel) to dig up the flowers.

_____ 10. That company manufactures men's and women's (appendage/apparel).

_____ 11. After vegetable scraps (decompose/decongest), you can put them on your garden as fertilizer.

_____ 12. Most bats are (nocturnal/noble) and sleep during the day.

_____ 13. We bought some (venerable/venetian) blinds for our windows instead of curtains.

_____ 14. The noisy class (exasperated/exaggerated) the teacher.

_____ 15. The prisoner was released on (parody/parole).

Name: _____

Learning New Words

Directions: Write a word from the box to complete each sentence. Use a dictionary to look up words you are unsure of.

bouquet	unconscious	inspire	disability
inherit	hovering	assault	enclosure
commotion	criticize		

1. He was knocked _____ by the blow to his head.

2. Megan never let her _____ stand in the way of accomplishing what she wanted.

3. The teacher burst into the noisy room and demanded to know what all the _____ was about.

4. He offered her a _____ of flowers as a truce after their argument.

5. The zoo was in the process of building a new _____ for the elephants.

6. The mother was _____ over her sick child.

7. The movie was meant to _____ people to do good deeds.

8. My friend will eventually _____ a fortune from his grandmother.

9. Not many people enjoy having someone _____ their work.

10. The female leopard led the _____ on the herd of zebras.

Name: _____

Learning New Words

Directions: Use a dictionary. Define the following words.
Then use each word in a sentence.

1. mechanical _____

_____

2. cashmere _____

_____

3. deplorable _____

_____

4. illusion _____

_____

5. rivalry _____

_____

6. traction _____

_____

7. whittle _____

_____

8. pageant _____

_____

9. nectarine _____

_____

10. javelin _____

_____

Grade 5 - Comprehensive Curriculum

Name: _____

Using a Thesaurus

A **thesaurus** is a type of reference book that lists words in alphabetical order followed by their synonyms and antonyms. **Synonyms** are words that mean the same. **Antonyms** are words that mean the opposite.

A thesaurus is an excellent tool for finding "just the right word." It is also a valuable resource for finding a variety of synonyms and/or antonyms to make your writing livelier.

Each main entry in a thesaurus consists of a word followed by the word's part of speech, its definition, an example, a list of related words and other information.

Here is a typical entry in a thesaurus, with an explanation of terms below:

SLOW
ADJ **SYN** deliberate, dilatory, laggard, leisurely, unhasty, unhurried
REL lateness, limited, measured, slowish, steady, unhurrying, slow-footed, plodding, pokey, straggling, snail-like **IDIOM** as slow as molasses in January; as slow as a turtle **CON** blitz, quick, rapid, swift **ANT** fast

ADJ means adjective

CON means contrasted words

SYN means synonym

ANT means antonym

REL means related words

idiom means a common phrase that is not literal

Directions: Use the thesaurus entry to answer the questions.

1. What is the antonym listed for **slow**? _____

2. How many contrasting words are listed for **slow**? _____

3. How many synonyms are listed for **slow**? _____

4. What is **slow** compared to in the two idioms listed? _____

5. What is the last related word listed for **slow**? _____

Name: _____

Using a Thesaurus to Find Synonyms

A thesaurus can help you find synonyms.
Example:
FIND:
VERB **SYN** locate, discover, detect, uncover, see, etc.

Directions: Use a thesaurus. Replace each word in bold with a synonym.

1. My father does not like our **artificial** Christmas tree.

   _____

2. The **fabulous** home sat on a large hill overlooking a wooded ravine.

   _____

3. My dog is allowed to be **loose** if someone is home.

   _____

4. A **peaceful** rally was held to bring attention to the needs of the homeless.

   _____

5. The artist completed his **sketch** of the girl.

   _____

6. The **timid** boy could not bring himself to speak to the man at the counter.

   _____

7. My family is cutting down the **timber** at the back of our property.

   _____

8. Her necklace was very **attractive**.

   _____

9. The girl looked hopelessly at her **clothes** and moaned that she had nothing to wear.

   _____

10. The team's **feat** of winning 20 games in a row was amazing.

    _____

Grade 5 - Comprehensive Curriculum

Name: _____

Using a Thesaurus

Directions: Use a thesaurus to list as many synonyms (SYN) as possible for the following words.

1. calm _____

2. hunt _____

3. quilt _____

4. tender _____

5. vacate _____

Directions: Use a thesaurus to list as many related words (REL) as possible for the following words.

6. value _____

7. difference _____

8. enable _____

Directions: Use a thesaurus to list one idiom for each of the following words.

9. beauty _____

10. cake _____

dog

pooch

canine

puppy

cur

bow wow

mongrel

mutt

Name: _____

Using a Thesaurus to Find Antonyms

Antonyms are words that mean the opposite. Antonyms can also be found in a thesaurus. They are identified by the abbreviation **ANT**.

Examples:

FOUND:
VERB **ANT** misplaced, gone, lost, missing, mislaid, etc.

RIDDLE:
NOUN **ANT** key, solution, answer, etc.

ANCIENT:
ADJECTIVE **ANT** new, recent, current, etc.

Directions: Use a thesaurus to replace each word in bold with an antonym.

_____ 1. Today's weather will undoubtedly be very **humid**.

_____ 2. Can you **give** my sister a napkin?

_____ 3. The man **insulted** me by laughing at my artwork.

_____ 4. I thought the rules for the classroom were too **lax**.

_____ 5. The broken leg was quite **painful**.

_____ 6. We made great **progress** last night on the parade float.

_____ 7. The girl received a **reward** for returning the lost wallet.

_____ 8. The teacher asked us to **separate** the types of art brushes.

_____ 9. The home was decorated in a **simple** manner.

_____ 10. They became very **tense** during the earthquake.

_____ 11. Mr. Kurtzman gave us a math test **today**.

_____ 12. My father loves hiking in the **hills**.

_____ 13. Stephen ran over my **new** red bike.

Comprehension: Word Origins

Did you ever wonder why we call our mid-day meal "lunch"? Or where the name "Abraham" came from? Or why one of our lovely eastern states is called "Vermont"?

These and other words have a history. The study of where words came from and how they began is called **etymology** (ett-a-mol-o-gee).

The word **lunch** comes from the Spanish word **longja**, which means "a slice of ham." Long ago, Spanish people ate a slice of ham for their mid-day meal. Eventually, what they ate became the word for the meal itself. Still later, it came to be pronounced "lunch" in English.

Abraham also has an interesting history. Originally, it came from the Hebrew word **avarahem**. Abraham means "father of many."

City and state names are often based on the names of Native American tribes or describe the geography of the area. **Vermont** is actually made from two French words. **Vert** is French for "green." **Mont** is French for "mountain."

Directions: Answer these questions about word origins.

1. What is the study of the history and origin of words? _____

2. From which language did the word **lunch** come? _____

3. What is the French word for "green"? _____

4. **Vermont** comes from two words of what language?

   ☐ Spanish   ☐ English   ☐ French

5. Which is not correct about the origin of names of cities and states?

   ☐ They describe geography.

   ☐ They name Native American tribes.

   ☐ They are mostly French in origin.

Comprehension and Context

Comprehension is understanding what is seen, heard or read.

Context is the rest of the words in a sentence or the sentences before or after a word. Context can help with comprehension.

Context clues help you figure out the meaning of a word by relating it to other words in the sentence.

Directions: Use the context clues in the sentences to find the meanings of the bold words.

1. Jane was a **wizard** at games. She mastered them in no time and seldom lost.

   ☐ evil magician   ☐ gifted person   ☐ average player

2. The holiday was so special that she was sure she'd never forget it. The memory would be **imprinted** forever on her mind.

   ☐ found   ☐ weighed   ☐ fixed

3. "John will believe anything anyone tells him," his teacher said. "He's a very **impressionable** young man."

   ☐ easily influenced   ☐ unhappy   ☐ unintelligent

4. "Do you really think it's **prudent** to spend all your money on clothes?" his mother asked crossly.

   ☐ foolish   ☐ wise   ☐ funny

5. "Your plan has **merit**," Elizabeth's father said. "Let me give it some thought."

   ☐ value   ☐ awards   ☐ kindness

6. John was very **gregarious** and loved being around people.

   ☐ shy   ☐ outgoing   ☐ unfriendly

Name: _____

Classifying

Classifying means putting items into categories based on similar characteristics.

Example: Apple pie, cookies and ice cream could be classified as desserts.

Directions: Cross out the word in each group that does not belong. Then add a word of your own that does belong. The first one has been done for you.

1. wren   robin   ~~feather~~
   sparrow   eagle   **bluebird** _____

2. sofa   stool   chair
   carpet   bench   _____

3. lettuce   salad   corn
   broccoli   spinach   _____

4. pencil   chalk   crayon
   pen   drawing   _____

5. perch   shark   penguin
   bass   tuna   _____

6. rapid   quick   unhurried
   swift   speedy   _____

7. lemon   daisy   melon
   lime   grapefruit   _____

Directions: Write a category name above each group of words. Then write a word of your own that belongs in each group.

_____   _____
blizzard   ankle
hurricane   shin
thunder   thigh

_____   _____

_____   _____
antenna   hockey
speaker   ice skating
battery   bobsledding

_____   _____

Classifying

Directions: Write three objects which could belong in each category.

1. whales _____ _____ _____

2. songs _____ _____ _____

3. sports stars _____ _____ _____

4. fruit _____ _____ _____

5. schools _____ _____ _____

6. teachers _____ _____ _____

7. tools _____ _____ _____

8. friends _____ _____ _____

9. books _____ _____ _____

10. mammals _____ _____ _____

11. fish _____ _____ _____

12. desserts _____ _____ _____

13. cars _____ _____ _____

14. hobbies _____ _____ _____

15. vegetables _____ _____ _____

16. insects _____ _____ _____

Name: _____

Classifying: Regional Forecast

Directions: Read the forecast. Then write words in the correct categories.

The very warm, early spring weather will continue to spread along the East Coast today. With some sunshine, afternoon temperatures will climb to 90 degrees in many places. Columbia, South Carolina and neighboring areas could reach 100 degrees. Showers are expected from Washington, D.C. to New York City. Severe thunderstorms are likely in Virginia and North Carolina. Central South Carolina will be under a tornado watch during the afternoon.

Cities

_____

_____

_____

States

_____

_____

_____

Weather Conditions

_____

_____

_____

_____

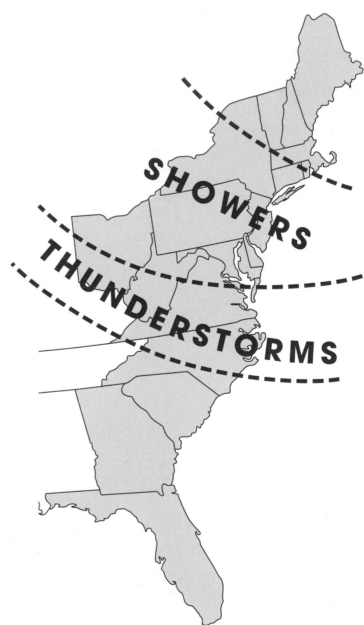

Name: _____

Analogies

An **analogy** is a way of comparing objects to show how they relate.

Example: Nose is to smell as tongue is to taste.

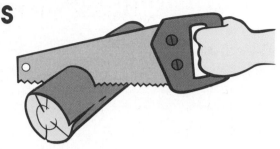

Directions: Write the correct word on the blank to fill in the missing part of each analogy. The first one has been done for you.

1. <u>Scissors</u> are to paper as saw is to wood.   fold   (scissors)   thin

2. Man is to boy as woman is to _____ .   mother   girl   lady

3. _____ is to cellar as sky is to ground.   down   attic   up

4. Rag is to dust as _____ is to sweep.   floor   straw   broom

5. Freezer is to cold as stove is to _____ .   cook   hot   recipe

6. Car is to _____ as book Is to bookshelf.   ride   gas   garage

7. Window is to _____ as car is to metal.   glass   clear   house

8. Eyes are to seeing as feet are to _____ .   legs   walking   shoes

9. Gas is to car as _____ is to lamp.   electricity   plug   cord

10. Refrigerator is to food as _____ is to clothes.   fold   material   closet

11. Floor is to down as ceiling is to _____ .   high   over   up

12. Pillow is to soft as rock is to _____ .   dirt   hard   hurt

13. Carpenter is to house as poet is to _____ .   verse   novel   writing

14. Lamp is to light as clock is to _____ .   time   hands   numbers

15. _____ is to hand as sole is to foot.   wrist   finger   palm

Analogies

Directions: Write your own words on the blanks to complete each analogy. The first one has been done for you.

1. Fuse is to firecracker as wick is to _candle_ .

2. Wheel is to steering as _____ is to stopping.

3. Scissors are to _____ as needles are to sew.

4. Water is to skiing as rink is to _____ .

5. Steam shovel is to dig as tractor is to _____ .

6. Stick is to hockey as _____ is to baseball.

7. Watch is to television as _____ is to radio.

8. _____ are to goose as children are to child.

9. Multiply is to multiplication as _____ is to subtraction.

10. Milk is to cow as egg is to _____ .

11. Yellow is to banana as _____ is to tomato.

12. _____ is to slow as day is to night.

13. Pine is to tree as _____ is to flower.

14. Zipper is to jacket as _____ is to shirt.

15. Museum is to painting as library is to _____ .

16. Petal is to flower as branch is to _____ .

17. Cow is to barn as car is to _____ .

18. Dresser is to bedroom as _____ is to kitchen.

19. Teacher is to _____ as doctor is to patient.

20. Ice is to cold as fire is to _____ .

Name: _____

Synonym and Antonym Analogies

Analogies are a way of comparing items to show how they are related. Analogies can show different types of relationships. Two relationships analogies might show are synonyms or antonyms.

Examples:
    Antonyms: hot is to cold as happy is to sad
    Synonyms: happy is to glad as run is to jog

You can write an analogy this way:
    slow:fast::up:down
You read it this way:
    slow is to fast as up is to down

Directions: Write **S** for synonym or **A** for antonym in the blanks in front of each analogy. Then complete the analogies by choosing a word from the box.

| life | run | comforter | fail | photograph |
| above | feline | play | drape | different |

_____ 1. dog:canine::cat: _____

_____ 2. coat:parka::curtain: _____

_____ 3. asleep:awake::work: _____

_____ 4. ground:sky::below: _____

_____ 5. freeze:thaw::stroll: _____

_____ 6. dangerous:treacherous::picture: _____

_____ 7. ancient:old::bedspread: _____

_____ 8. win:lose::succeed: _____

_____ 9. manmade:artificial::unique: _____

_____ 10. wealthy:poor::death: _____

Grade 5 - Comprehensive Curriculum

Name: _____

Part/Whole and Cause/Effect Analogies

Other types of analogies are part to whole and cause and effect.

Example:
Part to whole: fingers:hand::toes:foot
Cause and effect: rain:flood::matches:fire

Directions: Write **P** for part to whole or **C** for cause and effect in the blanks in front of each analogy. Then complete the analogies by choosing a word from the box.

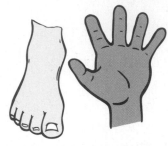

tree	bike	punishment	stomachache
beach	laugh	fingers	hawk
pencil	blizzard		

_____ 1. hair:head::fingernails: _____

_____ 2. germ:virus::misbehavior: _____

_____ 3. fall:injury::overeating: _____

_____ 4. keyboard:computer::wheels: _____

_____ 5. tongue:shoe::sand: _____

_____ 6. practice:win::joke: _____

_____ 7. read:learn::snow: _____

_____ 8. pouch:kangaroo::beak: _____

_____ 9. leaf:plant::bark:

_____

_____ 10. ink:pen::lead:

_____

Name: _____

Facts and Opinions

A **fact** is information that can be proved.

Example: Hawaii is a state.

An **opinion** is a belief. It tells what someone thinks. It cannot be proved.

Example: Hawaii is the prettiest state.

Directions: Write **f** (fact) or **o** (opinion) on the line by each sentence. The first one has been done for you.

_____f_____ 1. Hawaii is the only island state.

_____ 2. The best fishing Is in Michigan.

_____ 3. It is easy to find a job in Wyoming.

_____ 4. Trenton is the capital of New Jersey.

_____ 5. Kentucky is nicknamed the Bluegrass State.

_____ 6. The friendliest people In the United States live in Georgia.

_____ 7. The cleanest beaches are In California.

_____ 8. Summers are most beautiful In Arizona.

_____ 9. Only one percent of North Dakota is forest or woodland.

_____ 10. New Mexico produces almost half of the nation's uranium.

_____ 11. The first shots of the Civil War were fired in South Carolina on April 12, 1861.

_____ 12. The varied geographical features of Washington include mountains, deserts, a rainforest and a volcano.

_____ 13. In 1959, Alaska and Hawaii became the 49th and 50th states admitted to the Union.

_____ 14. Wyandotte Cave, one of the largest caves in the United States, is in Indiana.

Directions: Write one fact and one opinion about your own state.

Fact: _____

_____

Opinion: _____

_____

Name: _____

Facts and Opinions

A **fact** is a statement based on truth. It can be proven. **Opinions** are the beliefs of an individual that may or may not be true.

Examples:
   Fact: Alaska is a state.
   Opinion: Alaska is the most magnificent state.

Directions: Write **F** if the statement is a fact. Write **O** if the statement is an opinion.

1. _____ The Grand Canyon is the most scenic site in the United States.

2. _____ Dinosaurs roamed Earth millions of years ago.

3. _____ Scientists have discovered how to clone sheep.

4. _____ All people should attend this fair.

5. _____ Purebreds are the best dogs to own because they are intelligent.

6. _____ Nobody likes being bald.

7. _____ Students should be required to get straight A's to participate in extracurricular activities.

8. _____ Reading is an important skill that is vital in many careers.

9. _____ Snakes do not make good pets.

10. _____ Many books have been written about animals.

11. _____ Thomas Edison invented the lightbulb.

12. _____ Most people like to read science fiction.

13. _____ Insects have three body parts.

Name: _____

Facts and Opinions

Directions: Read the articles about cats. List the facts and opinions.

Cats make the best pets. Domestic or house cats were originally produced by crossbreeding several varieties of wild cats. They were used in ancient Egypt to catch rats and mice, which were overrunning bins of stored grain. Today they are still the most useful domestic animal.

Facts:

_____

_____

_____

Opinions:

_____

_____

It is bad luck for a black cat to cross your path. This is one of the many legends about cats. In ancient Egypt, for example, cats were considered sacred, and often were buried with their masters. During the Middle Ages, cats often were killed for taking part in what people thought were evil deeds. Certainly, cats sometimes do bring misfortune.

Facts:

_____

_____

_____

Opinions:

_____

_____

Grade 5 - Comprehensive Curriculum

Name: _____

Facts and Opinions

Directions: Write nine statements that are facts and nine statements that are opinions.

FACTS

1. _____
2. _____
3. _____
4. _____
5. _____
6. _____
7. _____
8. _____
9. _____

OPINIONS

1. _____
2. _____
3. _____
4. _____
5. _____
6. _____
7. _____
8. _____
9. _____

Cause and Effect

A **cause** is an event or reason which has an effect on something else.

Example:
The heavy rains produced flooding in Chicago.
Heavy rains were the **cause** of the flooding in Chicago.

An **effect** is an event that results from a cause.

Example:
Flooding in Chicago was due to the heavy rains.
Flooding was the **effect** caused by the heavy rains.

Directions: Read the paragraphs. Complete the charts by writing the missing cause (reason) or effect (result).

Club-footed toads are small toads that live in the rainforests of Central and South America. Because they give off a poisonous substance on their skins, other animals cannot eat them.

Cause:	Effect:
They give off a poisonous substance.	_____

Civets (siv its) are weasel-like animals. The best known of the civets is the mongoose, which eats rats and snakes. For this reason, it is welcome around homes in its native India.

Cause:	Effect:
_____	It is welcome around homes in its native India.

Bluebirds can be found in most areas of the United States. Like other members of the thrush family of birds, young bluebirds have speckled breasts. This makes them difficult to see and helps them hide from their enemies. The Pilgrims called them "blue robins" because they are much like the English robin. They are the same size and have the same red breast and friendly song as the English robin.

Cause:	Effect:
Young bluebirds have speckled breasts.	_____
_____	The Pilgrims called them "blue robins."

Name: _____

Review

Directions: Write the answers.

1. Define classifying.

   _____

2. Add words to these classifications:

   meat:
   hamburger
   steak
   sirloin tip
   _____

   _____

   music groups:
   the Pointer Sisters
   the Beatles
   _____

   _____

   breakfast drinks:
   orange juice
   cranberry juice
   grapefruit juice
   _____

   _____

   colors:
   blue
   fuschia
   melon
   _____

   _____

3. What is an analogy? _____

4. Give an example of an analogy. _____

5. Write two sentences that are facts.

   _____

   _____

6. Write two sentences that are opinions.

   _____

   _____

7. Write an example of cause and effect. Underline the cause. Circle the effect.

   _____

   _____

Name: _____

Review

Directions: Write three statements about yourself that are facts.

1. _____

2. _____

3. _____

Directions: Write three statements about yourself that are opinions.

4. _____

5. _____

6. _____

Directions: Write a category name for each set of words.

7. Arizona, Wisconsin, Texas _____

8. mouse, rat, squirrel _____

9. saddle, reins, halter _____

Directions: Finish the analogies with words from the box.
Not all words will be used.

10. look:see::kind:

_____

11. bald:hairy::difficult:

_____

12. insomnia:nightmares::crumbs:

_____

13. engine:car::heart:

_____

friend
nice
ants
pretzels
human
hard
easy
alone

Grade 5 - Comprehensive Curriculum

Name: _____

Main Idea

The **main idea** is the most important idea, or main point, in a sentence, paragraph or story.

Directions: Read the paragraphs below. For each paragraph, underline the sentence that tells the main idea.

Sometimes people think they have to choose between exercise and fun. For many people, it is more fun to watch television than to run 5 miles. Yet, if you don't exercise, your body gets soft and out of shape. You move more slowly. You may even think more slowly. But why do something that isn't fun? Well, there are many ways to exercise and have fun.

One family solved the exercise problem by using their TV. They hooked up the television to an electric generator. The generator was operated by an exercise bike. Anyone who wanted to watch TV had to ride the bike. The room with their television in it must have been quite a sight!

Think of the times when you are just "hanging out" with your friends. You go outside and jump rope, play ball, run races, and so on. Soon you are all laughing and having a good time. Many group activities can provide you with exercise and be fun, too.

Maybe there aren't enough kids around after school for group games. Perhaps you are by yourself. Then what? You can get plenty of exercise just by walking, biking or even dancing. In the morning, walk the long way to the bus. Ride your bike to and from school. Practice the newest dance by yourself. Before you know it, you will be the fittest dancer of all your friends!

Directions: Write other ideas you have for combining fun and exercise below.

_____

_____

_____

_____

_____

_____

_____

Name: _____

Reading Skills: Skimming

Skimming an article means to read quickly, looking for headings and key words to give an overall idea of the content of an article or to find a particular fact. When skimming for answers, read the questions first. Then look for specific words that will help locate the answers.

Directions: Skim the paragraph to answer this question.

1. What "marvel" is the paragraph about?_____

In America, there is so much magnificent scenery. Perhaps the most stunning sight of all is the Grand Canyon. This canyon is in northern Arizona. It is the deepest, widest canyon on Earth. The Grand Canyon is 217 miles long, 4 to 18 miles wide and, in some places, more than a mile deep. The rocks at the bottom of the steep walls are at least 500 million years old. Most of the rocks are sandstone, limestone and shale. By studying these rocks, scientists know that this part of the world was once under the sea.

Directions: Skim the paragraph again to find the answers to these questions.

1. How deep are the lowest points in the Grand Canyon?

   _____

2. How old are the rocks at the bottom of the Grand Canyon?

   _____

3. What kinds of rocks would you find in the Grand Canyon?

   _____

4. What do these rocks tell us?

   _____

Grade 5 - Comprehensive Curriculum

Reading Skills: Maps

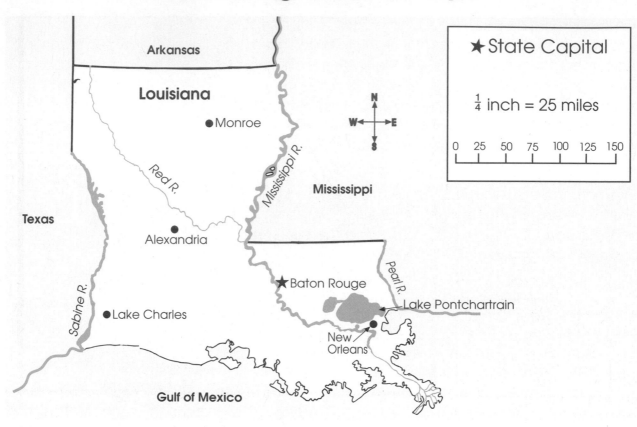

Directions: Use this map to answer the questions.

1. What state borders Louisiana to the north?

   _____

2. What is the state capital of Louisiana?

   _____

3. What cities are located near Lake Pontchartrain?

   _____

4. In which direction would you be traveling if you drove from Monroe to Alexandria?

   _____

5. About how far is it from Alexandria to Lake Charles?

   _____

6. Besides Arkansas, name one other state that borders Louisiana.

   _____

Reading Skills: Maps

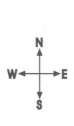

Directions: Use this map of Columbus, Ohio, to answer the questions.

1. Does Highway 104 run east and west or north and south?

    _____

2. What is the name of the freeway numbered 315?

    _____

3. Which is farther south, Bexley or Whitehall?

    _____

4. What two freeways join near the Port Columbus International Airport?

    _____

5. Which two suburbs are farther apart, Dublin and Upper Arlington or Dublin and Worthington?

    _____

6. In which direction would you be traveling if you drove from Grove City to Worthington?

    _____

Sequencing: Maps

Directions: Read the information about planning a map.

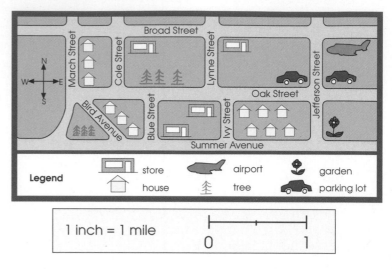

Maps have certain features that help you to read them. A **compass rose** points out directions. Color is often used so you can easily see where one area (such as a county, state or country) stops and the next starts.

To be accurate, a map must be drawn to scale. The **scale** of a map shows how much area is represented by a given measurement. The scale can be small: one inch = one mile; or large: one inch = 1,000 miles.

Symbols are another map tool. An airplane may represent an airport. Sometimes a symbol does not look like what it represents. Cities are often represented by dots. A map **legend** tells what each symbol means.

One of the best ways to learn about maps is to make one of your own. You may be surprised at how much you learn about your neighborhood, too. You will need a large piece of paper, a ruler, a pencil and colored pencils.

You will need to choose the area you want to map out. It is important to decide on the scale for your map. It could be small: one inch = three feet, if you are mapping out your own backyard. Be sure to include symbols, like a picnic table to represent a park or a flag to represent a school. Don't forget to include the symbols and other important information in your legend.

Directions: Number in order the steps to making your own map.

_____ Figure out the scale that will work best for your map.

_____ Obtain a large piece of paper, ruler, pencil and colored pencils.

_____ Make a legend explaining the symbols you used.

_____ Draw your map!

_____ Draw symbols to represent features of the area you are mapping.

_____ Decide on the area you want to map out.

Name: _____

Creating a Map

Directions: In the space below, draw a map of your street or town. Be sure to include a compass rose, scale, symbols and a map legend.

Grade 5 - Comprehensive Curriculum

Name: _____

Following Directions

Directions: Read and follow the directions.

1. Draw a vertical line from the top mid-point of the square to the bottom mid-point of the square.
2. Draw a diagonal line from top left to bottom right of the square.
3. In each of the two triangles, draw a heart.
4. Draw a picture of a cat's face below the square.
5. Draw a horizontal line from the left mid-point to the right mid-point of the square.
6. Draw two intersecting lines in each of the two smaller squares so they are equally divided into four quadrants.
7. Draw a triangle-shaped roof on the square.
8. Draw a circle next to each heart.
9. Write your name in the roof section of your drawing.

Name: _____

Following Directions: Continents

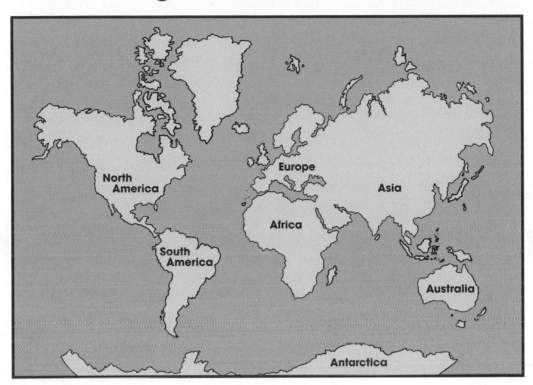

Directions: Read the facts about the seven continents and follow the directions.

1. Asia is the largest continent. It has the largest land mass and the largest population. Draw a star on Asia.
2. Africa is the second largest continent. Write a **2** on Africa.
3. Australia is the smallest continent in area: 3 million square miles, compared to 17 million square miles for Asia. Write **3,000,000** on Australia.
4. Australia is not a very crowded continent, but it does not rank lowest in population. That honor goes to Antarctica, which has no permanent population at all! This ice-covered continent is too cold for life. Write **zero** on Antarctica.
5. Australia and Antarctica are the only continents entirely separated by water. Draw circles around Australia and Antarctica.
6. North America and South America are joined together by a narrow strip of land. It is called Central America. Write an **N** on North America, an **S** on South America and a **C** on Central America.
7. Asia and Europe are joined together over such a great distance that they are sometimes called one continent. The name given to it is Eurasia. Draw lines under the names of the two continents in Eurasia.

Reading a Recipe

Directions: Read the recipe. Then answer the questions.

Graham Cracker Smoothies

Graham crackers

Icing:
  2 T. peanut butter
  2 T. butter
  2 c. powdered sugar
  milk

Break graham crackers in half. Mix peanut butter, butter and powdered sugar with a spoon. Add enough milk to make creamy icing. Stir vigorously until no lumps remain. Spread on graham cracker half and top with another graham cracker half, sandwich style. Enjoy!
The smoothie icing will keep in the refrigerator for two days.

1. What do these abbreviations stand for?

    T. _____

    c. _____

2. Number the steps in the correct order.

    ___ Spread icing on graham crackers.

    ___ Add milk and stir until creamy.

    ___ Break graham crackers in half.

    ___ Eat and enjoy.

    ___ Mix the peanut butter, butter and powdered sugar together.

3. Why is it important to follow the correct sequence when cooking?

    _____

Name: _____

Reading Skills: Labels

Labels provide information about products.

Directions: Read the label on the medicine bottle. Answer the questions.

> **Remember:** Children should never take medicines without their parents' knowledge and consent.

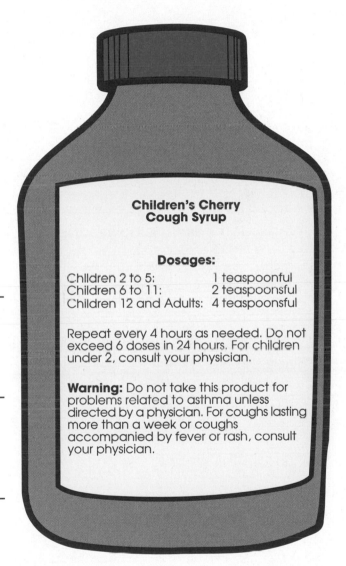

Children's Cherry Cough Syrup

Dosages:
Children 2 to 5: 1 teaspoonful
Children 6 to 11: 2 teaspoonsful
Children 12 and Adults: 4 teaspoonsful

Repeat every 4 hours as needed. Do not exceed 6 doses in 24 hours. For children under 2, consult your physician.

Warning: Do not take this product for problems related to asthma unless directed by a physician. For coughs lasting more than a week or coughs accompanied by fever or rash, consult your physician.

1. What is the dosage, or amount to be taken, for a three-year-old child?

_____

2. How often can you take this medicine if it is needed?

_____

3. How many times a day can you take this medicine?

_____

4. What should you do before taking the medicine if you have a rash in addition to your cough?

_____

5. Will this medicine help you if you are sneezing?

_____

6. What is the dosage for an adult?

_____

Name: _____

Reading Skills: Newspapers

Directions: Write the answers.

1. What is the name of your daily local newspaper?

   _____

2. List the sections included in your local newspaper.

   _____

3. What sections of the newspaper do you read on a regular basis?

   _____

4. Ask a parent which sections he or she reads on a regular basis.

   _____

5. Find the editorial section of your newspaper. An editorial is the opinion of one person.
   Write the main idea of one editorial. _____

   _____

   _____

   _____

6. If you could work at a newspaper, which job would you like? Why?

   _____

   _____

   _____

Directions: Read a copy of *USA Today*. You can find a copy in most libraries. Compare it to your local paper.

7. How are they alike? _____

   _____

8. How are they different? _____

   _____

Name: _____

Reading Skills: A Newspaper Index

An **index** is a listing in a book, magazine or newspaper that tells where to find items or information.

Newspapers provide many kinds of information. You can read about national events, local news, the weather and sports. You will also find opinions, feature stories, advice columns, comics, entertainment, recipes, advertisements and more. A guide that tells you where to find different types of information in a newspaper is called a **newspaper index**. An index of the newspaper usually appears on the front page.

Directions: Use the newspaper index to answer the questions.

Business.......................... 8	Local News........................... 5–7
Classified Ads................18–19	National News 1–4
Comics 20	Radio-TV 17
Editorials 9	Sports 11–13
Entertainment.................14–16	Weather 10

1. Where would you look for results of last night's basketball games?

   Section: _____ Page(s) _____

2. Where would you find your favorite cartoon strip?

   Section: _____ Page(s) _____

3. Where would you find opinions of upcoming elections?

   Section: _____ Page(s) _____

4. Where would you look to locate a used bicycle to buy?

   Section: _____ Page(s) _____

5. Where would you find out if you need to wear your raincoat tomorrow?

   Section: _____ Page(s) _____

6. Where would you find the listing of tonight's TV shows?

   Section: _____ Page(s) _____

7. Which would be first, a story about the president's trip to Europe or a review of the newest movie?

   _____

Name: _____

Reading Skills: Classified Ads

A **classified ad** is an advertisement in a newspaper or magazine offering a product or service for sale or rent.

Example: For Sale: Used 26" 30-speed bike. $100.
Call 555-5555.

Directions: Read these advertisements. Answer the questions.

Pet Sitter
Going on Vacation?
Away for the Weekend?
I am 14 years old and have experience caring for dogs and cats. Your home or mine.
Excellent References.
Call Sally Trent
Phone: 999-8250

1.

Yard Work
Breaking Your Back?
Give Mike and Jane a crack!
Mowing, raking, trash hauled.
References provided.
Call 555-9581.

2.

Pet Sitter:
Going on vacation?
Away for the weekend?
I am 14 years old and
have experience caring
for dogs and cats.
Your home or mine.
Excellent references.
Call Sally Trent.
Phone: 999-8250.

3.

Singing Lessons
for All Ages!
Be popular at parties!
Fulfill your dreams!
20 years coaching
experience.
Madame Rinaud . . .
Coach to the Stars.
555-5331.

1. What is promised in the third ad?_____

2. Is it fact or opinion?_____

3. What fact is offered in the third ad? _____

4. Give an example of a slogan, or easy-to-remember phrase, that appears in one of

   the ads._____

5. Which ad gives the most facts?_____

6. Which ad is based mostly on opinion?_____

Reading Skills: Classified Ads

Directions: Write a classified ad for these topics. Include information about the item, a phone number and an eye-catching title.

1. An ad to wash cars

_____

_____

_____

2. An ad for free puppies

_____

_____

_____

3. An ad for something you would like to sell

_____

_____

_____

4. An ad to sell your house

_____

_____

_____

_____

Reading Skills: Schedules

A **schedule** lists events or programs by time, date and place or channel.

Example:

Packer Preseason Games

August 14	7 P.M.	NY Jets at Green Bay
August 23	7 P.M.	Denver Broncos at Madison
August 28	3 P.M.	Saints at New Orleans
September 2	Noon	Miami Dolphins at Green Bay

Directions: Use this newspaper television schedule to answer the questions.

Evening

6:00 3 Let's Talk! Guest: Animal expert Jim Porter
      5 Cartoons
      8 News
      9 News
7:00 3 Farm Report
      5 Movie. *A Laugh a Minute* (1955) James
         Rayburn. Comedy about a boy who wants to join the circus.
      8 Spin for Dollars!
      9 Cooking with Cathy. Tonight: Chicken with mushrooms
7:30 3 Double Trouble (comedy). The twins disrupt the high school dance.
      8 Wall Street Today: Stock Market Report
8:00 3 NBA Basketball. Teams to be announced.
      8 News Special. "Saving Our Waterways: Pollution in the Mississippi."
      9 Movie. *At Day's End* (1981). Michael Collier, Julie Romer. Drama set
         in World War II.

1. What two stations have the news at 6:00? _____

2. What time would you turn on the television to watch a funny movie?_____
   What channel?_____

3. What could you watch if you are a sports fan? _____
   What time and channel is it on?_____

4. Which show title sounds like it could be a game show?_____

5. What show might you want to watch if you are interested in the environment?

   _____

   What time and channel is it on?_____

Name: _____

Review

Directions: Write the answers.

1. What is the purpose of a classified ad? _____

2. Skim your local newspaper. List at least six categories of classified ads.

   _____   _____

   _____   _____

   _____   _____

3. What sections are included in the index of your local newspaper?

   _____

4. What four pieces of information should a television program schedule contain?

   _____   _____

   _____   _____

5. What information is present on a medicine bottle?

   _____   _____

   _____   _____

6. Why is it important for medicine labels to include warnings?

   _____

   _____

   _____

Using Prior Knowledge: Books

Directions: Before reading about books in the following section, answer these questions.

1. What books have you read recently?

_____

_____

2. Write a summary of one of the books you listed above.

_____

_____

_____

_____

_____

_____

3. Define the following types of books and, if possible, give an example of each.

biography: _____

_____

fiction: _____

_____

mystery: _____

_____

nonfiction: _____

_____

Name: _____

Context Clues: Remember Who You Are

Directions: Read each paragraph. Then use context clues to figure out the meanings of the bold words.

During the 1940s, Esther Hautzig lived in the town of Vilna, which was then part of Poland. Shortly after the **outbreak** of World War II, she and her family were **deported** to Siberia by Russian communists who hated Jews. She told what happened to her and other Polish Jews in a book. The book is called *Remember Who You Are: Stories About Being Jewish*.

1. Choose the correct definition of **deported**.

☐ sent away   ☐ asked to go   ☐ invited to visit

2. Choose the correct definition of **outbreak**.

☐ a sudden occurrence   ☐ to leave suddenly

Remember Who You Are: Stories About Being Jewish is a nonfiction book that tells true stories. An interesting **fiction** book is *Leave the Cooking to Me* by Judie Angell. It tells the story of a girl named Shirley, who learns about cooking from her best friend's mother. Shirley gets very good at making fancy food. Most young people have a hard time finding jobs that pay well, but Shirley's cooking skills help her land a **lucrative** summer job.

3. Choose the correct definition of **fiction**.

☐ stories that are true   ☐ stories that are not true

4. Choose the correct definition of **lucrative**.

☐ interesting   ☐ profitable   ☐ nearby

Comprehension: Books and More Books!

Variety is said to be the spice of life. Where books are concerned, variety is the key to reading pleasure. There is a type of book that appeals to every reader.

Each year, hundreds of new books are published for children. A popular series of books for girls between the ages of 8 and 12 is *Sweet Valley Kids*, written by Francine Pascal. All of Pascal's books are fictional stories about children who live in the town of Sweet Valley.

If you like legends, an interesting book is *Dream Wolf* by Paul Goble. *Dream Wolf* is a retelling of an old Native American legend. Legends are stories passed down from one generation to another that may or may not be true. Some of them are scary! *The Legend of Sleepy Hollow*, for example, is about a headless horseman. Other legends are about a person's brave or amazing deeds. For example, there are many legends about Robin Hood, who stole from the rich and gave to the poor.

Many people like to read nonfiction books, which are about things that really exist or really happened. Many children who like nonfiction choose books about animals, careers, sports and hobbies. Those interested in information about Native Americans might like to read these books: *The Navajos* by Peter Iverson, *The Yakima* by Helen Schuster and *The Creek* by Michael Green. The titles of these nonfiction books are names of Native American tribes.

Directions: Answer these questions about different types of books.

1. What is the name of Francine Pascal's book series? _____

2. What legend is about a headless horseman? _____

3. Which of the following is not correct about legends?

☐ Legends are passed down through the generations.

☐ All legends are scary.

☐ Some legends are about people who did braves things.

Comprehension: Help for the Homeless

In Dayton, Ohio, a bookstore called Books & Co. launched a program to educate the public about the needs of homeless people. The program was built around profits from sales of a book called *Louder Than Words*. The book is a collection of 22 short stories by such noted authors as Louise Erdrich and Anne Tyler.

Many of the authors helped promote the book by coming to the bookstore to autograph copies of *Louder Than Words*. All profits from the sale of the book were donated to a fund that provides food and housing for homeless people.

The fund for the homeless is managed by a nonprofit organization called Share Our Strength. Located in Washington, D.C., the organization distributes the money to food banks and shelters for homeless people around the United States.

By the end of 1990, $50,000 had been raised for the homeless from the sale of *Louder Than Words*. Other bookstore owners learned about the success of Books & Co. in raising money for the homeless. They were impressed! Now, bookstores in these other cities are running fund-raising efforts of their own: Ann Arbor, Michigan; Columbus, Ohio; Taos, New Mexico; and Minneapolis, Minnesota.

Directions: Answer these questions about how booksellers have helped raise funds for the homeless.

1. How many short stories are in the book *Louder Than Words*? _____

2. What is the name of the organization that distributes money to homeless shelters

   around the country? _____

3. Name two authors whose stories are included in *Louder Than Words*.

   _____

4. Share Our Strength is located in what city?

   ☐ Portland, OR   ☐ Minneapolis, MN   ☐ Washington, D.C.

5. In what city is Books & Co. located?

   ☐ Columbus, OH   ☐ Dayton, OH   ☐ Taos, NM

Name: _____

Fact or Opinion?

Directions: Read the paragraphs below. Then, in the corresponding numbered blanks, write whether each numbered sentence is a fact or an opinion.

Have you ever seen *Reading Rainbow* on your local public television station? **(1)** It's a show about books, and its host is LeVar Burton. **(2)** LeVar is very handsome and the show is great!

Some books that have been featured on the show are *I Can Be an Oceanographer* by Paul Sipiera, *Soccer Sam* by Jean Marzolla, *Redbird* by Patrick Fort and *Miss Nelson Has a Field Day* by Harry Allard. **(3)** *Miss Nelson Has a Field Day* sounds like the most interesting book of all!

(4) On *Reading Rainbow,* children give informal book reports about books they have read. **(5)** All the children are adorable! In about 1 minute, each child describes his or her book. **(6)** While the child is talking, pictures of some of the pages from the book are shown. **(7)** Seeing the pictures will make you want to read the book. A few books are described on each show. **(8)** Other activities include trips with LeVar to places the books tell about. **(9)** Every child should make time to watch *Reading Rainbow!* **(10)** It's a fabulous show!

1. _____

2. _____

3. _____

4. _____

5. _____

6. _____

7. _____

8. _____

9. _____

10. _____

Context Clues: Kids' Books Are Big Business

Between 1978 and 1988, the number of children's books published in the United States doubled. The publishing industry, which prints, promotes and sells books, does not usually move this fast. Why? Because if publishers print too many books that don't sell, they lose money. They like to wait, if they can, to see what the "public demand" is for certain types of books. Then they accept manuscripts from writers who have written the types of books the public seems to want. More than 4,600 children's books were

published in 1988, because publishers thought they could sell that many titles. Many copies of each title were printed and sold to bookstores and libraries. The publishers made good profits and, since then, the number of children's books published each year has continued to grow.

The title of a recent new book for children is *The Wild Horses of Sweetbriar* by Natalie Kinsey-Warnock. It is the story of a girl and a band of wild horses that lived on an island off the coast of Massachusetts in 1903. The story sounds very exciting! Wild horses can be quite dangerous. The plot of *The Wild Horses of Sweetbriar* is probably filled with danger and suspense.

Directions: Answer these questions about how interest in writing, reading and selling children's books has grown.

1. Use context clues to choose the correct definition of **industry**.

☐ booksellers   ☐ writers   ☐ entire business

2. If 4,600 books were sold in 1988, how many books were sold in 1978? _____

3. The number of children's books published
   in the United States doubled between 1978 and 1988.   Fact   Opinion

4. *The Wild Horses of Sweetbriar* is the story of a girl and a
   band of wild horses that lived on an island in 1903.   Fact   Opinion

5. The story sounds very exciting!   Fact   Opinion

6. The plot of *The Wild Horses of Sweetbriar* is probably
   filled with danger and suspense.   Fact   Opinion

Name: _____

Review

Directions: Follow the instructions below.

1. Write a summary of the selection "Help for the Homeless" (page 91).

   _____

   _____

   _____

2. What skills must a writer have in order to produce a book?

   _____

   _____

   _____

3. Define the following words from this section.

   appeal: _____

   legend: _____

   deed: _____

   generation: _____

   profit: _____

   distribute: _____

   suspense: _____

   manuscript: _____

4. Interview the members of your family. Ask each person his/her favorite book title and the reason he/she enjoyed it. Then, summarize your findings in a paragraph.

   _____

   _____

   _____

   _____

READING COMPREHENSION

Name: _____

Using Prior Knowledge: Music

Using **prior knowledge** means being able to use what one already knows to find an answer or get information.

Directions: Before reading about music in the following section, answer these questions.

1. In your opinion, why is music important to people?

_____

_____

_____

2. Name as many styles of music as you can.

_____

_____

_____

3. What is your favorite type of music? Why?

_____

_____

_____

4. If you could choose a musical instrument to play, what would it be? Why?

_____

_____

_____

5. Name a famous musician and describe what you know about him/her.

_____

_____

_____

_____

Main Idea: Where Did Songs Come From?

Historians say the earliest music was probably connected to religion. Long ago, people believed the world was controlled by a variety of gods. Singing was among the first things humans did to show respect to the gods.

Singing is still an important part of most religions. Buddhists (bood-ists), Christians and Jews all use chants and/or songs in their religious ceremonies. If you have ever sung a song—religious or otherwise—you know that singing is fun. The feeling of joy that comes from singing must also have made ancient people feel happy.

Another time people sang was when they worked. Egyptian slaves sang as they carried the heavy stones to build the pyramids. Soldiers sang as they marched into battle. Farmers sang one song as they planted and another when they harvested. Singing made the work less burdensome. People used the tunes to pace themselves. Sometimes they followed Instructions through songs. For example, "Yo-oh, heave ho!/Yo-oh, heave ho!" was sung when sailors pulled on a ship's ropes to lift the sails. **Heave** means "to lift," and that is what they did as they sang the song. The song helped sailors work together and pull at the same time. This made the task easier.

Directions: Answer these questions about music.

1. Circle the main idea:

   Singing is fun, and that is why early people liked it so much.

   Singing began as a way to show respect to the gods and is still an important part of most religious ceremonies.

   Traditionally, singing has been important as a part of religious ceremonies and as inspiration to workers.

2. Besides religious ceremonies, what other activity fostered singing? _____

   _____

3. When did farmers sing two different songs? _____

4. How did singing "Yo-oh, heave ho!" help sailors work? _____

   _____

Name: _____

Comprehension: Facts About Folk Music

Folk music literally means music "of the folks," and it belongs to everyone. The names of the musicians who composed most folk music have long been forgotten. Even so, folk music has remained popular because it tells about the lives of people. Usually, the tune is simple, and even though folk songs often have many verses, the words are easy to remember. Do you know the words to "She'll Be Comin' 'Round the Mountain"?

Although no one ever says who "she" is, the verses tell you that she will be "riding six white horses" and that "we'll go out to greet her." The song also describes what will be eaten when she comes (chicken and dumplings) and what those singing will be wearing (red pajamas).

"Clementine" is a song that came out of the California gold rush in the mid-1800s. It tells the story of a woman who was "lost and gone forever" when she was killed. ("In a cavern, in a canyon, excavating for a mine/Met a miner '49er and his daughter, Clementine.")

Another famous folk song is "Swing Low, Sweet Chariot." This song was sung by slaves in the United States and today is sung by people of all races. The words "Swing low, sweet chariot, coming for to carry me home . . . " describe the soul being united with God after death. Like other folk songs that sprang from slaves, "Swing Low, Sweet Chariot" is simple, moving and powerful.

Directions: Answer these questions about folk music.

1. What is the purpose of folk music? _____

_____

2. What food is sung about in "She'll Be Comin' 'Round the Mountain"? _____

_____

3. Where did Clementine live?

☐ Florida ☐ Mississippi ☐ California

4. Where in the United States do you think "Swing Low, Sweet Chariot" was first sung?

☐ the North ☐ the West ☐ the South

Recalling Details: Woodwinds

There are four kinds of woodwind instruments in modern bands. They are flutes, oboes, clarinets and bassoons. They are called "woodwind" instruments for two sensible reasons. In the beginning, they were all made of wood. Also, the musician's breath, or "wind," was required to play them.

Although they are all woodwinds, these instruments look different and are played differently. To play an oboe, the musician blows through a mouthpiece on the front of the instrument. The mouthpiece, called a reed, is made of two flat pieces of a kind of wood called cane. Clarinet players also blow into a reed mouthpiece. The clarinet has only one reed in its mouthpiece.

To play the flute, the musician blows across a hole near one end of the instrument. The way the breath is aimed helps to make the flute's different sounds. The bassoon is the largest woodwind instrument. Bassoon players blow through a mouthpiece that goes through a short metal pipe before it goes into the body of the bassoon. It makes a very different sound from the clarinet or the oboe.

Woodwind instruments also have keys—but not the kind of keys that open locks. These keys are more like levers that the musician pushes up and down. The levers cover holes. When the musician pushes down on a lever, it closes that hole. When he/she lifts his/her finger, it opens the hole. Different sounds are produced by controlling the amount of breath, or "wind," that goes through the holes.

Directions: Answer these questions about woodwind instruments.

1. What instruments are in the woodwind section?_____

2. Why are some instruments called woodwinds?_____

_____

3. How is a flute different from the other woodwinds?_____

4. What happens when a musician pushes down on a woodwind key?_____

_____

5. How would a woodwind musician open the holes on his/her instrument?

_____

Comprehension: Harp Happenings

If you have ever heard a harpist play, you know what a lovely sound a harp makes. Music experts say the harp is among the oldest of instruments. It probably was invented several thousand years ago in or near Egypt.

The first harps are believed to have been made by stretching a string tightly between an empty tortoise shell and a curved pole. The empty shell magnified the sound the string made when it was plucked. More strings were added later so that more sounds could be made. Over the centuries, the shape of the harp gradually was changed into that of the large, graceful instruments we recognize today.

Here is how a harpist plays a harp. First, he/she leans the harp against his/her right shoulder. Then, the harpist puts his/her hands on either side of the harp and plucks its strings with both hands.

A harp has seven pedals on the bottom back. The audience usually cannot see these pedals. Most people are surprised to learn about them. The pedals are connected to the strings. Stepping on a particular pedal causes certain strings to tighten. The tightening and loosening of the strings makes different sounds; so does the way the strings are plucked with the hands.

At first glance, harps look like simple instruments. Actually, they are rather complicated and difficult to keep in tune. A harpist often spends as long as half an hour before a performance tuning his/her harp's strings so it produces the correct sounds.

Directions: Answer these questions about harps.

1. When were harps invented? _____

2. Where were harps invented? _____

3. What is a person called who plays the harp? _____

4. The harpist leans the harp against his/her

☐ right shoulder. ☐ left shoulder. ☐ left knee.

5. How many pedals does a harp have?

☐ five ☐ six ☐ seven

6. Harps are easy to play.

☐ yes ☐ no

Name: _____

Comprehension: Brass Shows Class

If you like band music, you probably love the music made by brass instruments. Bright, loud, moving and magnificent—all these words describe the sounds made by brass.

Some of the earliest instruments were horns. Made from hollowed-out animal horns, these primitive instruments could not possibly have made the rich sounds of modern horns that are made of brass.

Most modern brass bands have three instruments—tubas, trombones and trumpets. Combined, these instruments can produce stirring marches, as well as haunting melodies. The most famous composer for brass instruments was John Phillip Sousa. Born in Washington, D.C., in 1854, Sousa was a military band conductor and composer. He died in 1932, but his music is still very popular today. One of Sousa's most famous tunes for military bands is "Stars and Stripes Forever."

Besides composing band music, Sousa also invented a practical band instrument—the sousaphone. The sousaphone is a huge tuba that makes very low noises. Because of the way it curls around the body, a sousaphone is easier to carry than a tuba, especially when the musician must march. This is exactly why John Phillip Sousa invented it!

Directions: Answer these questions about brass instruments.

1. Who invented the sousaphone? _____

2. What were the first horns made from? _____

3. Where was John Phillip Sousa born? _____

4. When did John Phillip Sousa die? _____

5. Why did Sousa invent the sousaphone? _____

_____

6. What types of instruments make up a modern brass band? _____

_____

Comprehension: Violins

If you know anything about violin music, chances are you have heard the word **Stradivarius** (Strad-uh-vary-us). Stradivarius is the name for the world's most magnificent violins. They are named after their creator, Antonio Stradivari.

Stradivari was born in northern Italy and lived from 1644 to 1737. Cremona, the town he lived in, was a place where violins were manufactured. Stradivari was very young when he learned to play the violin. He grew to love the instrument so much that he began to make them himself.

Violins were new instruments during Stradivari's time. People made them in different sizes and shapes and of different types of wood. Stradivari is said to have been very particular about the wood he selected for his violins. He took long walks alone in the forest to find just the right tree. He is also said to have used a secret and special type of varnish to put on the wood. Whatever the reasons, his violins are the best in the world.

Stradivari put such care and love into his violins that they are still used today. Many of these are in museums. But some wealthy musicians, who can afford the thousands and thousands of dollars they cost, own Stradivarius violins.

Stradivari passed his methods on to his sons. But the secrets of making Stradivarius violins seem to have died out with the family. Their rarity, as well as their mellow sound, make Stradivarius violins among the most prized instruments in the world.

Directions: Answer these questions about Stradivarius violins.

1. Where did Stradivari live? _____

2. Why did he begin making violins? _____

3. Why are Stradivarius violins special? _____

   _____

4. Where can Stradivarius violins be found today? _____

   _____

5. How did Stradivari select the wood for his violins? _____

   _____

6. Who else knew Stradivari's secrets for making such superior violins?_____

Name: _____

Review

Directions: Complete the following exercises.

1. Write a four-sentence summary of the selection "Where Did Songs Come From?" (page 97).

   _____

   _____

   _____

   _____

2. Describe the main difference between a clarinet and an oboe.

   _____

   _____

3. How do the keys of woodwind instruments work?

   _____

   _____

4. Write a summary of the history of the harp.

   _____

   _____

   _____

5. Define the following words from the selection "Facts About Folk Music" (page 98).

   verses: _____

   excavating: _____

   chariot: _____

   composed: _____

Using Prior Knowledge: Art

Directions: Before reading about art in the following section, answer these questions.

1. Write a short paragraph about a famous artist of your choice.

_____

_____

_____

2. Many artists paint realistic scenes. Other artists paint imaginary scenes. Which do you prefer? Why?

_____

_____

3. Although we often think of art as painting and drawing, art also includes sculpture, fabric weavings and metalwork. Are you talented at a particular type of art? If so, what type? If not, what would you like to learn?

_____

_____

_____

4. Why are art museums important to society?

_____

_____

_____

5. Why do you think some artwork is worth so much money? Would you pay several thousand dollars for a piece of artwork? Why or why not?

_____

_____

_____

Main Idea: Creating Art

No one knows exactly when the first human created the first painting. Crude drawings and paintings on the walls of caves show that humans have probably always expressed themselves through art. These early cave pictures show animals being hunted, people dancing and other events of daily life. The simplicity of the paintings reflect the simple lifestyles of these primitive people.

The subjects of early paintings also help to make another important point. Art is not created out of nothing. The subjects an artist chooses to paint reflect the history, politics and culture of the time and place in which he/she lives. An artist born and raised in New York City, for example, is not likely to paint scenes of the Rocky Mountains. An artist living in the Rockies is not likely to paint pictures of city life.

Of course, not all paintings are realistic. Many artists choose to paint pictures that show their own "inner vision" as opposed to what they see with their eyes. Many religious paintings of earlier centuries look realistic but contain figures of angels. These paintings combine the artist's inner vision of angels with other things, such as church buildings, that can be seen.

Directions: Answer these questions about creating art.

1. Circle the main idea:

   Art was important to primitive people because it showed hunting and dancing scenes, and is still important today.

   Through the ages, artists have created paintings that reflect the culture, history and politics of the times, as well as their own inner visions.

2. Why is an artist living in the Rocky Mountains less likely to paint city scenes?

   _____

   _____

3. In addition to what they see with their eyes, what do some artists' paintings also show?

   _____

   _____

Name: _____

Comprehension: Leonardo da Vinci

Many people believe that Leonardo da Vinci, an Italian artist and inventor who lived from 1452 to 1519, was the most brilliant person ever born. He was certainly a man ahead of his time! Records show that da Vinci loved the earth and was curious about everything on it.

To learn about the human body, he dissected corpses to find out what was inside. In the 15th and 16th centuries, dissecting the dead was against the laws of the Catholic church. Leonardo was a brave man!

He was also an inventor. Leonardo invented a parachute and designed a type of helicopter—5 centuries before airplanes were invented! Another of da Vinci's major talents was painting. You have probably seen a print, or copy, of one of his most famous paintings. It is called *The Last Supper*, and shows Jesus eating his final meal with his disciples. It took da Vinci 3 years to paint *The Last Supper*. The man who hired da Vinci to do the painting was upset. He went to da Vinci to ask why it was taking so long. The problem, said da Vinci, was that in the painting, Jesus has just told the disciples that one of them would betray him. He wanted to get their expressions exactly right as each cried out, "Lord, am I the one?"

Another famous painting by da Vinci is called the *Mona Lisa*. Have you seen a print of this painting? Maybe you have been lucky enough to see the original hanging in a Paris art museum called the Louvre (Loov). If so, you know that Mona Lisa has a wistful expression on her face. The painting is a real woman, the wife of an Italian merchant. Art historians believe she looks wistful because one of her children had recently died.

Directions: Answer these questions about Leonardo da Vinci.

1. How old was da Vinci when he died? _____

2. Name two of da Vinci's inventions. _____

3. Name two famous paintings by da Vinci. _____

4. In which Paris museum does *Mona Lisa* hang? ☐ Lourre ☐ Loure ☐ Louvre

Name: _____

Context Clues: Leonardo da Vinci

Directions: Read the sentences below. Use context clues to figure out the meaning of the bold words.

1. Some people are **perplexed** when they look at *The Last Supper*, but others understand it immediately.

   ☐ unhappy   ☐ happy   ☐ puzzled

2. Because his model felt **melancholy** about the death of her child, da Vinci had music played to lift her spirits as he painted the *Mona Lisa*.

   ☐ sad   ☐ unfriendly   ☐ hostile

3. Because da Vinci's work is so famous, many people **erroneously** assume that he left behind many paintings. In fact, he left only 20.

   ☐ rightly   ☐ correctly   ☐ wrongly

4. Leonardo da Vinci was not like most other people. He didn't care what others thought of him—he led an interesting and **unconventional** life.

   ☐ dull   ☐ not ordinary   ☐ ordinary

5. The **composition** of *The Last Supper* is superb. All the parts of the painting seem to fit together beautifully.

   ☐ the picture frame   ☐ parts of the picture

6. Leonardo's **genius** set him apart from people with ordinary minds. He never married, he had few friends and he spent much of his time alone.

   ☐ great mental abilities   ☐ great physical abilities

   ☐ improper way to do things   ☐ proper way to do things

7. Because he was a loner, da Vinci worried no one would come to his funeral when he died. In his will, he set aside 70 cents each to hire 60 **mourners** to accompany his body to his grave.

   ☐ friends   ☐ people who grieve   ☐ people who smile

Comprehension: Michelangelo

Another famous painter of the late 14th and early 15th centuries was Michelangelo Buonarroti. Michelangelo, who lived from 1475 to 1564, was also an Italian. Like da Vinci, his genius was apparent at a young age. When he was 13, the ruler of his hometown of Florence, Lorenzo Medici (Muh-dee-chee), befriended Michelangelo and asked him to live in the palace. There Michelangelo studied sculpture and met many artists.

By the time he was 18, Michelangelo was a respected sculptor. He created one of his most famous religious sculptures, the *Pieta* (pee-ay-tah), when he was only 21. Then the Medici family abruptly fell from power and Michelangelo had to leave Florence.

Still, his work was well known and he was able to make a living. In 1503, Pope Julius II called Michelangelo to Rome. He wanted Michelangelo to paint the tomb where he would someday be buried. Michelangelo preferred sculpting to painting, but no one turned down the pope! Before Michelangelo finished his painting, however, the pope ordered Michelangelo to begin painting the ceiling of the Sistine Chapel inside the Vatican. (The Vatican is the palace and surrounding area where the pope lives in Rome.)

Michelangelo was very angry! He did not like to paint. He wanted to create sculptures. But no one turns down the pope. After much complaining, Michelangelo began work on what would be his most famous project.

Directions: Answer these questions about Michelangelo.

1. How old was Michelangelo when he died? _____

2. What was the first project Pope Julius II asked Michelangelo to paint?

_____

3. What is the Vatican? _____

4. What was the second project the pope asked Michelangelo to do?

☐ paint his tomb's ceiling   ☐ paint the Sistine Chapel's ceiling

Comprehension: Rembrandt

Most art critics agree that Rembrandt (Rem-brant) was one of the greatest painters of all time. This Dutch artist, who lived from 1606 to 1669, painted some of the world's finest portraits.

Rembrandt, whose full name was Rembrandt van Rijn, was born in Holland to a wealthy family. He was sent to a fine university, but he did not like his studies. He only wanted to paint. He sketched the faces of people around him. During his lifetime, Rembrandt painted 11 portraits of his father and nearly as many of his mother. From the beginning, the faces of old people fascinated him.

When he was 25, Rembrandt went to paint in Amsterdam, a large city in Holland where he lived for the rest of his life. There he married a wealthy woman named Saskia, whom he loved deeply. She died from a disease called tuberculosis (ta-bur-ku-lo-sis) after only 8 years, leaving behind a young son named Titus (Ty-tuss).

Rembrandt was heartbroken over his wife's death. He began to spend all his time painting. But instead of painting what his customers wanted, he painted exactly the way he wanted. Unsold pictures filled his house. They were wonderful paintings, but they were not the type of portraits people wanted. Rembrandt could not pay his debts. He and his son were thrown into the streets. The creditors took his home, his possessions and his paintings. One of the finest painters on Earth was treated like a criminal.

Directions: Answer these questions about Rembrandt.

1. How old was Rembrandt when he died? _____

2. In what city did he spend most of his life? _____

3. How many children did Rembrandt have? _____

4. Rembrandt's wife was named

☐ Sasha. ☐ Saskia. ☐ Saksia.

5. These filled his house after his wife's death.

☐ friends ☐ customers ☐ unsold paintings

Name: _____

Review

Directions: Follow the instructions below.

1. Write a one-sentence main idea for the selection "Leonardo da Vinci" (page 106).

   _____

   _____

2. Write a summary of the selection "Leonardo da Vinci" (page 106).

   _____

   _____

   _____

3. Complete the sequence of events from the selection "Michelangelo" (page 108).

   1) Michelangelo was born in 1475 in Italy.

   2) _____

   3) _____

   4) _____

   5) _____

   6) _____

   7) _____

4. Define the following words from this section.

   crude: _____

   dissect: _____

   disciples: _____

   merchant: _____

   wistful: _____

Using Prior Knowledge: Big Cats

Directions: Before reading about big cats in the following section, answer these questions.

1. Name at least four big wild cats.

   _____   _____

   _____   _____

2. Compare and contrast a house cat with a wild cat.

   _____

   _____

   _____

   _____

3. What impact might the expansion of human population and housing have on big cats?

   _____

   _____

   _____

4. Do you have a cat? What are the special qualities of this pet? Write about your cat's name and its personality traits. If you don't have a cat, write about a cat you would like to have.

   _____

   _____

   _____

   _____

Comprehension: Jaguars

The jaguar is a large cat, standing up to 2 feet tall at the shoulder. Its body can reach 73 inches long, and the tail can be another 30 inches long. The jaguar is characterized by its yellowish-red coat covered with black spots. The spots themselves are made up of a central spot surrounded by a circle of spots.

Jaguars are not known to attack humans, but some ranchers claim that jaguars attack their cattle. This claim has given jaguars a bad reputation.

The jaguar can be found in southern North America, but is most populous in Central and South America. Jaguars are capable climbers and swimmers, and they eat a wide range of animals.

Female jaguars have between one and four cubs after a gestation of 93 to 105 days. Cubs stay with the mother for 2 years. Jaguars are known to have a life expectancy of at least 22 years.

Directions: Use context clues for these definitions.

1. populous: _most popular_

2. reputation: _How you are known_

3. gestation: _the amount of time it stays in the mother's tummy._

Directions: Answer these questions about jaguars.

4. Describe the spots on a jaguar's coat.

_____

_____

5. Why would it be to a jaguar's advantage to have spots on its coat?

_____

_____

Name: _____

Comprehension: Leopards

The leopard is a talented nocturnal hunter and can see very well in the dark. Because of its excellent climbing ability, the leopard is able to stalk and kill monkeys and baboons. Leopards are also known to consume mice, porcupines and fruit.

Although the true leopard is characterized by a light beige coat with black spots, some leopards can be entirely black. These leopards are called black panthers. Many people refer to other cat species as leopards. Cheetahs are sometimes referred to as hunting leopards. The clouded leopard lives in southeastern Asia and has a grayish spotted coat. The snow leopard, which has a white coat, lives in Central Asia. A leopard's spots help to camouflage (cam-o-floj) it as it hunts.

True leopards can grow to over 6 feet long, not including their 3-foot-long tail. Leopards can be found in Africa and Asia.

Directions: Use context clues for these definitions.

1. consume: _____

2. ability: _____

3. nocturnal: _____

Directions: Answer these questions about leopards.

4. List three differences between the leopard and the jaguar.

_____

_____

_____

_____

_____

_____

5. What makes a leopard able to hunt monkeys and baboons?

_____

Grade 5 - Comprehensive Curriculum

Comprehension: Lynxes

Lynxes are strange-looking cats with very long legs and large paws. Their bodies are a mere 51 inches in length, and they have short little tails. Most lynxes have a clump of hair that extends past the tip of their ears.

Lynxes not only are known to chase down their prey, but also to leap on them from a perch above the ground. They eat small mammals and birds, as well as an occasional deer.

There are four types of lynxes. Bobcats can be found in all areas of the United States except the Midwest. The Spanish lynx is an endangered species. The Eurasian lynx, also known as the northern lynx, and the Canadian lynx are two other kinds of lynxes.

Directions: Use context clues for these definitions.

1. prey: _____

2. perch: _____

Directions: Answer these questions about lynxes.

3. What are the four types of lynxes? _____

_____

4. Use the following words in a sentence of your own.

mammal _____

endangered _____

5. Do you believe it is important to classify animals as "endangered" to protect a species that is low in population? Explain your answer.

_____

_____

_____

Name: _____

Comprehension: Pumas

The puma is a cat most recognized by the more popular names of "cougar" or "mountain lion." Just like other large cats, the puma is a carnivore. It feeds on deer, elk and other mammals. It can be found in both North and South America.

Pumas have small heads with a single black spot above each eye. The coat color ranges from bluish-gray (North America) to reddish-brown (South America). The underside of the body, as well as the throat and muzzle, are white. The puma's body can be almost 6 feet long, not including the tail.

Female pumas give birth to two to four young. When first born, pumas have brown spots on their backs, and their tails are lined with dark brown rings.

As with the jaguar, pumas are blamed for killing cattle. Because of this, pumas are either nonexistent in some areas or are endangered.

Directions: Answer these questions about pumas.

1. What is a muzzle? _____

2. As the population increases in North America, predict what might happen to pumas.

   _____

   _____

   _____

3. What are two other popular names for the puma? _____

4. What other cat besides the puma is blamed for killing cattle? _____

5. Reviewing the sizes of cats discussed so far, write their names in order, from smallest to largest.

   1)_____   2)_____

   3)_____   4)_____

Comprehension: Tigers

Tigers live on the continent of Asia. The tiger is the largest cat, often weighing over 500 pounds. Its body can grow to be 9 feet long and the tail up to 36 inches in length.

There are three types of tigers. The Siberian tiger is very rare and has a yellow coat with dark stripes. The Bengal tiger can be found in southeastern Asia and central India. Its coat is more orange and its stripes are darker. There is a tiger that lives on the island of Sumatra as well. It is smaller and darker in color than the Bengal tiger.

Tigers lead solitary lives. They meet with other tigers only to mate and share food or water. Tigers feed primarily on deer and cattle but are also known to eat fish and frogs. If necessary, tigers will also eat dead animals.

Female tigers bear one to six cubs at a time. The cubs stay with their mother for almost 2 years before going out on their own.

Because tiger parts are in high demand for use in Chinese medicine and recipes, tigers have been hunted almost to extinction. All tigers are currently listed as endangered.

Directions: Use context clues for these definitions.

1. rare:_____

2. solitary:_____

3. extinction:_____

Directions: Answer these questions about tigers.

4. Why have tigers been hunted almost to extinction?

_____

_____

5. Name the three types of tigers.

_____

Comprehension: Lions

The lion, often referred to as the king of beasts, once commanded a large territory. Today, their territory is very limited. Lions are savanna-dwelling animals, which has made them easy targets for hunters. The increasing population of humans and their livestock has also contributed to the lion's decreased population.

Lions are heavy cats. Males weigh over 500 pounds and can grow to be over 8 feet in length, with a tail over 36 inches long. Males are characterized by a long, full mane that covers the neck and most of the head and shoulders. Females do not have a mane and are slightly smaller in size. Both males and females have beige coats, hooked claws and powerful jaws. Their roars can be heard up to 5 miles away!

Lions tend to hunt in the evening and spend the day sleeping. They prefer hunting zebra or giraffe but will eat almost anything. A lion is capable of eating over 75 pounds of meat at a single kill and then going a week without eating again. Generally, female lions do the hunting, and the males come to share the kill.

Lions live in groups called prides. Each pride has between 4 and 37 lions. Females bear one to four cubs approximately every 2 years.

Directions: Answer these questions about lions.

1. What are the differences between male and female lions? _____

_____

2. Why would living on a savanna make the lion an "easy target"? _____

_____

Directions: Use context clues for these definitions.

3. pride: _____

4. territory: _____

5. savanna: _____

6. capable: _____

Review

Directions: Follow the instructions below.

1. Choose any two big cats from this section and compare them.

_____

_____

_____

_____

2. Why are each of these big cats endangered or decreasing in number?

_____

_____

_____

3. What can be done to get these big cats off the endangered list?

_____

_____

_____

4. Now that you have read about big cats, compare and contrast them with a house cat. What do you know now that you didn't know before reading this section?

_____

_____

_____

_____

_____

Name: _____

Using Prior Knowledge: Farm Animals

Directions: Before reading about farm animals in the following section, answer these questions.

1. List at least nine types of farm animals by mother and baby names.

   Example: sow—piglet.

   _____   _____   _____

   _____   _____   _____

   _____   _____   _____

2. If you owned a large ranch, what type of livestock would you enjoy keeping? Why?

   _____

   _____

3. Some animals routinely give birth to twins, triplets or larger litters. Which animals give birth to more than one baby at a time?

   _____

   _____

4. Would you enjoy living on a farm? Why or why not?

   _____

   _____

   _____

5. What is the importance of raising livestock today?

   _____

   _____

   _____

Comprehension: All About Sheep

Did you ever wonder what really happened to the tails of Little Bo-Peep's sheep? Here's the real story.

When sheep are born, they are called lambs. Lambs are born with long tails. A few days after lambs are born, the shepherd cuts off their tails. Because they get dirty, the lambs' long tails can pick up lots of germs. Cutting them off helps to prevent disease. The procedure is called "docking." This is probably what happened to Bo-Peep's sheep! Another shepherd must have cut their tails off without telling her.

Little lambs are cute. A lamb grows inside its mother for 150 days before it is born. This is called the "gestation period." Some types of sheep, such as hill sheep, give birth to one lamb at a time. Other types of sheep, such as lowland sheep, give birth to two or three lambs at a time.

After it is born, it takes a lamb 3 or 4 days to recognize its mother. Once it does, it stays close to her until it is about 3 weeks old. After that, the lamb becomes friendly toward other lambs.

Young lambs then form play groups. They chase each other in circles. They butt into each other. Like children, they pretend to fight. When play gets too rough, the lambs run back to their mothers for protection.

Lambs follow their mothers as they graze on grass. Usually, sheep move in single file behind an older female sheep. Female sheep are called ewes. The ewes teach their lambs how to keep themselves clean. This is called "grooming." Sheep groom only their faces. Here is how they do it: They lick one of their front legs, then they rub their faces against the spot they have licked.

Directions: Follow the instructions below.

1. Define the word **docking**. _____

2. Name a type of sheep that gives birth to one lamb at a time. _____

3. Name a type of sheep that gives birth to two or three lambs at a time.

_____

4. Female sheep are called

☐ grazers. ☐ ewes. ☐ dockers.

5. Lambs begin playing in groups when they are

☐ 2 weeks old. ☐ 3 weeks old. ☐ 4 weeks old.

Name: _____

Comprehension: Pigs Are Particular

Have you ever wondered why pigs wallow in the mud? It's not because they are dirty animals. Pigs have no sweat glands. They can't sweat, so they roll in the mud to cool themselves. The next time you hear anyone who's hot say, "I'm sweating like a pig!" be sure to correct him/her. Humans can sweat but pigs cannot.

Actually, pigs are particular about their pens. They are very clean animals. They prefer to sleep in clean, dry places. They move their bowels and empty their bladders in another area. They do not want to get their homes dirty.

Another misconception about pigs is that they are smooth. Only cartoon pigs are pink, smooth and shiny-looking. The skin of real pigs is covered with bristles—small, stiff hairs. Their bristles protect their tender skin. When pigs are slaughtered, their bristles are sometimes made into hair brushes or clothes brushes.

Female pigs are called sows. Sows have babies twice a year and give birth to 10 to 14 piglets at a time. The babies have a "gestation period" of 16 weeks before they are born.

All the piglets together are called a "litter." Newborn piglets are on their tiny feet within a few minutes after birth. Can you guess why? They are hungrily looking for their mother's teats so they can get milk. As they nurse, piglets snuggle in close to their mother's belly to keep warm.

Directions: Answer these questions about pigs.

1. Why do pigs wallow in mud? _____

2. How long is the gestation period for pigs? _____

3. What are pig bristles used for? _____

4. Tell two reasons pigs are on their feet soon after they are born.

1) _____ 2) _____

5. A female pig is called a

☐ bristle.   ☐ piglet.   ☐ sow.

6. Together, the newborn piglets are called a

☐ group.   ☐ family.   ☐ litter.

Context Clues: No Kidding About Goats

Goats are independent creatures. Unlike sheep, which move easily in herds, goats cannot be driven along by a goatherd. They must be moved one or two at a time. Moving a big herd of goats can take a long time, so goatherds must be patient people.

Both male and female goats can have horns, but some goats don't have them at all. Male goats have longer and bushier beards than females. Males goats also have thicker and shaggier coats than females. During breeding season, when goats mate to produce babies, male goats have a very strong smell.

Goats are kept in paddocks with high fences. The fences are high because goats are good jumpers. They like to nibble on hedges and on the tips of young trees. They can cause a lot of damage this way! That is why many farmers keep their goats in a paddock.

Baby goats are called "kids," and two or three at a time are born to the mother goat. Farmers usually begin to bottle-feed kids when they are a few days old. They milk the mother goat and keep the milk. Goat's milk is much easier to digest than cow's milk, and many people think it tastes delicious.

Directions: Answer these questions about goats.

1. Use context clues to choose the correct definition of **goatherd**.

   ☐ person who herds goats ☐ goats in a herd ☐ person who has heard of goats

2. Use context clues to choose the correct definition of **paddock**.

   ☐ pad   ☐ fence   ☐ pen

3. Use context clues to choose the correct definition of **nibble**.

   ☐ take small bites   ☐ take small drinks   ☐ take little sniffs

4. Use context clues to choose the correct definition of **delicious**.

   ☐ delicate   ☐ tasty   ☐ terrible

Name: _____

Comprehension: Cows Are Complicated

If you believe cows have four stomachs, you're right! It sounds incredible, but it's true.

Here are the "hows" and "whys" of a cow's digestive system. First, it's important to know that cows do not have front teeth. They eat grass by wrapping their tongues around it and pulling it from the ground. They do have back teeth, but still they cannot properly chew the grass.

Cows swallow grass without chewing it. When it's swallowed, the grass goes into the cow's first stomach, called a "rumen" (roo-mun). There it is broken up by the digestive juices and forms into a ball of grass. This ball is called a "cud." The cow is able to bring the cud back up into its mouth. Then the cow chews the cud into a pulp with its back teeth and re-swallows it.

After it is swallowed the second time, the cud goes into the cow's second stomach. This second stomach is called the "reticulum" (re-tick-u-lum). The reticulum filters the food to sort out any small stones or other non-food matter. Then it passes the food onto the cow's third stomach. The third stomach is called the "omasum" (oh-mass-um).

From there, any food that is still undigested is sent back to the first stomach so the cow can bring it back up into her mouth and chew it some more. The rest goes into the cow's fourth stomach. The fourth stomach is called the "abomasum" (ab-oh-ma-sum). Digesting food that can be turned into milk is a full-time job for cows!

Directions: Answer these questions about cows.

1. List in order the names of a cow's four stomachs.

   1) _____   2) _____   3) _____   4) _____

2. What is the name of the ball of grass a cow chews on? _____

3. A cow has no

   ☐ front teeth.   ☐ back teeth.   ☐ fourth stomach.

4. Which stomach acts as a filter for digestion?

   ☐ reticulum   ☐ rumen   ☐ abomasum

Context Clues: Dairy Cows

Some cows are raised for their beef. Other cows, called dairy cows, are raised for their milk. A dairy cow cannot produce any milk until after its first calf is born. Cows are not mature enough to give birth until they are 2 years old. A cow's gestation period is 40 weeks long, and she usually gives birth to one calf. Then she produces a lot of milk to feed it. When the calf is 2 days old, the dairy farmer takes the calf away from its mother. After that, the cow is milked twice a day.

The dairy cow's milk comes from the large, smooth udder beneath her body. The udder has four openings called "teats." To milk the cow, the farmer grasps a teat and squeezes it with his thumb and forefinger. Then he gently but firmly pulls his hand down the teat to squeeze the milk out. Milking machines that are hooked to the cow's teats duplicate this action and can milk many cows quickly.

A dairy cow's milk production is not at the same level all the time. When the cow is pregnant, milk production gradually decreases. For 2 months before her calf is born, a cow is said to be "dry" and is not milked. This happens because, like humans, much of the cow's food is actually being used to nourish the unborn calf.

Farmers give the cow extra food at this time to make sure the mother and unborn calf are well-nourished. Again, like humans, well-nourished mother cows are more likely to produce healthy babies.

Directions: Answer these questions about dairy cows.

1. Use context clues to choose the correct definition of **grasp**.

   ☐ pull firmly   ☐ hold firmly   ☐ hold gently

2. Use context clues to choose the correct definition of **duplicate**.

   ☐ correct   ☐ make   ☐ copy

3. Use context clues to choose the correct definition of **decrease**.

   ☐ become more   ☐ become less   ☐ become quicker

4. Use context clues to choose the correct definition of **nourish**.

   ☐ to be happy   ☐ to be friendly   ☐ to feed

Comprehension: Chickens

Have you ever heard the expression "pecking order"? In the pecking order of a school, the principal is at the top of the order. Next comes the assistant principal, then the teachers and students.

In the pecking order of chickens, the most aggressive chicken is the leader. The leader is the hen that uses her beak most often to peck the chickens she bosses. These chickens, in turn, boss other chickens by pecking them, and so on. Chickens can peck all others who are "below" them in the pecking order. They never peck "above" themselves by pecking their bosses.

Answer these questions about chickens.

1. Put this pecking order of four chickens in order.

   _____ This chicken pecks numbers 3 and 4 but never 1.

   _____ No one pecks this chicken. She's the top boss.

   _____ This chicken can't peck anyone.

   _____ This chicken pecks chicken number 4.

2. Use context clues to figure out the definition of **aggressive**. _____

   _____

   _____

3. Who is at the top of the pecking order in a school? _____

   _____

Review

Directions: Follow the instructions for each section.

1. Write a summary of the selection "All About Sheep" (page 120).

   _____

   _____

   _____

2. What is the purpose of a pig's bristles?

   _____

   _____

   _____

3. Write a summary of the selection "No Kidding About Goats" (page 122).

   _____

   _____

   _____

4. What is the purpose of a cow's four stomachs?

   _____

   _____

   _____

5. How do chickens establish leaders and followers?

   _____

   _____

   _____

6. What is a "cud"?

   _____

   _____

Using Prior Knowledge: Stamp Collecting

Directions: Before reading about stamp collecting in the following section, answer these questions.

1. Why do you think people collect stamps?

_____

_____

_____

2. What hobby do you most enjoy? Why?

_____

_____

_____

3. Name at least six famous people who have been pictured on a stamp.

_____   _____

_____   _____

_____   _____

4. Why do you think the postal service issues many different stamps each year? Why not just issue one stamp?

_____

_____

_____

5. The postal service recently introduced self-stick stamps. What are the benefits of these stamps? Do you think these create any drawbacks for collectors?

_____

_____

_____

Fact or Opinion?

Directions: Read the paragraphs below. Then, in the corresponding numbered blanks, write whether each numbered sentence is a fact or an opinion.

(1) An important rule for stamp collectors to follow is never to handle stamps with their fingers. (2) Instead, to keep the stamps clean, collectors use stamp tongs to pick up stamps. (3) Stamps are stored by being placed on mounts. (4) Stamp mounts are plastic holders that fit around the stamp and keep it clean. (5) The backs of the mounts are sticky, so they can be stuck onto a stamp album page. (6) What a great idea!

(7) The stamps are mounted in stamp albums that have either white or black pages. (8) Some people prefer black pages, claiming that the stamps "show" better. (9) Some people prefer white pages, claiming that they give the album a cleaner look. (10) I think this foolish bickering over page colors is ridiculous!

1. _____

2. _____

3. _____

4. _____

5. _____

6. _____

7. _____

8. _____

9. _____

10. _____

Comprehension: More Stamp Collecting

Many people collect stamps in blocks of four. Each stamp in the block is stuck to the other stamps along the edges. Collectors do not tear the stamps apart from one another. They buy blocks of stamps bearing new designs directly from the post office. Then they mount the blocks of stamps and place them in their albums.

Collectors also get their stamps off of envelopes. This is a bit tricky, because the stamps are glued on. Usually, collectors soak the stamps in warm water to loosen the glue. Then they gently pull the stamps from the paper and let them dry before mounting them.

Some beginners start their collections by buying a packet of mixed stamps. The packets, or bags, contain a variety of different stamps. Beginners buy these packets from companies that supply stamps to philatelists (fuh-lay-tell-lists). Philately (fuh-lay-tell-lee) is the collection and study of postage stamps. Philatelists are the people who collect and study them.

Packets of stamps usually contain stamps from many different countries. Often, they contain duplicates of some of the stamps. Suppliers usually don't sort the stamps that go into the packets for beginners. They leave that for beginning philatelists to enjoy!

Directions: Answer these questions about stamp collecting.

1. Name three places some people get stamps. _____

_____

2. What is the word that describes the collection and study of stamps? _____

3. What are people called who collect and study stamps? _____

4. The bag that a mixture of stamps comes in is called a

☐ postal bag.   ☐ packet.   ☐ philatelist.

5. Do stamp mixtures usually include only U.S. stamps?

☐ Yes   ☐ No

Recalling Details: Philately Abbreviations

Like other hobbies, philately has its own jargon and symbols. Collectors and dealers know what they mean, but "outsiders" would be puzzled if they saw the following abbreviations without their definitions. Read them carefully, then refer to them when answering the questions below.

Avg. — average condition

blk. — block of four stamps

C — cancelled (used) stamp

OG — original gum

(glue on back of stamp)

G — good condition

M — mint (excellent and unused) condition

s — single stamp

U — used stamp

VF — very fine condition

Wmk — watermark (can occur when water is used to remove stamp from envelope)

Directions: Answer these questions about the abbreviations used by stamp dealers and collectors.

1. If a philatelist wrote the following description, what would he/she mean?

   I have a blk. in VF. _____

   _____

2. What does this mean? **s with OG, condition M** _____

   _____

3. What other abbreviation would most likely be used do describe a used (U) stamp?

   _____

4. What does this mean? **s in Avg. with Wmk** _____

   _____

5. Which is more valuable, a rare stamp in **M** or **VF** condition? _____

6. Would you rather own a single U stamp or a blk. in M? _____

Comprehension: Faces on Stamps

If anyone ever tries to sell you a stamp with a picture of former Vice President Dan Quayle on it, just say no! In the United States, only people who have died can have their pictures on stamps. That is why the singer Elvis Presley's face appeared on stamps only after he died.

Many U.S. presidents' faces have been on postage stamps, as have pictures of the faces of other important people in U.S. history. Some people's faces have been on many different stamps. Through the years, George Washington and Benjamin Franklin have been on dozens of different types of stamps!

Other people whose pictures have been on stamps include John Quincy Adams, the sixth president of the United States; Jane Addams, a U.S. social worker and writer; Louisa May Alcott, author of *Little Women* and many other books; Clara Barton, nurse and founder of the American Red Cross; Alexander Graham Bell, inventor of the telephone; and poet, Emily Dickinson. These are only a few of the hundreds of famous Americans whose faces have appeared on U.S. postage stamps.

Directions: Answer these questions about some of the people whose faces have appeared on U.S. stamps.

1. Name six occupations of people whose faces have appeared on postage stamps.

   President, social worker, author, nurse, inventor, poet.

   _____

2. What two people's pictures have appeared on more stamps than on any others?

   George Washington and Benjamin Franklin.

3. Why can't Dan Quayle's face appear on a postage stamp? _No, because only_

   people who have died can.

4. Which person featured on a postage stamp was a social worker?

   ☐ Clara Barton   ☐ Louisa May Alcott   ☑ Jane Addams

5. Which person featured on a postage stamp was an inventor?

   ☐ Emily Dickinson   ☑ Alexander Graham Bell   ☐ John Quincy Adams

Comprehension: Valuable Stamps

Most people collect stamps as a hobby. They spend small sums of money to get the stamps they want, or they trade stamps with other collectors. They rarely make what could be considered "big money" from their philately hobby.

A few collectors are in the business of philately as opposed to the hobby. To the people who can afford it, some stamps are worth big money. For example, a U.S. airmail stamp with a face value of 24 cents when it was issued in 1918 is now worth more than $35,000 if a certain design appears on the stamp. Another stamp, the British Guiana, an ugly stamp that cost only a penny when it was issued, later sold for $280,000!

The Graf Zeppelin is another example of an ugly stamp that became valuable. Graf Zeppelin is the name of a type of airship, similar to what we now call a "blimp," invented around the turn of the century. Stamps were issued to mark the first roundtrip flight the *Zeppelin* made between two continents. A set of three of these stamps cost $4.55 when they were issued. The stamps were ugly and few of them sold. The postal service destroyed the rest. Now, because they are rare, each set of the Graf Zeppelin stamps is worth hundreds of dollars.

Directions: Answer these questions about valuable stamps.

1. What is the most valuable stamp described? _____

2. For how much did this stamp originally sell? _____

3. What did a collector later pay for it? _____

4. The Graf Zeppelin stamps originally sold for $4.55 for a set of

   ☐ four.   ☐ six.   ☐ three.

5. Which stamp did the postal service destroy because it didn't sell?

   ☐ British Guiana   ☐ Graf Zeppelin   ☐ British Zeppelin

Name: _____

Fact or Opinion?

Directions: Read the paragraphs below. Then, in the corresponding numbered blanks, write whether each numbered sentence is a fact or an opinion.

(1) Nearly every valuable stamp on Earth has been counterfeited (coun-ter-fit-tid) at one time or another. (2) A "counterfeit" is a fake that looks nearly identical to the original. (3) It takes a lot of nerve to try to pass off counterfeits as the real thing. (4) Counterfeiting is big business, especially with stamps from overseas. (5) Because a collector often has no original for comparison, he/she can be easily fooled by a good counterfeit!

(6) One way people can make sure a stamp is real is to have it checked by a company that authenticates (aw-then-ti-kates) stamps. (7) To "authenticate" means to prove the stamp is real. (8) Of course, there is a fee for this service. (9) But I think paying a reasonable fee is worth what collectors get in return. (10) Those counterfeiters should be locked up forever!

1. _____

2. _____

3. _____

4. _____

5. _____

6. _____

7. _____

8. _____

9. _____

10. _____

Comprehension: Stamp Value

It's nearly impossible to predict which stamps will rise in value. Why? Because the value is based on the law of supply and demand. How much does someone or a group of "someones" want for a particular stamp? If many people want a stamp, the value will increase, especially if few of the stamps exist.

However, collectors are also always on the lookout for things that can lower the value of a stamp. Are the stamp's perforations (per-four-ay-shuns) torn along the edges? (Perforations are ragged edges where stamps tear apart.) Is there a watermark on the stamp? Has the gum worn off the back? All these things can make a stamp less valuable.

Directions: Answer these questions about determining the value of stamps.

1. Name three things that can lower the value of a stamp.

_____

_____

2. Collecting stamps is a fascinating hobby.   Fact   Opinion

3. What is one thing the value of stamps is based upon? _____

4. What will happen if many people want a rare stamp?_____

_____

5. Explain how to spot a stamp that will become valuable. _____

_____

_____

_____

Name: _____

Review

Directions: Follow the instructions below.

1. Define the following words from this section.

mount: _____

bickering: _____

philately: _____

counterfeit: _____

authenticate: _____

perforations: _____

2. Choose two of the words above and use each in a sentence.

1)_____

2)_____

3. Write a one-sentence main idea for the selection "Stamp Value" (page 134).

_____

_____

4. Write a summary of the selection "Faces on Stamps" (page 131).

_____

_____

_____

5. Write a summary of the selection "More Stamp Collecting" (page 129).

_____

_____

_____

Using Prior Knowledge: Cooking

Before reading about cooking in the following section, answer these questions.

1. What is your favorite recipe? Why?

   _____

   _____

   _____

2. What do you most like to cook? Why?

   _____

   _____

   _____

3. Have you tried food from cultures other than your own? If so, which type of food do you like most? Why?

   _____

   _____

   _____

4. Why is it important to follow the correct sequence when preparing a recipe?

   _____

   _____

   _____

5. What safety precautions must be followed when working in a kitchen?

   _____

   _____

   _____

Following Directions: Chunky Tomato and Green Onion Sauce

Following directions means to do what the directions say to do, step by step, in the correct order.

Directions: Read the recipe for chunky tomato and green onion sauce. Answer the questions below.

Ingredients:

- 2 tablespoons corn oil

- 2 cloves of garlic, finely chopped

- $1\frac{1}{2}$ pounds plum tomatoes, cored, peeled, seeded, then coarsely chopped

- 3 green onions, cut in half lengthwise, then thinly sliced

- salt

- freshly ground pepper

Heat oil in a heavy skillet over medium heat. Add garlic and cook until yellow, about 1 minute. Stir in tomatoes. Season with salt and pepper. Cook until thickened, about 10 minutes. Stir in green onions and serve.

1. What is the last thing the cook does to prepare the tomatoes before cooking them?

_____

2. What kind of oil does the cook heat in the heavy skillet? _____

3. How long should the garlic be cooked? _____

4. What does the cook do to the tomatoes right before removing the seeds?

_____

5. Is the sauce served hot or cold? _____

Comprehension: Cooking With Care

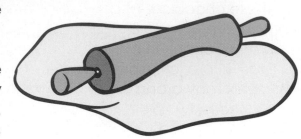

People are so busy these days that many have no time to cook. This creates a problem, because most families love home cooking! The food tastes good and warm, and a family meal brings everyone together. In some families, meals are often the only times everyone sees one another at the same time.

Another reason people enjoy home cooking is that it is often a way of showing love. A parent who bakes a batch of chocolate chip cookies isn't just satisfying a child's sweet tooth. He/she is sending a message. The message says, "I care about you enough to spend an hour making cookies that you will eat up in 15 minutes if I let you!"

There's also something about the smell of good cooking that appeals to people of all ages. It makes most of us feel secure and loved—even if we are the ones doing the cooking! Next time you smell a cake baking, stop for a moment and pay attention to your mood. Chances are, the good smell is making you feel happy.

Real estate agents know that good cooking smells are important. They sometimes advise people whose homes are for sale to bake cookies or bread if prospective buyers are coming to see the house. The good smells make the place "feel like home." These pleasant smells help convince potential buyers that the house would make a good home for their family, too!

Directions: Answer these questions about good cooking.

1. Why do fewer people cook nowadays? _____

2. Why are family meals important? _____

3. What do homemade cookies do besides satisfy a child's sweet tooth?

_____

4. Real estate agents often advise home sellers holding open houses to

   ☐ clean the garage.   ☐ bake cookies or bread.

5. The smell of baking at open houses may encourage buyers to

   ☐ bake cookies.   ☐ buy the house.   ☐ bake bread.

Sequencing: Chocolate Chunk Cookies

These chocolate chunk cookies require only five ingredients. Before you combine them, preheat the oven to 350 degrees. Preheating the oven to the correct temperature is always step number one in baking.

Now, into a large mixing bowl, empty an $18\frac{1}{4}$-ounce package of chocolate fudge cake mix (any brand). Add a 10-ounce package of semi-sweet chocolate, broken into small pieces, two $5\frac{1}{8}$-ounce packages of chocolate fudge pudding mix (any brand) and $1\frac{1}{2}$ cups chopped walnuts.

Use a large wooden spoon to combine the ingredients. When they are well-mixed, add $1\frac{1}{2}$ cups mayonnaise and stir thoroughly. Shape the dough into small balls and place the balls 2 inches apart on an ungreased cookie sheet. Bake 12 minutes. Cool and eat!

Directions: Number in correct order the steps for making chocolate chunk cookies.

_____ Place $1\frac{1}{2}$ cups of mayonnaise in the bowl.

_____ Shape dough into small balls and place them on a cookie sheet.

_____ Empty the package of chocolate fudge cake mix into the bowl.

_____ Bake the dough for 12 minutes.

_____ Place two $5\frac{1}{8}$-ounce packages of chocolate fudge pudding in the bowl.

_____ Put $1\frac{1}{2}$ cups chopped walnuts in the bowl.

_____ Preheat the oven to 350 degrees.

_____ Place the 10-ounce package of semi-sweet chocolate pieces in the bowl.

_____ Stir everything thoroughly.

Comprehension: Eating High-Fiber Foods

Have you heard your parents or other adults talk about "high-fiber" diets? Foods that are high in fiber, like oats and other grains, are believed to be very healthy. Here's why: The fiber adds bulk to the food the body digests and helps keep the large intestines working properly. Corn, apples, celery, nuts and other chewy foods also contain fiber that helps keep the body's systems for digesting and eliminating food working properly.

Researchers at the University of Minnesota have found another good reason to eat high-fiber food, especially at breakfast. Because fiber is bulky, it absorbs a lot of liquid in the stomach. As it absorbs the liquid, it swells. This "fools" the stomach into thinking it's full. As a result, when lunchtime comes, those who have eaten a high-fiber breakfast are not as hungry. They eat less food at lunch. Without much effort on their parts, dieters eating a high-fiber breakfast can lose weight.

The university researchers say a person could lose 10 pounds in a year just by eating a high-fiber breakfast! This is good news to people who are only slightly overweight and want an easy method for losing that extra 10 pounds.

Directions: Answer these questions about eating high-fiber foods.

1. Why is fiber healthy? _____

_____

2. How does fiber "fool" the stomach? _____

_____

3. How does "fooling" the stomach help people lose weight? _____

_____

4. How many pounds could a dieter eating a high-fiber breakfast lose in a year?

☐ 20 pounds   ☐ 30 pounds   ☐ 10 pounds

5. The university that did the research is in which state?

☐ Michigan   ☐ Minnesota   ☐ Montana

Main Idea: New Corn

I will clothe myself in spring clothing

And visit the slopes of the eastern hill.

By the mountain stream, a mist hovers,

Hovers a moment and then scatters.

Then comes a wind blowing from the south

That brushes the fields of new corn.

Directions: Answer these questions about this ancient poem, which is translated from Chinese.

1. Circle the main idea:

   The poet will dress comfortably and go to where the corn grows so he/she can enjoy the beauty of nature.

   The poet will dress comfortably and visit the slopes of the eastern hill, where he/she will plant corn.

2. From which direction does the wind blow? _____

3. Where does the mist hover? _____

4. What do you think the poet means by "spring clothing"? _____

_____

Comprehension: The French Eat Differently

Many people believe that French people are very different from Americans. This is certainly true where eating habits are concerned! According to a report by the World Health Organization, each year the French people eat four times more butter than Americans. The French also eat twice as much cheese! In addition, they eat more vegetables, potatoes, grain and fish.

Yet, despite the fact that they eat larger amounts of these foods, the French take in about the same number of calories each day as Americans. (French and American men consume about 2,500 calories daily. French and American women take in about 1,600 calories daily.)

How can this be? If the French are eating more of certain types of foods, shouldn't this add up to more calories? And why are so few French people overweight compared to Americans? The answer—Americans consume 18 times more refined sugar than the French and drink twice as much whole milk!

Although many Americans believe the French end each meal with grand and gooey desserts, this just isn't so. Except for special occasions, dessert in a typical French home consists of fresh fruit or cheese. Many American families, on the other hand, like to end their meals with a bowl or two of ice cream or another sweet treat.

It's believed that this difference in the kind of calories consumed—rather than in the total number of calories taken in—is what causes many Americans to be chubby and most French people to be thin.

Directions: Answer these questions about the eating habits of French and American people.

1. How many calories does the average French man eat each day? _____

2. How much whole milk does the average French person drink compared to the average

American? _____

3. How much more refined sugar do Americans eat than the French?

☐ 2 times more ☐ 18 times more ☐ 15 times more

4. What do French families usually eat for dessert?

☐ refined sugar ☐ ice cream ☐ fruit and cheese

Name: _____

Comprehension: Chinese Cabbage

Many Americans enjoy Chinese food. In big cities, like New York and Chicago, many Chinese restaurants deliver their food in small boxes to homes. It's just like ordering a pizza! Then the people who ordered the "take-out" food simply open it, put it on their plates and eat it while it's hot.

Because it tastes so good, many people are curious about the ingredients in Chinese food. Siu choy and choy sum are two types of Chinese cabbage that many people enjoy eating. Siu choy grows to be 2 to 3 feet! Of course, it is chopped into small pieces before it is cooked and served. Its leaves are light green and soft. It is not crunchy like American cabbage. Siu choy is used in soups and stews. Sometimes it is pickled with vinegar and other ingredients and served as a side dish to other courses.

Choy sum looks and tastes different from siu choy. Choy sum grows to be only 8 to 10 inches. It is a flowering cabbage that grows small yellow flowers. The flowers are "edible," which means they can be eaten. Its leaves are long and bright green. After Its leaves are boiled for 4 minutes, choy sum is often served as a salad. Oil and oyster sauce are mixed together and poured over choy sum as a salad dressing.

Directions: Answer these questions about Chinese cabbage.

1. Which Chinese cabbage grows small yellow flowers?_____

2. Which Chinese cabbage is served as a salad?_____

3. Is siu choy crunchy? _____

4. What ingredients are in the salad dressing used on choy sum?

_____

5. To what size does siu choy grow? _____

6. Name two main dishes in which siu choy is used. _____

Review

Here's a recipe for a special mashed potato treat that serves two people. The recipe is fast and easy to follow, and the results are delicious!

Begin by peeling two large potatoes and cooking them in a pot of boiling water. When a fork or knife inserted into them pulls out easily, you will know they are done. Then take them from the pot and drain them well. Place them in a large mixing bowl and add 2 tablespoons of milk and 2 tablespoons of butter. Mash with a potato masher until the lumps are gone.

In a skillet, melt a tablespoon of butter and add one bunch of chopped green onions. Cook them about 1 minute. Add them to the potatoes and mix gently. Season with salt and pepper and add more butter if desired. Serve and eat!

Directions: Answer these questions about how to make mashed potatoes with green onions.

1. Circle the main idea:

   This recipe is fast and easy, and the potatoes are delicious.

   This recipe has only four ingredients (plus salt and pepper).

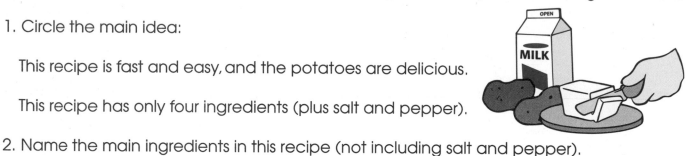

2. Name the main ingredients in this recipe (not including salt and pepper).

   _____

3. How many people does this recipe serve? _____

4. Number in order the steps for making mashed potatoes with green onions.

   _____ Cook the chopped green onions for 1 minute.

   _____ Peel two potatoes.

   _____ Season with salt and pepper and serve.

   _____ Put the cooked potatoes in a bowl with milk and butter, then mash.

   _____ Add the onions to the mashed potatoes.

   _____ Boil the potatoes until they are done.

Name: _____

Using Prior Knowledge: Greek and Roman Mythology

Directions: Before reading about Greek and Roman mythology in the following section, answer these questions.

1. Hercules is a man from Greek and Roman mythology. Write a short paragraph describing what you know about Hercules.

   _____

   _____

   _____

2. Can you think of anything today that derived its name from a Greek or Roman myth?

   _____

   _____

   _____

3. Compare and contrast what you know of Greek and Roman beliefs about mythology with your beliefs.

   _____

   _____

   _____

   _____

   _____

   _____

4. Many constellations are named after gods, goddesses and mythical creatures. Name at least six.

   _____   _____   _____

   _____   _____   _____

Comprehension: Roman Legends

Long ago, people did not know as much about science and astronomy as they do today. When they did not understand something, they thought the "gods" were responsible. The ancient Romans believed there were many gods and that each god or goddess (a female god) was responsible for certain things.

For example, the Romans believed Ceres (Sir-eez) was the goddess who made flowers, plants, trees and other things grow. She was a lot like what people today refer to as Mother Nature. Ceres was also responsible for the good weather that made crops grow. You can see why Ceres was such an important goddess to the ancient Romans.

Apollo was the god of the sun. People believed he used his chariot to pull the sun up each day and take it down at night. Apollo was extremely good-looking. His home was a golden palace near the sun surrounded by fluffy white clouds. Apollo had to work every single day, but he lived a wonderful life.

Jupiter was the most important god of all. He was the god who ruled all of the other gods, as well as the people. Jupiter was also called Jove. Maybe you have heard someone use the exclamation, "By Jove!" That person is talking about Jupiter! The word **father** is derived from the word **Jupiter**. Although he did not really exist, Jupiter influenced our language.

Directions: Answer these questions about Roman legends.

1. What imaginary figure is Ceres compared to today? _____

2. Where did Apollo live? _____

3. The word **father** is derived from the name of this god:

☐ Ceres   ☐ Apollo   ☐ Jupiter

4. Which is not true of Apollo?   ☐ He had to work every day.

                                      ☐ He lived in a mountain cave.

                                      ☐ He was very handsome.

Comprehension: Apollo and Phaethon

Apollo, the sun god, had a son named Phaethon (Fay-a-thun). Like most boys, Phaethon was proud of his father. He liked to brag to his friends about Apollo's important job, but no one believed that the great Apollo was his father.

Phaethon thought of a way to prove to his friends that he was telling the truth. He went to Apollo and asked if he could drive the chariot of the sun. If his friends saw him making the sun rise and set, they would be awestruck!

Apollo did not want to let Phaethon drive the chariot. He was afraid Phaethon was not strong enough to control the horses. But Phaethon begged until Apollo gave in. "Stay on the path," Apollo said. "If you dip too low, the sun will catch the earth on fire. If you go too high, people will freeze."

Unfortunately, Apollo's worst fears came true. Phaethon could not control the horses. He let them pull the chariot of the sun too close to the earth. To keep the earth from burning, Jupiter, father of the gods, sent a thunderbolt that hit Phaethon and knocked him from the driver's seat. When Phaethon let go of the reins, the horses pulled the chariot back up onto the proper path. Phaethon was killed as he fell to earth. His body caught fire and became a shooting star.

Directions: Answer these questions about the Roman legend of Apollo and his son.

1. Who did not believe Apollo was Phaethon's father? _____

2. What did Phaethon do to prove Apollo was his father? _____

_____

3. Why did Jupiter send a lightning bolt? _____

_____

4. Which was not a warning from Apollo to Phaethon?

☐ Don't go too close to the earth. It will burn up.

☐ Don't pet the horses. They will run wild.

☐ Don't go too far from the earth. It will freeze.

Context Clues: Mighty Hercules

Some people lift weights to build their strength. But Hercules (Her-cu-lees) had a different idea. He carried a calf on his shoulders every day. As the calf grew, it got heavier, and Hercules got stronger. Eventually, Hercules could carry a full-grown bull!

Hercules used his enormous strength to do many kind things. He became famous. Even the king had heard of Hercules! He called for Hercules to kill a lion that had killed many people in his kingdom. Hercules tracked the lion to its den and strangled it. Then Hercules made clothes for himself from the lion's skin. This kind of apparel was unusual, and soon Hercules was recognized everywhere he went. Hercules was big and his clothes made it easy to pick him out in a crowd!

The king asked Hercules to stay in his kingdom and help protect the people who lived there. Hercules performed many feats of strength and bravery. He caught a golden deer for the king. The deer had outrun everyone else. Then Hercules killed a giant, a dragon and other dangerous creatures. Hercules became a hero and was known throughout the kingdom.

Directions: Answer these questions about Hercules.

1. Use context clues to choose the correct definition of **enormous**.

   ☐ huge   ☐ tiny   ☐ smart

2. Use context clues to choose the correct definition of **strangle**.

   ☐ beat   ☐ choke   ☐ tickle

3. Use context clues to choose the correct definition of **den**.

   ☐ pond   ☐ hutch   ☐ home

4. Use context clues to choose the correct definition of **apparel**.

   ☐ appearance   ☐ clothing   ☐ personality

5. Use context clues to choose the correct definition of **feat**.

   ☐ trick   ☐ treat   ☐ act

Comprehension: Ceres and Venus

Remember Ceres? She was like Mother Nature to the ancient Romans.

Ceres made the flowers, plants and trees grow. She made crops come up and rain fall. Ceres was a very important goddess. The ancient Romans depended on her for many things.

Although the gods and goddesses were important, they had faults like ordinary people. They argued with one another. Sometimes they got mad and lost their tempers. This is what happened to Ceres and another goddess named Venus (Veen-us). Venus, who was the goddess of love and beauty, got mad at Ceres. She decided to hurt Ceres by causing Pluto, gloomy god of the underworld, to fall in love with Ceres' daughter, Proserpine (Pro-sur-pin-ay).

To accomplish this, Venus sent her son Cupid to shoot Pluto with his bow and arrow. Venus told Cupid that the man shot by this arrow would then fall in love with the first woman he saw. Venus instructed Cupid to make sure that woman was Ceres' daughter. Cupid waited with his bow and arrow until Pluto drove by Ceres' garden in his chariot. In the garden was Proserpine. Just as Pluto's chariot got near her, Cupid shot his arrow.

Ping! The arrow hit Pluto. It did not hurt, but it did its job well. Pluto fell instantly in love with poor Proserpine, who was quietly planting flowers. Pluto was not a gentleman. He did not even introduce himself! Pluto swooped down and carried Proserpine off in his chariot before she could call for help.

Directions: Answer these questions about Ceres and Venus.

1. With whom was Venus angry? _____

2. How did Venus decide to get even? _____

_____

3. Ceres' daughter's name was

☐ Persperpine.　　　☐ Prosperline.　　　☐ Proserpine.

4. Venus' son's name was

☐ Apollo.　　　☐ Cupid.　　　☐ Persperpine.

Comprehension: Proserpine and Pluto

Proserpine was terrified in Pluto's palace in the underworld. She missed her mother, Ceres, and would not stop crying.

When Ceres discovered her daughter was missing, she searched the whole Earth looking for her. Of course, she did not find her. Ceres was so unhappy about Proserpine's disappearance that she refused to do her job, which was to make things grow. When Ceres did not work, rain could not fall and crops could not grow. Finally, Ceres went to Jupiter for help.

Jupiter was powerful, but so was Pluto. Jupiter told Ceres he could get Proserpine back from Pluto if she had not eaten any of Pluto's food. As it turned out, Proserpine had eaten something. She had swallowed six seeds from a piece of fruit. Because he felt sorry for the people on Earth who were suffering, Pluto told Jupiter that Proserpine could return temporarily to Ceres so she would cheer up and make crops grow again. But Pluto later came back for Proserpine and forced her to spend six months each year with him in the underworld— one month for each seed she had eaten. Every time she returned to the underworld, Ceres mourned and refused to do her job. This is how the Romans explained the seasons—when Proserpine is on Earth with Ceres, it is spring and summer; when Proserpine goes to the underworld, it is fall and winter.

Directions: Answer these questions about Proserpine and Pluto.

1. What happened to Ceres when Pluto took her daughter? _____

_____

2. Whom did Ceres ask for help to get her daughter back? _____

3. Why did Proserpine have to return to Pluto's underworld? _____

_____

4. How long did Proserpine have to stay in the underworld each time she returned?

_____

Comprehension: Orpheus Saves the Day

Orpheus (Or-fee-us) was a talented Greek musician. Once, by playing beautiful music on his lyre (ly-er), he caused a ship that was stuck in the sand to move into the water. (A lyre is a stringed instrument that looks like a small harp and fits in the musician's lap.) The song was about how wonderful it was to sail upon the sea. The ship itself must have thought the song was wonderful, too, because it slipped into the water and sailed away!

There was a reason the ship understood Orpheus' song. Inside the ship was a piece of wood that a goddess had given to the captain of the ship. The captain's name was Jason. Once, Jason had helped an old woman across a deep river. He later learned that the old woman was a goddess. To thank him, the goddess gave Jason a piece of wood that could talk. She told him to use the wood when he built a new ship. If he ever got stuck while building the ship and did not know what to do, the goddess told Jason to ask the wood.

Several times, Jason and his crew got instructions from the wood. Finally, the ship was finished. It was beautiful and very large. Because it was so big, Jason and his men were unable to move it into the water. They called on Hercules for help, and even he could not make it budge. That's when Orpheus saved the day with his lyre.

Directions: Answer these questions about Orpheus' amazing talent.

1. Who owned the ship that was stuck? _____

2. Where was the ship stuck? _____

3. Why did the ship get stuck? _____

4. A lyre looks like what other instrument?

   ☐ harmonica   ☐ guitar   ☐ harp

5. Who did Jason first ask for help to move the ship?

   ☐ Orpheus   ☐ Hercules   ☐ Jupiter

Grade 5 - Comprehensive Curriculum

Review

Directions: Follow the instructions below.

1. Define the following words from this section.

   astronomy: _____

   reins: _____

   lyre: _____

   centaur: _____

   minotaur: _____

   myth: _____

2. Choose two words from above and use each in a sentence.

   1)_____

   2)_____

3. Write a summary of the selection "Mighty Hercules" (page 148).

   _____

   _____

   _____

   _____

4. Complete the sequence of events from the selection "Proserpine and Pluto" (page 150).

   1) Pluto fell in love with Proserpine and kidnapped her in his chariot.

   2) _____

   3) _____

   4) _____

   5) _____

Name: _____

Using Prior Knowledge: Famous Ships

Directions: Before reading about famous ships in the following section, answer these questions.

1. Look up the following terms in a dictionary and write their definitions.

   vessel: _____

   bow: _____

   stern: _____

   poop deck: _____

   hull: _____

   caravel: _____

   mast: _____

   frigate: _____

   lateen: _____

   spar: _____

   fore: _____

   aft: _____

2. Have you ever been on a large ship? If so, describe the experience. If not, on what kind of ship or boat would you like to ride? Why?

   _____

   _____

   _____

3. Name at least one famous ship and write what you know about it.

   _____

   _____

   _____

Comprehension: The *Constitution*

The *Constitution*, or "Old Ironsides," was built by the United States Navy in 1798. Its success in battle made it one of the most famous vessels in the United States. The *Constitution*'s naval career began with the war with Tripoli from 1803 to 1804. Later, it was also used in the War of 1812. During this war, it was commanded by Isaac Hull. The *Constitution* won a 30-minute battle with the British ship, *Guerriere*, in August of 1812. The *Guerriere* was nearly demolished. Later that same year, the *Constitution* was used to capture a British frigate near Brazil.

The *Constitution* was taken out of service in 1829 and was rebuilt many times over the years. Today, it is on display at the Boston Navy Yard.

Directions: Answer these questions about the *Constitution*.

1. What is the main idea of the selection? _____

_____

2. Which ship was almost demolished by the *Constitution*? _____

3. In which two wars was the *Constitution* used? _____

4. Where is the *Constitution* now on display? _____

5. Complete the following time line with dates and events described above.

_____   _____   _____   _____   _____

├────┼────────┼────────┼────────┼────────┼────┤

Comprehension: The *Santa Maria, Niña* and *Pinta*

When Christopher Columbus decided to attempt a voyage across the ocean, the ships he depended upon to take him there were called "caravels." A caravel is a small sailing ship built by Spain and Portugal in the 15th and 16th centuries. The caravels Columbus used to sail to the New World were named the *Santa Maria, Niña,* and *Pinta*.

The ships were not very large. It is believed the *Santa Maria* was only 75 to 90 feet long, and the *Niña* and *Pinta* were only about 70 feet long. Caravels typically had three to four masts with sails attached. The foremast carried a square sail, while the others were more triangular in shape. These triangular-shaped sails were called "lateen sails."

These three small ships were quite seaworthy and proved excellent ships for Columbus. They got him where he wanted to go.

Directions: Answer these questions about the *Santa Maria, Niña* and *Pinta*.

1. What is a lateen sail? _____

2. What is the main idea of the selection? _____

_____

_____

3. What is a caravel? _____

4. Where did Columbus sail in his caravels? _____

5. Do some research and compare a 15th-century caravel with a ship built in the 20th century.

_____

_____

_____

_____

Comprehension: The *Lusitania*

The *Lusitania* was a British passenger steamship. It became famous when it was torpedoed and sunk by the Germans during World War I. On May 7, 1915, the *Lusitania* was traveling off the coast of Ireland when a German submarine fired on it without warning. The ship stood no chance of surviving the attack and sunk in an astonishing 20 minutes. 1,198 people perished, of whom 128 were American citizens. At the time the ship was torpedoed, the United States was not yet involved in the war. Public opinion over the attack put pressure on President Woodrow Wilson to declare war on Germany. The Germans proclaimed that the *Lusitania* was carrying weapons for the use of the allies.

This claim was later proven to be true. President Wilson demanded that the German government apologize for the sinking and make amends. Germany did not accept responsibility but did promise to avoid sinking any more passenger ships without first giving a warning.

Directions: Answer these questions about the *Lusitania*.

1. What does **proclaimed** mean? _____

2. What does **perished** mean? _____

3. What does **amends** mean? _____

4. What does **allies** mean? _____

5. If the *Lusitania* was carrying arms, do you think the Germans had a right to sink it? Why or why not?

_____

_____

_____

_____

Comprehension: The *Titanic*

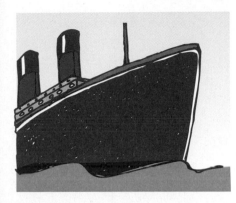

The British passenger ship, *Titanic*, debuted in the spring of 1912. It was billed as an unsinkable ship due to its construction. It had 16 watertight compartments that would hold the ship afloat even in the event that four of the compartments were damaged.

But on the evening of April 14, 1912, during *Titanic*'s first voyage, its design proved unworthy. Just before midnight, *Titanic* struck an iceberg, which punctured 5 of the 16 compartments. The ship sunk in a little under 3 hours. Approximately 1,513 of the over 2,220 people onboard died. Most of these people died because there weren't enough lifeboats to accommodate everyone onboard. These people were left floating in the water. Many died from exposure, since the Atlantic Ocean was near freezing in temperature. It was one of the worst ocean disasters in history.

Because of the investigations that followed the *Titanic* disaster, the passenger ship industry instituted many reforms. It is now required that there is ample lifeboat space for all passengers and crew. An international ice patrol and full-time radio coverage were also instituted to prevent such disasters in the future.

Directions: Answer these questions about the *Titanic*.

1. How did most of the 1,513 people onboard the *Titanic* die? _____

2. Why did this "unsinkable" ship sink? _____

_____

3. What changes have been made in ship safety as a result of the *Titanic* tragedy?

_____

_____

4. There have been many attempts to rescue artifacts from the *Titanic*. But many families of the dead wish the site to be left alone, as it is the final resting place of their relatives. They feel burial sites should not be disrupted. Do you agree or disagree? Why?

_____

_____

_____

Venn Diagram: *Lusitania* and *Titanic*

A **Venn diagram** is used to chart information that shows similarities and differences between two things.

Example:

Dogs	Both	Cats
bark	good pets	one size
dependent	can live inside or outside	kill mice
large and small breeds	have fur	can use litterbox
protect the home	four legs	independent

Directions: Complete the Venn diagram for the *Lusitania* and the *Titanic*.

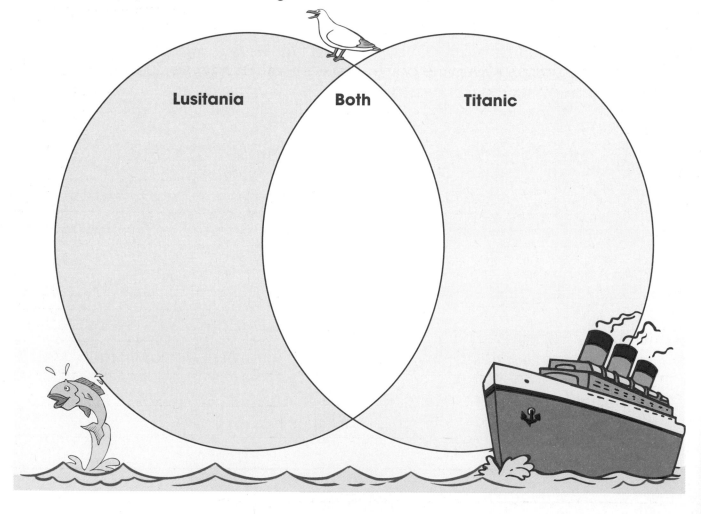

Comprehension: The *Monitor* and the *Virginia*

During the Civil War, it became customary to cover wooden warships with iron. This increased their durability and made them more difficult to sink. Two such ships were built using iron. They were the *Monitor* and the *Virginia*.

Most people are more familiar with the name the *Merrimack*. The *Merrimack* was a U.S. steam frigate that had been burnt and sunk by Union forces when the Confederates were forced to abandon their navy yard. The Confederate Navy raised the hull of the *Merrimack* and rebuilt her as the ironclad *Virginia*.

Both the *Monitor* and the *Virginia* engaged in battle on March 9, 1962. After several hours of battle, the bulky *Virginia* had no choice but to withdraw in order to avoid the lowering tides. This battle, called Hampton Roads, was considered to be a tie between the two ships.

Although both ships survived the battle, they were later destroyed. Two months later, the *Virginia* was sunk by her crew to avoid capture. The *Monitor* sunk on December 31, 1862, during a storm off the coast of North Carolina.

Directions: Use context clues for these definitions.

1. customary: _____

2. durability: _____

3. ironclad: _____

Directions: Answer these questions about the *Monitor* and the *Virginia*.

4. Who won the battle between the *Virginia* and the *Monitor*? _____

5. Why would lowering tides present danger to a ship? _____

_____

6. Describe how each ship was finally destroyed. _____

_____

_____

_____

Review

1. Use the Venn diagram you completed comparing the *Lusitania* and the *Titanic* (page 158) to write a two-paragraph compare/contrast essay about the two ships. Describe their similarities in the first paragraph and their differences in the second.

_____

_____

_____

_____

_____

_____

_____

_____

2. Describe the differences in the structure of the following ships: *Santa Maria*, *Monitor* and *Titanic*.

_____

_____

_____

_____

_____

3. Why did people think the *Titanic* was unsinkable? After the ship actually did sink, how do you think this affected the way people thought about new technology?

_____

_____

_____

_____

_____

_____

Name: _____

Reading Comprehension: Railroads

Directions: Read the information about railroads. Then answer the questions.

As early as the 1550s, a rough form of railroad was already being used in parts of Europe. Miners in England and other areas of western Europe used horse- or mule-drawn wagons on wooden tracks to pull loads out of mines. With these tracks, the horses could pull twice as much weight as they could without them. No one could have known then that one day this simple idea would change the world.

There were many developments along the way that helped make railroads a practical and valuable form of transportation. Two of the most important were the iron track and the "flanged" wheel, which has a rim around it to hold it onto the track. The most important invention was the steam engine by James Watt in 1765.

The first railroads in the United States were built during the late 1820s and caused a lot of excitement. They were faster than other forms of travel, and they could provide service year-round, unlike boats and stagecoaches. Trains were soon the main means of travel in the U.S.

Railroads played a major part in the Industrial Revolution—the years of change when machines were first used to do work that had been done by hand for many centuries. Trains provided cheaper rates and quicker service for transporting goods. Because manufacturers could ship their goods over long distances, they could sell their products all over the nation instead of only in the surrounding cities and towns. This meant greater profits for the companies. Trains also brought people into the cities to work in factories.

1. What was the source of power for the earliest railroads? _____

_____

2. What were three important developments that made railroads a practical means of transportation?

_____

_____

_____

3. What is meant by the Industrial Revolution? _____

_____

4. What were two ways that railroads changed life in America?_____

_____

Main Idea: Locomotives

Directions: Read the information about locomotives. Then answer the questions.

In the 1800s, the steam locomotive was considered by many to be a symbol of the new Industrial Age. It was, indeed, one of the most important inventions of the time. Over the years, there have been many changes to the locomotive. One of the most important has been its source of power. During its history, the locomotive has gone from steam to electric to diesel power.

The first railroads used horses or mules for power, but the development of the steam locomotive made railroads a practical means of transportation. The first steam locomotive was built in 1804 in Great Britain by Richard Trevithick. It could haul 50,000 pounds, but it was not very successful because it was so heavy it caused the tracks to fall apart. However, it encouraged other engineers to try to build steam locomotives. Two of the most important men to accept the challenge were George Stephenson and his son, Robert. Robert once won a contest to build the best locomotive. *The Rocket*, as he called it, had a top speed of 29 miles per hour.

In America, developments in steam engines were close behind those of the British. In 1830, Peter Cooper's tiny locomotive, called *Tom Thumb*, lost a famous race against a horse-drawn coach. In spite of the loss, it still convinced railroad officials that steam power was more practical than horsepower.

Just before the turn of the century, the electric locomotive was widely used. At its peak in the 1940s, U.S. railroads had 2,400 miles of electric routes.

The diesel locomotive was invented in the 1890s by Rudolf Diesel, a German engineer. The power of this locomotive was supplied by a diesel fuel engine. The diesel locomotive is still used today. It costs about twice as much as a steam locomotive to build, but it is much cheaper to operate.

1. What is the main idea of this selection?
    ___ The steam locomotive was considered a symbol of the Industrial Age.
    ✓ Over the years, there have been many changes to the locomotive.

2. Who built the first steam locomotive in 1804?
    Richard Trevithick

3. How fast could *The Rocket* travel?
    29 miles an hour

4. Who built the locomotive called *Tom Thumb*?
    Peter Cooper

5. *Tom Thumb* was in a race against a horse-drawn coach. Which won?
    horse-drawn coach

6. What kind of fuel does a diesel engine use?
    diesel fuel

Name: _____

Review

Directions: Define these words as used in the selections "Railroads" and "Locomotives."

1. flanged wheel _____

   _____

2. transportation _____

3. profit _____

4. locomotive _____

5. diesel _____

6. engineer _____

Directions: Use information from the selection "Locomotives" to create a time line of the invention of locomotives.

7. _____

Directions: Write your answer in a complete sentence.

8. The world is going through another "revolution" in industry today. What new technology is leading this change and how might it affect workers in the future?

   _____

   _____

   _____

Name: _____

Reading Comprehension: Railroad Pioneer

Directions: Read the information about railroad pioneers. Then answer the questions by circling **Yes** or **No**.

George Stephenson was born in Wylam, England, in 1781. His family was extremely poor. When he was young, he didn't go to school but worked in the coal mines. In his spare time, he taught himself to read and write. After a series of explosions in the coal pits, Stephenson built a miner's safety lamp. This helped bring him to the attention of the owners of the coal mines. They put him in charge of all the machinery.

In 1812, Stephenson became an engine builder for the mines. The owners were interested in locomotives because the cost of horse feed was so high. They wanted Stephenson to build a locomotive to pull the coal cars from the mines. His first locomotive, The *Blucher*, was put on the rails in 1814.

Stephenson was a good engineer, and he was fortunate to work for a rich employer. Between 1814 and 1826, Stephenson was the only man in Great Britain building locomotives.

When the Stockholm and Darlington Railway, the first public railroad system, was planned, Stephenson was named company engineer. He convinced the owners to use steam power instead of horses. He built the first locomotive on the line. *The Locomotion*, as it was called, was the best locomotive that had been built anywhere in the world up to that time. Over the years, Stephenson was responsible for many other important developments in locomotive design, such as improved cast-iron rails and wheels, and the first steel springs strong enough to carry several tons.

Stephenson was convinced that the future of railroads lay in steam power. His great vision of what the railroad system could become was a driving force in the early years of its development.

1. George Stephenson was an excellent student in school.   Yes   No

2. Stephenson's first invention was a miner's safety lamp.   Yes   No

3. Between 1814 and 1826, Stephenson was one of many engineers building locomotives in Great Britain.   Yes   No

4. The Stockholm and Darlington Railway was the first public railroad system.   Yes   No

5. The first locomotive on the Stockholm and Darlington line was *The Locomotion*, built by Stephenson.   Yes   No

6. Stephenson's ideas did not influence the development of the railroad system.   Yes   No

Name: _____

Tall Tales

A **tall tale** is a fictional story with exaggerated details and a "super" hero. The main character in a tall tale is much larger, stronger, smarter or better than a real person. Tall tales may be unbelievable, but they are fun to hear.

America had nearly 200,000 miles of railroad track by 1900. Because of the rapid growth and the excitement over the railroads, many colorful tall tales about railroad heroes and their adventures were told.

Directions: Read the story about John Henry. Then answer the questions.

A Steel-Driving Man

On the night John Henry was born, forked lightning split the air and the earth shook. He weighed 44 pounds at birth, and the first thing he did was reach for a hammer hanging on the wall. "He's going to be a steel-driving man," his father told his mother.

One night, John Henry dreamed he was working on a railroad. Every time his hammer hit a spike, the sky lit up with the sparks. "I dreamed that the railroad was going to be the end of me, and I'd die with a hammer in my hand," he said. When John Henry grew up he did work for the railroad. He was the fastest, most powerful steel-driving man in the world.

In about 1870, the steam drill was invented. One day the company at the far end of a tunnel tried it out. John Henry's company, working at the other end, continued to use men to do the drilling. There was much bragging from both companies as to which was faster. Finally, they decided to have a contest. John Henry was matched against the best man with a steam drill.

John Henry swung a 20-pound hammer in each hand. The sparks flew so fast and hot that they burned his face. At the end of the day, the judges said John Henry had beaten the steam drill by 4 feet!

That night, John Henry said, "I was a steel-driving man." Then he laid down and closed his eyes forever.

1. How much was John Henry said to have weighed at birth? _____
2. Why did his father think he would be a steel-driving man? _____
3. What invention was John Henry in a contest against? _____
4. Why was the contest held? _____
5. What tools did John Henry use in the contest? _____
6. Who won the contest? _____
7. What happened to John Henry after the contest? _____

Tall Tales

Directions: Write a tall tale about yourself. Be sure to make it a fantastic and incredible story!

_____

_____

_____

_____

_____

_____

_____

_____

_____

_____

_____

_____

_____

_____

_____

Directions: Reread your tall tale. Does it make sense? Check and correct spelling and grammar mistakes. Does your story fit the category of tall tale?

Context Clues: Passenger Cars

Directions: Read the information about passenger cars. Use context clues to determine the meaning of words in bold. Check the correct answers.

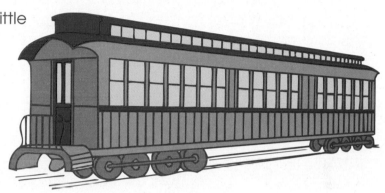

Early railroad passenger cars were little more than stagecoaches fitted with special wheels to help them stay on the tracks. They didn't hold many passengers, and because they were made out of wood, they were fire **hazards**. They also did not hold up very well if the train came off the track or had a **collision** with another train.

In the United States, it wasn't long before passenger cars were lengthened to hold more people. Late in the 1830s, Americans were riding in **elongated** cars with double seats on either side of a center aisle. By the early 1900s, most cars were made of metal instead of wood.

Sleeping and dining cars were introduced in the United States by the early 1860s. Over the next 25 years other improvements were made, including electric lighting, steam heat and covered **vestibules** that allowed passengers to walk between cars. All of these **luxuries** helped make railroad travel much more comfortable.

1. Based on the other words in the sentence, what is the correct definition of **hazards**?

    ____ engines   ____ risks   ____ stations

2. Based on the other words in the sentence, what is the correct definition of **collision**?

    ____ crash   ____ race   ____ track

3. Based on the other words in the sentence, what is the correct definition of **elongated**?

    ____ wooden   ____ new   ____ lengthened

4. Based on the other words in the sentence, what is the correct definition of **vestibules**?

    ____ passageways   ____ cars   ____ depots

5. Based on the other words in the sentence, what is the correct definition of **luxuries**?

    ____ additions   ____ things offering the greatest comfort   ____ inventions

Reading Skills: Railroads

Directions: Read the information about railroads. Then answer the questions.

When railroads became the major means of transportation, they replaced earlier forms of travel, like the stagecoach. Railroads remained the unchallenged leader for a hundred years. Beginning in the early 1900s, railroads faced **competition** from newer forms of transportation.

Today, millions of people have their own automobiles. Buses offer inexpensive travel between cities. Large trucks haul goods across the country. Airplanes provide quick transportation over long distances. The result has been a sharp drop in the use of trains.

Today, nearly all railroads face serious problems that threaten to drive them out of business. But railroads still provide low-cost, fuel-saving transportation that will remain important. One gallon of diesel fuel will haul about four times as much by railroad as by truck. In a time when the world is concerned about saving fuel, this is but one area in which the railroads still have much to offer.

1. What is the main idea of this selection?

    ____ When railroads became the major means of transportation, they replaced earlier forms of travel.
    ____ Beginning in the early 1900s, railroads have faced competition from newer forms of transportation.

2. Based on the other words in the sentence, what is the correct definition of **competition**?

    ____ businesses trying to get the same customers
    ____ problems
    ____ support

3. What are four newer forms of transportation that have challenged railroads?

    _____

4. One gallon of diesel fuel will haul about twice as much by railroad as by truck.   Yes   No

Reading Comprehension: Printing

Directions: Read the information about printing. Then answer the questions.

When people talk about printing, they usually mean making exact copies of an original document, such as a newspaper, magazine or an entire book. The inventions that have allowed us to do this are some of the most important developments in history. Look around you at the many examples of printed materials. Can you imagine life without them?

Until the thirteenth century, all material had to be printed by hand, one copy at a time. To make a copy of a book took much time and effort.

The oldest known example of a printed book was made in China in 848 A.D. by Wang Chieh, who carved each page of a book by hand onto a block of wood. He then put ink on the wood and pressed it on paper. The idea of printing with wood blocks spread to Europe. The letters in these block books were made to look handwritten.

In about 1440, a German goldsmith named Johann Gutenberg developed the idea of movable type. He invented separate letters made of metal for printing. The letters could be joined together to make words and sentences. Ink was applied to the letters to print many copies of the same material. Because they were made of metal, the letters could be used over and over. This wonderful invention made it possible to have more printed material at a lower cost.

Gutenberg had other ideas that were important to printing. He developed a special type of ink that would stick to the new metal letters. Gutenberg's ideas were so successful that the process of printing went almost unchanged for more than 300 years.

1. In what country was the oldest known printed book made?

   _____

2. Who made the first printed book?

   _____

3. What is "movable type"?

   _____

4. Who developed the idea of movable type?

   _____

5. What was another important invention of Gutenberg?

   _____

Reading Comprehension: Newspapers

Directions: Read the information about
newspapers. Then answer the questions.

    Newspapers keep us informed about what is going
on in the world. They entertain, educate and examine
the events of the day. For millions of people worldwide,
newspapers are an important part of daily life.

    Newspapers are published at various intervals, but they usually
come out daily or weekly. Of the nearly 60,000 newspapers published
around the world, about 2,600 are published in the United States.
More than half—about 1800—of them are dailies.

    Some newspapers have many subscribers—people who pay
to have each edition delivered to them. *The Wall Street Journal*
and *USA Today* each have about two million subscribers.
There are many, many newspapers with only a few thousand
subscribers. These include small-town weeklies and special-interest
papers, like those written for people who enjoy the same hobby.

    Newspapers provide a service to the community by providing information at little cost.
But newspaper publishing is a business, so like other businesses, newspapers need to make
money. They can keep the cost to subscribers low and still stay in business by selling space
to businesses and individuals who want to advertise products or services. In most newspapers,
between one-third and two-thirds of the paper is taken up by advertising.

1. About how many newspapers are published worldwide?

    _____

2. What services do newspapers provide?

    _____

3. What are subscribers?

    _____

4. How often are most newspapers published?

    _____

5. What do newspapers do to keep the cost to the reader low, but still make money?

    _____

6. In most newspapers, about how much of the paper is taken up by advertising?

    _____

Reading Comprehension: Newspapers

Directions: Read the information about the first newspapers. Then answer the questions.

Long ago, town criers walked through cities reading important news to the people. The earliest newspapers were probably handwritten notices posted in towns for the public to read.

The first true newspaper was a weekly paper started in Germany in 1609. It was called *The Strassburg Relation*. The Germans were pioneers in newspaper publishing. Johann Gutenberg, the man who developed movable type, was German.

One of the first English-language newspapers, *The London Gazette*, was first printed in England in 1665. Gazette is an old English word that means "official publication." Many newspapers today still use the word gazette in their names.

In America, several papers began during colonial days. The first successful one, *The Boston News-Letter*, began printing in 1704. It was very small—about the size of a sheet of notebook paper with printing on both sides.

An important date in newspaper publishing was 1833. In that year, *The New York Sun* became the first penny newspaper. The paper actually did cost only a penny. The penny newspapers were similar to today's papers: they printed news while it was still new, they were the first to print advertisements and to sell papers in newsstands, and they were the first to be delivered to homes.

1. How were the earliest newspapers different from today's newspapers?

   _____

2. In what year and where was the first true newspaper printed?

   _____

3. What was the name of the first successful newspaper in America?

   _____

4. Why was 1833 important in newspaper publishing?

   _____

5. List four ways penny newspapers were like the newspapers of today.

   _____

   _____

   _____

   _____

Reading Comprehension: Newspaper Jobs

Directions: Read the information about jobs at a newspaper. Then answer the questions.

It takes an army of people to put out one of the big daily newspapers. Three separate departments are needed to make a newspaper operate smoothly: editorial, mechanical and business.

The editorial department is the one most people think about first. That is the news-gathering part of the newspaper. The most familiar job in this department is that of the reporter—the person who obtains information for a story and writes it. A photographer takes pictures to go along with the reporter's story.

Editors are the decision-makers. There are many editors at a large newspaper. They assign stories to reporters, read the stories to be certain they are correct and decide where and if the stories should appear in the paper. The most important stories go on the front page. There are also photo editors who choose which pictures will appear in the paper. Other workers in the editorial department include artists, copy editors, proofreaders and cartoonists.

The biggest job in the mechanical department is printing the paper. Most large newspapers have their own printing presses. Some small papers send their work to outside printing shops. After an issue, or edition, is printed, it is ready to be sold or "circulated" to the public.

Circulation of the paper is one of the jobs of the business department. This department also sells advertising space. This is very important for newspapers. Many papers make more money selling advertising space than selling newspapers. The business department also takes care of normal business jobs, like paying employees, paying bills and keeping records.

1. What are the three main departments at a newspaper?

   _____

2. Who gets the information for a story and writes it?

   _____

3. Who are the decision-makers at a newspaper?

   _____

4. What is the biggest job for the mechanical department?

   _____

5. What is the most important job of the business department?

   _____

Name: _____

Reading Comprehension: News Stories

Directions: Read the information about news stories. Then draw an **X** on the line to show the corrct meaning of the bold word.

Here is an example of how a story gets into the newspaper:

Let's imagine that a city bus has turned over in a ditch, injuring some of the passengers. An **eyewitness** calls the newspaper. The editor assigns a reporter to go to the scene. The reporter talks to the passengers, driver and witnesses who saw the accident. She finds out what they saw and how they feel, writing down their comments or tape recording their answers. At the same time, a photographer is busy taking pictures.

If there isn't time for the reporter to go back to the newsroom, she could call and **dictate** the story to a copytaker who types the story into a computer. Many reporters use portable computers which allow them to write the story on the spot and then send it back to the office over the telephone by modem.

Next, an editor reads the story, checking facts, grammar and spelling. Meanwhile, the photographer's film is developed and a picture is chosen.

The story is set in print. On most newspapers today, this is done with a computer. The computer makes sets of columns of type, which are pasted onto a sheet of paper exactly the same size as a newspaper page. A **proofreader** checks the story for mistakes. The newspaper is now ready for printing. The presses begin to run.

Miles of paper are turned into thousands of printed, cut and folded newspapers. They are counted, put into bundles and placed in waiting trucks. Within a few hours, people can read about the bus accident in their daily newspaper.

1. Based on the other words in the sentence, what is the correct definition of **eyewitness**?

   _____ a reporter

   _____ a person who saw what happened

   _____ a lawyer

2. Based on the other words in the sentence, what is the correct definition of **dictate**?

   _____ govern without regard for what people want

   _____ use a dictionary

   _____ read a story word for word for someone else to write

3. Based on the other words in the sentence, what is the correct definition of **proofreader**?

   _____ person who checks for mistakes

   _____ person who shows proof he has read a book

   _____ a teacher

Reading Comprehension: News Services

Directions: Read the information about news services. Then answer the questions.

When people read daily newspapers, they expect to see current news from all over the world. Some newspapers have offices or reporters in Washington, D.C. and other major cities around the world. Most newspapers rely on news services for international news. News services are organizations that gather and sell news to papers, radio and television stations. They are sometimes referred to as "wire services," because they originally sent stories over telegraph or Teletype lines, or "wires."

The two largest news services are the Associated Press and United Press International. Stories sent by these services have their initials—AP or UPI—at the beginning of the article. All large American newspapers are members of either the AP or UPI service.

At one time, people had to wait for messengers to arrive by foot, horse or ship to learn the news. By the time it reached a newspaper, news could be months old.

Gathering news from around the world became much faster after the invention of the telegraph, Teletype, telephone and transatlantic cable. Today, satellites, computer modems and fax machines can send stories, pictures and even videos around the world in seconds.

1. What is another name for news service organizations?

   _____

2. What are the two largest news service organizations?

   _____

3. What are three inventions that have speeded up worldwide news-gathering?

   _____

4. Why do newspapers use news services?

   _____

5. How was news delivered before the invention of modern communication devices?

   _____

Name: _____

Reading Comprehension: Samuel Clemens

Directions: Read the information about Samuel Clemens.

Samuel Langhorne Clemens was born in Florida, Missouri, in 1835. In his lifetime, he gained worldwide fame as a writer, lecturer and humorist.

Clemens first worked for a printer when he was only 12 years old. Soon after that he worked on his brother's newspaper.

Clemens traveled frequently and worked as a printer in New York, Philadelphia, St. Louis and Cincinnati. On a trip to New Orleans in 1857, he learned the difficult art of steamboat **piloting**. Clemens loved piloting and later used it as a background for some of his books, including *Life on the Mississippi*.

A few years later, Clemens went to Nevada with his brother and tried gold mining. When this proved unsuccessful, he went back to writing for newspapers. At first he signed his humorous pieces with the name "Josh." In 1863, he began signing them Mark Twain. The words "mark twain" were used by riverboat pilots to mean two fathoms (12 feet) deep, water deep enough for steamboats. From then on, Clemens used this now-famous **pseudonym** for all his writing.

As Mark Twain, he received attention from readers all over the world. His best-known works include *Tom Sawyer* and *The Adventures of Huckleberry Finn*. These two books about boyhood adventures remain popular with readers of all ages.

Directions: Check the correct answer.

1. Based on the other words In the sentence, what is the correct definition of **pseudonym**?
   _____ book title
   _____ a made-up name used by an author
   _____ a humorous article

2. Based on the other words in the sentence, what is the correct definition of **piloting**?
   _____ driving an airplane
   _____ steering a steamboat on a river
   _____ being a train engineer

Directions: Write the answers.

3. Under what name did Samuel Clemens write his books?

   _____

4. What do the words "mark twain" mean?

   _____

5. Besides author, list two other jobs held by Mark Twain.

   _____

6. List two of the best-known books written by Mark Twain.

   _____

Review

Directions: Write the answers.

1. What are two ways newspapers earn money?

   _____

   _____

2. What was Mark Twain's real name?

   _____

3. Name six jobs at a newspaper.

   _____

   _____

   _____

   _____

   _____

   _____

4. What is the purpose of the Associated Press and the United Press International?

   _____

   _____

   _____

   _____

   _____

Directions: Use dates from the articles "Printing" and "Newspapers" to create a time line of the development of newspapers.

_____

Recognizing Details: The Coldest Continent

Directions: Read the information about Antarctica. Then answer the questions.

Antarctica lies at the South Pole and is the coldest continent. It is without sunlight for months at a time. Even when the sun does shine, its angle is so slanted that the land receives little warmth. Temperatures often drop to 100 degrees below zero, and a fierce wind blows almost endlessly. Most of the land is covered by snow heaped thousands of feet deep. The snow is so heavy and tightly packed that it forms a great ice cap covering more than 95 percent of the continent.

Considering the conditions, it is no wonder there are no towns or cities in Antarctica. There is no permanent population at all, only small scientific research stations. Many teams of explorers and scientists have braved the freezing cold since Antarctica was sighted in 1820. Some have died in their effort, but a great deal of information has been learned about the continent.

From fossils, pieces of coal and bone samples, we know that Antarctica was not always an ice-covered land. Scientists believe that 200 million years ago it was connected to southern Africa, South America, Australia and India. Forests grew in warm swamps, and insects and reptiles thrived there. Today, there are animals that live in and around the waters that border the continent. In fact, the waters surrounding Antarctica contain more life than oceans in warmer areas of the world.

1. Where is Antarctica?_____

2. How much of the continent is covered by an ice cap?_____

3. When was Antarctica first sighted by explorers?_____

4. What clues indicate that Antarctica was not always an ice-covered land?

_____

5. Is Antarctica another name for the North Pole?   Yes   No

Reading Comprehension: The Arctic Circle

Directions: Read the article about the Arctic Circle. Then answer the questions.

On the other side of the globe from Antarctica, at the northernmost part of the Earth, is another icy land. This is the Arctic Circle. It includes the North Pole itself and the northern fringes of three continents—Europe, Asia and North America, including the state of Alaska—as well as Greenland and other islands.

The seasons are opposite at the two ends of the Earth. When it is summer in Antarctica, it is winter in the Arctic Circle. In both places, there are very long periods of sunlight in summer and very long nights in the winter. On the poles themselves, there are six full months of sunlight and six full months of darkness each year.

Compared to Antarctica, the summers are surprisingly mild in some areas of the Arctic Circle. Much of the snow cover may melt, and temperatures often reach 50 degrees in July. Antarctica is covered by water—frozen water, of course—so nothing can grow there. Plant growth is limited in the polar regions not only by the cold, but also by wind, lack of water and the long winter darkness.

In the far north, willow trees grow but only become a few inches high! The annual rings, the circles within the trunk of a tree that show its age and how fast it grows, are so narrow in those trees that you need a microscope to see them.

A permanently frozen layer of soil, called "permafrost," keeps roots from growing deep enough into the ground to anchor a plant. Even if a plant could survive the cold temperatures, it could not grow roots deep enough or strong enough to allow the plant to get very big.

1. What three continents have land included in the Arctic Circle?

    _____   _____   _____

2. Is the Arctic Circle generally warmer or colder than Antarctica?

    _____

3. What is "permafrost"? _____

4. Many tall pine trees grow in the Arctic Circle.   Yes   No

Main Idea: The Polar Trail

Directions: Read the information about explorers to Antarctica.

A recorded sighting of Antarctica, the last continent to be discovered, was not made until the early nineteenth century. Since then, many brave explorers and adventurers have sailed south to conquer the icy land. Their achievements once gained as much world attention as those of the first astronauts.

Long before the continent was first spotted, the ancient Greeks suspected there was a continent at the bottom of the Earth. Over the centuries, legends of the undiscovered land spread. Some of the world's greatest seamen tried to find it, including Captain James Cook in 1772.

Cook was the first to sail all the way to the solid field of ice that surrounds Antarctica every winter. In fact, he sailed all the way around the continent but never saw it. Cook went farther south than anyone had ever gone. His record lasted 50 years.

Forty years after Cook, a new kind of seamen sailed the icy waters. They were hunters of seals and whales. Sailing through unknown waters in search of seals and whales, these men became explorers as well as hunters. The first person known to sight Antarctica was an American hunter, 21-year-old Nathaniel Brown Palmer in 1820.

Directions: Draw an **X** on the blank for the correct answer.

1. The main idea is:
   _____ Antarctica was not sighted until the early nineteenth century.
   _____ Many brave explorers and adventurers have sailed south to conquer the icy land.

2. The first person to sail to the ice field that surrounds Antarctica was:
   _____ Nathaniel Brown Palmer
   _____ Captain James Cook
   _____ Neal Armstrong

3. His record for sailing the farthest south stood for:
   _____ 40 years
   _____ 50 years
   _____ 500 years

4. The first person known to sight Antarctica was:
   _____ an unknown ancient Greek
   _____ Captain James Cook
   _____ Nathaniel Brown Palmer

5. His profession was:
   _____ hunter
   _____ ship captain
   _____ explorer

Grade 5 - Comprehensive Curriculum

Reading Skills: Research

To learn more about the explorers to Antarctica, reference sources like encyclopedias, CD-ROMs, the Internet and history books are excellent sources for finding more information.

Directions: Use reference sources to learn more about Captain James Cook and Captain James Clark Ross. Write an informational paragraph about each man.

1. Captain James Cook

_____

_____

_____

_____

_____

_____

2. Captain James Clark Ross

_____

_____

_____

_____

_____

_____

3. What dangers did both these men and their teams face in their attempts to reach the South Pole?

_____

_____

_____

_____

_____

Name: _____

Recognizing Details: The Frozen Continent

Directions: Read the information about explorers. Then answer the questions.

By the mid-1800s, most of the seals of Antarctica had been killed. The seal hunters no longer sailed the icy waters. The next group of explorers who took an interest in Antarctica were scientists. Of these, the man who took the most daring chances and made the most amazing discoveries was British Captain James Clark Ross.

Ross first made a name for himself sailing to the north. In 1831, he discovered the North Magnetic Pole—one of two places on Earth toward which a compass needle points. In 1840, Ross set out to find the South Magnetic Pole. He made many marvelous discoveries, including the Ross Sea, a great open sea beyond the ice packs that stopped other explorers, and the Ross Ice Shelf, a great floating sheet of ice bigger than all of France!

The next man to make his mark exploring Antarctica was British explorer Robert Falcon Scott. Scott set out in 1902 to find the South Pole. He and his team suffered greatly, but they were able to make it a third of the way to the pole. Back in England, Scott was a great hero. In 1910, he again attempted to become the first man to reach the South Pole. But this time he had competition: an explorer from Norway, Roald Amundsen, was also leading a team to the South Pole.

It was a brutal race. Both teams faced many hardships, but they pressed on. Finally, on December 14, 1911, Amundsen became the first man to reach the South Pole. Scott arrived on January 17, 1912. He was bitterly disappointed at not being first. The trip back was even more horrible. None of the five men in the Scott expedition survived.

1. After the seal hunters, who were the next group of explorers interested in Antarctica?

   _____

2. What great discovery did James Ross make before ever sailing to Antarctica?

   _____

3. What were two other great discoveries made by James Ross?

   _____   _____

4. How close did Scott and his team come to the South Pole in 1902?

   _____

5. Who was the first person to reach the South Pole?_____

Grade 5 - Comprehensive Curriculum

Reading Comprehension: Polar Bears

Directions: Read the information about polar bears. Then answer the questions by circling **Yes** or **No**.

Some animals are able to survive the cold weather and difficult conditions of the snow and ice fields in the Arctic polar regions. One of the best known is the polar bear.

Polar bears live on the land and the sea. They may drift hundreds of miles from land on huge sheets of floating ice. They use their great paws to paddle the ice along. Polar bears are excellent swimmers, too. They can cross great distances of open water. While in the water, they feed mostly on fish and seals.

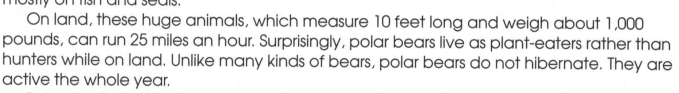

On land, these huge animals, which measure 10 feet long and weigh about 1,000 pounds, can run 25 miles an hour. Surprisingly, polar bears live as plant-eaters rather than hunters while on land. Unlike many kinds of bears, polar bears do not hibernate. They are active the whole year.

Baby polar bears are born during the winter. At birth, they are pink and almost hairless. These helpless cubs weigh only two pounds—less than one-third the size of most human infants. The mother bears raise their young in dens dug in snowbanks. By the time they are 10 weeks old, polar bear cubs are about the size of puppies and have enough white fur to protect them in the open air. The mothers give their cubs swimming, hunting and fishing lessons. By the time autumn comes, the cubs are left to survive on their own.

1. Polar bears can live on the land and the sea.   Yes   No

2. Polar bears are excellent swimmers.   Yes   No

3. Polar bears hibernate in the winter.   Yes   No

4. A newborn polar bear weighs more than a newborn human baby.   Yes   No

5. Mother polar bears raise their babies in caves.   Yes   No

6. Father polar bears give the cubs swimming lessons.   Yes   No

Context Clues: Seals

Directions: Read the information about seals. Use context clues to determine the meaning of the bold words. Check the correct answers.

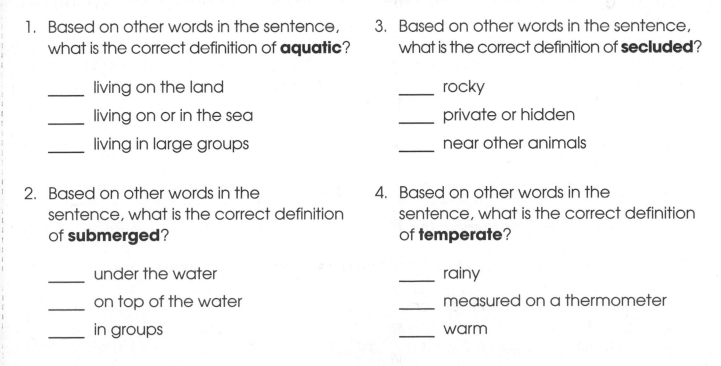

Seals are **aquatic** mammals that also live on land at times. Some seals stay in the sea for weeks or months at a time, even sleeping in the water. When seals go on land, they usually choose **secluded** spots to avoid people and other animals.

The 31 different kinds of seals belong to a group of animals often called pinnipeds meaning "fin-footed." Their fins, or flippers, make them very good swimmers and divers. Their nostrils close tightly when they dive. They have been known to stay **submerged** for as long as a half-hour at a time!

Seals are warm-blooded animals that can adjust to various temperatures. They live in both **temperate** and cold climates. Besides their fur to keep them warm, seals have a thick layer of fat, called blubber, to protect them against the cold. It is harder for seals to cool themselves in hot weather than to warm themselves in cold weather. They can sometimes become so overheated that they die.

1. Based on other words in the sentence, what is the correct definition of **aquatic**?

    ____ living on the land

    ____ living on or in the sea

    ____ living in large groups

2. Based on other words in the sentence, what is the correct definition of **submerged**?

    ____ under the water

    ____ on top of the water

    ____ in groups

3. Based on other words in the sentence, what is the correct definition of **secluded**?

    ____ rocky

    ____ private or hidden

    ____ near other animals

4. Based on other words in the sentence, what is the correct definition of **temperate**?

    ____ rainy

    ____ measured on a thermometer

    ____ warm

Name: _____

Reading Comprehension: Walruses

Directions: Read the information about walruses. Then answer the questions.

A walrus is actually a type of seal that lives only in the Arctic Circle. It has two huge upper teeth, or tusks, which it uses to pull itself out of the water or to move over the rocks on land. It also uses its tusks to dig clams, one of its favorite foods, from the bottom of the sea. On an adult male walrus, the tusks may be three and a half feet long!

A walrus has an unusual face. Besides its long tusks, it has a big, bushy mustache made up of hundreds of movable, stiff bristles. These bristles also help the walrus push food into its mouth. Except for small wrinkles in the skin, a walrus has no outer ears.

Like a seal, the walrus uses its flippers to help it swim. Its front flippers serve as paddles, and while swimming, it swings the back of its huge body from side to side. A walrus looks awkward using its flippers to walk on land, but don't be fooled! A walrus can run as fast as a man.

Baby walruses are born in the early spring. They stay with their mothers until they are two years old. There is a good reason for this—they must grow little tusks, at least three or four inches long, before they can catch their own food from the bottom of the sea. Until then, they must stay close to their mothers to eat. A young walrus that is tired from swimming will climb onto its mother's back for a ride, holding onto her with its front flippers.

1. The walrus is a type of seal found only _____.

2. List two ways the walrus uses its tusks.

_____   _____

3. A walrus cannot move quickly on land.	Yes	No
4. A walrus has a large, bushy mustache.	Yes	No
5. A baby walrus stays very close to its mother until it is two years old.	Yes	No
6. Baby walruses are born late in fall.	Yes	No

Main Idea: Penguins

Directions: Read the information about penguins.

People are amused by the funny, duck-like waddle of penguins and by their appearance because they seem to be wearing little tuxedos. Penguins are among the best-liked animals on Earth, but are also a most misunderstood animal. People may have more wrong ideas about penguins than any other animal.

For example, many people are surprised to learn that penguins are really birds, not mammals. Penguins do not fly, but they do have feathers, and only birds have feathers. Also, like other birds, penguins build nests and their young hatch from eggs. Because of their unusual looks, though, you would never confuse them with any other bird!

Penguins are also thought of as symbols of the polar regions, but penguins do not live north of the equator, so you would not find a penguin on the North Pole. Penguins don't live at the South Pole, either. Only two of the seventeen **species** of penguins spend all of their lives on the frozen continent of Antarctica. You would be just as likely to see a penguin living on an island in a warm climate as in a cold area.

Directions: Draw an **X** on the blank for the correct answer.

1. The main idea is:

 _____ Penguins are among the best-liked animals on earth.
 _____ The penguin is a much misunderstood animal.

2. Penguins live

 _____ only at the North Pole.
 _____ only at the South Pole.
 _____ only south of the equator.

3. Based on the other words in the sentence, what is the correct definition of the word **species**?

 _____ number
 _____ bird
 _____ a distinct kind

Directions: List three ways penguins are like other birds.

_____

Name: _____

Review

Directions: Write your answers on the lines.

1. Which contains the South Pole—the Arctic or Antarctica?
   _____

2. Would you like to live in either the Arctic or Antarctica?
   Why or why not?
   _____
   _____

3. What adaptations would people who live (even for a short time) in these areas have to make?
   _____
   _____

4. What characteristics are common to animals who live in the polar regions?
   _____
   _____

5. Name two animals that live in the polar regions.
   _____   _____

6. Write three facts you learned about one of the animals that live in the polar regions.
   _____
   _____
   _____

7. On each of the poles, there are six months of sunlight and six months of darkness each year. How do you think this would affect you?
   _____
   _____

8. Write three facts you learned about explorers to the North or South Pole regions.
   _____
   _____
   _____

Name: _____

Reading Comprehension: The Desert

Directions: Read the information about the desert. Then answer the questions by circling **Yes** or **No**.

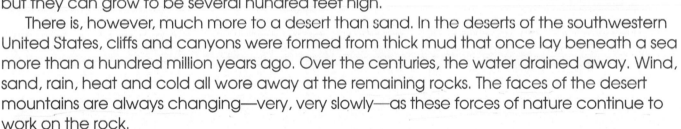

Deserts are found where there is little rainfall or where the rainfall for a whole year falls in only a few weeks' time. Ten inches of rain may be enough for many plants to survive if the rain is spread throughout the year. If the 10 inches of rain falls during one or two months and the rest of the year is dry, those plants may not be able to survive and a desert may form.

When people think of deserts, they may think of long stretches of sand. Sand begins as tiny pieces of rock that get smaller and smaller as wind and weather wear them down. Sand dunes, or hills of drifting sand, are formed as winds move the sand across the desert. Grain by grain, the dunes grow over the years, always shifting with the winds and changing shape. Most dunes are only a few feet tall, but they can grow to be several hundred feet high.

There is, however, much more to a desert than sand. In the deserts of the southwestern United States, cliffs and canyons were formed from thick mud that once lay beneath a sea more than a hundred million years ago. Over the centuries, the water drained away. Wind, sand, rain, heat and cold all wore away at the remaining rocks. The faces of the desert mountains are always changing—very, very slowly—as these forces of nature continue to work on the rock.

Most deserts have a surprising variety of life. There are plants, animals and insects that have adapted to life in the desert. During the heat of the day, a visitor may see very few signs of living things, but as the air begins to cool in the evening, the desert comes to life. As the sun begins to rise again in the sky, the desert once again becomes quiet and lonely.

1. Deserts are found where there is little rainfall or where the rainfall for a whole year falls in only a few weeks.   Yes   No

2. Sand begins as tiny pieces of rock that get smaller and smaller as wind and weather wear them down.   Yes   No

3. Sand dunes were formed from thick mud that once lay beneath a sea more than a hundred million years ago.   Yes   No

4. The faces of the desert mountains can never change.   Yes   No

Reading Comprehension: Desert Weather

Directions: Read the information about desert weather. Then answer the questions.

One definition of a desert is an area that has, on average, less than 10 inches of rain a year. Many deserts have far less than that. Death Valley in California and Nevada, for example, averages fewer than 2 inches of rain each year. The driest of all deserts is the Atacama Desert in Chile, where no rain has been known to fall in 400 years!

Some deserts have a regular rainy season each year, but usually desert rainfall is totally unpredictable. An area may have no rainfall for many years. Sometimes a passing cloud may look like it will send relief to the waiting land, but only a "ghost rain" falls. This means that the hot, dry air dries up the raindrops long before they ever reach the ground.

The temperature in the desert varies greatly. The daytime temperatures in the desert frequently top 120 degrees. In Death Valley, temperatures have been known to reach 190 degrees! In most parts of the world, moisture in the air works like a blanket to hold the heat of the day close to the Earth at night. But, because it has so little moisture, the desert has no such blanket. As a result, nighttime temperatures are very chilly. Temperatures have been known to drop 50 or even 100 degrees at night in the desert.

1. On the average, how much rainfall is there in a year in a desert?

   Less than 10 inches.

2. Where is the driest desert in the world? _chile_

3. What is a "ghost rain"? _the earth is to hot and when the rain evaporates touch the groud it goes away_

4. In other parts of the world, what works as a "blanket" to hold the heat of the day close to the Earth at night? _moisture_

5. What happens to the temperature in the desert at night?

   the desert temp. drops to very chilly.

Name: _____

Review

Directions: Write a three-sentence summary of these selections which includes the main idea.

1. "The Desert"

_____

_____

_____

_____

2. "Desert Weather"

_____

_____

_____

_____

Directions: Define these words. Then use them in sentences of your own.

3. dunes _____

_____

4. canyon _____

_____

5. adapt _____

_____

6. average _____

_____

7. unpredictable _____

_____

Context Clues: Desert Plants

Directions: Read the information about desert plants. Use context clues to determine the meaning of the bold words. Check the correct answers.

Desert plants have special features, or adaptations, that allow them to **survive** the harsh conditions of the desert. A cactus stores water in its tissues when it rains. It then uses this supply of water during the long dry season. The tiny needles on some kinds of **cacti** may number in the tens of thousands. These sharp thorns protect the cactus. They also form tiny shadows in the sunlight that help keep the plant from getting too hot.

Other plants are able to live by dropping their leaves. This cuts down on the **evaporation** of their water supply in the hot sun. Still other plants survive as seeds, protected from the sun and heat by tough seed coats. When it rains, the seeds **sprout** quickly, bloom and produce more seeds that can **withstand** long dry spells.

Some plants spread their roots close to the Earth's surface to quickly gather water when it does rain. Other plants, such as the mesquite, have roots that grow 50 or 60 feet below the ground to reach underground water supplies.

1. Based on the other words in the sentence, what is the correct definition of **survive**?

   ____ continue to live
   ____ bloom in the desert
   ____ flower

2. Based on the other words in the sentence, what is the correct definition of **evaporation**?

   ____ water loss from heat
   ____ much-needed rainfall
   ____ boiling

3. Based on the other words in the sentence, what is the correct definition of **withstand**?

   ____ put up with
   ____ stand with another
   ____ take from

4. Based on the other words in the sentence, what is the correct definition of **cacti**?

   ____ a type of sand dune
   ____ more than one cactus
   ____ a caravan of camels

5. Based on the other words in the sentence, what is the correct definition of **sprout**?

   ____ a type of bean that grows only in the desert
   ____ begin to grow
   ____ a small flower

Recognizing Details: The Cactus Family

Directions: Read the information about cacti. Pay close attention to details. Answer the questions.

Although cacti are the best-known desert plants, they don't live only in hot, dry places. While cacti are most likely to be found in the desert areas of Mexico and the southwestern United States, they can by seen as far north as Nova Scotia, Canada. Certain types of cacti can live even in the snow!

Desert cacti are particularly good at surviving very long dry spells. Most cacti have a very long root system so they can absorb as much water as possible. Every available drop of water is taken into the cactus and held in its fleshy stem. A cactus stem can hold enough water to last for 2 years or longer.

A cactus may be best known for its spines. Although a few kinds of cacti don't have spines, the stems of most types are covered with these sharp needles. The spines have many uses for a cactus. They keep animals from eating the cactus. They collect raindrops and dew. The spines also help keep the plant cool by forming shadows in the sun and by trapping a layer of air close to the plant. They break up the desert winds that dry out the cactus.

Cacti come in all sizes and shapes. The biggest type In North America is the saguaro. It can weigh 12,000 to 14,000 pounds and grow to be 50 feet tall. A saguaro can last several years without water, but it will grow only after summer rains. In May and June, white blossoms appear. Many kinds of birds nest in these enormous cacti: white-winged doves, woodpeckers, small owls, thrashers and wrens all build nests in the saguaro.

1. Where are you most likely to find a cactus growing?

   _____

2. How long can most cacti survive without water?

   _____

3. What are two ways the spines help a cactus?

   _____

4. What is the biggest cactus in North America?

   _____

5. What animals live in a saguaro cactus?

   _____

Review

Directions: Write a three-sentence summary of these selections. Refer to the reading selections for review if necessary.

1. "Desert Plants"

   _____
   _____
   _____

2. "The Cactus Family"

   _____
   _____
   _____

Directions: Describe the adaptations these plants have made to survive in the desert.

3. cacti _____
   _____

4. mesquite _____
   _____

5. saguaro cactus _____

Directions: Answer these questions.

6. What is the purpose of cactus spines? _____
   _____

7. Why does the mesquite have long roots? _____
   _____

Directions: Define these words. Then use them in sentences of your own.

8. evaporation _____
   _____

9. spine _____
   _____

Reading Comprehension: Lizards

Directions: Read the information about lizards. Then answer the questions.

Lizards are reptiles, related to snakes, turtles, alligators and crocodiles. Like other reptiles, lizards are cold-blooded. This means their body temperature changes with that of their surroundings. However, by changing their behavior throughout the day they can keep their temperature fairly constant.

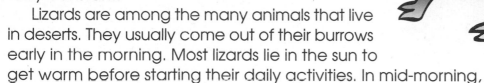

Lizards are among the many animals that live in deserts. They usually come out of their burrows early in the morning. Most lizards lie in the sun to get warm before starting their daily activities. In mid-morning, they hunt for food. If it becomes too hot, lizards can raise their tails and bodies off the ground to help cool off. At mid-day, they return to their burrows or crawl under rocks for several hours. Late in the day, they again lie in the sun to absorb heat before the chilly desert night falls.

Like all animals, lizards have ways of protecting themselves. Some types of lizards have developed a most unusual defense. If a hawk or other animal grabs one of these lizards by its tail, the tail will break off. The tail will continue to wiggle around to distract the attacker while the lizard runs away. A month or two later, the lizard grows a new tail.

There are about 3,000 kinds of lizards, and all of them can bite, but only two types of lizards are poisonous: the Gila monster of the southwestern United States and the Mexican bearded lizard. Both are short-legged, thick-bodied reptiles with fat tails. These lizards do not attack people and will not bite them unless they are attacked.

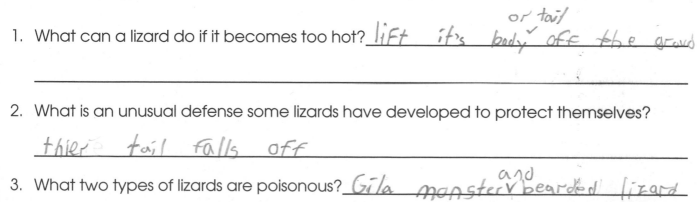

1. What can a lizard do if it becomes too hot? lift it's body *or tail* off the ground

_____

2. What is an unusual defense some lizards have developed to protect themselves?

thier tail falls off

3. What two types of lizards are poisonous? Gila monster *and* bearded lizard

_____

Main Idea: People in the Desert

Directions: Read the information about people in the desert. Then answer the questions.

Long before Europeans came to live in America, Native Americans had discovered ways of living in the desert. Some of these Native Americans were hunters or belonged to wandering tribes that stayed in the desert for only short periods of time. Others learned to farm and live in villages. They made their houses of trees, clay and brush.

The desert met all of their needs for life: food, water, skins for clothing, materials for tools, weapons and shelter. For meat, the desert offered deer, birds and rabbits for hunting. When these animals were hard to find, the Native Americans would eat mice and lizards. Many desert plants, such as the prickly pear and mesquite, provided moisture, fruit and seeds that could be eaten.

The first Europeans in the American deserts were searching for furs and metals, like silver and gold. They explored, but did not settle in the desert. The early pioneers were usually unsuccessful at living in the desert. They found the great heat and long dry periods too difficult. When they moved away, they left behind empty mining camps, houses and sheds that slowly fell apart in the sun and wind.

1. What is the main idea of this selection?

   _____ Before Europeans came to live in America, Native Americans had discovered ways of successfully living in the desert.

   _____ Some Native Americans were hunters or belonged to wandering tribes who stayed in the desert for only short periods of time.

2. Who were the first people to live in the deserts of North America?

   _____

3. What did the Native Americans use to make their houses in the desert?

   _____

4. What kinds of food did the Native Americans find in the desert?

   _____

5. What were the first Europeans who came to the desert looking for?

   _____

Name: _____

Main Idea: Camels

Directions: Read the information about camels. Then answer the questions.

Camels are well suited to desert life. They can cope with infrequent supplies of food and water, blazing heat during the day, low temperatures at night and sand blown by high winds.

There are two kinds of camels: the two-humped bactrian and the one-humped dromedary. The dromedary is the larger of the two. It has coarse fur on its back that helps protect it from the sun's rays. The hair on its stomach and legs is short to prevent overheating. When camels **molt** in the spring, their wool can be collected in tufts from the bushes and ground.

The legs of the dromedary are much longer than those of the bactrian. Animals that live in very hot countries tend to have longer legs. This gives them a larger area of body surface from which heat can escape. Bactrian camels live in the deserts of central Asia where winters are bitterly cold, so they are not as tall as dromedaries.

Both kinds of camels have pads on their feet that keep them from sinking into the sand as they walk. A camel's long neck allows it to reach the ground to drink water and eat grass without having to bend its legs. It also can reach up to eat leaves from trees.

Camels do not store water in their humps as many people believe. The hump is for fat storage. When there is plenty of food, the camel's hump swells and feels firm. During the dry season when there is little food, the fat is used up and the hump shrinks and becomes soft.

1. What is the main idea of this selection?

   _____ Camels are well suited to desert life.

   _____ There are two kinds of camels.

2. Based on the other words in the sentence, what is the correct definition of **molt**?

   _____ turns into a butterfly

   _____ sheds its hair

   _____ becomes overheated

3. What are the two kinds of camels? _____

4. Why don't camels sink into the sand when they walk? _____

_____

5. What is the purpose of a camel's hump? _____

Review

Directions: Write your answers in complete sentences.

1. Describe how the cold-blooded lizard regulates its body temperature.

   _____

   _____

   _____

   _____

2. What is the main idea of the selection "Lizards"?

   _____

   _____

3. Describe how Native Americans adapted to life in the desert.

   _____

   _____

   _____

   _____

4. Why do you think early pioneers were unsuccessful at desert living?

   _____

   _____

   _____

   _____

5. Describe the adaptations of camels for successful desert habitation.

   _____

   _____

   _____

Name: _____

Reading Comprehension: Desert Lakes

Directions: Read the information about lakes in the desert. Then answer the questions.

A few deserts have small permanent lakes. While they may be a welcome sight in the desert, the water in them is not fit for drinking. They are salt lakes. Rain from nearby higher land keeps these lakes supplied with water, but the lakes are blocked in with nowhere to drain. Over the years, mineral salts collect in the water and build up to a high level, making the water undrinkable.

Most desert lakes are only temporary. Occasional rains may fill them to depths of several feet, but in a matter of weeks or months, all the water has been dried up by the heat and sun. The dried lake beds that remain are called **playas**. Some playas are simply areas of sun-baked mud; others are covered with a sparkling layer of salt.

Perhaps the most unusual desert lake is in central Australia. It is called Lake Eyre. It is a huge lake—nearly 3,600 square miles in area—but it is almost totally dry most of the time. Since it was discovered in 1840, it has been filled only two times. Both times, the lake completely dried up again within a few years.

1. Why is the water in a desert lake not fit for drinking?

   _____

2. Why are the lakes in the desert salt lakes?

   _____

3. Why are most desert lakes only temporary?

   _____

4. What is a **playa**? _____

5. What is the name of the unusual desert lake in central Australia?

   _____

6. How big is this desert lake? _____

Name: _____

Review

Directions: Write your answers in complete sentences.

1. What is a desert?
   _____
   _____

2. Name a desert in the United States and tell where it is.
   _____
   _____

3. What special characteristics must an animal have to survive in the desert?
   _____
   _____
   _____

4. What special characteristics must a plant have to survive in the desert?
   _____
   _____
   _____

5. What differences exist between animals whose habitat is the polar regions and animals whose habitat is the desert regions?
   _____
   _____
   _____
   _____
   _____

6. Would you like to visit the desert? Why or why not?
   _____
   _____
   _____
   _____

ENGLISH

Metaphor:
Don't be a crab!
Simile:
The wet floor was as slippery as an eel.

Name: _____

Nouns

A **noun** is a word that names a person, place or thing.

Examples:
> **person** — friend
> **place** — home
> **thing** — desk

Nouns are used many ways in sentences. They can be the subjects of sentences.

Example: Noun as subject: Your high-topped **sneakers** look great with that outfit.

Nouns can be direct objects of a sentence. The **direct object** follows the verb and completes its meaning. It answers the question **who** or **what**.

Example: Noun as direct object: Shelly's family bought a new **car**.

Nouns can be indirect objects. An **indirect object** comes between the verb and the direct object and tells **to whom** or **for whom** something was done.

Example: Noun as indirect object: She gave **Tina** a big hug.

Directions: Underline all the nouns. Write **S** above the noun if it is a subject, **DO** if it is a direct object or **IO** if it is an indirect object. The first one has been done for you.

          S   DO

1. Do <u>alligators</u> eat <u>people</u>?

2. James hit a home run, and our team won the game.

3. The famous actor gave Susan his autograph.

4. Eric loaned Keith his bicycle.

5. The kindergarten children painted cute pictures.

6. Robin sold David some chocolate chip cookies.

7. The neighbors planned a going-away party and bought a gift.

8. The party and gift surprised Kurt and his family.

9. My scout leader told our group a funny joke.

10. Karen made her little sister a clown costume.

Name: _____

Nouns

Directions: Write 10 nouns for each category.

People

1. _____
2. _____
3. _____
4. _____
5. _____
6. _____
7. _____
8. _____
9. _____
10. _____

Places

1. _____
2. _____
3. _____
4. _____
5. _____
6. _____
7. _____
8. _____
9. _____
10. _____

Things

1. _____
2. _____
3. _____
4. _____
5. _____

6. _____
7. _____
8. _____
9. _____
10. _____

PERSON PLACE THING

Name: _____

Proper and Common Nouns

Proper nouns name specific people, places or things.

Examples: Washington, D.C., Thomas Jefferson, Red Sea

Common nouns name nonspecific people, places or things.

Examples: man, fortress, dog

Directions: Underline the proper nouns and circle the common nouns in each sentence.

1. My friend, Josephine, loves to go to the docks to watch the boats sail into the harbor.

2. Josephine is especially interested in the boat named *Maiden Voyage*.

3. This boat is painted red with yellow stripes and has several large masts.

4. Its sails are white and billow in the wind.

5. At Misty Harbor, many boats are always sailing in and out.

6. The crews on the boats rush from bow to stern working diligently to keep the sailboats moving.

7. Josephine has been invited aboard *Maiden Voyage* by its captain.

8. Captain Ferdinand knew of her interest in sailboats, so he offered a tour.

9. Josephine was amazed at the gear aboard the boat and the skills of the crew.

10. It is Josephine's dream to sail the Atlantic Ocean on a boat similar to *Maiden Voyage*.

11. Her mother is not sure of this dangerous dream and urges Josephine to consider safer dreams.

12. Josephine thinks of early explorers like Christopher Columbus, Amerigo Vespucci and Leif Ericson.

13. She thinks these men must have been brave to set out into the unknown waters of the world.

14. Their boats were often small and provided little protection from major ocean storms.

15. Josephine believes that if early explorers could challenge the rough ocean waters, she could, too.

Abstract and Concrete Nouns

Concrete nouns name something that can be touched or seen.
Abstract nouns name an idea, a thought or a feeling which cannot
be touched or seen.

Examples:
    concrete nouns: house, puppy, chair
    abstract nouns: love, happiness, fear

Directions: Write **concrete** or **abstract** in the blank after each noun.

1. loyalty_____

2. light bulb _____

3. quarter _____

4. hope _____

5. satellite _____

6. ability _____

7. patio _____

8. door _____

9. allegiance _____

10. Cuba _____

11. Michael Jordan _____

12. friendship _____

13. telephone _____

14. computer _____

Directions: Write eight nouns for each category.

Concrete	Abstract
1. _____	1. _____
2. _____	2. _____
3. _____	3. _____
4. _____	4. _____
5. _____	5. _____
6. _____	6. _____
7. _____	7. _____
8. _____	8. _____

Name: _____

Verbs

A **verb** tells what something does or that something exists.

Examples:
Tim **has shared** his apples with us.
Those apples **were** delicious.
I hope Tim **is bringing** more apples tomorrow.
Tim **picked** the apples himself.

Directions: Underline the verbs.

1. Gene moved here from Philadelphia.

2. Now he is living in a house on my street.

3. His house is three houses away from mine.

4. I have lived in this house all my life.

5. I hope Gene will like this town.

6. I am helping Gene with his room.

7. He has a lot of stuff!

8. We are painting his walls green.

9. He picked the color himself.

10. I wonder what his parents will say.

Directions: Write verbs to complete these sentences.

11. We _____ some paintbrushes.

12. Gene already _____ the paint.

13. I _____ my old clothes.

14. There _____ no furniture in his room right now.

15. It _____ several hours to paint his whole room.

Verbs

A **verb** is the action word in a sentence. It tells what the subject does (**build**, **laugh**, **express**, **fasten**) or that it exists (**is**, **are**, **was**, **were**).

Examples: Randy **raked** the leaves into a pile.
I **was** late to school today.

Directions: In the following sentences, write verbs that make sense.

1. The quarterback _____ the ball to the receiver.

2. My mother _____ some cookies yesterday.

3. John _____ newspapers to make extra money.

4. The teacher _____ the instructions on the board.

5. Last summer, our family _____ a trip to Florida to visit relatives.

Sometimes, a verb can be two or more words. Verbs used to "support" other verbs are called **helping verbs**.

Examples: We **were** listening to music in my room.
Chris **has been** studying for over 2 hours.

Directions: In the following sentences, write helping verbs along with the correct form of the given verbs. The first one has been done for you.

1. Michelle (write) ____**is writing**____ a letter to her grandmother right now.

2. My brother (have) _____ trouble with his math homework.

3. When we arrived, the movie (start) _____ already.

4. My aunt (live) _____ in the same house for 30 years.

5. Our football team (go) _____ to win the national championship this year.

6. My sister (talk) _____ on the phone all afternoon!

7. I couldn't sleep last night because the wind (blow) _____ so hard.

8. Last week, Pat was sick, but now he (feel) _____ much better.

9. Tomorrow, our class (have) _____ a bake sale.

10. Mr. Smith (collect) _____ stamps for 20 years.

Name: _____

Verb Tenses

Verbs have different forms to show whether something already happened, is happening right now or will happen.

Examples:
   Present tense: I **walk**.
   Past tense: I **walked**.
   Future tense: I **will walk**.

Directions: Write **PAST** if the verb is past tense, **PRES** for present tense or **FUT** for future tense. The first one has been done for you.

PRES 1. My sister Sara works at the grocery store.

_____ 2. Last year, she worked in an office.

_____ 3. Sara is going to college, too.

_____ 4. She will be a dentist some day.

_____ 5. She says studying is difficult.

_____ 6. Sara hardly studied at all in high school.

_____ 7. I will be ready for college in a few years.

_____ 8. Last night, I read my history book for 2 hours.

Directions: Complete these sentences using verbs in the tenses listed. The first one has been done for you.

   9. take: future tense   My friends and I **will take** a trip.

  10. talk: past tense   We _____ for a long time about where to go.

  11. want: present tense   Pam _____ to go to the lake.

  12. want: past tense   Jake _____ to go with us.

  13. say: past tense   His parents _____ no.

  14. ride: future tense   We _____ our bikes.

  15. pack: past tense   Susan and Jared already _____ lunches for us.

Name: _____

Verb Tenses

The past tense of many verbs is formed by adding **ed**.

Examples:
    remember + **ed** = remembered
    climb + **ed** = climbed

If a verb ends in **e**, drop the **e** before adding **ed**.

Examples:

Present	Past
phone	phoned
arrive	arrived

If a verb ends in **y**, change the **y** to **i** before adding **ed**.

Examples:

Present	Past
carry	carried
try	tried

If a verb ends in a short vowel followed by a single consonant, double the final consonant.

Examples:

Present	Past
trip	tripped
pop	popped

Directions: Circle the misspelled verb in each sentence and write it correctly in the blank.

1. They stopped at our house and then hurryed home. _____

2. I scrubed and mopped the floor. _____

3. The coach nameed the five starting players. _____

4. He popped the potatoes into the oil and fryed them. _____

5. I accidentally droped my papers on the floor. _____

6. I had hopeed you could go climbing with me. _____

7. He triped on the rug. _____

8. The baby cryed and screamed all night. _____

9. I moped the mess up after the glass dropped on the floor. _____

10. First, she frowned, and then she smileed. _____

Name: _____

Writing: Verb Forms

Present-tense verbs tell what is happening right now. To form present-tense verbs, use the "plain" verbs or use **is** or **are** before the verb and add **ing** to the verb.

Examples: We **eat**. We **are eating**.
He **serves**. He **is serving**.

Directions: Complete each sentence with the correct verb form, telling what is happening right now. Read carefully, as some sentences already have **is** or **are**.

Examples: Scott is (loan) <u>loaning</u> Jenny his math book.
Jenny (study) <u>is studying</u> for a big math test.

1. The court is (release) _____ the prisoner early.

2. Jonah and Jill (write) _____ their notes in code.

3. Are you (vote) _____ for Baxter?

4. The girls are (coax) _____ the dog into the bathtub.

5. The leaves (begin) _____ to fall from the trees.

6. My little brother (stay) _____ at his friend's house tonight.

7. Is she (hide) _____ behind the screen?

To tell what already happened, or in the **past tense**, add **ed** to many verbs or use **was** or **were** and add **ing** to the verb.

Example: I **watched**. I **was watching**.

Directions: Complete each sentence with the correct verb form. This time, tell what already happened.

Examples: We (walk) <u>walked</u> there yesterday.
They were (talk) <u>talking</u>.

1. The government was (decrease) _____ our taxes.

2. Was anyone (cheat) _____ in this game?

3. We were (try) _____ to set goals for the project.

Name: _____

Writing: Future-Tense Verbs

Future-tense verbs tell about things that will happen in the future. To form future-tense verbs, use **will** before the verb.

Example: Tomorrow I **will walk** to school.

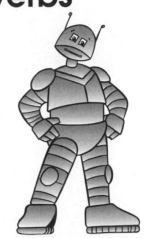

When you use **will**, you may also have to add a helping verb and the ending **ing**.

Example: Tomorrow I **will be walking** to school.

Directions: Imagine what the world will be like 100 years from now. Maybe you think robots will be doing our work for us, or that people will be living on the moon. What will our houses look like? What will school be like? Write a paragraph describing what you imagine. Be sure to use future-tense verbs.

_____

_____

_____

_____

_____

_____

_____

_____

_____

_____

_____

Grade 5 - Comprehensive Curriculum

Principal Parts of Verbs

Verbs have three principal parts. They are **present**, **past** and **past participle**.

Regular verbs form the past tense by adding **ed** to the present tense.

The past participle is formed by using the past tense verb with a helping verb: **has**, **have** or **had**.

Directions: Write the correct form of each verb. The first one has been done for you.

Present	Past	Past Participle
1. look	<u>looked</u>	<u>have/has/had looked</u>
2. _____	planned	_____
3. _____	_____	has/have/had closed
4. wash	_____	_____
5. _____	prepared	_____
6. _____	_____	has/have/had provided
7. invite	_____	_____
8. _____	discovered	_____
9. approve	_____	_____
10. _____	searched	_____
11. establish	_____	_____
12. _____	_____	has/have/had formed
13. _____	pushed	_____
14. travel	_____	_____

Name: _____

Irregular Verbs

Irregular verbs change completely in the past tense. Unlike regular verbs, the past tense forms of irregular verbs are not formed by adding **ed**.

Examples:

Chung **eats** the cookies.
Chung **ate** them yesterday.
Chung **has eaten** them for weeks.

Present Tense	Past Tense	Past Participle
begin	began	has/have/had begun
speak	spoke	has/have/had spoken
drink	drank	has/have/had drunk
know	knew	has/have/had known
eat	ate	has/have/had eaten
wear	wore	has/have/had worn

Directions: Rewrite these sentences once using the past tense and again using the past participle of each verb.

1. Todd begins football practice this week.

   _____

   _____

2. She wears her hair in braids.

   _____

   _____

3. I drink two glasses of milk.

   _____

   _____

4. The man is speaking to us.

   _____

   _____

5. The dogs are eating.

   _____

   _____

Grade 5 - Comprehensive Curriculum

Name: _____

Irregular Verbs

The past participle form of an irregular verb needs a helping verb.

Examples:

Present	Past	Past Participle
begin	began	has/have/had begun
drive	drove	has/have/had driven

present, past and past participle

Directions: Write the past and past participle form of these irregular verbs. Use a dictionary if you need help.

Present	Past	Past Participle
1. speak	_____	_____
2. break	_____	_____
3. beat	_____	_____
4. dream	_____	_____
5. tear	_____	_____
6. forget	_____	_____
7. lead	_____	_____
8. stand	_____	_____
9. sting	_____	_____
10. freeze	_____	_____
11. grow	_____	_____
12. lose	_____	_____
13. run	_____	_____
14. meet	_____	_____
15. sit	_____	_____
16. do	_____	_____

Name: _____

"Be" as a Helping Verb

A **helping verb** tells when the action of a sentence takes place. The helping verb **be** has several forms: **am**, **is**, **are**, **was**, **were** and **will**. These helping verbs can be used in all three tenses.

Examples:
   Past tense: Ken **was** talking. We **were** eating.
   Present tense: I **am** coming. Simon **is** walking. They **are** singing.
   Future tense: I **will** work. The puppies **will** eat.

In the present and past tense, many verbs can be written with or without the helping verb **be**. When the verb is written with a form of **be**, add **ing**. **Was** and **is** are used with singular subjects. **Were** and **are** are used with plural subjects.

Examples:
   Present tense: Angela **sings**. Angela **is singing**. The children **sing**. They **are singing**.
   Past tense: I **studied**. I **was studying**. They **studied**. They **were studying**.

The helping verb **will** is always needed for the future tense, but the **ing** ending is not used with **will**. **Will** is both singular and plural.

Examples:
   Future tense: I **will eat**. We **will watch**.

Directions: Underline the helping verbs.

1. Brian is helping me with this project.
2. We are working together on it.
3. Susan was painting the background yesterday.
4. Matt and Mike were cleaning up.
5. Tomorrow, we will present our project to the class.

Directions: Rewrite the verbs using a helping verb. The first one has been done for you.

6. Our neighborhood plans a garage sale.   _____is planning_____

7. The sale starts tomorrow.   _____

8. My brother Doug and I think about things we sell.   _____

9. My grandfather cleans out the garage.   _____

10. Doug and I help him.   _____

Name: _____

"Be" as a Linking Verb

A **linking verb** links a noun or adjective in the predicate to the subject. Forms of the verb **be** are the most common linking verbs. Linking verbs can be used in all three tenses.

Examples:
   Present: My father **is** a salesman.
   Past: The store **was** very busy last night.
   Future: Tomorrow **will be** my birthday.

In the first sentence, **is** links the subject (father) with a noun (salesman). In the second sentence, **was** links the subject (store) with an adjective (busy). In the third sentence, **will be** links the subject (tomorrow) with a noun (birthday).

Directions: Circle the linking verbs. Underline the two words that are linked by the verb. The first one has been done for you.

1. Columbus (is) the capital of Ohio.

2. By bedtime, Nicole was bored.

3. Andy will be the captain of our team.

4. Tuesday is the first day of the month.

5. I hate to say this, but we are lost.

6. Ask him if the water is cold.

7. By the time I finished my paper, it was late.

8. Spaghetti is my favorite dinner.

9. The children were afraid of the big truck.

10. Karen will be a good president of our class.

11. These lessons are helpful.

12. Was that report due today?

Name: _____

"Be" as a Linking or Helping Verb

Directions: Write **H** if the form of **be** is used as a helping verb or **L** if it is used as a linking verb.

_____ 1. Mary Beth was watching for the mail.

_____ 2. The mail was late, as usual.

_____ 3. Her friends were calling her to come to the park.

_____ 4. "We will be missed by everyone at the park," they said.

_____ 5. Still, Mary Beth was hopeful as she waited.

_____ 6. She knew her brother was sending her a letter.

_____ 7. He was a soldier in the army.

_____ 8. He was homesick for his family, so he wrote every day.

Directions: Write two sentences using a form of **be** as a helping verb.

9. _____

_____

10. _____

_____

Directions: Write two sentences using a form of **be** as a linking verb.

11. _____

_____

12. _____

_____

Name: _____

Transitive and Intransitive Verbs

An **intransitive verb** can stand alone in the predicate because its meaning is complete. In the examples below, notice that each short sentence is a complete thought.

Examples: Intransitive verbs: The tree **grows**. The mouse **squeaked**. The deer **will run**.

A **transitive verb** needs a direct object to complete its meaning. The meaning of a sentence with a transitive verb is not complete without a direct object.

Examples: Transitive verbs: The mouse **wants** seeds. The deer **saw** the hunter. The tree **will lose** its leaves.

The direct object **seeds** tells what the mouse wants. **Leaves** tells what the tree will lose and **hunter** tells what the deer saw.

Both transitive and intransitive verbs can be in the past, present or future tense.

Directions: Underline the verb in each sentence. Write **I** if the sentence has an intransitive verb or **T** if it has a transitive verb.

_____ 1. The snake slid quietly along the ground.

_____ 2. The snake scared a rabbit.

_____ 3. The rabbit hopped quickly back to its hole.

_____ 4. Safe from the snake, the rabbit shivered with fear.

_____ 5. In the meantime, the snake caught a frog.

_____ 6. The frog was watching flies and didn't see the snake.

Directions: Complete these sentences with intransitive verbs.

7. Our friends _____

8. The movie _____

Directions: Complete these sentences with transitive verbs and direct objects.

9. My family _____

10. The lightning _____

Name: _____

Which Noun Is the Subject?

Usually, the noun that is the subject will come at the beginning of the sentence.

Examples: The [truck] turned quickly around the corner.
[Kevin] stayed home from school yesterday.

Sometimes, other words will come before the subject. When this happens, remember to look for who or what the sentence is about.

Example: After school, [Katie] usually walks to the library.

The sentence is about Katie, not school.

Directions: In the sentences below, circle the nouns that are subjects. Some sentences have more than one subject, and they will not always be at the beginning of the sentence.

1. Mark and I helped the teacher clean the classroom.

2. In the morning, my mother cooks breakfast for the whole family.

3. To finish the project, Ann had to stay up very late last night.

4. After the storm, power lines were down all over the city.

5. Oranges and grapefruits grow very well in Florida.

6. During the summer, squirrels work hard to gather nuts for the winter.

7. While skiing last weekend, my neighbor fell and broke his leg.

8. Pictures and posters cover all the walls of our classroom.

9. To save gas, my father takes the bus to work instead of driving.

10. In my opinion, dogs and cats make the best pets.

Grade 5 - Comprehensive Curriculum

Name: _____

Subjects and Verbs

Directions: Underline the subject and verb in each sentence below. Write **S** over the subject and **V** over the verb. If the verb is two words, mark them both.

Examples:
$$\overset{S}{\underline{Dennis}} \ \overset{V}{\underline{was}} \ \overset{V}{\underline{drinking}} \text{ some punch.}$$

$$\text{The } \overset{S}{\underline{punch}} \ \overset{V}{\underline{was}} \text{ too sweet.}$$

1. Hayley brags about her dog all the time.

2. Mrs. Thomas scrubbed the dirt off her car.

3. Then her son rinsed off the soap.

4. The teacher was flipping through the cards.

5. Jenny's rabbit was hungry and thirsty.

6. Your science report lacks a little detail.

7. Chris is stocking the shelves with cans of soup.

8. The accident caused a huge dent in our car.

Just as sentences can have two subjects, they can also have two verbs.

Example:
$$\overset{S}{\underline{Jennifer}} \text{ and } \overset{S}{\underline{Amie}} \ \overset{V}{\underline{fed}} \text{ the dog and } \overset{V}{\underline{gave}} \text{ him clean water.}$$

Directions: Underline all the subjects and verbs in these sentences. Write **S** over the subjects and **V** over the verbs.

1. Mom and Dad scrubbed and rinsed the basement floor.

2. The men came and stocked the lake with fish.

3. Someone broke the window and ran away.

4. Carrie punched a hole in the paper and threaded yarn through the hole.

5. Julie and Pat turned their bikes around and went home.

Name: _____

Writing: Subjects and Verbs

Directions: Make each group of words below into a sentence by adding a subject, a verb, or a subject and a verb. Then write **S** over each subject and **V** over each verb.

Example: the dishes in the sink

        S   V

The dishes in the sink were dirty.

1. a leash for your pet

_____

2. dented the table

_____

3. a bowl of punch for the party

_____

4. rinsed the soap out

_____

5. a lack of chairs

_____

6. bragging about his sister

_____

7. the stock on the shelf

_____

8. with a flip of the wrist

_____

Name: _____

Writing: Subjects and Verbs

Directions: Decide which words in the box are subjects (nouns) and which are verbs. Write each word under the correct heading. Then match each subject with a verb to make a sentence. Use each subject and verb only once. The first one has been done for you.

dog	~~girls~~	~~walked~~	barked	honked
flew	car	played	neighbor	teacher
wrote	mowed	Marcus	birds	

Subjects	**Verbs**
girls	walked
_____	_____
_____	_____
_____	_____
_____	_____
_____	_____
_____	_____

1. <u>The tired girls walked slowly home from school.</u>

2. _____

3. _____

4. _____

5. _____

6. _____

7. _____

Name: _____

Indirect Objects

An **indirect object** is a word or words that come between the verb and the direct object. An indirect object tells **to whom** or **for whom** something has been done. Indirect objects are always nouns or pronouns.

Examples:

She cooked **me** a great dinner. **Me** is the indirect object. It tells **for whom** something was cooked.

Give the **photographer** a smile. **Photographer** is the indirect object. It tells **to whom** the smile should be given.

Directions: Circle the indirect objects. Underline the direct objects.

1. Marla showed me her drawing.

2. The committee had given her an award for it.

3. The principal offered Marla a special place to put her drawing.

4. While babysitting, I read Timmy a story.

5. He told me the end of the story.

6. Then I fixed him some hot chocolate.

7. Timmy gave me a funny look.

8. Why didn't his mother tell me?

9. Hot chocolate gives Timmy a rash.

10. Will his mom still pay me three dollars for watching him?

Directions: Write indirect objects to complete these sentences.

11. I will write _____ a letter.

12. I'll give _____ part of my lunch.

13. Show _____ your model.

14. Did you send _____ a card?

15. Don't tell _____ my secret.

Direct and Indirect Objects

Directions: Underline the direct objects. Circle the indirect objects.

1. Please give him a note card.

2. My father told me a secret.

3. I carefully examined the dinosaur bones.

4. Joseph decorated the banquet hall for the wedding.

5. Every night, I telephone my grandmother.

6. The head of the company offered my father a new position.

7. Too much pizza can give you a stomachache.

8. Will you draw me a picture?

9. This new computer gives me a headache!

10. Thomas discovered a new entrance to the cave.

11. He showed me the rare penny.

12. While watching television, I wrote Maria a letter.

13. Mrs. Fetters will pay me ten dollars for shoveling her sidewalk this winter.

14. The teacher handed her class a surprise quiz.

15. I like to drink iced tea on summer days.

16. Mom bought Sharon new school supplies for kindergarten.

17. I had to pay the library a fine for overdue books.

18. My family enjoys playing football.

19. Each night my mom reads me one chapter of a novel.

20. The teacher gave us our report cards.

Prepositions

A **preposition** is a word that comes before a noun or pronoun and shows the relationship of that noun or pronoun to other words in the sentence.

The **object of a preposition** is a noun or pronoun that follows a preposition and completes its meaning. A **prepositional phrase** includes a preposition and the object(s) of the preposition.

Examples:

The girl **with red hair** spoke first.
With is the preposition.
Hair is the object of the preposition.
With red hair is a prepositional phrase.

In addition to being subjects, direct and indirect objects and nouns and pronouns can also be objects of prepositions.

Prepositions						
across	behind	from	near	over	to	on
by	through	in	around	off	with	of
after	before	for	between	beyond	at	into

Directions: Underline the prepositional phrases in these sentences. Circle the prepositions. The first sentence has been done for you.

1. The name (of) our street is Redsail Court.
2. We have lived in our house for three years.
3. In our family, we eat a lot of hamburgers.
4. We like hamburgers on toasted buns with mustard.
5. Sometimes we eat in the living room in front of the TV.
6. In the summer, we have picnics in the backyard.
7. The ants crawl into our food and into our clothes.
8. Behind our house is a park with swings.
9. Kids from the neighborhood walk through our yard to the park.
10. Sometimes they cut across Mom's garden and stomp on her beans.
11. Mom says we need a tall fence without a gate.
12. With a fence around our yard, we could get a dog!

Pronouns

A **pronoun** is a word used in place of a noun. Instead of repeating a noun again and again, use a pronoun.

Examples:
I	you	he	she	them	us
me	your	him	her	they	it
my	our	his	we	their	its

Each pronoun takes the place of a certain noun. If the noun is singular, the pronoun should be singular. If the noun is plural, the pronoun should be plural.

Examples: John told **his** parents **he** would be late.
The girls said **they** would ride **their** bikes.

Directions: In the sentences below, draw an arrow from each pronoun to the noun it replaces.

Example: Gail needs the salt. Please pass it to her.

1. The workers had faith they would finish the house in time.

2. Kathy fell and scraped her knees. She put bandages on them.

3. The teacher told the students he wanted to see their papers.

Directions: Cross out some nouns and write pronouns to replace them.

his
Example: Dan needed a book for ~~Dan's~~ book report.

1. Brian doesn't care about the style of Brian's clothes.

2. Joy dyed Joy's jeans to make the jeans dark blue.

3. Faith said Faith was tired of sharing a bedroom with Faith's two sisters. Faith wanted a room of Faith's own.

4. Bathe babies carefully so the soap doesn't get in the babies' eyes and make the babies cry.

5. When the children held up the children's pictures, we could see the pride in the children's eyes.

Name: _____

Singular and Plural Pronouns

Directions: Rewrite the sentences so the pronouns match the nouns they replace in gender and number. Change the verb form if necessary. The first one has been done for you.

1. Canada geese are the best-known geese in North America. It was here when the first settlers came from Europe.

   <u>Canada geese are the best-known geese in North America. They were here when the first settlers came from Europe.</u>

2. A Canada goose has a white patch from their chin to a spot behind their eyes.

   _____
   _____

3. Canada geese can harm farmland when it grazes in fields.

   _____
   _____

4. Geese have favorite fields where it likes to stop and eat.

   _____
   _____

5. While most of the flock eats, some geese stand guard. He warns if there is any danger.

   _____
   _____

6. Each guard gets their turn to eat, too.

   _____
   _____

7. Female geese usually lay five or six eggs, but she may lay as many as eleven.

   _____
   _____

8. While the female goose sits on the eggs, the male goose guards their mate.

   _____
   _____

Possessive Pronouns

A **possessive pronoun** shows ownership. A possessive pronoun can be used with the name of what is owned or by itself.

Examples:
> This is **my** book. The book is **mine**.
> This is **your** sandwich. It is **yours**.
> This is **our** room. The room is **ours**.

The possessive pronouns are **my**, **your**, **our**, **his**, **her**, **their**, **its**, **mine**, **yours**, **ours**, **hers** and **theirs**. Possessive pronouns do not have apostrophes.

Directions: Complete the sentences with the correct possessive pronouns.

1. I entered _____ picture in the contest. That farm scene is _____.

2. Shelby entered _____ picture, too. Do you see _____?

3. Hal didn't finish _____ drawing. He left _____ at home.

4. Did you enter _____ clay pot? That looks like _____.

5. One picture has fallen off _____ stand.

6. Brian and Kendell worked together on a chalk drawing. That sketch by the doorway

    is _____.

7. The judges have made _____ choices.

8. We both won! They picked both of _____!

9. Here come the judges with our ribbons in _____ hands.

10. Your ribbon is the same as _____.

Name: _____

Writing: Possessive Pronouns

A **possessive pronoun** shows ownership. Instead of writing "That is Jill's book," write "That is her book" or "That is hers." Instead of "I lost my pencil," write "I lost mine." Use possessive pronouns to name what is possessed.

Examples: my (book)   our (car)   your (hat)   his (leg)
        her (hair)   their (group)   its (team)

Use **mine**, **ours**, **yours**, **his**, **hers** and **theirs** when you do not name what is possessed. Notice that possessive pronouns don't use apostrophes.

Directions: Complete these sentences with the correct possessive pronoun.

Example: This book belongs to Jon. It is _____ his _____.

1. I brought my lunch. Did you bring _____ ?

2. I can't do my homework. I wonder if Nancy figured out _____ .

3. Jason saved his candy bar, but I ate _____ .

4. Our team finished our project, but the other team didn't finish _____ .

5. They already have their assignment. When will we get _____?

It's easy to confuse the possessive pronoun **its** with the contraction for **it is**, which is spelled **it's**. The apostrophe in **it's** shows that the **i** in **is** has been left out.

Directions: Write **its** or **it's** in each sentence below.

Examples: The book has lost its cover. It's going to rain soon.

1. _____ nearly time to go.

2. The horse hurt _____ leg.

3. Every nation has _____ share of problems.

4. What is _____ name?

5. I think _____ too warm to snow.

6. The teacher said _____ up to us.

Indefinite Pronouns

Indefinite pronouns often end with **body**, **one** or **thing**.

Examples:
 Everybody is going to be there.
 No one wants to miss it.

Indefinite pronouns do not change form when used as subjects or objects. They are always singular.

Example:
 Incorrect: Everyone must bring **their** own lunches.
 Correct: All students must bring **their** own lunches.
  Everyone must bring **his or her** own lunch.
  Everyone must bring **a** lunch.

Directions: Write twelve indefinite pronouns by matching a word from column A with a word from column B.

Column A
any
every
no
some

Column B
thing
one
body

1. _____

2. _____

3. _____

4. _____

5. _____

6. _____

7. _____

8. _____

9. _____

10. _____

11. _____

12. _____

Directions: Write all the indefinite pronouns that would make sense in the sentence below.
 _____ can come.

13. _____

Directions: Rewrite this sentence correctly.

14. Everybody has their books.

_____

Interrogative and Relative Pronouns

An **interrogative pronoun** is used when asking a question. The interrogative pronouns are **who**, **what** and **which**. Use **who** when referring to people. Use **what** when referring to things. **Which** can be used to refer to people or things.

Directions: Circle the interrogative pronouns. Write whether the pronoun refers to people or things.

1. Who brought this salad for the picnic?

   _____

2. Which car will we drive to the movies?

   _____

3. Which girl asked the question?

   _____

4. What time is it?

   _____

5. What will we do with the leftover food?

   _____

6. Who is going to the swim meet?

   _____

Relative pronouns refer to the noun or pronoun which comes before them. The noun or pronoun to which it refers is called the **antecedent**. The relative pronouns are **who**, **whom**, **which** and **that**. **Who** and **whom** refer to people. **Which** refers to things or animals. **That** can refer to people, animals or things.

Directions: Circle the relative pronouns and underline the antecedents.

1. My dog, which is very well-behaved, never barks.

2. The story was about a girl who wanted a horse of her own.

3. The bookcase, which was full, toppled over during the night.

4. The man to whom I spoke gave me complicated directions.

5. The book that I wanted had already been checked out of the library.

Gender and Number of Pronouns

Pronouns that identify males are **masculine gender**. The masculine pronouns are **he**, **his** and **him**. Pronouns that identify females are **feminine gender**. The feminine pronouns are **she**, **her** and **hers**. Pronouns that identify something that is neither male nor female are **neuter gender**. The neuter pronouns are **it** and **its**.

The plural pronouns **they** and **them** are used for masculine, feminine or neuter gender.

Examples:

Noun	Pronoun	Noun	Pronoun
boot	it	woman	she
man	he	John's	his
travelers	they	dog's	its

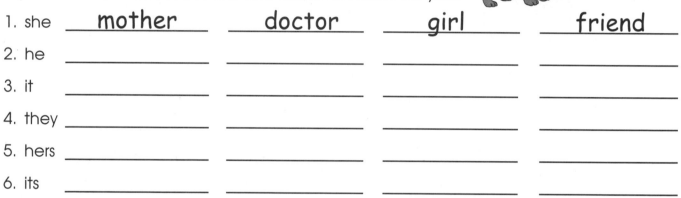

Directions: List four nouns that each pronoun could replace in a sentence. The first one has been done for you.

1. she   mother   doctor   girl   friend
2. he   _____   _____   _____   _____
3. it   _____   _____   _____   _____
4. they   _____   _____   _____   _____
5. hers   _____   _____   _____   _____
6. its   _____   _____   _____   _____

Singular pronouns take the place of singular nouns. Plural pronouns take the place of plural nouns. The singular pronouns are **I**, **me**, **mine**, **he**, **she**, **it**, **its**, **hers**, **his**, **him**, **her**, **you** and **yours**. The plural pronouns are **we**, **you**, **yours**, **they**, **theirs**, **ours**, **them** and **us**.

Directions: Write five sentences. Include a singular and a plural pronoun in each sentence.

1. _____
2. _____
3. _____
4. _____
5. _____

Writing: Pronouns

Sometimes, matching nouns and pronouns can be difficult.

Example: A teacher should always be fair to their students.

Teacher is singular, but **their** is plural, so they don't match. Still, we can't say "A teacher should always be fair to his students," because teachers are both men and women. "His or her students" sounds awkward. One easy way to handle this is to make **teacher** plural so it will match **their**.

Example: Teachers should always be fair to their students.

Directions: Correct the problems in the following sentences by crossing out the incorrect words and writing in the correct nouns and pronouns. (If you make the noun plural, make the verb plural, too.)

its

Examples: Ron's school won ~~their~~ basketball game.

cats are

You can tell If ~~a cat is~~ angry by watching their tails.

1. A student should try to praise their friends' strong points.

2. The group finished their work on time in spite of the deadline.

3. A parent usually has a lot of faith in their children.

4. The company paid their workers once a week.

5. The train made their daily run from Chicago to Detroit.

6. Each student should have a title on their papers.

Directions: Complete these sentences with the correct pronouns.

1. Simon fell out of the tree and scraped _____ arm.

2. The citizens felt a deep pride in _____ community.

3. Heather and Sheila wear _____ hair in the same style.

4. I dyed some shirts, but _____ didn't turn out right.

5. The nurse showed the mother how to bathe _____ baby.

6. Our school made $75 from _____ carnival.

Name: _____

Pronouns as Subjects

A **pronoun** is a word that takes the place of a noun. The pronouns **I, we, he, she, it, you** and **they** can be the subjects of a sentence.

Examples:
> **I** left the house early.
> **You** need to be more careful.
> **She** dances well.

A pronoun must be singular if the noun it replaces is singular. A pronoun must be plural if the noun it replaces is plural. **He**, **she** and **it** are singular pronouns. **We** and **they** are plural pronouns. **You** is both singular and plural.

Examples:
> Tina practiced playing the piano. **She** plays well.
> Jim and I are studying Africa. **We** made a map of it.
> The children clapped loudly. **They** liked the clown.

Directions: Write the correct pronouns.

1. Bobcats hunt at night. _____ are not seen during the day.

2. The mother bobcat usually has babies during February or March. _____ may have two litters a year.

3. The father bobcat stays away when the babies are first born. Later, _____ helps find food for them.

4. We have a new assignment. _____ is a project about bobcats.

5. My group gathered pictures of bobcats. _____ made a display.

6. Jennifer wrote our report. _____ used my notes.

Directions: Circle the pronouns that do not match the nouns they replace. Then write the correct pronouns on the lines.

7. Two boys saw a bobcat. He told us what happened. _____

8. Then we saw a film. They showed bobcats climbing trees. _____

Pronouns as Direct Objects

The pronouns **me**, **you**, **him**, **her**, **it**, **us** and **them** can be used as direct objects.

Examples:
I heard Grant. Grant heard **me**.
We like the teacher. The teacher likes **us**.
He saw the dog. The dog saw **him**.

A pronoun used as a direct object must be plural if the noun is plural and singular if the noun is singular.

Directions: Write the correct pronouns.

1. Goldfish come from China. The Chinese used to eat _____ like trout.

2. The prettiest goldfish were kept as pets. The Chinese put _____ in small bowls and ponds.

3. My sister, brother and I have goldfish. Grandpa took _____ to the store to get them.

4. They come to the top when I am around. I think they like _____ .

5. My sister's fish was white. She kept _____ for 3 weeks.

6. She claimed the fish splashed _____ when she fed it.

Directions: Circle pronouns that do not match the nouns they replace. Rewrite the sentences using the correct pronouns. Change the verbs after the pronouns if necessary.

7. Goldfish often die because kids don't feed it.

_____

8. Some goldfish live a long time because it is well cared for.

_____

9. A wild goldfish will eat anything they think looks good.

_____

10. Birds eat wild goldfish. It likes the young ones best.

_____

Name: _____

Pronouns as Indirect Objects and Objects of Prepositions

The pronouns **me**, **you**, **him**, **her**, **it**, **us** and **them** can be used as indirect objects and objects of prepositions.

Examples:

> **Pronouns as indirect objects:** Shawn showed **me** his new bike. The teacher gave **us** two more days to finish our reports.
>
> **Pronouns as objects of prepositions:** It's your turn after **her**. I can't do it without **them**.

A pronoun used as an indirect object or an object of a preposition must be singular if the noun it replaces is singular and plural if the noun it replaces is plural.

Directions: Write the correct pronouns. Above the pronoun, write **S** if it is the subject, **DO** if it is the direct object, **IO** if it is the indirect object or **OP** if it is the object of a preposition.

1. Markos is coming to our party. I gave _____ the directions.

2. Janelle and Eldon used to be his friends. Is he still friends with _____?

3. Kevin and I like each other, but _____ are too young to go steady.

4. We listened closely while she told _____ what happened to _____.

5. My brother hurt his hand, but I took care of _____.

6. A piece of glass cut him when _____ dropped _____.

7. When Annalisa won the race, the coach gave _____ a trophy.

8. We were hot and sweaty, but a breeze cooled _____ off.

Pronouns

Subjects:	he	she	it	you	I	they	we
Objects:	him	her	it	you	me	them	us
Possessive:	his	her	its	your	my	their	our
Possessive:	his	hers	its	yours	mine	theirs	ours
Indefinite:	everyone	nobody	something	(and others)			

Directions: Complete these sentences with the correct pronouns from the box. Above each pronoun, write how it is used: **S** for subject, **DO** for direct object, **IO** for indirect object, **OP** for object of a preposition, **PP** for possessive pronoun or **IP** for indefinite pronoun.

1. Last week, we had a food drive at _____ church.

2. _____ in our Sunday school class helped collect food.

3. I walked down my street and asked _____ neighbors for food.

4. They gave _____ cans and boxes of food.

5. Kelly came with _____ and helped _____ carry all of _____.

6. Paul had brought his old red wagon from _____ house.

7. When I saw it, _____ wished I had brought _____.

8. Kelly and _____ had to put _____ cans in grocery bags.

9. Those bags were really heavy when _____ were full.

10. When I picked one up, _____ tore and the cans fell out!

11. Jeremy's sister gave _____ a ride around the neighborhood.

12. Walking made Kelly and _____ hungry.

Review

Directions: Write a noun for each possessive pronoun.

1. my _____   5. our _____

2. his _____   6. her _____

3. your _____   7. its _____

4. their _____

Directions: Use these indefinite pronouns in sentences.

8. everyone _____

9. nobody _____

10. something _____

Directions: Use these interrogative pronouns in sentences.

11. who _____

12. what _____

13. which _____

Directions: Use these relative pronouns in sentences.

14. who _____

15. whom _____

16. which _____

17. that _____

who   whom   which   that

Name: _____

Adjectives

An **adjective** describes a noun or pronoun. There are three types of adjectives. They are **positive**, **comparative** and **superlative**.

Examples:

Positive	Comparative	Superlative
big	bigger	biggest
beautiful	more beautiful	most beautiful
bright	less bright	least bright

Directions: Write the comparative and superlative forms of these adjectives.

Positive	Comparative	Superlative
1. happy	_____	_____
2. kind	_____	_____
3. sad	_____	_____
4. slow	_____	_____
5. low	_____	_____
6. delicious	_____	_____
7. strong	_____	_____
8. straight	_____	_____
9. tall	_____	_____
10. humble	_____	_____
11. hard	_____	_____
12. clear	_____	_____
13. loud	_____	_____
14. clever	_____	_____

Name: _____

Writing: Comparatives

Comparatives are forms of adjectives or adverbs used to compare different things. With adjectives, you usually add **er** to the end to make a comparative. If the adjective ends in **y**, drop the **y** and add **ier**.

Examples:

Adjective	Comparative
tall	taller
easy	easier

With adverbs, you usually add **more** before the word to make a comparative.

Examples:

Adverb	Comparative
quickly	more quickly
softly	more softly

Directions: Using the given adjective or adverb, write a sentence comparing the two nouns.

Example: clean   my room   my sister's room

My room is always cleaner than my sister's room.

1. cold   Alaska   Florida

_____

2. neatly   Maria   her brother

_____

3. easy   English   Math

_____

4. scary   book   movie

_____

5. loudly   the drummer   the guitarist

_____

6. pretty   autumn   winter

_____

"Good" and "Bad"

When the adjectives **good** and **bad** are used to compare things, the entire word changes.

Examples:

	Comparative	Superlative
good	better	best
bad	worse	worst

Use the comparative form of an adjective to compare two people or objects. Use the superlative form to compare three or more people or objects.

Examples:

This is a **good** day.
Tomorrow will be **better** than today.
My birthday is the **best** day of the year.

This hamburger tastes **bad**.
Does it taste **worse** than the one your brother cooked?
It's the **worst** hamburger I have ever eaten.

Directions: Write the correct words in the blanks to complete these sentences.

_____   1. Our team just had its bad/worse/worst season ever.

_____   2. Not everything about our team was bad/worse/worst, though.

_____   3. Our pitcher was good/better/best than last year.

_____   4. Our catcher is the good/better/best in the league.

_____   5. We had good/better/best uniforms, like we do every year.

_____   6. I think we just needed good/better/best fielders.

_____   7. Next season we'll do good/better/best than this one.

_____   8. We can't do bad/worse/worst than we did this year.

_____   9. I guess everyone has one bad/worse/worst year.

_____   10. Now that ours is over, we'll get good/better/best.

Name: _____

Demonstrative and Indefinite Adjectives

A **demonstrative adjective** identifies a particular person, place or thing. **This**, **these**, **that** and **those** are demonstrative adjectives.

Examples:

    this pen   **these** earrings
    that chair   **those** books

An **indefinite adjective** does not identify a particular person, place or thing but rather a group or number. **All**, **any**, **both**, **many**, **another**, **several**, **such**, **some**, **few** and **more** are indefinite adjectives.

Examples:

    all teachers   **any** person
    both girls   **many** flowers
    another man   **more** marbles

Directions: Use each noun in a sentence with a demonstrative adjective.

1. dishes _____

2. clothes _____

3. cats _____

4. team _____

5. apples _____

6. stereo _____

7. mountain _____

Directions: Use each noun in a sentence with an indefinite adjective.

8. reporters _____

9. decisions _____

10. papers _____

11. pears _____

12. occupations _____

13. friends _____

Name: _____

Interrogative and Possessive Adjectives

An **interrogative adjective** is used when asking a question. The interrogative adjectives are **what** and **which**.

Examples:

What kind of haircut will you get?
Which dog snarled at you?

A **possessive adjective** shows ownership. The possessive adjectives are **our**, **your**, **her**, **his**, **its**, **my** and **their**.

Examples:

That is **my** dog.
He washed **his** jeans.
Our pictures turned out great.

Directions: Write six sentences containing interrogative adjectives and six sentences containing possessive adjectives.

Interrogative Adjectives

1. _____

2. _____

3. _____

4. _____

5. _____

6. _____

Possessive Adjectives

1. _____

2. _____

3. _____

4. _____

5. _____

6. _____

Prepositional Phrases as Adjectives

An adjective can be one word or an entire prepositional phrase.

Examples:
The **new** boy **with red hair**
The **tall** man **in the raincoat**
The **white** house **with green shutters**

Directions: Underline the prepositional phrases used as adjectives.

1. The boy in the blue cap is the captain.

2. The house across the street is 100 years old.

3. Jo and Ty love cookies with nuts.

4. I lost the book with the green cover.

5. Do you know the girl in the front row?

6. I like the pony with the long tail.

7. The dog in that yard is not friendly.

8. The picture in this magazine looks like you.

Directions: Complete these sentences with prepositional phrases used as adjectives.

9. I'd like a hamburger _____.

10. Did you read the book _____?

11. The dog _____ is my favorite.

12. The woman _____ is calling you.

13. I bought a shirt _____.

14. I'm wearing socks _____.

15. I found a box _____.

Adverbs

Adverbs modify verbs. Adverbs tell **when**, **where** or **how**. Many, but not all adverbs, end in **ly**.

Adverbs of time answer the questions **how often** or **when**.

Examples:
The dog escapes its pen **frequently**.
Smart travelers **eventually** will learn to use travelers' checks.

Adverbs of place answer the question **where**.

Example: The police pushed bystanders **away** from the accident scene.

Adverbs of manner answer the questions **how** or **in what manner**.

Example: He **carefully** replaced the delicate vase.

Directions: Underline the verb in each sentence. Circle the adverb. Write the question each adverb answers on the line.

1. My grandmother walks gingerly to avoid falls.

_____

2. The mice darted everywhere to escape the cat.

_____

3. He decisively moved the chess piece.

_____

4. Our family frequently enjoys a night at the movies.

_____

5. Later, we will discuss the consequences of your behavior.

_____

6. The audience glanced up at the balcony where the noise originated.

_____

7. The bleachers are already built for the concert.

_____

8. My friend and I study daily for the upcoming exams.

_____

Adverbs

Like adjectives, adverbs have types of comparison. They are positive, comparative and superlative.

Examples:

Positive	**Comparative**	**Superlative**
expertly	more expertly	most expertly
soon	sooner	soonest

Directions: Underline the adverb in each sentence. Then write the type of comparison on the line.

1. The car easily won the race. _____

2. Our class most eagerly awaited the return of our test. _____

3. My ice cream melted more quickly than yours. _____

4. Frances awoke early the first day of school. _____

5. He knows well the punishment for disobeying his parents. _____

6. There is much work to be done on the stadium project. _____

7. The child played most happily with the building blocks. _____

8. This article appeared more recently than the other. _____

Directions: Write the comparative and superlative forms of these adverbs.

Positive	**Comparative**	**Superlative**
9. hard	_____	_____
10. impatiently	_____	_____
11. anxiously	_____	_____
12. suddenly	_____	_____
13. far	_____	_____
14. long	_____	_____

Name: _____

Prepositional Phrases as Adverbs

An adverb can be one word or an entire prepositional phrase.

Examples:
    They'll be here **tomorrow**.
    They always come **on time**.
    Move it **down**.
    Put it **under the picture**.
    Drive **carefully**.
    He drove **with care**.

Directions: Underline the adverb or prepositional phrase used as an adverb in each sentence. In the blank, write **how**, **when** or **where** to tell what the adverb or prepositional phrase explains.

1. Don't go swimming without a buddy.   _____

2. Don't go swimming alone.   _____

3. I wish you still lived here.   _____

4. I wish you still lived on our street.   _____

5. I will eat lunch soon.   _____

6. I will eat lunch in a few minutes.   _____

7. He will be here in a few hours.   _____

8. He will be here later.   _____

9. I'm going outside.   _____

10. I'm going in the backyard.   _____

11. She smiled happily.   _____

12. She smiled with happiness.   _____

Writing: Adjectives and Adverbs

An **adjective** is a describing word. It describes nouns. Adjectives can tell:
- Which one or what kind — the dog's **floppy** ears, the **lost** child
- How many — **three** wagons, **four** drawers

An **adverb** is also a describing word. It describes verbs, adjectives or other adverbs. Adverbs can tell:
- How — ran **quickly**, talked **quietly**
- When — finished **prompty**, came **yesterday**
- Where — lived **there**, drove **backward**
- How often — sneezed **twice**, **always** wins

Directions: The adjectives and adverbs are bold in the sentences below. Above each, write **ADJ** for adjective or **ADV** for adverb. Then draw an arrow to the noun the adjective describes or to the verb the adverb describes.

ADJ   ADV

Example: A girl in a **green** jacket **quickly** released the birds into the sky.

1. An **old** mayor was elected **twice**.

2. He **carefully** put the **tall** screen between our desks.

3. The **new** boy in our class moved **here** from Phoenix.

4. **Today**, our **soccer** team **finally** made its **first** goal.

5. The woman **gently** coaxed the **frightened** kitten out of the tree.

Directions: Use adjectives and adverbs to answer the questions below.

Example: The boy talked. (Which boy? How?)
   The nervous boy talked loudly.

1. The plant grew. (Which plant? How?)

   _____

2. The birds flew. (How many? What kind? Where?)

   _____

Name: _____

Writing: Adjectives and Adverbs

Adjectives and adverbs make sentences more interesting. Often, we can make adverbs from adjectives by adding **ly** to the end.

Examples:

Adjectives	Adverbs
quick	quickly
brief	briefly

If an adjective ends with a **y**, change the **y** to an **i** before adding **ly**.

Examples:

Adjectives	Adverbs
messy	messily
noisy	noisily

Directions: Write a new sentence using each subject and adjective below. Then add **ly** to the adjective and write a new sentence using the adverb.

Example: teacher — brief
  a. The teacher gave a **brief** talk about using lab equipment.
  b. The teacher spoke **briefly** about using lab equipment.

1. sister — quiet

   a. _____

   b. _____

2. children — excited

   a. _____

   b. _____

3. players — tired

   a. _____

   b. _____

4. snow — soft

   a. _____

   b. _____

Placement of Adjective and Adverb Phrases

Adjectives and adverbs, including prepositional phrases, should be placed as close as possible to the words they describe to avoid confusion.

Example:
   Confusing: The boy under the pile of leaves looked for the ball.
                  (Is the boy or the ball under the pile of leaves?)
   Clear: The boy looked under the pile of leaves for the ball.

Directions: Rewrite each sentence by moving the prepositional phrase closer to the word or words it describes. The first one has been done for you.

1. A bird at the pet store bit me in the mall.

   A bird at the pet store in the mall bit me.

2. The woman was looking for her dog in the large hat.

   _____

3. This yard would be great for a dog with a fence.

   _____

4. The car hit the stop sign with the silver stripe.

   _____

5. My cousin with a big bow gave me a present.

   _____

6. The house was near some woods with a pond.

   _____

7. I'll be back to wash the dishes in a minute.

   _____

8. We like to eat eggs in the morning with toast.

   _____

9. He bought a shirt at the new store with short sleeves.

   _____

10. We live in the house down the street with tall windows.

   _____

Name: _____

Writing: Parts of Speech Story

Directions: Play the following game with a partner. In the story below, some of the words are missing. Without letting your partner see the story, ask him/her to provide a word for each blank. Each word should be a noun, verb, adjective or adverb, as shown. Then read the story aloud. It might not make sense, but it will make you laugh!

Last night, as I was _____ through the _____ , a
          (verb + ing)   (noun)

_____ _____ fell from the ceiling and landed on my
  (adjective)   (noun)

head! "Yikes!" I shrieked. I _____ _____ through the
                            (past-tense verb)   (adverb)

_____ , trying to get rid of the thing. Finally, it fell off, and it started
   (noun)

_____ around the _____ . I tried to hit it with a _____ ,
 (verb + ing)   (noun)   (noun)

but it was too _____ . I _____ managed to _____
               (adjective)   (adverb)   (verb)

it out of the house, where it quickly climbed the nearest _____ .
                                                            (noun)

Grade 5 - Comprehensive Curriculum

Writing: Parts of Speech

Directions: Write each word from the box in the column that names its part of speech. Some words can be listed in two columns.

ADJ   ADV

Example: a chair **behind** me   he was walking **behind** me

code	young	slowly	today	finally	screen
thirsty	praise	loan	broken	decrease	slowly
nearby	twenty	Monday	town	faithful	red
coax	goal	bathe	release	cheat	there

Noun	**Verb**	**Adjective**	**Adverb**
_____	_____	_____	_____
_____	_____	_____	_____
_____	_____	_____	_____
_____	_____	_____	_____
_____	_____	_____	_____
_____	_____	_____	_____

Directions: Write four sentences, using at least three words from the box in each one. Mark each word as a noun (**N**), verb (**V**), adjective (**ADJ**) or adverb (**ADV**).

        ADJ   ADV   N

Example: Twenty people **slowly** walked through the **town**.

_____

_____

_____

_____

Conjunctions

A **conjunction** joins words or groups of words in a sentence. The most commonly used conjunctions are **and**, **but** and **or**.

Examples: My brother **and** I each want to win the trophy.
Tonight, it will rain **or** sleet.
I wanted to go to the party, **but** I got sick.

Directions: Circle the conjunctions.

1. Dolphins and whales are mammals.

2. They must rise to the surface of the water to breathe, or they will die.

3. Dolphins resemble fish, but they are not fish.

4. Sightseeing boats are often entertained by groups of dolphins or whales.

5. Whales appear to effortlessly leap out of the water and execute flips.

6. Both whale and dolphin babies are born alive.

7. The babies are called calves and are born in the water, but must breathe air within a few minutes of birth.

8. Sometimes an entire pod of whales will help a mother and calf reach the surface to breathe.

9. Scientists and marine biologists have long been intrigued by these ocean animals.

10. Whales and dolphins do not seem to be afraid of humans or boats.

Directions: Write six sentences using conjunctions.

11. _____

12. _____

13. _____

14. _____

15. _____

16. _____

Writing: Conjunctions

Too many short sentences make writing seem choppy. Short sentences can be combined to make writing flow better. Words used to combine sentences are called **conjunctions**.

Examples: but, before, after, because, when, or, so, and

Directions: Use **or**, **but**, **before**, **after**, **because**, **when**, **and** or **so** to combine each pair of sentences. The first one has been done for you.

1. I was wearing my winter coat. I started to shiver.

     I was wearing my winter coat, but I started to shiver.

2. Animals all need water. They may perish without it.

   _____

3. The sun came out. The ice began to thaw.

   _____

4. The sun came out. The day was still chilly.

   _____

5. Will the flowers perish? Will they thrive?

   _____

6. The bear came closer. We began to feel threatened.

   _____

7. Winning was a challenge. Our team didn't have much experience.

   _____

8. Winning was a challenge. Our team was up to it.

   _____

Directions: Write three sentences of your own. Use a conjunction in each sentence.

_____

_____

_____

Name: _____

Statements and Questions

A **statement** is a sentence that tells something. It ends with a period (.).

A **question** is a sentence that asks something. It ends with a question mark (?).

Examples:
   Statement: Shari is walking to school today.
   Question: Is Shari walking to school today?

In some questions, the subject comes between two parts of the verb. In the examples below, the subjects are underlined. The verbs and the rest of the predicates are bold.

Examples:
   Is <u>Steve</u> **coming with us**?
   <u>Who</u> **will be there**?
   Which one did <u>you</u> **select**?

To find the predicate, turn a question into a statement.

Example: Is Steve coming with us? Steve is coming with us.

Directions: Write **S** for statement or **Q** for question. Put a period after the statements and a question mark after the questions.

_____ 1. Today is the day for our field trip

_____ 2. How are we going to get there

_____ 3. The bus will take us

_____ 4. Is there room for everyone

_____ 5. Who forgot to bring a lunch

_____ 6. I'll save you a seat

Directions: Circle the subjects and underline all parts of the predicates.

7. Do you like field trips?

8. Did you bring your coat?

9. Will it be cold there?

10. Do you see my gloves anywhere?

11. Is anyone sitting with you?

12. Does the bus driver have a map?

13. Are all the roads this bumpy?

Grade 5 - Comprehensive Curriculum

Name: _____

Statements and Questions

Directions: Write 10 statements and 10 questions.

Statements

1. _____
2. _____
3. _____
4. _____
5. _____
6. _____
7. _____
8. _____
9. _____
10. _____

Questions

1. _____
2. _____
3. _____
4. _____
5. _____
6. _____
7. _____
8. _____
9. _____
10. _____

Commands, Requests and Exclamations

A **command** is a sentence that orders someone to do something. It ends with a period or an exclamation mark (!).

A **request** is a sentence that asks someone to do something. It ends with a period or a question mark (?).

An **exclamation** is a sentence that shows strong feeling. It ends with an exclamation mark (!).

Examples:
   Command: Stay in your seat.
   Request: Would you please pass the salt?
          Please pass the salt.
   Exclamation: Call the police!

In the first and last two sentences in the examples, the subject is not stated. The subject is understood to be **you**.

Directions: Write **C** if the sentence is a command, **R** if it is a request and **E** if it is an exclamation. Put the correct punctuation at the end of each sentence.

C _____ 1. Look both ways before you cross the street

C _____ 2. Please go to the store and buy some bread for us

E _____ 3. The house is on fire

R _____ 4. Would you hand me the glue

E _____ 5. Don't step there

C _____ 6. Write your name at the top of the page

C _____ 7. Please close the door

R _____ 8. Would you answer the phone

E _____ 9. Watch out

C _____ 10. Take one card from each pile

Name: _____

Commands, Requests and Exclamations

Directions: Write six sentences for each type listed.

Command

1. _____
2. _____
3. _____
4. _____
5. _____
6. _____

Request

1. _____
2. _____
3. _____
4. _____
5. _____
6. _____

Exclamation

1. _____
2. _____
3. _____
4. _____
5. _____
6. _____

Name: _____

Commas

Commas are used to separate items in a series. Both examples below are correct. A final comma is optional.

Examples:
    The fruit bowl contains oranges, peaches, pears, and apples.
    The fruit bowl contains oranges, peaches, pears and apples.

Commas are also used to separate geographical names and dates.

Examples:
    Today's date is January 13, 2000.
    My grandfather lives in Tallahassee, Florida.
    I would like to visit Paris, France.

Directions: Place commas where needed in these sentences.

1. I was born on September 21 1992.
2. John's favorite sports include basketball football hockey and soccer.
3. The ship will sail on November 16 2004.
4. My family and I vacationed in Salt Lake City Utah.
5. I like to plant beans beets corn and radishes in my garden.
6. Sandy's party will be held in Youngstown Ohio.
7. Periods commas colons and exclamation marks are types of punctuation.
8. Cardinals juncos blue jays finches and sparrows frequent our birdfeeder.
9. My grandfather graduated from high school on June 4 1962.
10. The race will take place in Burlington Vermont.

Directions: Write a sentence using commas to separate words in a series.

11. _____

Directions: Write a sentence using commas to separate geographical names.

12. _____

Directions: Write a sentence using commas to separate dates.

13. _____

Commas

Commas are used to separate a noun or pronoun in a direct address from the rest of the sentence. A noun or pronoun in a **direct address** is one that names or refers to the person addressed.

Examples:

John, this room is a mess!
This room**, John,** is a disgrace!
Your room needs to be more organized**, John**.

Commas are used to separate an appositive from the rest of the sentence. An **appositive** is a word or words that give the reader more information about a previous noun or pronoun.

Examples:

My teacher, **Ms. Wright**, gave us a test.
Thomas Edison, **the inventor of the lightbulb**, was an interesting man.

Directions: Place commas where needed in these sentences. Then write **appositive** or **direct address** on the line to explain why the commas were used.

1. Melissa do you know the answer? _____

2. John the local football hero led the parade through town._____

3. Cancun a Mexican city is a favorite vacation destination._____

4. Please help me move the chair Gail._____

5. My great-grandfather an octogenarian has witnessed many events._____

6. The president of the company Madison Fagan addressed his workers._____

7. My favorite book *Anne of Green Gables* is a joy to read._____

8. Your painting Andre shows great talent._____

Name: _____

Punctuation

Directions: Add commas where needed. Put the correct punctuation at the end of each sentence.

1. My friend Jamie loves to snowboard

2. Winter sports such as hockey skiing and skating are fun

3. Oh what a lovely view

4. The map shows the continents of Asia Africa Australia and Antarctica

5. My mother a ballet dancer will perform tonight

6. What will you do tomorrow

7. When will the plane arrive at the airport

8. Jason do you know what time it is

9. Friends of ours the Watsons are coming for dinner

10. Margo look out for that falling rock

11. The young child sat reading a book

12. Who wrote this letter

13. My sister Jill is very neat

14. The trampoline is in our backyard

15. We will have chicken peas rice and salad for dinner

16. That dog a Saint Bernard looks dangerous

Quotation Marks

When a person's exact words are used in a sentence, **quotation marks** (" ") are used to identify those words. Commas are used to set off the quotation from the rest of the sentence. End punctuation is placed inside the final quotation mark.

Examples:
"When are we leaving?" Joe asked.
Marci shouted, "Go, team!"

When a sentence is interrupted by words that are not part of the quotation (he said, she answered, etc.), they are not included in the quotation marks. Note how commas are used in the next example.

Example: "I am sorry," the man announced, "for my rude behavior."

Directions: Place quotation marks, commas and other punctuation where needed in the sentences below.

1. Watch out yelled Dad.

2. Angela said I don't know how you can eat Brussels sprouts, Ted

3. Put on your coats said Mom. We'll be leaving in 10 minutes

4. Did you hear the assignment asked Joan.

5. Jim shouted This game is driving me up the wall

6. After examining our dog, the veterinarian said He looks healthy and strong

7. The toddlers both wailed We want ice cream

8. The judge announced to the swimmers Take your places

9. Upon receiving the award, the actor said I'd like to thank my friends and family

10. These are my favorite chips said Becky.

11. This test is too hard moaned the class.

12. When their relay team came in first place, the runners shouted, Hooray

13. Where shall we go on vacation this year Dad asked.

14. As we walked past the machinery, the noise was deafening. Cover your ears said Mom.

15. Fire yelled the chef as his pan ignited.

16. I love basketball my little brother stated.

Name: _____

Capitalization/Punctuation

Directions: Rewrite the paragraphs below, adding punctuation where it is needed. Capitalize the first word of each sentence and all other words that should be capitalized.

most countries have laws that control advertising in norway no ads at all are allowed on radio or TV in the united states ads for alcoholic drinks, except beer and wine, are not permitted on radio or TV england has a law against advertising cigarettes on TV what do you think about these laws should they be even stricter

_____

_____

_____

_____

my cousin jeff is starting college this fall he wants to be a medical doctor, so he's going to central university the mayor of our town went there mayor stevens told jeff all about the university our town is so small that everyone knows what everyone else is doing is your town like that

_____

_____

_____

_____

my grandparents took a long vacation last year grandma really likes to go to the atlantic ocean and watch the dolphins my grandfather likes to fish in the ocean my aunt went with them last summer they all had a party on the fourth of july

_____

_____

_____

Grade 5 - Comprehensive Curriculum

Capitalization

Directions: Write **C** if capital letters are used correctly or **X** if they are used incorrectly.

_____ 1. Who will win the election for Mayor in November?

_____ 2. Tom Johnson used to be a police officer.

_____ 3. He announced on monday that he wants to be mayor.

_____ 4. My father said he would vote for Tom.

_____ 5. Mom and my sister Judy haven't decided yet.

_____ 6. They will vote at our school.

_____ 7. Every Fall and Spring they put up voting booths there.

_____ 8. I hope the new mayor will do something about our river.

_____ 9. That River is full of chemicals.

_____ 10. I'm glad our water doesn't come from Raven River.

_____ 11. In late Summer, the river actually stinks.

_____ 12. Is every river in our State so dirty?

_____ 13. Scientists check the water every so often.

_____ 14. Some professors from the college even examined it.

_____ 15. That is getting to be a very educated River!

★ ★ ★ Vote ★ ★ ★

TOM JOHNSON

for Mayor

Directions: Write sentences that include:

16. A person's title that should be capitalized.

_____

17. The name of a place that should be capitalized.

_____

18. The name of a time (day, month, holiday) that should be capitalized.

_____

"Who" Clauses

A **clause** is a group of words with a subject and a verb. When the subject of two sentences is the same person or people, the sentences can sometimes be combined with a "who" clause.

Examples:
Mindy likes animals. Mindy feeds the squirrels.
Mindy, **who likes animals**, feeds the squirrels.

A "who" clause is set off from the rest of the sentence with commas.

Directions: Combine the pairs of sentences, using "who" clauses.

1. Teddy was late to school. Teddy was sorry later.

   _____

2. Our principal is retiring. Our principal will be 65 this year.

   _____

3. Michael won the contest. Michael will receive an award.

   _____

4. Charlene lives next door. Charlene has three cats.

   _____

5. Burt drew that picture. Burt takes art lessons.

   _____

6. Marta was elected class president. Marta gave a speech.

   _____

7. Amy broke her arm. Amy has to wear a cast for 6 weeks.

   _____

8. Dr. Bank fixed my tooth. He said it would feel better soon.

   _____

"Which" Clauses

When the subject of two sentences is the same thing or things, the sentences can sometimes be combined with a "which" clause.

Examples:
> The guppy was first called "the millions fish." The guppy was later named after Reverend Robert Guppy in 1866.
> The guppy, **which was first called "the millions fish,"** was later named after Reverend Robert Guppy in 1866.

A "which" clause is set off from the rest of the sentence with commas.

Directions: Combine the pairs of sentences using "which" clauses.

1. Guppies also used to be called rainbow fish. Guppies were brought to Germany in 1908.

   _____

2. The male guppy is about 1 inch long. The male is smaller than the female.

   _____

3. The guppies' colors range from red to violet. The colors are brighter in the males.

   _____

4. Baby guppies hatch from eggs inside the mothers' bodies. The babies are born alive.

   _____

5. The young are usually born at night. The young are called "fry."

   _____

6. Female guppies have from 2 to 50 fry at one time. Females sometimes try to eat their fry!

   _____

7. These fish have been studied by scientists. The fish actually like dirty water.

   _____

8. Wild guppies eat mosquito eggs. Wild guppies help control the mosquito population.

   _____

Name: _____

"Who" and "Which" Clauses

Directions: Combine the pairs of sentences using "who" or "which" clauses.

1. Bullfrogs are rarely found out of the water. They live near ponds and streams.

   _____

   _____

2. These frogs grow about eight inches long. These frogs can jump three feet.

   _____

   _____

3. Mark Twain was a famous writer. He wrote a story about a frog-jumping contest.

   _____

   _____

4. This story took place in California. This story started an annual frog-jumping contest there.

   _____

   _____

5. The contest has rules and judges. The contest allows each frog to make three leaps.

   _____

   _____

6. The judges watch carefully. They measure each frog's leap.

   _____

   _____

7. Bullfrogs eat many insects. Bullfrogs also eat small snakes.

   _____

   _____

8. Scientists study what frogs eat. Scientists know bullfrogs can catch birds.

   _____

   _____

"That" Clauses

When the subject of two sentences is the same thing or things, the sentences can sometimes be combined with a "that" clause. We use **that** instead of **which** when the clause is very important in the sentence.

Examples:

    The store is near our house. The store was closed.
    The store **that is near our house** was closed.

The words "**that is near our house**" are very important in the combined sentence. They tell the reader which store was closed. A "that" clause is not set off from the rest of the sentence with commas.

Examples:

    Pete's store is near our house. Pete's store was closed.
    Pete's store, which is near our house, was closed.

The words "**which is near our house**" are not important to the meaning of the combined sentence. The words **Pete's store** already told us which store was closed.

Directions: Combine the pairs of sentences using "that" clauses.

1. The dog lives next door. The dog chased me.

    _____

2. The bus was taking us to the game. The bus had a flat tire.

    _____

3. The fence is around the school. The fence is painted yellow.

    _____

4. The notebook had my homework in it. The notebook is lost.

    _____

5. A letter came today. The letter was from Mary.

    _____

6. The lamp was fixed yesterday. The lamp doesn't work today.

    _____

7. The lake is by our cabin. The lake is filled with fish.

    _____

Name: _____

"That" and "Which" Clauses

Directions: Combine the pairs of sentences using either a "that" or a "which" clause.

1. The TV show was on at 8:00 last night. The TV show was funny.

   _____

2. *The Snappy Show* was on at 8:00 last night. *The Snappy Show* was funny.

   _____

3. The Main Bank is on the corner. The Main Bank is closed today.

   _____

4. The bank is on the corner. The bank is closed today.

   _____

5. The bus takes Dad to work. The bus broke down.

   _____

6. The Broad Street bus takes Dad to work. The Broad Street bus broke down.

   _____

Name: _____

Combining Sentences

Not every pair of sentences can be combined with "who," "which" or "that" clauses. These sentences can be combined in other ways, either with a conjunction or by renaming the subject.

Examples:

Tim couldn't go to sleep. Todd was sleeping soundly.
Tim couldn't go to sleep, **but** Todd was sleeping soundly.

The zoo keeper fed the baby ape. A crowd gathered to watch.
When the zoo keeper fed the baby ape, a crowd gathered to watch.

Directions: Combine each pair of sentences using "who," "which" or "that" clauses, by using a conjunction or by renaming the subject.

1. The box slipped off the truck. The box was filled with bottles.

   _____

2. Carolyn is our scout leader. Carolyn taught us a new game.

   _____

3. The girl is 8 years old. The girl called the emergency number when her grandmother fell.

   _____

4. The meatloaf is ready to eat. The salad isn't made yet.

   _____

5. The rain poured down. The rain canceled our picnic.

   _____

6. The sixth grade class went on a field trip. The school was much quieter.

   _____

"Who's" and "Whose"

Who's is a contraction for **who is**.

Whose is a possessive pronoun.

Examples:
   Who's going to come?
   Whose shirt is this?

To know which word to use, substitute the words "who is." If the sentence makes sense, use **who's**.

Directions: Write the correct words to complete these sentences.

_____ 1. Do you know who's/whose invited to the party?

_____ 2. I don't even know who's/whose house it will be at.

_____ 3. Who's/Whose towel is on the floor?

_____ 4. Who's/Whose going to drive us?

_____ 5. Who's/Whose ice cream is melting?

_____ 6. I'm the person who's/whose gloves are lost.

_____ 7. Who's/Whose in your group?

_____ 8. Who's/Whose group is first?

_____ 9. Can you tell who's/whose at the door?

_____ 10. Who's/Whose friend are you?

_____ 11. Who's/Whose cooking tonight?

_____ 12. Who's/Whose cooking do you like best?

Name: _____

"Their," "There" and "They're"

Their is a possessive pronoun meaning "belonging to them."

There is an adverb that indicates place.

They're is a contraction for **they are**.

Examples:
Ron and Sue took **their** dog to the park.
They like to go **there** on Sunday afternoon.
They're probably going back next Sunday, too.

Directions: Write the correct words to complete these sentences.

_____ 1. All the students should bring their/there/they're books to class.

_____ 2. I've never been to France, but I hope to travel their/there/they're someday.

_____ 3. We studied how dolphins care for their/there/they're young.

_____ 4. My parents are going on vacation next week, and their/there/they're taking my sister.

_____ 5. Their/There/They're was a lot of food at the party.

_____ 6. My favorite baseball team lost their/there/they're star pitcher this year.

_____ 7. Those peaches look good, but their/there/they're not ripe yet.

_____ 8. The book is right their/there/they're on the table.

"Teach" and "Learn"

Teach is a verb meaning "to explain something." Teach is an irregular verb. Its past tense is **taught**.

Learn is a verb meaning "to gain information."

Examples:
Carrie will **teach** me how to play the piano.
Yesterday she **taught** me "Chopsticks."

I will **learn** a new song every week.
Yesterday I **learned** to play "Chopsticks."

Directions: Write the correct words to complete these sentences.

_____ 1. My brother taught/learned me how to ice skate.

_____ 2. With his help, I taught/learned in three days.

_____ 3. First, I tried to teach/learn skating from a book.

_____ 4. I couldn't teach/learn that way.

_____ 5. You have to try it before you can really teach/learn how to do it.

_____ 6. Now I'm going to teach/learn my cousin.

_____ 7. My cousin already taught/learned how to roller skate.

_____ 8. I shouldn't have any trouble teaching/learning her how to ice skate.

_____ 9. Who taught/learned you how to skate?

_____ 10. My brother taught/learned Mom how to skate, too.

_____ 11. My mother took longer to teach/learn it than I did.

_____ 12. Who will he teach/learn next?

_____ 13. Do you know anyone who wants to teach/learn how to ice skate?

_____ 14. My brother will teach/learn you for free.

_____ 15. You should teach/learn how to ice skate in the wintertime, though. The ice is a little thin in the summer!

"Lie" and "Lay"

Lie is a verb meaning "to rest." Lie is an intransitive verb that doesn't need a direct object.

Lay is a verb meaning "to place or put something down." Lay is a transitive verb that requires a direct object.

Examples:
> **Lie** here for a while. (**Lie** has no direct object; **here** is an adverb.)
> **Lay** the book here. (**Lay** has a direct object: **book**.)

Lie and lay are especially tricky because they are both irregular verbs. Notice the past tense of lie is lay!

Present tense	ing form	Past tense	Past participle
lie	lying	lay	has/have/had lain
lay	laying	laid	has/have/had laid

Examples:

I **lie** here today.	I **lay** the baby in her bed.
I **lay** here yesterday.	I will be **laying** her down in a minute.
I **was lying** there for three hours.	I **laid** her in her bed last night, too.

Directions: Write the correct words to complete these sentences.

_____ 1. Shelly lies/lays a blanket on the grass.

_____ 2. Then she lies/lays down in the sun.

_____ 3. Her dog lies/lays there with her.

_____ 4. Yesterday, Shelly lay/laid in the sun for an hour.

_____ 5. The workers are lying/laying bricks for a house.

_____ 6. Yesterday, they lay/laid a ton of them.

_____ 7. They lie/lay one brick on top of the other.

_____ 8. The bricks just lie/lay in a pile until the workers are ready for them.

_____ 9. At lunchtime, some workers lie/lay down for a nap.

_____ 10. Would you like to lie/lay bricks?

_____ 11. Last year, my uncle lay/laid bricks for his new house.

_____ 12. He was so tired every day that he lay/laid down as soon as he finished.

"Rise" and "Raise"

Rise is a verb meaning "to get up" or "to go up." Rise is an intransitive verb that doesn't need a direct object.

Raise is a verb meaning "to lift" or "to grow." Raise is a transitive verb that requires a direct object.

Examples:
> The curtain **rises**.
> The girl **raises** her hand.

Raise is a regular verb. Rise is irregular.

Present tense	Past tense	Past participle
rise	rose	has/have/had risen
raise	raised	has/have/had raised

Examples:
> The sun **rose** this morning.
> The boy **raised** the window higher.

Directions: Write the correct words to complete these sentences.

_____ 1. This bread dough rises/raises in an hour.

_____ 2. The landlord will rise/raise the rent.

_____ 3. The balloon rose/raised into the sky.

_____ 4. My sister rose/raised the seat on my bike.

_____ 5. The baby rose/raised the spoon to his mouth.

_____ 6. The eagle rose/raised out of sight.

_____ 7. The farmer rises/raises pigs.

_____ 8. The scouts rose/raised the flag.

_____ 9. When the fog rose/raised, we could see better.

_____ 10. The price of ice cream rose/raised again.

_____ 11. The king rose/raised the glass to his lips.

_____ 12. Rise/Raise the picture on that wall higher.

Name: _____

"All Right," "All Ready" and "Already"

All right means "well enough" or "very well." Sometimes **all right** is incorrectly spelled. **Alright** is not a word.

Example:
   Correct: We'll be all right when the rain stops.
   Incorrect: Are you feeling **alright** today?

All ready is an adjective meaning "completely ready."

Already is an adverb meaning "before this time" or "by this time."

Examples:
   Are you **all ready** to go?
   He was **already** there when I arrived.

Directions: Write the correct words to complete these sentences.

_____ 1.   The children are all ready/already for the picnic.

_____ 2.   Ted was all ready/already late for the show.

_____ 3.   Is your sister going to be all right/alright?

_____ 4.   I was all ready/already tired before the race began.

_____ 5.   Joan has all ready/already left for the dance.

_____ 6.   Will you be all right/alright by yourself?

_____ 7.   We are all ready/already for our talent show.

_____ 8.   I all ready/already read that book.

_____ 9.   I want to be all ready/already when they get here.

_____ 10.   Dad was sick, but he's all right/alright now.

_____ 11.   The dinner is all ready/already to eat.

_____ 12.   Cathy all ready/already wrote her report.

"Accept" and "Except"/"Affect" and "Effect"

Accept is a verb meaning "to receive."

Except can be used as a verb or a preposition. As a verb, it means "to leave out."
As a preposition, it means "excluding."

Examples:

I will **accept** the invitation to the dinner dance.
No one **except** Robert will receive an award.

Affect is a verb meaning "to impress one's thoughts or feelings."

Effect can be used as a noun or a verb. As a verb, it means
"to accomplish." As a noun, it means "the result of an action."

Examples:

Her attitude may **affect** her performance on the test.
He **effected** several changes during his first few months as governor.
The **effects** of the storm will be felt for some time.

Directions: Write the correct words to complete these sentences.

_____ 1. My partner and I will work to affect/effect attitudes toward rainforest renewal.

_____ 2. He courageously accepted/excepted the challenge of a chess duel.

_____ 3. The affect/effect of the strike by truck drivers was felt nationwide.

_____ 4. The new CEO of the company sought to affect/effect a change in company morale.

_____ 5. Everyone accept/except Marlene will attend the game.

_____ 6. My grandmother will never accept/except the fact that she can no longer drive.

_____ 7. Accept/Except for this chewing incident, my puppy has been well-behaved.

_____ 8. The sights of the war affected/effected soldiers for the rest of their lives.

_____ 9. What affect/effect will the drop in the stock market have on the average person?

_____ 10. The affect/effect of the wind was devastating.

_____ 11. How will cheating on a test affect/effect your reputation?

_____ 12. I would like to go to the park on any day accept/except Monday.

Review

Directions: Use each of these words correctly in a sentence of your own.

1. good _____

2. bad _____

3. who's _____

4. whose _____

5. their _____

6. there _____

7. they're _____

8. teach _____

9. learn _____

10. lie _____

11. lay _____

12. rise _____

13. raise _____

14. all ready _____

15. already _____

16. all right _____

17. accept _____

18. except _____

19. affect _____

20. effect _____

WRITING

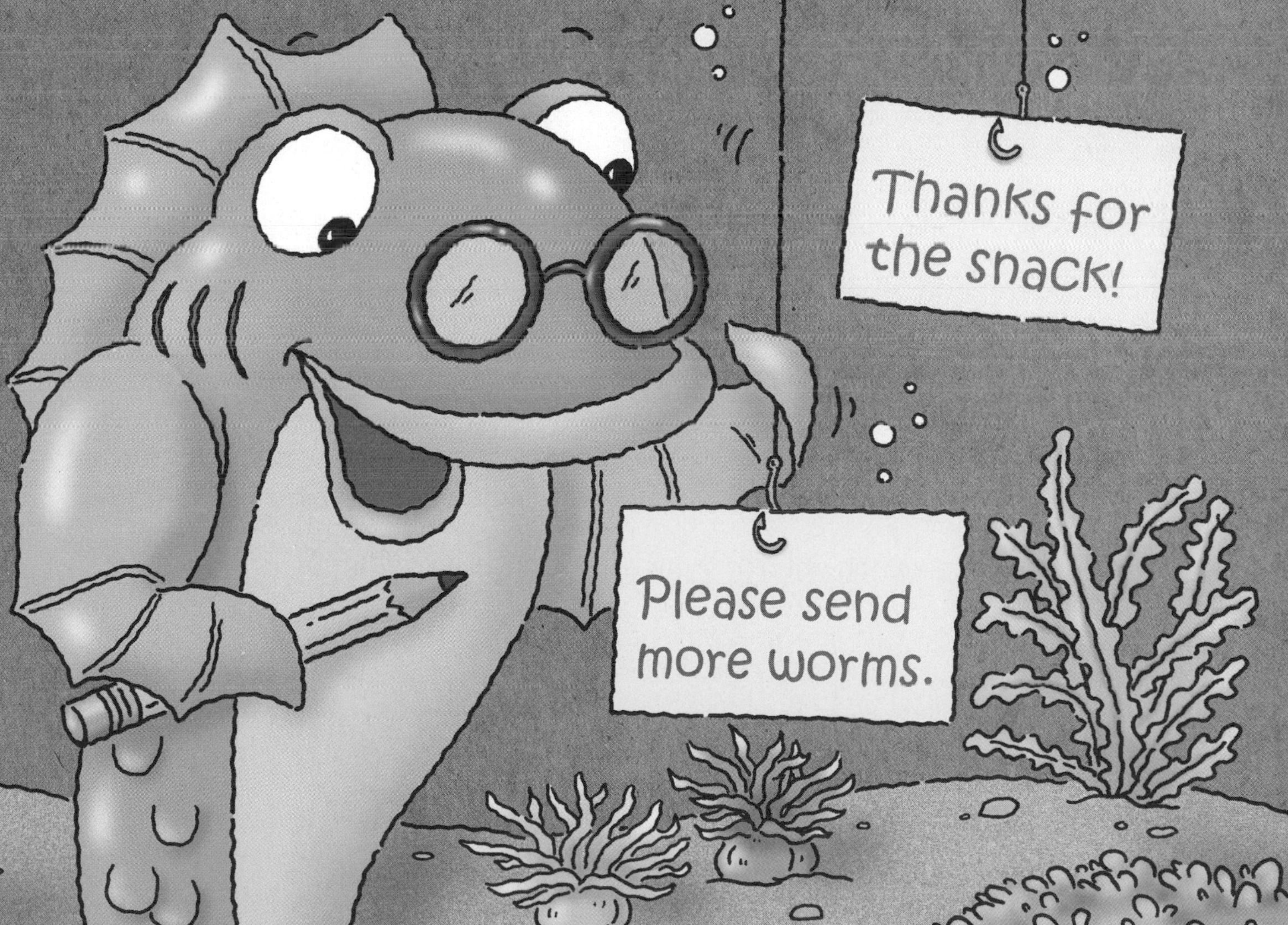

Writing: Topic Sentences

The topic sentence in a paragraph usually comes first. Sometimes, however, the topic sentence can come at the end or even in the middle of a paragraph. When looking for the topic sentence, try to find the one that tells the main idea of a paragraph.

Directions: Read the following paragraphs and underline the topic sentence in each.

The maple tree sheds its leaves every year. The oak and elm trees shed their leaves, too. Every autumn, the leaves on these trees begin changing color. Then, as the leaves gradually begin to die, they fall from the trees. Trees that shed their leaves annually are called deciduous trees.

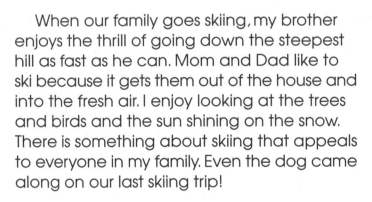

When our family goes skiing, my brother enjoys the thrill of going down the steepest hill as fast as he can. Mom and Dad like to ski because it gets them out of the house and into the fresh air. I enjoy looking at the trees and birds and the sun shining on the snow. There is something about skiing that appeals to everyone in my family. Even the dog came along on our last skiing trip!

If you are outdoors at night and there is traffic around, you should always wear bright clothing so that cars can see you. White is a good color to wear at night. If you are riding a bicycle, be sure it has plenty of reflectors, and if possible, headlamps as well. Be especially careful when crossing the street, because sometimes drivers cannot see you in the glare of their headlights. Being outdoors at night can be dangerous, and it is best to be prepared!

Writing: Supporting Sentences

A **paragraph** is a group of sentences that tell about one topic. The **topic sentence** in a paragraph usually comes first and tells the main idea of the paragraph. **Supporting sentences** follow the topic sentence and provide details about the topic.

Directions: Write at least three supporting sentences for each topic sentence below.

Example: Topic Sentence: Carly had an accident on her bike.
Supporting Sentences: She was on her way to the store to buy some bread. A car came weaving down the road and scared her. She rode her bike off the road so the car wouldn't hit her. Now, her knee is scraped, but she's all right.

1. I've been thinking of ways I could make some more money after school.

_____

_____

_____

2. In my opinion, cats (dogs, fish, etc.) make the best pets.

_____

_____

_____

3. My life would be better if I had a(n) (younger sister, younger brother, older sister, older brother).

_____

_____

_____

4. I'd like to live next door to a (swimming pool, video store, movie theater, etc.).

_____

_____

_____

Writing: Building Paragraphs

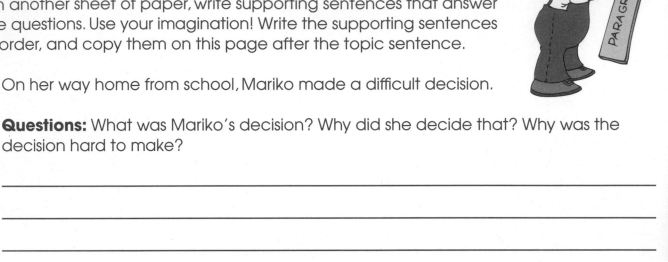

Directions: Read the groups of topic sentences and questions below. On another sheet of paper, write supporting sentences that answer the questions. Use your imagination! Write the supporting sentences in order, and copy them on this page after the topic sentence.

1. On her way home from school, Mariko made a difficult decision.

   Questions: What was Mariko's decision? Why did she decide that? Why was the decision hard to make?

   _____

   _____

   _____

   _____

2. Suddenly, Conrad thought of a way to clear up all the confusion.

   Questions: What was the confusion about? How was Conrad involved in it? What did he do to clear it up?

   _____

   _____

   _____

   _____

3. Bethany used to feel awkward at the school social activities.

   Questions: Why did Bethany feel awkward before? How does she feel now? What happened to change the way she feels?

   _____

   _____

   _____

   _____

Name: _____

Writing: Sequencing

When writing paragraphs, it is important to write events in the correct order. Think about what happens first, next, later and last.

Directions: The following sentences tell about Chandra's day, but they are all mixed up. Read each sentence and number them in the order in which they happened.

_____ She arrived at school and went to her locker to get her books.

_____ After dinner, she did the dishes, then read a book for a while.

_____ Chandra brushed her teeth and put on her pajamas.

_____ She rode the bus home, then she fixed herself a snack.

_____ She ate breakfast and went out to wait for the bus.

_____ Chandra woke up and picked out her clothes for school.

_____ She met her friend Sarah on the way to the cafeteria.

_____ She worked on homework and watched TV until her mom called her for dinner.

Directions: Write a short paragraph about what you did today. Use words like **first**, **next**, **then**, **later** and **finally** to indicate the order in which you did things.

_____

_____

_____

_____

_____

_____

_____

_____

_____

_____

_____

Sequencing

Sequencing means to place events in order from beginning to end or first to last.

Example:

    To send a letter, you must:
    Get paper, pencil or pen, an envelope and a stamp.
    Write the letter.
    Fold the letter and put it in the envelope.
    Address the envelope correctly.
    Put a stamp on the envelope.
    Put the envelope in the mailbox or take
        it to the Post Office.

Directions: Write the sequence for making a
peanut butter and jelly sandwich.

You get Jelly and peanutbutter and bread
and spread the jelly on the bread and
spread the peanutbutter on the bread and
there you go time to eat!

_____

_____

_____

Directions: After you finish, try making the sandwich **exactly** the way you wrote the steps.
Did you leave out any steps? Which ones?

_____

_____

_____

Does a particular section you wrote require a better explanation? Clarify your explanation
by adding missing information.

_____

_____

_____

Author's Purpose

Authors write to fulfill one of three purposes: to **inform**, to **entertain** or to **persuade**.

Authors who write to inform are providing facts for the reader in an informational context.

Examples: Encyclopedia entries and newspaper articles

Authors who write to entertain are hoping to provide enjoyment for the reader.

Examples: Funny stories and comics

Authors who write to persuade are trying to convince the reader to believe as they believe.

Examples: Editorials and opinion essays

Directions: Read each paragraph. Write **inform**, **entertain** or **persuade** on the line to show the author's purpose.

1. The whooping crane is a migratory bird. At one time, this endangered bird was almost extinct. These large white cranes are characterized by red faces and trumpeting calls. Through protection of both the birds and their habitats, the whooping crane is slowly increasing in number.

    _____

2. It is extremely important that all citizens place bird feeders in their yards and keep them full for the winter. Birds that spend the winter in this area are in danger of starving due to lack of food. It is every citizen's responsibility to ensure the survival of the birds.

    _____

3. Imagine being able to hibernate like a bear each winter! Wouldn't it be great to eat to your heart's content all fall? Then, sometime in late November, inform your teacher that you will not be attending school for the next few months because you'll be resting and living off your fat? Now, that would be the life!

    _____

4. Bears, woodchucks and chipmunks are not the only animals that hibernate. The queen bumblebee also hibernates in winter. All the other bees die before winter arrives. The queen hibernates under leaves in a small hole. She is cold-blooded and therefore is able to survive slightly frozen.

    _____

Name: _____

Author's Purpose

Directions: Write a paragraph of your own for each purpose. The paragraph can be about any topic.

1. to inform

    _____

    _____

    _____

    _____

2. to persuade

    _____

    _____

    _____

    _____

3. to entertain

    _____

    _____

    _____

    _____

Directions: Reread your paragraphs. Do they make sense? Check for grammar, spelling and punctuation errors and make corrections where needed.

Name: _____

Descriptive Sentences

Descriptive sentences give readers a vivid image and enable them to imagine a scene clearly.

Example:
   Nondescriptive sentence: There were grapes in the bowl.
   Descriptive sentence: The plump purple grapes in the bowl looked tantalizing.

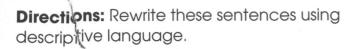

Directions: Rewrite these sentences using descriptive language.

1. The dog walked in its pen.

   _____

2. The turkey was almost done.

   _____

3. I became upset when my computer wouldn't work.

   _____

4. Jared and Michelle went to the ice-cream parlor.

   _____

5. The telephone kept ringing.

   _____

6. I wrote a story.

   _____

7. The movie was excellent.

   _____

8. Dominique was upset that her friend was ill.

   _____

Grade 5 - Comprehensive Curriculum

Name: _____

Writing: Descriptive Details

A writer creates pictures in a reader's mind by telling him/her how something looks, sounds, feels, smells or tastes. For example, compare **A** and **B** below. Notice how the description in **B** makes you imagine how the heavy door and the cobweb would feel and how the broken glass would look and sound as someone walked on it.

A. I walked into the house.

B. I pushed open the heavy wooden door of the old house. A cobweb brushed my face, and broken glass, sparkling like ice, crushed under my feet.

Directions: Write one or two sentences about each topic below. Add details that will help your reader see, hear, feel, smell or taste what you are describing.

1. Your favorite dinner cooking

   _____

   _____

2. Old furniture

   _____

   _____

3. Wind blowing in the trees

   _____

   _____

4. A tired stranger

   _____

   _____

5. Wearing wet clothes

   _____

   _____

6. A strange noise somewhere in the house

   _____

   _____

Writing: Descriptive Details

Directions: For each topic sentence below, write three or four supporting sentences. Include details about how things look, sound, smell, taste or feel. Don't forget to use adjectives, adverbs, similes and metaphors.

Example: After my dog had his bath, I couldn't believe how much better he looked. His fur, which used to be all matted and dirty, was as clean as new snow. He still felt a little damp when I scratched behind his ears. The smell from rolling in our garbage was gone, too. He smelled like apples now because of the shampoo.

1. My little cousin's birthday party was almost over.

_____

_____

_____

2. I always keep my grandpa company while he bakes bread.

_____

_____

_____

3. By the end of our day at the beach, I was a mess.

_____

_____

_____

4. Early morning is the best time to go for a bike ride.

_____

_____

_____

Name: _____

Personal Narratives

A **personal narrative** tells about a person's own experiences.

Directions: Read the example of a personal narrative. Write your answers in complete sentences.

My Worst Year

When I look back on that year, I can hardly believe that one person could have such terrible luck for a whole year. But then again, I should have realized that if things could begin to go wrong in January, it didn't bode well for the rest of the year.

It was the night of January 26. One of my best friends was celebrating her birthday at the local roller-skating rink, and I had been invited. The evening began well enough with pizza and laughs. I admit I have never been a cracker jack roller skater, but I could hold my own. After a few minutes of skating, I decided to exit the rink for a cold soda.

Unfortunately, I did not notice the trailing ribbons of carpet which wrapped around the wheel of my skate, yanking my left leg from under me. My leg was broken. It wasn't just broken in one place but in four places! At the hospital, the doctor set the bone and put a cast on my leg. Three months later, I felt like a new person.

Sadly, the happiness wasn't meant to last. Five short months after the final cast was removed, I fell and broke the same leg again. Not only did it rebreak but it broke in the same four places! We found out later that it hadn't healed correctly. Three months later, it was early December and the end of a year I did not wish to repeat.

1. List the sequence of events in this personal narrative.

   _____

   _____

   _____

   _____

2. From reading the personal narrative, what do you think were the author's feelings toward the events that occurred?

   _____

   _____

Name: _____

Personal Narratives

A **narrative** is a spoken or written account of an actual event. A **personal narrative** tells about your own experience. It can be written about any event in your life and may be serious or comical.

When writing a personal narrative, remember to use correct sentence structure and punctuation. Include important dates, sights, sounds, smells, tastes and feelings to give your reader a clear picture of the event.

Directions: Write a personal narrative about an event in your life that was funny.

_____

_____

_____

_____

_____

_____

_____

_____

_____

_____

_____

_____

_____

_____

_____

Grade 5 - Comprehensive Curriculum

Complete the Story

Directions: Read the beginning of this story. Then complete the story with your own ideas.

It was a beautiful summer day in June when my family and I set off on vacation. We were headed for Portsmouth, New Hampshire. There we planned to go on a whale-watching ship and perhaps spy a humpback whale or two. However, there were many miles between our home and Portsmouth.

We camped at many lovely parks along the way to New Hampshire. We stayed in the Adirondack Mountains for a few days and then visited the White Mountains of Vermont before crossing into New Hampshire.

My family enjoys tent camping. My dad says you can't really get a taste of the great outdoors in a pop-up camper or RV. I love sitting by the fire at night, gazing at the stars and listening to the animal noises.

The trip was going well, and everyone was enjoying our vacation. We made it to Portsmouth and were looking forward to the whale-watching adventure. We arrived at the dock a few minutes early. The ocean looked rough, but we had taken seasickness medication. We thought we were prepared for any kind of weather.

_____

_____

_____

_____

_____

_____

_____

_____

_____

Name: _____

Writing Fiction

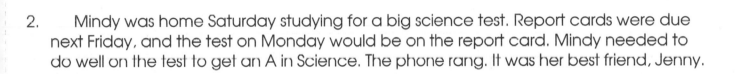

Directions: Use descriptive writing to complete each story. Write at least five sentences.

1.   It was a cold, wintry morning in January. Snow had fallen steadily for 4 days. I was staring out my bedroom window when I saw the bedraggled dog staggering through the snow.

_____

_____

_____

_____

_____

_____

2.   Mindy was home Saturday studying for a big science test. Report cards were due next Friday, and the test on Monday would be on the report card. Mindy needed to do well on the test to get an A in Science. The phone rang. It was her best friend, Jenny.

_____

_____

_____

_____

_____

_____

3.   Martin works every weekend delivering newspapers. He wakes up at 5:30 A.M. and begins his route at 6:00 A.M. He delivers 150 newspapers on his bike. He enjoys his weekend job because he is working toward a goal.

_____

_____

_____

_____

_____

_____

Grade 5 - Comprehensive Curriculum

Name: _____

Writing: Point of View

People often have different opinions about the same thing. This is because each of us has a different "point of view." **Point of view** is the attitude someone has about a particular topic as a result of his or her personal experience or knowledge.

Directions: Read the topic sentence below about the outcome of a basketball game. Then write two short paragraphs, one from the point of view of a player for the Reds and one from the point of view of a player for the Cowboys. Be sure to give each person's opinion of the outcome of the game.

Topic Sentence: In the last second of the basketball game between the Reds and the Cowboys, the Reds scored and won the game.

Terry, a player for the Reds . . . _____

_____

_____

Chris, a player for the Cowboys . . . _____

_____

_____

Directions: Here's a different situation. Read the topic sentence, and then write three short paragraphs from the points of view of Katie, her dad and her brother.

Topic Sentence: Katie's dog had chewed up another one of her father's shoes.

Katie . . . _____

_____

Katie's father . . . _____

_____

Katie's brother Mark, who would rather have a cat . . . _____

_____

Friendly Letters

A **friendly letter** has these parts: return address, date, greeting, body, closing and signature.

Directions: Read this letter. Then label the parts of the letter.

_____ ⟶ 222 West Middle Street
Boise, Idaho 33444
May 17, 1999 ⟵ _____

Dear Blaine, ⟵ _____

    Hello! I know I haven't written in several weeks, but I've been very busy with school and baseball practice. How have you been? How is the weather in Boston? It is finally getting warm in Boise.
    As I mentioned, I am playing baseball this year. My team is called the Rockets, and we are really good. We have a terrific coach. We practice two nights a week and play games on the weekends. Are you playing baseball?
    I can hardly wait to visit you this summer. I can't believe I'll be flying on an airplane and staying with you and your family for 2 weeks! There is probably a lot to do in Boston. When you write, tell me some ideas you have for the 2 weeks.

_____ ⟶ Your friend,

_____ ⟶ Mason

Envelopes should follow this format:

Mason Fitch
222 West Middle Street
Boise, ID 33444

                 Blaine Morgan
                 111 E. 9th Street, Apt 22B
                 Boston, MA 00011

Name: _____

Friendly Letters

Directions: Write a friendly letter. Then address the envelope.

Name: _____

Writing: Supporting Your Opinion

Directions: Decide what your opinion is on each topic below. Then write a paragraph supporting your opinion. Begin with a topic sentence that tells the reader what you think. Add details in the next three or four sentences that show why you are right.

Example: Whether kids should listen to music while they do homework

Kids do a better job on their homework
if they listen to music. The music makes
the time more enjoyable. It also drowns
out the sounds of the rest of the family.
If things are too quiet while kids do
homework, every little sound distracts them.

1. Whether young people should have a choice about going to school, no matter how old they are

   _____

   _____

   _____

2. Whether all parents should give their children the same amount of money for an allowance

   _____

   _____

   _____

3. Whether you should tell someone if you doubt he/she is telling the truth

   _____

   _____

   _____

Writing From a Prompt: An Opinion Essay

Directions: Write an opinion essay in response to the prompt.

Writing Prompt: Think about rainforests. What is the importance of preserving the rainforests of the world? What problems could arise if there were no longer any rainforest areas? What problems could arise for humans due to the preservation of rainforests? How do rainforests affect you?

_____

_____

_____

_____

_____

_____

_____

_____

_____

_____

Directions: When you finish writing, reread your essay. Use this checklist to help make corrections.

☐ I have used correct spelling, grammar and punctuation.

☐ I have no sentence fragments.

☐ My essay makes sense.

☐ I wrote complete sentences.

☐ I have no run-on sentences.

☐ I answered the prompt.

Writing a Summary

A **summary** is a short description of what a selection or book is about.

Directions: Read the following selection and the example summary.

Fads of the 1950s

A fad is a practice or an object that becomes very popular for a period of time. Recent popular fads include yo-yos and Beanie Babies®. In the 1950s, there were many different fads, including coonskin caps, hula hoops and 3-D movies.

Coonskin caps were made popular by the weekly television show about Davy Crockett, which began in December of 1954. Not only did Davy's hat itself become popular but anything with Davy Crockett on it was in hot demand.

Also popular were hula hoops. They were produced by the Wham-O company in 1958. The company had seen similar toys in Australia. Hula hoops were priced at $1.98, and over 30 million hoops were sold within 6 months.

Another fad was the 3-D movie. When television sets began to appear in every American home, the movie industry began to suffer financially. Movie companies rushed to produce 3-D movies, and movie-goers once more flocked to theaters. The first 3-D movie was shown in Los Angeles on November 26, 1952. People loved the special Polaroid® glasses and scenes in the movie that seemed to jump out at them. As with the hula hoop and Davy Crockett, people soon tired of 3-D movies, and they became old news as they were replaced by new fads.

Summary

Over the years, many fads have become popular with the American public. During the 1950s, three popular fads were the hula hoop, Davy Crockett and 3-D movies. Davy Crockett's coonskin cap became a fad with the beginning of the weekly television show. Hula hoops were sold by the millions, and 3-D movies were enjoyed by people everywhere. However, like all fads, interest in these items soon died out.

Name: _____

Writing a Summary

Directions: Read the following selection. Using page 309 as a guide, write a summary of the selection.

Man's First Flights

In the first few years of the 20th century, the majority of people strongly believed that man could not and would not ever be able to fly. There were a few daring individuals who worked to prove the public wrong.

On December 8, 1903, Samuel Langley attempted to fly his version of an airplane from the roof of a houseboat on the Potomac River. Langley happened to be the secretary of the Smithsonian Institution, so his flight was covered not only by news reporters but also by government officials. Unfortunately, his trip met with sudden disaster when his aircraft did a nose dive into the river.

Nine days later, brothers Orville and Wilbur Wright attempted a flight. They had assembled their aircraft at their home in Dayton, Ohio, and shipped it to Kitty Hawk, North Carolina. On December 17, the Wright brothers made several flights, the longest one lasting an incredible 59 seconds. Since the Wright brothers had kept their flight attempts secret, their miraculous flight was only reported by two newspapers in the United States.

_____

_____

_____

_____

_____

_____

_____

Name: _____

Comparing and Contrasting

When writing comparison/contrast essays, it is helpful to write one paragraph which contains all the similarities and another paragraph which contains all the differences.

Directions: Write an essay in response to the prompt.

Writing Prompt: Think of your brother, sister or a friend. What similarities are there between you and this person? What differences are there?

_____

_____

_____

_____

_____

_____

_____

_____

_____

_____

_____

_____

_____

Directions: When you finish writing, reread your essay. Use this checklist to help make corrections.

☐ My essay makes sense.

☐ I listed at least two similarities and two differences.

☐ My sentences are correctly written.

☐ I used correct spelling, grammar and punctuation.

Grade 5 - Comprehensive Curriculum

Advantages and Disadvantages

As in the comparison/contrast essay, it is easiest to put all of the advantages in one paragraph and the disadvantages in another paragraph.

Directions: Write an essay in response to the prompt.

Writing Prompt: Think about what a society would be like if all people had the same skin tone, hair color, eye color, height and weight. What would the benefits of living in such a society be? Would there be any disadvantages? What would they be?

_____

_____

_____

_____

_____

_____

_____

_____

_____

_____

_____

_____

_____

Directions: When you finish writing, reread your essay. Use this checklist to help make corrections.

☐ My essay makes sense.

☐ I used correct spelling, grammar and punctuation.

☐ I answered the writing prompt.

☐ I have varied sentence length.

Name: _____

Newswriting

Newswriting is a style of writing used by newspaper reporters and other journalists who write for periodicals. **Periodicals** are newspapers, magazines and newsletters that are published regularly.

Magazine and newspaper writers organize their ideas and their writing around what is called "the five W's and the H" — who, what, when, where, why and how. As they conduct research and interview people for articles, journalists keep these questions in mind.

Directions: Read a newspaper article of your choice. Use the information you read to answer the questions.

Who
Who is involved? _____

Who is affected? _____

Who is responsible? _____

What
What is the event or subject? _____

What exactly has happened? _____

_____

When
When did this happen? _____

Where
Where did it happen? _____

_____

Why
Why did it happen? _____

Why will readers care? _____

_____

How
How did it happen? _____

_____

Name: _____

Newswriting: Inverted Pyramid Style

Newspaper reporters organize their news stories in what is called the **inverted pyramid** style. The inverted pyramid places the most important facts at the beginning of the story—called the lead (LEED)—and the least important facts at the end.

There are two practical reasons for this approach:

1) If the story must be shortened by an editor, he or she simply cuts paragraphs from the end of the story rather than rewriting the entire story.

2) Because newspapers contain so much information, few people read every word of every newspaper story. Instead, many readers skim headlines and opening paragraphs. The inverted pyramid style of writing enables readers to quickly get the basics of what the story is about without reading the entire story.

Directions: Read the news story. Then answer the questions.

> Cleveland—Ohio State University student John Cook is within one 36-hole match of joining some of amateur golf's top performers. The 21-year-old Muirfield Village Golf Club representative will try for his second straight U.S. Amateur championship Sunday against one of his California golf buddies, Mark O'Meara, over the 6,837-yard Canterbury Golf Club course. Starting times are 8 a.m. and 12:30 p.m.
>
> "Winning the U.S. Amateur once is a great thrill," said Cook after Saturday's breezy 5-3 semifinal decision over Alabama's Cecil Ingram III. "But winning the second time is something people don't very often do."

1. Who is the story about? _____

2. The "dateline" at the beginning of a news article tells where the event happened and where the reporter wrote the story. Where was the story about John Cook written?

_____

3. What is Cook trying to accomplish? _____

_____

4. Who did Cook beat on Saturday? _____

5. Which of the above paragraphs could be cut by an editor? _____

Writing: Just the Facts

Some forms of writing, such as reports and essays, contain opinions that are supported by the writer. In other kinds of writing, however, it is important to stick to the facts. Newspaper reporters, for example, must use only facts when they write their stories.

Directions: Read the following newspaper story about a fire, and underline the sentences or parts of sentences that are opinions. Then rewrite the story in your own words, giving only the facts.

At around 10:30 p.m. last night, a fire broke out in a house at 413 Wilshire Boulevard. The house is in a very nice neighborhood, surrounded by beautiful trees. The family of four who lives in the house was alerted by smoke alarms, and they all exited the house safely, although they must have been very frightened. Firefighters arrived on the scene at approximately 10:45 p.m., and it took them over 3 hours to extinguish the blaze. The firefighters were very courageous. The cause of the fire has not yet been determined, although faulty electric wiring is suspected. People should have their electric wiring checked regularly. The family is staying with relatives until repairs to their home can be made, and they are probably very anxious to move back into their house.

_____

_____

_____

_____

_____

_____

_____

_____

_____

_____

Name: _____

Writing: You're the Reporter

Directions: Now, write your own short newspaper story about an interesting event that occurred at your school or in your neighborhood. Find out who and what the story is about, where and when it happened, and why and how it happened. Take some notes, interview some of the people involved and write your story. Give your story a title, and remember to stick to the facts! In the box, draw a picture (or "photo") to go with your story.

_____

_____

_____

_____

_____

_____

_____

_____

_____

_____

_____

_____

_____

_____

_____

_____

Writing: Personification

Sometimes writers use descriptions like: The fire engine **screamed** as it rushed down the street. The sun **crawled** slowly across the sky. We know that fire engines do not really scream, and the sun does not really crawl. Writers use descriptions like these to make their writing more interesting and vivid. When a writer gives an object or animal human qualities, it is called **personification**.

Directions: For each object below, write a sentence using personification. The first one has been done for you.

1. the barn door

   The old, rusty barn door groaned loudly when I pushed it open.

2. the rain

   _____

3. the pickup truck

   _____

4. the radiator

   _____

5. the leaves

   _____

6. the television

   _____

7. the kite

   _____

8. the river

   _____

Name: _____

Similes

A **simile** is a comparison of two things that have something in common but are really very different. The words **like** and **as** are used in similes.

Examples:
   The baby was **as** happy **as** a lark.
   She is **like** a ray of sunshine to my tired eyes.

Directions: Choose a word from the box to complete each comparison. The first one has been done for you.

tack	grass	fish	mule	ox	rail	hornet	monkey

1. as stubborn as a _mule_____
2. as strong as an _____
3. swims like a _____
4. as sharp as a _____
5. as thin as a _____
6. as mad as a _____
7. climbs like a _____
8. as green as _____

Directions: Use your own words to complete these similes.

9. as _____ as a tack
10. _____ like a bird
11. as hungry as a _____
12. as white as _____

13. as light as a _____
14. as _____ as honey
15. _____ like a snake
16. as cold as _____

Directions: Use your own similes to complete these sentences.

17. Our new puppy sounded _____.
18. The clouds were _____.
19. Our new car is _____.
20. The watermelon tasted _____.

Name: _____

Writing: Common Similes

There are many similes that are used often in the English language. For example, "as frightened as a mouse" is a very common simile. Can you think of others?

Directions: Match the first part of each common simile to the second part. The first one has been done for you.

as slippery as	a mule
as smart as	a statue
as sly as	a rock
as still as	a bee
as quick as	an eel
as slow as	a pancake
as busy as	a whip
as cold as	a turtle
as flat as	a fox
as stubborn as	lightning
as hungry as	ice
as hard as	a bear

Directions: Write sentences using these common similes.

1. eats like a bird

_____

2. fits like a glove

_____

3. sits there like a bump on a log

_____

4. like a bull in a china shop

_____

5. works like a charm

_____

Grade 5 - Comprehensive Curriculum

Name: _____

Metaphors

A **metaphor** makes a direct comparison between two unlike things. A noun must be used in the comparison. The words **like** and **as** are not used.

Examples:
   Correct: The exuberant puppy was a **bundle of energy**.
   Incorrect: The dog is **happy**. (**Happy** is an adjective.)

Directions: Circle the two objects being compared.

1. The old truck was a heap of rusty metal.

2. The moon was a silver dollar in the sky.

3. Their vacation was a nightmare.

4. That wasp is a flying menace.

5. The prairie was a carpet of green.

6. The flowers were jewels on stems.

7. This winter, our pond is glass.

8. The clouds were marshmallows.

Directions: Complete the metaphor in each sentence.

9. The ruby was _____.

10. The hospital is _____.

11. The car was _____.

12. This morning when I awoke, I was _____.

13. When my brother is grumpy, he is _____.

14. Her fingers on the piano keys were _____.

Name: _____

Writing: Similes and Metaphors

Using **similes** and **metaphors** makes writing interesting. They are ways of describing things. **Similes** are comparisons that use **like** or **as**.

Examples: She looked like a frightened mouse.
She looked as frightened as a mouse.

Metaphors are direct comparisons that do not use **like** or **as**.

Example: She was a frightened mouse.

Directions: Rewrite each sentence two different ways to make them more interesting. In the first sentence (a), add at least one adjective and one adverb. In the second sentence (b), compare something in the sentence to something else, using a simile or metaphor.

Example: The baby cried.
a. The sick baby cried softly all night.
b. The baby cried louder and louder, like a storm gaining strength.

1. The stranger arrived.

   a. _____

   b. _____

2. The dog barked.

   a. _____

   b. _____

3. The children danced.

   a. _____

   b. _____

4. The moon rose.

   a. _____

   b. _____

Name: _____

Writing: Similes and Metaphors in Poetry

Many poems use similes and metaphors to create a more interesting description of what the poem is about.

Directions: Read the following poems and underline any similes or metaphors you see.

Flint

An emerald is as green as grass,
    A ruby red as blood;
A sapphire shines as blue as heaven;
    A flint lies in the mud.

A diamond is a brilliant stone,
    To catch the world's desire;
An opal holds a fiery spark;
    But a flint holds fire.

                            —Christina Rossetti

The Night Is a Big Black Cat

The night is a big black cat
        The moon is her topaz eye,
The stars are the mice she hunts at night,
        In the field of the sultry sky.

                            —G. Orr Clark

Directions: Now, write your own poem, using at least one simile and one metaphor.

_____

_____

_____

_____

_____

_____

_____

_____

_____

_____

Name: _____

Writing: Rhyming Words

Words that share the same vowel sound in their last syllables are **rhyming words**. Rhyming words can have the same number of syllables, like **spike** and **hike**, or different numbers of syllables, like **tent** and **excellent** or **nation** and **conversation**.

Directions: Write words that rhyme with the words below and have the number of syllables shown. The first one has been done for you.

1. table _____unable_____ (3)

2. green _____ (3)

3. instead _____ (1)

4. store _____ (2)

5. remember _____ (3)

6. concentration _____ (4)

7. stars _____ (2)

8. giraffe _____ (1)

9. neighbor _____ (2)

10. berry _____ (4)

11. dog _____ (3)

12. bath _____ (1)

13. celebration _____ (4)

14. master _____ (2)

15. baby _____ (2)

They share the same vowel sound in their last syllables.

spike
hike
like
Mike

Name: _____

Writing: Poetry

Directions: For the first group of poems below, both lines should rhyme. The first line is given. Complete each poem, using one of the given rhyming words, or use one of your own. Make sure to add the correct punctuation.

Example: mile   Kevin James has a certain style.
          pile
          dial   <u>To get his way, he'd walk a mile.</u>

ape   Mindy Lou got a very bad scrape!
grape
cape   _____

hide   Sometimes you have to swallow your pride.
fried
cried   _____

Directions: Complete these poems, using one of the given words, or use one of your own. Each poem should have four lines. The second and fourth lines should rhyme.

Example: cape   Kenny skidded on his bike.
          tape   And got himself all **scraped**.
          grape   Now his bike has a flat tire,
                     And his whole leg is **taped**.

I   I put some water in a bucket
cry   And then threw in some **dye**.
my   _____

        _____

file   Kelly got her hair cut,
dial   But I don't like the **style**.
Nile   _____

        _____

ride   When Billy Joe didn't win the race,
hide   It really hurt his **pride**.
cried   _____

        _____

Name: _____

Haiku

Haiku is a form of unrhymed Japanese poetry. Haiku have three lines. The first line has five syllables, the second line has seven syllables and the third line has five syllables.

Example:

The Fall

Leaves fall from the trees.
Do they want to leave their home?
They float on the breeze.

Directions: Write a haiku about nature. Write the title on the first line. Then illustrate your haiku.

Nature _____

_____

_____

_____

Lantern

Lantern is another type of five-line Japanese poetry. It takes the shape of a Japanese lantern. Each line must contain the following number of syllables.

Line 1:   1 syllable
Line 2:   2 syllables
Line 3:   3 syllables
Line 4:   4 syllables
Line 5:   1 syllable

Example:
Cats—
Stealthy
wild creatures
want to be your
pet.

Directions: Write and illustrate your own lantern.

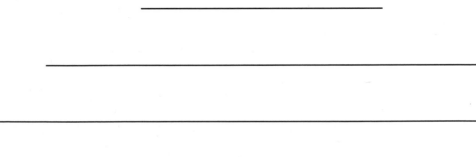

Alliterative Poetry

Alliteration is the repetition of a consonant sound in a group of words.

Example: Barney Bear bounced a ball.

Alliterative story poems can be fun to read and write. Any of several rhyming patterns can be used. Possibilities include:
Every two lines rhyme.
Every other line rhymes.
The first line rhymes with the last line and the two middle lines rhyme with each other.
All four lines rhyme.

Example:
Thomas Tuttle tries to dine,
On turkey, tea and treats so fine.
Thomas eats tomatoes and tortellini,
He devours tuna and tettrazini.

When tempting tidbits fill the table,
Thomas tastes as much as he is able,
He stuffs himself from top to toes,
Where he puts it, goodness knows!

Directions: Write an alliterative story poem using any rhyming pattern listed above. Your poem should be at least four lines long.

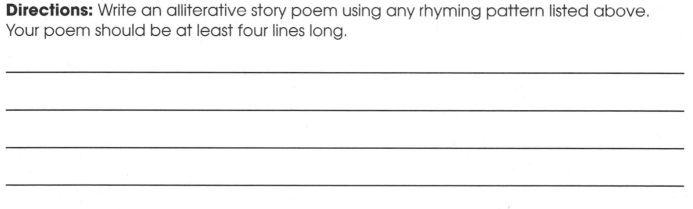

_____

_____

_____

_____

_____

_____

_____

How to Write a Book Report

Writing a book report should not be a chore. Instead, consider it an opportunity to share the good news about a book you have enjoyed. Simply writing, "I really liked this book. You will, too!" is not enough. You need to explain what makes the book worth reading.

Like other essays, book reports have three parts. An essay is a short report that presents the personal views of the writer. The three parts of an essay (and a book report) are introduction, body and conclusion.

The **introduction** to a book report should be a full paragraph that will capture the interest of your readers. The **body** paragraphs contain the main substance of your report. Include a brief overview of the plot of your book, along with supporting details that make it interesting. In the **conclusion**, summarize the central ideas of your report. Sum up why you would or would not recommend it to others.

Directions: Answer these questions about writing book reports.

1. Which of these introductory sentences is more interesting?

   ☐ Richie, a 12-year-old runaway, cries himself to sleep every night in the bowling alley where he lives.

   ☐ Many children run away from home, and this book is about one of them, a boy named Richie.

2. In a report on a fiction book about runaways, where would these sentences go?

   "Richie's mother is dead. He and his father don't get along."

   ☐ introduction

   ☐ conclusion

3. In the same report, where would these sentences go?

   "Author Clark Howard has written a sad and exciting book about runaways that shows how terrible the life of a runaway can be. I strongly recommend the book to people of all ages."

   ☐ body

   ☐ conclusion

Book Report: A Book I Devoured

Directions: Follow the writing prompts to write a short book report on a book you truly enjoyed.

Recently, I read a book I could not put down.

Its title is _____

One reason I "devoured" this book was _____

_____

_____

If I could be one of the characters, I'd be _____ because _____

_____

_____

_____

My favorite part of the story was when _____

_____

_____

_____

_____

_____

_____

_____

_____

Name: _____

Book Report: Comparing Two Books

Directions: Follow the writing prompts to write a short book report comparing two books on the same subject.

Two books I recently read on the same subject

are _____

by _____

and _____

by _____

I liked _____ better because _____

_____

_____

_____

The best part of this book was when _____

_____

_____

_____

_____

_____

_____

Even though I did not like it as well, one good thing I can say about the other book is

_____

_____

_____

Reference Sources: Languages, Social Studies

Reference sources are books and other materials which provide facts and information. Dictionaries, encyclopedias and nonfiction books are reference books. Magazine and newspaper articles, the Internet and computer CD's are also reference sources.

There are many other kinds of reference sources on specific topics. Some of these are listed below by the topics covered.

Language:
1. *The American Heritage Dictionary*
2. *The Dictionary of Contemporary Slang* by Jonathan Green
3. *The Misspeller's Dictionary* by Peter and Craig Norback
4. *Dictionary of Foreign Terms* by C. O. Mawson
5. *Webster's Dictionary of Synonyms*

Social Studies:
1. *The Black American Reference Book* by Mabel M. Smythe
2. *The Encyclopedia of Drug Abuse* by Robert O'Brien and Sidney Cohen
3. *Women's Rights Almanac* by Nancy Gager
4. *Encyclopedia of Psychology* by Raymond J. Corsini
5. *Webster's New Geographical Dictionary*

Directions: Answer the questions.

1. Which book would be the best source for finding the meaning of the Spanish term, *que pasa*?

_____

2. Which book would be the best source of information on Martin Luther King, Jr.?

_____

3. Where would you find information on cocaine use in the U.S.?

_____

4. Which book would have information on equal employment opportunities for women?

_____

5. Where would you look for a list of terms that mean the same as **incredible**?

_____

Reference Sources:
General, Science and Technology

These reference sources are listed by the topics covered.

General:
1. *Books in Print*
2. *International Who's Who*
3. *World Book Encyclopedia* (on computer CD)
4. *Rand McNally Contemporary World Atlas*
5. *Statistical Abstract of the United States*

Science and Technology:
1. *A Field Guide to Rocks and Minerals* by Frederick H. Pough
2. *Grzimek's Animal Life Encyclopedia*
3. *Living Plants of the World* by Lorus and Margery Milne
4. *Scientific American Library Guide to the Universe* (on computer CD)
5. *Your Vital Statistics: The Ultimate Book About the Average Human Being* by Gyles Brandreth

Directions: Answer the questions.

1. Which reference source would you check to find a map of Poland?

   _____

2. Which source would you consult to find the most recent statistics on the number of single parents in the United States?

   _____

3. Where would you find the most complete information on the Milky Way and other galaxies?

   _____

4. Where would you find the most complete information about a rock crystal called quartz?

   _____

5. Where would you find the most complete information on the chancellor of Germany?

   _____

Using the Library Catalog

Directions: Read about library catalogs. Use this information to answer the questions on the next page.

A **library catalog** lists on separate index cards, or in a computer file, all the books, videos, CD's, etc. in the library's collection. There are three ways to find a particular book: by title, by author or by subject.

Library catalogs that are on cards provide three different cards for each book—one for each of the ways the book is filed. Computerized library catalogs also list books in the same three ways. Usually, you simply type the title, author or subject in the appropriate box on the screen. A list of books by that author, title or subject will appear on the screen.

In both card and computerized catalogs, authors are filed alphabetically by last name.

Information on cards in a card catalog is arranged somewhat the same as information on a computerized catalog screen.

Title card

371.3	Coping With Study Strategies
Be	**Bergreen, Gary**
	N.Y., The Rosen Publishing Group, 1990
	137p.: ill.

Author card

371.3	**Bergreen, Gary**
Be	Coping With Study Strategies
	N.Y., The Rosen Publishing Group, 1990
	137p.: ill.

Subject card

371.3	STUDY SKILLS
Be	**Bergreen, Gary**
	Coping With Study Strategies
	N.Y., The Rosen Publishing Group, 1990
	137p.: ill.

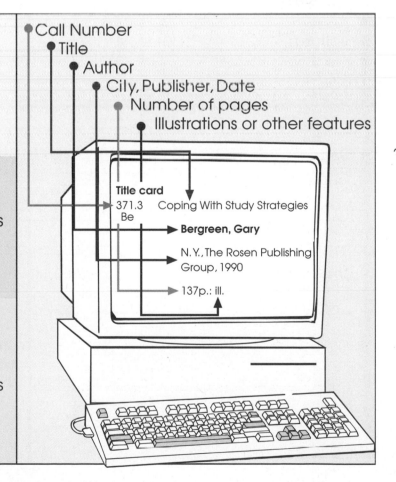

- Call Number
- Title
- Author
- City, Publisher, Date
- Number of pages
- Illustrations or other features

Title card
371.3 Coping With Study Strategies
Be
Bergreen, Gary
N.Y., The Rosen Publishing Group, 1990
137p.: ill.

Name: _____

Using the Library Catalog

The **call number** for a book is printed on its spine and also appears in the library catalog. Nonfiction books are shelved in order by call number.

Directions: Use what you learned about library catalogs to answer these questions.

1. What should you type into a library's computerized catalog for a listing of all the books the library has on birds? _____

2. What should you type into the library's computerized catalog for a list of all the books by Louisa May Alcott? _____

3. What should you type into the library's computerized catalog to see if the library owns a book called *Birds of North America*? _____

4. According to the card catalog card shown on the previous page, what company published the book *Coping With Study Strategies*? _____

5. Under what subject is *Coping With Study Strategies* listed? _____

6. What is the call number for *Coping With Study Strategies*? _____

7. What are three ways to find a book in the library? _____

_____

8. How are authors' names listed in library catalogs? _____

_____

9. Besides the call number, title and author, what are three other types of information given for a book in a library catalog?

_____

_____

_____

Name: _____

Library Research

Directions: Read about doing research in a library. Then answer the questions.

Step 1: Look in a general encyclopedia, such as *Encyclopedia Americana* or *World Book*, for background information on your topic. Use the index volume to locate the main article and all related articles. Look at the suggested cross-references that direct you to other sources. Also, check for a bibliography at the end of the article for clues to other sources. A **bibliography** lists all the books and magazines used to write the article.

Step 2: Use a special encyclopedia for more specific information or for definitions of special terms. The *Encyclopedia of Education, International Encyclopedia of the Social Sciences* and the *Encyclopedia of Bioethics* are examples of special encyclopedias.

Step 3: Look for a general book on your topic using the subject headings in the library catalog. Be sure to note the copyright date (date published) on all books you select. For current topics such as medical research or computers, you will want to use only the most recently published and up-to-date sources.

Step 4: Use *Facts on File* to pinpoint specific facts or statistics related to your topic. *Facts on File* is a weekly summary of national and international news.

Step 5: An index helps you locate magazine articles on your topic. To find the most current information, try the *Reader's Guide to Periodical Literature*. The *Guide* lists articles by subject published during a particular month, the magazines containing the articles and the date and page numbers of the articles.

1. Name two general encyclopedias. _____

   _____

2. Name three special encyclopedias. _____

   _____

   _____

3. Which reference book contains a weekly summary of national and international news?

   _____

Library Research

Directions: Read the remaining steps for doing library research. Then answer the questions.

Step 6: Newspaper indexes will direct you to newspaper articles related to your topic. See *The New York Times Index* for national and international coverage of a topic or event. If you are researching a local subject or event, ask the librarian if indexes for the local newspapers are available.

Step 7: Ask the librarian if the library keeps "clip files" of articles on particular topics. Clip files contain articles librarians have cut out and saved in folders. Consulting a clip file can sometimes save time because the librarian has already done the research and filed it together in one place!

Step 8: If your research topic is a person—for example, President Bill Clinton—a good source is *Current Biography.* This reference contains long articles about people in the news. Another source is *Biography Index,* which will direct you to articles in magazines and newspapers.

Step 9: If you need to locate statistics—for example, how many students play a certain school sport—check the *World Almanac and Book of Facts* or *Statistical Abstract of the United States.* The *Abstract* contains government statistics on education, politics and many other subjects.

Step 10: For detailed instructions about writing your paper, check one of these references: *Elements of Style* by Strunk and White or *A Manual for Writers of Term Papers, Theses, and Dissertations* by Kate Turabian.

1. What index should you consult if you're researching an article about water pollution in your town?

   _____

2. What is a "clip file"? _____

   _____

   _____

3. What are two sources of information on people in the news?

   _____

   _____

Using the *Reader's Guide to Periodical Literature*

Here is an example of a *Reader's Guide to Periodical Literature* entry for an article in *Discover* magazine. An explanation of terms follows the entry.

Science
  Science experiments for young people
  M. Watson, il *Discover* 11:33-7 Ja '90

Science is the topic under which the article (one of many) is listed.
Science experiments for young people is the title of the article.
M. Watson is the author of the article.
il means the article is illustrated.
Discover is the magazine where you will find the article.
11:33-7 means the article is in volume 11 on pages 33 to 37.
Ja '90 means the article was in the January 1990
   issue of the magazine.

Directions: Circle the correct answers.

1. An **O 18, 1998** listing in the *Reader's Guide* means:

   The article can be ordered on October 18, 1998.

   The article was published on October 18, 1998.

   The article was written on October 18, 1998.

2. An **il** listing in an article about birds means:

   The article contains pictures of birds.

   The article is about ill birds.

   The author's last name is il.

3. How many pages are contained
   in a listing that reads 12:32-41?

   Eight

   Forty-one

   Ten

Fiction, Nonfiction and Biographies

Fiction books are stories that are not based on facts or real events. They are based on the imagination of the author.

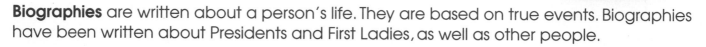

Examples: picture books and novels

Nonfiction books are about facts or events that actually occurred.

Examples: reference books and history books

Biographies are written about a person's life. They are based on true events. Biographies have been written about Presidents and First Ladies, as well as other people.

Directions: Use your library to answer the following questions.

1. What are the titles and authors of three fiction books? _____

_____

_____

2. What are the titles and authors of three nonfiction books? _____

_____

_____

3. What are the call numbers of the three nonfiction books you listed? _____

_____

Directions: Use the library catalog to locate two biographies of each of the people listed. Write the titles, authors and call numbers.

4. Abraham Lincoln _____

5. George Washington Carver _____

6. John F. Kennedy _____

7. Princess Diana _____

8. Pocahontas _____

Book Search: Fiction

Have you ever been on a scavenger hunt? Usually, when you go on a scavenger hunt, you need to find unusual items on a list. This scavenger hunt will take place at your library. Instead of finding unusual items, you will need to find books.

Directions: Find these books at your library. They will be in alphabetical order by the author's last name in the picture book section of the children's department. Then answer the questions.

Author: Margaret Wise Brown   **Title:** *Goodnight Moon*

1. Where is the cow jumping over the moon? _____

2. What is the old lady whispering? _____

3. How many kittens are in the story? _____

Author: Audrey Wood   **Title:** *Napping House*

4. In the beginning, what is everyone in the house doing? _____

5. What kind of flea is in this story? _____

6. What breaks at the end of the story? _____

Author: Audrey Wood   **Title:** *Heckedy Peg*

7. Who is Heckedy Peg?

_____

8. What did Heckedy Peg lose?

_____

_____

9. What two things does the mother tell her children not to do?

_____

_____

Name: _____

Book Search: Nonfiction

Directions: Look in your library catalog to find the types of nonfiction books listed. Then go to the shelf in the nonfiction section and locate the books. Write the information requested for each book.

A book about gorillas

Title: _____

Author: _____

Call number: _____

First sentence in book: _____

A book about the solar system

Title: _____

Author: _____

Call number: _____

Last sentence in book: _____

A book about baseball

Title: _____

Author: _____

Call number: _____

Color of book's cover: _____

A book about flowers

Title: _____

Author: _____

Call Number: _____

Name of a flower pictured in book: _____

Name: _____

Book Search: Biographies

Biographies may be located in the 920 section in your library or may be filed by call number according to subject.

Directions: Use the library catalog and the actual books to answer these questions.

1. How many books can you find about Elizabeth Blackwell? _____

2. What is the title of one of the books? _____

3. How many books can you find about Kareem Abdul-Jabar? _____

4. What are the titles, authors and call numbers of three books about George Washington?

_____

_____

_____

5. What are the titles, authors and call numbers of three books about Martin Luther King, Jr.?

_____

_____

_____

6. What are the titles, authors and call numbers of three books about Eleanor Roosevelt?

_____

_____

_____

7. What are the titles, authors and call numbers of three books about Marie Curie?

_____

_____

_____

Name: _____

Reports: Choosing a Topic

Directions: Read about how to write a report. Then answer the questions.

A report is a written paper based on the writer's research. It is logically organized and, if it is a good report, presents information in an interesting way. Reports can focus on many different topics. A social studies report may provide information about a city or state. A science report may explain why the oceans are polluted.

If possible, choose a topic you're interested in. Sometimes a teacher assigns a general topic to the whole class, such as the solar system. This is a very broad topic, so you must first narrow it to a smaller topic about which you can write an interesting four- or five-page report. For example, your report could be on "The Sun, the Center of the Solar System" or "Jupiter, the Jumbo Planet."

A narrower topic gives your paper a better focus. Be careful not to make your topic too narrow, because then you may not be able to find much information about it for your report.

The inverted pyramid on the right shows how to narrow your topic from the general, at the top of the pyramid, to the specific, at the bottom.

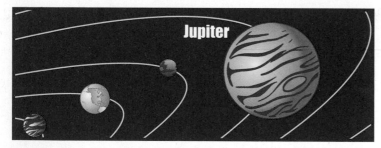

The solar system

Planets in the solar system

Jupiter, the jumbo planet

Directions: Select a topic for a paper you will write. You may choose one of these topics or select one of your own. Then answer the questions.

| American wars | Games | Presidents | States |
| Famous American women | Solar system | Sports heroes | Ecology |

1. What is a report? _____

_____

2. Which general topic did you choose? _____

3. What specific topic will you write about? _____

_____

Name: _____

Reports: Doing Research

Directions: Review the information on pages 335 and 336 about doing library research. Then read about how to do research for a report and answer the questions.

Before starting your report, locate the most likely places to find relevant information for your research. Ask the librarian for help if necessary. A good report will be based on at least three or four sources, so it's important to find references that provide varied information.

Is the topic a standard one, such as a report on the skeletal system? A general encyclopedia, such as *World Book*, is a good place to begin your research. Remember to use the encyclopedia's index to find related entries. For related entries on the skeletal system, you could check the index for entries on bones, health and the musculo-skeletal system. The index entry will show which encyclopedia number and pages to read to find information related to each entry topic.

Does your report require current statistics and/or facts? *Facts on File* and *Editorial Research Reports* are two sources for statistics. Ask the librarian to direct you to more specialized reference sources, such as *The People's Almanac* or *The New Grove Dictionary of Music and Musicians* which are related specifically to your topic.

For current magazine articles, see the *Reader's Guide to Periodical Literature*, which lists the names and page numbers of magazine articles related to a variety of topics. If you need geographical information about a country, check an atlas such as the *Rand McNally Contemporary World Atlas*.

1. How many reference sources should you consult before writing your report? _____

2. What are two references that provide statistics and facts? _____

_____

3. Where will you find a listing of magazine articles? _____

_____

4. Where should you look for geographical information? _____

_____

5. If you're stumped or don't know where to begin, who can help? _____

_____

Name: _____

Reports: Taking Notes

Directions: Read about taking notes for your report. Use the "index card" below to write a sample note from one of your reference sources.

When gathering information for a report, it is necessary to take notes. You'll need to take notes when you read encyclopedia entries, books and magazine or newspaper articles related to your topic.

Before you begin gathering information for a report, organize your thoughts around the who, what, when, where, why and how questions of your topic. This organized approach will help direct you to the references that best answer these questions. It will also help you select and write in your notes only useful information.

There are different ways of taking notes. Some people use notebook paper. If you write on notebook paper, put a heading on each page. Write only notes related to each heading on specific pages. Otherwise, your notes will be disorganized, and it will be difficult to begin writing your paper.

Many people prefer to put their notes on index cards. Index cards can be easily sorted and organized when you begin writing your report and are helpful when preparing an outline. If you use index cards for your notes, put one fact on each card.

Take several notes from each reference source you use. Having too many notes is better than not having enough information when you start to write your report.

_____

_____

_____

_____

_____

_____

_____

_____

_____

Name: _____

Encyclopedia Skills: Taking Notes

A **biography** is a written report of a person's life. It is based on facts and actual events. To prepare to write a biographical essay, you could look up information about the person in an encyclopedia.

Directions: Select one of the people listed below. Read about that person in an encyclopedia. Take notes to prepare for writing a biographical essay. Then use your notes to answer the questions.

Babe Ruth

Mikhail Baryshnikov

Golda Meir

Dolly Madison

Pearl S. Buck

Billie Jean King

Willie Mays

Woodrow Wilson

Charles Darwin

Marie Curie

My Notes:

1. Where and when was he/she born? _____

2. If deceased, when did the person die? _____

3. When and why did he/she first become famous? _____

_____

_____

4. What are some important points about this person's career?

_____

_____

_____

_____

_____

_____

Reports: Making an Outline

An outline will help you organize your ideas before you begin writing your report.

Title
I. First Main Idea
   A. A supporting idea or fact
   B. Another supporting idea or fact
      1. An example or related fact
      2. An example or related fact
II. Second Main Idea
   A. A supporting idea or fact
   B. Another supporting idea or fact
III. Third Main Idea
   A. A supporting idea or fact
   B. Another supporting idea or fact

Directions: Use information from your notes to write an outline for your report. Follow the above format, but expand your outline to include as many main ideas, facts and examples as necessary.

_____

_____

_____

_____

_____

_____

_____

_____

_____

Reports: Writing the Paper

Directions: Read more about writing a report. Then write your report.

Before you begin, be certain you clearly understand what is expected. How long should your report be? Must it be typed? Can it be written in pen? Should it be double-spaced?

Begin the first draft of your report with a general introduction of your topic. In the introduction, briefly mention the main points you will write about. One paragraph is usually enough to introduce your paper.

Next, comes the body of your report. Start a new paragraph for each main point. Include information that supports that point. If you are writing a long report, you may need to write a new paragraph for each supporting idea and/or each example. Follow your outline to be certain you cover all points. Depending on the number of words required to cover your topic, the body of the report will be anywhere from three or four paragraphs to several pages long.

In one or two concluding paragraphs, briefly summarize the main points you wrote about in the body of the report and state any conclusions you have drawn as a result of your research.

Once you finish the first draft, you will need to edit and rewrite your report to make it read smoothly and correct errors. You may need to rewrite your report more than once to make it the best it can be.

If possible, put the report aside for a day or two before you rewrite it so you can look at it with fresh eyes and a clear mind. Professional writers often write several drafts, so don't be discouraged about rewrites! Rewriting and editing are the keys to good writing—keys that every writer, no matter how old or experienced, relies on.

Directions: Circle the words in the puzzle related to writing a report.

K	K	N	K	T	O	P	I	C	D	T	B
L	D	O	B	T	T	O	D	P	T	D	O
I	N	T	R	O	D	U	C	T	I	O	N
E	N	E	R	G	D	E	E	O	O	O	N
D	W	S	R	G	E	Y	C	P	C	X	R
S	A	F	E	A	T	T	E	I	E	Y	O
R	W	A	Q	U	B	W	P	C	D	G	F
L	I	C	O	N	C	L	U	S	I	O	N
O	U	T	L	I	N	E	U	T	T	E	D
R	E	S	E	A	R	C	H	R	E	S	E

topic
facts
outline
introduction
body
conclusion
notes
research
edit

Name: _____

Review

1. Why should you narrow your topic when writing a report?

☐ So you can include specific, relevant information.

☐ So you can write a short paper.

☐ So you can use only one reference book.

2. Which of the following is not a reference book?

☐ *Facts on File*

☐ *Rand McNally Contemporary World Atlas*

☐ *Flowers For Cosmo*

☐ *World Book Encyclopedia*

3. Writing an outline for your report will help you

☐ narrow your topic.

☐ gather many notes.

☐ get organized and follow a plan.

☐ broaden your topic.

4. Which of the following is not a part of a finished report?

☐ Introduction

☐ Conclusion

☐ Body

☐ Outline

5. When taking notes, index cards will help you

☐ check spelling, grammar and punctuation.

☐ organize your writing later.

☐ find things quickly on the shelves.

☐ transfer facts to your notebook.

Editing

To **edit** means to revise and correct written work. Learning how to edit your work will help you become a better writer. First, you should write a rough draft of your paper, then edit it to make it better. Remember these things when writing your rough draft:

► **Do not overcrowd your page.** Leave space between every line and at the sides of your pages to make notes and changes.

► **Write so you can read it.** Don't be sloppy just because you're only writing a rough draft.

► **Number your pages.** This will help you keep everything in order.

► **Write on only one side of the page.** This gives you plenty of space if you want to make changes or add information between paragraphs.

► **Use the same size notebook paper for all drafts.** If all pages are the same size, you're less likely to lose any.

Before turning in your report or paper, ask yourself these questions:

► **Have I followed my outline?**

► **Have I told the who, what, when, where, why and how?**

► **Have I provided too much information?** (Good writers are concise. Don't repeat yourself after you have made a point.)

► **Do I still have unanswered questions?** (If you have questions, you can bet your readers will also. Add the missing information.)

It is always a good idea to let a day or so pass before rereading your paper and making final corrections. That way you will see what you actually wrote, instead of what you **think** you wrote.

When you edit your work, look for:

► **Correct grammar.**

► **Correct spelling.** Use the dictionary if you are not 100 percent sure.

► **Correct punctuation.**

► **Complete sentences.** Each should contain a complete thought.

Directions: Answer these questions about editing by writing **T** for true or **F** for false.

___ 1. When you are editing, you should look for correct grammar and spelling.

___ 2. Editors do not look for complete sentences.

___ 3. Editors do not have to read each word of a story.

___ 4. It is best to use both sides of a sheet of paper when writing the rough draft of your report.

___ 5. It does not matter how neat your first draft is.

___ 6. Editors make sure that sentences are punctuated correctly.

Name: _____

Editing

Editors and proofreaders use certain marks to note the changes that need to be made. In addition to circling spelling errors and fixing capitalization mistakes, editors and proofreaders also use the following marks to indicate other mistakes that need to be corrected.

the	Delete.	∧	Insert a comma.
a nt	Remove the space.	◡	Insert an apostrophe.
In#this	Insert a space.	◡◡	Insert quotation marks.
is∧	Insert a word.	⊙	Insert a period.

Directions: Use editing marks to correct the errors in these sentences. Then write the sentences correctly on the lines.

1. Mr. Ramsey was a man who liked to do nothing

_____

2. Lili a young hawaiian girl, liked to swim in the sea.

_____

3. Youngsters who play baseballalways have a favorite player.

_____

4. Too many people said, That movie was terrible."

_____

5. I didn't wantto go to the movie with sally

_____

6. Prince charles always wants to play polo

_____

7. The little boy's name was albert leonard longfellow

_____

Name: _____

Editing

Directions: Use editing marks to show the changes that need to be made in the following sentences.

1. billy bob branstool was was the biggest bully at our school

2. mr. Smith told my mother that i was not a good student

3. I heard your mom say, "give your mother a kiss.

4. david and justin liked reading about dinosaurs especially tyrannosaurus rex.

5. milton said to to mabel "maybe we can play tomorrow."

6. lisa and Phil knew the answers to the questions but they would not raise hands

7. too many people were going to see the movie so we decided to go get pizza instead

8. tillie's aunt teresa was coming to visit for the month of may

9. we lived in a small town called sophia, north carolina, for 20 days before we decided to move away.

10. little people do not always live under bridges but sometimes little fish do.

11. i was reading the book called, *haunting at midnight.*

12. kevin and i decided that we would be detective bob and detective joe.

13. there were thirteen questions on the test. kevin missed all but the first one

14. thirty of us were going on a fieldtrip when suddenly the teachertold the bus driver to turn around.

Editing

⌒not⌒is⌒	Flip the words around; transpose.
wa⌒n⌒l⌒ut	Flip letters around; transpose.
¶That was when Peter began talking.	Indent the paragraph or start a new paragraph.
with you.⌐The movie we went to see was good.	Move text down to line below.
There were no people there. ⌐ Jason thought we should go.	Move text up to line above.

Directions: Use editing marks to edit this story.

The Fallen Log

There was once a log on the floor of a very damp and eerie forest two men came upon the log and sat down for a rest. these two men, leroy and larry, did not know that someone could hear every word they said. "I'm so tired, moaned larry, as he began unlacing his heavy hikingboots. "and my feet hurt, too."

"Quit complaining" friend his said. We've got miles to walk before we'll find the cave with the hidden treasure. besides, if you think you're tired at look feet my. with that he kicked off his tennis shoe and discovered a very red big toe. "i think i won't be able to go any farther.

"Sh-h-h, already!" the two men heard a voice. "enough about feet, enough!" Larry and Leroy began loking around them. theycouldn't see anyone, though. "I'm in hree the voice said hoarsely.

Editing

Directions: Use editing marks to edit the continuing story of Larry and Leroy.

Larry and Leroy

larry and leroy jumped up from the log as soon as they realized that they were sitting on something that had a voice. "Hey, that was fast, said the voice. "How did you figure out where i was?"

By this time larry and leroy felt a little silly. Theycertainly didn't want to talk to a log. they looked at each other and then back at the log again. together they turned around and started walking down the path that had brought them to this point in the forest. "Hey were are you going?" the voice called.

"Well, i-i-i don't know," Larry replied, wondering if he sould be answering a log. "Who are you?"

"I'm a tiny elf who has been lostin this tree foryears," said the voice.

"Sure you are," replied larr. with that he and lroy began running for their lives.

Grade 5 - Comprehensive Curriculum

Name: _____

Editing

Directions: Draw a line from the editing mark on the left to its meaning on the right.

comp‌lain   Close up a word

The two boys came to class.   Insert an apostrophe
The girls, though,

¶This is the best pie ever.   Insert a comma

this   Delete a word

copy editor   Transpose words

We went zoo to the   Transpose letters

There were two of us in the house.   Insert a space

Once upon a time, there were   Capitalize

leonardo da vinci   Move text down to line below

Thomas was the best.   Change letter to lower-case

The two girls came to class. The two   Start a new paragraph
boys never came back until the
principal left.

Now I will end the story   Move text up to line above

                    was
My mother the best lady I know   Insert a period
              ^

This is my mothers hat.   Insert a word

Name: _____

Review

Directions: Use editing marks to edit the story. Also watch for and change:
Important details that may have been left out.
Places where the wording could be livelier.
Information that is not related to the story.

My friend Annie and I decided to go windsurfing one day. We gathered up our equipment—our windsuring boards and sails—and headed down to the lake. The air was coolthat day so annie and I didn't wear our bathing suits. we were just in cut-off shorts and t-shirts.

Ittook us a few minutes to get our windsails puttogether. Thiswas the first time Annie and I had ever did this alone. Usually ourbig brothers helped us. They had to be in school, though, and and annie and I don't so we decidedto try the sport alone.

Annie's smile was ok. But I was glad the sun was shining brightly.It made It feel like it was warming outside that it reallywas. "Are you sure we should do this?" said annie, just as I was pulling my windsurf board down to the water. "It will be fine, I assured her. I had candy in my mouth.

I put my toe into the lake.

"Wow is it cold!" I yelled back to Annie. She pulled her windsurf board down beside mine. Hers was orange, blue and yellow. Mine was just purple and green. I finally got inot the water with my board Annie was right beside me. We got onto our boards and finally, both of us were standing up. But our windsails wouldn't move. Then Annie and I realized there was no wind that day!

Grade 5 - Comprehensive Curriculum

Name: _____

Proofreading

Proofreading or "proofing" means to carefully look over what has been written, checking for spelling, grammar, punctuation and other errors. At a newspaper, this is the job of a copyeditor. All good writers carefully proofread and correct their own work before turning it in to a copyeditor—or a teacher.

Here are three common proofreading marks:

Correct spelling   ^{dog} d̶o̶t̶

Replace with lower-case letter   A̸

Replace with upper-case letter   a̲

Directions: Carefully read the following paragraphs. Use proofreading marks to mark errors in the second paragraph. Correct all errors. The first sentence has been done for you.

     A six-^{alarm} a̶l̶u̶r̶m̶ fire at 2121 w̲indsor Terrace on the northeast

side awoke apartment /Residents at 3 A.M. yesterday morning.

Elven people were in the biulding. No one was hurt in the

blase, which caused $200,000 of property damage.

     Proporty manager Jim smith credits a perfectly Functioning smoke alurm

system for waking residents so they could get out safely. A springkler system

were also in plase. "There was No panick," Smith said proudly. "Everone was calm

and Orderly."

Name: _____

Proofreading

Directions: Proofread the news article. Mark and correct the 20 errors in capitalization and spelling.

Be Wise When Buying a Car

Each year, about five percent of the U.S. popalation buys a new car, acording to J.D. Link and Associates, a New York-based auto industry reseerch company.

"A new car is the second most expenseve purchase most people Ever make," says Link. "it's amazing how litle reseerch people do before they enter the car showroom."

Link says reseerch is the most impotant Thing a new car buyer can do to pertect himself or herself. That way, he or she wil get the Best car at the best price.

"the salesman is not trying to get You the best deal," says Link. "he's trying to get himself the best deal. Bee smart! Read up on new cars in magazines like *Car and Driver* and *motortrend* before you talk to a saleman!"

Name: _____

Editing: Check Your Proofreading Skills

Directions: Read about the things you should remember when you are revising your writing. Then follow the instructions to revise the paper below.

After you have finished writing your rough draft, you should reread it later to determine what changes you need to make to ensure it's the best possible paper you are capable of writing.

Check yourself by asking the following questions:
Does my paper stick to the topic?
Have I left out any important details?
Can I make the writing more lively?
Have I made errors in spelling, punctuation or capitalization?
Is there any information that should be left out?

Directions: Revise the following story by making changes to correct spelling, punctuation and capitalization; add details; and cross out words or sentences that do not stick to the topic.

Hunting for Treasure

No one really believes me when I tell them that I'm a tresure

hunter. But, really, i am. It isn't just any treasure that I like

to hunt, though. I like treasures related to coins. Usually

when I go treasure huting I go alone. I always wear my blue

coat.

One day my good friend Jesse wanted to come with me. Why

would you want to do that?" I said. "Because I like coins, too,"

he replied. What Jesse did not know was that the Coins that I

dig to find are not the coins that just anyone collects.

The coins i like are special. They are coins that have been

buried in dirt for years!

Ancient Egypt

Have you ever wished you could visit Egypt for a first-hand look at the pyramids and ancient mummies? For most people, learning about Egypt is the closest they will come to visiting these ancient sites.

Directions: Test your knowledge about Egypt by writing as many of the answers as you can.

1. Write a paragraph describing what you already know about Egypt.

_____

_____

_____

_____

_____

_____

2. Name at least two famous Egyptian kings or queens. _____

_____

3. What was the purpose of a pyramid? _____

_____

_____

4. What was the purpose of mummification? _____

_____

_____

5. What major river runs through Egypt? _____

Name: _____

Taking Notes: Egyptian Mummies

Taking notes is the process of writing important points to remember, such as taking notes from material prepared by your teacher or from what is discussed in class or from an article you read. Taking notes is useful when preparing for a test or when writing a report. When taking notes, follow these steps:

1. Read the article carefully.
2. Select one or two important points from each paragraph.
3. Write your notes in your own words.
4. Reread your notes to be sure you understand what you have written.
5. Abbreviate words to save time.

Directions: Read about Egyptian mummies. Select one or two important points from each paragraph. Write your notes in your own words.

> After the Egyptians discovered that bodies buried in the hot, dry sand of the desert became mummified, they began searching for ways to improve the mummification process. The use of natron became a vital part of embalming.
>
> Natron is a type of white powdery salt found in oases throughout Egypt. An oasis is a place in the desert where underground water rises to the surface. This water contains many types of salts, including table salt. It also contained natron. As the water evaporated in the hot sun of the desert, the salts were left behind. Natron was then collected for use in the mummification process.
>
> The body was dried in natron for up to 40 days. The natron caused the body to shrink and the skin to become leathery. For thousands of years, natron was a vital ingredient in preserving the bodies of kings, queens and other wealthy Egyptian citizens.

Sample notes:

Paragraph 1   <u>Bodies buried in hot dry sand became mummified.</u>
              <u>Natron is vital for embalming.</u>

Paragraph 2   _____

              _____

Paragraph 3   _____

              _____

Outlining

Outlining is a way to organize information before you write an essay or informational paragraph. Outlining helps you understand the information you read.

This sample form will help you get started. When outlining, you can add more main points, more smaller points and/or more examples.

Title
I. First Main Idea
   A. A smaller idea
      1. An example
      2. An example
   B. Another smaller idea
II. Second Main Idea
   A. A smaller idea
   B. Another smaller idea
      1. An example
      2. An example
III. Third Main Idea
   A. A smaller idea
   B. A smaller idea

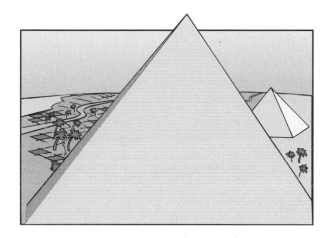

Directions: Read about building pyramids. Then complete the outline on the next page.

The process of building pyramids began as a way to honor a king or queen. Since the Egyptians believed in an afterlife, they thought it only fitting for their kings and queens to have elaborate burial tombs filled with treasures to enjoy in the afterlife. Thus, the idea of the pyramid was born.

At first pyramids were not built as they are known today. In the early stages of the Egyptian dynasty, kings were entombed in a *mastaba*. Mastabas were tombs made of mud-dried bricks. They formed a rectangular tomb with angled sides and a flat roof.

Later, as the Egyptian kingdom became more powerful, kings felt they needed grander tombs. The step pyramid was developed. These pyramids were made of stone rather than mud and were much taller. A large mastaba was built on the ground. Then, four more mastabas (each smaller than the previous) were stacked on top.

Finally, the pyramids took the shape that is familiar today. They were constructed with a flat bottom and four slanting sides which ascended to a final point. One of the tallest is over 400 feet high. These pyramids were also built of stone and were finished with an exterior of white limestone.

Name: _____

Outlining: Egyptian Pyramids

Directions: Complete the outline. Then answer the question.

_____
(title)

I. Mastabas

   A. _____

   B. _____

   C. _____

II. Step pyramids

   A. _____

   B. _____

   C. _____

III. Pyramids

   A. _____

   B. _____

   C. _____

What do you find is the most interesting aspect about the pyramids of ancient Egypt? Why?

_____

_____

_____

_____

_____

_____

_____

Summarizing

A **summary** includes the main points from an article, book or speech.

Example:

Tomb robbing was an important business in ancient Egypt. Often entire families participated in the plunder of tombs. These robbers may have been laborers, officials, tomb architects or guards, but they all probably had one thing in common. They were involved in the building or designing of the tomb or they wouldn't have had the knowledge necessary to successfully rob the burial sites. Not only did tomb robbing ensure a rich life for the robbers but it also enabled them to be buried with many riches themselves.

Summary:

Tomb robbing occurred in ancient Egypt. The robbers stole riches to use in their present lives or in their burials. Tomb robbers usually had some part in the building or design of the tomb. This allowed them to find the burial rooms where the treasures were stored.

Directions: Read about life in ancient Egypt. Then write a three- to five-sentence summary.

Egyptologists have learned much from the pyramids and mummies of ancient Egypt from the items left by grave robbers.

Women of ancient Egypt wore makeup to enhance their features. Dark colored minerals called *kohl* were used as eyeliner and eye shadow. Men also wore eyeliner. Women used another mineral called *ocher* on their cheeks and lips to redden them. Henna, a plant which produces an orange dye, tinted the fingernails, the palms of their hands and the soles of their feet.

Perfume was also important in ancient Egypt. Small cones made of wax were worn on top of the head. These cones contained perfume oils. The sun slowly melted the wax, and the perfume would scent the hair, head and shoulders.

_____

_____

_____

_____

Name: _____

Summarizing: King Tut

Directions: Read about King Tut. Then write a five- to seven-sentence summary.

King Tutankhamen (TO-TAN-KO-MEN) became king of Egypt when he was only nine years old. Known today as "King Tut," he died in 1355 B.C. when he was 18. Because King Tut died so young, not much is known about what he did while he was king.

After his death, Tut's body was "mummified" and buried in a pyramid in the Valley of the Kings in Egypt. Many other kings of ancient Egypt were buried there also.

In 1922, King Tut became famous when an Englishman named Howard Carter discovered and explored his tomb. The king's mummy, wearing a gold mask decorated with precious stones, was found intact. Amazingly, all King Tut's riches were still in his tomb. His was the only one in the Valley of the Kings that had not been discovered and robbed.

The King's tomb contained four rooms. One contained his mummy. The other rooms were filled with beautiful furniture, including King Tut's throne. Also found in Tut's tomb were more than 3,000 objects, like clothes, jewelry, wine, food—and a trumpet that could still be played. Obviously, King Tut planned to live royally in the next world!

_____

_____

_____

_____

_____

_____

_____

_____

_____

_____

Name: _____

Place Value

The place value of a digit or numeral is shown by where it is in the number. In the number 1,234, 1 has the place value of thousands, 2 is hundreds, 3 is tens and 4 is ones.

Example: 1,250,000,000

   Read: One billion, two hundred fifty million

   Write: 1,250,000,000

Billions			Millions			Thousands			Ones		
h	t	o	h	t	o	h	t	o	h	t	o
		1,		2	5	0,	0	0	0,	0	0	0

Directions: Read the words. Then write the numbers.

twenty million, three hundred four thousand _____

five thousand, four hundred twenty-three _____

one hundred fifty billion, eight million,
one thousand, five hundred _____

sixty billion, seven hundred million,
one hundred thousand, three hundred twelve _____

four hundred million, fifteen thousand,
seven hundred one _____

six hundred ninety-nine million, four thousand,
nine hundred forty-two _____

Here's a game to play with a partner.

Write a ten-digit number using each digit, 0 to 9, only once. Do not show the number to your partner. Give clues like: "There is a five in the hundreds place." The clues can be given in any order. See if your partner can write the same number you have written.

Place Value

Directions: Draw a line to connect each number to its correct written form.

1. 791,000	Three hundred fifty thousand
2. 350,000	Seventeen million, five hundred thousand
3. 17,500,000	Seven hundred ninety-one thousand
4. 3,500,000	Seventy thousand, nine hundred ten
5. 70,910	Three million, five hundred thousand
6. 35,500,000	Seventeen billion, five hundred thousand
7. 17,000,500,000	Thirty-five million, five hundred thousand

Directions: Look carefully at this number: 2,071,463,548. Write the numeral for each of the following places.

8. _____ ten thousands

9. _____ millions

10. _____ hundreds

11. _____ billions

12. _____ hundred thousands

13. _____ ten millions

14. _____ one thousands

15. _____ hundred millions

2,342

Addition

Addition is "putting together" two or more numbers to find the sum.

Directions: Add. Fill the backpacks with the right answers.

38
+ 92
130

71
+ 48
119

43
+ 62
105

56
+ 14
70

87
+ 13
100

24
+ 39
63

15
+ 67
82

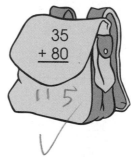
83
+ 47
130

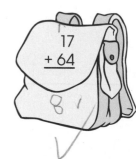
35
+ 80
115

17
+ 64
81

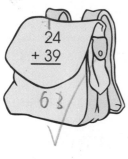
95
+ 25
120

54
+ 19
73

61
+ 77
138

42
+ 89
131

37
+ 97
134

62
+ 39
101

18
+ 43
61

27
+ 94
121

11
+ 89
100

48
+ 58
106

Addition

Teachers of an Earth Science class planned to take 50 students on an overnight hiking and camping experience. After planning the menu, they went to the grocery store for supplies.

Breakfast	Lunch	Dinner	Snacks
bacon	hot dogs/buns	pasta	crackers
eggs	apples	sauce	marshmallows
bread	chips	garlic bread	chocolate bars
cereal	juice	salad	cocoa mix
juice	granola bars	cookies	
$34.50	$ 52.15	$ 47.25	$ 23.40

Directions: Answer the questions. Write the total amount spent on food for the trip.

What information do you need to answer the question? _____

_____

What is the total? _____

Directions: Add.

462 + 574	918 + 359	527 + 582	386 + 745	295 + 764
397 + 448	524 + 725	906 + 337	750 + 643	891 + 419
1,568 + 2,341	3,214 + 2,896	5,147 + 4,285	7,259 + 2,451	9,317 + 3,583

Name: _____

Addition

Directions: Add.

1. Tourists travel to national parks to see the many animals which live there. Park Rangers estimate 384 buffalo, 282 grizzly bears and 426 deer are in the park. What is the total number of buffalo, bears and deer estimated in the park?

   _____

2. Last August, 2,248 visitors drove motor homes into the campgrounds for overnight camping. 647 set up campsites with tents. How many campsites were there altogether in August?

   _____

3. During a 3-week camping trip, Tom and his family hiked 42 miles, took a 126-mile long canoeing trip and drove their car 853 miles. How many miles did they travel in all?

   _____

4. Old Faithful is a geyser which spouts water high into the air. 10,000 gallons of water burst into the air regularly. Two other geysers spout 2,400 gallons of water during each eruption. What is the amount of water thrust into the air during one cycle?

   _____

5. Yellowstone National Park covers approximately 2,221,772 acres of land. Close by, the Grand Tetons cover approximately 310,350 acres. How many acres of land are there in these two parks?

   _____

6. Hiking trails cover 486 miles, motor routes around the north rim total 376 miles, and another 322 miles of road allow visitors to follow a loop around the southern part of the park. How many miles of trails and roadways are there?

   _____

Name: _____

Addition

Bob the butcher is popular with the dogs in town. He was making a delivery this morning when he noticed he was being followed by two dogs. Bob tried to climb a ladder to escape from the dogs. Solve the following addition problems and shade in the answers on the ladder. If all the numbers are shaded when the problems have been solved, Bob made it up the ladder. Some answers may not be on the ladder.

1.
```
    986,145
    621,332
+   200,008
  1807,485
```

2.
```
  1,873,402
    925,666
+     4,689
  2,803,757
```

3.
```
    506,328
    886,510
+   342,225
   1735,063
```

4.
```
     43,015
  2,811,604
+   987,053
  3,841,672
```

5.
```
     18,443
    300,604
+   999,999
  1,319,046
```

6.
```
      8,075
     14,608
+    33,914
     56,597
```

7.
```
      9,162
      7,804
+   755,122
    772,088
```

8.
```
     88,714
    213,653
+ 5,441,298
```

9.
```
  3,244,662
  1,986,114
+   521,387
```

10.
```
      4,581
     22,983
+ 5,618,775
  5,646,329
```

11.
```
    818,623
        926
+ 3,260,004
```

12.
```
     80,436
      9,159
+ 3,028,761
```

Ladder (right side):
- 5. 1,319,046
- 2. 2,803,757
- 5,743,665
- 3,118,356
- 6. 56,597
- 4,079,553
- 1. 1,807,485
- 2,943,230
- 18,344,666
- 3. 1,735,063
- 5,752,163
- 896,316
- 4. 3,841,672
- 10. 5,646,339

Does Bob make it? _____

Grade 5 - Comprehensive Curriculum

Subtraction

Subtraction is "taking away" one number from another to find the difference between the two numbers.

Directions: Subtract.

76 − 23	93 − 14	68 − 25	49 − 17	88 − 39	54 − 25

Brent saved $75.00 of the money he earned delivering the local newspaper in his neighborhood. He wanted to buy a new bicycle that cost $139.00. How much more would he need to save in order to buy the bike?

_____

38 − 29	74 − 25	67 − 49	92 − 35	43 − 26	85 − 37

When Brent finally went to buy the bicycle, he saw a light and basket for the bike. He decided to buy them both. The light was $5.95 and the basket was $10.50. He gave the clerk a twenty dollar bill his grandmother had given him for his birthday. How much change did he get back?

_____

Subtraction

When working with larger numbers, it is important to keep the numbers lined up according to place value.

Subtract.

```
  398          543          491
- 149        - 287        - 311


  786        1,825        4,172
- 597        - 495        - 2,785


8,391       63,852       24,107       52,900
-5,492      -34,765      -19,350      -43,081
```

Eagle Peak is the highest mountain peak at Yellowstone National Park. It is 11,353 feet high. The next highest point at the park is Mount Washburn. It is 10,243 feet tall. How much higher is Eagle Peak?

_____

The highest mountain peak in North America is Mount McKinley, which stretches 20,320 feet toward the sky. Two other mountain ranges in North America have peaks at 10,302 feet and 8,194 feet. What is the greatest difference between the peaks?

_____

Name: _____

Checking Subtraction

You can check your subtraction by using addition.

Example:
$$34,436$$
$$- 12,264$$
$$22,172$$

Check:
$$22,172$$
$$+ 12,264$$
$$34,436$$

Directions: Subtract. Then check your answers by adding.

15,326 – 11,532	Check:	28,615 – 25,329	Check:
96,521 – 47,378	Check:	46,496 – 35,877	Check:
77,911 – 63,783	Check:	156,901 –112,732	Check:
395,638 –187,569	Check:	67,002 – 53,195	Check:
16,075 –15,896	Check:	39,678 –19,769	Check:
84,654 – 49,997	Check:	12,335 –10,697	Check:

During the summer, 158,941 people visited Yellowstone National Park. During the fall, there were 52,397 visitors. How many more visitors went to the park during the summer than the fall?

_____

Name: _____

Addition and Subtraction

Directions: Check the answers. Write **T** if the answer is true and **F** if it is false.

Example:
$$
\begin{array}{r} 48{,}973 \\ -\ 35{,}856 \\ \hline 13{,}118 \end{array}
$$
Check: **F**
$$
\begin{array}{r} 35{,}856 \\ +13{,}118 \\ \hline 48{,}974 \end{array}
$$

$$
\begin{array}{r} 18{,}264 \\ +\ 17{,}893 \\ \hline 36{,}157 \end{array}
$$
Check: _____

$$
\begin{array}{r} 458{,}342 \\ -\ 297{,}652 \\ \hline 160{,}680 \end{array}
$$
Check: _____

$$
\begin{array}{r} 39{,}854 \\ +\ 52{,}713 \\ \hline 92{,}577 \end{array}
$$
Check: _____

$$
\begin{array}{r} 631{,}928 \\ -\ 457{,}615 \\ \hline 174{,}313 \end{array}
$$
Check: _____

$$
\begin{array}{r} 14{,}389 \\ +\ 93{,}587 \\ \hline 107{,}976 \end{array}
$$
Check: _____

$$
\begin{array}{r} 554{,}974 \\ -\ 376{,}585 \\ \hline 178{,}389 \end{array}
$$
Check: _____

$$
\begin{array}{r} 87{,}321 \\ -\ 62{,}348 \\ \hline 24{,}973 \end{array}
$$
Check: _____

$$
\begin{array}{r} 109{,}568 \\ +\ 97{,}373 \\ \hline 206{,}941 \end{array}
$$
Check: _____

Directions: Read the story problem. Write the equation and check the answer.

A camper hikes 53,741 feet out into the wilderness. On his return trip he takes a shortcut, walking 36,752 feet back to his cabin. The shortcut saves him 16,998 feet of hiking. True or False?

Grade 5 - Comprehensive Curriculum

Addition and Subtraction

Directions: Add or subtract to find the answers.

Eastland School hosted a field day. Students could sign up for a variety of events. 175 students signed up for individual races. Twenty two-person teams competed in the mile relay and 36 kids took part in the high jump. How many students participated in the activities?

_____

Westmore School brought 42 students and 7 adults to the field day event. Northern School brought 84 students and 15 adults. There was a total of 300 students and 45 adults at the event. How many were from other schools?

_____

The Booster Club sponsored a concession stand during the day. Last year, they made $1,000 at the same event. This year they hoped to earn at least $1,250. They actually raised $1,842. How much more did they make than they had anticipated?

_____

Each school was awarded a trophy for participating in the field day's activities. The Booster Club planned to purchase three plaques as awards, but they only wanted to spend $150. The first place trophy they selected was $68. The second place award was $59. How much would they be able to spend on the third place award if they stay within their budgeted amount?

_____

The Booster Club decided to spend $1,000 to purchase several items for the school with the money they had earned. Study the list of items suggested and decide which combination of items they could purchase.

A. Swing set $425 _____

B. Sliding board $263 _____

C. Scoreboard $515 _____

D. Team uniforms $180 _____

Name: _____

Rounding

Rounding a number means to express it to the nearest ten, hundred, thousand and so on. When rounding a number to the nearest ten, if the number has five or more ones, round up. Round down if the number has four or fewer ones.

Examples:

Round to the nearest ten:	84	⟶	80	86 ⟶	90
Round to the nearest hundred:	187	⟶	200	120 ⟶	100
Round to the nearest thousand:	981	⟶	1,000	5,480 ⟶	5,000

Directions: Round these numbers to the nearest ten.

87 ⟶ _____   53 ⟶ _____   48 ⟶ _____   32 ⟶ _____   76 ⟶ _____

Directions: Round these numbers to the nearest hundred.

168 ⟶ _____   243 ⟶ _____   591 ⟶ _____   743 ⟶ _____   493 ⟶ _____

Directions: Round these numbers to the nearest thousand.

895 ⟶ _____   3,492 ⟶ _____   7,521 ⟶ _____   14,904 ⟶ _____   62,387 ⟶ _____

City Populations	
City	Population
Cleveland	492,801
Seattle	520,947
Omaha	345,033
Kansas City	443,878
Atlanta	396,052
Austin	514,013

Directions: Use the city population chart to answer the questions.

Which cities have a population of about 500,000?

_____

Which city has a population of about 350,000?

_____

How many cities have a population of about 400,000? _____

Which ones? _____

_____

Estimating

To **estimate** means to give an approximate rather than an exact answer. Rounding each number first makes it easy to estimate an answer.

Example:

$$93 \rightarrow 90$$
$$\underline{+ 48} \quad \underline{+ 50}$$
$$140$$

$$321 \rightarrow 300$$
$$\underline{+ 597} \quad \underline{+ 600}$$
$$900$$

$$1,859 \rightarrow 2,000$$
$$\underline{- 997} \quad \underline{- 1,000}$$
$$1,000$$

Directions: Estimate the sums and differences by rounding the numbers first.

68 $\rightarrow$ $\underline{+ 34}$	12 $\rightarrow$ $\underline{+ 98}$	89 $\rightarrow$ $\underline{+ 23}$
638 $\rightarrow$ $\underline{- 395}$	281 $\rightarrow$ $\underline{- 69}$	271 $\rightarrow$ $\underline{- 126}$
$1,532$ $\rightarrow$ $\underline{- 998}$	$8,312$ $\rightarrow$ $\underline{- 4,789}$	$6,341$ $\rightarrow$ $\underline{+ 9,286}$

Bonnie has $50 to purchase tennis shoes, a tennis racquet and tennis balls. Does she have enough money?

$23.00

$16.00

$3.00

_____

Name: _____

Rounding and Estimating

Rounding numbers and estimating answers is an easy way of finding the approximate answer without writing out the problem or using a calculator.

Directions: Circle the correct answer.

Round to the nearest **ten**:

$73 \longrightarrow$ 70
80

$48 \longrightarrow$ 40
50

$65 \longrightarrow$ 60
70

$85 \longrightarrow$ 80
90

$92 \longrightarrow$ 90
100

$37 \longrightarrow$ 30
40

Round to the nearest **hundred**:

$139 \longrightarrow$ 100
200

$782 \longrightarrow$ 700
800

$390 \longrightarrow$ 300
400

$640 \longrightarrow$ 600
700

$525 \longrightarrow$ 500
600

$457 \longrightarrow$ 400
500

Round to the nearest **thousand**:

$1,375 \longrightarrow$ 1,000
2,000

$21,800 \longrightarrow$ 21,000
22,000

$36,240 \longrightarrow$ 36,000
37,000

Sam wanted to buy a new computer. He knew he only had about $1,200 to spend. Which of the following ones could he afford to buy?

 $1,165

 $1,279

 $1,249

If Sam spent $39 on software for his new computer, $265 for a printer and $38 for a cordless mouse, about how much money did he need?

_____

Name: _____

Prime Numbers

Example: 3 is a prime number 3 ÷ 1 = 3 and 3 ÷ 3 = 1

Any other divisor will result in a mixed number or fraction.

A **prime number** is any number greater than 1 that can only be divided by itself and the number 1.

A **composite number** is not a prime number. That is, it can be divided evenly by numbers other than itself and 1.

A prime number is a positive whole number which can be divided evenly only by itself or one.

Directions: Write the first 15 prime numbers. Test by dividing by 2 and by 3.

Prime Numbers:

_____ _____ _____ _____ _____

_____ _____ _____ _____ _____

_____ _____ _____ _____ _____

How many prime numbers are there between 0 and 100? _____

Name: _____

Prime Numbers

Directions: Circle the prime numbers.

71	3	82	20	43	69
128	97	23	111	75	51
13	44	137	68	171	83
61	21	77	101	34	16
2	39	92	17	52	29
19	156	63	99	27	147
121	25	88	12	87	55
57	7	139	91	9	37
67	183	5	59	11	95

Grade 5 - Comprehensive Curriculum

Multiples

A **multiple** is the product of a specific number and any other number. When you multiply two numbers, the answer is called the **product**.

Example:

The multiples of 2 are 2 (2 x 1), 4 (2 x 2), 6, 8, 10, 12, and so on.

The **least common multiple** (LCM) of two or more numbers is the smallest number other than 0 that is a multiple of each number.

Example:

Multiples of 3 are 3, 6, 9, 12, 15, 18, 21, 24, etc.
Multiples of 6 are 6, 12, 18, 24, 30, 36, 42, etc.
Multiples that 3 and 6 have in common are 6, 12, 18, 24.
The LCM of 3 and 6 is 6.

Directions: Write the first nine multiples of 3, 4, and 6. Write the LCM.

3: _____ , _____ , _____ , _____ , _____ , _____ , _____ , _____ , _____

4: _____ , _____ , _____ , _____ , _____ , _____ , _____ , _____ , _____

6: _____ , _____ , _____ , _____ , _____ , _____ , _____ , _____ , _____

LCM = _____

Directions: Write the first nine multiples of 2 and 5. Write the LCM.

2: _____ , _____ , _____ , _____ , _____ , _____ , _____ , _____ , _____

5: _____ , _____ , _____ , _____ , _____ , _____ , _____ , _____ , _____

LCM = _____

Directions: Find the LCM for each pair of numbers.

7 and 3 _____   4 and 6 _____   6 and 9 _____

5 and 15 _____   5 and 4 _____   3 and 18 _____

Directions: Fill in the missing numbers.

30 has multiples of 5 and _____ , of 2 and _____ , of 3 and _____ .

Factors

Factors are the numbers multiplied together to give a product. The **greatest common factor** (GCF) is the largest number for a set of numbers that divides evenly into each number in the set.

Example:

The factors of 12 are 3 x 4, 2 x 6 and 1 x 12.

We can write the factors like this: 3, 4, 2, 6, 12, 1.

The factors of 8 are 2, 4, 8, 1.

The common factors of 12 and 8 are 2 and 4 and 1.

The GCF of 12 and 8 is 4.

Directions: Write the factors of each pair of numbers. Then write the common factors and the GCF.

12: _____ , _____ , _____ , _____ , _____ , _____

15: _____ , _____ , _____ , _____

The common factors of 12 and 15 are _____ , _____ .

The GCF is _____ .

20: _____ , _____ , _____ , _____ , _____ , _____

10: _____ , _____ , _____ , _____

The common factors of 10 and 20 are _____ , _____ , _____ , _____ .

The GCF is _____ .

32: _____ , _____ , _____ , _____ , _____ , _____

24: _____ , _____ , _____ , _____ , _____ , _____ , _____ , _____

The common factors of 24 and 32 are _____ , _____ , _____ , _____ .

The GCF is _____ .

Directions: Write the GCF for the following pairs of numbers.

28 and 20 _____   42 and 12 _____

36 and 12 _____   20 and 5 _____

Name: _____

Factor Trees

A **factor tree** shows the prime factors of a number. A prime number, such as 7, has for its factors only itself and 1.

Example:

30 = 3 x 2 x 5.

3, 2, and 5 are prime numbers.

Directions: Fill in the numbers in the factor trees.

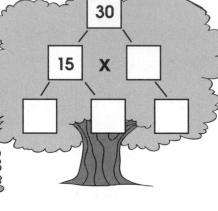

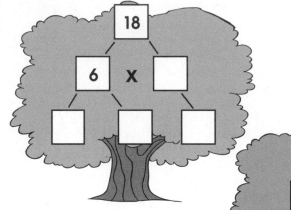

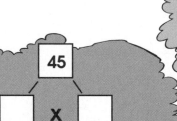

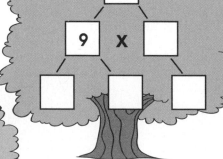

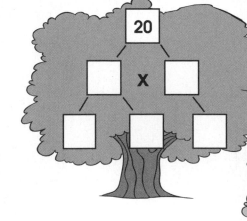

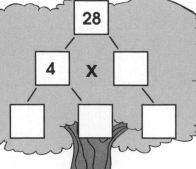

Name: _____

Factor Trees

Directions: Fill in the numbers in the factor trees. The first one has been done for you.

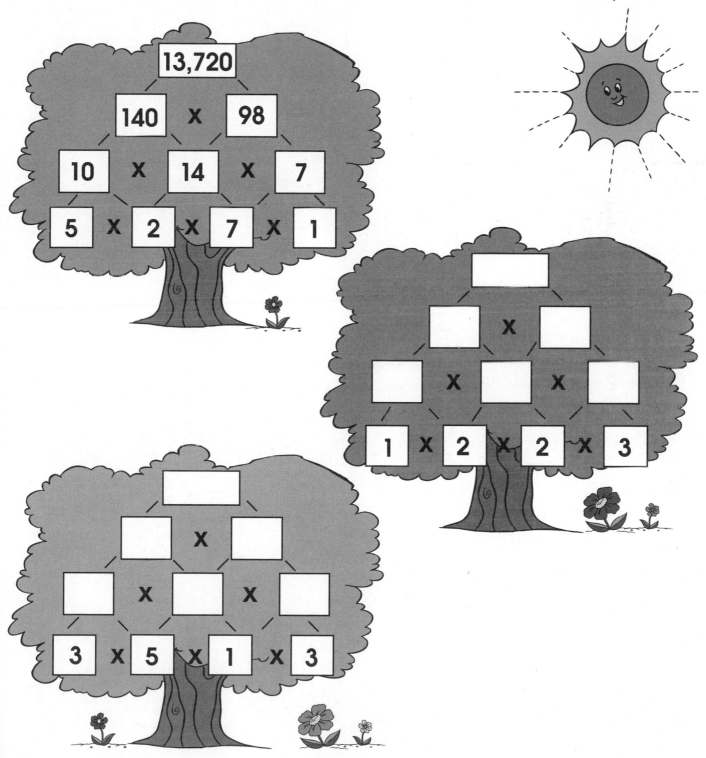

Grade 5 - Comprehensive Curriculum

Name: _____

Greatest Common Factor

Directions: Write the greatest common factor for each set of numbers.

10 and 35 _____

2 and 10 _____

42 and 63 _____

16 and 40 _____

25 and 55 _____

12 and 20 _____

14 and 28 _____

8 and 20 _____

6 and 27 _____

15 and 35 _____

18 and 48 _____

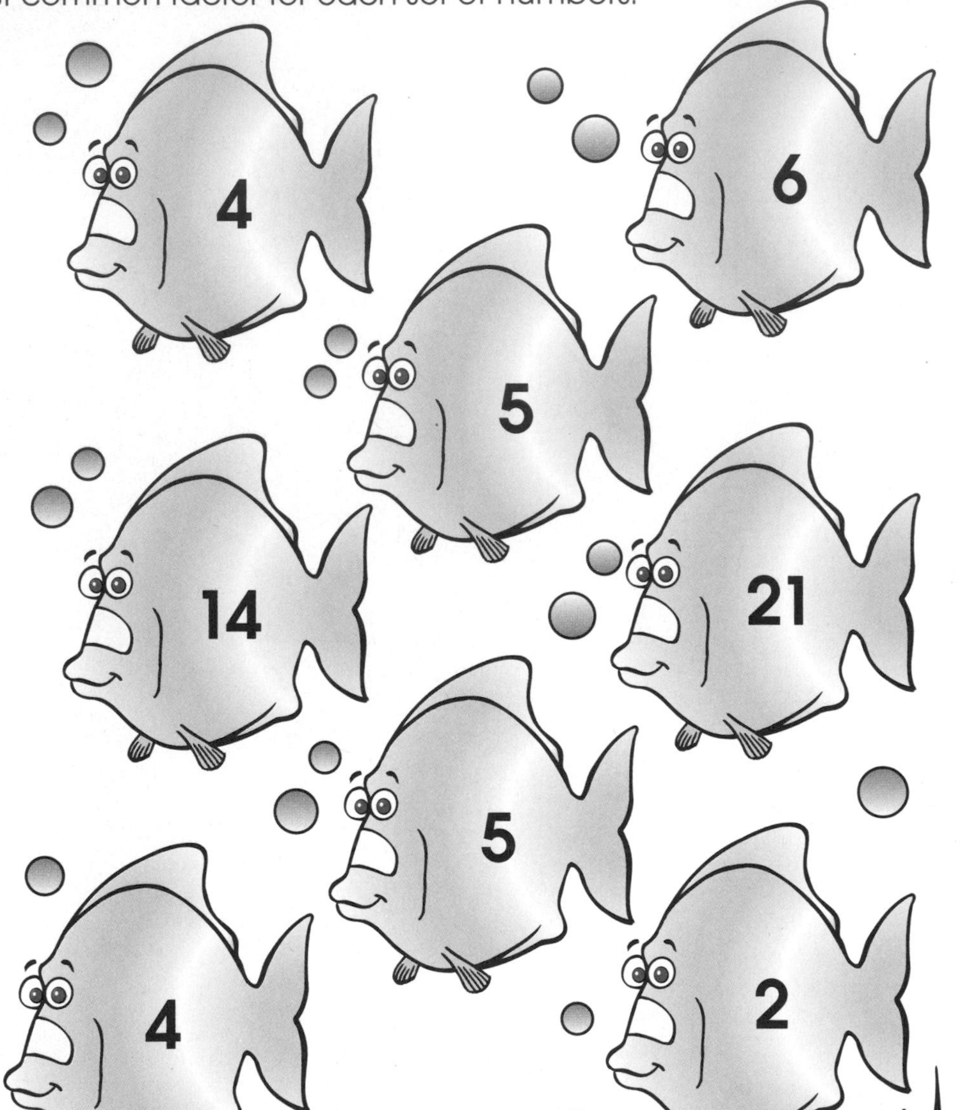

Name: _____

Least Common Multiple

Directions: Write the least common multiple for each pair of numbers.

12 and 7 _____

2 and 4 _____

22 and 4 _____

6 and 10 _____

3 and 7 _____

6 and 8 _____

5 and 10 _____

8 and 12 _____

9 and 15 _____

7 and 5 _____

3 and 8 _____

9 and 4 _____

Name: _____

Multiplication

Multiplication is a process of quick addition of a number a certain number of times.

Example: 3 x 15 = 45   is the same as adding   15 + 15 + 15 = 45
                             15 three times.

Directions: Multiply.

32	48	26	19	63
x 3	x 7	x 5	x 6	x 2

251	523	915	431	275
x 4	x 8	x 3	x 7	x 3

412	643	526	742
x 21	x 17	x 22	x 35

256	874	372	951
x 74	x 15	x 45	x 34

Cathy is on the cross country team. She runs 3 miles every day except on her birthday. How many miles does she run each year?

_____

Name: _____

Multiplication

Be certain to keep the proper place value when multiplying by tens and hundreds.

Examples:

```
    143              250
  x 262            x 150
    286             000
    858            1250
    286            250
   37,466         37,500
```

Directions: Multiply.

```
    701              621              348              597
  x 308            x 538            x 200            x 424
```

```
    537              416              682              180
  x 189            x 727            x 472            x 340
```

```
    878              267              893              907
  x 638            x 196            x 214            x 428
```

An airplane flies 720 trips a year between the cities of Chicago and Columbus. Each trip is 375 miles. How many miles does the airplane fly each year?

_____

Name: _____

Division

Division is the reverse of multiplication. It is the process of dividing a number into equal groups of smaller numbers.

Directions: Divide.

Greg had 936 marbles to share with his two brothers. If the boys divided them evenly, how many will each one get? _____

The marbles Greg kept were four different colors: blue, green, red and orange. He had the same number of each color. He divided them into two groups. One group had only orange marbles. The rest of the marbles were in the other group. How many marbles did he have in each group? orange _____ others _____

The **dividend** is the number to be divided by another number. In the problem 28 ÷ 7 = 4, 28 is the dividend.

The **divisor** is the number by which another number is divided. In the problem 28 ÷ 7 = 4, 7 is the divisor.

The **quotient** is the answer in a division problem. In the problem 28 ÷ 7 = 4, 4 is the quotient.

The **remainder** is the number left over in the quotient of a division problem. In the problem 29 ÷ 7 = 4 r1, 1 is the remainder.

Directions: Write the answers.

In the problem 25 ÷ 8 = 3 r1 . . .

What is the divisor? _____   What is the remainder? _____

What is the quotient? _____   What is the dividend? _____

Directions: Divide.

$$9\overline{)2,025} \qquad 6\overline{)2,508} \qquad 3\overline{)225} \qquad 5\overline{)400} \qquad 2\overline{)1,156}$$

Division

The remainder in a division problem must always be less than the divisor.

Example:

```
       244 r 23
26 ) 6,367
     5 2
     116
     104
      127
      104
       23
```

Directions: Divide.

53) 1,220   37) 1,528   83) 6,270   26) 3,618

14) 389   29) 2,645   60) 8,010   57) 5,406

35) 2,546   43) 492   83) 4,608   19) 185

The Oregon Trail is 2,197 miles long. How long would it take a
covered wagon traveling 20 miles a day to complete the trip?

_____

Checking Division

Answers in division problems can be checked by multiplying.

Example:

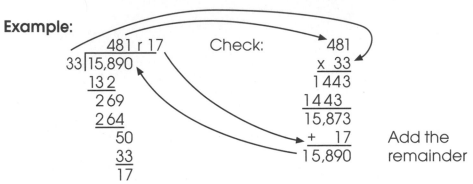

$$\begin{array}{r} 481 \text{ r } 17 \\ 33\overline{)15,890} \\ \underline{132} \\ 269 \\ \underline{264} \\ 50 \\ \underline{33} \\ 17 \end{array}$$

Check:
$$\begin{array}{r} 481 \\ \times\ 33 \\ \hline 1443 \\ 1443 \\ \hline 15,873 \\ +\ 17 \\ \hline 15,890 \end{array}$$

Add the remainder

Directions: Divide and check your answers.

$61\overline{)2,736}$ Check:	$73\overline{)86,143}$ Check:
$59\overline{)9,390}$ Check:	$43\overline{)77,141}$ Check:
$33\overline{)82,050}$ Check:	$93\overline{)84,039}$ Check:

Denny has a baseball card collection. He has 13,789 cards. He wants to put the cards in a scrapbook that holds 15 cards on a page. How many pages does Denny need in his scrapbook? _____

Name: _____

Multiplication and Division

Directions: Multiply or divide to find the answers.

Brianne's summer job is mowing lawns for three of her neighbors. Each lawn takes about 1 hour to mow and needs to be done once every week. At the end of the summer, she will have earned a total of $630. She collected the same amount of money from each job. How much did each neighbor pay for her summer lawn service?

_____

If the mowing season lasts for 14 weeks, how much will Brianne earn for each job each week? _____

If she had worked for two more weeks, how much would she have earned? _____

Brianne agreed to shovel snow from the driveways and sidewalks for the same three neighbors. They agreed to pay her the same rate. However, it only snowed seven times that winter. How much did she earn shoveling snow? _____

What was her total income for both jobs? _____

Directions: Multiply or divide.

12 ⟌ 7,476   23 ⟌ 21,620   40 ⟌ 32,600

32 x 45 = _____   28 x 15 = _____   73 x 14 = _____   92 x 30 = _____

Name: _____

Adding and Subtracting Like Fractions

A **fraction** is a number that names part of a whole. Examples of fractions are $\frac{1}{2}$ and $\frac{1}{3}$. **Like fractions** have the same **denominator**, or bottom number. Examples of like fractions are $\frac{1}{4}$ and $\frac{3}{4}$.

To add or subtract fractions, the denominators must be the same. Add or subtract only the **numerators**, the numbers above the line in fractions.

Example:

numerators
denominators $\quad \frac{5}{8} - \frac{1}{8} = \frac{4}{8}$

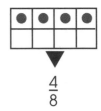

$\frac{5}{8}$ $\qquad$ $\frac{1}{8}$ $\qquad$ $\frac{4}{8}$

Directions: Add or subtract these fractions.

$\frac{6}{12} - \frac{3}{12} =$	$\frac{4}{9} + \frac{1}{9} =$	$\frac{1}{3} + \frac{1}{3} =$	$\frac{5}{11} + \frac{4}{11} =$
$\frac{3}{5} - \frac{1}{5} =$	$\frac{5}{6} - \frac{2}{6} =$	$\frac{3}{4} - \frac{2}{4} =$	$\frac{5}{10} + \frac{3}{10} =$
$\frac{3}{8} + \frac{2}{8} =$	$\frac{1}{7} + \frac{4}{7} =$	$\frac{2}{20} + \frac{15}{20} =$	$\frac{11}{15} - \frac{9}{15} =$

Directions: Color the part of each pizza that equals the given fraction.

$\frac{2}{4}$ $\qquad$ + $\qquad$ $\frac{1}{4}$ $\qquad$ =

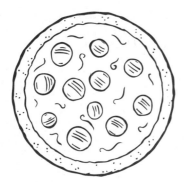  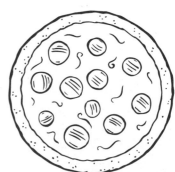

Name: _____

Adding and Subtracting Unlike Fractions

Unlike fractions have different denominators. Examples of unlike fractions are $\frac{1}{4}$ and $\frac{2}{5}$. To add or subtract fractions, the denominators must be the same.

Example:

Step 1: Make the denominators the same by finding the least common denominator. The LCD of a pair of fractions is the same as the least common multiple (LCM) of their denominators.

$$\frac{1}{3} + \frac{1}{4} =$$

Multiples of 3 are 3, 6, 9, **12**, 15.
Multiples of 4 are 4, 8, **12**, 16.
LCM (and LCD) = 12

Step 2: Multiply by a number that will give the LCD. The numerator and denominator must be multiplied by the same number.

A. $\frac{1}{3} \times \frac{4}{4} = \frac{4}{12}$ **B.** $\frac{1}{4} \times \frac{3}{3} = \frac{3}{12}$

Step 3: Add the fractions. $\frac{1}{3} + \frac{1}{4} = \frac{4}{12} + \frac{3}{12} = \frac{7}{12}$

Directions: Follow the above steps to add or subtract unlike fractions. Write the LCM.

$\frac{2}{4} + \frac{3}{8} =$ LCM = _____	$\frac{3}{6} + \frac{1}{3} =$ LCM = _____	$\frac{4}{5} - \frac{1}{4} =$ LCM = _____
$\frac{2}{3} + \frac{2}{9} =$ LCM = _____	$\frac{4}{7} - \frac{2}{14} =$ LCM = _____	$\frac{7}{12} - \frac{2}{4} =$ LCM = _____

The basketball team ordered two pizzas. They left $\frac{1}{3}$ of one and $\frac{1}{4}$ of the other. How much pizza was left?

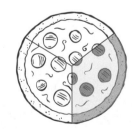 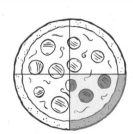

_____

Reducing Fractions

A fraction is in lowest terms when the GCF of both the numerator and denominator is 1. These fractions are in lowest possible terms: $\frac{2}{3}$, $\frac{5}{8}$ and $\frac{99}{100}$.

Example: Write $\frac{4}{8}$ in lowest terms.

Step 1: Write the factors of 4 and 8.

Factors of 4 are **4**, 2, 1.

Factors of 8 are 1, 8, 2, **4**.

Step 2: Find the GCF: 4.

Step 3: Divide both the numerator and denominator by 4.

Directions: Write each fraction in lowest terms.

$\frac{6}{8}$ = _____ lowest terms $\frac{9}{12}$ = _____ lowest terms

factors of 6: 6, 1, 2, 3   factors of 9: ____ , ____ , ____   _____ GCF

factors of 8: 8, 1, 2, 4   factors of 12: ____ , ____ , ____ , ____ , ____ , ____   _____ GCF

$\frac{2}{6}$ =	$\frac{10}{15}$ =	$\frac{8}{32}$ =	$\frac{4}{10}$ =
$\frac{12}{18}$ =	$\frac{6}{8}$ =	$\frac{4}{6}$ =	$\frac{3}{9}$ =

Directions: Color the pizzas to show that $\frac{4}{6}$ in lowest terms is $\frac{2}{3}$.

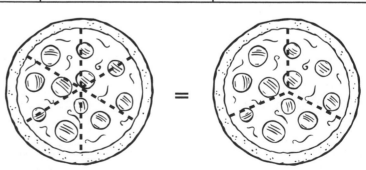

Name: _____

Improper Fractions

An **improper fraction** has a numerator that is greater than its denominator. An example of an improper fraction is $\frac{7}{6}$. An improper fraction should be reduced to its lowest terms.

Example: $\frac{5}{4}$ is an improper fraction because its numerator is greater than its denominator.

Step 1: Divide the numerator by the denominator: $5 \div 4 = 1$, r1

Step 2: Write the remainder as a fraction: $\frac{1}{4}$

$\frac{5}{4} = 1\frac{1}{4}$ $1\frac{1}{4}$ is a mixed number—a whole number and a fraction.

Directions: Follow the steps above to change the improper fractions to mixed numbers.

$\frac{9}{8} =$	$\frac{11}{5} =$	$\frac{5}{3} =$	$\frac{7}{6} =$	$\frac{8}{7} =$	$\frac{4}{3} =$
$\frac{21}{5} =$	$\frac{9}{4} =$	$\frac{3}{2} =$	$\frac{9}{6} =$	$\frac{25}{4} =$	$\frac{8}{3} =$

Sara had 29 duplicate stamps in her stamp collection. She decided to give them to four of her friends. If she gave each of them the same number of stamps, how many duplicates will she have left? _____

Name the improper fraction in this problem. _____

What step must you do next to solve the problem? _____

_____

Write your answer as a mixed number. _____

How many stamps could she give each of her friends? _____

Grade 5 - Comprehensive Curriculum

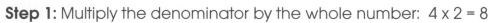

Mixed Numbers

A **mixed number** is a whole number and a fraction together. An example of a mixed number is $2\frac{3}{4}$. A mixed number can be changed to an improper fraction.

Example: $2\frac{3}{4}$

Step 1: Multiply the denominator by the whole number: $4 \times 2 = 8$

Step 2: Add the numerator: $8 + 3 = 11$

Step 3: Write the sum over the denominator: $\frac{11}{4}$

Directions: Follow the steps above to change the mixed numbers to improper fractions.

$3\frac{2}{3} =$	$6\frac{1}{5} =$	$4\frac{7}{8} =$	$2\frac{1}{2} =$
$1\frac{4}{5} =$	$5\frac{3}{4} =$	$7\frac{1}{8} =$	$9\frac{1}{9} =$
$8\frac{1}{2} =$	$7\frac{1}{6} =$	$5\frac{3}{5} =$	$9\frac{3}{8} =$
$12\frac{1}{5} =$	$25\frac{1}{2} =$	$10\frac{2}{3} =$	$14\frac{3}{8} =$

Adding Mixed Numbers

To add mixed numbers, first find the least common denominator.

Always reduce the answer to lowest terms.

Example:

$$5 \frac{1}{4} \longrightarrow 5 \frac{3}{12}$$

$$+ 6 \frac{1}{3} \longrightarrow + 6 \frac{4}{12}$$

$$11 \frac{7}{12}$$

Directions: Add. Reduce the answers to lowest terms.

$$8 \frac{1}{2}$$
$$+ 7 \frac{1}{4}$$

$$5 \frac{1}{4}$$
$$+ 2 \frac{3}{8}$$

$$9 \frac{3}{10}$$
$$+ 7 \frac{1}{5}$$

$$8 \frac{1}{5}$$
$$+ 6 \frac{7}{10}$$

$$4 \frac{4}{5}$$
$$+ 3 \frac{3}{10}$$

$$3 \frac{1}{2}$$
$$+ 7 \frac{1}{4}$$

$$4 \frac{1}{2}$$
$$+ 1 \frac{1}{3}$$

$$6 \frac{1}{12}$$
$$+ 3 \frac{3}{4}$$

$$5 \frac{1}{3}$$
$$+ 2 \frac{3}{9}$$

$$6 \frac{1}{3}$$
$$+ 2 \frac{2}{5}$$

$$2 \frac{2}{7}$$
$$+ 4 \frac{1}{14}$$

$$3 \frac{1}{2}$$
$$+ 3 \frac{1}{4}$$

The boys picked $3 \frac{1}{2}$ baskets of apples. The girls picked $5 \frac{1}{2}$ baskets. How many baskets of apples did the boys and girls pick in all?

_____

Subtracting Mixed Numbers

To subtract mixed numbers, first find the least common denominator. Reduce the answer to its lowest terms.

Directions: Subtract. Reduce to lowest terms.

Example:

$$6 \frac{5}{8} \rightarrow 6 \frac{10}{16}$$
$$- 3 \frac{4}{16} \rightarrow - 3 \frac{4}{16}$$
$$3 \frac{6}{16} = 3 \frac{3}{8}$$

$$2 \frac{3}{7}$$
$$- 1 \frac{1}{14}$$

$$7 \frac{2}{3}$$
$$- 5 \frac{1}{8}$$

$$6 \frac{3}{4}$$
$$- 2 \frac{3}{12}$$

$$9 \frac{5}{12}$$
$$- 5 \frac{9}{24}$$

$$5 \frac{1}{2}$$
$$- 3 \frac{1}{3}$$

$$7 \frac{3}{8}$$
$$- 5 \frac{1}{6}$$

$$8 \frac{3}{8}$$
$$- 6 \frac{5}{12}$$

$$11 \frac{5}{6}$$
$$- 7 \frac{1}{12}$$

$$9 \frac{3}{5}$$
$$- 7 \frac{1}{15}$$

$$4 \frac{4}{5}$$
$$- 2 \frac{1}{4}$$

$$9 \frac{2}{3}$$
$$- 4 \frac{1}{6}$$

$$14 \frac{3}{8}$$
$$- 9 \frac{3}{16}$$

The Rodriguez Farm has $9 \frac{1}{2}$ acres of corn. The Johnson Farm has $7 \frac{1}{3}$ acres of corn. How many more acres of corn does the Rodriguez Farm have? _____

Name: _____

Comparing Fractions

Directions: Use the symbol > (greater than), < (less than) or = (equal to) to show the relationship between each pair of fractions.

$\frac{1}{2}$ _____ $\frac{1}{3}$ $\frac{2}{5}$ _____ $\frac{3}{7}$ $\frac{3}{8}$ _____ $\frac{2}{4}$

$\frac{3}{4}$ _____ $\frac{6}{8}$ $\frac{2}{3}$ _____ $\frac{4}{5}$ $\frac{3}{9}$ _____ $\frac{1}{3}$

$\frac{3}{12}$ _____ $\frac{1}{4}$ $\frac{2}{14}$ _____ $\frac{1}{7}$ $\frac{5}{15}$ _____ $\frac{2}{3}$

If Kelly gave $\frac{1}{3}$ of a pizza to Holly and $\frac{1}{5}$ to Diane, how much did she have left?

_____

Holly decided to share $\frac{1}{2}$ of her share of the pizza with Deb. How much did each of them actually get?

_____

Grade 5 - Comprehensive Curriculum

Name: _____

Ordering Fractions

When putting fractions in order from smallest to largest or largest to smallest, it helps to find a common denominator first.

Example:

$$\frac{1}{3} \; , \; \frac{1}{2} \quad \text{changed to} \quad \frac{2}{6} \; , \; \frac{3}{6}$$

Directions: Put the following fractions in order from least to largest value.

Least   Largest

$\dfrac{1}{2}$ $\dfrac{2}{7}$ $\dfrac{4}{5}$ $\dfrac{1}{3}$ _____ _____ _____ _____

$\dfrac{3}{12}$ $\dfrac{3}{6}$ $\dfrac{1}{3}$ $\dfrac{3}{4}$ _____ _____ _____ _____

$\dfrac{2}{5}$ $\dfrac{4}{15}$ $\dfrac{3}{5}$ $\dfrac{5}{15}$ _____ _____ _____ _____

$3\dfrac{4}{5}$ $3\dfrac{2}{5}$ $\dfrac{9}{5}$ $3\dfrac{1}{5}$ _____ _____ _____ _____

$9\dfrac{1}{3}$ $9\dfrac{2}{3}$ $9\dfrac{9}{12}$ $8\dfrac{2}{3}$ _____ _____ _____ _____

$5\dfrac{8}{12}$ $5\dfrac{5}{12}$ $5\dfrac{4}{24}$ $5\dfrac{3}{6}$ _____ _____ _____ _____

$4\dfrac{3}{5}$ $5\dfrac{7}{15}$ $6\dfrac{2}{5}$ $5\dfrac{1}{5}$ _____ _____ _____ _____

Four dogs were selected as finalists at a dog show. They were judged in four separate categories. One received a perfect score in each area. The dog with a score closest to four is the winner. Their scores are listed below. Which dog won the contest? _____

Dog A $3\dfrac{4}{5}$ Dog B $3\dfrac{2}{3}$ Dog C $3\dfrac{5}{15}$ Dog D $3\dfrac{9}{12}$

Multiplying Fractions

To multiply fractions, follow these steps:

$\frac{1}{2}$ x $\frac{3}{4}$ =   **Step 1:** Multiply the numerators.   1 x 3 = $\frac{3}{8}$
                  Step 2: Multiply the denominators.   2 x 4 = 8

When multiplying a fraction by a whole number, first change the whole number to a fraction.

Example:

$\frac{1}{2}$ x 8 = $\frac{1}{2}$ x $\frac{8}{1}$ = $\frac{8}{2}$ = 4   reduced to lowest terms

Directions: Multiply. Reduce your answers to lowest terms.

$\frac{3}{4}$ x $\frac{1}{6}$ =	$\frac{1}{2}$ x $\frac{5}{8}$ =	$\frac{2}{3}$ x $\frac{1}{6}$ =	$\frac{2}{3}$ x $\frac{1}{2}$ =
$\frac{5}{6}$ x 4 =	$\frac{3}{8}$ x $\frac{1}{16}$ =	$\frac{1}{5}$ x 5 =	$\frac{7}{8}$ x $\frac{3}{4}$ =
$\frac{7}{11}$ x $\frac{1}{3}$ =	$\frac{2}{9}$ x $\frac{9}{4}$ =	$\frac{1}{3}$ x $\frac{1}{3}$ x $\frac{1}{3}$ =	$\frac{1}{8}$ x $\frac{1}{4}$ x $\frac{1}{2}$ =

Jennifer has 10 pets. Two-fifths of the pets are cats, one-half are fish and one-tenth are dogs. How many of each pet does she have?

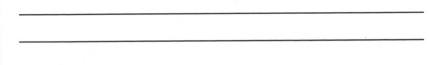

_____

_____

_____

Name: _____

Multiplying Mixed Numbers

Multiply mixed numbers by first changing them to improper fractions. Always reduce your answers to lowest terms.

Example:

$$2\frac{1}{3} \times 1\frac{1}{8} = \frac{7}{3} \times \frac{9}{8} = \frac{63}{24} = 2\frac{15}{24} = 2\frac{5}{8}$$

Directions: Multiply. Reduce to lowest terms.

$4\frac{1}{4} \times 2\frac{1}{5} =$	$1\frac{1}{3} \times 3\frac{1}{4} =$	$1\frac{1}{9} \times 3\frac{3}{5} =$
$1\frac{6}{7} \times 4\frac{1}{2} =$	$2\frac{3}{4} \times 2\frac{3}{5} =$	$4\frac{2}{3} \times 3\frac{1}{7} =$
$6\frac{2}{5} \times 2\frac{1}{8} =$	$3\frac{1}{7} \times 4\frac{5}{8} =$	$7\frac{3}{8} \times 2\frac{1}{9} =$

Sunnyside Farm has two barns with 25 stalls in each barn.
Cows use $\frac{3}{5}$ of the stalls, and horses use the rest.

How many stalls are for cows? _____

How many are for horses? _____

(Hint: First, find how many total stalls are in the two barns.)

Name: _____

Dividing Fractions

To divide fractions, follow these steps:

$$\frac{3}{4} \div \frac{1}{4} =$$

Step 1: "Invert" the divisor. That means to turn it upside down.

$$\frac{3}{4} \div \frac{4}{1}$$

Step 2: Multiply the two fractions:

$$\frac{3}{4} \times \frac{4}{1} = \frac{12}{4}$$

Step 3: Reduce the fraction to lowest terms by dividing the denominator into the numerator.

$$12 \div 4 = 3$$

$$\frac{3}{4} \div \frac{1}{4} = 3$$

Directions: Follow the above steps to divide fractions.

$\frac{1}{4} \div \frac{1}{5} =$	$\frac{1}{3} \div \frac{1}{12} =$	$\frac{3}{4} \div \frac{1}{3} =$
$\frac{5}{12} \div \frac{1}{3} =$	$\frac{3}{4} \div \frac{1}{6} =$	$\frac{2}{9} \div \frac{2}{3} =$
$\frac{3}{7} \div \frac{1}{4} =$	$\frac{2}{3} \div \frac{4}{6} =$	$\frac{1}{8} \div \frac{2}{3} =$
$\frac{4}{5} \div \frac{1}{3} =$	$\frac{4}{8} \div \frac{1}{2} =$	$\frac{5}{12} \div \frac{6}{8} =$

Grade 5 - Comprehensive Curriculum

Dividing Whole Numbers by Fractions

Follow these steps to divide a whole number by a fraction:

$$8 \div \frac{1}{4} =$$

Step 1: Write the whole number as a fraction:

$$\frac{8}{1} \div \frac{1}{4} =$$

Step 2: Invert the divisor.

$$\frac{8}{1} \div \frac{4}{1} =$$

Step 3: Multiply the two fractions:

$$\frac{8}{1} \times \frac{4}{1} = \frac{32}{1}$$

Step 4: Reduce the fraction to lowest terms by dividing the denominator into the numerator: $32 \div 1 = 32$

Directions: Follow the above steps to divide a whole number by a fraction.

$6 \div \frac{1}{3} =$	$4 \div \frac{1}{2} =$	$21 \div \frac{1}{3} =$
$8 \div \frac{1}{2} =$	$3 \div \frac{1}{6} =$	$15 \div \frac{1}{7} =$
$9 \div \frac{1}{5} =$	$4 \div \frac{1}{9} =$	$12 \div \frac{1}{6} =$

Three-fourths of a bag of popcorn fits into one bowl.
How many bowls do you need if you have six bags of popcorn? _____

Name: _____

Decimals

A **decimal** is a number with one or more places to the right of a decimal point.

Examples: 6.5 and 2.25

Fractions with denominators of 10 or 100 can be written as decimals.

Examples:

$\dfrac{7}{10}$ = 0.7 $\quad$ $\underline{0}_{\text{ones}}$. $\underline{7}_{\text{tenths}}$ $\underline{0}_{\text{hundredths}}$

$1\dfrac{52}{100}$ = 1.52 $\quad$ $\underline{1}_{\text{ones}}$. $\underline{5}_{\text{tenths}}$ $\underline{2}_{\text{hundredths}}$

Directions: Write the fractions as decimals.

$\dfrac{1}{2}$ = $\dfrac{}{10}$ = 0. _____

$\dfrac{2}{5}$ = $\dfrac{}{10}$ = 0. _____

$\dfrac{1}{5}$ = $\dfrac{}{10}$ = 0. _____

$\dfrac{3}{5}$ = $\dfrac{}{10}$ = 0. _____

			1/10
	1/4	1/5	1/10
1/2		1/5	1/10
	1/4		1/10
		1/5	1/10
	1/4	1/5	1/10
1/2			1/10
	1/4	1/5	1/10

$\dfrac{63}{100}$ =	$2\dfrac{8}{10}$ =	$38\dfrac{4}{100}$ =	$6\dfrac{13}{100}$ =
$\dfrac{1}{4}$ =	$\dfrac{2}{5}$ =	$\dfrac{1}{50}$ =	$\dfrac{100}{200}$ =
$5\dfrac{2}{100}$ =	$\dfrac{4}{25}$ =	$15\dfrac{3}{5}$ =	$\dfrac{3}{100}$ =

Name: _____

Decimals and Fractions

Directions: Write the letter of the fraction that is equal to the decimal.

0.25 = _____

0.5 = _____

0.7 = _____

0.8 = _____

0.37 = _____

0.2 = _____

0.65 = _____

0.75 = _____

0.6 = _____

0.12 = _____

0.33 = _____

0.95 = _____

0.24 = _____

0.3 = _____

0.4 = _____

A. $\dfrac{33}{100}$

B. $\dfrac{3}{4}$

C. $\dfrac{13}{20}$

D. $\dfrac{3}{5}$

E. $\dfrac{3}{25}$

F. $\dfrac{19}{20}$

G. $\dfrac{1}{4}$

H. $\dfrac{2}{5}$

I. $\dfrac{3}{10}$

J. $\dfrac{37}{100}$

K. $\dfrac{1}{5}$

L. $\dfrac{1}{2}$

M. $\dfrac{6}{25}$

N. $\dfrac{4}{5}$

O. $\dfrac{7}{10}$

Name: _____

Adding and Subtracting Decimals

Add and subtract with decimals the same way you do with whole numbers. Keep the decimal points lined up so that you work with hundreths, then tenths, then ones, and so on.

Directions: Add or subtract. Remember to keep the decimal point in the proper place.

$$
\begin{array}{r} 0.5 \\ +\ 0.8 \\ \hline \end{array}
\qquad
\begin{array}{r} 0.35 \\ +\ 0.25 \\ \hline \end{array}
\qquad
\begin{array}{r} 47.5 \\ -\ 32.7 \\ \hline \end{array}
\qquad
\begin{array}{r} 85.7 \\ -\ 9.8 \\ \hline \end{array}
$$

$$
\begin{array}{r} 13.90 \\ +\ 4.23 \\ \hline \end{array}
\qquad
\begin{array}{r} 9.53 \\ -\ 8.16 \\ \hline \end{array}
\qquad
\begin{array}{r} 72.8 \\ -\ 63.9 \\ \hline \end{array}
\qquad
\begin{array}{r} 6.43 \\ +\ 4.58 \\ \hline \end{array}
$$

$$
\begin{array}{r} 638.07 \\ -\ 19.34 \\ \hline \end{array}
\qquad
\begin{array}{r} 811.060 \\ +\ 78.430 \\ \hline \end{array}
\qquad
\begin{array}{r} 521.09 \\ -\ 148.75 \\ \hline \end{array}
$$

$$
\begin{array}{r} 916.635 \\ +\ 172.136 \\ \hline \end{array}
\qquad
\begin{array}{r} 287.768 \\ -\ 63.951 \\ \hline \end{array}
\qquad
\begin{array}{r} 467.05 \\ -\ 398.19 \\ \hline \end{array}
$$

Sean ran a 1-mile race in 5.58 minutes. Carlos ran it in 6.38 minutes. How much less time did Sean need?

_____

Grade 5 - Comprehensive Curriculum

Name: _____

Multiplying Decimals

Multiply with decimals the same way you do with whole numbers. The decimal point moves in multiplication. Count the number of decimal places in the problem and use the same number of decimal places in your answer.

Example:

```
   3.5
 x 1.5
 1 7 5
 3 5
 5.2 5
```

Directions: Multiply.

2.5 x .9	67.4 x 2.3	83.7 x 9.8	13.35 x 3.06

9.06 x 2.38	28.97 x 5.16	33.41 x .93	28.7 x 11.9

The jet flies 1.5 times faster than the plane with a propeller. The propeller plane flies 165.7 miles per hour. How fast does the jet fly?

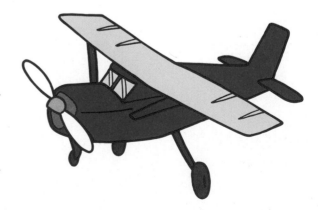

_____

Name: _____

Dividing With Decimals

When the dividend has a decimal, place the decimal point for the answer directly above the decimal point in the dividend. The first one has been done for you.

$$
\begin{array}{r}
12.5 \\
3\,\overline{)37.5} \\
-3 \\
\hline
07 \\
-6 \\
\hline
15 \\
-15 \\
\hline
0
\end{array}
$$

$4\,\overline{)34.4}$

$2\,\overline{)31.6}$

$3\,\overline{)131.4}$

$5\,\overline{)187.5}$

$7\,\overline{)181.3}$

$6\,\overline{)340.8}$

$9\,\overline{)294.3}$

$3\,\overline{)135.6}$

$5\,\overline{)264.5}$

$2\,\overline{)134.6}$

$8\,\overline{)754.4}$

$5\,\overline{)35.25}$

$7\,\overline{)79.45}$

$9\,\overline{)28.71}$

$36\,\overline{)199.44}$

Grade 5 - Comprehensive Curriculum

Dividing Decimals by Decimals

When the divisor has a decimal point you must eliminate it before dividing. You can do this by moving the decimal point to the right to create a whole number. You must also move the decimal point the same number of spaces to the right in the dividend.

Sometimes you need to add zeros to do this.

Example:

$$0.25\overline{)85.50}$$ changes to

$$\begin{array}{r} 342 \\ 25\overline{)8550} \\ -75 \\ \hline 105 \\ -100 \\ \hline 50 \\ 50 \\ \hline 0 \end{array}$$

Directions: Divide.

$0.3\overline{)27.9}$ $0.6\overline{)42.6}$ $0.9\overline{)81.9}$ $0.7\overline{)83.3}$

$0.4\overline{)23.2}$ $0.7\overline{)56.7}$ $1.2\overline{)10.8}$ $2.2\overline{)138.6}$

$12.6\overline{)5,670}$ $4.7\overline{)564}$ $8.6\overline{)842.8}$ $3.7\overline{)2,009.1}$

$5.9\overline{)1,917.5}$ $4.3\overline{)1,376}$ $2.9\overline{)922.2}$ $2.7\overline{)5613.3}$

Geometry

Geometry is the branch of mathematics that has to do with points, lines and shapes.

Directions: Use the Glossary on pages 446–455 if you need help. Write the word from the box that is described below.

triangle	square	cube	angle
line	ray	segment	rectangle

a collection of points on a straight path
that goes on and on in opposite directions _____

a figure with three sides and three corners _____

a figure with four equal sides
and four corners _____

part of a line that has one end point
and goes on and on in one direction _____

part of a line having two end points _____

a space figure with six square faces _____

two rays with a common end point _____

a figure with four corners and four sides _____

Name: _____

Geometry

Review the definitions on the previous page before completing the problems below.

Directions: Identify the labeled section of each of the following diagrams.

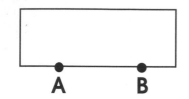

AB = _____

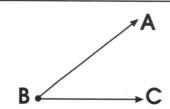

ABC = _____

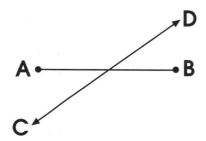

AB = _____

CD = _____

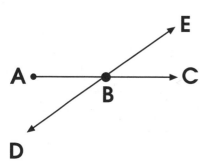

AC = _____

AB = _____

EBC = _____

BC = _____

Name: _____

Circumference

The **radius** of a circle is the distance from the center of the circle to its outside edge. The diameter equals two times the radius.

Find the circumference by multiplying π (3.14) times the diameter or by multiplying π (3.14) times 2r (2 times the radius).

$C = π \times d$ or $C = π \times 2r$

Directions: Write the missing radius, diameter or circumference.

radius ___3___
diameter _____
circumference _____

radius _____
diameter ___14___
circumference _____

radius _____
diameter ___12___
circumference _____

radius ___2___
diameter _____
circumference _____

radius _____
diameter ___8___
circumference _____

radius ___5___
diameter _____
circumference _____

Diameter, Radius and Circumference

C = π x d or C = π x 2r

Directions: Write the missing radius, diameter or circumference.

Katie was asked to draw a circle on the playground for a game during recess. If the radius of the circle needed to be 14 inches, how long is the diameter? _____

What is the circumference? _____

A friend told her that more kids could play the game if they enlarged the circle. She had a friend help her. They made the diameter of the circle 45 inches long.

What is the radius? _____

What is the circumference? _____

Jamie was creating an art project. He wanted part of it to be a sphere. He measured 24 inches for the diameter.

What would the radius of the sphere be? _____

Find the circumference. _____

Unfortunately, Jamie discovered that he didn't have enough material to create a sphere that large, so he cut the dimensions in half. What are the new dimensions for his sphere?

Radius _____

Diameter _____

Circumference _____

Name: _____

Triangle Angles

A **triangle** is a figure with three corners and three sides. Every triangle contains three angles. The sum of the angles is always 180°, regardless of the size or shape of the triangle.

If you know two of the angles, you can add them together, then subtract the total from 180 to find the number of degrees in the third angle.

Directions: Find the number of degrees in the third angle of each triangle.

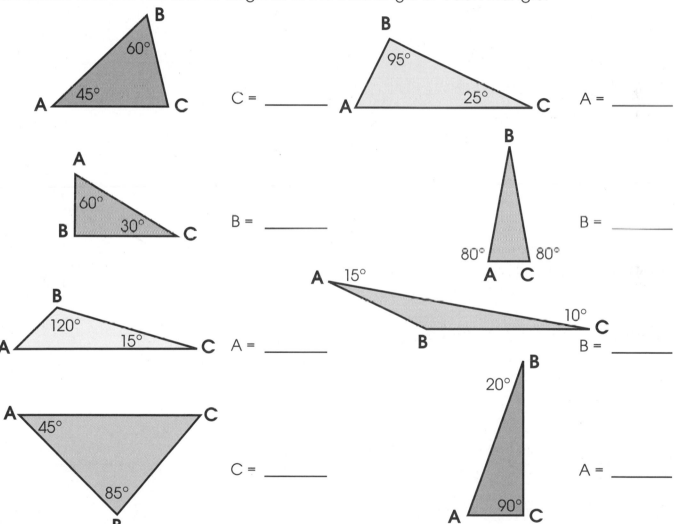

C = _____

A = _____

B = _____

B = _____

A = _____

B = _____

C = _____

A = _____

A = _____

B = _____

Grade 5 - Comprehensive Curriculum

Area of a Triangle

The area of a triangle is found by multiplying $\frac{1}{2}$ times the base times the height.

$A = \frac{1}{2} \times b \times h$

Example:

$\overline{CD}$ is the height.   4 in.

$\overline{AB}$ is the base.   8 in.

Area = $\frac{1}{2} \times 4 \times 8 = \frac{32}{2}$ = 16 sq. in.

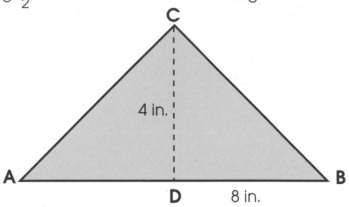

Directions: Find the area of each triangle.

4 in.

2 in.

A = _____

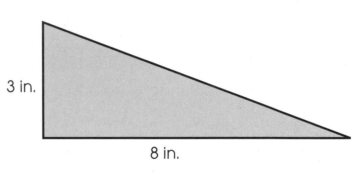

3 in.

8 in.

A = _____

9 in.

4 in.

A = _____

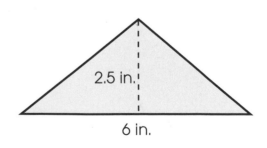

2.5 in.

6 in.

A = _____

Name: _____

Space Figures

Space figures are figures whose points are in more than one plane. Cubes and cylinders are space figures.

 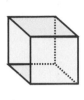 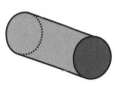 

| **rectangular prism** | **cone** | **cube** | **cylinder** | **sphere** | **pyramid** |

A **prism** has two identical, parallel bases.

All of the faces on a **rectangular prism** are rectangles.

A **cube** is a prism with six identical, square faces.

A **pyramid** is a space figure whose base is a polygon and whose faces are triangles with a common vertex—the point where two rays meet.

A **cylinder** has a curved surface and two parallel bases that are identical circles.

A **cone** has one circular, flat face and one vertex.

A **sphere** has no flat surface. All points are an equal distance from the center.

Directions: Circle the name of the figure you see in each of these familiar objects

cone   sphere   cylinder

cone   sphere   cylinder

cube   rectangular prism   pyramid

cone   pyramid   cylinder

Name: _____

Length

Inches, feet, yards and miles are used to measure length in the United States.

12 inches = 1 foot (ft.)

3 feet = 1 yard (yd.)

36 inches = 1 yard

1,760 yards = 1 mile (mi.)

Directions: Circle the best unit to measure each object. The first one has been done for you.

the length of a	(inches)	feet	yards	miles
the height of a	inches	feet	yards	miles
the length of a	inches	feet	yards	miles
distance to the	inches	feet	yards	miles
the height of a	inches	feet	yards	miles
the length of a field	inches	feet	yards	miles

Length

Directions: Use a ruler to find the shortest paths. Round your measurement to the nearest quarter inch. Then convert to yards using the scale.

Scale: 1 inch = 100 yards

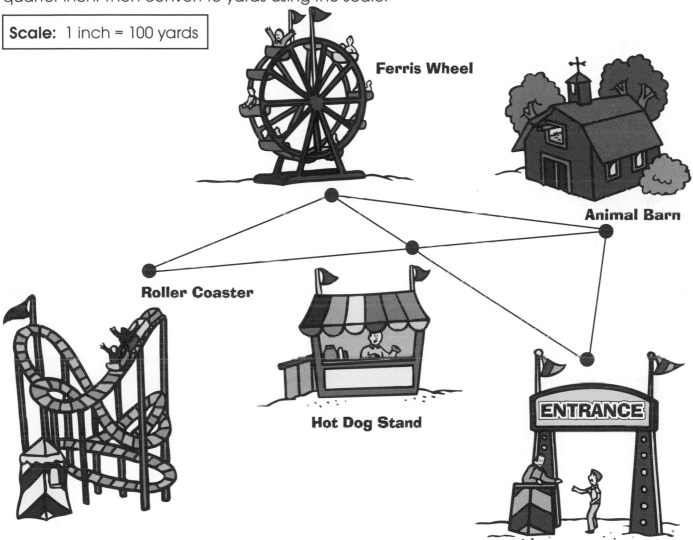

Ferris Wheel

Animal Barn

Roller Coaster

Hot Dog Stand

ENTRANCE

Hot dog stand to the roller coaster . . .　_____

The Ferris wheel to the animal barn . . .　_____

Entrance to roller coaster . . .　_____

Animal barn to hot dog stand . . .　_____

Ferris wheel to roller coaster to entrance . . .　_____

Length: Metric

Millimeters, centimeters, meters and **kilometers** are used to measure length in the metric system.

> 1 meter = 39.37 inches
>
> 1 kilometer = about $\frac{5}{8}$ mile
>
> 10 millimeters = 1 centimeter (cm)
>
> 100 centimeters = 1 meter (m)
>
> 1,000 meters = 1 kilometer (km)

Directions: Circle the best unit to measure each object. The first one has been done for you.

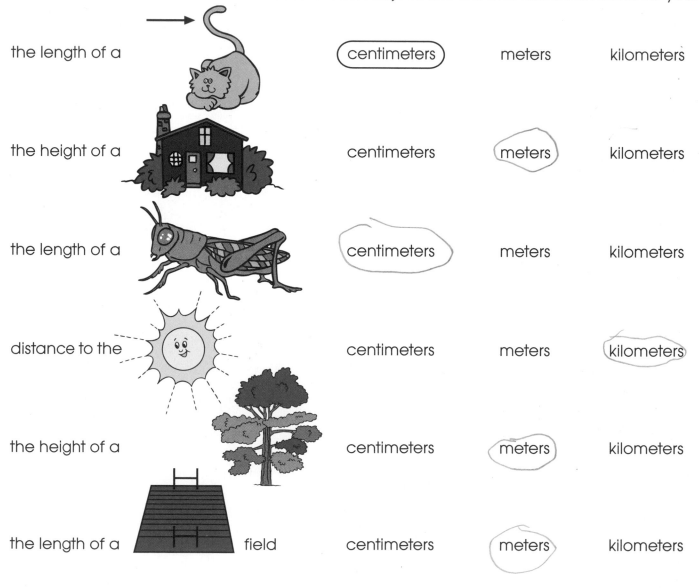

	centimeters	meters	kilometers
the length of a	**(centimeters)**	meters	kilometers
the height of a	centimeters	**meters**	kilometers
the length of a	**centimeters**	meters	kilometers
distance to the	centimeters	meters	**kilometers**
the height of a	centimeters	**meters**	kilometers
the length of a field	centimeters	**meters**	kilometers

Name: _____

Weight

Ounces, **pounds** and **tons** are used to measure weight in the United States.

16 ounces = 1 pound (lb.)
2,000 pounds = 1 ton (tn.)

Directions: Circle the most reasonable estimate for the weight of each object. The first one has been done for you.

10 ounces   (10 pounds)   10 tons

6 ounces   (6 pounds)   6 tons

2 ounces   2 pounds   (2 tons)

(3 ounces)   3 pounds   3 tons

1,800 ounces   (1,800 pounds)   1,800 tons

20 ounces   20 pounds   (20 tons)

(1 ounce)   1 pound   1 ton

Grade 5 - Comprehensive Curriculum

Weight: Metric

Grams and **kilograms** are units of weight in the metric system. A paper clip weighs about 1 gram. A kitten weighs about 1 kilogram.

1 kilogram (kg) = about 2.2 pounds

1,000 grams (g) = 1 kilogram

Directions: Circle the best unit to weigh each object.

kilogram
gram

kilogram
gram

kilogram
gram

kilogram
gram

kilogram
gram

kilogram
gram

kilogram
gram

kilogram
gram

kilogram
gram

kilogram
gram

Name: _____

Capacity

The **fluid ounce**, **cup**, **pint**, **quart** and **gallon** are used to measure capacity in the United States.

1 cup

1 pint

1 quart

1 half gallon

1 gallon

> 8 fluid ounces (fl. oz.) = 1 cup (c.)
> 2 cups = 1 pint (pt.)
> 2 pints = 1 quart (qt.)
> 2 quarts = 1 half gallon ($\frac{1}{2}$ gal.)
> 4 quarts = 1 gallon (gal.)

Directions: Convert the units of capacity.

13 gal. = _____ qt.   10 pt. = _____ c.   12 c. = _____ pt.

4 gal. = _____ qt.   16 qt. = _____ gal.   5 c. = _____ pt.

36 pt. = _____ gal.   12 qt. = _____ pt.   6 gal. = _____ pt.

16 c. = _____ qt.   32 oz. = _____ c.   16 oz. = _____ pt.

Grade 5 - Comprehensive Curriculum

Capacity: Metric

Milliliters and liters are units of capacity in the metric system. A can of soda contains about 350 milliliters of liquid. A large plastic bottle contains 1 liter of liquid. A liter is about a quart.

1,000 milliliters (mL) = 1 liter (L)

Directions: Circle the best unit to measure each liquid.

milliliters
liters

milliliters
liters

milliliters
liters

milliliters
liters

milliliters
liters

milliliters
liters

milliliters
liters

milliliters
liters

milliliters
liters

milliliters
liters

Comparing Measurements

Directions: Use the symbols greater than (>), less than (<) or equal to (=) to complete each statement.

10 inches   _____   10 centimeters

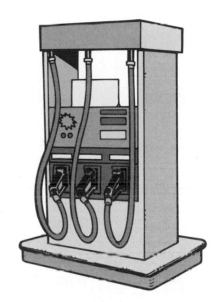

40 feet   _____   120 yards

25 grams   _____   25 kilograms

16 quarts   _____   4 gallons

2 liters   _____   2 milliliters

16 yards   _____   6 meters

3 miles   _____   3 kilometers

20 centimeters   _____   20 meters

85 kilograms   _____   8 grams

2 liters   _____   1 gallon

Name: _____

Temperature: Fahrenheit

Degrees Fahrenheit (°F) is a unit for measuring temperature.

Directions: Write the temperature in degrees Fahrenheit (°F).

Example:

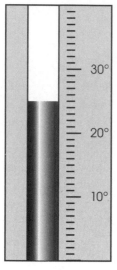

$\underline{25°F}$

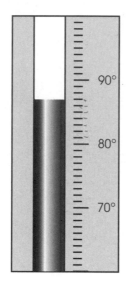

$\underline{87°F}$

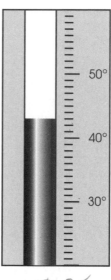

$\underline{43°F}$

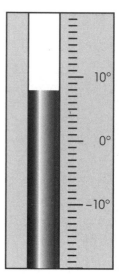

_____

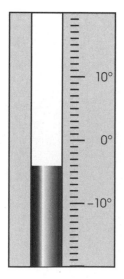

_____

_____

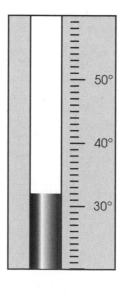

_____

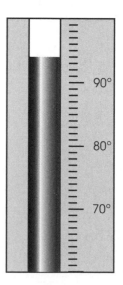

_____

Name: _____

Temperature: Celsius

Degrees Celsius (°C) is a unit for measuring temperature in the metric system.

Directions: Write the temperature in degrees Celsius (°C).

Example:

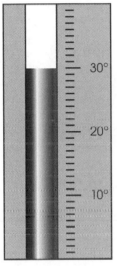

30°C

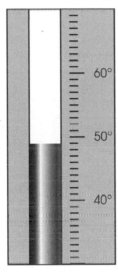

_____

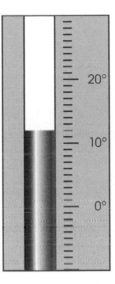

_____

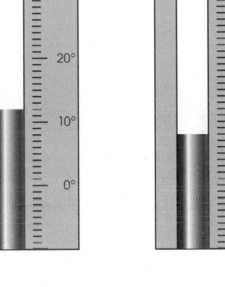

_____

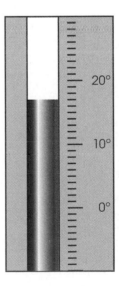

_____

_____

_____

_____

Grade 5 - Comprehensive Curriculum

Name: _____

Review

Directions: Write the best unit to measure each item: inch, foot, yard, mile, ounce, pound, ton, fluid ounce, cup, pint, quart or gallon.

distance from New York to Chicago _____

weight of a goldfish _____

height of a building _____

water in a large fish tank _____

glass of milk _____

weight of a whale _____

length of a pencil _____

distance from first base to second base _____

distance traveled by a space shuttle _____

length of a soccer field _____

amount of paint needed to cover a house _____

material needed to make a dress _____

Ratio

A **ratio** is a comparison of two quantities.

Ratios can be written three ways: 2 to 3 or 2 : 3 or $\frac{2}{3}$. Each ratio is read: two to three.

Example:

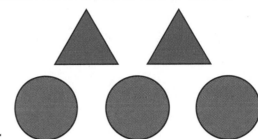

The ratio of triangles to circles is 2 to 3.
The ratio of circles to triangles is 3 to 2.

Directions: Write the ratio that compares these items.

ratio of tulips to cacti _____

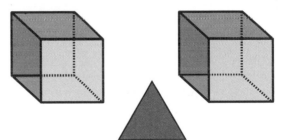

ratio of cubes to triangles _____

ratio of pens to pencils _____

Percent

Percent is a ratio meaning "per hundred." It is written with a % sign. 20% means 20 percent or 20 per hundred.

Example:

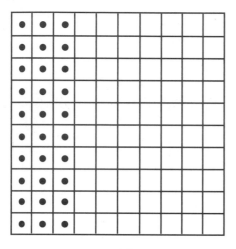

ratio = $\frac{30}{100}$

percent = 30%

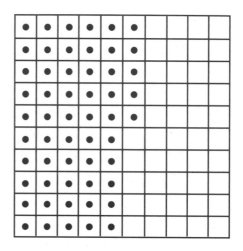

ratio = _____

percent = _____

Directions: Write the percent for each ratio.

$\frac{7}{100}$ =	$\frac{38}{100}$ =
$\frac{63}{100}$ =	$\frac{3}{100}$ =
$\frac{40}{100}$ =	$\frac{1}{5}$ =

Book Sale

The school received 100 books for the Book Fair. It sold 43 books.

What is the percent of books sold to books received? _____

Name: _____

Probability

Probability is the ratio of favorable outcomes to possible outcomes of an experiment.

Vehicle	Number Sold
4 door	26
2 door	18
Sport	7
Van	12
Wagon	7
Compact	5
Total	75

Example:

This table records vehicle sales for 1 month. What is the probability of a person buying a van?

number of vans sold = 12   total number of cars = 75

The probability that a person will choose a van is 12 in 75 or $\frac{12}{75}$.

Directions: Look at the chart of flowers sold in a month. What is the probability that a person will buy each?

Roses   _____

Tulips   _____

Violets _____

Orchids _____

Flowers	Number Sold
Roses	48
Tulips	10
Violets	11
Orchids	7
Total	76

How would probability help a flower store owner keep the correct quantity of each flower in the store?

_____

_____

_____

Grade 5 - Comprehensive Curriculum

Name: _____

Using Calculators to Find Percent

A **calculator** is a machine that rapidly does addition, subtraction, multiplication, division and other mathematical functions.

Example:

Carlos got 7 hits in 20 "at bats."

$$\frac{7}{20} = \frac{35}{100} = 35\%$$

To use a calculator:

Step 1: Press 7.

Step 2: Press the ÷ symbol.

Step 3: Press 20.

Step 4: Press the = symbol.

Step 5: 0.35 appears.
0.35 = 35%.

Directions: Use a calculator to find the percent of hits to the number of "at bats" for each baseball player. Round your answer to two digits. If your calculator displays the answer 0.753, round it to 0.75 or 75%.

Player	Hits	At Bats	Percent
Carlos	7	20	35%
Troy	3	12	_____
Sasha	4	14	_____
Dan	8	18	_____
Jaye	5	16	_____
Keesha	9	17	_____
Martin	11	16	_____
Robi	6	21	_____
Devan	4	15	_____

Who is most likely to get a hit? _____

Finding Percents

Find percent by dividing the number you have by the number possible.

Example:

15 out of 20 possible:

$$20 \overline{)15.00} = \frac{0.75}{} = 75\%$$

$$\begin{array}{r} 0.75 \\ 20\overline{)15.00} \\ -140 \\ \hline 100 \\ \underline{100} \end{array} = 75\%$$

Annie has been keeping track of the scores she earned on each spelling test during the grading period.

Directions: Find out each percentage grade she earned. The first one has been done for you.

Week	Number Correct		Total Number of Words	Score in Percent
1	14	(out of)	20	70%
2	16		20	_____
3	18		20	_____
4	12		15	_____
5	16		16	_____
6	17		18	_____
Review Test	51		60	_____

If Susan scored 5% higher than Annie on the review test, how many words did she get right? _____

Carrie scored 10% lower than Susan on the review test. How many words did she spell correctly? _____

Of the 24 students in Annie's class, 25% had the same score as Annie. Only 10% had a higher score. What percent had a lower score? _____

Is that answer possible? _____

Why? _____

Name: _____

Locating Points on a Grid

To locate points on a grid, read the first coordinate and follow it to the second coordinate.

Example: C, 3

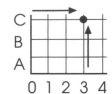

Directions: Maya is new in town. Help her learn the way around her new neighborhood. Place the following locations on the grid below.

Grocery	C, 10
Home	B, 2
School	A, 12
Playground	B, 13
Library	D, 6
Bank	G, 1
Post Office	E, 7
Ice-Cream Shop	D, 3

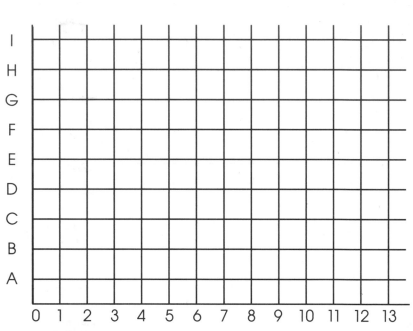

Is her home closer to the bank or the grocery? _____

Does she pass the playground on her way to school? _____

If she needs to stop at the library after school, will she
be closer to home or farther away? _____

Comma: A punctuation mark that tells a reader where to pause when reading a sentence.

Command: A sentence that orders someone to do something. It ends with a period (.) or exclamation mark (!).

Common Noun: A noun which names a nonspecific person, place or thing.

Comparative: A form of adjective or adverb used to compare things. Examples: Adjective—quick, quicker; Adverb—quickly, more quickly.

Compound Predicate: A predicate with two or more verbs joined with a conjunction.

Compound Subject: A subject with two or more nouns or pronouns joined by a conjunction.

Comprehension: Understanding what is seen, heard or read.

Conclusion: The final one or two paragraphs of a report which sum up the main ideas and restate any conclusions the writer has drawn as a result of research.

Concrete Noun: A noun that names something that can be touched or seen.

Cone: A space figure having one circular surface, one flat face and one vertex.

Congruent Figures: Figures having identical shapes but different orientations, that is, facing in different directions.

Conjunction: A word used to join words or groups of words in a sentence or to combine sentences. Examples: and, or, but, because.

Consonants: Letters in the alphabet that are not vowels.

Context: The rest of the words in a sentence or the sentences before or after a word that help show its meaning.

Context Clue: A way to determine the meaning of new words by relating them to other words in the sentence.

Cube: A space figure with six square faces.

Cup (c.): A measurement of capacity equal to 8 fluid ounces.

Cylinder: A space figure with a curved surface and two parallel bases that are identical circles.

Decimal: A number with one or more places to the right of a decimal point, such as 6.5 or 2.25.

Demonstrative Adjective: An adjective that identifies a particular person, place or thing. Examples: this, these, that and those.

Denominator: The number below the fraction bar in a fraction.

Descriptive Sentence: A sentence that gives readers a vivid image and enables them to imagine a scene clearly.

Diameter: A line segment that passes through the center of a circle and has both end points on the circle.

Dictionary: A reference book which lists words in alphabetical order and gives their definitions, pronunciation and parts of speech. Some dictionaries provide illustrations and further information about words.

Digraph: Two letters pronounced as one sound. Examples: sh—shell, ch—chew, th—thin.

Direct Address: A noun or pronoun that names or refers to the person addressed. Example: John, are you ready yet?

Direct Object: A word that follows a verb and completes its meaning. Example: I called Mary.

Dividend: The number that is divided by another number (the divisor) in a division problem. In the problem $28 \div 7 = 4$, 28 is the dividend.

Division: The process of dividing a number into equal groups of smaller numbers.

Divisor: The number by which another number (the dividend) is divided in a division problem. In the problem $28 \div 7 = 4$, 7 is the divisor.

Editing: Revising and correcting written work.

Effect: An event that results from a cause.

Encyclopedia: A set of reference books or a CD which provides information about different subjects in alphabetical order.

Estimate: To give an approximate rather than an exact answer.

Exclamation: A sentence that shows strong feeling or excitement. It ends with an exclamation mark (!).

Fact: Information that can be proven true.

Factors: The numbers multiplied together to give a product.

Fahrenheit: A measurement of temperature using units called degrees Fahrenheit.

Fiction: Books that are not based on facts or real events.

Fluid Ounce (fl. oz.): A measure of capacity equal to $\frac{1}{8}$ of a cup.

Following Directions: Doing what the directions say to do, step by step, in the correct order.

Foot (ft.): A measurement of length equal to 12 inches.

Fraction: A number that names part of a whole. It is usually shown as one number (the part) above a second number (the whole), with a horizontal line between. Examples: $\frac{1}{2}$ and $\frac{1}{4}$

Fragment: A sentence that does not contain both a subject and a predicate.

Future-Tense Verb: A verb that tells about something that will happen in the future.

Gallon (gal.): A measurement of capacity equal to 4 quarts.

Geometry: The branch of mathematics that has to do with points, lines and shapes.

Gram (g): A metric measurement of weight. 1,000 grams = 1 kilogram.

Graph: A drawing that shows information about changes in numbers.

Greatest Common Factor (GCF): The largest number that is a factor of every number in a given set of numbers. Example: The greatest common factor of 9, 15, and 27 is 3 (3 x 3 = 9, 3 x 5 = 15, and 3 x 9 = 27), while the GCF of 9, 15, and 25 is 1.

Guide Words: Words that appear at the top of a dictionary page to indicate the first and last words, alphabetically, found on that page.

Haiku: A three-line, unrhymed Japanese verse with five, seven and five syllables.

Helping Verb: A verb used to "support" another verb. Examples: is helping; are working.

Homographs: Words that have the same spelling but different meanings and pronunciations.

Homophones: Words that are pronounced the same but are spelled differently and have different meanings.

Idiom: A figure of speech that has a meaning different from the literal one.

Improper Fraction: A fraction in which the numerator is greater than its denominator.

Inch: A measurement of length. 12 inches = 1 foot.

Indefinite Adjective: An adjective that does not identify a particular person, place or thing but rather a group or number.

Indefinite Pronoun: A pronoun that ends with body, one or thing. Examples: all, any, both, many.

Index: The section in the back of an encyclopedia or nonfiction book that indicates the page number and/or volume where information on a specific topic can be found.

Indirect Object: Words that come between the verb and the direct object.

Indirect objects tell to whom or for whom something is done.
Example: She cooked me a great dinner.

Interrogative Adjective: An adjective that is used when asking a question. What and which are interrogative adjectives.

Interrogative Pronoun: A pronoun that is used when asking a question. such as who, what and which.

Intransitive Verb: A verb that can stand alone in the predicate because its meaning is complete.

Introduction: A paragraph at the beginning of a report that states the main parts to be covered in the report.

Inverted Pyramid: A style of newswriting that places the most important facts at the beginning of the article.

Irregular Verb: A verb which changes completely in the past tense. Example: eat—ate.

Kilogram (kg): A metric measurement of weight equal to 1,000 grams. 1 kilogram = about 2.2 pounds

Kilometer (km): A metric measure of distance equal to 1,000 meters or about $\frac{5}{8}$ mile.

Lantern: A five-line Japanese verse in the shape of a lantern. Each line must contain a specific number of syllables.

Least Common Denominator (LCD): The least common multiple of the denominators in a given set of fractions.

Least Common Multiple (LCM): The smallest number other than 0 which is a multiple of each number in a given set of more numbers.
Example: The least common multiple of 3, 5, and 6 is 30 (3 x 10, 5 x 6, 6 x 5).

Library Catalog: A listing on separate index cards or in a computer file of all the books, videos, CDs, etc., in a library collection. Materials are listed by title, by author and by subject.

Like Fractions: Fractions with the same denominator, or bottom number.

Line: A collection of points on a straight path that goes on and on in opposite directions.

Linking Verb: A verb that links a noun or adjective in the predicate to the subject.

Liter (L): A metric measurement of capacity equal to about 1 quart.

Main Idea: The most important idea, or main point, in a sentence, paragraph or story.

Metaphor: A direct comparison between two unlike things that doesn't use the words like or as. Example: She was a frightened mouse.

Meter (m): A metric measurement of length equal to 39.37 inches.

Mile (mi.): A measurement of distance equal to 1,760 yards.

Milliliter (mL): A metric measurement of capacity. 1,000 milliliters = 1 liter.

Millimeter (mm): A metric measurement of length equal to $\frac{1}{1000}$ of a meter. 10 millimeters = 1 centimeter.

Mixed Number: A number written as a whole number and a fraction.

Multiple: The product of a specific number and any other number.
Example: The multiples of 2 are 2 (2 x 1), 4 (2 x 2), 6, 8, 10, 12, and so on.

Multiplication: The process of quick addition of a number a certain number of times.

Narrative: A spoken or written account of an actual event.

Newswriting: A style of writing used by newspaper reporters and other journalists who write for periodicals.

Nonfiction: Books based on facts or events that actually occurred.

Noun: A word that names a person, place or thing.

Numerator: The number above the fraction bar in a fraction.

Object of a Preposition: A noun or pronoun that follows a preposition and completes its meaning.

Opinion: Information that tells what someone thinks or believes about something or someone.

Ounce (oz.): A measurement of weight. 16 ounces = 1 pound.

Outlining: A way to organize information in preparation for writing a paper or a report.

Paragraph: A group of related sentences about a topic.

Past-Tense Verb: A verb that tells what already happened.

Percent: A ratio which means "per hundred."

Perimeter: The distance around an object found by adding the lengths of the sides.

Periodicals: Newspapers, magazines and newsletters that are published regularly.

Personal Narrative: Tells about a person's own experiences.

Personification: A figure of speech in which an object or animal is given human qualities. Example: The wind sighed and moaned.

Pi (π): A symbol representing a number equal to approximately 3.14.

Pint (pt.): A measurement of capacity equal to 2 cups.

Place Value: The value of a digit as representing ones, tens, hundreds, and so on, according to its position, or place, in a number.

Point of View: The attitude someone has about a particular topic as a result of his or her personal experience or knowledge.

Possessive Adjective: An adjective that shows ownership. Examples: our, your, her, his, its, my and their.

Possessive Pronoun: A pronoun that shows ownership. Examples: his, theirs, its.

Pound (lb.): A measurement of weight equal to 16 ounces.

Predicate: The part of the sentence that tells what the subject does, did or is doing.

Prefix: A syllable added to the beginning of a word that changes the word's meaning.

Preposition: A word that comes before a noun or pronoun and shows the relationship of that noun or pronoun to other words in the sentence.

Prepositional Phrase: Includes a preposition and the object(s) of the preposition.

Present-Tense Verb: A verb that tells what is happening now.

Prime Number: A positive whole number which can be divided evenly only by itself or one.

Prior Knowledge: What one already knows.

Prism: A space figure with two identical, parallel bases.

Probability: The ratio of favorable outcomes to possible outcomes of an experiment.

Product: The quantity that results from multiplying two or more numbers.

Pronoun: A word used in place of a noun. Examples: Wanda—her; Brian—him.

Proofreading: Carefully checking over what has been written for spelling, grammar, punctuation and other errors.

Proper Noun: A noun which names a specific person, place or thing.

Pyramid: A space figure whose base is a polygon and whose faces are triangles with a common vertex—the point where two rays meet.

Quart (qt.): A measurement of capacity equal to 4 cups or 2 pints.

Question: A sentence that asks something. It ends with a question mark (?).

Quotation Marks: Punctuation marks used to identify a person's exact words used in a sentence.

Quotient: The answer found by dividing one number by another number.

Radius: A line segment with one end point on the circle and the other end point at the center.

Ratio: A comparison of two quantities.

Ray: A part of a line with one end point that goes on and on in one direction.

Recalling Details: Being able to pick out and remember the who, what, when, where, why and how of what has been read.

Rectangle: A figure with four equal angles and four sides, having the sides opposite each other of equal length.

Rectangular Prism: A space figure with six sides, or faces, all of which are rectangles.

Reference Sources: Nonfiction books and other materials which provide facts and information.

Relative Pronoun: A pronoun which refers to the nouns which come before it. Examples: who, whom, which and that.

Remainder: The number left over in the quotient of a division problem.

Report Writing: Researching and collecting information about a particular topic and writing about it.

Request: A sentence that asks someone to do something. It ends with a period (.) or question mark (?).

Rhyming Words: Words that share the same vowel sound in their last syllables. Example: cane and explain.

Root Word: The common stem that gives related words their basic meanings. Example: The root word of arrangement is arrange.

Rounding: Expressing a number to the nearest ten, hundred, thousand, and so on. Examples: round 18 up to 20; round 113 down to 100.

Run-on Sentence: Two or more sentences which are joined together without correct punctuation.

Segment: A part of a line having two end points.

Sentence: A group of words that expresses a complete thought.

Sequencing: Placing events or objects in the correct order.

Similar Figures: Figures having the same shape but different sizes.

Simile: A comparison using the words like or as. Example: She looked as frightened as a mouse.

Skimming: To read quickly, looking for headings and key words, in order to identify the overall idea of the material's content or to find a particular fact.

Space Figures: Figures whose points are in more than one plane.

Sphere: A space figure with no flat surface. All points are an equal distance from the center.

Square: A figure with four equal sides and four equal angles.

Statement: A sentence that tells something. It ends with a period (.).

Subject: The part of a sentence that tells whom or what the sentence is about.

Subtraction: The process of "taking away" one number from another. It is used to find the difference between two numbers.

Suffix: A syllable at the end of a word that changes its meaning.

Summarizing: Writing a short report containing only the main points found in an article, book or speech.

Summary: A short description of what a selection or book is about.

Superlative: A form of adjectives or adverbs which compare by pointing out the most extreme case. Examples: tallest, softest, most important.

Supporting Sentences: The sentences in a paragraph that follow the topic sentence and provide details about the topic.

Syllable: A word part with only one vowel sound.

Symmetrical Figure: A figure that can be divided equally into two identical parts.

Synonym: A word that means the same or nearly the same as another word. Example: jump and hop.

Taking Notes: The process of writing important information from a story, article or lecture that can be used later when writing a report or taking a test.

Tall Tale: A fictional story with exaggerated details.

Thesaurus: A type of reference book that lists words in alphabetical order followed by their synonyms and antonyms. Some types of thesauri also list idioms, related words, examples and other information.

Ton (tn.): A measurement of weight equal to 2,000 pounds.

Topic Sentence: The sentence that tells the main idea of a paragraph.

Transitive Verb: A verb that needs a direct object to complete its meaning.

Triangle: A figure with three sides and three angles.

Unlike Fractions: Fractions with different denominators, or bottom numbers.

Venn Diagram: A diagram used to chart information comparing two things, showing their similarities and differences.

Verb: The action word in a sentence that tells what the subject does or that it exists.

Volume: The number of cubic units inside a space figure.

Vowels: The letters a, e, i, o, u and sometimes y.

Word Family: A group of words based on the same word. Example: play—playful, playground, playing.

Yard (yd.): A measurement of distance equal to 3 feet.

Page 6

Spelling: Digraphs

A **digraph** is two consonants pronounced as one sound.

Examples: sh as in **shell**, **ch** as in **chew**, **th** as in **thin**.

Directions: Write **sh**, **ch** or **th** to complete each word below.

1. **th** reaten
2. **ch** ill
3. **sh** ock
4. **sh** iver
5. **th** aw
6. **ch** allenge
7. peri **sh**
8. **sh** ield
9. **ch** art
10. **th** rive

Directions: Complete these sentences with a word, or form of the word, from the list above.

1. A trip to the South Pole would really be a (**ch**) __challenge__ .
2. The ice there never (**th**) __thaws__ because the temperature averages –50°C.
3. How can any living thing (**th**) __thrive__ or even live when it's so cold?
4. With 6 months of total darkness and those icy temperatures, any plants would soon (**sh**) __perish__ .
5. Even the thought of that numbing cold makes me (**sh**) __shiver__ .
6. The cold and darkness (**th**) __threaten__ the lives of explorers.
7. The explorers take along maps and (**ch**) __charts__ to help them find their way.
8. Special clothing helps protect and (**sh**) __shield__ them from the cold.
9. Still, the weather must be a (**sh**) __shock__ at first.
10. Did someone leave a door open? Suddenly I feel a (**ch**) __chill__ .

Page 7

Spelling: Listening for Sounds

Not every word spelled with **ow** is pronounced **ou** as in **powder** and **however**. In the same way, not every word spelled with **ou** is pronounced **ou** as in **amount** and **announce**. The letters **ou** can be pronounced a number of ways.

Directions: Write the word from the box that rhymes with each of the words or phrases below. Some words are used twice.

| doubt | amount | avoid | annoy | announce |
| choice | poison | powder | soil | however |

joys in	__poison__	two counts	__announce__
shout	__doubt__	loyal	__soil__
a boy	__annoy__	crowd her	__powder__
employed	__avoid__	Joyce	__choice__
now never	__however__	a count	__amount__
voice	__choice__	employ	__annoy__
a bounce	__announce__	louder	__powder__
enjoyed	__avoid__	trout	__doubt__

Page 8

Spelling: The j and ch Sounds

The **j** sound can be spelled with a **j** as in **jump**, with a **g** before **e** or **i** as in **agent** and **giant**, or with **ge** at the end of a word as in **page**.

The **ch** sound is often spelled with the letters **ch** but can also be spelled with a **t** before **u**, as in **nature**.

Directions: Use words from the box to complete the exercises below.

| statue | imagination | jealous | future | arrangements |
| furniture | stranger | project | justice | capture |

1. Say each word and then write it in the correct row, depending on whether it has the **j** or **ch** sound.

j __imagination__ __stranger__ __jealous__
__project__ __justice__ __arrangements__

ch __statue__ __furniture__ __future__ __capture__

2. Write a word from the box that belongs to the same word family as each word below.

imagine __imagination__   arranging __arrangements__
strangely __stranger__   furnish __furniture__
just __justice__   jealousy __jealous__

Directions: Complete each sentence with a word containing the given sound.

1. What is your group's (**j**) __project__ this week?
2. There is a (**ch**) __statue__ of George Washington in front of our school.
3. She used her (**j**) __imagination__ to solve the problem.
4. My sister keeps rearranging the (**ch**) __furniture__ in our room.

Page 9

Spelling: Words With Silent Letters

Some letters in words are not pronounced, such as the **s** in **island**, the **t** in **listen**, the **k** in **knee**, the **h** in **hour** and the **w** in **write**.

Directions: Use words from the box to complete the exercises below.

| wrinkled | honest | aisle | knife | wrist |
| rhyme | exhaust | glisten | knowledge | wrestle |

1. Write each word beside its silent letter. Two words have two silent letters—write them twice.

s __aisle__
t __glisten__ __wrestle__
h __rhyme__ __honest__ __exhaust__
w __wrinkle__ __wrist__ __wrestle__ __knowledge__
k __knife__ __knowledge__

2. Write in the missing letter or letters for each word.

w res **t** le   ex **h** aust   **k** nife   glis **t** en   ai **s** le
k nowledge   **w** rinkle   r **h** yme   **h** onest   **w** rist

Directions: Complete each sentence with a word that has the given silent letter. Use each word only once.

1. He always tells the truth. He's very (**h**) __honest__ .
2. I like (**s**) __aisle__ seats in airplanes.
3. I need a sharper (**k**) __knife__ to cut this bread.
4. I think a long hike might (**h**) __exhaust__ me.
5. Did you sleep in that shirt? It is so (**w**) __wrinkled__ !
6. The snow seemed to (**t**) __glisten__ in the sunlight.
7. To play tennis, you need a strong (**w**) __wrist__ .

Page 10

Spelling: Syllables

A **syllable** is a part of a word with only one vowel sound. Some words have only one syllable, like **cat**, **leaf** and **ship**. Some words have two or more syllables. **Be-lief** and **trac-tor** have two syllables, **to-ge-ther** and **ex-cel-lent** have three syllables and **con-ver-sa-tion** has four syllables. Some words can have six or more syllables! The word **ex-tra-ter-res-tri-al**, for example, has six syllables.

Directions: Follow the instructions below.

1. Count the syllables in each word below, and write the number of syllables on the line.

a. badger __2__
b. location __3__
c. award __2__
d. national __3__
e. necessary __4__
f. grease __1__
g. relationship __4__
h. communication __5__
i. government __3__
j. Braille __1__

2. Write four words with four syllables each in the blanks.

a. __Answers will vary.__   c. _____
b. _____   d. _____

3. Write one word with five syllables and one with six syllables. If you need help, use a dictionary.

Five syllables: __Answers will vary.__
Six syllables: _____

Page 11

Writing: Sounding Out Syllables

Directions: Use words from the box to complete the exercises below.

| decision | division | pressure | addition | ancient |
| subtraction | confusion | multiplication | social | correction |

1. Write each word in the row showing the correct number of syllables.

Two: __pressure__ __social__ __ancient__
Three: __decision__ __division__ __addition__
__subtraction__ __confusion__ __correction__
Five: __multiplication__

2. Write in the missing syllables for each word.

s o cial   sub **t r a c** tion   mul **t i** pli **ca** tion   pres **s u r e**
di **v i** sion   an **c i e n t**   deci **s i o n**   ad **d i** tion
c o n fusion   cor **r e c** tion

3. Beside each word below, write a word with the same number of syllables. Use each word from the box only once.

Answers may include:

daily __pressure__   challenging __addition__
syllable __decision__   election __correction__
decreasing __subtraction__   threaten __ancient__
advantage __division__   shivering __confusion__
title __social__   experimenting __multiplication__

Page 12

Writing: Word Families

A **word family** is a group of words based on the same word. For example, **playful**, **playground** and **playing** are all based on the word **play**.

Directions: Use words from the box to complete the exercises below.

| decision | division | pressure | addition | create |
| subtraction | confusion | multiplication | social | correction |

1. Write the word that belongs to the same word family as each word below.

correctly __correction__   confused __confusion__

divide __division__   subtracting __substraction__

pressing __pressure__   society __social__

multiply __multiplication__   decide __decision__

added __addition__   creativity __create__

2. Complete each sentence by writing the correct form of the given word.

Example: Have you (decide) __decided__ what to do? Did you make a (decide) __decision__ yet?

I am (add) __adding__ the numbers right now. Would you check my

(add) __addition__ ?

This problem has me (confuse) __confused__ . Can you clear up my

(confuse) __confusion__ ?

This is a (press) __pressing__ problem. We feel (press) __pressure__

to solve it right away.

Is he (divide) __dividing__ by the right number? Will you help him with his

(divide) __division__ ?

Try to answer (correct) __correctly__ . Then you won't have to make any

(correct) __corrections__ on your paper later on.

Page 13

Writing: Word Families

Directions: Write the word that belongs to the same word family as each word below.

| doubt | amount | avoid | annoy | announce |
| choice | poison | powder | soil | however |

avoidance __avoid__   annoyance __annoy__

doubtful __doubt__   soiled __soil__

announcement __announce__   poisonous __poison__

choose __choice__   amounted __amount__

powdery __powder__   whenever __however__

Directions: Complete each sentence by writing the correct form of the given word.

Example: Are you (doubt) __doubting__ my word? You never (doubt) __doubted__ it before.

1. The teacher is (announce) __announcing__ the next test. Did you hear what he (announce) __announced__ ?

2. This stream was (poison) __poisoned__ by a chemical from a factory nearby.

3. Is the chemical (poison) __poisoning__ any other water supply? How many (poison) __poisons__ does the factory produce?

4. My cat always (annoy) __annoys__ our dog.

5. Last night, Carrie (annoy) __annoyed__ Lucas for hours.

6. I think Carrie is (avoid) __avoiding__ me. Yesterday, she (avoid) __avoided__ walking home with me.

Page 14

Spelling: Double Consonants

When adding endings such as **ng** and **ed** to verbs, use the following rule: Double the final consonant of verbs that have short vowel sounds and end with only one consonant. For example, **rip** becomes **ripped** and **beg** becomes **begging**. However, do not double the final consonant in words that end in double consonants. For example, **rock** ends with two consonants, **ck**. So even though it has a short vowel sound, **rock** becomes **rocked**.

Directions: Add **ed** to the verbs below. Remember, when a verb ends with **e**, drop the **e** before adding an ending (**taste**, **tasting**). The first one has been done for you.

top	__topped__	rip	__ripped__
pet	__petted__	punch	__punched__
sob	__sobbed__	rinse	__rinsed__
brag	__bragged__	stock	__stocked__
scrub	__scrubbed__	lack	__lacked__
flip	__flipped__	dent	__dented__

Directions: Add **ing** to the verbs below. The first one has been done for you.

flap	__flapping__	snack	__snacking__
scrub	__scrubbing__	flip	__flipping__
stock	__stocking__	rinse	__rinsing__
dent	__denting__	brag	__bragging__
pet	__petting__	lack	__lacking__
sob	__sobbing__	punch	__punching__

Page 15

Writing: Verb Forms

Directions: In the following story, some of the verbs are missing. Write the proper form of the verbs shown, adding **ed** or **ing** when necessary.

What's Your Verb Form?

Yesterday, I was (brag) __bragging__ to my brother about how much I (help) __helped__ our mother around the house. I had (scrub) __scrubbed__ the kitchen floor, (wipe) __wiped__ off all the counters and (rinse) __rinsed__ out the sink. I was (pour) __pouring__ the dirty water out of the bucket when our mother came in. She looked around the kitchen and (smile) __smiled__ . "Who did all this work?" she (ask) __asked__ .

I was (get) __getting__ ready to tell her what I had done when my brother (interrupt) __interrupted__ me. "We both did! We've been (work) __working__ very hard!" he said. "He's not (tell) __telling__ the truth!" I said to Mom. "I did everything!" My brother (glare) __glared__ at me.

"Is that true?" asked Mom. My brother (look) __looked__ at the floor and (nod) __nodded__ . He was (think) __thinking__ about all the trouble he would get into. Instead, Mom smiled again. "Well, that's okay," she said. "The rest of the house needs to be (clean) __cleaned__ , too. You can get (start) __started__ right away!"

Page 16

Spelling: Math Plurals

To make most nouns plural, add **s**. When a noun ends with **s, ss, sh, ch** or **x**, add **es**: bus—buses, cross—crosses, brush—brushes, church—churches, box—boxes. When a noun ends with a consonant and **y**, change the **y** to **i** and add **es**: berry—berries. For some words, instead of adding **s** or **es**, the spelling of the word changes: man—men, mouse—mice.

Directions: Write the correct plural or singular form of the words in these math problems. Write whether the problem requires addition (**A**), subtraction (**S**), multiplication (**M**) or division (**D**). The first one has been done for you.

1. 3 (box) __boxes__ – 2 (box) __boxes__ = __1 box__ S
2. 2 (supply) __supplies__ + 5 (supply) __supplies__ = __7 supplies__ A
3. 4 (copy) __copies__ x 2 (copy) __copies__ = __8 copies__ M
4. 6 (class) __classes__ + 2 (class) __classes__ = __3 classes__ D
5. 5 (factory) __factories__ – 3 (factory) __factories__ = __2 factories__ S
6. 3 (daisy) __daisies__ x 3 (daisy) __daisies__ = __9 daisies__ M
7. 8 (sandwich) __sandwiches__ + 4 (sandwich) __sandwiches__ = __12 sandwiches__ A
8. 3 (child) __children__ – 1 (child) __child__ = __2 children__ S
9. 10 (brush) __brushes__ + 5 (brush) __brushes__ = __2 brushes__ D
10. 4 (goose) __geese__ + 1 (goose) __goose__ = __5 geese__ A
11. 3 (mouse) __mice__ + 1 (mouse) __mouse__ = __4 mice__ A

Page 17

Spelling: More Plurals

Remember, in some words, an **f** changes to a **v** to make the plural form.

Examples: life — lives   wife — wives   knife — knives   leaf — leaves

Directions: Complete these sentences by writing the correct plural form of the given word. Also, circle the spelling errors and write the words correctly on the lines to the right.

1. The (leaf) __leaves__ are dry and (rinkled). __wrinkled__
2. The (knife) __knives__ (glisened) in the sun. __glistened__
3. I think the (child) __children__ in this school are (honist). __honest__
4. The (supply) __supplies__ were stacked in the (isle). __aisle__
5. (mouse) __Mice__ (rimes) with twice. __rhymes__
6. Some people feel (exausted) all their (life) __lives__ . __exhausted__
7. The (class) __classes__ were trying to gain more (knowlege) about Olympic athletes. __knowledge__
8. The kittens were (wresling) in the (bush) __bushes__ . __wrestling__
9. Jamie nearly broke his (rist) trying to carry all those (box) __boxes__ . __wrist__
10. Some kings had several (wife) __wives__ who (new) about each other. __knew__
11. (Daisy) __Daisies__ are (knot) expensive. __not__
12. (Right) your name on both (copy) __copies__ . __Write__
13. We watched the (monkey) __monkeys__ play on the swings for (ours). __hours__
14. Do you like (strawberry) __strawberries__ (hole) or sliced? __whole__

Page 18

Spelling: Finding Mistakes

Directions: Circle the four spelling mistakes in each paragraph. Then write the words correctly on the lines below.

Last (nite) our family went to a nice restaurant. As we were (lookking) at the menus, a waiter walked in from the (kichen) carrying a large tray of food. As he walked by us, he (triped) and the tray went flying! The food flew all over our table and all over us, too!

night	looking
tripped	kitchen

Last week, my dad was washing the car, our dog Jack (dicided) to help. He stuck his nose in the (pale) of soapy water, and it (tiped) over and soaked him! As he shook himself off, the water from his fur went all over the car. "Look!" Dad (laffed) "Jack is doing his part!"

decided	pail
tipped	laughed

For our next (feild) trip, my class is going to the zoo. We have been studying about animals in (sceince) class. I'm very (eksited) to see the elephants, but my (freind) Karen really wants to see the monkeys. She has been to the zoo before, and she says the monkeys are the most fun to watch.

field	science
excited	friend

It seems the rain will never stop! It has been (rainning) for seven days now, and the sky is always dark and (cloudy) Everyone at school is in a bad mood, because we have to stay inside during (resess) Will we ever see the (son) again?

raining	cloudy
recess	sun

Page 19

Spelling: Finding Mistakes

Directions: Circle the four spelling mistakes in each paragraph. Then write the misspelled words correctly on the lines below.

According to the newspaper, a man came into the store and stood near a clerk. The clerk was (stocking) the shelves with watches. Then the man suddenly (grabed) several watches and raced out of the store. The clerk shouted, "Stop him! He's (robbing) us!" The police searched for the man, but they still (lak) a suspect.

stocking	grabbed
robbing	lack

Tony always (braged) about the tricks he could do with his skateboard. One day, he (tried) to skate up a ramp and jump over three bikes. Well, he landed on the last bike and (dentted) it. The last I saw Tony, he was (runing) down the street. The owner of the bike was (chasing) him.

bragged	dented
running	chasing

One day, I was (peting) my dog when I felt something sticky in his (fur) It was time for a bath! I put him in a (tub) of water and (scrubbed) as best I could. Then (rinced) the soap out of his fur. He jumped out of the tub, soaking wet, and rolled in some (dirt) I sighed and (draged) him back into the tub. This dog makes me tired sometimes!

petting	scrubbed
rinsed	dragged

Last night, my little sister started (braging) about how fast she (could) wash the dishes. I told her to prove it. (It was my turn to do the dishes.) She started (fliping) the dishes around in the sink, washing them as fast as she could. I noticed she was (rinseing) only about half of them. Finally, it happened. She (droped) a cup on the floor. Dad made me finish the dishes, but at least she did some of them.

bragging	flipping
rinsing	dropped

Page 20

Spelling: Finding Mistakes

Directions: Circle the four spelling mistakes in each paragraph. Write the words correctly on the lines below.

Some (poisins) that kill insects can also (threten) people. Often these (pouders) and sprays are used on corn, beans and other plants we eat. Unless these plants are well (scrubed) we may eat a small amount of the poison.

poisons	threaten	powders	scrubbed

Sometimes the poison is (put) into the (soyl) and moves into the plant through its roots. Then it stays in the plant in (spyte) of all our (rinseing) All we can do is (avoyd) eating food that has been grown this way. (Howver) that also means we have to (expect) more insects in our food. (Its) a hard (chioce) Some people (dout) that a little bit of (poison) will hurt them, while others have made a (dicision) to grow their own food.

soil	spite	rinsing	avoid
However	It's	choice	doubt
	poison	decision	

Yesterday, the teacher (annonced) a new (projict) She (chalenged) us to think of a new (arrangement) for the (furnichure) in the room. We (voated) to put the chairs in groups. Then Brian said it would be easier to (cheet) that way. I was (annoyd) I told him we had more (pryde) than that!

announced	project	challenged
arrangement	furniture	voted
cheat	annoyed	pride

Page 21

Spelling: Proofreading Practice

Directions: Circle the six spelling and pronoun mistakes in each paragraph. Write the words correctly on the lines below.

Jenna always (braged) about being ready to meet (any) (challenge) or reach any (gole) When it was (time) for our class to (elekt) (it's) new officers, Jenna said we should (voat) for her to be president.

bragged	challenge	goal
elect	its	vote

Simon wanted to be (ours) president, too. He tried to (coaks) everyone to vote for (his) He even (lowned) kids money to get their votes! Well, Jenna may have too much (pryde) in herself, but I like her in (spit) of that. At least she didn't try to buy our votes!

our	coax	him
loaned	pride	spite

(Its) true that Jenna tried other ways to get us to vote for (her) She (scrubbed) the chalkboards even though it was my (dayly) job for that week. One day, I saw her (rinseing) out the paintbrushes when it was Peter's turn to do it. Then she made sure we knew about her good deeds so we would (praize) her.

It's	her	scrubbed
daily	rinsing	praise

We held the election, but I was (shoked) when the teacher (releesed) the results. Simon won! I wondered if he (cheated) somehow. I feel like our class was (robbed) Now Simon is the one who's (braging) about how great he is. I wish he knew the (titel) of president doesn't mean anything if no one wants to be around you!

shocked	released	cheated
robbed	bragging	title

Page 22

Adding Suffixes

A **suffix** is a syllable at the end of a word that changes its meaning. The suffixes **ant** and **ent** mean a person or thing that does something.

Examples:
A person who occupies a place is an **occupant**.
A person who obeys is **obedient**.

A **root word** is the common stem that gives related words their basic meanings.

When a word ends in silent **e**, keep the **e** before adding a suffix beginning with a consonant. Drop the **e** before adding a suffix beginning with a vowel.

Examples:
announce + ment = **announcement**
announce + ing = **announcing**

Announce is the root word in this example.

Directions: Combine each root word and suffix to make a new word. The first one has been done for you.

Root word	Suffix	New word
observe	ant	observant
contest	ant	contestant
please	ant	pleasant
preside	ent	president
differ	ent	different

Directions: Use the meanings in parentheses to complete the sentences with one of the above new words. The first one has been done for you.

1. To be a good scientist, you must be very **observant**. (pay careful attention)
2. Her perfume had a strong but very **pleasant** smell. (nice)
3. Because the bridge was out, we had to find a **different** route home. (not the same)
4. The game show **contestant** jumped up and down when she won the grand prize. (person who competes)
5. Next week we will elect a new student council **president**. (highest officer)

Page 23

Adding Suffixes

The suffix **less** means without; **ative** means having the nature of or relating to; **ive** means having or tending to be.

Examples:
Faultless means without fault or blame.
Formative means something that can be formed or molded.
Corrective means something that fixes a problem.

Directions: Combine each root word and suffix to form a new word. The first one has been done for you.

Root word	Suffix	New word
sleep	less	sleepless
imagine	ative	imaginative
talk	ative	talkative
impress	ive	impressive
attract	ive	attractive

Directions: Use the meanings in parentheses to complete the sentences with one of the above new words.

1. The night before his birthday, Michael spent a **sleepless** night. (wide awake)
2. Our history teacher is a rather **talkative** man who likes to tell jokes and stories. (fond of speaking)
3. That book has such an **imaginative** plot! (showing creativity)
4. Monica thought the dress in the store window was very **attractive**. (pleasing)
5. The high school basketball team was **impressive** in its Friday night game, beating their rivals by 30 points. (making an impact on the mind or emotions)

Page 24

Adding Prefixes

A **prefix** is a syllable at the beginning of a word that changes its meaning. The prefixes **il, im, in** and **ir** all mean not.

Examples:
Illogical means not logical or practical.
Impossible means not possible.
Invisible means not visible.
Irrelevant means not relevant or practical.

Directions: Divide each word into its prefix and root word. The first one has been done for you.

	Prefix	Root Word
illogical	il	logical
impatient	im	patient
immature	im	mature
incomplete	in	complete
insincere	in	sincere
irresponsible	ir	responsible
irregular	ir	regular

Directions: Use the meanings in parentheses to complete the sentences with one of the above words.

1. I had to turn in my assignment **incomplete** because I was sick last night. (not finished)
2. It was **illogical** for Jimmy to give me his keys because he can't get into his house without them. (not practical)
3. Sue and Joel were **irresponsible** to leave their bikes out in the rain. (not doing the right thing)
4. I sometimes get **impatient** waiting for my ride to school. (restless)
5. The boys sounded **insincere** when they said they were sorry. (not honest)
6. These towels didn't cost much because they are **irregular**. (not straight or even)

Page 25

Adding Prefixes

The prefix **pre** means before. The prefix **re** means again.

Examples:
Preview means to see in advance.
Redo means to do again.

Directions: Write sentences using these words with prefixes.

1. prefix _____

2. redirect _____

3. regain _____

4. pre____ *Answers will vary.*

5. reorg____

6. prepackage _____

7. redistribute _____

8. precook _____

Page 26

Synonyms

A **synonym** is a word with the same or similar meaning as another word.

Examples: bucket — pail   happy — cheerful   dirty — messy

Directions: Match the words on the left with their synonyms on the right. The first one has been done for you.

tired	beverage
start	notice
get	boring
fire	busy
dull	sleepy
big	couch
noisy	receive
crowded	begin
sofa	loud
drink	halt
sign	large
stop	flames

Directions: Rewrite the sentences below using synonyms for the bold words.

1. Because the road was **rough**, we had a **hard** time riding our bikes on it.

2. After the accident, the driver appeared ___ ___ ran to call an ambulance.   *Sentences will vary.*

3. Yesterday eve ___ ool to pick up litter, and now the school yard is **nice** and **clea**

Page 27

Synonyms

Directions: Circle a word or a phrase in each sentence that is a synonym for a word in the box. Write the synonym on the line.

challenged	shocked	thaw	chart	frighten
perish	chill	shivering	thrive	shield

Example: The writing was in an (old) code.   **ancient**

1. A fish out of water will quickly (die)   **perish**
2. The ice carving is beginning to (melt)   **thaw**
3. I was (amazed) when I saw how he looked.   **shocked**
4. The puppy was (trembling) with excitement.   **shivering**
5. Ferns need moisture to (grow well)   **thrive**
6. Are you trying to (scare) me?   **frighten**
7. Let the salad (get cold) in the refrigerator.   **chill**
8. She tried to (protect) him from the truth.   **shield**
9. He made a (list) of different kinds of birds.   **chart**
10. They (dared) us to enter the contest.   **challenged**

Directions: Write your own sentences using five words from the box. If you're not sure what a word means, look it up in a dictionary.

Sentences will vary.

Page 28

Finding Synonyms

Directions: Circle a word, or group of words, in each sentence that is a synonym for a word in the box. Write the synonym on the line.

furniture	imagination	jealous	future	arrangements
	stranger	project	justice	capture

Example: She will (lend) me her book.   **loan**

1. He tried to (catch) the butterfly.   **capture**
2. No one knows what will happen in the (time to come)   **future**
3. They are loading the (chairs and tables and beds) into the moving van.   **furniture**
4. We almost finished our team (assignment)   **project**
5. They made (plans) to have a class party.   **arrangements**
6. Penny made a (model) of a horse.   **statue**
7. The accused man asked the judge for (fairness)   **justice**

Directions: Write your own sentences for these words: **stranger, imagination, jealous.** Then choose one other word from the box and use it in a sentence. Make each sentence at least ten words long. The sentences should show that you know what the word means.

1. _____
2. _____   *Sentences will vary.*
3. _____
4. _____

Page 29

Synonyms

Synonyms are words that mean the same or nearly the same.

Examples:
small and **little**
big and **large**
bright and **shiny**
unhappy and **sad**

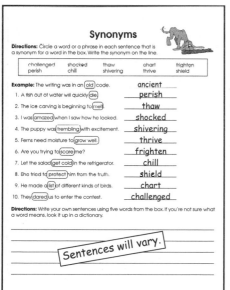

Directions: Write a synonym for each word. Then use it in a sentence. Use a dictionary if you are unsure of the meaning of a word.

1. cup _____
2. book _____
3. looking glass _____
4. hop _____
5. discover _____   *Answers will vary.*
6. plan _____
7. lamp _____
8. friend _____
9. discuss _____
10. rotate _____

Page 30

Antonyms

An **antonym** is a word with the opposite meaning of another word.

Examples: hot — cold
up — down
start — stop

Directions: Match the words on the left with their antonyms on the right. The first one has been done for you.

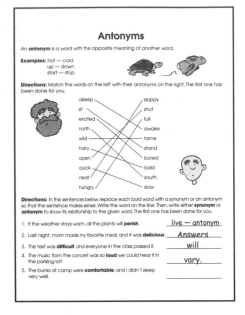

asleep — sloppy
sit — shut
excited — full
north — awake
wild — tame
hairy — stand
open — bored
quick — bald
neat — south
hungry — slow

Directions: In the sentences below, replace each bold word with a synonym or an antonym so that the sentence makes sense. Write the word on the line. Then, write either **synonym** or **antonym** to show its relationship to the given word. The first one has been done for you.

1. If the weather stays warm, all the plants will **perish**.   live — antonym
2. Last night, mom made my favorite meal, and it was **delicious**.   Answers
3. The test was **difficult**, and everyone in the class passed it.   will
4. The music from the concert was so **loud** we could hear it in the parking lot!   vary.
5. The bunks at camp were **comfortable**, and I didn't sleep very well.

Page 31

Finding Antonyms

Directions: Write a word that is an antonym for each bold word in the sentences below.

1. Jared made his way **quickly** through the crowd.
2. My friends and I arrived **late** to the party.
3. My sister loves to watch airpla_____
4. The teacher seem_____ this morning.
5. When are you go_____ **gin** your project? _____

Antonyms will vary.

Directions: Write antonyms for the following words on the lines. Then write a short paragraph using all the words you wrote.

dirty _____   whisper _____
old _____   carefully _____
down _____   night _____
sit _____   happy _____

Paragraphs and answers will vary.

Page 32

Antonyms

Antonyms are words that mean the opposite.

Examples:
tall and **short**
high and **low**
top and **bottom**

Directions: Write an antonym for each word. Then use it in a sentence. Use a dictionary if you are unsure of the meaning of a word.

1. tired _____
2. bright _____
3. sparkling _____
4. tame _____
5. fresh _____
6. elegant _____
7. real _____
8. odd _____
9. unruly _____
10. valor _____

Answers will vary.

Page 33

Homophones

Homophones are words that sound alike but have different spellings and meanings. The words **no** and **know** are homophones. They sound alike, but their spellings and meanings are very different.

Directions: Use words from the box to complete the exercises below.

| hour | wring | knot | whole | knew |
| wrap | knight | piece | write | |

1. Write each word beside its homophone.

peace   piece   new   knew   ring   wring
hole   whole   rap   wrap   night   knight
not   knot   right   write   our   hour

2. Write three words that have a silent **k**.   knight   knot   knew
3. Write one word that has a silent **h**.   hour

Directions: Circle the misused homophones in each sentence. Then rewrite the sentences, using the correct homophones.

1. By the time (knight) fell, I (new) she was (knot) coming.
   By the time night fell, I knew she was not coming.
2. I would never have any (piece) until I (new) the (hole) story.
   I would never have any peace until I knew the whole story.
3. He spent an (our) (righting) down what had happened.
   He spent an hour writing down what had happened.
4. I could see (write) through the (whole) in the (night's) armor.
   I could see right through the hole in the knight's armor.

Page 34

Homophones

Homophones are words that are pronounced the same but are spelled differently and have different meanings.

Example: to, two, too

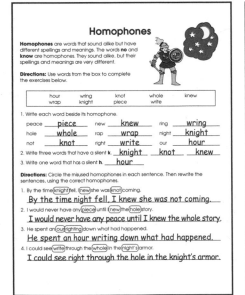

Directions: Use these homophones in sentences of your own.

1. forth _____
2. fourth _____
3. shown _____
4. shone _____
5. they're _____
6. their _____
7. there _____
8. not _____
9. knot _____

Answers will vary.

Page 35

Homophones

Directions: Complete the story below by writing the correct homophones for the words in parentheses.

Last Saturday, I went to (meat) __meet__ my friend, Andrea, at the mall.

When I got there, I noticed she looked a little (pail) __pale__ .

"What's wrong?" I asked her.

She (side) __sighed__ . "I'm (knot) __not__ feeling so (grate) __great__ ," she said. "I don't (no) __know__ what's wrong with me."

"Maybe you (knead) __need__ to take some aspirin," I said. "Let's go to the drugstore. It's this (weigh) __way__ ."

As we were walking, we passed a (flour) __flower__ shop, and I bought (sum) __some__ roses for my mother. Then we found the drugstore, and Andrea bought some aspirin and took (too) __two__ of them. An (our) __hour__ later, she felt much better.

That (knight) __night__ , I gave the roses to my mother. "You shouldn't (waist) __waste__ your money on (presence) __presents__ for me!" she said, but she was smiling. I (new) __knew__ she was pleased.

"That's okay, Mom. I wanted to buy them for you," I said. "But now I'm broke. How about a (lone) __loan__ ?"

Page 36

Homographs

Homographs are words that have the same spelling but different meanings and pronunciations.

pres´ent	n.	a gift
pre sent´	v.	to introduce or offer to view
rec´ord	n.	written or official evidence
re cord´	v.	to keep an account of
wind	n.	air in motion
wind	v.	to tighten the spring by turning a key
wound	n.	an injury in which the skin is broken
wound	v.	past tense of wind

Directions: Write the definition for the bold word in each sentence.

1. I would like to **present** our new student council president, Mindy Hall.
   to introduce
2. The store made a **record** of all my payments.
   written evidence
3. **Wind** the music box to hear the song.
   to tighten the spring by turning a key
4. His **wound** was healing quickly.
   an injury
5. The **wind** knocked over my bicycle.
   air in motion
6. I bought her a birthday **present** with my allowance.
   a gift

Page 37

Similes

A **simile** uses the words **like** or **as** to compare two things.

Examples:
The snow glittered **like** diamonds.
He was **as** slow **as** a turtle.

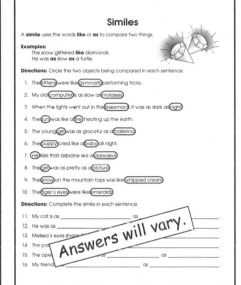

Directions: Circle the two objects being compared in each sentence.

1. The (kittens) were like (gymnasts) performing tricks.
2. My old (computer) is as slow as (molasses).
3. When the lights went out in the (basement), it was as dark as (night).
4. The (sun) was like a (fire) heating up the earth.
5. The young (girl) was as graceful as a (ballerina).
6. The (puppy) cried like a (baby) all night.
7. (He) flies that airplane like a (daredevil).
8. The (girl) was as pretty as a (picture).
9. The (snow) on the mountain tops was like (whipped cream).
10. The (tiger's eyes) were like (emeralds).

Directions: Complete the simile in each sentence.

11. My cat is as _____ as _____.
12. He was as _____.
13. Melissa's eyes shone _____

Answers will vary.

14. The _____
15. The ope _____ as _____ as _____
16. My friend _____ as _____

Page 38

Metaphors

A **metaphor** is a direct comparison between two things. The words **like** or **as** are not used in a metaphor.

Example: The sun is a **yellow ball** in the sky.

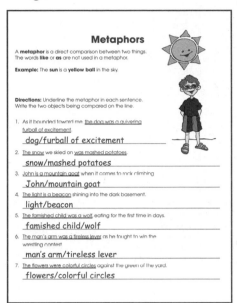

Directions: Underline the metaphor in each sentence. Write the two objects being compared on the line.

1. As it bounded toward me the dog was a quivering furball of excitement.
   dog/furball of excitement
2. The snow we skied on was mashed potatoes.
   snow/mashed potatoes
3. John is a mountain goat when it comes to rock climbing.
   John/mountain goat
4. The light is a beacon shining into the dark basement.
   light/beacon
5. The famished child was a wolf, eating for the first time in days.
   famished child/wolf
6. The man's arm was a tireless lever as he fought to win the wrestling contest.
   man's arm/tireless lever
7. The flowers were colorful circles against the green of the yard.
   flowers/colorful circles

Page 39

Idioms

An **idiom** is a phrase that says one thing but actually means something quite different.

Example: A **horse of a different color** means something quite unusual.

Directions: Write the letter of the correct meaning for each bold phrase. The first one has been done for you.

a. refusal to see or listen
b. misbehaving, acting in a wild way
c. made a thoughtless remark
d. lost an opportunity
e. got angry
f. pay for
g. unknowing
h. feeling very sad
i. get married
j. excited and happy

_f_ 1. My parents will **foot the bill** for my birthday party.
_i_ 2. Tony and Lisa will finally **tie the knot** in June.
_h_ 3. Sam was **down in the dumps** after he wrecked his bicycle.
_c_ 4. Sarah **put her foot in her mouth** when she was talking to our teacher.
_d_ 5. I really **missed the boat** when I turned down the chance to work after school.
_a_ 6. I got the **brush-off** from Susan when I tried to ask her where she was last night.
_g_ 7. Mickey is **in the dark** about our plans to throw a surprise birthday party for him.
_b_ 8. The children were **bouncing off the walls** when the baby-sitter tried to put them to bed.
_j_ 9. The students were **flying high** on the last day of school.
_e_ 10. My sister **lost her cool** when she discovered I had spilled chocolate milk on her new sweater.

Page 40

Idioms

An **idiom** is a figure of speech that has a meaning different from the literal one.

Example:
Dad is **in the doghouse** because he was late for dinner.
Meaning: Dad is in trouble because he was late for dinner.

Directions: Write the meanings of the idioms in bold.

1. He was a **bundle of nerves** waiting for his test scores.
   very nervous
2. It was **raining cats and dogs**.
   raining very hard
3. My friend and I decided to **bury the hatchet** after our argument.
   make peace
4. He gave me the **cold shoulder** when I spoke to him.
   ignored
5. My mom **blew up** when she saw my poor report card.
   got very upset
6. I was **on pins and needles** before my skating performance.
   nervous and anxious
7. When the student didn't answer, the teacher asked, "**Did the cat get your tongue?**"
   Why are you not speaking?
8. The city **rolled out the red carpet** for the returning Olympic champion.
   welcomed
9. They hired a clown for the young boy's birthday party to help **break the ice**.
   put everyone at ease

Page 41

Review

Directions: Circle the word or phrase that best defines the bold words.

1. The woman has a very **pleasant** smile.
   loud   (nice)   strange
2. He had a very **imaginative** excuse for not turning in his homework.
   (creative)   difficult to believe   acceptable
3. I didn't get credit for my answer on the test because it was **incomplete**.
   not correct   too short   (not finished)
4. Will you **wind** the music box for the baby?
   air in motion   injury in which the skin is broken
   (tighten the spring by turning a key)
5. To enroll in the school, you must bring your birth certificate or some other legal **record** for identification.
   to keep an account   a flat disk that plays music
   (written or official evidence)
6. We use the crystal **pitcher** when we have company.
   printed likeness of a person or object
   baseball team member   (container for pouring)
7. This block is as **light as a feather**!
   very heavy   (not heavy at all)   bright
8. The whole family was there when Bill and Lynn **tied the knot** last weekend.
   were caught in a trap   bought a house   (got married)
9. I will have to **foot the bill** for the damage you caused.
   kick   (pay for)   seek payment
10. Carol **lost her cool** when the party was called off.
    (got angry)   had a fever   went home
11. The kite **soared like an eagle**.
    flapped and fluttered   (glided along high in the air)
    crashed to the ground

Grade 5 - Comprehensive Curriculum

Page 42

Review

Directions: Write a synonym for each word.

1. amusing _____ 3. terrifying _____
2. prison _____ 4. flee _____

Directions: Write an antonym for each word.

5. insult _____ 7. discourage _____
6. famine _____

Directions: Write a _____ *Answers will vary.*

9. _____

Directions: W_____ containing a simile.

10. _____

Directions: Write a sentence containing a metaphor.

11. _____

Directions: Write the letter of the correct meaning for the idiom in each sentence.

a. made a thoughtless remark
b. lost an opportunity
c. pay for
d. feeling very sad
e. excited and happy

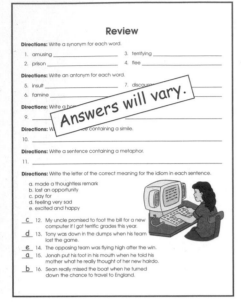

_c_ 12. My uncle promised to foot the bill for a new computer if I got terrific grades this year.

_d_ 13. Tony was down in the dumps when his team lost the game.

_e_ 14. The opposing team was flying high after the win.

_a_ 15. Jonah put his foot in his mouth when he told his mother what he really thought of her new hairdo.

_b_ 16. Sean really missed the boat when he turned down the chance to travel to England.

Page 43

Using a Dictionary

Directions: Read about dictionaries. Then answer the questions.

Dictionaries are books that give definitions of words. Dictionaries list words in alphabetical order. **Guide words** at the top of each page show the first and last words listed on the page. All other words on the page are listed in alphabetical order between the guide words. This helps you locate the word you want quickly and easily.

In addition to definitions, dictionaries also show the following: how to pronounce, or say, each word; the individual syllables found in each word; the part of speech for each word; and the plural form or verb forms if the base word changes.

Some dictionaries provide considerably more information. For example, *The Tormont Webster's Illustrated Encyclopedic Dictionary* includes many color illustrations of terms, a pronunciation key on every other page and two pages of introductory information on how to use the dictionary effectively.

Other highlights of the *Tormont Webster* are **historic labels** that tell the history of words no longer in common use; **geographic labels** that tell in what part of the world uncommon words are used; **stylistic labels** that tell whether a word is formal, informal, humorous or a slang term; and **field labels** that tell what field of knowledge—such as medicine—the word is used in.

1. Where are guide words found? _at the top of each page_

2. What is the purpose of guide words? _They show the first and last words listed on the page._

3. Which label tells if a word is a slang term? _stylistic_

4. Which label tells the history of a word? _historic_

5. Which type of information is not provided for each word in the dictionary?

☐ definition
☐ part of speech
☑ picture

Page 44

Using a Dictionary

Directions: Use the dictionary entry below to answer the questions.

ad·he·sive (ad-he'-siv) adj. 1. Tending to adhere; sticky. 2. Gummed so as to adhere. n. 3. An adhesive substance such as paste or glue. **ad·he·sive·ly** adv. **ad·he·sive·ness** n.

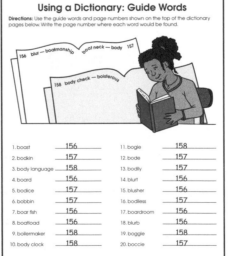

1. Based on the first definition of **adhesive**, what do you think **adhere** means? _to stick to something_

2. Which definition of **adhesive** is used in this sentence? The tape was so adhesive that we couldn't peel it loose. _tending to adhere, sticky_

3. Which part of speech is **adhesive** used in this sentence? We put a strong adhesive on the package to keep is sealed. _noun_

4. How many syllables does **adhesive** have? _three_

5. Is **adhesive** used as a noun or an adjective in this sentence? The adhesive we chose to use was not very gummy. _noun_

6. Adhesive and variations of the word can be used as what parts of speech? _noun, adjective, adverb_

Directions: Write sentences using these words.

7. adhesiveness _____

8. adhesively _____ *Answers will vary.*

9. adhere _____

Page 45

Using the Dictionary

Guide words are the words that appear at the top of dictionary pages. They show the first and last words on each page.

Directions: Read the guide words on each dictionary page below. Then look around for objects whose names come between the guide words. Write the names of the objects, and then number them in alphabetical order.

Answers will vary.

babble	buzz	magic	myself

cabin	cycle	pea	puzzle

dairy	dwarf	scar	sword

feast	future	tack	truth

Page 46

Using a Dictionary: Guide Words

Directions: Use the guide words and page numbers shown on the top of the dictionary pages below. Write the page number where each word would be found.

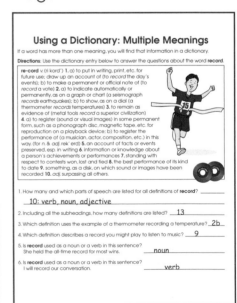

156 blur — boatmanship   boat neck — body 157

158 body check — boisterous

1. boast _156_   11. bogie _158_
2. bodkin _157_   12. bode _157_
3. body language _158_   13. bodily _157_
4. board _156_   14. blurt _156_
5. bodice _157_   15. blusher _156_
6. bobbin _157_   16. bodless _157_
7. boar fish _156_   17. boardroom _156_
8. boatload _156_   18. blurb _156_
9. boilermaker _158_   19. boggle _158_
10. body clock _158_   20. boccie _157_

Page 47

Using a Dictionary: Multiple Meanings

If a word has more than one meaning, you will find that information in a dictionary.

Directions: Use the dictionary entry below to answer the questions about the word **record**.

re·cord v. (ri kord') 1. a) to put in writing, print, etc. for future use; draw up an account of (to *record* the day's events); b) to make a permanent or official note of (to *record* a vote) 2. a) to indicate automatically or permanently, as on a graph or chart (a seismograph *records* earthquakes); b) to show, as on a dial (a thermometer *records* temperatures) 3. to remain as evidence of (metal tools *record* a superior civilization) 4. a) to register (sound or visual images) in some permanent form, such as a phonograph disc, magnetic tape, etc. for reproduction on a playback device; b) to register the performance of (a musician, actor, composition, etc.) in this way. (for n. & adj. rek' erd) 5. an account of facts or events preserved, esp. in writing 6. information or knowledge about a person's achievements or performances 7. standing with respect to contests won, lost and tied 8. the best performance of its kind to date 9. something, as a disk, on which sound or images have been recorded 10. *adj.* surpassing all others.

1. How many and which parts of speech are listed for all definitions of **record**? _10: verb, noun, adjective_

2. Including all the subheadings, how many definitions are listed? _13_

3. Which definition uses the example of a thermometer recording a temperature? _2b_

4. Which definition describes a record you might play to listen to music? _9_

5. Is **record** used as a noun or a verb in this sentence? She held the all-time record for most wins. _noun_

6. Is **record** used as a noun or a verb in this sentence? I will record our conversation. _verb_

Page 48

Multiple Meanings

Directions: Circle the correct definition of the bold word in each sentence. The first one has been done for you.

1. Try to **flag** down a car to get us some help!
   - **to signal to stop**
   - cloth used as symbol

2. We listened to the **band** play the National Anthem.
   - **group of musicians**
   - a binding or tie

3. He was the **sole** survivor of the plane crash.
   - bottom of the foot
   - **one and only**

4. I am going to **pound** the nail with this hammer.
   - **to hit hard**
   - a unit of weight

5. He lived on what little **game** he could find in the woods.
   - **animals for hunting**
   - form of entertainment

6. We are going to **book** the midnight flight from Miami.
   - **to reserve in advance**
   - a written work

7. The **pitcher** looked toward first base before throwing the ball.
   - **baseball team member**
   - container for pouring

8. My grandfather and I played a **game** of checkers last night.
   - animals for hunting
   - **form of entertainment**

9. They raise the **flag** over City Hall every morning.
   - to signal to stop
   - **cloth used as symbol**

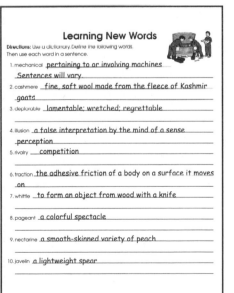

Page 49

Using a Dictionary: Choosing the Correct Word

Directions: Use a dictionary to look up the words in parenthesis. Then write the correct words in the blanks.

1. gallery — 1. Our class visited an art (galley/**gallery**) last week to learn about paintings and sculptures.
2. scrutinize — 2. He didn't (**scrutinize**/scruple) his essay very carefully before handing it in.
3. pliable — 3. She squeezed the clay in her hands until it became (plentiful/**pliable**).
4. laudable — 4. The quarterback's (**laudable**/laughable) performance helped his team win the game.
5. astronomy — 5. The science that deals with the universe beyond Earth's atmosphere is known as (**astronomy**/astrology).
6. grateful — 6. My mother was (**grateful**/graphic) that I helped her with the dishes.
7. tangible — 7. The police did not have any (tantamount/**tangible**) evidence that the man was guilty.
8. unfortunate — 8. It was very (**unfortunate**/unfamiliar) that she broke her arm right before the big game.
9. trowel — 9. The gardener was using a (trough/**trowel**) to dig up the flowers.
10. apparel — 10. That company manufactures men's and women's (appendage/**apparel**).
11. decompose — 11. After vegetable scraps (**decompose**/decongest), you can put them on your garden as fertilizer.
12. nocturnal — 12. Most bats are (**nocturnal**/noble) and sleep during the day.
13. venetian — 13. We bought some (venerable/**venetian**) blinds for our windows instead of curtains.
14. exasperated — 14. The noisy class (**exasperated**/exaggerated) the teacher.
15. parole — 15. The prisoner was released on (parody/**parole**).

Page 50

Learning New Words

Directions: Write a word from the box to complete each sentence. Use a dictionary to look up words you are unsure of.

bouquet	unconscious	inspire	disability
inherit	hovering	assault	enclosure
commotion	criticize		

1. He was knocked **unconscious** by the blow to his head.
2. Megan never let her **disability** stand in the way of accomplishing what she wanted.
3. The teacher burst into the noisy room and demanded to know what all the **commotion** was about.
4. He offered her a **bouquet** of flowers as a truce after their argument.
5. The zoo was in the process of building a new **enclosure** for the elephants.
6. The mother was **hovering** over her sick child.
7. The movie was meant to **inspire** people to do good deeds.
8. My friend will eventually **inherit** a fortune from his grandmother.
9. Not many people enjoy having someone **criticize** their work.
10. The female leopard led the **assault** on the herd of zebras.

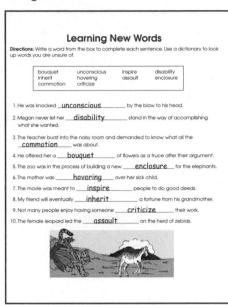

Page 51

Learning New Words

Directions: Use a dictionary. Define the following words. Then use each word in a sentence.

1. mechanical **pertaining to or involving machines**
   Sentences will vary.
2. cashmere **fine, soft wool made from the fleece of Kashmir goats**
3. deplorable **lamentable; wretched; regrettable**
4. illusion **a false interpretation by the mind of a sense perception**
5. rivalry **competition**
6. traction **the adhesive friction of a body on a surface it moves on**
7. whittle **to form an object from wood with a knife**
8. pageant **a colorful spectacle**
9. nectarine **a smooth-skinned variety of peach**
10. javelin **a lightweight spear**

Page 52

Using a Thesaurus

A **thesaurus** is a type of reference book that lists words in alphabetical order followed by their synonyms and antonyms. **Synonyms** are words that mean the same. **Antonyms** are words that mean the opposite.

A thesaurus is an excellent tool for finding "just the right word." It is also a valuable resource for finding a variety of synonyms and/or antonyms to make your writing livelier.

Each main entry in a thesaurus consists of a word followed by the word's part of speech, its definition, an example, a list of related words and other information.

Here is a typical entry in a thesaurus, with an explanation of terms below:

SLOW
ADJ **SYN** deliberate, dilatory, laggard, leisurely, unhasty, unhurried **REL** lateness, limited, measured, slowish, steady, unhurrying, slow-footed, plodding, pokey, straggling, snail-like **IDIOM** as slow as molasses in January; as slow as a turtle **CON** blitz, quick, rapid, swift **ANT** fast

ADJ means adjective
CON means contrasted words
SYN means synonym
ANT means antonym
REL means related words
idiom means a common phrase that is not literal

Directions: Use the thesaurus entry to answer the questions.

1. What is the antonym listed for **slow**? **fast**
2. How many contrasting words are listed for **slow**? **4**
3. How many synonyms are listed for **slow**? **6**
4. What is **slow** compared to in the two idioms listed? **molasses, turtle**
5. What is the last related word listed for **slow**? **snail-like**

Page 53

Using a Thesaurus to Find Synonyms

A thesaurus can help you find synonyms.
Example:
FIND:
VERB **SYN** locate, discover, detect, uncover, see, etc.

Directions: Use a thesaurus. Replace each word in bold with a synonym. **Sample answers:**

1. My father does not like our **artificial** Christmas tree.
   take
2. The **fabulous** home sat on a large hill overlooking a wooded ravine.
   terrific
3. My dog is allowed to be **loose** if someone is home.
   free
4. A **peaceful** rally was held to bring attention to the needs of the homeless.
   nonviolent
5. The artist completed his **sketch** of the girl.
   drawing
6. The **timid** boy could not bring himself to speak to the man at the counter.
   shy
7. My family is cutting down the **timber** at the back of our property.
   trees
8. Her necklace was very **attractive**.
   pretty
9. The girl looked hopelessly at her **clothes** and moaned that she had nothing to wear.
   apparel
10. The team's **feat** of winning 20 games in a row was amazing.
    accomplishment

Grade 5 - Comprehensive Curriculum

Page 54

Using a Thesaurus

Directions: Use a thesaurus to list as many synonyms (SYN) as possible for the following words. **Answers will vary but may include:**

1. calm __placid, serene, tranquil, peaceful__
2. hunt __chase, stalk, follow, pursue__
3. quilt __coverlet, comforter, goosedown__
4. tender __gentle, kind, affectionate, merciful__
5. vacate __abandon, evacuate, leave, quit__

Directions: Use a thesaurus to list as many related words (REL) as possible for the following words.

6. value __importance, goodness, measurement, approbation__
7. __disagreement, unconformity, change, deviation, inequality__
8. enable __empower, allow, permit__

Directions: Use a thesaurus to list one idiom for each of the following words.

9. beauty __Beauty is only skin deep.__
10. cake __You can't have your cake and eat it too.__

dog
pooch
canine
puppy
cur
bow wow
mongrel
mutt

Page 55

Using a Thesaurus to Find Antonyms

Antonyms are words that mean the opposite. Antonyms can also be found in a thesaurus. They are identified by the abbreviation ANT.

Examples:

FOUND:
VERB **ANT** misplaced, gone, lost, missing, mislaid, etc.

RIDDLE:
NOUN **ANT** key, solution, answer, etc.

ANCIENT:
ADJECTIVE **ANT** new, recent, current, etc.

Directions: Use a thesaurus to replace each word in bold with an antonym.
Sample answers:

1. Today's weather will undoubtedly be very **humid**. __dry__
2. Can you **give** my sister a napkin? __take__
3. The man **insulted** me by laughing at my artwork. __complimented__
4. I thought the rules for the classroom were too **lax**. __strict__
5. The broken leg was quite **painful**. __painless__
6. We made great **progress** last night on the parade float. __delay__
7. The girl received a **reward** for returning the lost wallet. __penalty__
8. The teacher asked us to **separate** the types of art brushes. __combine__
9. The home was decorated in a **simple** manner. __extravagant__
10. They became very **tense** during the earthquake. __relaxed__
11. Mr. Kurtzman gave us a math test **today**. __yesterday__
12. My father loves hiking in the **hills**. __valleys__
13. Stephen ran over my **new** red bike. __old__

Page 56

Comprehension: Word Origins

Did you ever wonder why we call our mid-day meal "lunch"? Or where the name "Abraham" came from? Or why one of our lovely eastern states is called "Vermont"?

These and other words have a history. The study of where words came from and how they began is called **etymology** (ett-a-mol-o-gee).

The word **lunch** comes from the Spanish word **longia**, which means "a slice of ham." Long ago, Spanish people ate a slice of ham for their mid-day meal. Eventually, what they ate became the word for the meal itself. Still later, it came to be pronounced "lunch" in English.

Abraham also has an interesting history. Originally, it came from the Hebrew word **avarahem**. Abraham means "father of many."

City and state names are often based on the names of Native American tribes or describe the geography of the area. **Vermont** is actually made from two French words. **Vert** is French for "green." **Mont** is French for "mountain."

Directions: Answer these questions about word origins.

1. What is the study of the history and origin of words? __etymology__
2. From which language did the word **lunch** come? __Spanish__
3. What is the French word for "green"? __vert__
4. Vermont comes from two words of what language?
   - [ ] Spanish
   - [ ] English
   - [x] French
5. Which is not correct about the origin of names of cities and states?
   - [ ] They describe geography.
   - [ ] They name Native American tribes.
   - [x] They are mostly French in origin.

Page 57

Comprehension and Context

Comprehension is understanding what is seen, heard or read.

Context is the rest of the words in a sentence or the sentences before or after a word. Context can help with comprehension.

Context clues help you figure out the meaning of a word by relating it to other words in the sentence.

Directions: Use the context clues in the sentences to find the meanings of the bold words.

1. Jane was a **wizard** at games. She mastered them in no time and seldom lost.
   - [ ] evil magician
   - [x] gifted person
   - [ ] average player

2. The holiday was so special that she was sure she'd never forget it. The memory would be **imprinted** forever on her mind.
   - [ ] found
   - [ ] weighed
   - [x] fixed

3. "John will believe anything anyone tells him," his teacher said. "He's a very **impressionable** young man."
   - [x] easily influenced
   - [ ] unhappy
   - [ ] unintelligent

4. "Do you really think it's **prudent** to spend all your money on clothes?" his mother asked crossly.
   - [ ] foolish
   - [x] wise
   - [ ] funny

5. "Your plan has **merit**," Elizabeth's father said. "Let me give it some thought."
   - [x] value
   - [ ] awards
   - [ ] kindness

6. John was very **gregarious** and loved being around people.
   - [ ] shy
   - [x] outgoing
   - [ ] unfriendly

Page 58

Classifying

Classifying means putting items into categories based on similar characteristics.

Example: Apple pie, cookies and ice cream could be classified as desserts.

Directions: Cross out the word in each group that does not belong. Then add a word of your own that does belong. The first one has been done for you.

1. wren / robin / ~~feather~~ / sparrow / eagle __bluebird__
2. sofa / stool / carpet / bench / chair
3. lettuce / salad / broccoli
4. pencil / pen
5. perch / tuna / bass / penguin
6. rapid / quick / swift / speedy / unhurried
7. lemon / daisy / lime / grapefruit __melon__

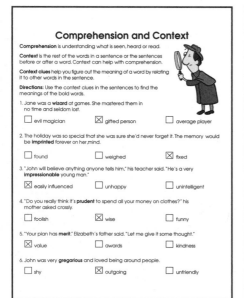

Directions: Write [a word] in each group of words. Then write a word of your own that [belongs].

Sample answers:

Weather	Parts of a Leg
blizzard	ankle
hurricane	shin
thunder	thigh
__tornado__	__knee__

radio parts	Winter Sports
antenna	hockey
speaker	ice skating
battery	bobsledding
__knob__	__skiing__

Page 59

Classifying — Sample Answers:

Directions: Write three objects which could belong in each category.

1. whales	humpback	blue	killer
2. songs	Happy Birthday	Blue Suede Shoes	Are You Sleeping?
3. sports stars	Michael Jordan	Steffi Graf	Mark Martin
4. fruit	apple	lemon	banana
5. schools	Lincoln High	Harvard	UCLA
6. teachers	Ms. McCall	Mr. Springer	Dr. Burns
7. tools	hammer	broom	ax
8. friends	Mary	Sue	Jon
9. books	Huckleberry Finn	Wrinkle in Time	Watership Down
10. mammals	bear	bat	people
11. fish	bass	cod	shark
12. desserts	cookies	cake	pie
13. cars	Ford	Chevy	VW
14. hobbies	collect stamps	painting	gardening
15. vegetables	potatoes	spinach	eggplant
16. insects	bee	wasp	hornet

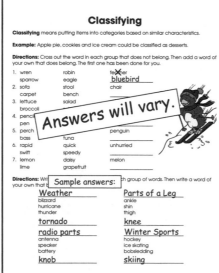

Page 60

Classifying: Regional Forecast

Directions: Read the forecast. Then write words in the correct categories.

The very warm, early spring weather will continue to spread along the East Coast today. With some sunshine, afternoon temperatures will climb to 90 degrees in many places. Columbia, South Carolina and neighboring areas could reach 100 degrees. Showers are expected from Washington, D.C. to New York City. Severe thunderstorms are likely in Virginia and North Carolina. Central South Carolina will be under a tornado watch during the afternoon.

Cities
Columbia
Washington, D.C.
New York City

States
South Carolina
Virginia
North Carolina

Weather Conditions
sunshine
showers
thunderstorms
tornado watch

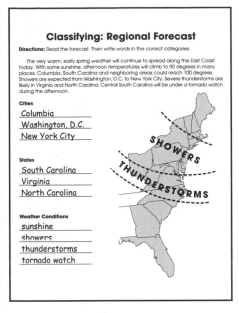

Page 61

Analogies

An **analogy** is a way of comparing objects to show how they relate.

Example: Nose is to smell as tongue is to taste.

Directions: Write the correct word on the blank to fill in the missing part of each analogy. The first one has been done for you.

1. **Scissors** are to paper as saw is to wood. — fold / (scissors) / thin
2. Man is to boy as woman is to **girl**. — mother / (girl) / lady
3. **Attic** is to cellar as sky is to ground. — down / (attic) / up
4. Rag is to dust as **broom** is to sweep. — floor / straw / (broom)
5. Freezer is to cold as stove is to **hot**. — cook / (hot) / recipe
6. Car is to **garage** as book is to bookshelf. — ride / gas / (garage)
7. Window is to **glass** as car is to metal. — (glass) / clear / house
8. Eyes are to seeing as feet are to **walking**. — legs / (walking) / shoes
9. Gas is to car as **electricity** is to lamp. — (electricity) / plug / cord
10. Refrigerator is to food as **closet** is to clothes. — fold / material / (closet)
11. Floor is to down as ceiling is to **up**. — high / over / (up)
12. Pillow is to soft as rock is to **hard**. — dirt / (hard) / hurt
13. Carpenter is to house as poet is to **verse**. — (verse) / novel / writing
14. Lamp is to light as clock is to **time**. — (time) / hands / numbers
15. **Palm** is to hand as sole is to foot. — wrist / finger / (palm)

Page 62

Answers will vary. **Analogies**
Examples given.

Directions: Write your own words on the blanks to complete each analogy. The first one has been done for you.

1. Fuse is to firecracker as wick is to **candle**.
2. Wheel is to steering as **brake** is to stopping.
3. Scissors are to **cut** as needles are to sew.
4. Water is to skiing as rink is to **skating**.
5. Steam shovel is to dig as tractor is to **plow**.
6. Stick is to hockey as **bat** is to baseball.
7. Watch is to television as **listen** is to radio.
8. **Geese** are to goose as children are to child.
9. Multiply is to multiplication as **subtract** is to subtraction.
10. Milk is to cow as egg is to **hen**.
11. Yellow is to banana as **red** is to tomato.
12. **Fast** is to slow as day is to night.
13. Pine is to tree as **daisy** is to flower.
14. Zipper is to jacket as **button** is to shirt.
15. Museum is to painting as library is to **book**.
16. Petal is to flower as branch is to **tree**.
17. Cow is to barn as car is to **garage**.
18. Dresser is to bedroom as **stove** is to kitchen.
19. Teacher is to **student** as doctor is to patient.
20. Ice is to cold as fire is to **hot**.

Page 63

Synonym and Antonym Analogies

Analogies are a way of comparing items to show how they are related. Analogies can show different types of relationships. Two relationships analogies might show are synonyms or antonyms.

Examples:
Antonyms: hot is to cold as happy is to sad
Synonyms: happy is to glad as run is to jog

You can write an analogy this way:
slow:fast::up:down
You read it this way:
slow is to fast as up is to down

Directions: Write **S** for synonym or **A** for antonym in the blanks in front of each analogy. Then complete the analogies by choosing a word from the box.

| life | run | comforter | fail | photograph |
| above | feline | play | drape | different |

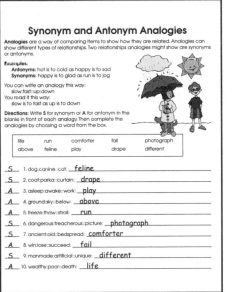

- **S** 1. dog:canine::cat: **feline**
- **S** 2. coat:parka::curtain: **drape**
- **A** 3. asleep:awake::work: **play**
- **A** 4. ground:sky::below: **above**
- **A** 5. freeze:thaw::stroll: **run**
- **S** 6. dangerous:treacherous::picture: **photograph**
- **S** 7. ancient:old::bedspread: **comforter**
- **A** 8. win:lose::succeed: **fail**
- **S** 9. manmade:artificial::unique: **different**
- **A** 10. wealthy:poor::death: **life**

Page 64

Part/Whole and Cause/Effect Analogies

Other types of analogies are part to whole and cause and effect.

Example:
Part to whole: fingers:hand::toes:foot
Cause and effect: rain:flood::matches:fire

Directions: Write **P** for part to whole or **C** for cause and effect in the blanks in front of each analogy. Then complete the analogies by choosing a word from the box.

tree	bike	punishment	stomachache
beach	laugh	fingers	hawk
pencil	blizzard		

- **P** 1. hair:head::fingernails: **fingers**
- **C** 2. germ:virus::misbehavior: **punishment**
- **C** 3. fall:injury::overeating: **stomachache**
- **P** 4. keyboard:computer::wheels: **bike**
- **P** 5. tongue:shoe::sand: **beach**
- **C** 6. practice:win::joke: **laugh**
- **C** 7. read:learn::snow: **blizzard**
- **P** 8. pouch:kangaroo::beak: **hawk**
- **P** 9. leaf:plant::bark: **tree**
- **P** 10. ink:pen::lead: **pencil**

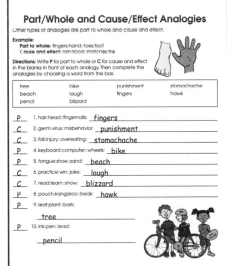

Page 65

Facts and Opinions

A **fact** is information that can be proved.

Example: Hawaii is a state.

An **opinion** is a belief. It tells what someone thinks. It cannot be proved.

Example: Hawaii is the prettiest state.

Directions: Write **f** (fact) or **o** (opinion) on the line by each sentence. The first one has been done for you.

- **f** 1. Hawaii is the only island state.
- **o** 2. The best fishing is in Michigan.
- **o** 3. It is easy to find a job in Wyoming.
- **f** 4. Trenton is the capital of New Jersey.
- **f** 5. Kentucky is nicknamed the Bluegrass State.
- **o** 6. The friendliest people in the United States live in Georgia.
- **o** 7. The cleanest beaches are in California.
- **o** 8. Summers are most beautiful in Arizona.
- **f** 9. Only one percent of North Dakota is forest or woodland.
- **f** 10. New Mexico produces almost half of the nation's uranium.
- **f** 11. The first shots of the Civil War were fired in South Carolina on April 12, 1861.
- **f** 12. The varied geographical features of Washington include mountains, deserts, a rainforest and a volcano.
- **f** 13. In 1959, Alaska and Hawaii became the 49th and 50th states admitted to the Union.
- **f** 14. Wyandotte Cave, one of the largest caves in the United States, is in Indiana.

Directions: Write one fact and one opinion about your own state.

Fact: _____

Answers will vary.

Opinion: _____

Grade 5 - Comprehensive Curriculum

Page 66

Facts and Opinions

A **fact** is a statement based on truth. It can be proven. **Opinions** are the beliefs of an individual that may or may not be true.

Examples:
Fact: Alaska is a state.
Opinion: Alaska is the most magnificent state.

Directions: Write **F** if the statement is a fact. Write **O** if the statement is an opinion.

1. _O_ The Grand Canyon is the most scenic site in the United States.
2. _F_ Dinosaurs roamed Earth millions of years ago.
3. _F_ Scientists have discovered how to clone sheep.
4. _O_ All people should attend this fair.
5. _O_ Purebreds are the best dogs to own because they are intelligent.
6. _O_ Nobody likes being bald.
7. _O_ Students should be required to get straight A's to participate in extracurricular activities.
8. _F_ Reading is an important skill that is vital in many careers.
9. _O_ Snakes do not make good pets.
10. _F_ Many books have been written about animals.
11. _F_ Thomas Edison invented the lightbulb.
12. _O_ Most people like to read science fiction.
13. _F_ Insects have three body parts.

Page 67

Facts and Opinions

Directions: Read the articles about cats. List the facts and opinions.

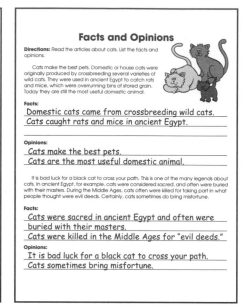

Cats make the best pets. Domestic or house cats were originally produced by crossbreeding several varieties of wild cats. They were used in ancient Egypt to catch rats and mice, which were overrunning bins of stored grain. Today they are still the most useful domestic animal.

Facts:
Domestic cats came from crossbreeding wild cats.
Cats caught rats and mice in ancient Egypt.

Opinions:
Cats make the best pets.
Cats are the most useful domestic animal.

It is bad luck for a black cat to cross your path. This is one of the many legends about cats. In ancient Egypt, for example, cats were considered sacred, and often were buried with their masters. During the Middle Ages, cats often were killed for taking part in what people thought were evil deeds. Certainly, cats sometimes do bring misfortune.

Facts:
Cats were sacred in ancient Egypt and often were buried with their masters.
Cats were killed in the Middle Ages for "evil deeds."

Opinions:
It is bad luck for a black cat to cross your path.
Cats sometimes bring misfortune.

Page 68

Facts and Opinions

Directions: Write nine statements that are facts and nine statements that are opinions.

FACTS
1. _____
2. _____
3. _____
4. _____
5. _____
6. _____
7. _____
8. _____
9. _____

OPINIONS
1. _____
2. _____
3. _____
4. _____
5. _____
6. _____
7. _____
8. _____
9. _____

Answers will vary.

Page 69

Cause and Effect

A **cause** is an event or reason which has an effect on something else.

Example:
The heavy rains produced flooding in Chicago.
Heavy rains were the **cause** of the flooding in Chicago.

An **effect** is an event that results from a cause.

Example:
Flooding in Chicago was due to the heavy rains.
Flooding was the **effect** caused by the heavy rains.

Directions: Read the paragraphs. Complete the charts by writing the missing cause (reason) or effect (result).

Club-footed toads are small toads that live in the rainforests of Central and South America. Because they give off a poisonous substance on their skins, other animals cannot eat them.

Cause:
They give off a poisonous substance.

Effect:
Other animals cannot eat them.

Civets (siv its) are weasel-like animals. The best known of the civets is the mongoose, which eats rats and snakes. For this reason, it is welcome around homes in its native India.

Cause:
It eats rats and snakes.

Effect:
It is welcome around homes in its native India.

Bluebirds can be found in most areas of the United States. Like other members of the thrush family of birds, young bluebirds have speckled breasts. This makes them difficult to see and helps them hide from their enemies. The Pilgrims called them "blue robins" because they are much like the English robin. They are the same size and have the same red breast and friendly song as the English robin.

Cause:
Young bluebirds have speckled breasts.
They are much like English robins.

Effect:
It helps them hide from enemies.
The Pilgrims called them "blue robins."

Page 70

Review

Directions: Write the answers.

1. Define classifying. _putting items into categories based on similar characteristics_
2. Add words to these classifications:

meat:
hamburger
steak
sirloin tip

music groups:
the Pointer Sisters
the Beatles

Answers will vary.

bre___
or___
cra___
gra___ juice

fuschia
melon

3. What is an analogy? _a way of comparing objects to show how they relate_
4. Give an example of an analogy. _____
5. Write two sentences that are facts. _____
6. Write two sentences that are opinions. _____
7. Write an example of cause and effect. Underline the cause. Circle the effect. _____

Page 71

Review

Directions: Write three statements about yourself that are facts.
1. _____
2. _____
3. _____

Directions: Write three statements ___ that are opinions.
4. _____
5. _____
6. _____

Answers will vary.

Directions: Write a category name for each set of words. **Sample answers:**

7. Arizona, Wisconsin, Texas _states_
8. mouse, rat, squirrel _rodents_
9. saddle, reins, halter _horse equipment_

Directions: Finish the analogies with words from the box. Not all words will be used.

10. look:see::kind:
nice
11. bald:hairy::difficult:
easy
12. insomnia:nightmares::crumbs:
pretzels
13. engine:car::heart:
human

friend
nice
ants
pretzels
human
hard
easy
alone

Page 72

Main Idea

The **main idea** is the most important idea, or main point, in a sentence, paragraph or story.

Directions: Read the paragraphs below. For each paragraph, underline the sentence that tells the main idea.

Sometimes people think they have to choose between exercise and fun. For many people, it is more fun to watch television than to run 5 miles. Yet, if you don't exercise, your body gets soft and out of shape. You move more slowly. You may even think more slowly. But why do something that isn't fun? Well, there are many ways to exercise and have fun.

One family solved the exercise problem by using their TV. They hooked up the television to an electric generator. The generator was operated by an exercise bike. Anyone who wanted to watch TV had to ride the bike. The room with their television in it must have been quite a sight!

Think of the times when you are just "hanging out" with your friends. You go outside and jump rope, play ball, run races, and so on. Soon you are all laughing and having a good time. Many group activities can provide you with exercise and be fun, too.

Maybe there aren't enough kids around after school for group games. Perhaps you are by yourself. Then what? You can get plenty of exercise just by walking, biking or even dancing. In the morning, walk the long way to the bus. Ride your bike to and from school. Practice the newest dance by yourself. Before you know it, you will be the fittest dancer of all your friends!

Directions: Write other ideas you have for combining fun and exercise below.

Answers will vary.

Page 73

Reading Skills: Skimming

Skimming an article means to read quickly, looking for headings and key words to give an overall idea of the content of an article or to find a particular fact. When skimming for answers, read the questions first. Then look for specific words that will help locate the answers.

Directions: Skim the paragraph to answer this question.

1. What "marvel" is the paragraph about? _Grand Canyon_

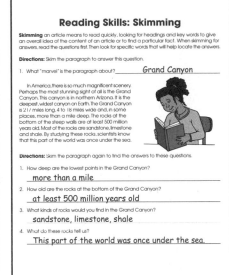

In America, there is so much magnificent scenery. Perhaps the most stunning sight of all is the Grand Canyon. This canyon is in northern Arizona. It is the deepest, widest canyon on Earth. The Grand Canyon is 217 miles long, 4 to 18 miles wide and, in some places, more than a mile deep. The rocks at the bottom of the steep walls are at least 500 million years old. Most of the rocks are sandstone, limestone and shale. By studying these rocks, scientists know that this part of the world was once under the sea.

Directions: Skim the paragraph again to find the answers to these questions.

1. How deep are the lowest points in the Grand Canyon?
   more than a mile
2. How old are the rocks at the bottom of the Grand Canyon?
   at least 500 million years old
3. What kinds of rocks would you find in the Grand Canyon?
   sandstone, limestone, shale
4. What do these rocks tell us?
   This part of the world was once under the sea.

Page 74

Reading Skills: Maps

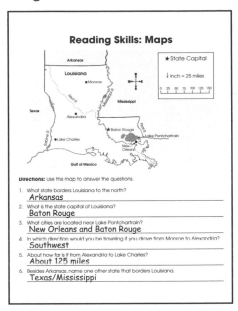

Directions: Use this map to answer the questions.

1. What state borders Louisiana to the north?
   Arkansas
2. What is the state capital of Louisiana?
   Baton Rouge
3. What cities are located near Lake Pontchartrain?
   New Orleans and Baton Rouge
4. In which direction would you be traveling if you drove from Monroe to Alexandria?
   Southwest
5. About how far is it from Alexandria to Lake Charles?
   About 125 miles
6. Besides Arkansas, name one other state that borders Louisiana.
   Texas/Mississippi

Page 75

Reading Skills: Maps

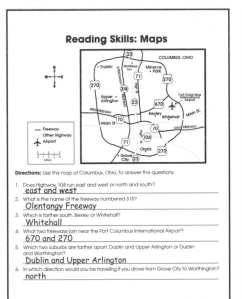

Directions: Use this map of Columbus, Ohio, to answer the questions.

1. Does Highway 104 run east and west or north and south?
   east and west
2. What is the name of the freeway numbered 315?
   Olentangy Freeway
3. Which is farther south, Bexley or Whitehall?
   Whitehall
4. What two freeways join near the Port Columbus International Airport?
   670 and 270
5. Which two suburbs are farther apart, Dublin and Upper Arlington or Dublin and Worthington?
   Dublin and Upper Arlington
6. In which direction would you be traveling if you drove from Grove City to Worthington?
   north

Page 76

Sequencing: Maps

Directions: Read the information about planning a map.

Maps have certain features that help you to read them. A **compass rose** points out directions. Color is often used so you can easily see where one area (such as a county, state or country) stops and the next starts.

To be accurate, a map must be drawn to scale. The **scale** of a map shows how much area is represented by a given measurement. The scale can be small: one inch = one mile; or large: one inch = 1,000 miles.

Symbols are another map tool. An airplane may represent an airport. Sometimes a symbol does not look like what it represents. Cities are often represented by dots. A map **legend** tells what each symbol means.

One of the best ways to learn about maps is to make one of your own. You may be surprised at how much you learn about your neighborhood, too. You will need a large piece of paper, a ruler, a pencil and colored pencils.

You will need to choose the area you want to map out. It is important to decide on the scale for your map. It could be small: one inch = three feet, if you are mapping out your own backyard. Be sure to include symbols, like a picnic table to represent a park or a flag to represent a school. Don't forget to include the symbols and other important information in your legend.

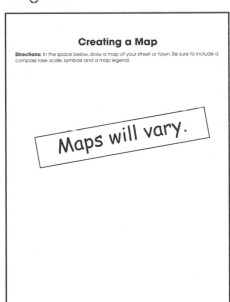

Directions: Number in order the steps to making your own map.

3 Figure out the scale that will work best for your map.
1 Obtain a large piece of paper, ruler, pencil and colored pencils.
5 Make a legend explaining the symbols you used.
6 Draw your map!
4 Draw symbols to represent features of the area you are mapping.
2 Decide on the area you want to map out.

Page 77

Creating a Map

Directions: In the space below, draw a map of your street or town. Be sure to include a compass rose, scale, symbols and a map legend.

Maps will vary.

Grade 5 - Comprehensive Curriculum

Page 78

Following Directions

Directions: Read and follow the directions.

1. Draw a vertical line from the top mid-point of the square to the bottom mid-point of the square.
2. Draw a diagonal line from top left to bottom right of the square.
3. In each of the two triangles, draw a heart.
4. Draw a picture of a cat's face below the square.
5. Draw a horizontal line from the left mid-point to the right mid-point of the square.
6. Draw two intersecting lines in each of the two smaller squares so they are equally divided into four quadrants.
7. Draw a triangle-shaped roof on the square.
8. Draw a circle next to each heart.
9. Write your name in the roof section of your drawing.

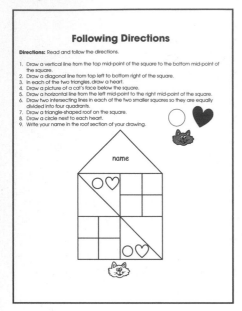

Page 79

Following Directions: Continents

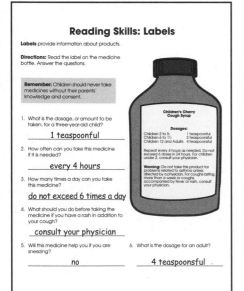

Directions: Read the facts about the seven continents and follow the directions.

1. Asia is the largest continent. It has the largest land mass and the largest population. Draw a star on Asia.
2. Africa is the second largest continent. Write a **2** on Africa.
3. Australia is the smallest continent in area: 3 million square miles, compared to 17 million square miles for Asia. Write **3,000,000** on Australia.
4. Australia is not a very crowded continent, but it does not rank lowest in population. That honor goes to Antarctica, which has no permanent population at all! This ice-covered continent is too cold for life. Write **zero** on Antarctica.
5. Australia and Antarctica are the only continents entirely separated by water. Draw circles around Australia and Antarctica.
6. North America and South America are joined together by a narrow strip of land. It is called Central America. Write an **N** on North America, an **S** on South America and a **C** on Central America.
7. Asia and Europe are joined together over such a great distance that they are sometimes called one continent. The name given to it is Eurasia. Draw lines under the names of the two continents in Eurasia.

Page 80

Reading a Recipe

Directions: Read the recipe. Then answer the questions.

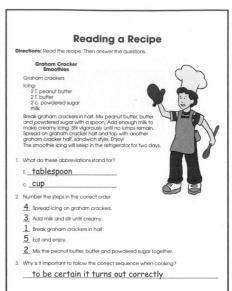

Graham Cracker Smoothies

Graham crackers
Icing:
  2 T. peanut butter
  2 T. butter
  2 c. powdered sugar
  milk

Break graham crackers in half. Mix peanut butter, butter and powdered sugar with a spoon. Add enough milk to make creamy icing. Stir vigorously until no lumps remain. Spread on graham cracker half and top with another graham cracker half, sandwich style. Enjoy!
The smoothie icing will keep in the refrigerator for two days.

1. What do these abbreviations stand for?

   T. _tablespoon_

   c. _cup_

2. Number the steps in the correct order.

   _4_ Spread icing on graham crackers.

   _3_ Add milk and stir until creamy.

   _1_ Break graham crackers in half.

   _5_ Eat and enjoy.

   _2_ Mix the peanut butter, butter and powdered sugar together.

3. Why is it important to follow the correct sequence when cooking?

   to be certain it turns out correctly

Page 81

Reading Skills: Labels

Labels provide information about products.

Directions: Read the label on the medicine bottle. Answer the questions.

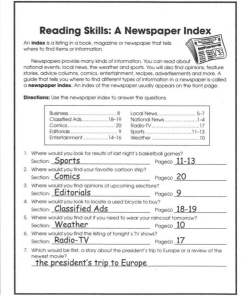

Remember: Children should never take medicines without their parents' knowledge and consent.

1. What is the dosage, or amount to be taken, for a three-year-old child?

   1 teaspoonful

2. How often can you take this medicine if it is needed?

   every 4 hours

3. How many times a day can you take this medicine?

   do not exceed 6 times a day

4. What should you do before taking the medicine if you have a rash in addition to your cough?

   consult your physician

5. Will this medicine help you if you are sneezing?

   _no_

6. What is the dosage for an adult?

   4 teaspoonsful

Page 82

Reading Skills: Newspapers

Directions: Write the answers.

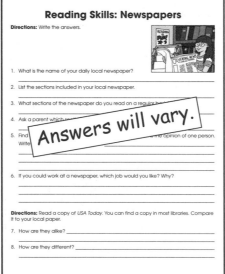

1. What is the name of your daily local newspaper?

2. List the sections included in your local newspaper.

3. What sections of the newspaper do you read on a regular basis?

4. Ask a parent which se~~ctions~~

5. Find ~~...~~ the opinion of one person. Write ~~...~~

Answers will vary.

6. If you could work at a newspaper, which job would you like? Why?

Directions: Read a copy of *USA Today*. You can find a copy in most libraries. Compare it to your local paper.

7. How are they alike? _____

8. How are they different? _____

Page 83

Reading Skills: A Newspaper Index

An **index** is a listing in a book, magazine or newspaper that tells where to find items or information.

Newspapers provide many kinds of information. You can read about national events, local news, the weather and sports. You will also find opinions, feature stories, advice columns, comics, entertainment, recipes, advertisements and more. A guide that tells you where to find different types of information in a newspaper is called a **newspaper index**. An index of the newspaper usually appears on the front page.

Directions: Use the newspaper index to answer the questions.

Business	8	Local News	5–7
Classified Ads	18–19	National News	1–4
Comics	20	Radio-TV	17
Editorials	9	Sports	11–13
Entertainment	14–16	Weather	10

1. Where would you look for results of last night's basketball games?
   Section: _Sports_   Page(s) _11–13_

2. Where would you find your favorite cartoon strip?
   Section: _Comics_   Page(s) _20_

3. Where would you find opinions of upcoming elections?
   Section: _Editorials_   Page(s) _9_

4. Where would you look to locate a used bicycle to buy?
   Section: _Classified Ads_   Page(s) _18–19_

5. Where would you find out if you need to wear your raincoat tomorrow?
   Section: _Weather_   Page(s) _10_

6. Where would you find the listing of tonight's TV shows?
   Section: _Radio-TV_   Page(s) _17_

7. Which would be first, a story about the president's trip to Europe or a review of the newest movie?
   the president's trip to Europe

Page 84

Reading Skills: Classified Ads

A **classified ad** is an advertisement in a newspaper or magazine offering a product or service for sale or rent.

Example: For Sale: Used 26" 30-speed bike. $100. Call 555-5555.

Directions: Read these advertisements. Answer the questions.

Pet Sitter
Going on Vacation?
Away for the Weekend?
I am 14 years old and have experience caring for dogs and cats in your home or mine.
Excellent References.
Call Sally Trent
Phone: 999-8250

1.
Yard Work
Breaking Your Back?
Give Mike and Jane a crack! Mowing, raking, trash hauled. References provided.
Call 555-9581.

2.
Pet Sitter:
Going on vacation? Away for the weekend? I am 14 years old and have experience caring for dogs and cats. Your home or mine. Excellent references.
Call Sally Trent.
Phone: 999-8250.

3.
Singing Lessons for All Ages!
Be popular at parties! Fulfill your dreams! 20 years coaching experience. Madame Rinaud . . . Coach to the Stars. 555-5331.

1. What is promised in the third ad? _popularity and fulfillment of dreams_
2. Is it fact or opinion? _opinion_
3. What fact is offered in the third ad? _20 years coaching experience_
4. Give an example of a slogan, or easy-to-remember phrase, that appears in one of the ads. _Example: Yard work breaking your back? Give Mike and Jane a crack!_
5. Which ad gives the most facts? _#2_
6. Which ad is based mostly on opinion? _#3_

Page 85

Reading Skills: Classified Ads

Directions: Write a classified ad for these topics. Include information about the item, a phone number and an eye-catching title.

1. An ad to wash cars

2. An ad for free puppies

3. An ad for somet... _Answers will vary._

4. An ad to sell your house

Page 86

Reading Skills: Schedules

A **schedule** lists events or programs by time, date and place or channel.

Example:

Packer Preseason Games

August 14	7 P.M.	NY Jets at Green Bay
August 23	7 P.M.	Denver Broncos at Madison
August 28	3 P.M.	Saints at New Orleans
September 2	Noon	Miami Dolphins at Green Bay

Directions: Use this newspaper television schedule to answer the questions.

Evening
6:00 ⑤ Let's Talk! Guest: Animal expert Jim Porter
⑥ Cartoons
⑧ News
⑨ News
7:00 ⑤ Farm Report
⑥ Movie. *A Laugh a Minute* (1955) James Rayburn. Comedy about a boy who wants to join the circus.
⑧ Spin for Dollars!
⑨ Cooking with Cathy. Tonight: Chicken with mushrooms
7:30 ⑤ Double Trouble (comedy). The twins disrupt the high school dance.
⑧ Wall Street Today: Stock Market Report
8:00 ⑤ NBA Basketball. Teams to be announced.
⑧ News Special. "Saving Our Waterways: Pollution in the Mississippi."
⑨ Movie. *At Day's End* (1981). Michael Collier, Julie Romer. Drama set in World War II.

1. What two stations have the news at 6:00? _8 and 9_
2. What time would you turn on the television to watch a funny movie? _7:00 P.M._ What channel? _5_
3. What could you watch if you are a sports fan? _NBA Basketball_ What time and channel is it on? _8:00 P.M. Channel 3_
4. Which show title sounds like it could be a game show? _Spin for Dollars!_
5. What show might you want to watch if you are interested in the environment? _"Saving Our Waterways: Pollution in the Mississippi"_ What time and channel is it on? _8:00 P.M. Channel 8_

Page 87

Review

Directions: Write the answers.

1. What is the purpose of a classified ad? _to sell an item or service_
2. Skim your local newspaper. List at least six categories of classified ads.
Answers may include:
cars/trucks   _antiques_
furniture   _computers_
real estate   _help wanted_
3. What sections are included in the index of your local newspaper?
Answers will vary.
4. What four pieces of information should a television program schedule contain?
day   _program name_
time   _channel_
5. What information is present on a medicine bottle?
dosage by age   _product name_
warning   _frequency and maximum dose_
6. Why is it important for medicine labels to include warnings?
so people know when to consult a physician

Page 88

Using Prior Knowledge: Books

Directions: Before reading about books in the following section, answer these questions.

1. What books have you read recently?

2. Write a summary of one of th... _Answers will vary._

3. Define the following types of books and, if possible, give an example of each.
biography: _story of a person's life, told by another_ _Examples will vary._
fiction: _non-factual literature_
mystery: _dealing with a puzzling event_
nonfiction: _a literary work other than fiction_

Page 89

Context Clues: Remember Who You Are

Directions: Read each paragraph. Then use context clues to figure out the meanings of the bold words.

During the 1940s, Esther Hautzig lived in the town of Vilna, which was then part of Poland. Shortly after the **outbreak** of World War II, she and her family were **deported** to Siberia by Russian communists who hated Jews. She told what happened to her and other Polish Jews in a book. The book is called *Remember Who You Are: Stories About Being Jewish*.

1. Choose the correct definition of **deported**.
☒ sent away   ☐ asked to go   ☐ invited to visit

2. Choose the correct definition of **outbreak**.
☒ a sudden occurrence   ☐ to leave suddenly

Remember Who You Are: Stories About Being Jewish is a nonfiction book that tells true stories. An interesting **fiction** book is *Leave the Cooking to Me* by Judie Angell. It tells the story of a girl named Shirley, who learns about cooking from her best friend's mother. Shirley gets very good at making fancy food. Most young people have a hard time finding jobs that pay well, but Shirley's cooking skills help her land a **lucrative** summer job.

3. Choose the correct definition of **fiction**.
☐ stories that are true   ☒ stories that are not true

4. Choose the correct definition of **lucrative**.
☐ interesting   ☒ profitable   ☐ nearby

Page 90

Comprehension: Books and More Books!

Variety is said to be the spice of life. Where books are concerned, variety is the key to reading pleasure. There is a type of book that appeals to every reader.

Each year, hundreds of new books are published for children. A popular series of books for girls between the ages of 8 and 12 is *Sweet Valley Kids*, written by Francine Pascal. All of Pascal's books are fictional stories about children who live in the town of Sweet Valley.

If you like legends, an interesting book is *Dream Wolf* by Paul Goble. *Dream Wolf* is a retelling of an old Native American legend. Legends are stories passed down from one generation to another that may or may not be true. Some of them are scary! *The Legend of Sleepy Hollow*, for example, is about a headless horseman. Other legends are about a person's brave or amazing deeds. For example, there are many legends about Robin Hood, who stole from the rich and gave to the poor.

Many people like to read nonfiction books, which are about things that really exist or really happened. Many children who like nonfiction choose books about animals, careers, sports and hobbies. Those interested in information about Native Americans might like to read these books: *The Navajos* by Peter Iverson, *The Yakima* by Helen Schuster and *The Creek* by Michael Green. The titles of these nonfiction books are names of Native American tribes.

Directions: Answer these questions about different types of books.

1. What is the name of Francine Pascal's book series? <u>Sweet Valley Kids</u>

2. What legend is about a headless horseman? <u>Legend of Sleepy Hollow</u>

3. Which of the following is not correct about legends?

☐ Legends are passed down through the generations.

☒ All legends are scary.

☐ Some legends are about people who did braves things.

Page 91

Comprehension: Help for the Homeless

In Dayton, Ohio, a bookstore called Books & Co. launched a program to educate the public about the needs of homeless people. The program was built around profits from sales of a book called *Louder Than Words*. The book is a collection of 22 short stories by such noted authors as Louise Erdrich and Anne Tyler.

Many of the authors helped promote the book by coming to the bookstore to autograph copies of *Louder Than Words*. All profits from the sale of the book were donated to a fund that provides food and housing for homeless people.

The fund for the homeless is managed by a nonprofit organization called Share Our Strength. Located in Washington, D.C., the organization distributes the money to food banks and shelters for homeless people around the United States.

By the end of 1990, $50,000 had been raised for the homeless from the sale of *Louder Than Words*. Other bookstore owners learned about the success of Books & Co. in raising money for the homeless. They were impressed! Now, bookstores in these other cities are running fund-raising efforts of their own: Ann Arbor, Michigan; Columbus, Ohio; Taos, New Mexico; and Minneapolis, Minnesota.

Directions: Answer these questions about how booksellers have helped raise funds for the homeless.

1. How many short stories are in the book *Louder Than Words*? <u>22</u>

2. What is the name of the organization that distributes money to homeless shelters around the country? <u>Share Our Strength</u>

3. Name two authors whose stories are included in *Louder Than Words*.

<u>Louise Erdich and Anne Tyler</u>

4. Share Our Strength is located in what city?

☐ Portland, OR   ☐ Minneapolis, MN   ☒ Washington, D.C.

5. In what city is Books & Co. located?

☐ Columbus, OH   ☒ Dayton, OH   ☐ Taos, NM

Page 92

Fact or Opinion?

Directions: Read the paragraphs below. Then, in the corresponding numbered blanks, write whether each numbered sentence is a fact or an opinion.

Have you ever seen *Reading Rainbow* on your local public television station? **(1)** It's a show about books, and its host is LeVar Burton. **(2)** LeVar is very handsome and the show is great!

Some books that have been featured on the show are *I Can Be an Oceanographer* by Paul Sipiera, *Soccer Sam* by Jean Marzollo, *Redbird* by Patrick Fort and *Miss Nelson Has a Field Day* by Harry Allard. **(3)** *Miss Nelson Has a Field Day* sounds like the most interesting book of all!

(4) On *Reading Rainbow*, children give informal book reports about books they have read. **(5)** All the children are adorable! In about 1 minute, each child describes his or her book. **(6)** While the child is talking, pictures of some of the pages from the book are shown. **(7)** Seeing the pictures will make you want to read the book. A few books are described on each show. **(8)** Other activities include trips with LeVar to places the books tell about. **(9)** Every child should make time to watch *Reading Rainbow*! **(10)** It's a fabulous show!

1. <u>fact</u>
2. <u>opinion</u>
3. <u>opinion</u>
4. <u>fact</u>
5. <u>opinion</u>
6. <u>fact</u>
7. <u>opinion</u>
8. <u>fact</u>
9. <u>opinion</u>
10. <u>opinion</u>

Page 93

Context Clues: Kids' Books Are Big Business

Between 1978 and 1988, the number of children's books published in the United States doubled. The publishing industry, which prints, promotes and sells books, does not usually move this fast. Why? Because if publishers print too many books that don't sell, they lose money. They like to wait, if they can, to see what the "public demand" is for certain types of books. Then they accept manuscripts from writers who have written the types of books the public seems to want. More than 4,600 children's books were published in 1988, because publishers thought they could sell that many titles. Many copies of each title were printed and sold to bookstores and libraries. The publishers made good profits and, since then, the number of children's books published each year has continued to grow.

The title of a recent new book for children is *The Wild Horses of Sweetbriar* by Natalie Kinsey-Warnock. It is the story of a girl and a band of wild horses that lived on an island off the coast of Massachusetts in 1903. The story sounds very exciting! Wild horses can be quite dangerous. The plot of *The Wild Horses of Sweetbriar* is probably filled with danger and suspense.

Directions: Answer these questions about how interest in writing, reading and selling children's books has grown.

1. Use context clues to choose the correct definition of **industry**.

☐ booksellers   ☐ writers   ☒ entire business

2. If 4,600 books were sold in 1988, how many books were sold in 1978? <u>2,300</u>

3. The number of children's books published in the United States doubled between 1978 and 1988. — (Fact)   Opinion

4. *The Wild Horses of Sweetbriar* is the story of a girl and a band of wild horses that lived on an island in 1903. — (Fact)   Opinion

5. The story sounds very exciting! — Fact   (Opinion)

6. The plot of *The Wild Horses of Sweetbriar* is probably filled with danger and suspense. — Fact   (Opinion)

Page 94

Review

Directions: Follow the instructions below.

1. Write a summary of the selection "Help for the Homeless" (page 91).

2. What skills must a writer have in order to produce a book?

3. Define the following words.

appeal:

legend:

deed:

generation:

profit:

distribute:

suspense:

manuscript:

> Answers will vary.

4. Interview the members of your family. Ask each person his/her favorite book title and the reason he/she enjoyed it. Then, summarize your findings in a paragraph.

Page 96

Using Prior Knowledge: Music

Using **prior knowledge** means being able to use what one already knows to find an answer or get information.

Directions: Before reading about music in the following section, answer these questions.

1. In your opinion, why is music important to people?

2. Name as many styles of music as you can.

3. What is your favo[rite]

> Answers will vary.

4. If you could choose a musical instrument to play, what would it be? Why?

5. Name a famous musician and describe what you know about him/her.

Page 97

Main Idea: Where Did Songs Come From?

Historians say the earliest music was probably connected to religion. Long ago, people believed the world was controlled by a variety of gods. Singing was among the first things humans did to show respect to the gods.

Singing is still an important part of most religions. Buddhists (bood-ists), Christians and Jews all use chants and/or songs in their religious ceremonies. If you have ever sung a song—religious or otherwise—you know that singing is fun. The feeling of joy that comes from singing must also have made ancient people feel happy.

Another time people sang was when they worked. Egyptian slaves sang as they carried the heavy stones to build the pyramids. Soldiers sang as they marched into battle. Farmers sang one song as they planted and another when they harvested. Singing made the work less burdensome. People used the tunes to pace themselves. Sometimes they followed instructions through songs. For example, "Yo-oh, heave ho!/Yo-oh, heave ho!" was sung when sailors pulled on a ship's ropes to lift the sails. **Heave** means "to lift," and that is what they did as they sang the song. The song helped sailors work together and pull at the same time. This made the task easier.

Directions: Answer these questions about music.

1. Circle the main idea:

   Singing is fun, and that is why early people liked it so much.

   Singing began as a way to show respect to the gods and is still an important part of most religious ceremonies.

   (Traditionally, singing has been important as a part of religious ceremonies and as inspiration to workers.)

Sample answers:

2. Besides religious ceremonies, what other activity fostered singing? working, marching into battle, planting, harvesting
3. When did farmers sing two different songs? planting and harvesting
4. How did singing "Yo-oh, heave ho!" help sailors work? The song helped them work together to pull the ropes at the same time.

Page 98

Comprehension: Facts About Folk Music

Folk music literally means music "of the folks," and it belongs to everyone. The names of the musicians who composed most folk music have long been forgotten. Even so, folk music has remained popular because it tells about the lives of people. Usually, the tune is simple, and even though folk songs often have many verses, the words are easy to remember. Do you know the words to "She'll Be Comin' 'Round the Mountain"?

Although no one ever says who "she" is, the verses tell you that she will be "riding six white horses" and that "we'll go out to greet her." The song also describes what will be eaten when she comes (chicken and dumplings) and what those singing will be wearing (red pajamas).

"Clementine" is a song that came out of the California gold rush in the mid-1800s. It tells the story of a woman who was "lost and gone forever" when she was killed. ("In a cavern, in a canyon, excavating for a mine/Met a miner '49er and his daughter, Clementine.")

Another famous folk song is "Swing Low, Sweet Chariot." This song was sung by slaves in the United States and today is sung by people of all races. The words "Swing low, sweet chariot, coming for to carry me home . . ." describe the soul being united with God after death. Like other folk songs that sprang from slaves, "Swing Low, Sweet Chariot" is simple, moving and powerful.

Directions: Answer these questions about folk music.

1. What is the purpose of folk music? It tells about people's lives.
2. What food is sung about in "She'll Be Comin' 'Round the Mountain"? chicken and dumplings
3. Where did Clementine live?
   ☐ Florida ☐ Mississippi ☒ California
4. Where in the United States do you think "Swing Low, Sweet Chariot" was first sung?
   ☐ the North ☐ the West ☒ the South

Page 99

Recalling Details: Woodwinds

There are four kinds of woodwind instruments in modern bands. They are flutes, oboes, clarinets and bassoons. They are called "woodwind" instruments for two sensible reasons. In the beginning, they were all made of wood. Also, the musician's breath, or "wind," was required to play them.

Although they are all woodwinds, these instruments look different and are played differently. To play an oboe, the musician blows through a mouthpiece on the front of the instrument. The mouthpiece, called a reed, is made of two flat pieces of a kind of wood called cane. Clarinet players also blow into a reed mouthpiece. The clarinet has only one reed in its mouthpiece.

To play the flute, the musician blows across a hole near one end of the instrument. The way the breath is aimed helps to make the flute's different sounds. The bassoon is the largest woodwind instrument. Bassoon players blow through a mouthpiece that goes through a short metal pipe before it goes into the body of the bassoon. It makes a very different sound from the clarinet or the oboe.

Woodwind instruments also have keys—but not the kind of keys that open locks. These keys are more like levers that the musician pushes up and down. The levers cover holes. When the musician pushes down on a lever, it closes that hole. When he/she lifts his/her finger, it opens the hole. Different sounds are produced by controlling the amount of breath, or "wind," that goes through the holes.

Directions: Answer these questions about woodwind instruments.

1. What instruments are in the woodwind section? oboe, clarinet, flute, bassoon
2. Why are some instruments called woodwinds? In the beginning, they were all made of wood. They require "breath" to play them.
3. How is a flute different from the other woodwinds? It does not have a mouthpiece.
4. What happens when a musician pushes down on a woodwind key? It covers a hole in the instrument.
5. How would a woodwind musician open the holes on his/her instrument? lift his/her finger

Page 100

Comprehension: Harp Happenings

If you have ever heard a harpist play, you know what a lovely sound a harp makes. Music experts say the harp is among the oldest of instruments. It probably was invented several thousand years ago in or near Egypt.

The first harps are believed to have been made by stretching a string tightly between an empty tortoise shell and a curved pole. The empty shell magnified the sound the string made when it was plucked. More strings were added later so that more sounds could be made. Over the centuries, the shape of the harp gradually was changed into that of the large, graceful instruments we recognize today.

Here is how a harpist plays a harp. First, he/she leans the harp against his/her right shoulder. Then, the harpist puts his/her hands on either side of the harp and plucks its strings with both hands.

A harp has seven pedals on the bottom back. The audience usually cannot see these pedals. Most people are surprised to learn about them. The pedals are connected to the strings. Stepping on a particular pedal causes certain strings to tighten. The tightening and loosening of the strings makes different sounds; so does the way the strings are plucked with the hands.

At first glance, harps look like simple instruments. Actually, they are rather complicated and difficult to keep in tune. A harpist often spends as long as half an hour before a performance tuning his/her harp's strings so it produces the correct sounds.

Directions: Answer these questions about harps.

1. When were harps invented? several thousand years ago
2. Where were harps invented? in or near Egypt
3. What is a person called who plays the harp? harpist
4. The harpist leans the harp against his/her
   ☒ right shoulder. ☐ left shoulder. ☐ left knee.
5. How many pedals does a harp have?
   ☐ five ☐ six ☒ seven
6. Harps are easy to play.
   ☐ yes ☒ no

Page 101

Comprehension: Brass Shows Class

If you like band music, you probably love the music made by brass instruments. Bright, loud, moving and magnificent—all these words describe the sounds made by brass.

Some of the earliest instruments were horns. Made from hollowed-out animal horns, these primitive instruments could not possibly have made the rich sounds of modern horns that are made of brass.

Most modern brass bands have three instruments—tubas, trombones and trumpets. Combined, these instruments can produce stirring marches, as well as haunting melodies. The most famous composer for brass instruments was John Phillip Sousa. Born in Washington, D.C., in 1854, Sousa was a military band conductor and composer. He died in 1932, but his music is still very popular today. One of Sousa's most famous tunes for military bands is "Stars and Stripes Forever."

Besides composing band music, Sousa also invented a practical band instrument—the sousaphone. The sousaphone is a huge tuba that makes very low noises. Because of the way it curls around the body, a sousaphone is easier to carry than a tuba, especially when the musician must march. This is exactly why John Phillip Sousa invented it!

Directions: Answer these questions about brass instruments.

1. Who invented the sousaphone? John Phillip Sousa
2. What were the first horns made from? hollowed-out animal horns
3. Where was John Phillip Sousa born? Washington, D.C.
4. When did John Phillip Sousa die? 1932
5. Why did Sousa invent the sousaphone? It was easier to carry than a tuba.
6. What types of instruments make up a modern brass band? tubas, trombones and trumpets

Page 102

Comprehension: Violins

If you know anything about violin music, chances are you have heard the word **Stradivarius** (Strad-uh-vary-us). Stradivarius is the name for the world's most magnificent violins. They are named after their creator, Antonio Stradivari.

Stradivari was born in northern Italy and lived from 1644 to 1737. Cremona, the town he lived in, was a place where violins were manufactured. Stradivari was very young when he learned to play the violin. He grew to love the instrument so much that he began to make them himself.

Violins were new instruments during Stradivari's time. People made them in different sizes and shapes and of different types of wood. Stradivari is said to have been very particular about the wood he selected for his violins. He took long walks alone in the forest to find just the right tree. He is also said to have used a secret and special type of varnish to put on the wood. Whatever the reasons, his violins are the best in the world.

Stradivari put such care and love into his violins that they are still used today. Many of these are in museums. But some wealthy musicians, who can afford the thousands and thousands of dollars they cost, own Stradivarius violins.

Stradivari passed his methods on to his sons. But the secrets of making Stradivarius violins seem to have died out with the family. Their rarity, as well as their mellow sound, make Stradivarius violins among the most prized instruments in the world.

Directions: Answer these questions about Stradivarius violins.

1. Where did Stradivari live? Cremona
2. Why did he begin making violins? because he loved them so much
3. Why are Stradivarius violins special? He used special wood and varnish.
4. Where can Stradivarius violins be found today? museums and some wealthy musicians
5. How did Stradivari select the wood for his violins? He took long walks alone in the forest to find just the right tree.
6. Who else knew Stradivari's secrets for making such superior violins? his sons

471 Grade 5 - Comprehensive Curriculum

Page 103

Review

Directions: Complete the following exercises.

1. Write a four-sentence summary of the selection "Where Did Songs Come From?" (page 97).

Answers will vary.

2. Describe the main difference between a clarinet and an oboe.

The oboe has two reeds in its mouthpiece while the clarinet has only one.

3. How do the keys of woodwind instruments work?

The keys are like levers that, when pressed, cover a hole in the instrument. This changes the sound.

4. Write a summary of the history of the harp.

Answers will vary.

5. Define the following words from the selection "Facts About Folk Music" (page 98).

verses: *stanza of a poem or a song*

excavating: *make a hole or channel by digging*

chariot: *two-wheeled vehicle drawn by a horse*

composed: *created in music or writing*

Page 104

Using Prior Knowledge: Art

Directions: Before reading about art in the following section, answer these questions.

1. Write a short paragraph about a famous artist of your choice.

2. Many artists paint realistic scenes. Other artists paint imaginary scenes. Which do you prefer? Why?

3. Although we often think ~~...~~ ~~...~~ pture, fabric weavings a~~...~~ ~~...~~ what type? If not, what ~~...~~

Answers will vary.

4. Why are art museums important to society?

5. Why do you think some artwork is worth so much money? Would you pay several thousand dollars for a piece of artwork? Why or why not?

Page 105

Main Idea: Creating Art

No one knows exactly when the first human created the first painting. Crude drawings and paintings on the walls of caves show that humans have probably always expressed themselves through art. These early cave pictures show animals being hunted, people dancing and other events of daily life. The simplicity of the paintings reflect the simple lifestyles of these primitive people.

The subjects of early paintings also help to make another important point. Art is not created out of nothing. The subjects an artist chooses to paint reflect the history, politics and culture of the time and place in which he/she lives. An artist born and raised in New York City, for example, is not likely to paint scenes of the Rocky Mountains. An artist living in the Rockies is not likely to paint pictures of city life.

Of course, not all paintings are realistic. Many artists choose to paint pictures that show their own "inner vision" as opposed to what they see with their eyes. Many religious paintings of earlier centuries look realistic but contain figures of angels. These paintings combine the artist's inner vision of angels with other things, such as church buildings, that can be seen.

Directions: Answer these questions about creating art.

1. Circle the main idea:

Art was important to primitive people because it showed hunting and dancing scenes.

⟨Through the ages, artists have created paintings that reflect the culture, history and politics of the times, as well as their own inner visions.⟩

2. Why is an artist living in the Rocky Mountains less likely to paint city scenes?

Artists usually portray something that is part of their lives.

3. In addition to what they see with their eyes, what do some artists' paintings also show?

their inner feelings or visions

Page 106

Comprehension: Leonardo da Vinci

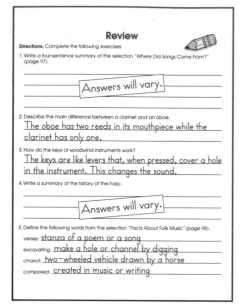

Many people believe that Leonardo da Vinci, an Italian artist and inventor who lived from 1452 to 1519, was the most brilliant person ever born. He was certainly a man ahead of his time! Records show that da Vinci loved the earth and was curious about everything on it.

To learn about the human body, he dissected corpses to find out what was inside. In the 15th and 16th centuries, dissecting the dead was against the laws of the Catholic church. Leonardo was a brave man!

He was also an inventor. Leonardo invented a parachute and designed a type of helicopter—5 centuries before airplanes were invented! Another of da Vinci's major talents was painting. You have probably seen a print, or copy, of one of his most famous paintings. It is called *The Last Supper*, and shows Jesus eating his final meal with his disciples. It took da Vinci 3 years to paint *The Last Supper*. The man who hired da Vinci to do the painting was upset. He went to da Vinci to ask why it was taking so long. The problem, said da Vinci, was that in the painting, Jesus has just told the disciples that one of them would betray him. He wanted to get their expressions exactly right as each cried out, "Lord, am I the one?"

Another famous painting by da Vinci is called the *Mona Lisa*. Have you seen a print of this painting? Maybe you have been lucky enough to see the original hanging in a Paris art museum called the Louvre (Loov). If so, you know that Mona Lisa has a wistful expression on her face. The painting is a real woman, the wife of an Italian merchant. Art historians believe she looks wistful because one of her children had recently died.

Directions: Answer these questions about Leonardo da Vinci.

1. How old was da Vinci when he died? 67

2. Name two of da Vinci's inventions. parachute and helicopter

3. Name two famous paintings by da Vinci. Mona Lisa, The Last Supper

4. In which Paris museum does *Mona Lisa* hang? ☐ Lourre ☐ Loure ☒ Louvre

Page 107

Context Clues: Leonardo da Vinci

Directions: Read the sentences below. Use context clues to figure out the meaning of the bold words.

1. Some people are **perplexed** when they look at *The Last Supper*, but others understand it immediately.

☐ unhappy ☐ happy ☒ puzzled

2. Because his model felt **melancholy** about the death of her child, da Vinci had music played to lift her spirits as he painted the *Mona Lisa*.

☒ sad ☐ unfriendly ☐ hostile

3. Because da Vinci's work is so famous, many people **erroneously** assume that he left behind many paintings. In fact, he left only 20.

☐ rightly ☐ correctly ☒ wrongly

4. Leonardo da Vinci was not like most other people. He didn't care what others thought of him—he led an interesting and **unconventional** life.

☐ dull ☒ not ordinary ☐ ordinary

5. The **composition** of *The Last Supper* is superb. All the parts of the painting seem to fit together beautifully.

☐ the picture frame ☒ parts of the picture

6. Leonardo's **genius** set him apart from people with ordinary minds. He never married, he had few friends and he spent much of his time alone.

☒ great mental abilities ☐ great physical abilities
☐ improper way to do things ☐ proper way to do things

7. Because he was a loner, da Vinci worried no one would come to his funeral when he died. In his will, he set aside 70 each to hire 60 **mourners** to accompany his body to his grave.

☐ friends ☒ people who grieve ☐ people who smile

Page 108

Comprehension: Michelangelo

Another famous painter of the late 14th and early 15th centuries was Michelangelo Buonarroti. Michelangelo, who lived from 1475 to 1564, was also an Italian. Like da Vinci, his genius was apparent at a young age. When he was 13, the ruler of his hometown of Florence, Lorenzo Medici (Muh-dee-chee), befriended Michelangelo and asked him to live in the palace. There Michelangelo studied sculpture and met many artists.

By the time he was 18, Michelangelo was a respected sculptor. He created one of his most famous religious sculptures, the *Pieta* (pee-ay-tah), when he was only 21. Then the Medici family abruptly fell from power and Michelangelo had to leave Florence.

Still, his work was well known and he was able to make a living. In 1503, Pope Julius II called Michelangelo to Rome. He wanted Michelangelo to paint the tomb where he would someday be buried. Michelangelo preferred sculpting to painting, but no one turned down the pope! Before Michelangelo finished his painting, however, the pope ordered Michelangelo to begin painting the ceiling of the Sistine Chapel inside the Vatican. (The Vatican is the palace and surrounding area where the pope lives in Rome.)

Michelangelo was very angry! He did not like to paint. He wanted to create sculptures. But no one turns down the pope. After much complaining, Michelangelo began work on what would be his most famous project.

Directions: Answer these questions about Michelangelo.

1. How old was Michelangelo when he died? 89

2. What was the first project Pope Julius II asked Michelangelo to paint?

his tomb

3. What is the Vatican? palace and grounds where the Pope lives

4. What was the second project the pope asked Michelangelo to do?

☐ paint his tomb's ceiling ☒ paint the Sistine Chapel's ceiling

Page 109

Comprehension: Rembrandt

Most art critics agree that Rembrandt (Rem-brant) was one of the greatest painters of all time. This Dutch artist, who lived from 1606 to 1669, painted some of the world's finest portraits.

Rembrandt, whose full name was Rembrandt van Rijn, was born in Holland to a wealthy family. He was sent to a fine university, but he did not like his studies. He only wanted to paint. He sketched the faces of people around him. During his lifetime, Rembrandt painted 11 portraits of his father and nearly as many of his mother. From the beginning, the faces of old people fascinated him.

When he was 25, Rembrandt went to paint in Amsterdam, a large city in Holland where he lived for the rest of his life. There he married a wealthy woman named Saskia, whom he loved deeply. She died from a disease called tuberculosis (ta-bur-ku-lo-sis) after only 8 years, leaving behind a young son named Titus (Ty-tuss).

Rembrandt was heartbroken over his wife's death. He began to spend all his time painting. But instead of painting what his customers wanted, he painted exactly the way he wanted. Unsold pictures filled his house. They were wonderful paintings, but they were not the type of portraits people wanted. Rembrandt could not pay his debts. He and his son were thrown into the streets. The creditors took his home, his possessions and his paintings. One of the finest painters on Earth was treated like a criminal.

Directions: Answer these questions about Rembrandt.

1. How old was Rembrandt when he died? **63**

2. In what city did he spend most of his life? **Amsterdam**

3. How many children did Rembrandt have? **one**

4. Rembrandt's wife was named
☐ Sasha. ☒ Saskia. ☐ Saksia.

5. These filled his house after his wife's death.
☐ friends ☐ customers ☒ unsold paintings

Page 110

Review

Directions: Follow the instructions below.

1. Write a one-sentence main idea for the selection "Leonardo da Vinci" (page 106).

2. Write a summary of the selection "Leonardo da Vinci" (page 106).

3. Complete the sequence of events from the selection "Michelangelo" (page 108).
1) Michelangelo
2)
3)
4)
5)
6)
7)

4. Define the following words from this section.
crude:
dissect:
disciples:
merchant:
wistful:

Answers will vary.

Page 111

Using Prior Knowledge: Big Cats

Directions: Before reading about big cats in the following section, answer these questions.

1. Name at least four big wild cats.

2. Compare and contrast a house cat with a wild cat.

3. What impact do humans have on big cats?

4. Do you have a cat? What are the special qualities of this pet? Write about your cat's name and its personality traits. If you don't have a cat, write about a cat you would like to have.

Answers will vary.

Page 112

Comprehension: Jaguars

The jaguar is a large cat, standing up to 2 feet tall at the shoulder. Its body can reach 73 inches long, and the tail can be another 30 inches long. The jaguar is characterized by its yellowish-red coat covered with black spots. The spots themselves are made up of a central spot surrounded by a circle of spots.

Jaguars are not known to attack humans, but some ranchers claim that jaguars attack their cattle. This claim has given jaguars a bad reputation.

The jaguar can be found in southern North America, but is most populous in Central and South America. Jaguars are capable climbers and swimmers, and they eat a wide range of animals.

Female jaguars have between one and four cubs after a gestation of 93 to 105 days. Cubs stay with the mother for 2 years. Jaguars are known to have a life expectancy of at least 22 years.

Directions: Use context clues for these definitions.

1. populous:
2. reputation:
3. gestation:

Answers will vary.

Directions: Answer these questions about jaguars.

4. Describe the spots on a jaguar's coat.
a central spot surrounded by a circle of spots

5. Why would it be to a jaguar's advantage to have spots on its coat?
Answers will vary.

Page 113

Comprehension: Leopards

The leopard is a talented nocturnal hunter and can see very well in the dark. Because of its excellent climbing ability, the leopard is able to stalk and kill monkeys and baboons. Leopards are also known to consume mice, porcupines and fruit.

Although the true leopard is characterized by a light beige coat with black spots, some leopards can be entirely black. These leopards are called black panthers. Many people refer to other cat species as leopards. Cheetahs are sometimes referred to as hunting leopards. The clouded leopard lives in southeastern Asia and has a grayish spotted coat. The snow leopard, which has a white coat, lives in Central Asia. A leopard's spots help to camouflage (cam-o-flaj) it as it hunts.

True leopards can grow to over 6 feet long, not including their 3 foot long tail. Leopards can be found in Africa and Asia.

Directions: Use context clues for these definitions.

1. consume:
2. ability:
3. nocturnal:

Answers will vary.

Directions: Answer these questions about leopards.

4. List three differences between the leopard and the jaguar.
1. Leopards live in Africa and Asia, while jaguars live in Central and South America.
2. Leopards are light beige with black spots; jaguars are yellowish-red with black spots.
3. Leopards have black spots; jaguars have a central spot surrounded by a circle of spots.

5. What makes a leopard able to hunt monkeys and baboons?
It has excellent climbing ability.

Page 114

Comprehension: Lynxes

Lynxes are strange looking cats with very long legs and large paws. Their bodies are a mere 51 inches in length, and they have short little tails. Most lynxes have a clump of hair that extends past the tip of their ears.

Lynxes not only are known to chase down their prey, but also to leap on them from a perch above the ground. They eat small mammals and birds, as well as an occasional deer.

There are four types of lynxes. Bobcats can be found in all areas of the United States except the Midwest. The Spanish lynx is an endangered species. The Eurasian lynx, also known as the northern lynx, and the Canadian lynx are two other kinds of lynxes.

Directions: Use context clues for these definitions.

1. prey:
2. perch:

Answers will vary.

Directions: Answer these questions about lynxes.

3. What are the four types of lynxes? **bobcats, Spanish lynx, Eurasian lynx, Canadian lynx**

4. Use the following words in a sentence of your own.
mammal
endangered

Answers will vary.

5. Do you believe it is important to classify animals as "endangered" to protect a species that is low in population? Explain your answer.

Answers will vary.

Page 115

Comprehension: Pumas

The puma is a cat most recognized by the more popular names of "cougar" or "mountain lion." Just like other large cats, the puma is a carnivore. It feeds on deer, elk and other mammals. It can be found in both North and South America.

Pumas have small heads with a single black spot above each eye. The coat color ranges from bluish-gray (North America) to reddish-brown (South America). The underside of the body, as well as the throat and muzzle, are white. The puma's body can be almost 6 feet long, not including the tail.

Female pumas give birth to two to four young. When first born, pumas have brown spots on their backs, and their tails are lined with dark brown rings.

As with the jaguar, pumas are blamed for killing cattle. Because of this, pumas are either nonexistent in some areas or are endangered.

Directions: Answer these q[uestions].

1. What is a muzzle? *Answers will vary.*

2. As the population increases in North America, predict what might happen to pumas.

Answers will vary.

3. What are two other popular names for the puma? cougar, mountain lion
4. What other cat besides the puma is blamed for killing cattle? jaguar
5. Reviewing the sizes of cats discussed so far, write their names in order, from smallest to largest.

1) lynx   2) puma
3) leopard   4) jaguar

Page 116

Comprehension: Tigers

Tigers live on the continent of Asia. The tiger is the largest cat, often weighing over 500 pounds. Its body can grow to be 9 feet long and the tail up to 36 inches in length.

There are three types of tigers. The Siberian tiger is very rare and has a yellow coat with dark stripes. The Bengal tiger can be found in southeastern Asia and central India. Its coat is more orange and its stripes are darker. There is a tiger that lives on the island of Sumatra as well. It is smaller and darker in color than the Bengal tiger.

Tigers lead solitary lives. They meet with other tigers only to mate and share food or water. Tigers feed primarily on deer and cattle but are also known to eat fish and frogs. If necessary, tigers will also eat dead animals.

Female tigers bear one to six cubs at a time. The cubs stay with their mother for almost 2 years before going out on their own.

Because tiger parts are in high demand for use in Chinese medicine and recipes, tigers have been hunted almost to extinction. All tigers are currently listed as endangered.

Directions: Use context clues for these definitions.

1. rare:
2. solitary: *Answers will vary.*
3. extinction:

Directions: Answer these questions about tigers.

4. Why have tigers been hunted almost to extinction?
Their body parts are used in Chinese medicine and recipes.

5. Name the three types of tigers.
Siberian, Bengal and Sumatran

Page 117

Comprehension: Lions

The lion, often referred to as the king of beasts, once commanded a large territory. Today, their territory is very limited. Lions are savanna-dwelling animals, which has made them easy targets for hunters. The increasing population of humans and their livestock has also contributed to the lion's decreased population.

Lions are heavy cats. Males weigh over 500 pounds and can grow to be over 8 feet in length, with a tail over 36 inches long. Males are characterized by a long, full mane that covers the neck and most of the head and shoulders. Females do not have a mane and are slightly smaller in size. Both males and females have beige coats, hooked claws and powerful jaws. Their roars can be heard up to 5 miles away!

Lions tend to hunt in the evening and spend the day sleeping. They prefer hunting zebra or giraffe but will eat almost anything. A lion is capable of eating over 75 pounds of meat at a single kill and then going a week without eating again. Generally, female lions do the hunting, and the males come to share the kill.

Lions live in groups called prides. Each pride has between 4 and 37 lions. Females bear one to four cubs approximately every 2 years.

Directions: Answer these questions about lions.

1. What are the differences between male and female lions? Male lions have a mane of hair and are larger in size.

2. Why would living on a savanna make the lion an "easy target"?

Directions: Use cont[ext]...

3. pride: *Answers will vary.*
4. territory:
5. savanna:
6. capable:

Page 118

Review

Directions: Follow the instructions below.

1. Choose any two big cats from this section and compare them.

2. Why are each of these big cats endangered or decreasing in number?

Answers will vary.

3. What can b[e]... [endang]ered list?

4. Now that you have read about big cats, compare and contrast them with a house cat. What do you know now that you didn't know before reading this section?

Page 119

Using Prior Knowledge: Farm Animals

Directions: Before reading about farm animals in the following section, answer these questions.

1. List at least nine types of farm animals by mother and baby names.

Example: sow—piglet.

2. If you owned a large ranch, what type of livestock would you enjoy keeping? Why?

3. Some anim[als]... *Answers will vary.* ...[ani]mals give birth to more tha[n]...

4. Would you enjoy living on a farm? Why or why not?

5. What is the importance of raising livestock today?

Page 120

Comprehension: All About Sheep

Did you ever wonder what really happened to the tails of Little Bo-Peep's sheep? Here's the real story.

When sheep are born, they are called lambs. Lambs are born with long tails. A few days after lambs are born, the shepherd cuts off their tails. Because they get dirty, the lambs' long tails can pick up lots of germs. Cutting them off helps to prevent disease. The procedure is called "docking." This is probably what happened to Bo-Peep's sheep! Another shepherd must have cut their tails off without telling her.

Little lambs are cute. A lamb grows inside its mother for 150 days before it is born. This is called the "gestation period." Some types of sheep, such as hill sheep, give birth to one lamb at a time. Other types of sheep, such as lowland sheep, give birth to two or three lambs at a time.

After it is born, it takes a lamb 3 or 4 days to recognize its mother. Once it does, it stays close to her until it is about 3 weeks old. After that, the lamb becomes friendly toward other lambs.

Young lambs then form play groups. They chase each other in circles. They butt into each other. Like children, they pretend to fight. When play gets too rough, the lambs run back to their mothers for protection.

Lambs follow their mothers as they graze on grass. Usually, sheep move in single file behind an older female sheep. Female sheep are called ewes. The ewes teach their lambs how to keep themselves clean. This is called "grooming." Sheep groom only their faces. Here is how they do it: They lick one of their front legs, then they rub their faces against the spot they have licked.

Directions: Follow the instructions below.

1. Define the word **docking**. to cut off the lamb's tail
2. Name a type of sheep that gives birth to one lamb at a time. hill sheep
3. Name a type of sheep that gives birth to two or three lambs at a time.
lowland sheep
4. Female sheep are called
☐ grazers.   ☒ ewes.   ☐ dockers.
5. Lambs begin playing in groups when they are
☐ 2 weeks old.   ☒ 3 weeks old.   ☐ 4 weeks old.

ANSWER KEY

Page 121

Comprehension: Pigs Are Particular

Have you ever wondered why pigs wallow in the mud? It's not because they are dirty animals. Pigs have no sweat glands. They can't sweat. Other cows are not driven themselves. The next time you hear anyone who's hot say, "I'm sweating like a pig!" be sure to correct him/her. Humans can sweat but pigs cannot.

Actually, pigs are particular about their pens. They are very clean animals. They prefer to sleep in clean, dry places. They move their bowels and empty their bladders in another area. They do not want to get their homes dirty.

Another misconception about pigs is that they are smooth. Only cartoon pigs are pink, smooth and shiny-looking. The skin of real pigs is covered with bristles—small, stiff hairs. Their bristles protect their tender skin. When pigs are slaughtered, their bristles are sometimes made into hairbrushes or clothes brushes.

Female pigs are called sows. Sows have babies twice a year and give birth to 10 to 14 piglets at a time. The babies have a "gestation period" of 16 weeks before they are born.

All the piglets together are called a "litter." Newborn piglets are on their tiny feet within a few minutes after birth. Can you guess why? They are hungrily looking for their mother's teats so they can get milk. As they nurse, piglets snuggle in close to their mother's belly to keep warm.

Directions: Answer these questions about pigs.

1. Why do pigs wallow in mud? **to cool off**

2. How long is the gestation period for pigs? **16 weeks**

3. What are pig bristles used for? **hairbrushes or clothes brushes**

4. Tell two reasons pigs are on their feet soon after they are born.
1) **to get milk** 2) **to get warm**

5. A female pig is called a ☐ bristle. ☐ piglet. ☒ sow.

6. Together, the newborn piglets are called a ☐ group. ☐ family. ☒ litter.

Page 122

Context Clues: No Kidding About Goats

Goats are independent creatures. Unlike sheep, which move easily in herds, goats cannot be driven along by a goatherd. They must be moved one or two at a time, so goatherds must be patient people.

Both male and female goats can have horns, but some goats don't have them at all. Male goats have beards but females do not. Male goats also have thicker and shaggier coats than females. During breeding season, when goats mate to produce babies, male goats have a very strong smell.

Goats are kept in paddocks with high fences. The fences are high because goats are good jumpers. They like to nibble on hedges and on the tips of young trees. They can cause a lot of damage this way! That is why many farmers keep their goats in a paddock.

Baby goats are called "kids," and two or three at a time are born to the mother goat. Farmers usually begin to bottle-feed kids when they are a few days old. They milk the mother goat and keep the milk. Goat's milk is much easier to digest than cow's milk, and many people think it tastes delicious.

Directions: Answer these questions about goats.

1. Use context clues to choose the correct definition of **goatherd**.
☒ person who herds goats ☐ goats in a herd ☐ person who has heard of goats

2. Use context clues to choose the correct definition of **paddock**.
☐ pad ☐ fence ☒ pen

3. Use context clues to choose the correct definition of **nibble**.
☒ take small bites ☐ take small drinks ☐ take little sniffs

4. Use context clues to choose the correct definition of **delicious**.
☐ delicate ☒ tasty ☐ terrible

Page 123

Comprehension: Cows Are Complicated

If you believe cows have four stomachs, you're right! It sounds incredible, but it's true.

Here are the "hows" and "whys" of a cow's digestive system. First, it's important to know that cows do not have front teeth. They eat grass by wrapping their tongues around it and pulling it from the ground. They do have back teeth, but still they cannot properly chew the grass.

Cows swallow grass without chewing it. When it's swallowed, the grass goes into the cow's first stomach, called a "rumen" (roo-mun). There it is broken up by the digestive juices and forms into a ball of grass. This ball is called a "cud." The cow is able to bring the cud back up into its mouth and re-swallows it.

After it is swallowed the second time, the cud goes into the cow's second stomach. This second stomach is called the "reticulum" (re-tick-u-lum). The reticulum filters the food to sort out any small stones or other non-food matter. Then it passes the food onto the cow's third stomach. The third stomach is called the "omasum" (oh-mass-um).

From there, any food that is still undigested is sent back to the first stomach so the cow can bring it back up into her mouth and chew it some more. The rest goes into the cow's fourth stomach. The fourth stomach is called the "abomasum" (ab-oh-ma-sum). Digesting food that can be turned into milk is a full-time job for cows!

Directions: Answer these questions about cows.

1. List in order the names of a cow's four stomachs.
1) **rumen** 2) **reticulum** 3) **omasum** 4) **abomasum**

2. What is the name of the ball of grass a cow chews on? **cud**

3. A cow has no
☒ front teeth. ☐ back teeth. ☐ fourth stomach.

4. Which stomach acts as a filter for digestion?
☒ reticulum ☐ rumen ☐ abomasum

Page 124

Context Clues: Dairy Cows

Some cows are raised for their beef. Other cows, called dairy cows, are raised for their milk. A dairy cow cannot produce any milk until after its first calf is born. Cows are not mature enough to give birth until they are 2 years old. A cow's gestation period is 40 weeks long, and she usually gives birth to one calf. Then she produces a lot of milk to feed it. When the calf is 2 days old, the dairy farmer takes the calf away from its mother. After that, the cow is milked twice a day.

The dairy cow's milk comes from the large, smooth udder beneath her body. The udder has four openings called "teats." To milk the cow, the farmer grasps a teat and squeezes it with his thumb and forefinger. Then he gently but firmly pulls his hand down the teat to squeeze the milk out. Milking machines that are hooked to the cow's teats duplicate this action and can milk many cows quickly.

A dairy cow's milk production is not at the same level all the time. When the cow is pregnant, milk production gradually decreases. For 2 months before her calf is born, a cow is said to be "dry" and is not milked. This happens because, like humans, much of the cow's food is actually being used to nourish the unborn calf.

Farmers give the cow extra food at this time to make sure the mother and unborn calf are well-nourished. Again, like humans, well-nourished mother cows are more likely to produce healthy babies.

Directions: Answer these questions about dairy cows.

1. Use context clues to choose the correct definition of **grasp**.
☐ pull firmly ☒ hold firmly ☐ hold gently

2. Use context clues to choose the correct definition of **duplicate**.
☐ correct ☐ make ☒ copy

3. Use context clues to choose the correct definition of **decrease**.
☐ become more ☒ become less ☐ become quicker

4. Use context clues to choose the correct definition of **nourish**.
☐ to be happy ☐ to be friendly ☒ to feed

Page 125

Comprehension: Chickens

Have you ever heard the expression "pecking order"? In the pecking order of a school, the principal is at the top of the order. Next comes the assistant principal, then the teachers and students.

In the pecking order of chickens, the most aggressive chicken is the leader. The leader is the hen that uses her beak most often to peck the chickens she bosses. These chickens, in turn, boss other chickens by pecking them, and so on. Chickens can peck all others who are "below" them in the pecking order. They never peck "above" themselves by pecking their bosses.

Answer these questions about chickens.

1. Put this pecking order of four chickens in order.
2 This chicken pecks numbers 3 and 4 but never 1.
1 No one pecks this chicken. She's the top boss.
4 This chicken can't peck anyone.
3 This chicken pecks chicken number 4.

2. Use context clues to figure out the definition of **aggressive**.
Answers will vary.

3. Who is at the top of the pecking order in a school? **Answers may include:**
principal

Page 126

Review

Directions: Follow the instructions for each section.

1. Write a summary of the selection "All About Sheep" (page 120).
Answers will vary.

2. What is the purpose of a pig's bristles?
The bristles protect their skin.

3. Write a summary of the selection "No Kidding About Goats" (page 122).
Answers will vary.

4. What is the purpose of a cow's four stomachs?
digest food that can be turned into milk

5. How do chickens establish leaders and followers?
Chickens peck each other to determine dominance. Chickens will only peck another chicken who is "below" them.

6. What is a "cud"?
the ball of grass formed by the rumen

Page 127

Using Prior Knowledge: Stamp Collecting

Directions: Before reading about stamp collecting in the following section, answer these questions.

1. Why do you think people collect stamps?

2. What hobby do you most enjoy? Why?

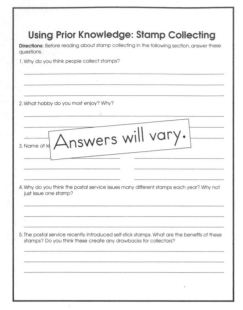

Answers will vary.

3. Name at le

4. Why do you think the postal service issues many different stamps each year? Why not just issue one stamp?

5. The postal service recently introduced self-stick stamps. What are the benefits of these stamps? Do you think these create any drawbacks for collectors?

Page 128

Fact or Opinion?

Directions: Read the paragraphs below. Then, in the corresponding numbered blanks, write whether each numbered sentence is a fact or an opinion.

(1) An important rule for stamp collectors to follow is never to handle stamps with their fingers. (2) Instead, to keep the stamps clean, collectors use stamp tongs to pick up stamps. (3) Stamps are stored by being placed on mounts. (4) Stamp mounts are plastic holders that fit around the stamp and keep it clean. (5) The backs of the mounts are sticky, so they can be stuck onto a stamp album page. (6) What a great idea!

(7) The stamps are mounted in stamp albums that have either white or black pages. (8) Some people prefer black pages, claiming that the stamps "show" better. (9) Some people prefer white pages, claiming that they give the album a cleaner look. (10) I think this foolish bickering over page colors is ridiculous!

1. fact
2. fact
3. fact
4. fact
5. fact
6. opinion
7. fact
8. opinion
9. opinion
10. opinion

Page 129

Comprehension: More Stamp Collecting

Many people collect stamps in blocks of four. Each stamp in the block is stuck to the other stamps along the edges. Collectors do not tear the stamps apart from one another. They buy blocks of stamps bearing new designs directly from the post office. Then they mount the blocks of stamps and place them in their albums.

Collectors also get their stamps off of envelopes. This is a bit tricky, because the stamps are glued on. Usually, collectors soak the stamps in warm water to loosen the glue. Then they gently pull the stamps from the paper and let them dry before mounting them.

Some beginners start their collections by buying a packet of mixed stamps. The packets, or bags, contain a variety of different stamps. Beginners buy these packets from companies that supply stamps to philatelists (fuh-lay-tell-lists). Philately (fuh-lay-tell-lee) is the collection and study of postage stamps. Philatelists are the people who collect and study them.

Packets of stamps usually contain stamps from many different countries. Often, they contain duplicates of some of the stamps. Suppliers usually don't sort the stamps that go into the packets for beginners. They leave that for beginning philatelists to enjoy!

Directions: Answer these questions about stamp collecting.

1. Name three places some people get stamps. post office, old envelopes and buy them

2. What is the word that describes the collection and study of stamps? philately

3. What are people called who collect and study stamps? philatelists

4. The bag that a mixture of stamps comes in is called a

☐ postal bag.　☒ packet.　☐ philatelist.

5. Do stamp mixtures usually include only U.S. stamps?

☐ Yes　☒ No

Page 130

Recalling Details: Philately Abbreviations

Like other hobbies, philately has its own jargon and symbols. Collectors and dealers know what they mean, but "outsiders" would be puzzled if they saw the following abbreviations without their definitions. Read them carefully, then refer to them when answering the questions below.

Avg. — average condition

blk. — block of four stamps

C — cancelled (used) stamp

OG — original gum

　　(glue on back of stamp)

G — good condition

M — mint (excellent and unused) condition

s — single stamp

U — used stamp

VF — very fine condition

Wmk — watermark (can occur when water is used to remove stamp from envelope)

Directions: Answer these questions about the abbreviations used by stamp dealers and collectors.

1. If a philatelist wrote the following description, what would he/she mean?

I have a blk. in VF. I have a block of four stamps in very fine conditions.

2. What does this mean? **s with OG, condition M** single stamp with the original gum on the back in excellent and unused condition

3. What other abbreviation would most likely be used do describe a used (U) stamp? C (cancelled)

4. What does this mean? **s in Avg. with Wmk** a single stamp in average condition with a watermark

5. Which is more valuable, a rare stamp in **M** or **VF** condition? M (mint)

6. Would you rather own a single U stamp or a blk. in M? a blk. in M

Page 131

Comprehension: Faces on Stamps

If anyone ever tries to sell you a stamp with a picture of former Vice President Dan Quayle on it, just say no! In the United States, only people who have died can have their pictures on stamps. That is why the singer Elvis Presley's face appeared on stamps only after he died.

Many U.S. presidents' faces have been on postage stamps, as have pictures of the faces of other important people in U.S. history. Some people's faces have been on many different stamps. Through the years, George Washington and Benjamin Franklin have been on dozens of different types of stamps!

Other people whose pictures have been on stamps include John Quincy Adams, the sixth president of the United States; Jane Addams, a U.S. social worker and writer; Louisa May Alcott, author of *Little Women* and many other books; Clara Barton, nurse and founder of the American Red Cross; Alexander Graham Bell, inventor of the telephone; and poet, Emily Dickinson. These are only a few of the hundreds of famous Americans whose faces have appeared on U.S. postage stamps.

Directions: Answer these questions about some of the people whose faces have appeared on U.S. stamps.

1. Name six occupations of people whose faces have appeared on postage stamps. president, writer, entertainer, nurse, inventor, social worker

2. What two people's pictures have appeared on more stamps than on any others? George Washington, Benjamin Franklin

3. Why can't Dan Quayle's face appear on a postage stamp? He is still alive and people must be dead to appear on a U.S. stamp.

4. Which person featured on a postage stamp was a social worker?

☐ Clara Barton　☐ Louisa May Alcott　☒ Jane Addams

5. Which person featured on a postage stamp was an inventor?

☐ Emily Dickinson　☒ Alexander Graham Bell　☐ John Quincy Adams

Page 132

Comprehension: Valuable Stamps

Most people collect stamps as a hobby. They spend small sums of money to get the stamps they want, or they trade stamps with other collectors. They rarely make what could be considered "big money" from their philately hobby.

A few collectors are in the business of philately as opposed to the hobby. To the people who can afford it, some stamps are worth big money. For example, a U.S. airmail stamp with a face value of 24 cents when it was issued in 1918 is now worth more than $35,000 if a certain design appears on the stamp. Another stamp, the British Guiana, an ugly stamp that cost only a penny when it was issued, later sold for $280,000!

The Graf Zeppelin is another example of an ugly stamp that became valuable. Graf Zeppelin is the name of a type of airship, similar to what we now call a "blimp," invented around the turn of the century. Stamps were issued to mark the first roundtrip flight the Zeppelin made between two continents. A set of three of these stamps cost $4.55 when they were issued. The stamps were ugly and few of them sold. The postal service destroyed the rest. Now, because they are rare, each set of the Graf Zeppelin stamps is worth hundreds of dollars.

Directions: Answer these questions about valuable stamps.

1. What is the most valuable stamp described? the British Guiana

2. For how much did this stamp originally sell? one penny

3. What did a collector later pay for it? $280,000

4. The Graf Zeppelin stamps originally sold for $4.55 for a set of

☐ four.　☐ six.　☒ three.

5. Which stamp did the postal service destroy because it didn't sell?

☐ British Guiana　☒ Graf Zeppelin　☐ British Zeppelin

Page 133

Fact or Opinion?

Directions: Read the paragraphs below. Then, in the corresponding numbered blanks, write whether each numbered sentence is a fact or an opinion.

(1) Nearly every valuable stamp on Earth has been counterfeited (coun-ter-fit-tid) at one time or another. (2) A "counterfeit" is a fake that looks nearly identical to the original. (3) It takes a lot of nerve to try to pass off counterfeits as the real thing. (4) Counterfeiting is big business, especially with stamps from overseas. (5) Because a collector often has no original for comparison, he/she can be easily fooled by a good counterfeit!

(6) One way people can make sure a stamp is real is to have it checked by a company that authenticates (aw-then-ti-kates) stamps. (7) To "authenticate" means to prove the stamp is real. (8) Of course, there is a fee for this service. (9) But I think paying a reasonable fee is worth what collectors get in return. (10) Those counterfeiters should be locked up forever!

1. fact
2. fact
3. opinion
4. fact
5. fact
6. fact
7. fact
8. fact
9. opinion
10. opinion

Page 134

Comprehension: Stamp Value

It's nearly impossible to predict which stamps will rise in value. Why? Because the value is based on the law of supply and demand. How much does someone or a group of "someones" want for a particular stamp? If many people want a stamp, the value will increase, especially if few of the stamps exist.

However, collectors are also always on the lookout for things that can lower the value of a stamp. Are the stamp's perforations (per-four-ay-shuns) torn along the edges? (Perforations are ragged edges where stamps tear apart.) Is there a watermark on the stamp? Has the gum worn off the back? All these things can make a stamp less valuable.

Directions: Answer these questions about determining the value of stamps.

1. Name three things that can lower the value of a stamp.
   a watermark, the gum is worn off the back, the perforations are torn

2. Collecting stamps is a fascinating hobby.   Fact   (Opinion)

3. What is one thing the value of stamps is based upon? supply and demand

4. What will happen if many people want a rare stamp? The value will increase.

5. Explain how to spot a stamp that will become valuable. It would be very difficult to predict future value. It depends on these variables—how many people want to own it and how many stamps are available.

Page 135

Review

Directions: Follow the instructions below.

1. Define the following words from this section.

   mount: _____
   bickering: _____
   philately: _____
   counterfeit: _____
   authenticate: _____
   perforations: _____

2. Choose two o[...]

   1) _____   Answers will vary.
   2) _____

3. Write a one-sentence main idea for the selection "Stamp Value" (page 134).
   _____

4. Write a summary of the selection "Faces on Stamps" (page 131).
   _____

5. Write a summary of the selection "More Stamp Collecting" (page 129).
   _____

Page 136

Using Prior Knowledge: Cooking

Before reading about cooking in the following section, answer these questions.

1. What is your favorite recipe? Why?
   _____

2. What do you most like to cook? Why?
   _____

3. Have you tr[...]   Answers will vary.   [...]ood do you like most? W[...]
   _____

4. Why is it important to follow the correct sequence when preparing a recipe?
   _____

5. What safety precautions must be followed when working in a kitchen?
   _____

Page 137

Following Directions: Chunky Tomato and Green Onion Sauce

Following directions means to do what the directions say to do, step by step, in the correct order.

Directions: Read the recipe for chunky tomato and green onion sauce. Answer the questions below.

Ingredients:
- 2 tablespoons corn oil
- 2 cloves of garlic, finely chopped
- 1½ pounds plum tomatoes, cored, peeled, seeded, then coarsely chopped
- 3 green onions, cut in half lengthwise, then thinly sliced
- salt
- freshly ground pepper

Heat oil in a heavy skillet over medium heat. Add garlic and cook until yellow, about 1 minute. Stir in tomatoes. Season with salt and pepper. Cook until thickened, about 10 minutes. Stir in green onions and serve.

1. What is the last thing the cook does to prepare the tomatoes before cooking them?
   chops them

2. What kind of oil does the cook heat in the heavy skillet? corn oil

3. How long should the garlic be cooked? about 1 minute

4. What does the cook do to the tomatoes right before removing the seeds?
   peels them

5. Is the sauce served hot or cold? hot

Page 138

Comprehension: Cooking With Care

People are so busy these days that many have no time to cook. This creates a problem, because most families love home cooking! The food tastes good and warm, and a family meal brings everyone together. In some families, meals are often the only times everyone sees one another at the same time.

Another reason people enjoy home cooking is that it is often a way of showing love. A parent who bakes a batch of chocolate chip cookies isn't just satisfying a child's sweet tooth. He/she is sending a message. The message says, "I care about you enough to spend an hour making cookies that you will eat up in 15 minutes if I let you!"

There's also something about the smell of good cooking that appeals to people of all ages. It makes most of us feel secure and loved—even if we are the ones doing the cooking! Next time you smell a cake baking, stop for a moment and pay attention to your mood. Chances are, the good smell is making you feel happy.

Real estate agents know that good cooking smells are important. They sometimes advise people whose homes are for sale to bake cookies or bread if prospective buyers are coming to see the house. The good smells make the place "feel like home." These pleasant smells help convince potential buyers that the house would make a good home for their family, too!

Directions: Answer these questions about good cooking.

1. Why do fewer people cook nowadays? They are too busy

2. Why are family meals important? They bring everyone together

3. What do homemade cookies do besides satisfy a child's sweet tooth?
   Someone cared enough to spend his/her time making them.

4. Real estate agents often advise home sellers holding open houses to
   ☐ clean the garage.   ☒ bake cookies or bread.

5. The smell of baking at open houses may encourage buyers to
   ☐ bake cookies.   ☒ buy the house.   ☐ bake bread.

Page 139

Sequencing: Chocolate Chunk Cookies

These chocolate chunk cookies require only five ingredients. Before you combine them, preheat the oven to 350 degrees. Preheating the oven to the correct temperature is always step number one in baking.

Now, into a large mixing bowl, empty an 18¼-ounce package of chocolate fudge cake mix (any brand). Add a 10-ounce package of semi-sweet chocolate, broken into small pieces, two 5⅛-ounce packages of chocolate fudge pudding mix (any brand) and 1½ cups chopped walnuts.

Use a large wooden spoon to combine the ingredients. When they are well-mixed, add 1½ cups mayonnaise and stir thoroughly. Shape the dough into small balls and place the balls 2 inches apart on an ungreased cookie sheet. Bake 12 minutes. Cool and eat!

Directions: Number in correct order the steps for making chocolate chunk cookies.

__6__ Place 1½ cups of mayonnaise in the bowl.

__8__ Shape dough into small balls and place them on a cookie sheet.

__2__ Empty the package of chocolate fudge cake mix into the bowl.

__9__ Bake the dough for 12 minutes.

__4__ Place two 5⅛-ounce packages of chocolate fudge pudding in the bowl.

__5__ Put 1½ cups chopped walnuts in the bowl.

__1__ Preheat the oven to 350 degrees.

__3__ Place the 10-ounce package of semi-sweet chocolate pieces in the bowl.

__7__ Stir everything thoroughly.

Page 140

Comprehension: Eating High-Fiber Foods

Have you heard your parents or other adults talk about "high-fiber" diets? Foods that are high in fiber, like oats and other grains, are believed to be very healthy. Here's why: The fiber adds bulk to the food the body digests and helps keep the large intestines working properly. Corn, apples, celery, nuts and other chewy foods also contain fiber that helps keep the body's systems for digesting and eliminating food working properly.

Researchers at the University of Minnesota have found another good reason to eat high-fiber food, especially at breakfast. Because fiber is bulky, it absorbs a lot of liquid in the stomach. As it absorbs the liquid, it swells. This "fools" the stomach into thinking it's full. As a result, when lunchtime comes, those who have eaten a high-fiber breakfast are not as hungry. They eat food at lunch. Without much effort on their parts, dieters eating a high-fiber breakfast can lose weight.

The university researchers say a person could lose 10 pounds in a year just by eating a high-fiber breakfast! This is good news to people who are only slightly overweight and want an easy method for losing that extra 10 pounds.

Directions: Answer these questions about eating high-fiber foods.

1. Why is fiber healthy? It adds bulk and helps the large intestine work properly.

2. How does fiber "fool" the stomach? It absorbs liquid and swells.

3. How does "fooling" the stomach help people lose weight? People feel full and aren't as hungry.

4. How many pounds could a dieter eating a high-fiber breakfast lose in a year?

☐ 20 pounds ☐ 30 pounds ☒ 10 pounds

5. The university that did the research is in which state?

☐ Michigan ☒ Minnesota ☐ Montana

Page 141

Main Idea: New Corn

I will clothe myself in spring clothing
And visit the slopes of the eastern hill,
By the mountain stream, a mist hovers,
Hovers a moment and then scatters,
Then comes a wind blowing from the south
That brushes the fields of new corn.

Directions: Answer these questions about this ancient poem, which is translated from Chinese.

1. Circle the main idea:

(The poet will dress comfortably and go to where the corn grows so he/she can enjoy the beauty of nature.)

The poet will dress comfortably and visit the slopes of the eastern hill, where he/she will plant corn.

2. From which direction does the wind blow? the south

3. Where does the mist hover? by the mountain stream

4. What do you think the poet means by "spring clothing"? Answers will vary.

Page 142

Comprehension: The French Eat Differently

Many people believe that French people are very different from Americans. This is certainly true where eating habits are concerned! According to a report by the World Health Organization, each year the French people eat four times more butter than Americans. The French also eat twice as much cheese! In addition, they eat more vegetables, potatoes, grain and fish.

Yet, despite the fact that they eat larger amounts of these foods, the French take in about the same number of calories each day as Americans. (French and American men consume about 2,500 calories daily. French and American women take in about 1,600 calories daily.)

How can this be? If the French are eating more of certain types of foods, shouldn't this add up to more calories? And why are so few French people overweight compared to Americans? The answer—Americans consume 18 times more refined sugar than the French and drink twice as much whole milk!

Although many Americans believe the French end each meal with grand and gooey desserts, this just isn't so. Except for special occasions, dessert in a typical French home consists of fresh fruit or cheese. Many American families, on the other hand, like to end their meals with a bowl or two of ice cream or another sweet treat.

It's believed that this difference in the kind of calories consumed—rather than in the total number of calories taken in—is what causes many Americans to be chubby and most French people to be thin.

Directions: Answer these questions about the eating habits of French and American people.

1. How many calories does the average French man eat each day? 2,500

2. How much whole milk does the average French person drink compared to the average American? half as much

3. How much more refined sugar do Americans eat than the French?

☐ 2 times more ☒ 18 times more ☐ 15 times more

4. What do French families usually eat for dessert?

☐ refined sugar ☐ ice cream ☒ fruit and cheese

Page 143

Comprehension: Chinese Cabbage

Many Americans enjoy Chinese food. In big cities, like New York and Chicago, many Chinese restaurants deliver their food in small boxes to homes. It's just like ordering a pizza! Then the people who ordered the "take-out" food simply open it, put it on their plates and eat it while it's hot.

Because it tastes so good, many people are curious about the ingredients in Chinese food. Siu choy and choy sum are two types of Chinese cabbage that many people enjoy eating. Siu choy grows to be 2 to 3 feet! Of course, it is chopped into small pieces before it is cooked and served. Its leaves are light green and soft. It is not crunchy like American cabbage. Siu choy is used in soups and stews. Sometimes it is pickled with vinegar and other ingredients and served as a side dish to other courses.

Choy sum looks and tastes different from siu choy. Choy sum grows to be only 8 to 10 inches. It is a flowering cabbage that grows small yellow flowers. The flowers are "edible," which means they can be eaten. Its leaves are long and bright green. After its leaves are boiled for 4 minutes, choy sum is often served as a salad. Oil and oyster sauce are mixed together and poured over choy sum as a salad dressing.

Directions: Answer these questions about Chinese cabbage.

1. Which Chinese cabbage grows small yellow flowers? choy sum

2. Which Chinese cabbage is served as a salad? choy sum

3. Is siu choy crunchy? no

4. What ingredients are in the salad dressing used on choy sum? oil and oyster sauce

5. To what size does siu choy grow? 2 to 3 feet

6. Name two main dishes in which siu choy is used. soups and stews

Page 144

Review

Here's a recipe for a special mashed potato treat that serves two people. The recipe is fast and easy to follow, and the results are delicious!

Begin by peeling two large potatoes and cooking them in a pot of boiling water. When a fork or knife inserted into them pulls out easily, you will know they are done. Then take them from the pot and drain them well. Place them in a large mixing bowl and add 2 tablespoons of milk and 2 tablespoons of butter. Mash with a potato masher until the lumps are gone.

In a skillet, melt a tablespoon of butter and add one bunch of chopped green onions. Cook them about 1 minute. Add them to the potatoes and mix gently. Season with salt and pepper and add more butter if desired. Serve and eat!

Directions: Answer these questions about how to make mashed potatoes with green onions.

1. Circle the main idea:

(This recipe is fast and easy, and the potatoes are delicious.)

This recipe has only four ingredients (plus salt and pepper).

2. Name the main ingredients in this recipe (not including salt and pepper). potatoes, milk, butter, green onions

3. How many people does this recipe serve? 2

4. Number in order the steps for making mashed potatoes with green onions.

__4__ Cook the chopped green onions for 1 minute.

__1__ Peel two potatoes.

__6__ Season with salt and pepper and serve.

__3__ Put the cooked potatoes in a bowl with milk and butter, then mash.

__5__ Add the onions to the mashed potatoes.

__2__ Boil the potatoes until they are done.

Page 145

Using Prior Knowledge: Greek and Roman Mythology

Directions: Before reading about Greek and Roman mythology in the following section, answer these questions.

1. Hercules is a man from Greek and Roman mythology. Write a short paragraph describing what you know about Hercules.

2. Can you think of anything today that derived its name from a Greek or Roman myth?

Answers will vary.

3. Compare and contrast what you know of Greek and Roman beliefs about mythology with your beliefs.

4. Many constellations are named after gods, goddesses and mythical creatures. Name at least six.

Page 146

Comprehension: Roman Legends

Long ago, people did not know as much about science and astronomy as they do today. When they did not understand something, they thought the "gods" were responsible. The ancient Romans believed there were many gods and that each god or goddess (a female god) was responsible for certain things.

For example, the Romans believed Ceres (Sir-eez) was the goddess who made flowers, plants, trees and other things grow. She was a lot like what people today refer to as Mother Nature. Ceres was also responsible for the good weather that made crops grow. You can see why Ceres was such an important goddess to the ancient Romans.

Apollo was the god of the sun. People believed he used his chariot to pull the sun up each day and take it down at night. Apollo was extremely good-looking. His home was a golden palace near the sun surrounded by fluffy white clouds. Apollo had to work every single day, but he lived a wonderful life.

Jupiter was the most important god of all. He was the god who ruled all of the other gods, as well as the people. Jupiter was also called Jove. Maybe you have heard someone use the exclamation, "By Jove!" That person is talking about Jupiter! The word **father** is derived from the word Jupiter. Although he did not really exist, Jupiter influenced our language.

Directions: Answer these questions about Roman legends.

1. What imaginary figure is Ceres compared to today? _Mother Nature_

2. Where did Apollo live? _a golden palace near the sun_

3. The word **father** is derived from the name of this god:

☐ Ceres ☐ Apollo ☒ Jupiter

4. Which is not true of Apollo? ☐ He had to work every day.
☒ He lived in a mountain cave.
☐ He was very handsome.

Page 147

Comprehension: Apollo and Phaethon

Apollo, the sun god, had a son named Phaethon (Fay-a-thun). Like most boys, Phaethon was proud of his father. He liked to brag to his friends about Apollo's important job, but no one believed that the great Apollo was his father.

Phaethon thought of a way to prove to his friends that he was telling the truth. He went to Apollo and asked if he could drive the chariot of the sun rise and set, they would be awestruck!

Apollo did not want to let Phaethon drive the chariot. He was afraid Phaethon was not strong enough to control the horses. But Phaethon begged until Apollo gave in. "Stay on the path," Apollo said. "If you dip too low, the sun will catch the earth on fire. If you go too high, people will freeze."

Unfortunately, Apollo's worst fears came true. Phaethon could not control the horses. He let them pull the chariot of the sun too close to the earth. To keep the earth from burning, Jupiter, father of the gods, sent a thunderbolt that hit Phaethon and knocked him from the driver's seat. When Phaethon let go of the reins, the horses pulled the chariot back up onto the proper path. Phaethon was killed as he fell to earth. His body caught fire and became a shooting star.

Directions: Answer these questions about the Roman legend of Apollo and his son.

1. Who did not believe Apollo was Phaethon's father? _Phaethon's friends_

2. What did Phaethon do to prove Apollo was his father? _drove the chariot of the sun_

3. Why did Jupiter send a lightning bolt? _to keep the earth from burning by knocking Phaethon from the driver's seat_

4. Which was not a warning from Apollo to Phaethon?

☐ Don't go too close to the earth. It will burn up.
☒ Don't pet the horses. They will run wild.
☐ Don't go too far from the earth. It will freeze.

Page 148

Context Clues: Mighty Hercules

Some people lift weights to build their strength. But Hercules (Her-cu-lees) had a different idea. He carried a calf on his shoulders every day. As the calf grew, it got heavier, and Hercules got stronger. Eventually, Hercules could carry a full-grown bull!

Hercules used his enormous strength to do many kind things. He became famous. Even the king had heard of Hercules! He called for Hercules to kill a lion that had killed many people in his kingdom. Hercules tracked the lion to its den and strangled it. Then Hercules made clothes for himself from the lion's skin. This kind of apparel was unusual, and soon Hercules was recognized everywhere he went. Hercules was big and his clothes made it easy to pick him out in a crowd!

The king asked Hercules to stay in his kingdom and help protect the people who lived there. Hercules performed many feats of strength and bravery. He caught a golden deer for the king. The deer had outrun everyone else. Then Hercules killed a giant, a dragon and other dangerous creatures. Hercules became a hero and was known throughout the kingdom.

Directions: Answer these questions about Hercules.

1. Use context clues to choose the correct definition of **enormous**.

☒ huge ☐ tiny ☐ smart

2. Use context clues to choose the correct definition of **strangle**.

☐ beat ☒ choke ☐ tickle

3. Use context clues to choose the correct definition of **den**.

☐ pond ☐ hutch ☒ home

4. Use context clues to choose the correct definition of **apparel**.

☐ appearance ☒ clothing ☐ personality

5. Use context clues to choose the correct definition of **feat**.

☐ trick ☐ treat ☒ act

Page 149

Comprehension: Ceres and Venus

Remember Ceres? She was like Mother Nature to the ancient Romans.

Ceres made the flowers, plants and trees grow. She made crops come up and rain fall. Ceres was a very important goddess. The ancient Romans depended on her for many things.

Although the gods and goddesses were important, they had faults like ordinary people. They argued with one another. Sometimes they got mad and lost their tempers. This is what happened to Ceres and another goddess named Venus (Veen-us). Venus, who was the goddess of love and beauty, got mad at Ceres. She decided to teach Ceres a lesson by causing Pluto, gloomy god of the underworld, to fall in love with Ceres' daughter, Proserpine (Pro-sur-pin-ay).

To accomplish this, Venus sent her son Cupid to shoot Pluto with his bow and arrow. Venus told Cupid that the man shot by this arrow would then fall in love with the first woman he saw. Venus instructed Cupid to make sure that woman was Ceres' daughter. Cupid waited with his bow and arrow until Pluto drove by Ceres' garden in his chariot. In the garden was Proserpine. Just as Pluto's chariot got near her, Cupid shot his arrow.

Ping! The arrow hit Pluto. It did not hurt, but it did its job well. Pluto fell instantly in love with poor Proserpine, who was quietly planting flowers. When Ceres did not even introduce himself! Pluto swooped down and carried Proserpine off in his chariot before she could stop him.

Directions: Answer these questions about Ceres and Venus.

1. With whom was Venus angry? _Ceres_

2. How did Venus decide to get even? _She made Pluto fall in love with Ceres' daughter._

3. Ceres' daughter's name was

☐ Perserpine. ☐ Prosperline. ☒ Proserpine.

4. Venus' son's name was

☐ Apollo. ☒ Cupid. ☐ Persperpine.

Page 150

Comprehension: Proserpine and Pluto

Proserpine was terrified in Pluto's palace in the underworld. She missed her mother, Ceres, and would not stop crying.

When Ceres discovered her daughter was missing, she searched the whole Earth looking for her. Of course, she did not find her. Ceres was so unhappy about Proserpine's disappearance that she refused to do her job, which was to make things grow. When Ceres did not work, rain could not fall and crops could not grow. Finally, Ceres went to Jupiter for help.

Jupiter was powerful, but so was Pluto. Jupiter told Ceres he could get Proserpine back from Pluto if she had not eaten any of Pluto's food. As it turned out, Proserpine had eaten something. She had swallowed six seeds from a piece of fruit. Because she felt sorry for the people on Earth who were suffering, Pluto told Jupiter that Proserpine could return temporarily to Ceres so she would cheer up and make crops grow again. But Pluto later came back for Proserpine and forced her to spend six months each year with him in the underworld—one month for each seed she had eaten. Every time she returned to the underworld, Ceres mourned and refused to do her job. This is how the Romans explained the seasons—when Proserpine is on Earth with Ceres, it is spring and summer; when Proserpine goes to the underworld, it is fall and winter.

Directions: Answer these questions about Proserpine and Pluto.

1. What happened to Ceres when Pluto took her daughter? _She was very unhappy and refused to do her job._

2. Whom did Ceres ask for help to get her daughter back? _Jupiter_

3. Why did Proserpine have to return to Pluto's underworld? _She had to spend one month there for each seed she had eaten._

4. How long did Proserpine have to stay in the underworld each time she returned?

six months

Page 151

Comprehension: Orpheus Saves the Day

Orpheus (Or-fee-us) was a talented Greek musician. Once, by playing beautiful music on his lyre (ly-er), he caused a ship that was stuck in the sand to move into the water. (A lyre is a stringed instrument that looks like a small harp and fits in the musician's lap.) The song was about how wonderful it was to sail upon the sea. The ship itself must have thought the song was wonderful, too, because it slipped into the water and sailed away!

There was a reason the ship understood Orpheus' song. Inside the ship was a piece of wood that a goddess had given to the captain of the ship. The captain's name was Jason. Once, Jason had helped an old woman across a deep river. He later learned that the old woman was a goddess. To thank him, the goddess gave Jason a piece of wood that could talk. She told him to use the wood when he built a new ship. If he ever got stuck while building the ship and did not know what to do, the goddess told Jason to ask the wood.

Several times, Jason and his crew got instructions from the wood. Finally, the ship was finished. It was beautiful and very large. Because it was so big, Jason and his men were unable to move it into the water. They called on Hercules for help, and even he could not make it budge. That's when Orpheus saved the day with his lyre.

Directions: Answer these questions about Orpheus' amazing talent.

1. Who owned the ship that was stuck? __Jason__
2. Where was the ship stuck? __in the sand__
3. Why did the ship get stuck? __It was too large to move.__
4. A lyre looks like what other instrument?
   ☐ harmonica   ☐ guitar   ☒ harp
5. Who did Jason first ask for help to move the ship?
   ☐ Orpheus   ☒ Hercules   ☐ Jupiter

Page 152

Review

Directions: Follow the instructions below.

1. Define the following words from this section.

astronomy: _____

reins: _____

lyre: _____

centaur: _____

minotaur: _____

myth: _____

2. Choose two words from ___ Answers will vary.
   1) _____
   2) _____
3. Write a summary of the selection "Mighty Hercules" (page 148).

_____
_____
_____

4. Complete the sequence of events from the selection "Proserpine and Pluto" (page 150).

1) Pluto fell in love with Proserpine and kidnapped her in his chariot.
2) _____
3) _____
4) _____
5) _____

Page 153

Using Prior Knowledge: Famous Ships

Directions: Before reading about famous ships in the following section, answer these questions.

1. Look up the following terms in a dictionary and write their definitions.

vessel: _____
bow: _____
stern: _____
poop deck: _____
hull: _____
caravel: _____
mast: _____
frigate: _____
lateen: _____   Answers will vary.
spar: _____
fore: _____
aft: _____

2. Have you ever been on a large ship? If so, describe the experience. If not, on what kind of ship or boat would you like to ride? Why?

_____
_____
_____

3. Name at least one famous ship and write what you know about it.

_____
_____

Page 154

Comprehension: The *Constitution*

The *Constitution*, or "Old Ironsides," was built by the United States Navy in 1798. Its success in battle made it one of the most famous vessels in the United States.

The *Constitution's* naval career began with the war with Tripoli from 1803 to 1804. Later, it was also used in the War of 1812. During this war, it was commanded by Isaac Hull. The *Constitution* won a 30-minute battle with the British ship, *Guerriere*, in August of 1812. The *Guerriere* was nearly demolished. Later that year, the *Constitution* was used to capture a British frigate near Brazil.

The *Constitution* was taken out of service in 1829 and was rebuilt many times over the years. Today, it is on display at the Boston Navy Yard.

Directions: Answer these questions about the *Constitution*.

1. What is the main idea of the ___
   Answers will vary.

2. Which ship was almost demolished by the *Constitution*? __Guerriere__
3. In which two wars was the *Constitution* used? __war with Tripoli, War of 1812__
4. Where is the *Constitution* now on display? __Boston Navy Yard__
5. Complete the following time line with dates and events described above.

Constitution was built	War with Tripoli	War of 1812 Battle-*Guerriere*	taken out of service	on display at Boston Navy Yard
1798	1803-1804	1812	1829	Today (2000)

Page 155

Comprehension: The *Santa Maria*, *Niña* and *Pinta*

When Christopher Columbus decided to attempt a voyage across the ocean, the ships he depended upon to take him there were called "caravels." A caravel is a small sailing ship built by Spain and Portugal in the 15th and 16th centuries. The caravels Columbus used to sail to the New World were named *Santa Maria*, *Niña*, and *Pinta*.

The ships were not very large. It is believed the *Santa Maria* was only 75 to 90 feet long, and the *Niña* and *Pinta* were only about 70 feet long. Caravels typically had three to four masts with sails attached. The foremast carried a square sail, while the others were more triangular in shape. These triangular-shaped sails were called "lateen sails."

These three small ships were quite seaworthy and proved excellent ships for Columbus. They got him where he wanted to go.

Directions: Answer these questions about the *Santa Maria*, *Niña* and *Pinta*.

1. What is a lateen sail? __triangular-shaped sail__
2. What is the main idea of the selection?

Answers will vary.

3. What is a caravel? __small sailing ship built by Portugal and Spain__
4. Where did Columbus sail in his caravels? __to the New World__
5. Do some research and compare a 15th-century caravel with a ship built in the 20th century.

Answers will vary.

Page 156

Comprehension: The *Lusitania*

The *Lusitania* was a British passenger steamship. It became famous when it was torpedoed and sunk by the Germans during World War I. On May 7, 1915, the *Lusitania* was traveling off the coast of Ireland when a German submarine fired on it without warning. The ship stood no chance of surviving the attack and sunk in an astonishing 20 minutes. 1,198 people perished, of whom 128 were American citizens. At the time the ship was torpedoed, the United States was not yet involved in the war. Public opinion over the attack put pressure on President Woodrow Wilson to declare war on Germany. The Germans proclaimed that the *Lusitania* was carrying weapons for the use of the allies.

This claim was later proven to be true. President Wilson demanded that the German government apologize for the sinking and make amends. Germany did not accept responsibility but did promise to avoid sinking any more passenger ships without first giving a warning.

Directions: Answer these questions about the *Lusitania*.

1. What does *proclaimed* mean? _____
2. What does *perished* mean? _____
3. What does ___
4. What does   Answers will vary.
5. If the *Lusitania* ___ carrying arms, do you think the Germans had a right to sink it? Why or why not?

_____
_____
_____

Page 157

Comprehension: The *Titanic*

The British passenger ship, *Titanic*, debuted in the spring of 1912. It was billed as an unsinkable ship due to its construction. It had 16 watertight compartments that would hold the ship afloat even in the event that four of the compartments were damaged.

But on the evening of April 14, 1912, during *Titanic's* first voyage, its design proved unworthy. Just before midnight, *Titanic* struck an iceberg, which punctured 5 of the 16 compartments. The ship sunk in a little under 3 hours. Approximately 1,513 of the over 2,220 people onboard died. Most of these people died because there weren't enough lifeboats to accommodate everyone onboard. These people were left floating in the water. Many died from exposure, since the Atlantic Ocean was near freezing in temperature. It was one of the worst ocean disasters in history.

Because of the investigations that followed the *Titanic* disaster, the passenger ship industry instituted many reforms. It is now required that there is ample lifeboat space for all passengers and crew. An international ice patrol and full-time radio coverage were also instituted to prevent such disasters in the future.

Directions: Answer these questions about the *Titanic*.

1. How did most of the 1,513 people onboard the *Titanic* die? __exposure to cold__

2. Why did this "unsinkable" ship sink? __An iceberg punctured too many__ __of its compartments.__

3. What changes have been made in ship safety as a result of the *Titanic* tragedy? __They must have enough lifeboats, international ice patrol,__ __full-time radio coverage.__

4. There have been many attempts to rescue artifacts from the *Titanic*. But many families of the dead wish the site to be left alone, as it is the final resting place of their relatives. They feel burial sites should not be disrupted. Do you agree or disagree? Why?

__Answers will vary.__

Page 158

Venn Diagram: *Lusitania* and *Titanic*

A **Venn diagram** is used to chart information that shows similarities and differences between two things.

Example:

Dogs	Both	Cats
bark	good pets	one size
dependent	can live inside or outside	kill mice
large and small breeds	have fur	can use litterbox
protect the home	four legs	independent

Directions: Complete the Venn diagram for the *Lusitania* and the *Titanic*.

Sample answers:

Lusitania
- Sunk by torpedo
- Many deaths because it sunk so fast
- Was carrying weapons for the allies in WWI

Both
- British passenger ship
- They sunk
- Many lives were lost

Titanic
- Sunk by iceberg
- Many deaths because there weren't enough lifeboats
- Many reforms were enacted after this disaster

Page 159

Comprehension: The *Monitor* and the *Virginia*

During the Civil War, it became customary to cover wooden warships with iron. This increased their durability and made them more difficult to sink. Two such ships were built using iron. They were the *Monitor* and the *Virginia*.

Most people are more familiar with the *Merrimack*. The *Merrimack* was a U.S. steam frigate that had been burnt and sunk by Union forces when the Confederates were forced to abandon their navy yard. The Confederate Navy raised the hull of the *Merrimack* and rebuilt her as the ironclad *Virginia*.

Both the *Monitor* and the *Virginia* engaged in battle on March 9, 1962. After several hours of battle, the bulky *Virginia* had no choice but to withdraw in order to avoid the lowering tides. This battle, called Hampton Roads, was considered to be a tie between the two ships.

Although both ships survived the battle, they were later destroyed. Two months later, the *Virginia* was sunk by her crew to avoid capture. The *Monitor* sunk on December 31, 1862, during a storm off the coast of North Carolina.

Directions: Use context clues for these definitions.

1. customary: _____
2. durability: _____ Answers will vary.
3. ironclad: _____

Directions: Answer these questions about the *Monitor* and the *Virginia*.

4. Who won the battle between the *Virginia* and the *Monitor*? __It was a tie.__

5. Why would lowering tides __Answers will vary.__

6. Describe how each ship was finally destroyed. __The *Virginia* was sunk__ __by its crew to avoid capture.__ __The *Monitor* sunk in a storm.__

Page 160

Review

1. Use the Venn diagram you completed comparing the *Lusitania* and the *Titanic* (page 158) to write a two-paragraph compare/contrast essay about the two ships. Describe their similarities in the first paragraph and their differences in the second.

__Answers will vary.__

2. Describe the differences in the structure of the following ships: *Santa Maria*, *Monitor* and *Titanic*.

__The *Santa Maria* was a relatively small sailing ship.__ __The *Monitor* was an iron-clad warship.__ __The *Titanic* was a luxury passenger ship built with 16__ __air-tight compartments to make it "unsinkable."__

3. Why did people think the *Titanic* was unsinkable? After the ship actually did sink, how do you think this affected the way people thought about new technology?

__The *Titanic* was constructed with 16 air-tight compartments.__

__Answers will vary.__

Page 161

Reading Comprehension: Railroads

Directions: Read the information about railroads. Then answer the questions.

As early as the 1550s, a rough form of railroad was already being used in parts of Europe. Miners in England and other areas of western Europe used horse- or mule-drawn wagons on wooden tracks to pull loads out of mines. With these tracks, the horses could pull twice as much weight as they could without them. No one could have known then that one day this simple idea would change the world.

There were many developments along the way that helped make railroads a practical and valuable form of transportation. Two of the most important were the iron track and the "flanged" wheel, which has a rim around it to hold it onto the track. The most important invention was the steam engine by James Watt in 1765.

The first railroads in the United States were built during the late 1820s and caused a lot of excitement. They were faster than other forms of travel, and they could provide service year-round, unlike boats and stagecoaches. Trains were soon the main means of travel in the U.S.

Railroads played a major part in the Industrial Revolution—the years of change when machines were first used to do work that had been done by hand for many centuries. Trains provided cheaper rates and quicker service for transporting goods. Because manufacturers could ship their goods over long distances, they could sell their products all over the nation instead of only in the surrounding cities and towns. This meant greater profits for the companies. Trains also brought people into the cities to work in factories.

1. What was the source of power for the earliest railroads? __horses or mules__

2. What were three important developments that made railroads a practical means of transportation?
   __iron track__
   __"flanged" wheels__
   __steam engine__

3. What is meant by the Industrial Revolution? __the years of change__ __from people-made to machine-made products__

4. What were two ways that railroads changed life in America? __They provided__ __more reliable and faster transportation for people and products.__

Page 162

Main Idea: Locomotives

Directions: Read the information about locomotives. Then answer the questions.

In the 1800s, the steam locomotive was considered by many to be a symbol of the new Industrial Age. It was, indeed, one of the most important inventions of the time. Over the years, there have been many changes to the locomotive. One of the most important has been its source of power. During its history, the locomotive has gone from steam to electric to diesel power.

The first railroads used horses or mules for power, but the development of the steam locomotive made railroads a practical means of transportation. The first steam locomotive was built in 1804 in Great Britain by Richard Trevithick. It could haul 50,000 pounds, but it was not very successful because it was so heavy it caused the tracks to fall apart. However, it encouraged other engineers to try to build steam locomotives. Two of the most important men to accept the challenge were George Stephenson and his son, Robert. Robert once won a contest to build the best locomotive. *The Rocket*, as he called it, had a top speed of 29 miles per hour.

In America, developments in steam engines were close behind those of the British. In 1830, Peter Cooper's tiny locomotive, called *Tom Thumb*, lost a famous race against a horse-drawn coach. In spite of the loss, it still convinced railroad officials that steam power was more practical than horsepower.

Just before the turn of the century, the electric locomotive was widely used. At its peak in the 1940s, U.S. railroads had 2,400 miles of electric routes.

The diesel locomotive was invented in the 1890s by Rudolf Diesel, a German engineer. The power of this locomotive was supplied by a diesel fuel engine. The diesel locomotive is still used today. It costs about twice as much as a steam locomotive to build, but it is much cheaper to operate.

1. What is the main idea of this selection?
   ___ The steam locomotive was considered a symbol of the Industrial Age.
   _X_ Over the years, there have been many changes to the locomotive.

2. Who built the first steam locomotive in 1804? __Richard Trevithick__

3. How fast could *The Rocket* travel? __29 miles per hour__

4. Who built the locomotive called *Tom Thumb*? __Peter Cooper__

5. *Tom Thumb* was in a race against a horse-drawn coach. Which won? __the horse-drawn coach__

6. What kind of fuel does a diesel engine use? __diesel fuel__

Page 163

Review

Directions: Define these words as used in the selections "Railroads" and "Locomotives."

1. flanged wheel __wheel which has a rim around it to hold it onto a track__
2. transportation __a way to move people and products from one place to another__
3. profit __money earned__
4. locomotive __a vehicle that pulls a train__
5. diesel __a type of fuel__
6. engineer __a person who drives a train__

Directions: Use information from the selection "Locomotives" to create a time line of the invention of locomotives.

7.

1804	early 1800s	1830	1890
George & Robert Stephenson build The Rocket	Tom Thumb built by Peter Cooper		diesel locomotive invented by Rudolf Diesel

First steam locomotive built in Great Britain by Richard Trevithick

Directions: Write your answer in a complete sentence.

8. The world is going through another "revolution" in industry today. What new technology is leading this change and how might it affect workers in the future?

__Answers will vary.__

Page 164

Reading Comprehension: Railroad Pioneer

Directions: Read the information about railroad pioneers. Then answer the questions by circling **Yes** or **No**.

George Stephenson was born in Wylam, England, in 1781. His family was extremely poor. When he was young, he didn't go to school but worked in the coal mines. In his spare time, he taught himself to read and write. After a series of explosions in the coal pits, Stephenson built a miner's safety lamp. This helped bring him to the attention of the owners of the coal mines. They put him in charge of all the machinery.

In 1812, Stephenson became an engine builder for the mines. The owners were interested in locomotives because the cost of horse feed was so high. They wanted Stephenson to build a locomotive to pull the coal cars from the mines. His first locomotive, The Blucher, was put on the rails in 1814.

Stephenson was a good engineer, and he was fortunate to work for a rich employer. Between 1814 and 1826, Stephenson was the only man in Great Britain building locomotives.

When the Stockholm and Darlington Railway, the first public railroad system, was planned, Stephenson was named company engineer. He convinced the owners to use steam power instead of horses. He built the first locomotive on the line. The Locomotion, as it was called, was the best locomotive that had been built anywhere in the world up to that time. Over the years, Stephenson was responsible for many other important developments in locomotive design, such as improved cast-iron rails and wheels, and the first steel springs strong enough to carry several tons.

Stephenson was convinced that the future of railroads lay in steam power. His great vision of what the railroad system could become was a driving force in the early years of its development.

1. George Stephenson was an excellent student in school. — Yes (No)
2. Stephenson's first invention was a miner's safety lamp. — (Yes) No
3. Between 1814 and 1826, Stephenson was one of many engineers building locomotives in Great Britain. — Yes (No)
4. The Stockholm and Darlington Railway was the first public railroad system. — (Yes) No
5. The first locomotive on the Stockholm and Darlington line was The Locomotion, built by Stephenson. — (Yes) No
6. Stephenson's ideas did not influence the development of the railroad system. — Yes (No)

Page 165

Tall Tales

A **tall tale** is a fictional story with exaggerated details and a "super" hero. The main character in a tall tale is much larger, stronger, smarter or better than a real person. Tall tales may be unbelievable, but they are fun to hear.

America had nearly 200,000 miles of railroad track by 1900. Because of the rapid growth and the excitement over the railroads, many colorful tall tales about railroad heroes and their adventures were told.

Directions: Read the story about John Henry. Then answer the questions.

A Steel-Driving Man

On the night John Henry was born, forked lightning split the air and the earth shook. He weighed 44 pounds at birth, and the first thing he did was reach for a hammer hanging on the wall. "He's going to be a steel-driving man," his father told his mother.

One night, John Henry dreamed he was working on a railroad. Every time his hammer hit a spike, the sky lit up with the sparks. "I dreamed that the railroad was going to be the end of me, and I'd die with a hammer in my hand," he said. When John Henry grew up he did work for the railroad. He was the fastest, most powerful steel-driving man in the world.

In about 1870, the steam drill was invented. One day the company at the far end of a tunnel tried it out. John Henry's company, working at the other end, continued to use men to do the drilling. There was much bragging from both companies as to which was faster. Finally, they decided to have a contest. John Henry was matched against the best man with a steam drill.

John Henry swung a 20-pound hammer in each hand. The sparks flew so fast and hot that they burned his face. At the end of the day, the judges said John Henry had beaten the steam drill by 4 feet!

That night, John Henry said, "I was a steel-driving man." Then he laid down and closed his eyes forever.

1. How much was John Henry said to have weighed at birth? __44 pounds__
2. Why did his father think he would be a __He reached for a hammer first.__
3. What invention was John Henry in a contest against? __steam drill__
4. Why was the contest held? __to see which was faster__
5. What tools did John Henry use in the contest? __two 20-pound hammers__
6. Who won the contest? __John Henry__
7. What happened to John Henry after the contest? __He died.__

Page 166

Tall Tales

Directions: Write a tall tale about yourself. Be sure to make it a fantastic and incredible story!

__Answers will vary.__

Directions: Reread your tall tale. Does it make sense? Check and correct spelling and grammar mistakes. Does your story fit the category of tall tale?

Page 167

Context Clues: Passenger Cars

Directions: Read the information about passenger cars. Use context clues to determine the meaning of words in bold. Check the correct answers.

Early railroad passenger cars were little more than stagecoaches fitted with special wheels to help them stay on the tracks. They didn't hold many passengers, and because they were made out of wood, they were fire **hazards**. They also did not hold up very well if the train came off the track or had a **collision** with another train.

In the United States, it wasn't long before passenger cars were lengthened to hold more people. Late in the 1830s, Americans were riding in **elongated** cars with double seats on either side of a center aisle. By the early 1900s, most cars were made of metal instead of wood.

Sleeping and dining cars were introduced in the United States by the early 1860s. Over the next 25 years other improvements were made, including electric lighting, steam heat and covered **vestibules** that allowed passengers to walk between cars. All of these **luxuries** helped make railroad travel much more comfortable.

1. Based on the other words in the sentence, what is the correct definition of **hazards**?
   ___ engines   _X_ risks   ___ stations
2. Based on the other words in the sentence, what is the correct definition of **collision**?
   _X_ crash   ___ race   ___ track
3. Based on the other words in the sentence, what is the correct definition of **elongated**?
   ___ wooden   ___ new   _X_ lengthened
4. Based on the other words in the sentence, what is the correct definition of **vestibules**?
   _X_ passageways   ___ cars   ___ depots
5. Based on the other words in the sentence, what is the correct definition of **luxuries**?
   ___ additions   _X_ things offering the greatest comfort   ___ inventions

Page 168

Reading Skills: Railroads

Directions: Read the information about railroads. Then answer the questions.

When railroads became the major means of transportation, they replaced earlier forms of travel, like the stagecoach. Railroads remained the unchallenged leader for a hundred years. Beginning in the early 1900s, railroads faced **competition** from newer forms of transportation.

Today, millions of people have their own automobiles. Buses offer inexpensive travel between cities. Large trucks haul goods across the country. Airplanes provide quick transportation over long distances. The result has been a sharp drop in the use of trains.

Today, nearly all railroads face serious problems that threaten to drive them out of business. But railroads still provide low-cost, fuel-saving transportation that will remain important. One gallon of diesel fuel will haul about four times as much by railroad as by truck. In a time when the world is concerned about saving fuel, this is but one area in which the railroads still have much to offer.

1. What is the main idea of this selection?
   ___ When railroads became the major means of transportation, they replaced earlier forms of travel.
   _X_ Beginning in the early 1900s, railroads have faced competition from newer forms of transportation.
2. Based on the other words in the sentence, what is the correct definition of **competition**?
   _X_ businesses trying to get the same customers
   ___ problems
   ___ support
3. What are four newer forms of transportation that have challenged railroads? __cars, trucks, buses, airplanes__
4. One gallon of diesel fuel will haul about twice as much by railroad as by truck. — Yes (No)

Page 169

Reading Comprehension: Printing

Directions: Read the information about printing. Then answer the questions.

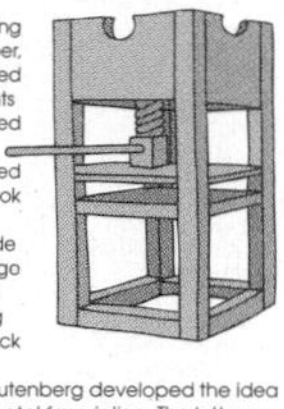

When people talk about printing, they usually mean making exact copies of an original document, such as a newspaper, magazine or an entire book. The inventions that have allowed us to do this are some of the most important developments in history. Look around you at the many examples of printed materials. Can you imagine life without them?

Until the thirteenth century, all material had to be printed by hand, one copy at a time. To make a copy of a book took much time and effort.

The oldest known example of a printed book was made in China in 848 A.D. by Wang Chieh, who carved each page of a book by hand onto a block of wood. He then put ink on the wood and pressed it on paper. The idea of printing with wood blocks spread to Europe. The letters in these block books were made to look handwritten.

In about 1440, a German goldsmith named Johann Gutenberg developed the idea of movable type. He invented separate letters made of metal for printing. The letters could be joined together to make words and sentences. Ink was applied to the letters to print many copies of the same material. Because they were made of metal, the letters could be used over and over. This wonderful invention made it possible to have more printed material at a lower cost.

Gutenberg had other ideas that were important to printing. He developed a special type of ink that would stick to the new metal letters. Gutenberg's ideas were so successful that the process of printing went almost unchanged for more than 300 years.

1. In what country was the oldest known printed book made?
   China
2. Who made the first printed book?
   Wang Chieh
3. What is "movable type"?
   separate letters made of metal for printing
4. Who developed the idea of movable type?
   Johann Gutenberg
5. What was another important invention of Gutenberg?
   special ink

Page 170

Reading Comprehension: Newspapers

Directions: Read the information about newspapers. Then answer the questions.

Newspapers keep us informed about what is going on in the world. They entertain, educate and examine the events of the day. For millions of people worldwide, newspapers are an important part of daily life.

Newspapers are published at various intervals, but they usually come out daily or weekly. Of the nearly 60,000 newspapers published around the world, about 2,600 are published in the United States. More than half—about 1800—of them are dailies.

Some newspapers have many subscribers—people who pay to have each edition delivered to them. *The Wall Street Journal* and *USA Today* each have about two million subscribers. There are many, many newspapers with only a few thousand subscribers. These include small-town weeklies and special-interest papers, like those written for people who enjoy the same hobby.

Newspapers provide a service to the community by providing information at little cost. But newspaper publishing is a business, so like other businesses, newspapers need to make money. They can keep the cost to subscribers low and still stay in business by selling space to businesses and individuals who want to advertise products or services. In most newspapers, between one-third and two-thirds of the paper is taken up by advertising.

1. About how many newspapers are published worldwide?
   nearly 60,000
2. What services do newspapers provide?
   entertain, educate, examine events
3. What are subscribers?
   people who pay to have newpapers delivered to them
4. How often are most newspapers published?
   daily
5. What do newspapers do to keep the cost to the reader low, but still make money?
   They sell space for ads.
6. In most newspapers, about how much of the paper is taken up by advertising?
   between one-third and two-thirds

Page 171

Reading Comprehension: Newspapers

Directions: Read the information about the first newspapers. Then answer the questions.

Long ago, town criers walked through cities reading important news to the people. The earliest newspapers were probably handwritten notices posted in towns for the public to read.

The first true newspaper was a weekly paper started in Germany in 1609. It was called *The Strassburg Relation*. The Germans were pioneers in newspaper publishing. Johann Gutenberg, the man who developed movable type, was German.

One of the first English-language newspapers, *The London Gazette*, was first printed in England in 1665. Gazette is an old English word that means "official publication." Many newspapers today still use the word gazette in their names.

In America, several papers began during colonial days. The first successful one, *The Boston News-Letter*, began printing in 1704. It was very small—about the size of a sheet of notebook paper with printing on both sides.

An important date in newspaper publishing was 1833. In that year, *The New York Sun* became the first penny newspaper. The paper actually did cost only a penny. The penny newspapers were similar to today's papers: they printed news while it was still new, they were the first to print advertisements and to sell papers in newsstands, and they were the first to be delivered to homes.

1. How were the earliest newspapers different from today's newspapers?
   They were handwritten notices posted in town.
2. In what year and where was the first true newspaper printed?
   1609 in Germany
3. What was the name of the first successful newspaper in America?
   The Boston News-Letter
4. Why was 1833 important in newspaper publishing?
   The first penny newspaper was published.
5. List four ways penny newspapers were like the newspapers of today.
   printed fresh news
   printed advertisements
   sold at newstands
   delivered to homes

Page 172

Reading Comprehension: Newspaper Jobs

Directions: Read the information about jobs at a newspaper. Then answer the questions.

It takes an army of people to put out one of the big daily newspapers. Three separate departments are needed to make a newspaper operate smoothly: editorial, mechanical and business.

The editorial department is the one most people think about first. That is the news-gathering part of the newspaper. The most familiar job in this department is that of the reporter—the person who obtains information for a story and writes it. A photographer takes pictures to go along with the reporter's story.

Editors are the decision-makers. There are many editors at a large newspaper. They assign stories to reporters, read the stories to be certain they are correct and decide where and if the stories should appear in the paper. The most important stories go on the front page. There are also photo editors who choose which pictures will appear in the paper. Other workers in the editorial department include artists, copy editors, proofreaders and cartoonists.

The biggest job in the mechanical department is printing the paper. Most large newspapers have their own printing presses. Some small papers send their work to outside printing shops. After an issue, or edition, is printed, it is ready to be sold or "circulated" to the public.

Circulation of the paper is one of the jobs of the business department. This department also sells advertising space. This is very important for newspapers. Many papers make more money selling advertising space than selling newspapers. The business department also takes care of normal business jobs, like paying employees, paying bills and keeping records.

1. What are the three main departments at a newspaper?
   editorial, mechanical, business
2. Who gets the information for a story and writes it?
   reporter
3. Who are the decision-makers at a newspaper?
   editors
4. What is the biggest job for the mechanical department?
   printing the paper
5. What is the most important job of the business department?
   selling advertising space

Page 173

Reading Comprehension: News Stories

Directions: Read the information about news stories. Then draw an **X** on the line to show the corrct meaning of the bold word.

Here is an example of how a story gets into the newspaper:

Let's imagine that a city bus has turned over in a ditch, injuring some of the passengers. An **eyewitness** calls the newspaper. The editor assigns a reporter to go to the scene. The reporter talks to the passengers, driver and witnesses who saw the accident. She finds out what they saw and how they feel, writing down their comments or tape recording their answers. At the same time, a photographer is busy taking pictures.

If there isn't time for the reporter to go back to the newsroom, she could call and **dictate** the story to a copytaker who types the story into a computer. Many reporters use portable computers which allow them to write the story on the spot and then send it back to the office over the telephone by modem.

Next, an editor reads the story, checking facts, grammar and spelling. Meanwhile, the photographer's film is developed and a picture is chosen.

The story is set in print. On most newspapers today, this is done with a computer. The computer makes sets of columns of type, which are pasted onto a sheet of paper exactly the same size as a newspaper page. A **proofreader** checks the story for mistakes. The newspaper is now ready for printing. The presses begin to run.

Miles of paper are turned into thousands of printed, cut and folded newspapers. They are counted, put into bundles and placed in waiting trucks. Within a few hours, people can read about the bus accident in their daily newspaper.

1. Based on the other words in the sentence, what is the correct definition of **eyewitness**?
   ______ a reporter
   __X__ a person who saw what happened
   ______ a lawyer
2. Based on the other words in the sentence, what is the correct definition of **dictate**?
   ______ govern without regard for what people want
   ______ use a dictionary
   __X__ read a story word for word for someone else to write
3. Based on the other words in the sentence, what is the correct definition of **proofreader**?
   __X__ person who checks for mistakes
   ______ person who shows proof he has read a book
   ______ a teacher

Page 174

Reading Comprehension: News Services

Directions: Read the information about news services. Then answer the questions.

When people read daily newspapers, they expect to see current news from all over the world. Some newspapers have offices or reporters in Washington, D.C. and other major cities around the world. Most newspapers rely on news services for international news. News services are organizations that gather and sell news to papers, radio and television stations. They are sometimes referred to as "wire services," because they originally sent stories over telegraph or Teletype lines, or "wires."

The two largest news services are the Associated Press and United Press International. Stories sent by these services have their initials—AP or UPI—at the beginning of the article. All large American newspapers are members of either the AP or UPI service.

At one time, people had to wait for messengers to arrive by foot, horse or ship to learn the news. By the time it reached a newspaper, news could be months old.

Gathering news from around the world became much faster after the invention of the telegraph, Teletype, telephone and transatlantic cable. Today, satellites, computer modems and fax machines can send stories, pictures and even videos around the world in seconds.

1. What is another name for news service organizations?
   wire services
2. What are the two largest news service organizations?
   Associated Press (AP) and United Press International (UPI)
3. What are three inventions that have speeded up worldwide news-gathering?
   telegraph, Teletype, telephone, transatlantic cable, satellites, computers, fax machines
4. Why do newspapers use news services?
   to obtain news from all over the world
5. How was news delivered before the invention of modern communication devices?
   by messengers on foot, horse or ship

Page 175

Reading Comprehension: Samuel Clemens

Directions: Read the information about Samuel Clemens.

Samuel Langhorne Clemens was born in Florida, Missouri, in 1835. In his lifetime, he gained worldwide fame as a writer, lecturer and humorist. Clemens first worked for a printer when he was only 12 years old. Soon after that he worked on his brother's newspaper.

Clemens traveled frequently and worked as a printer in New York, Philadelphia, St. Louis and Cincinnati. On a trip to New Orleans in 1857, he learned the difficult art of steamboat **piloting**. Clemens loved piloting and later used it as a background for some of his books, including *Life on the Mississippi.*

A few years later, Clemens went to Nevada with his brother and tried gold mining. When this proved unsuccessful, he went back to writing for newspapers. At first he signed his humorous pieces with the name "Josh." In 1863, he began signing them Mark Twain. The words "mark twain" were used by riverboat pilots to mean two fathoms (12 feet) deep, water deep enough for steamboats. From then on, Clemens used this now-famous **pseudonym** for all his writing.

As Mark Twain, he received attention from readers all over the world. His best-known works include *Tom Sawyer* and *The Adventures of Huckleberry Finn.* These two books about boyhood adventures remain popular with readers of all ages.

Directions: Check the correct answer.

1. Based on the other words in the sentence, what is the correct definition of **pseudonym**?
   ___ book title
   _X_ a made-up name used by an author
   ___ a humorous article

2. Based on the other words in the sentence, what is the correct definition of **piloting**?
   ___ driving an airplane
   _X_ steering a steamboat on a river
   ___ being a train engineer

Directions: Write the answers.

3. Under what name did Samuel Clemens write his books?
   Mark Twain
4. What do the words "mark twain" mean?
   two fathoms (12 feet)
5. Besides author, list two other jobs held by Mark Twain.
   reporter, pilot, printer, miner
6. List two of the best-known books written by Mark Twain.
   Tom Sawyer and The Adventures of Huckleberry Finn

Page 176

Review

Directions: Write the answers.

1. What are two ways newspapers earn money?
   sell subscriptions
   sell advertising space

2. What was Mark Twain's real name?
   Samuel Clemens

3. Name six jobs at a newspaper.
   Answers could include: reporter, editor, photographer, proofreader, copy taker, press operator, circulation director, sales, business director, etc.

4. What is the purpose of the Associated Press and the United Press International?
   to provide international news in a timely manner to newspapers, television and radio stations

Directions: Use dates from the articles "Printing" and "Newspapers" to create a time line of the development of newspapers.

848 AD	1440	1609	1665	1704	1833
first book printed in China	movable type invented in Germany	first true newspaper printed the Strassburg Relation	London Gazette first printed in England	First successful American paper, The Boston Herald	first penny newspaper published

Page 177

Recognizing Details: The Coldest Continent

Directions: Read the information about Antarctica. Then answer the questions.

Antarctica lies at the South Pole and is the coldest continent. It is without sunlight for months at a time. Even when the sun does shine, its angle is so slanted that the land receives little warmth. Temperatures often drop to 100 degrees below zero, and a fierce wind blows almost endlessly. Most of the land is covered by snow heaped thousands of feet deep. The snow is so heavy and tightly packed that it forms a great ice cap covering more than 95 percent of the continent.

Considering the conditions, it is no wonder there are no towns or cities in Antarctica. There is no permanent population at all, only small scientific research stations. Many teams of explorers and scientists have braved the freezing cold since Antarctica was sighted in 1820. Some have died in their effort, but a great deal of information has been learned about the continent.

From fossils, pieces of coal and bone samples, we know that Antarctica was not always an ice-covered land. Scientists believe that 200 million years ago it was connected to southern Africa, South America, Australia and India. Forests grew in warm swamps, and insects and reptiles thrived there. Today, there are animals that live in and around the waters that border the continent. In fact, the waters surrounding Antarctica contain more life than oceans in warmer areas of the world.

1. Where is Antarctica? **at the South Pole**
2. How much of the continent is covered by an ice cap? **more than 95%**
3. When was Antarctica first sighted by explorers? **1820**
4. What clues indicate that Antarctica was not always an ice-covered land?
   fossils, pieces of coal, bone samples
5. Is Antarctica another name for the North Pole? Yes (No)

Page 178

Reading Comprehension: The Arctic Circle

Directions: Read the article about the Arctic Circle. Then answer the questions.

On the other side of the globe from Antarctica, at the northernmost part of the Earth, is another icy land. This is the Arctic Circle. It includes the North Pole itself and the northern fringes of three continents—Europe, Asia and North America, including the state of Alaska—as well as Greenland and other islands.

The seasons are opposite at the two ends of the Earth. When it is summer in Antarctica, it is winter in the Arctic Circle. In both places, there are very long periods of sunlight in summer and very long nights in the winter. On the poles themselves, there are six full months of sunlight and six full months of darkness each year.

Compared to Antarctica, the summers are surprisingly mild in some areas of the Arctic Circle. Much of the snow cover may melt, and temperatures often reach 50 degrees in July. Antarctica is covered by water—frozen water, of course—so nothing can grow there. Plant growth is limited in the polar regions not only by the cold, but also by wind, lack of water and the long winter darkness.

In the far north, willow trees grow but only become a few inches high! The annual rings, the circles within the trunk of a tree that show its age and how fast it grows, are so narrow in those trees that you need a microscope to see them.

A permanently frozen layer of soil, called "permafrost," keeps roots from growing deep enough into the ground to anchor a plant. Even if a plant could survive the cold temperatures, it could not grow roots deep enough or strong enough to allow the plant to get very big.

1. What three continents have land included in the Arctic Circle?
   Europe **Asia** **North America**
2. Is the Arctic Circle generally warmer or colder than Antarctica?
   warmer
3. What is "permafrost"? **a permanently frozen layer of soil**
4. Many tall pine trees grow in the Arctic Circle. Yes (No)

Page 179

Main Idea: The Polar Trail

Directions: Read the information about explorers to Antarctica.

A recorded sighting of Antarctica, the last continent to be discovered, was not made until the early nineteenth century. Since then, many brave explorers and adventurers have sailed south to conquer the icy land. Their achievements once gained as much world attention as those of the first astronauts.

Long before the continent was first spotted, the ancient Greeks suspected there was a continent at the bottom of the Earth. Over the centuries, legends of the undiscovered land spread. Some of the world's greatest seamen tried to find it, including Captain James Cook in 1772.

Cook was the first to sail all the way to the solid field of ice that surrounds Antarctica every winter. In fact, he sailed all the way around the continent but never saw it. Cook went farther south than anyone had ever gone. His record lasted 50 years.

Forty years after Cook, a new kind of seamen sailed the icy waters. They were hunters of seals and whales. Sailing through unknown waters in search of seals and whales, these men became explorers as well as hunters. The first person known to sight Antarctica was an American hunter, 21-year-old Nathaniel Brown Palmer in 1820.

Directions: Draw an X on the blank for the correct answer.

1. The main idea is:
   ___ Antarctica was not sighted until the early nineteenth century.
   _X_ Many brave explorers and adventurers have sailed south to conquer the icy land.

2. The first person to sail to the ice field that surrounds Antarctica was:
   ___ Nathaniel Brown Palmer
   _X_ Captain James Cook
   ___ Neal Armstrong

3. His record for sailing the farthest south stood for:
   ___ 40 years
   _X_ 50 years
   ___ 500 years

4. The first person known to sight Antarctica was:
   ___ an unknown ancient Greek
   ___ Captain James Cook
   _X_ Nathaniel Brown Palmer

5. His profession was:
   _X_ hunter
   ___ ship captain
   ___ explorer

Page 180

Recognizing Details: The Frozen Continent

Directions: Read the information about explorers. Then answer the questions.

By the mid-1800s, most of the seals and bone of Antarctica had been killed. The seal hunters no longer sailed the icy waters. The next group of explorers who took an interest in Antarctica were scientists. Of these, the man who took the most daring chances and made the most amazing discoveries was British Captain James Clark Ross.

Ross first made a name for himself sailing to the north. In 1831, he discovered the North Magnetic Pole—one of two places on Earth toward which a compass needle points. In 1840, Ross set out to find the South Magnetic Pole. He made many marvelous discoveries, including the Ross Sea, a great open sea beyond the ice packs that stopped other explorers, and the Ross Ice Shelf, a great floating sheet of ice bigger than all of France!

The next man to make his mark exploring Antarctica was British explorer Robert Falcon Scott. Scott set out in 1902 to find the South Pole. He and his team suffered greatly, but they were able to make it a third of the way to the pole. Back in England, Scott was a great hero. In 1910, he again attempted to become the first man to reach the South Pole. But this time he had competition: an explorer from Norway, Roald Amundsen, was also leading a team to the South Pole.

It was a brutal race. Both teams faced many hardships, but they pressed on. Finally, on December 14, 1911, Amundsen became the first man to reach the South Pole. Scott arrived on January 17, 1912. He was bitterly disappointed at not being first. The trip back was even more horrible. None of the five men in the Scott expedition survived.

1. After the seal hunters, who were the next group of explorers interested in Antarctica?
   scientists
2. What great discovery did James Ross make before ever sailing to Antarctica?
   He discovered the North Magnetic Pole.
3. What were two other great discoveries made by James Ross?
   Ross Sea **Ross Ice Shelf**
4. How close did Scott and his team come to the South Pole in 1902?
   one-third of the way
5. Who was the first person to reach the South Pole? **Roald Amundsen**

ANSWER KEY

Page 181

Reading Skills: Research

To learn more about the explorers to Antarctica, reference sources like encyclopedias, CD-ROMs, the internet and history books are excellent sources for finding more information.

Directions: Use reference sources to learn more about Captain James Cook and Captain James Clark Ross. Write an informational paragraph about each man.

1. Captain James Cook

_____

_____

_____

2. Captain James Clark Ross

Answers will vary.

3. What dangers did both these men and their teams face in their attempts to reach the South Pole?

_____

Page 182

Reading Comprehension: Polar Bears

Directions: Read the information about polar bears. Then answer the questions by circling **Yes** or **No**.

Some animals are able to survive the cold weather and difficult conditions of the snow and ice fields in the Arctic polar regions. One of the best known is the polar bear.

Polar bears live on the land and the sea. They may drift hundreds of miles from land on huge sheets of floating ice. They use their great paws to paddle the ice along. Polar bears are excellent swimmers, too. They can cross great distances of open water. While in the water, they feed mostly on fish and seals.

On land, these huge animals, which measure 10 feet long and weigh about 1,000 pounds, can run 25 miles an hour. Surprisingly, polar bears live as plant-eaters rather than hunters while on land. Unlike many kinds of bears, polar bears do not hibernate. They are active the whole year.

Baby polar bears are born during the winter. At birth, they are pink and almost hairless. These helpless cubs weigh only two pounds—less than one-third the size of most human infants. The mother bears raise their young in dens dug in snowbanks. By the time they are 10 weeks old, polar bear cubs are about the size of puppies and have enough white fur to protect them in the open air. The mothers give their cubs swimming, hunting and fishing lessons. By the time autumn comes, the cubs are left to survive on their own.

1. Polar bears can live on the land and the sea. **(Yes)** No
2. Polar bears are excellent swimmers. **(Yes)** No
3. Polar bears hibernate in the winter. Yes **(No)**
4. A newborn polar bear weighs more than a newborn human baby. Yes **(No)**
5. Mother polar bears raise their babies in caves. Yes **(No)**
6. Father polar bears give the cubs swimming lessons. Yes **(No)**

Page 183

Context Clues: Seals

Directions: Read the information about seals. Use context clues to determine the meaning of the bold words. Check the correct answers.

Seals are **aquatic** mammals that also live on land at times. Some seals stay in the sea for weeks or months at a time, even sleeping in the water. When seals go on land, they usually choose **secluded** spots to avoid people and other animals.

The 31 different kinds of seals belong to a group of animals often called pinnipeds meaning "fin-footed." Their fins, or flippers, make them very good swimmers and divers. Their nostrils close tightly when they dive. They have been known to stay **submerged** for as long as a half-hour at a time!

Seals are warm-blooded animals that can adjust to various temperatures. They live in both **temperate** and cold climates. Besides their fur to keep them warm, seals have a thick layer of fat, called blubber, to protect them against the cold. It is harder for seals to cool themselves in hot weather than to warm themselves in cold weather. They can sometimes become so overheated that they die.

1. Based on other words in the sentence, what is the correct definition of **aquatic**?
   - _____ living on the land
   - **✓** living on or in the sea
   - _____ living in large groups

2. Based on other words in the sentence, what is the correct definition of **submerged**?
   - **✓** under the water
   - _____ on top of the water
   - _____ in groups

3. Based on other words in the sentence, what is the correct definition of **secluded**?
   - _____ rocky
   - **✓** private or hidden
   - _____ near other animals

4. Based on other words in the sentence, what is the correct definition of **temperate**?
   - _____ rainy
   - _____ measured on a thermometer
   - **✓** warm

Page 184

Reading Comprehension: Walruses

Directions: Read the information about walruses. Then answer the questions.

A walrus is actually a type of seal that lives only in the Arctic Circle. It has two huge upper teeth, or tusks, which it uses to pull itself out of the water or to move over the rocks on land. It also uses its tusks to dig clams, one of its favorite foods, from the bottom of the sea. On an adult male walrus, the tusks may be three and a half feet long!

A walrus has an unusual face. Besides its long tusks, it has a big, bushy mustache made up of hundreds of movable, stiff bristles. These bristles also help the walrus push food into its mouth. Except for small wrinkles in the skin, a walrus has no outer ears.

Like a seal, the walrus uses its flippers to help it swim. Its front flippers serve as paddles, and while swimming, it swings the back of its huge body from side to side. A walrus looks awkward using its flippers to walk on land, but don't be fooled! A walrus can run as fast as a man.

Baby walruses are born in the early spring. They stay with their mothers until they are two years old. There is a good reason for this—they must grow little tusks, at least three or four inches long, before they can catch their own food from the bottom of the sea. Until then, they must stay close to their mothers to eat. A young walrus that is tired from swimming will climb onto its mother's back for a ride, holding onto her with its front flippers.

1. The walrus is a type of seal found only ___ **in the Arctic Circle**

2. List two ways the walrus uses its tusks.
   to pull itself out of water ___ **to dig clams**

3. A walrus cannot move quickly on land. Yes **(No)**
4. A walrus has a large, bushy mustache. **(Yes)** No
5. A baby walrus stays very close to its mother until it is two years old. **(Yes)** No
6. Baby walruses are born late in fall. Yes **(No)**

Page 185

Main Idea: Penguins

Directions: Read the information about penguins.

People are amused by the funny, duck-like waddle of penguins and by their appearance because they seem to be wearing little tuxedos. Penguins are among the best-liked animals on Earth, but are also a most misunderstood animal. People may have more wrong ideas about penguins than any other animal.

For example, many people are surprised to learn that penguins are really birds, not mammals. Penguins do not fly, but they do have feathers, and only birds have feathers. Also, like other birds, penguins build nests and their young hatch from eggs. Because of their unusual looks, though, you would never confuse them with any other bird!

Penguins are also thought of as symbols of the polar regions, but penguins do not live north of the equator, so you would not find a penguin on the North Pole. Penguins don't live at the South Pole, either. Only two of the seventeen **species** of penguins spend all of their lives on the frozen continent of Antarctica. You would be just as likely to see a penguin living on an island in a warm climate as in a cold area.

Directions: Draw an **X** on the blank for the correct answer.

1. The main idea is:
   - _____ Penguins are among the best-liked animals on earth.
   - **X** The penguin is a much misunderstood animal.

2. Penguins live
   - _____ only at the North Pole.
   - _____ only at the South Pole.
   - **X** only south of the equator.

3. Based on the other words in the sentence, what is the correct definition of the word **species**?
   - _____ number
   - _____ bird
   - **X** a distinct kind

Directions: List three ways penguins are like other birds.
have feathers, lay eggs, build nests

Page 186

Review

Directions: Write your answers on the lines.

1. Which contains the South Pole—the Arctic or Antarctica?
   Antarctica

2. Would you like to live in either the Arctic or Antarctica? Why or why not?
   Answers may vary.

3. What adaptations would people who live (even for a short time) in these areas have to make?
   Answers may include: can handle cold and long periods of darkness

4. What characteristics are common to animals who live in the polar regions?
   thick coat of fur, ability to find food, layer of fat

5. Name two animals that live in the polar regions. **Answers may include:**
   polar bears ___ **walruses**

6. Write three facts you learned about one of the animals that live in the polar regions.
   _____

7. On each of the poles, there are six months of sunlight and darkness each year. How do you think this would affect...
   Answers will vary.

8. Write three ... explorers to the North or South Pole regions.
   _____

485

Grade 5 - Comprehensive Curriculum

Page 187

Reading Comprehension: The Desert

Directions: Read the information about the desert. Then answer the questions by circling **Yes** or **No**.

Deserts are found where there is little rainfall or where the rainfall for a whole year falls in only a few weeks' time. Ten inches of rain may be enough for many plants to survive if the rain is spread throughout the year. If the 10 inches of rain falls during one or two months and the rest of the year is dry, those plants may not be able to survive and a desert may form.

When people think of deserts, they may think of long stretches of sand. Sand begins as tiny pieces of rock that get smaller and smaller as wind and weather wear them down. Sand dunes, or hills of drifting sand, are formed as winds move the sand across the desert. Grain by grain, the dunes grow over the years, always shifting with the winds and changing shape. Most dunes are only a few feet tall, but they can grow to be several hundred feet high.

There is, however, much more to a desert than sand. In the deserts of the southwestern United States, cliffs and canyons were formed from thick mud that once lay beneath a sea more than a hundred million years ago. Over the centuries, the water drained away. Wind, sand, rain, heat and cold all wore away at the remaining rocks. The faces of the desert mountains are always changing—very, very slowly—as these forces of nature continue to work on the rock.

Most deserts have a surprising variety of life. There are plants, animals and insects that have adapted to life in the desert. During the heat of the day, a visitor may see very few signs of living things, but as the air begins to cool in the evening, the desert comes to life. As the sun begins to rise again in the sky, the desert once again becomes quiet and lonely.

1. Deserts are found where there is little rainfall or where the rainfall for a whole year falls in only a few weeks. **(Yes)**   No

2. Sand begins as tiny pieces of rock that get smaller and smaller as wind and weather wear them down. **(Yes)**   No

3. Sand dunes were formed from thick mud that once lay beneath a sea more than a hundred million years ago. Yes   **(No)**

4. The faces of the desert mountains can never change. Yes   **(No)**

Page 188

Reading Comprehension: Desert Weather

Directions: Read the information about desert weather. Then answer the questions.

One definition of a desert is an area that has, on average, less than 10 inches of rain a year. Many deserts have far less than that. Death Valley in California and Nevada, for example, averages fewer than 2 inches of rain each year. The driest of all deserts is the Atacama Desert in Chile, where no rain has been known to fall in 400 years!

Some deserts have a regular rainy season each year, but usually desert rainfall is totally unpredictable. An area may have no rainfall for many years. Sometimes a passing cloud may look like it will send relief to the waiting land, but only a "ghost rain" falls. This means that the hot, dry air dries up the raindrops long before they ever reach the ground.

The temperature in the desert varies greatly. The daytime temperatures in the desert frequently top 120 degrees. In Death Valley, temperatures have been known to reach 190 degrees! In most parts of the world, moisture in the air works like a blanket to hold the heat of the day close to the Earth at night. But, because it has so little moisture, the desert has no such blanket. As a result, nighttime temperatures are very chilly. Temperatures have been known to drop 50 or even 100 degrees at night in the desert.

1. On the average, how much rainfall is there in a year in a desert?
   less than 10 inches

2. Where is the driest desert in the world? _in Chile_

3. What is a "ghost rain"? _hot dry air dries up rain before it reaches the ground_

4. In other parts of the world, what holds the heat close to the Earth at night? _moisture in the air_

5. What happens to the temperature in the desert at night?
   it gets very chilly

Page 189

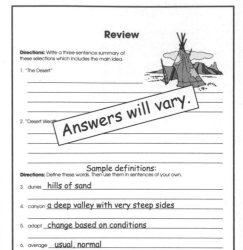

Review

Directions: Write a three-sentence summary of these selections which includes the main idea.

1. "The Desert"

2. "Desert Weather"

Answers will vary.

Directions: Define these words. Then use them in sentences of your own. _Sample definitions:_

3. dunes _hills of sand_

4. canyon _a deep valley with very steep sides_

5. adapt _change based on conditions_

6. average _usual, normal_

7. unpredictable _not known in advance_

Page 190

Context Clues: Desert Plants

Directions: Read the information about desert plants. Use context clues to determine the meaning of the bold words. Check the correct answers.

Desert plants have special features, or adaptations, that allow them to **survive** the harsh conditions of the desert. A cactus stores water in its tissues until it rains. It then uses this supply of water during the long dry season. The tiny needles on some kinds of **cacti** may number in the tens of thousands. These sharp thorns protect the cactus. They also form tiny shadows in the sunlight that help keep the plant from getting too hot.

Other plants are able to live by dropping their leaves. This cuts down on the **evaporation** of their water supply in the hot sun. Still other plants survive as seeds, protected from the sun and heat by tough seed coats. When it rains, the seeds **sprout** quickly, bloom and produce seeds that can **withstand** long dry spells.

Some plants spread their roots close to the Earth's surface to quickly gather water when it does rain. Other plants, such as the mesquite, have roots that grow 50 or 60 feet below the ground to reach underground water supplies.

1. Based on the other words in the sentence, what is the correct definition of **survive**?
   - ✓ continue to live
   - ___ bloom in the desert
   - ___ flower

2. Based on the other words in the sentence, what is the correct definition of **evaporation**?
   - ✓ water loss from heat
   - ___ much-needed rainfall
   - ___ boiling

3. Based on the other words in the sentence, what is the correct definition of **withstand**?
   - ✓ put up with
   - ___ stand with another
   - ___ take from

4. Based on the other words in the sentence, what is the correct definition of **cacti**?
   - ___ a type of sand dune
   - ✓ more than one cactus
   - ___ a caravan of camels

5. Based on the other words in the sentence, what is the correct definition of **sprout**?
   - ___ a type of bean that grows only in the desert
   - ✓ begin to grow
   - ___ a small flower

Page 191

Recognizing Details: The Cactus Family

Directions: Read the information about cacti. Pay close attention to details. Answer the questions.

Although cacti are the best-known desert plants, they don't live only in hot, dry places. While cacti are most likely to be found in the desert areas of Mexico and the southwestern United States, they can be seen as far north as Nova Scotia, Canada. Certain types of cacti can live even in the snow!

Desert cacti are particularly good at surviving very long dry spells. Most cacti have a very long root system so they can absorb as much water as possible. Every available drop of water is taken into the cactus and held in its fleshy stem. A cactus stem can hold enough water to last for 2 years or longer.

A cactus may be best known for its spines. Although a few kinds of cacti don't have spines, the stems of most types are covered with these sharp needles. The spines have many uses for a cactus. They keep animals from eating the cactus. They collect raindrops and dew. The spines also help keep the plant cool by forming shadows in the sun and by trapping a layer of air close to the plant. They break up the desert winds that dry out the cactus.

Cacti come in all sizes and shapes. The biggest type in North America is the saguaro. It can weigh 12,000 to 14,000 pounds and grow to be 50 feet tall. A saguaro can last several years without water, but it will grow only after summer rains. In May and June, white blossoms appear. Many kinds of birds nest in these enormous cacti: white-winged doves, woodpeckers, small owls, thrashers and wrens all build nests in the saguaro.

1. Where are you most likely to find a cactus growing?
   in deserts

2. How long can most cacti survive without water?
   2 years or longer

3. What are two ways the spines help a cactus?
   collect moisture, form cooling shadows, keep animals from eating the plant

4. What is the biggest cactus in North America?
   saguaro

5. What animals live in a saguaro cactus?
   doves, woodpeckers, owls, thrashers, wrens

Page 192

Review

Directions: Write a three-sentence summary of these selections. Refer to the reading selections for review if necessary.

1. "Desert Plants"

2. "The Cactus Family"

Answers will vary.

Directions: Describe the adaptations these plants have made to survive in the desert. _Sample answers:_

3. cacti _store water_

4. mesquite _long roots to reach underground water_

5. saguaro cactus _stores water, withstands drought_

Directions: Answer these questions.

6. What is the purpose of cactus spines? _collects moisture, protects cactus from being eaten_

7. Why does the mesquite have long roots? _to reach deep underground water supplies_

Directions: Define these words. Then use them in sentences of your own.

8. evaporation _water loss due to heat and/or wind_

9. spine _sharp needle-like growths on cacti_

Page 193

Reading Comprehension: Lizards

Directions: Read the information about lizards. Then answer the questions.

Lizards are reptiles, related to snakes, turtles, alligators and crocodiles. Like other reptiles, lizards are cold-blooded. This means their body temperature changes with that of their surroundings. However, by changing their behavior throughout the day they can keep their temperature fairly constant.

Lizards are among the many animals that live in deserts. They usually come out of their burrows early in the morning. Most lizards lie in the sun to get warm before starting daily activities. In mid-morning, they hunt for food. If it becomes too hot, lizards can raise their tails and bodies off the ground to help cool off. At mid-day, they return to their burrows or crawl under rocks for several hours. Late in the day, they again lie in the sun to absorb heat before the chilly desert night falls.

Like all animals, lizards have ways of protecting themselves. Some types of lizards have developed a most unusual defense. If a hawk or other animal grabs one of these lizards by its tail, the tail will break off. The tail will continue to wiggle around to distract the attacker while the lizard runs away. A month or two later, the lizard grows a new tail.

There are about 3,000 kinds of lizards, and all of them can bite, but only two types of lizards are poisonous: the Gila monster of the southwestern United States and the Mexican bearded lizard. Both are short-legged, thick-bodied reptiles with fat tails. These lizards do not attack people and will not bite them unless they are attacked.

1. What can a lizard do if it becomes too hot? __raise its tail and__
   __body off the ground, crawl in burrows or under rocks__
2. What is an unusual defense some lizards have developed to protect themselves?
   __tails will break off and distract predators__
3. What two types of lizards are poisonous? __Gila monster and__
   __Mexican bearded lizard__

Page 194

Main Idea: People in the Desert

Directions: Read the information about people in the desert. Then answer the questions.

Long before Europeans came to live in America, Native Americans had discovered ways of living in the desert. Some of these Native Americans were hunters or belonged to wandering tribes that stayed in the desert for only short periods of time. Others learned to farm and live in villages. They made their houses of trees, clay and brush.

The desert met all of their needs for life: food, water, skins for clothing, materials for tools, weapons and shelter. For meat, the desert offered deer, birds and rabbits for hunting. When those animals were hard to find, the Native Americans would eat mice and lizards. Many desert plants, such as the prickly pear and mesquite, provided moisture, fruit and seeds that could be eaten.

The first Europeans in the American deserts were searching for furs and metals, like silver and gold. They explored, but did not settle in the desert. The early pioneers were usually unsuccessful at living in the desert. They found the great heat and long dry periods too difficult. When they moved away, they left behind empty mining camps, houses and sheds that slowly fell apart in the sun and wind.

1. What is the main idea of this selection?
   __X__ Before Europeans came to live in America, Native Americans had discovered ways of living in the desert.
   ____ Some Native Americans were hunters or belonged to wandering tribes who stayed in the desert for only short periods of time.
2. Who were the first people to live in the deserts of North America?
   __Native Americans__
3. What did the Native Americans use to make their houses in the desert?
   __trees, clay and brush__
4. What kinds of food did the Native Americans find in the desert?
   __meat, desert plants__
5. What were the first Europeans who came to the desert looking for?
   __furs and metals (silver and gold)__

Page 195

Main Idea: Camels

Directions: Read the information about camels. Then answer the questions.

Camels are well suited to desert life. They can cope with infrequent supplies of food and water, blazing heat during the day, low temperatures at night and sand blown by high winds.

There are two kinds of camels: the two-humped bactrian and the one-humped dromedary. The dromedary is the larger of the two. It has coarse fur on its back that helps protect it from the sun's rays. The hair on its stomach and legs is short to prevent overheating. When camels **molt** in the spring, their wool can be collected in tufts from the bushes and ground.

The legs of the dromedary are much longer than those of the bactrian. Animals that live in very hot countries tend to have longer legs. This gives them a larger area of body surface from which heat can escape. Bactrian camels live in the deserts of central Asia where winters are bitterly cold, so they are not as tall as dromedaries.

Both kinds of camels have pads on their feet that keep them from sinking into the sand as they walk. A camel's long neck allows it to reach the ground to drink water and eat grass without having to bend its legs. It also can reach up to eat leaves from trees.

Camels do not store water in their humps as many people believe. The hump is for fat storage. When there is plenty of food, the camel's hump swells and feels firm. During the dry season when there is little food, the fat is used up and the hump shrinks and becomes soft.

1. What is the main idea of this selection?
   __X__ Camels are well suited to desert life.
   ____ There are two kinds of camels.
2. Based on the other words in the sentence, what is the correct definition of **molt**?
   ____ turns into a butterfly
   __X__ sheds its hair
   ____ becomes overheated
3. What are the two kinds of camels? __bactrian and dromedary__
4. Why don't camels sink into the sand when they walk?
   __They have pads on their feet.__
5. What is the purpose of a camel's hump? __to store fat__

Page 196

Review

Directions: Write your answers in complete sentences.

1. Describe how the cold-blooded lizard regulates its body temperature.
   __It lies in the sun to get warm in the morning.__
   __It raises its tail and body off the ground to cool off.__
   __It hides in burrows or under rocks to cool off.__
   __It lies in the sun late in the day to absorb warmth__
   __before night.__
2. What is the main idea of the selection "Lizards"?
   __Lizards have adapted to desert life in many ways.__
3. Describe how Native Americans adapted to life in the desert.
   __They made homes of available materials. They learned__
   __to find food, water, shelter and clothing.__
4. Why do you think early pioneers were unsuccessful at desert living?
   __Answers will vary.__
5. Describe the adaptations of camels for successful desert habitation.
   __They store fat in their humps, cope with little food__
   __or water, have longs legs for larger body surface, fur__
   __to protect from sun's rays, pads on feet, etc.__

Page 197

Reading Comprehension: Desert Lakes

Directions: Read the information about lakes in the desert. Then answer the questions.

A few deserts have small permanent lakes. While they may be a welcome sight in the desert, the water in them is not fit for drinking. They are salt lakes. Rain from nearby higher land keeps these lakes supplied with water, but the lakes are blocked in with nowhere to drain. Over the years, mineral salts collect in the water and build up to a high level, making the water undrinkable.

Most desert lakes are only temporary. Occasional rains may fill them to depths of several feet, but in a matter of weeks or months, all the water has been dried up by the heat and sun. The dried lake beds that remain are called **playas**. Some playas are simply areas of sun-baked mud; others are covered with a sparkling layer of salt.

Perhaps the most unusual desert lake is in central Australia. It is called Lake Eyre. It is a huge lake—nearly 3,600 square miles in area—but it is almost totally dry most of the time. Since it was discovered in 1840, it has been filled only two times. Both times, the lake completely dried up again within a few years.

1. Why is the water in a desert lake not fit for drinking?
   __It is salt water.__
2. Why are the lakes in the desert salt lakes?
   __Mineral salts collect there.__
3. Why are most desert lakes only temporary?
   __The water evaporates.__
4. What is a **playa**? __a dried lake bed__
5. What is the name of the unusual desert lake in central Australia?
   __Lake Eyre__
6. How big is this desert lake? __nearly 3,600 square miles__

Page 198

Review

Directions: Write your answers in complete sentences.

1. What is a desert?
   __A desert is an area where less__
   __than 10 inches of rain falls per year.__
2. Name a desert in the United States and tell where it is.
   __Answers will vary.__
3. What special characteristics must an animal have to survive in the desert?
   __It must be able to tolerate extremes of heat and__
   __cold, be able to protect itself from the sun's rays__
   __and be able to find or store food and water.__
4. What special characteristics must a plant have to survive in the desert?
   __It must have a way to collect or store moisture,__
   __withstand long dry periods and tolerate extremes__
   __of heat and cold.__
5. What differences exist between animals whose habitat is the polar regions and animals whose habitat is the desert regions?
   __Answers may include: Polar animals need warm fur__
   __or feathers, a layer of fat, the ability to tolerate__
   __cold and find food. Desert animals need to protect__
   __themselves from heat and find moisture when little__
   __exists.__
6. Would you like to visit the desert? Why or why not?
   __Answers will vary.__

Page 200

Nouns

A **noun** is a word that names a person, place or thing.

Examples:
person — friend
place — home
thing — desk

Nouns are used many ways in sentences. They can be the subjects of sentences.

Example: Noun as subject: Your high-topped **sneakers** look great with that outfit.

Nouns can be direct objects of a sentence. The **direct object** follows the verb and completes its meaning. It answers the question who or what.

Example: Noun as direct object: Shelly's family bought a new **car.**

Nouns can be indirect objects. An **indirect object** comes between the verb and the direct object and tells **to whom** or **for whom** something was done.

Example: Noun as indirect object: She gave **Tina** a big hug.

Directions: Underline all the nouns. Write **S** above the noun if it is a subject, **DO** if it is a direct object or **IO** if it is an indirect object. The first one has been done for you.

1. Do alligators eat people?
2. James hit a home run, and our team won the game.
3. The famous actor gave Susan his autograph.
4. Eric loaned Keith his bicycle.
5. The kindergarten children painted cute pictures.
6. Robin sold David some chocolate chip cookies.
7. The neighbors planned a going-away party and bought a gift.
8. The party and gift surprised Kurt and his family.
9. My scout leader told our group a funny joke.
10. Karen made her little sister a clown costume.

Page 201

Nouns

Directions: Write 10 nouns for each category.

Answers will vary, but may include:

People
1. boy
2. girl
3. child
4. adult
5. person
6. friend
7. neighbor
8. classmate
9. man
10. woman

Places
1. park
2. zoo
3. bridge
4. town
5. city
6. country
7. river
8. desert
9. ocean
10. forest

Things
1. cat
2. dog
3. ball
4. bat
5. cup
6. fork
7. table
8. pen
9. computer
10. ruler

Page 202

Proper and Common Nouns

Proper nouns name specific people, places or things.

Examples: Washington, D.C., Thomas Jefferson, Red Sea

Common nouns name nonspecific people, places or things.

Examples: man, fortress, dog

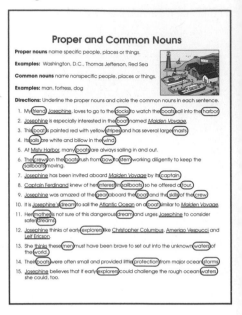

Directions: Underline the proper nouns and circle the common nouns in each sentence.

1. My friend, Josephine, loves to go to the docks to watch the boats sail into the harbor.
2. Josephine is especially interested in the boat named Maiden Voyage.
3. This boat is painted red with yellow stripes and has several large masts.
4. Its sails are white and billow in the wind.
5. At Misty Harbor, many boats are always sailing in and out.
6. The crew on the boats rush from bow to stern working diligently to keep the sailboats moving.
7. Josephine has been invited aboard Maiden Voyage by its captain.
8. Captain Ferdinand knew of her interest in sailboats so he offered a tour.
9. Josephine was amazed at the gear aboard the boat and the skills of the crew.
10. It is Josephine's dream to sail the Atlantic Ocean on a boat similar to Maiden Voyage.
11. Her mother is not sure of this dangerous dream and urges Josephine to consider safer dreams.
12. Josephine thinks of early explorers like Christopher Columbus, Amerigo Vespucci and Leif Ericson.
13. She thinks these men must have been brave to set out into the unknown waters of the world.
14. Their boats were often small and provided little protection from major ocean storms.
15. Josephine believes that if early explorers could challenge the rough ocean waters she could, too.

Page 203

Abstract and Concrete Nouns

Concrete nouns name something that can be touched or seen.
Abstract nouns name an idea, a thought or a feeling which cannot be touched or seen.

Examples:
concrete nouns: house, puppy, chair
abstract nouns: love, happiness, fear

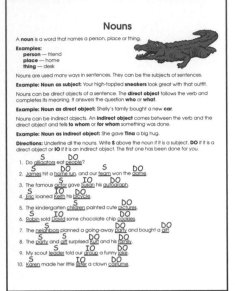

Directions: Write **concrete** or **abstract** in the blank after each noun.

1. loyalty — abstract
2. light bulb — concrete
3. quarter — concrete
4. hope — abstract
5. satellite — concrete
6. ability — abstract
7. patio — concrete
8. door — concrete
9. allegiance — abstract
10. Cuba — concrete
11. Michael Jordan — concrete
12. friendship — abstract
13. telephone — concrete
14. computer — concrete

Directions: Write eight nouns for each category.

Answers will vary, but may include:

Concrete
1. glass
2. battle
3. apple
4. pig
5. ruler
6. hand
7. page
8. paper

Abstract
1. love
2. faith
3. loneliness
4. fear
5. anger
6. joy
7. pride
8. shyness

Page 204

Verbs

A **verb** tells what something does or that something exists.

Examples:
Tim **has shared** his apples with us.
Those apples **were** delicious.
I hope Tim **is bringing** more apples tomorrow.
Tim **picked** the apples himself.

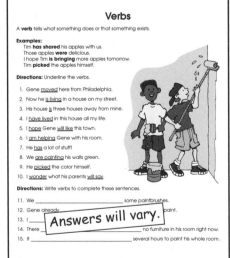

Directions: Underline the verbs.

1. Gene moved here from Philadelphia.
2. Now he is living in a house on my street.
3. His house is three houses away from mine.
4. I have lived in this house all my life.
5. I hope Gene will like this town.
6. I am helping Gene with his room.
7. He has a lot of stuff!
8. We are painting his walls green.
9. He picked the color himself.
10. I wonder what his parents will say.

Directions: Write verbs to complete these sentences.

11. We _____ some paintbrushes.
12. Gene already _____ paint.
13. I _____

Answers will vary.

14. There _____ no furniture in his room right now.
15. It _____ several hours to paint his whole room.

Page 205

Verbs

A **verb** is the action word in a sentence. It tells what the subject does (**build, laugh, express, fasten**) or that it exists (**is, are, was, were**).

Examples: Randy **raked** the leaves into a pile.
I **was** late to school today.

Answers may include:

Directions: In the following sentences, write verbs that make sense.

1. The quarterback ___threw___ the ball to the receiver.
2. My mother ___baked___ some cookies yesterday.
3. John ___sold___ newspapers to make extra money.
4. The teacher ___wrote___ the instructions on the board.
5. Last summer, our family ___took___ a trip to Florida to visit relatives.

Sometimes, a verb can be two or more words. Verbs used to "support" other verbs are called **helping verbs**.

Examples: We **were** listening to music in my room.
Chris **has been** studying for over 2 hours.

Directions: In the following sentences, write helping verbs along with the correct form of the given verbs. The first one has been done for you.

1. Michelle (write) ___is writing___ a letter to her grandmother right now.
2. My brother (have) ___is having___ trouble with his math homework.
3. When we arrived, the movie (start) ___had started___ already.
4. My aunt (live) ___has lived___ in the same house for 30 years.
5. Our football team (go) ___is going___ to win the national championship this year.
6. My sister (talk) ___has been talking___ on the phone all afternoon!
7. I couldn't sleep last night because the wind (blow) ___was blowing___ so hard.
8. Last week, Pat was sick, but now he (feel) ___is feeling___ much better.
9. Tomorrow, our class (have) ___will have___ a bake sale.
10. Mr. Smith (collect) ___has collected___ stamps for 20 years.

ANSWER KEY

Page 206

Verb Tenses

Verbs have different forms to show whether something already happened, is happening right now or will happen.

Examples:
- **Present tense:** I walk.
- **Past tense:** I walked.
- **Future tense:** I will walk.

Directions: Write PAST if the verb is past tense, PRES for present tense or FUT for future tense. The first one has been done for you.

PRES 1. My sister Sara works at the grocery store.
PAST 2. Last year, she worked in an office.
PRES 3. Sara is going to college, too.
FUT 4. She will be a dentist some day.
PRES 5. She says studying is difficult.
PAST 6. Sara hardly studied at all in high school.
FUT 7. I will be ready for college in a few years.
PAST 8. Last night, I read my history book for 2 hours.

Directions: Complete these sentences using verbs in the tenses listed. The first one has been done for you.

9. take: future tense — My friends and I **will take** a trip.
10. talk: past tense — We **talked** for a long time about where to go.
11. want: present tense — Pam **wants** to go to the lake.
12. want: past tense — Jake **wanted** to go with us.
13. say: past tense — His parents **said** no.
14. ride: future tense — We **will ride** our bikes.
15. pack: past tense — Susan and Jared already **packed** lunches for us.

Page 207

Verb Tenses

The past tense of many verbs is formed by adding **ed**.

Examples:
- remember + ed = remembered
- climb + ed = climbed

If a verb ends in **e**, drop the **e** before adding **ed**.

Examples:

Present	Past
phone	phoned
arrive	arrived

If a verb ends in **y**, change the **y** to **i** before adding **ed**.

Examples:

Present	Past
carry	carried
try	tried

If a verb ends in a short vowel followed by a single consonant, double the final consonant.

Examples:

Present	Past
trip	tripped
pop	popped

Directions: Circle the misspelled verb in each sentence and write it correctly in the blank.

1. They stopped at our house and then (hurryed) home. **hurried**
2. I (scrubed) and mopped the floor. **scrubbed**
3. The coach (nameed) the five starting players. **named**
4. He popped the potatoes into the oil and (fryed) them. **fried**
5. I accidentally (droped) my papers on the floor. **dropped**
6. I had (hopeed) you could go climbing with me. **hoped**
7. He (triped) on the rug. **tripped**
8. The baby (cryed) and screamed all night. **cried**
9. I (moped) the mess up after the glass dropped on the floor. **mopped**
10. First, she frowned, and then she (smileed) **smiled**

Page 208

Writing: Verb Forms

Present-tense verbs tell what is happening right now. To form present-tense verbs, use the "plain" verbs or use **is** or **are** before the verb and add **ing** to the verb.

Examples: We **eat**. We **are eating**.
He **serves**. He **is serving**.

Directions: Complete each sentence with the correct verb form, telling what is happening right now. Read carefully, as some sentences already have **is** or **are**.

Examples: Scott is (loan) loaning Jenny his math book.
Jenny (study) is studying for a big math test.

1. The court is (release) **releasing** the prisoner early.
2. Jonah and Jill (write) **are writing** their notes in code.
3. Are you (vote) **voting** for Baxter?
4. The girls are (coax) **coaxing** the dog into the bathtub.
5. The leaves (begin) **are beginning** to fall from the trees.
6. My little brother (stay) **is staying** at his friend's house tonight.
7. Is she (hide) **hiding** behind the screen?

To tell what already happened, or in the **past tense**, add **ed** to many verbs or use **was** or **were** and add **ing** to the verb.

Example: I watched. I was watching.

Directions: Complete each sentence with the correct verb form. This time, tell what already happened.

Examples: We (walk) walked there yesterday.
They were (talk) talking.

1. The government was (decrease) **decreasing** our taxes.
2. Was anyone (cheat) **cheating** in this game?
3. We were (try) **trying** to set goals for the project.

Page 209

Writing: Future-Tense Verbs

Future-tense verbs tell about things that will happen in the future. To form future-tense verbs, use **will** before the verb.

Example: Tomorrow I **will walk** to school.

When you use **will**, you may also have to add a helping verb and the ending **ing**.

Example: Tomorrow I **will be walking** to school.

Directions: Imagine what the world will be like 100 years from now. Maybe you think robots will be doing our work for us, or that people will be living on the moon. What will our houses look like? What will school be like? Write a paragraph describing what you imagine. Be sure to use future-tense verbs.

Paragraphs will vary.

Page 210

Principal Parts of Verbs

Verbs have three principal parts. They are **present**, **past** and **past participle**.

Regular verbs form the past tense by adding **ed** to the present tense.

The past participle is formed by using the past tense verb with a helping verb: **has**, **have** or **had**.

Directions: Write the correct form of each verb. The first one has been done for you.

	Present	Past	Past Participle
1.	look	looked	has/have/had looked
2.	plan	planned	has/have/had planned
3.	close	closed	has/have/had closed
4.	wash	washed	has/have/had washed
5.	prepare	prepared	has/have/had prepared
6.	provide	provided	has/have/had provided
7.	invite	invited	has/have/had invited
8.	discover	discovered	has/have/had discovered
9.	approve	approved	has/have/had approved
10.	search	searched	has/have/had searched
11.	establish	established	has/have/had established
12.	form	formed	has/have/had formed
13.	push	pushed	has/have/had pushed
14.	travel	traveled	has/have/had traveled

Page 211

Irregular Verbs

Irregular verbs change completely in the past tense. Unlike regular verbs, the past tense forms of irregular verbs are not formed by adding **ed**.

Examples:
Chung **eats** the cookies.
Chung **ate** them yesterday.
Chung **has eaten** them for weeks.

Present Tense	Past Tense	Past Participle
begin	began	has/have/had begun
speak	spoke	has/have/had spoken
drink	drank	has/have/had drunk
know	knew	has/have/had known
eat	ate	has/have/had eaten
wear	wore	has/have/had worn

Directions: Rewrite these sentences once using the past tense and again using the past participle of each verb.

1. Todd begins football practice this week.
   Todd began football practice this week.
   Todd has begun football practice this week.
2. She wears her hair in braids.
   She wore her hair in braids.
   She had worn her hair in braids.
3. I drink two glasses of milk.
   I drank two glasses of milk.
   I have drunk two glasses of milk.
4. The man is speaking to us.
   The man spoke to us.
   The man has spoken to us.
5. The dogs are eating.
   The dogs ate.
   The dogs have eaten.

Page 212

Irregular Verbs

The past participle form of an irregular verb needs a helping verb.

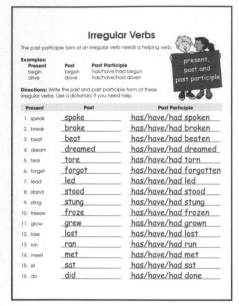

Examples:

Present	Past	Past Participle
begin	began	has/have/had begun
drive	drove	has/have/had driven

Directions: Write the past and past participle form of these irregular verbs. Use a dictionary if you need help.

	Present	Past	Past Participle
1.	speak	spoke	has/have/had spoken
2.	break	broke	has/have/had broken
3.	beat	beat	has/have/had beaten
4.	dream	dreamed	has/have/had dreamed
5.	tear	tore	has/have/had torn
6.	forget	forgot	has/have/had forgotten
7.	lead	led	has/have/had led
8.	stand	stood	has/have/had stood
9.	sting	stung	has/have/had stung
10.	freeze	froze	has/have/had frozen
11.	grow	grew	has/have/had grown
12.	lose	lost	has/have/had lost
13.	run	ran	has/have/had run
14.	meet	met	has/have/had met
15.	sit	sat	has/have/had sat
16.	do	did	has/have/had done

Page 213

"Be" as a Helping Verb

A **helping verb** tells when the action of a sentence takes place. The helping verb **be** has several forms: **am, is, are, was, were** and **will**. These helping verbs can be used in all three tenses.

Examples:
Past tense: Ken **was** talking. We **were** eating.
Present tense: I **am** coming. Simon **is** walking. They **are** singing.
Future tense: I **will** work. The puppies **will** eat.

In the present and past tense, many verbs can be written with or without the helping verb **be**. When the verb is written with a form of **be**, add **ing**. **Was** and **is** are used with singular subjects. **Were** and **are** are used with plural subjects.

Examples:
Present tense: Angela **sings**. Angela **is singing**. The children **sing**. They **are singing**.
Past tense: I **studied**. I **was studying**. They **studied**. They **were studying**.

The helping verb **will** is always needed for the future tense, but the **ing** ending is not used with **will**. **Will** is both singular and plural.

Examples:
Future tense: I **will** eat. We **will** watch.

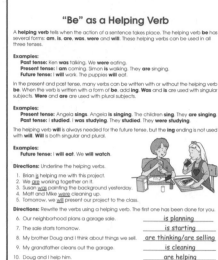

Directions: Underline the helping verbs.

1. Brian **is** helping me with this project.
2. We **are** working together on it.
3. Susan **was** painting the background yesterday.
4. Matt and Mike **were** cleaning up.
5. Tomorrow, we **will** present our project to the class.

Directions: Rewrite the verbs using a helping verb. The first one has been done for you.

6. Our neighborhood plans a garage sale. _is planning_
7. The sale starts tomorrow. _is starting_
8. My brother Doug and I think about things we sell. _are thinking/are selling_
9. My grandfather cleans out the garage. _is cleaning_
10. Doug and I help him. _are helping_

Page 214

"Be" as a Linking Verb

A **linking verb** links a noun or adjective in the predicate to the subject. Forms of the verb **be** are the most common linking verbs. Linking verbs can be used in all three tenses.

Examples:
Present: My father **is** a salesman.
Past: The store **was** very busy last night.
Future: Tomorrow **will be** my birthday.

In the first sentence, **is** links the subject (father) with a noun (salesman). In the second sentence, **was** links the subject (store) with an adjective (busy). In the third sentence, **will be** links the subject (tomorrow) with a noun (birthday).

Directions: Circle the linking verbs. Underline the two words that are linked by the verb. The first one has been done for you.

1. Columbus **is** the capital of Ohio.
2. By bedtime, Nicole **was** bored.
3. Andy **will be** the captain of our team.
4. Tuesday **is** the first day of the month.
5. I hate to say this, but we **are** lost.
6. Ask him if the water **is** cold.
7. By the time I finished my paper, it **was** late.
8. Spaghetti **is** my favorite dinner.
9. The children **were** afraid of the big truck.
10. Karen **will be** a good president of our class.
11. These lessons **are** helpful.
12. **Was** that report due today?

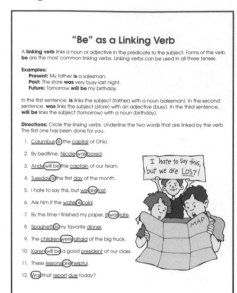

Page 215

"Be" as a Linking or Helping Verb

Directions: Write **H** if the form of **be** is used as a helping verb or **L** if it is used as a linking verb.

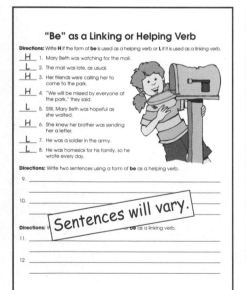

1. **H** Mary Beth was watching for the mail.
2. **L** The mail was late, as usual.
3. **H** Her friends were calling her to come to the park.
4. **H** "We will be missed by everyone at the park," they said.
5. **L** Still, Mary Beth was hopeful as she waited.
6. **H** She knew her brother was sending her a letter.
7. **L** He was a soldier in the army.
8. **L** He was homesick for his family, so he wrote every day.

Directions: Write two sentences using a form of **be** as a helping verb.

9. _____
10. _____

Sentences will vary.

Directions: Write ___ of **be** as a linking verb.

11. _____
12. _____

Page 216

Transitive and Intransitive Verbs

An **intransitive verb** can stand alone in the predicate because its meaning is complete. In the examples below, notice that each short sentence is a complete thought.

Examples: Intransitive verbs: The tree **grows**. The mouse **squeaked**. The deer **will run**.

A **transitive verb** needs a direct object to complete its meaning. The meaning of a sentence with a transitive verb is not complete without a direct object.

Examples: Transitive verbs: The mouse **wants** seeds. The deer **saw** the hunter. The tree **will lose** its leaves.

The direct object **seeds** tells what the mouse wants. **Leaves** tells what the tree will lose and **hunter** tells what the deer saw.

Both transitive and intransitive verbs can be in the past, present or future tense.

Directions: Underline the verb in each sentence. Write **I** if the sentence has an intransitive verb or **T** if it has a transitive verb.

1. **I** The snake slid quietly along the ground.
2. **T** The snake scared a rabbit.
3. **I** The rabbit hopped quickly back to its hole.
4. **I** Safe from the snake, the rabbit shivered with fear.
5. **T** In the meantime, the snake caught a frog.
6. **T** The frog was watching flies and didn't see the snake.

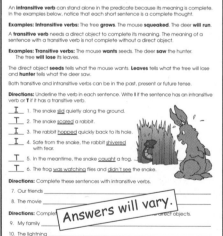

Directions: Complete these sentences with intransitive verbs.

7. Our friends _____
8. The movie _____

Directions: Complete ___ direct objects.

Answers will vary.

9. My family _____
10. The lightning _____

Page 217

Subjects and Predicates

The **subject** tells who or what a sentence is about. The **predicate** tells what the subject does, did or is doing. All complete sentences must have a subject and a predicate.

Examples:

Subject	Predicate
Hamsters	are common pets.
Pets	need special care.

Directions: Circle the subjects and underline the predicates.

1. Many children keep hamsters as pets.
2. Mice are good pets, too.
3. Hamsters collect food in their cheeks.
4. My sister sneezes around furry animals.
5. My brother wants a dog instead of a hamster.

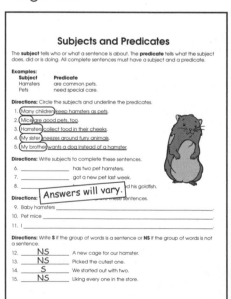

Directions: Write subjects to complete these sentences.

6. _____ has two pet hamsters.
7. _____ got a new pet last week.
8. _____ and his goldfish.

Directions: ___ these sentences.

Answers will vary.

9. Baby hamsters _____
10. Pet mice _____
11. I _____

Directions: Write **S** if the group of words is a sentence or **NS** if the group of words is not a sentence.

12. **NS** A new cage for our hamster.
13. **NS** Picked the cutest one.
14. **S** We started out with two.
15. **NS** Liking every one in the store.

ANSWER KEY

Page 218

Which Noun Is the Subject?

A **noun** is a word that names a person, place or thing.

Examples: Andy, Mrs. Henderson, doctor, child, house, shirt, dog, freedom, country

Often a noun is the subject of a sentence. The **subject** tells who or what the sentence is about. In this sentence, the subject is **Sara**: Sara drank some punch. A sentence can have several nouns, but they are not all subjects.

Directions: Underline each noun in the sentences below. Then circle the noun that is the subject of the sentence.

Example: Benny caught a huge fish in a small net.

1. Anna bragged about her big brother.
2. The car has a dent in the fender.
3. Our school won the city spirit award.
4. The cook scrubbed the pots and pans.
5. The quarter flipped onto the floor.
6. My sister rinsed her hair in the sink.
7. Our neighbor has 12 pets.
8. The cross country team ran 5 miles at practice.
9. Jo walked to the store on the corner.
10. A farmer stocks this pond with fish.

Directions: Each sentence below has two subjects. Underline all the nouns, as you did above. Then circle both subjects.

Example: Joe and Peter walked to school.

1. Apples and peaches grow in different seasons.
2. The chair and table matched the other furniture.

Page 219

Which Noun Is the Subject?

Usually, the noun that is the subject will come at the beginning of the sentence.

Examples: The truck turned quickly around the corner.

Kevin stayed home from school yesterday.

Sometimes, other words will come before the subject. When this happens, remember to look for who or what the sentence is about.

Example: After school, Katie usually walks to the library.

The sentence is about Katie, not school.

Directions: In the sentences below, circle the nouns that are subjects. Some sentences have more than one subject, and they will not always be at the beginning of the sentence.

1. Mark and I helped the teacher clean the classroom.
2. In the morning, my mother cooks breakfast for the whole family.
3. To finish the project, Ann had to stay up very late last night.
4. After the storm, power lines were down all over the city.
5. Oranges and grapefruits grow very well in Florida.
6. During the summer, squirrels work hard to gather nuts for the winter.
7. While skiing last weekend, my neighbor fell and broke his leg.
8. Pictures and posters cover all the walls of our classroom.
9. To save gas, my father takes the bus to work instead of driving.
10. In my opinion, dogs and cats make the best pets.

I come first!
Noun

Page 220

Subjects and Verbs

Directions: Underline the subject and verb in each sentence below. Write **S** over the subject and **V** over the verb. If the verb is two words, mark them both.

Examples:
S V
Dennis was drinking some punch.
S V
The punch was too sweet.

1. Hayley brags about her dog all the time.
2. Mrs. Thomas scrubbed the dirt off her car.
3. Then her son rinsed off the soap.
4. The teacher was flipping through the cards.
5. Jenny's rabbit was hungry and thirsty.
6. Your science report lacks a little detail.
7. Chris is stocking the shelves with cans of soup.
8. The accident caused a huge dent in our car.

Just as sentences can have two subjects, they can also have two verbs.

Example:
S S V V
Jennifer and Amie fed the dog and gave him clean water.

Directions: Underline all the subjects and verbs in these sentences. Write **S** over the subjects and **V** over the verbs.

1. Mom and Dad scrubbed and rinsed the basement floor.
2. The men came and stocked the lake with fish.
3. Someone broke the window and ran away.
4. Carrie punched a hole in the paper and threaded yarn through the hole.
5. Julie and Pat turned their bikes around and went home.

Page 221

Writing: Subjects and Verbs

Directions: Make each group of words below into a sentence by adding a subject, a verb, or a subject and a verb. Then write **S** over each subject and **V** over each verb.

Example: the dishes in the sink
S V
The dishes in the sink were dirty.

1. a leash for your pet
2. dented the table
3. a bowl of punch for the party
4. rinsed the soap
5. a lack
6. bragging about his sister
7. the stock on the shelf
8. with a flip of the wrist

Answers will vary.

Page 222

Writing: Subjects and Verbs

Directions: Decide which words in the box are subjects (nouns) and which are verbs. Write each word under the correct heading. Then match each subject with a verb to make a sentence. Use each subject and verb only once. The first one has been done for you.

dog	girls	walked	barked	honked
flew	car	played	neighbor	teacher
wrote	mowed	Marcus	birds	

Subjects	Verbs
girls	walked
dog	flew
car	wrote
Marcus	mowed
neighbor	played
birds	barked
teacher	honked

1. The tired girls walked slowly home from school.
2.
3.
4.
5.
6.
7.

Sentences will vary.

Page 223

Complete Sentences

A sentence which does not contain both a subject and a predicate is called a **fragment**.

Directions: Write **C** if the sentence is complete or **F** if it is a fragment.

1. C My mother and I hope to go to the mall this afternoon.
2. F To get shoes.
3. C We both need a new pair of tennis shoes.
4. F Maybe blue and white.
5. C Mom wants a pair of white shoes.
6. C That seems rather boring to me.
7. C There are many shoe stores in the mall.
8. F Sure to be a large selection.
9. C Tennis shoes are very expensive.
10. C My last pair cost $72.00!

Directions: Write the missing subject or predicate for these sentences.

11. _____ decided to go for hamburgers.
12. We _____
13. My parents _____
14. One day so _____
15. My favorite subject in school _____
16. _____ went fishing on Sunday.

Answers will vary.

Grade 5 - Comprehensive Curriculum

Page 224

Direct Objects

A **direct object** is a word or words that follow a transitive verb and complete its meaning. It answers the question **whom** or **what**. Direct objects are always nouns or pronouns.

Examples:
We built a **doghouse**. Doghouse is the direct object. It tells **what** we built.
I called **Mary**. Mary is the direct object. It tells **whom** I called.

Directions: Underline the direct objects.

1. Jean drew a <u>picture</u> of the doghouse.
2. Then we bought some <u>wood</u> at the store.
3. Erin measured each <u>board</u>.
4. Who will saw the <u>wood</u> into boards?
5. Chad hammered <u>nails</u> into the boards.
6. He accidentally hit his <u>thumb</u> with the hammer.
7. Kirsten found some <u>paint</u> in the basement.
8. Should we paint the <u>roof</u>?
9. Will you write Sparky's <u>name</u> above the door?
10. Spell his <u>name</u> correctly.

Directions: Write direct objects to complete these sentences.

11. I will write _____?
12. When we were finished, we put _____
13. We washed out _____
14. We threw away _____
15. Then, to celebrate, we ate _____

Answers will vary.

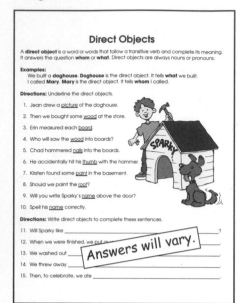

Page 225

Indirect Objects

An **indirect object** is a word or words that come between the verb and the direct object. An indirect object tells **to whom** or **for whom** something has been done. Indirect objects are always nouns or pronouns.

Examples:
She cooked **me** a great dinner. Me is the indirect object. It tells **for whom** something was cooked.
Give the **photographer** a smile. Photographer is the indirect object. It tells **to whom** the smile should be given.

Directions: Circle the indirect objects. Underline the direct objects.

1. Marla showed (me) her <u>drawing</u>.
2. The committee had given (her) an <u>award</u> for it.
3. The principal offered (Marla) a special <u>place</u> to put her drawing.
4. While babysitting, I read (Timmy) a <u>story</u>.
5. He told (me) the <u>end</u> of the story.
6. Then I fixed (him) some <u>hot chocolate</u>.
7. Timmy gave (me) a funny <u>look</u>.
8. Why didn't his mother tell (me)?
9. Hot chocolate gives (Timmy) a <u>rash</u>.
10. Will his mom still pay (me) three <u>dollars</u> for watching him?

Directions: Write indirect objects to complete these sentences.

11. I will write _____ a letter.
12. I'll give _____ part of my lunch.
13. Show _____ your model.
14. Did you send _____ a card?
15. Don't tell _____ my secret.

Answers will vary.

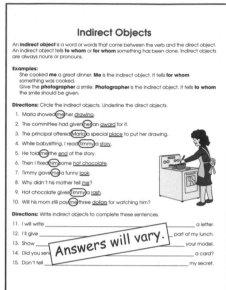

Page 226

Direct and Indirect Objects

Directions: Underline the direct objects. Circle the indirect objects.

1. Please give (him) a note <u>card</u>.
2. My father told (me) a <u>secret</u>.
3. I carefully examined the dinosaur <u>bones</u>.
4. Joseph decorated the banquet <u>hall</u> for the wedding.
5. Every night, I telephone my <u>grandmother</u>.
6. The head of the company offered (my father) a new <u>position</u>.
7. Too much pizza can give (you) a <u>stomachache</u>.
8. Will you draw (me) a <u>picture</u>?
9. This new computer gives (me) a <u>headache</u>!
10. Thomas discovered a new <u>entrance</u> to the cave.
11. He showed (me) the rare <u>penny</u>.
12. While watching television, I wrote (Marla) a <u>letter</u>.
13. Mrs. Fetters will pay (me) ten <u>dollars</u> for shoveling her sidewalk this winter.
14. The teacher handed her (class) a surprise <u>quiz</u>.
15. I like to drink <u>iced tea</u> on summer days.
16. Mom bought (Sharon) new school <u>supplies</u> for kindergarten.
17. I had to pay the (library) a <u>fine</u> for overdue books.
18. My family enjoys playing <u>football</u>.
19. Each night my mom reads (me) one <u>chapter</u> of a novel.
20. The teacher gave (us) our report <u>cards</u>.

Page 227

Prepositions

A **preposition** is a word that comes before a noun or pronoun and shows the relationship of that noun or pronoun to other words in the sentence.

The **object of a preposition** is a noun or pronoun that follows a preposition and completes its meaning. A **prepositional phrase** includes a preposition and the object(s) of the preposition.

Examples:
The girl **with red hair** spoke first.
With is the preposition.
Hair is the object of the preposition.
With red hair is a prepositional phrase.

In addition to being subjects, direct and indirect objects and nouns and pronouns can also be objects of prepositions.

Prepositions							
across	behind	from	near	over	to	with	on
by	before	for	between	beyond	at	into	
after							

Directions: Underline the prepositional phrases in these sentences. Circle the prepositions. The first sentence has been done for you.

1. The name (of) our <u>street</u> is Redsail Court.
2. We have lived (in) our house (for) three years.
3. (In) our family, we eat a lot (of) hamburgers.
4. We like hamburgers (on) toasted buns (with) mustard.
5. Sometimes we eat (in) the living room (in) front (of) the TV.
6. (In) the summer, we have picnics (in) the backyard.
7. The ants crawl (into) our food and (into) our clothes.
8. (Behind) our house is a park (with) swings.
9. Kids (from) the neighborhood walk (through) our yard (to) the park.
10. Sometimes they cut (across) Mom's garden and stomp (on) her beans.
11. Mom says we need a tall fence (without) a gate.
12. (With) a fence (around) our yard, we could get a dog!

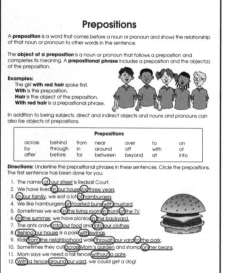

Page 228

Pronouns

A **pronoun** is a word used in place of a noun. Instead of repeating a noun again and again, use a pronoun.

Examples:
	I	you	he	she	them	us
me	your	him	her	they	it	
my	our	his	we	their	its	

Each pronoun takes the place of a certain noun. If the noun is singular, the pronoun should be singular. If the noun is plural, the pronoun should be plural.

Examples: John told **his** parents **he** would be late.
The girls said **they** would ride **their** bikes.

Directions: In the sentences below, draw an arrow from each pronoun to the noun it replaces.

Example: Gail needs the salt. Please pass it to her.

1. The workers had faith they would finish the house in time.
2. Kathy fell and scraped her knees. She put bandages on them.
3. The teacher told the students he wanted to see their papers.

Directions: Cross out some nouns and write pronouns to replace them.

Example: Dan needed a book for ~~Dan's~~ his book report.

1. Brian doesn't care about the style of ~~Brian's~~ his clothes.
2. Joy dyed ~~Joy's~~ her jeans to make ~~the jeans~~ them dark blue.
3. Faith said ~~Faith~~ she was tired of sharing a bedroom with ~~Faith's~~ her two sisters. ~~Faith~~ She wanted a room of ~~Faith's~~ her own.
4. Bathe babies carefully so the soap doesn't get in ~~the babies~~ their eyes and make ~~the babies~~ them cry.
5. When the children held up ~~the children's~~ their pictures, we could see the pride in ~~the children's~~ their eyes.

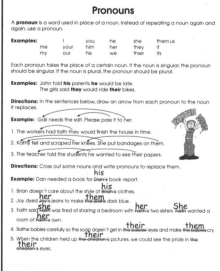

Page 229

Singular and Plural Pronouns

Directions: Rewrite the sentences so the pronouns match the nouns they replace in gender and number. Change the verb form if necessary. The first one has been done for you.

1. Canada geese are the best-known geese in North America. It was here when the first settlers came from Europe.
<u>Canada geese are the best-known geese in North America. They were here when the first settlers came from Europe.</u>

2. A Canada goose has a white patch from their chin to a spot behind their eyes.
<u>A Canada goose has a white patch from its chin to a spot behind its eyes.</u>

3. Canada geese can harm farmland when it grazes in fields.
<u>Canada geese can harm farmland when they graze in fields.</u>

4. Geese have favorite fields where it likes to stop and eat.
<u>Geese have favorite fields where they like to stop and eat.</u>

5. While most of the flock eats, some geese stand guard. He warns if there is any danger.
<u>While most of the flock eats, some geese stand guard. They warn if there is any danger.</u>

6. Each guard gets their turn to eat, too.
<u>Each guard gets its turn to eat, too.</u>

7. Female geese usually lay five or six eggs, but she may lay as many as eleven.
<u>Female geese usually lay five or six eggs, but they may lay as many as eleven.</u>

8. While the female goose sits on the eggs, the male goose guards their mate.
<u>While the female goose sits on the eggs, the male goose guards his mate.</u>

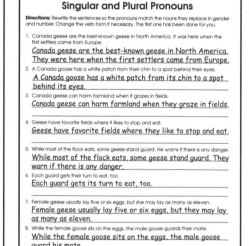

Page 230

Possessive Pronouns

A **possessive pronoun** shows ownership. A possessive pronoun can be used with the name of what is owned or by itself.

Examples:
This is **my** book. The book is **mine**.
This is **your** sandwich. It is **yours**.
This is **our** room. The room is **ours**.

The possessive pronouns are **my**, **your**, **our**, **his**, **her**, **their**, **its**, **mine**, **yours**, **ours**, **hers** and **theirs**. Possessive pronouns do not have apostrophes.

Directions: Complete the sentences with the correct possessive pronouns.

1. I entered __my__ picture in the contest. That farm scene is __mine__.
2. Shelby entered __her__ picture, too. Do you see __hers__?
3. Hal didn't finish __his__ drawing. He left __his__ at home.
4. Did you enter __your__ clay pot? That looks like __yours__.
5. One picture has fallen off __its__ stand.
6. Brian and Kendell worked together on a chalk drawing. That sketch by the doorway is __theirs__.
7. The judges have made __their__ choices.
8. We both won! They picked both of __ours__!
9. Here come the judges with our ribbons in __their__ hands.
10. Your ribbon is the same as __mine__.

Page 231

Writing: Possessive Pronouns

A **possessive pronoun** shows ownership. Instead of writing "That is Jill's book," write "That is her book" or "That is hers." Instead of "I lost my pencil," write "I lost mine." Use possessive pronouns to name what is possessed.

Examples: my (book)   our (car)   your (hat)   his (leg)
her (hair)   their (group)   its (team)

Use **mine**, **ours**, **yours**, **his**, **hers** and **theirs** when you do not name what is possessed. Notice that possessive pronouns don't use apostrophes.

Directions: Complete these sentences with the correct possessive pronoun.

Example: This book belongs to Jon. It is __his__.

1. I brought my lunch. Did you bring __yours__?
2. I can't do my homework. I wonder if Nancy figured out __hers__.
3. Jason saved his candy bar, but I ate __mine__.
4. Our team finished our project, but the other team didn't finish __theirs__.
5. They already have their assignment. When will we get __ours__?

It's easy to confuse the possessive pronoun **its** with the contraction for **it is**, which is spelled **it's**. The apostrophe in **it's** shows that the **i** in **is** has been left out.

Directions: Write **its** or **it's** in each sentence below.

Examples: The book has lost **its** cover. **It's** going to rain soon.

1. __It's__ nearly time to go.
2. The horse hurt __its__ leg.
3. Every nation has __its__ share of problems.
4. What is __its__ name?
5. I think __it's__ too warm to snow.
6. The teacher said __it's__ up to us.

Page 232

Indefinite Pronouns

Indefinite pronouns often end with **body**, **one** or **thing**.

Examples:
Everybody is going to be there.
No one wants to miss it.

Indefinite pronouns do not change form when used as subjects or objects. They are always singular.

Example:
Incorrect: Everyone must bring **their** own lunches.
Correct: **All students** must bring **their** own lunches.
Everyone must bring **his** or **her** own lunch.
Everyone must bring **a** lunch.

Directions: Write twelve indefinite pronouns by matching a word from column A with a word from column B.

Column A	Column B
any	thing
every	one
no	body
some	

1. __anything__
2. __anyone__
3. __anybody__
4. __everything__
5. __everyone__
6. __everybody__
7. __nothing__
8. __no one__
9. __nobody__
10. __something__
11. __someone__
12. __somebody__

Directions: Write all the indefinite pronouns that would make sense in the sentence below. _____ can come.

13. __Anyone, Anybody, Everyone, Everybody, No one, Nobody, Someone, Somebody__

Directions: Rewrite this sentence correctly.

14. Everybody has their books.
__Everybody has his or her books.__

Page 233

Interrogative and Relative Pronouns

An **interrogative pronoun** is used when asking a question. The interrogative pronouns are **who**, **what** and **which**. Use **who** when referring to people. Use **what** when referring to things. **Which** can be used to refer to people or things.

Directions: Circle the interrogative pronouns. Write whether the pronoun refers to people or things.

1. (Who) brought this salad for the picnic?
__people__
2. (Which) car will we drive to the movies?
__things__
3. (Which) girl asked the question?
__people__
4. (What) time is it?
__things__
5. (What) will we do with the leftover food?
__things__
6. (Who) is going to the swim meet?
__people__

Relative pronouns refer to the noun or pronoun which comes before them. The noun or pronoun to which it refers is called the **antecedent**. The relative pronouns are **who**, **whom**, **which** and **that**. **Who** and **whom** refer to people. **Which** refers to things or animals. **That** can refer to people, animals or things.

Directions: Circle the relative pronouns and underline the antecedents.

1. My dog (which) is very well-behaved, never barks.
2. The story was about a girl (who) wanted a horse of her own.
3. The bookcase (which) was full, toppled over during the night.
4. The man to (whom) I spoke gave me complicated directions.
5. The book (that) I wanted had already been checked out of the library.

Page 234

Gender and Number of Pronouns

Pronouns that identify males are **masculine gender**. The masculine pronouns are **he**, **his** and **him**. Pronouns that identify females are **feminine gender**. The feminine pronouns are **she**, **her** and **hers**. Pronouns that identify something that is neither male nor female are **neuter gender**. The neuter pronouns are **it** and **its**.

The plural pronouns **they** and **them** are used for masculine, feminine or neuter gender.

Examples:

Noun	Pronoun	Noun	Pronoun
boat	it	woman	she
man	he	John's	his
travelers	they	dog's	its

Directions: List four nouns that each pronoun could replace in a sentence. The first one has been done for you.

1. she __mother__ __doctor__ __girl__ __friend__
2. he __Answers will vary.__
3. it
4. they
5. hers
6. its

Singular pronouns take the place of singular nouns. Plural pronouns take the place of plural nouns. The singular pronouns are **I**, **me**, **mine**, **he**, **it**, **its**, **hers**, **his**, **him**, **her**, **you** and **yours**. The plural pronouns are **we**, **you**, **yours**, **they**, **theirs**, **ours**, **them** and **us**.

Directions: Write five sentences. Include a singular and a plural pronoun in each sentence.

1.
2.
3. __Sentences will vary.__
4.
5.

Page 235

Writing: Pronouns

Sometimes, matching nouns and pronouns can be difficult.

Example: A teacher should always be fair to their students.

Teacher is singular, but **their** is plural, so they don't match. Still, we can't say "A teacher should always be fair to his students," because teachers are both men and women. "His or her students" sounds awkward. One easy way to handle this is to make **teacher** plural so it will match **their**.

Example: Teachers should always be fair to their students.

Directions: Correct the problems in the following sentences by crossing out the incorrect words and writing in the correct nouns and pronouns. (If you make the noun plural, make the verb plural, too.)

Examples: Ron's school won ~~their~~ _its_ basketball game.
You can tell if ~~a cat is~~ _cats are_ angry by watching their tails.

1. ~~A student~~ _Students_ should try to praise their friends' strong points.
2. The group finished ~~their~~ _its_ work on time in spite of the deadline.
3. ~~A parent~~ _Parents_ usually ~~has~~ _have_ a lot of faith in their children.
4. The company paid ~~their~~ _its_ workers once a week.
5. The train made ~~their~~ _its_ daily run from Chicago to Detroit.
6. ~~Each student~~ _Students_ should have a title on their papers.

Directions: Complete these sentences with the correct pronouns.

1. Simon fell out of the tree and scraped __his__ arm.
2. The citizens felt a deep pride in __their__ community.
3. Heather and Sheila wear __their__ hair in the same style.
4. I dyed some shirts, but __they__ didn't turn out right.
5. The nurse showed the mother how to bathe __her__ baby.
6. Our school made $75 from __its__ carnival.

ANSWER KEY

Page 236

Pronouns as Subjects

A **pronoun** is a word that takes the place of a noun. The pronouns **I, we, he, she, it, you** and **they** can be the subjects of a sentence.

Examples:
I left the house early.
You need to be more careful.
She dances well.

A pronoun must be singular if the noun it replaces is singular. A pronoun must be plural if the noun it replaces is plural. **He, she** and **it** are singular pronouns. **We** and **they** are plural pronouns. **You** is both singular and plural.

Examples:
Tina practiced playing the piano. **She** plays well.
Jim and I are studying Africa. **We** made a map of it.
The children clapped loudly. **They** liked the clown.

Directions: Write the correct pronouns.

1. Bobcats hunt at night. __They__ are not seen during the day.
2. The mother bobcat usually has babies during February or March. __She__ may have two litters a year.
3. The father bobcat stays away when the babies are first born. Later, __he__ helps find food for them.
4. We have a new assignment. __It__ is a project about bobcats.
5. My group gathered pictures of bobcats. __We__ made a display.
6. Jennifer wrote our report. __She__ used my notes.

Directions: Circle the pronouns that do not match the nouns they replace. Then write the correct pronouns on the lines.

7. Two boys saw a bobcat. (He) told us what happened. __They__
8. Then we saw a film. (They) showed bobcats climbing trees. __It__

Page 237

Pronouns as Direct Objects

The pronouns **me, you, him, her, it, us** and **them** can be used as direct objects.

Examples:
I heard Grant. Grant heard **me**.
We like the teacher. The teacher likes **us**.
He saw the dog. The dog saw **him**.

A pronoun used as a direct object must be plural if the noun is plural and singular if the noun is singular.

Directions: Write the correct pronouns.

1. Goldfish come from China. The Chinese used to eat __them__ like trout.
2. The prettiest goldfish were kept as pets. The Chinese put __them__ in small bowls and ponds.
3. My sister, brother and I have goldfish. Grandpa took __us__ to the store to get them.
4. They come to the top when I am around. I think they like __me__.
5. My sister's fish was white. She kept __it__ for 3 weeks.
6. She claimed the fish splashed __her__ when she fed it.

Directions: Circle pronouns that do not match the nouns they replace. Rewrite the sentences using the correct pronouns. Change the verbs after the pronouns if necessary.

7. Goldfish often die because kids don't feed (it).
__Goldfish often die because kids don't feed them.__
8. Some goldfish live a long time because (it) is well cared for.
__Some goldfish live a long time because they are well cared for.__
9. A wild goldfish will eat anything (they) think looks good.
__A wild goldfish will eat anything it thinks looks good.__
10. Birds eat wild goldfish. (It) likes the young ones best.
__Birds eat wild goldfish. They like the young ones best.__

Page 238

Pronouns as Indirect Objects and Objects of Prepositions

The pronouns **me, you, him, her, it, us** and **them** can be used as indirect objects and objects of prepositions.

Examples:
Pronouns as indirect objects: Shawn showed **me** his new bike. The teacher gave **us** two more days to finish our reports.
Pronouns as objects of prepositions: It's your turn after **her**. I can't do it without **them**.

A pronoun used as an indirect object or an object of a preposition must be singular if the noun it replaces is singular and plural if the noun it replaces is plural.

Directions: Write the correct pronouns. Above the pronoun, write **S** if it is the subject, **DO** if it is the direct object, **IO** if it is the indirect object or **OP** if it is the object of a preposition.

1. Markos is coming to our party. I gave __him__ [IO] the directions.
2. Janelle and Eldon used to be his friends. Is he still friends with __them__ [OP]?
3. Kevin and I like each other, but __we__ [S] are too young to go steady.
4. We listened closely while she told __us__ [IO] what happened to __her__ [OP].
5. My brother hurt his hand, but I took care of __it__ [OP].
6. A piece of glass cut him when __he__ [S] dropped __it__ [DO].
7. When Annalisa won the race, the coach gave __her__ [IO] a trophy.
8. We were hot and sweaty, but a breeze cooled __us__ [DO] off.

Page 239

Pronouns

Subjects:	he	she	it	you	I	they	we
Objects:	him	her	it	you	me	them	us
Possessive:	his	her	its	your	my	their	our
Possessive:	his	hers	its	yours	mine	theirs	ours
Indefinite:	everyone	nobody	something	(and others)			

Directions: Complete these sentences with the correct pronouns from the box. Above each pronoun, write how it is used: **S** for subject, **DO** for direct object, **IO** for indirect object, **OP** for object of a preposition, **PP** for possessive pronoun or **IP** for indefinite pronoun.

1. Last week, we had a food drive at __our__ [PP] church.
2. __Everyone__ [IP] in our Sunday school class helped collect food.
3. I walked down my street and asked __our__ [PP] neighbors for food.
4. They gave __us__ [IO] cans and boxes of food.
5. Kelly came with __us__ [OP] and helped __us__ [DO] carry all of __them__ [OP].
6. Paul had brought his old red wagon from __his__ [PP] house.
7. When I saw it, __I__ [S] wished I had brought __mine__ [PP].
8. Kelly and __I__ [S] had to put __our__ [PP] cans in grocery bags.
9. Those bags were really heavy when __they__ [S] were full.
10. When I picked one up, __it__ [S] tore and the cans fell out!
11. Jeremy's sister gave __us__ [IO] a ride around the neighborhood.
12. Walking made Kelly and __me__ [DO] hungry.

Page 240

Review

Directions: Write a noun for each possessive pronoun.
1. my _____   5. our _____
2. his _____   6. her _____
3. your _____   7. its _____
4. their _____

Directions: Use these indefinite pronouns in sentences.
8. everyone _____
9. nobody _____
10. something _____

Directions: Use these _____
11. who _____
12. who _____
13. which _____

Answers will vary.

Directions: Use these relative pronouns in sentences.
14. who _____
15. whom _____
16. which _____
17. that _____

Page 241

Adjectives

An **adjective** describes a noun or pronoun. There are three types of adjectives. They are **positive, comparative** and **superlative.**

Examples:

Positive	Comparative	Superlative
big	bigger	biggest
beautiful	more beautiful	most beautiful
bright	less bright	least bright

Directions: Write the comparative and superlative forms of these adjectives.

Positive	Comparative	Superlative
1. happy	happier	happiest
2. kind	kinder	kindest
3. sad	sadder	saddest
4. slow	slower	slowest
5. low	lower	lowest
6. delicious	more delicious	most delicious
7. strong	stronger	strongest
8. straight	straighter	straightest
9. tall	taller	tallest
10. humble	more humble	most humble
11. hard	harder	hardest
12. clear	clearer	clearest
13. loud	louder	loudest
14. clever	more clever	most clever

Page 242

Writing: Comparatives

Comparatives are forms of adjectives or adverbs used to compare different things. With adjectives, you usually add **er** to the end to make a comparative. If the adjective ends in **y**, drop the **y** and add **ier**.

Examples:
tall — taller
easy — easier

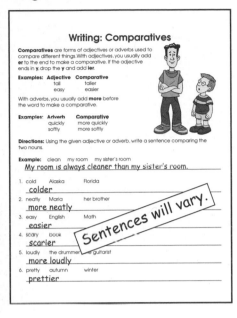

With adverbs, you usually add **more** before the word to make a comparative.

Examples:
Adverb	Comparative
quickly	more quickly
softly	more softly

Directions: Using the given adjective or adverb, write a sentence comparing the two nouns.

Example: clean   my room   my sister's room
My room is always cleaner than my sister's room.

1. cold   Alaska   Florida
   colder
2. neatly   Maria   her brother
   more neatly
3. easy   English   Math
   easier
4. scary   book
   scarier
5. loudly   the drummer   the guitarist
   more loudly
6. pretty   autumn   winter
   prettier

Sentences will vary.

Page 243

"Good" and "Bad"

When the adjectives **good** and **bad** are used to compare things, the entire word changes.

Examples:
	Comparative	Superlative
good	better	best
bad	worse	worst

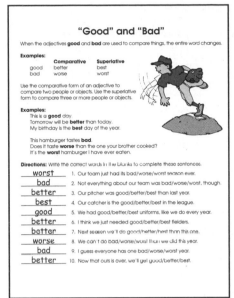

Use the comparative form of an adjective to compare two people or objects. Use the superlative form to compare three or more people or objects.

Examples:
This is a **good** day.
Tomorrow will be **better** than today.
My birthday is the **best** day of the year.

This hamburger tastes **bad**.
Does it taste **worse** than the one your brother cooked?
It's the **worst** hamburger I have ever eaten.

Directions: Write the correct words in the blanks to complete these sentences.

worst	1. Our team just had its bad/worse/worst season ever.
bad	2. Not everything about our team was bad/worse/worst, though.
better	3. Our pitcher was good/better/best than last year.
best	4. Our catcher is the good/better/best in the league.
good	5. We had good/better/best uniforms, like we do every year.
better	6. I think we just needed good/better/best fielders.
better	7. Next season we'll do good/better/best than this one.
worse	8. We can't do bad/worse/worst than we did this year.
bad	9. I guess everyone has one bad/worse/worst year.
better	10. Now that ours is over, we'll get good/better/best.

Page 244

Demonstrative and Indefinite Adjectives

A **demonstrative adjective** identifies a particular person, place or thing. **This**, **these**, **that** and **those** are demonstrative adjectives.

Examples:
this pen	**these** earrings
that chair	**those** books

An **indefinite adjective** does not identify a particular person, place or thing but rather a group or number. **All**, **any**, **both**, **many**, **another**, **several**, **such**, **some**, **few** and **more** are indefinite adjectives.

Examples:
all teachers	**any** person
both girls	**many** flowers
another man	**more** marbles

Directions: Use each noun in a sentence with a demonstrative adjective.

1. dishes
2. clothes
3. cats
4. team
5. apples
6. stereo
7. moun...

Sentences will vary.

Directions: ... with an indefinite adjective.

8. reported
9. decisions
10. papers
11. pears
12. occupations
13. friends

Page 245

Interrogative and Possessive Adjectives

An **interrogative adjective** is used when asking a question. The interrogative adjectives are **what** and **which**.

Examples:
What kind of haircut will you get?
Which dog snarled at you?

A **possessive adjective** shows ownership. The possessive adjectives are **our**, **your**, **her**, **his**, **its**, **my** and **their**.

Examples:
That is **my** dog.
He washed **his** jeans.
Our pictures turned out great.

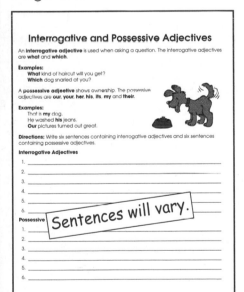

Directions: Write six sentences containing interrogative adjectives and six sentences containing possessive adjectives.

Interrogative Adjectives
1.
2.
3.
4.
5.
6.

Possessive
1.
2.
3.
4.
5.
6.

Sentences will vary.

Page 246

Prepositional Phrases as Adjectives

An adjective can be one word or an entire prepositional phrase.

Examples:
The new boy **with red hair**
The tall man **in the raincoat**
The white house **with green shutters**

Directions: Underline the prepositional phrases used as adjectives.

1. The boy in the blue cap is the captain.
2. The house across the street is 100 years old.
3. Jo and Ty love cookies with nuts.
4. I lost the book with the green cover.
5. Do you know the girl in the front row?
6. I like the pony with the long tail.
7. The dog in that yard is not friendly.
8. The picture in this magazine looks like you.

Directions: Complete these sentences with prepositional phrases used as adjectives.

9. I'd like a hamburger
10. Did you read the book
11. The dog ... is my favorite.
12. The woman ... is calling you.
13. I bought a s...
14. I'm wearing socks
15. I found a box

Answers will vary.

Page 247

Adverbs

Adverbs modify verbs. Adverbs tell **when**, **where** or **how**. Many, but not all adverbs, end in **ly**.

Adverbs of time answer the questions **how often** or **when**.

Examples:
The dog escapes its pen **frequently**.
Smart travelers **eventually** will learn to use travelers' checks.

Adverbs of place answer the question **where**.

Example: The police pushed bystanders **away** from the accident scene.

Adverbs of manner answer the question **how** or **in what manner**.

Example: He **carefully** replaced the delicate vase.

Directions: Underline the verb in each sentence. Circle the adverb. Write the question each adverb answers on the line.

1. My grandmother walks gingerly to avoid falls.
   how or in what manner
2. The mice darted everywhere to escape the cat.
   where
3. He decisively moved the chess piece.
   how or in what manner
4. Our family frequently enjoys a night at the movies.
   how often or when
5. Later we will discuss the consequences of your behavior.
   when
6. The audience glanced up at the balcony where the noise originated.
   where
7. The bleachers are already built for the concert.
   when
8. My friend and I study daily for the upcoming exams.
   how often or when

Grade 5 - Comprehensive Curriculum

Page 248

Adverbs

Like adjectives, adverbs have types of comparison. They are positive, comparative and superlative.

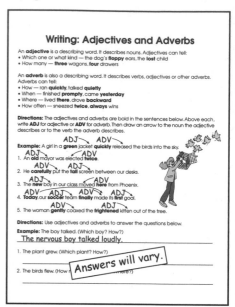

Examples:

Positive	Comparative	Superlative
expertly	more expertly	most expertly
soon	sooner	soonest

Directions: Underline the adverb in each sentence. Then write the type of comparison on the line.

1. The car _easily_ won the race. _positive_
2. Our class _most eagerly_ awaited the return of our test. _superlative_
3. My ice cream melted _more quickly_ than yours. _comparative_
4. Frances awoke _early_ the first day of school. _positive_
5. He knows _well_ the punishment for disobeying his parents. _positive_
6. There is _much_ work to be done on the stadium project. _positive_
7. The child played _most happily_ with the building blocks. _superlative_
8. This article appeared _more recently_ than the other. _comparative_

Directions: Write the comparative and superlative forms of these adverbs.

Positive	Comparative	Superlative
9. hard	harder	hardest
10. impatiently	more impatiently	most impatiently
11. anxiously	more anxiously	most anxiously
12. suddenly	more suddenly	most suddenly
13. far	farther	farthest
14. long	longer	longest

Page 249

Prepositional Phrases as Adverbs

An adverb can be one word or an entire prepositional phrase.

Examples:
They'll be here **tomorrow**.
They always come **on time**.
Move it **down**.
Put it **under the picture**.
Drive **carefully**.
He drove **with care**.

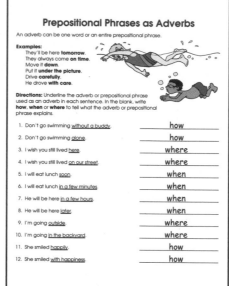

Directions: Underline the adverb or prepositional phrase used as an adverb in each sentence. In the blank, write **how, when** or **where** to tell what the adverb or prepositional phrase explains.

1. Don't go swimming _without a buddy_. _how_
2. Don't go swimming _alone_. _how_
3. I wish you still lived _here_. _where_
4. I wish you still lived _on our street_. _where_
5. I will eat lunch _soon_. _when_
6. I will eat lunch _in a few minutes_. _when_
7. He will be here _in a few hours_. _when_
8. He will be here _later_. _when_
9. I'm going _outside_. _where_
10. I'm going _in the backyard_. _where_
11. She smiled _happily_. _how_
12. She smiled _with happiness_. _how_

Page 250

Writing: Adjectives and Adverbs

An **adjective** is a describing word. It describes nouns. Adjectives can tell:
• Which one or what kind — the dog's **floppy** ears, the **lost** child
• How many — **three** wagons, **four** drawers

An **adverb** is also a describing word. It describes verbs, adjectives or other adverbs. Adverbs can tell:
• How — ran **quickly**, talked **quietly**
• When — finished **promptly**, came **yesterday**
• Where — lived **there**, drove **backward**
• How often — sneezed **twice**, **always** wins

Directions: The adjectives and adverbs are bold in the sentences below. Above each, write **ADJ** for adjective or **ADV** for adverb. Then draw an arrow to the noun the adjective describes or to the verb the adverb describes.

Example: A girl in a **green** jacket **quickly** released the birds into the sky.

1. An **old** mayor was elected **twice**.
2. He **carefully** put the **tall** screen between our desks.
3. The **new** boy in our class moved **here** from Phoenix.
4. **Today**, our soccer team **finally** made its **first** goal.
5. The woman **gently** coaxed the **frightened** kitten out of the tree.

Directions: Use adjectives and adverbs to answer the questions below.

Example: The boy talked. (Which boy? How?)
The nervous boy talked loudly.

1. The plant grew. (Which plant? How?)

2. The birds flew. (How?... where?)

Answers will vary.

Page 251

Writing: Adjectives and Adverbs

Adjectives and adverbs make sentences more interesting. Often, we can make adverbs from adjectives by adding **ly** to the end.

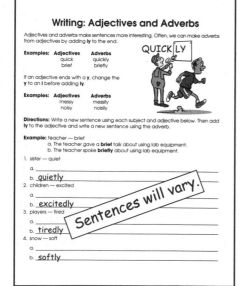

Examples:
Adjectives	Adverbs
quick	quickly
brief	briefly

If an adjective ends with a **y**, change the **y** to an **i** before adding **ly**.

Examples:
Adjectives	Adverbs
messy	messily
noisy	noisily

Directions: Write a new sentence using each subject and adjective below. Then add **ly** to the adjective and write a new sentence using the adverb.

Example: teacher — brief
 a. The teacher gave a **brief** talk about using lab equipment.
 b. The teacher spoke **briefly** about using lab equipment.

1. sister — quiet
 a.
 b. quietly
2. children — excited
 a.
 b. excitedly
3. players — tired
 a.
 b. tiredly
4. snow — soft
 a.
 b. softly

Sentences will vary.

Page 252

Placement of Adjective and Adverb Phrases

Adjectives and adverbs, including prepositional phrases, should be placed as close as possible to the words they describe to avoid confusion.

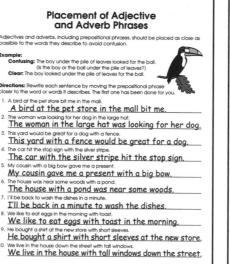

Example:
 Confusing: The boy under the pile of leaves looked for the ball. (Is the boy or the ball under the pile of leaves?)
 Clear: The boy looked under the pile of leaves for the ball.

Directions: Rewrite each sentence by moving the prepositional phrase closer to the word or words it describes. The first one has been done for you.

1. A bird at the pet store bit me in the mall.
 A bird at the pet store bit me in the mall.
2. The woman was looking for her dog in the large hat.
 The woman in the large hat was looking for her dog.
3. This yard would be great for a dog with a fence.
 This yard with a fence would be great for a dog.
4. The car hit the stop sign with the silver stripe.
 The car with the silver stripe hit the stop sign.
5. My cousin with a big bow gave me a present.
 My cousin gave me a present with a big bow.
6. The house was near some woods with a pond.
 The house with a pond was near some woods.
7. I'll be back to wash the dishes in a minute.
 I'll be back in a minute to wash the dishes.
8. We like to eat eggs in the morning with toast.
 We like to eat eggs with toast in the morning.
9. He bought a shirt at the new store with short sleeves.
 He bought a shirt with short sleeves at the new store.
10. We live in the house down the street with tall windows.
 We live in the house with tall windows down the street.

Page 253

Writing: Parts of Speech Story

Directions: Play the following game with a partner. In the story below, some of the words are missing. Without letting your partner see the story, ask him/her to provide a word for each blank. Each word should be a noun, verb, adjective or adverb, as shown. Then read the story aloud. It might not make sense, but it will make you laugh!

Last night, as I was _____ (verb + ing) _____ through the _____ (noun) _____ _____ (adjective) _____ (noun) fell from the _____ head! "Yikes!" I shrieked. I _____ (noun) _____ off, and it started _____ (verb) _____ (noun) I tried to hit it with a _____ (noun) but it was _____ (adjective) I _____ (adverb) managed to _____ (verb)

it out of the house, where it quickly climbed the nearest _____ (noun)

Answers will vary.

Page 254

Writing: Parts of Speech

Directions: Write each word from the box in the column that names its part of speech. Some words can be listed in two columns.

ADJ
Example: a chair **behind** me

ADV
he was walking **behind** me

code	young	slowly	today	finally	screen
thirsty	praise	loan	broken	decrease	slowly
nearby	twenty	Monday	town	faithful	red
coax	goal	bathe	release	cheat	there

Answers will vary but may include:

Noun	Verb	Adjective	Adverb
code	coax	thirsty	nearby
goal	praise	young	slowly
loan	cheat	twenty	today
Monday	bathe	broken	finally
screen	release	red	slowly
town	decrease	faithful	there

Directions: Write four sentences, using at least three words from the box in each one. Mark each word as a noun (**N**), verb (**V**), adjective (**ADJ**) or adverb (**ADV**).

ADJ   ADV   N
Example: **Twenty** people **slowly** walked through the **town**.

Sentences will vary.

Page 255

Conjunctions

A **conjunction** joins words or groups of words in a sentence. The most commonly used conjunctions are **and**, **but** and **or**.

Examples: My brother **and** I each want to win the trophy.
Tonight, it will rain **or** sleet.
I wanted to go to the party, **but** I got sick.

Directions: Circle the conjunctions.

1. Dolphins (and) whales are mammals.
2. They must rise to the surface of the water to breathe (or) they will die.
3. Dolphins resemble fish (but) they are not fish.
4. Sightseeing boats are often entertained by groups of dolphins (or) whales.
5. Whales appear to effortlessly leap out of the water (and) execute flips.
6. Both whale (and) dolphin babies are born alive.
7. The babies are called calves (and) are born in the water (but) must breathe air within a few minutes of birth.
8. Sometimes an entire pod of whales will help a mother (and) calf reach the surface to breathe.
9. Scientists (and) marine biologists have long been intrigued by these ocean animals.
10. Whales (and) dolphins do not seem to be afraid of humans (or) boats.

Directions: Write six sentences using conjunctions.

11. _____
12. _____
13. _____
14. _____
15. _____
16. _____

Sentences will vary.

Page 256

Writing: Conjunctions

Too many short sentences make writing seem choppy. Short sentences can be combined to make writing flow better. Words used to combine sentences are called **conjunctions**.

Examples: but, before, after, because, when, or, so, and

Directions: Use **or, but, before, after, because, when,** and **so** to combine each pair of sentences. The first one has been done for you.

1. I was wearing my winter coat. I started to shiver.
   I was wearing my winter coat, but I started to shiver.

2. Animals all need water. They may perish without it.

3. The sun came out. The ice began to thaw.

4. The sun came out. The day was still ch...

5. Will the flowers...

6. ...an to feel threatened.

7. Win... was a challenge. Our team didn't have much experience.

8. Winning was a challenge. Our team was up to it.

Sentences will vary.

Directions: Write three sentences of your own. Use a conjunction in each sentence.

Page 257

Statements and Questions

A **statement** is a sentence that tells something. It ends with a period (.).

A **question** is a sentence that asks something. It ends with a question mark (?).

Examples:
Statement: Shari is walking to school today.
Question: Is Shari walking to school today?

In some questions, the subject comes between two parts of the verb. In the examples below, the subjects are underlined. The verbs and the rest of the predicates are bold.

Examples:
Is Steve coming with us?
Who will be there?
Which one did you **select**?

To find the predicate, turn a question into a statement.

Example: Is Steve coming with us? Steve is coming with us.

Directions: Write **S** for statement or **Q** for question. Put a period after the statements and a question mark after the questions.

S 1. Today is the day for our field trip.
Q 2. How are we going to get there?
S 3. The bus will take us.
Q 4. Is there room for everyone?
Q 5. Who forgot to bring a lunch?
S 6. I'll save you a seat.

Directions: Circle the subjects and underline all parts of the predicates.

7. Do (you) like field trips?
8. Did (you) bring your coat?
9. Will (it) be cold there?
10. Do (you) see my gloves anywhere?
11. Is (anyone) sitting with you?
12. Does (the bus driver) have a map?
13. Are (all the roads) this bumpy?

Page 258

Statements and Questions

Directions: Write 10 statements and 10 questions.

Statements

1. _____
2. _____
3. _____
4. _____
5. _____
6. _____
7. _____
8. _____
9. _____
10. _____

Questions

1. _____
2. _____
3. _____
4. _____
5. _____
6. _____
7. _____
8. _____
9. _____
10. _____

Sentences will vary.

Page 259

Commands, Requests and Exclamations

A **command** is a sentence that orders someone to do something. It ends with a period or an exclamation mark (!).

A **request** is a sentence that asks someone to do something. It ends with a period or a question mark (?).

An **exclamation** is a sentence that shows strong feeling. It ends with an exclamation mark (!).

Examples:
Command: Stay in your seat.
Request: Would you please pass the salt?
Please pass the salt.
Exclamation: Call the police!

In the first and last two sentences in the examples, the subject is not stated. The subject is understood to be **you**.

Directions: Write **C** if the sentence is a command, **R** if it is a request and **E** if it is an exclamation. Put the correct punctuation at the end of each sentence.

C 1. Look both ways before you cross the street.
R 2. Please go to the store and buy some bread for us.
E 3. The house is on fire!
R 4. Would you hand me the glue?
C 5. Don't step there.
C 6. Write your name at the top of the page.
R 7. Please close the door.
R 8. Would you answer the phone?
E 9. Watch out!
C 10. Take one card from each pile.

Page 266

Run-On Sentences

A **run-on sentence** occurs when two or more sentences are joined together without the correct punctuation. A run-on sentence must be divided into two or more separate sentences.

Example:
Run-on: On Tuesday my family went to the amusement park but unfortunately it rained and we got wet and it took hours for our clothes to dry.

Correct: On Tuesday my family went to the amusement park. Unfortunately, it rained and we got wet. It took hours for our clothes to dry.

Directions: Rewrite these run-on sentences correctly.

1. I have a dog named Boxer and a cat named Phoebe and they are both well-behaved and friendly.

   I have a dog named Boxer and a cat named Phoebe. They are both friendly and well-behaved.

2. Jacob's basketball coach makes the team run for 20 minutes each practice and then he makes them play a full game and afterwards he makes them do 50 push-ups and 100 sit-ups.

   Jacob's basketball coach makes the team run for 20 minutes each practice. Then he makes them play a full game. Afterwards, he makes them do 50 push-ups and 100 sit-ups.

3. My family members each enjoy different hobbies Mom likes to paint Dad likes to read I like to play sports and my younger sister likes to build model airplanes although I think they are too hard.

   My family members each enjoy different hobbies. Mom likes to paint. Dad likes to read. I like to play sports. My younger sister likes to build model airplanes, although I think they are too hard.

Page 267

Commas

Commas are used to separate items in a series. Both examples below are correct. A final comma is optional.

Examples:
The fruit bowl contains oranges, peaches, pears, and apples.
The fruit bowl contains oranges, peaches, pears and apples.

Commas are also used to separate geographical names and dates.

Examples:
Today's date is January 13, 2000.
My grandfather lives in Tallahassee, Florida.
I would like to visit Paris, France.

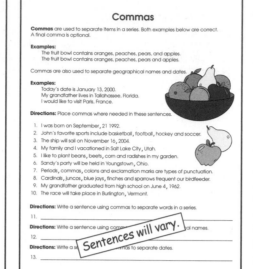

Directions: Place commas where needed in these sentences.

1. I was born on September, 21 1992.
2. John's favorite sports include basketball, football, hockey and soccer.
3. The ship will sail on November 16, 2004.
4. My family and I vacationed in Salt Lake City, Utah.
5. I like to plant beans, beets, corn and radishes in my garden.
6. Sandy's party will be held in Youngstown, Ohio.
7. Periods, commas, colons and exclamation marks are types of punctuation.
8. Cardinals, juncos, blue jays, finches and sparrows frequent our birdfeeder.
9. My grandfather graduated from high school on June 4, 1962.
10. The race will take place in Burlington, Vermont.

Directions: Write a sentence using commas to separate words in a series.

11. _____

Directions: Write a sentence using com___ ___al names.

12. _____

Directions: Write a s___ ___mas to separate dates.

13. _____

Sentences will vary.

Page 268

Commas

Commas are used to separate a noun or pronoun in a direct address from the rest of the sentence. A noun or pronoun in a **direct address** is one that names or refers to the person addressed.

Examples:
John, this room is a mess!
This room, **John,** is a disgrace!
Your room needs to be more organized, **John.**

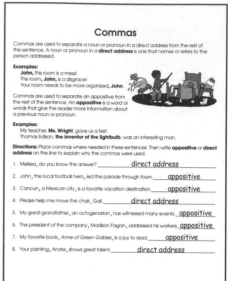

Commas are used to separate an appositive from the rest of the sentence. An **appositive** is a word or words that give the reader more information about a previous noun or pronoun.

Examples:
My teacher, **Ms. Wright,** gave us a test.
Thomas Edison, **the inventor of the lightbulb,** was an interesting man.

Directions: Place commas where needed in these sentences. Then write **appositive** or **direct address** on the line to explain why the commas were used.

1. Melissa, do you know the answer? _____ direct address
2. John, the local football hero, led the parade through town. _____ appositive
3. Cancun, a Mexican city, is a favorite vacation destination. _____ appositive
4. Please help me move the chair, Gail. _____ direct address
5. My great-grandfather, an octogenarian, has witnessed many events. _____ appositive
6. The president of the company, Madison Fagan, addressed his workers. _____ appositive
7. My favorite book, Anne of Green Gables, is a joy to read. _____ appositive
8. Your painting, Andre, shows great talent. _____ direct address

Page 269

Combining Sentences

When the subjects are the same, sentences can be combined by using appositives.

Examples:
Tony likes to play basketball. Tony is my neighbor.
Tony, **my neighbor,** likes to play basketball.

Ms. Herman was sick today. Ms. Herman is our math teacher.
Ms. Herman, **our math teacher,** was sick today.

Appositives are set off from the rest of the sentence with commas.

Directions: Use commas and appositives to combine the pairs of sentences.

1. Julie has play practice today. Julie is my sister.
   Julie, my sister, has play practice today.

2. Greg fixed my bicycle. Greg is my cousin.
   Greg, my cousin, fixed my bicycle.

3. Mr. Scott told us where to meet. Mr. Scott is our coach.
   Mr. Scott, our coach, told us where to meet.

4. Tiffany is moving to Detroit. Tiffany is my neighbor.
   Tiffany, my neighbor, is moving to Detroit.

5. Kyle has the flu. Kyle is my brother.
   Kyle, my brother, has the flu.

6. My favorite football team is playing tonight. Houston is my favorite team.
   My favorite football team, Houston, is playing tonight.

7. Bonnie Pryor will be at our school next week. Bonnie Pryor is a famous author.
   Bonnie Pryor, a famous author, will be at our school next week.

8. Our neighborhood is having a garage sale. Our neighborhood is the North End.
   Our neighborhood, the North End, is having a garage sale.

Page 270

Writing: Using Commas Correctly

A **comma** tells a reader where to pause when reading a sentence. Use commas when combining two or more *complete* sentences with a joining word.

Examples: We raked the leaves, and **we put them into bags.**
Brian dressed quickly, but **he still missed the school bus.**

Do not use commas if you are not combining complete sentences.

Examples: We raked the leaves and **put them into bags.**
Brian dressed quickly but **still missed the school bus.**

If either part of the sentence does not have both a subject and a verb, do not use a comma.

Directions: Read each sentence below and decide whether or not it needs a comma. If it does, rewrite the sentence, placing the comma correctly. If it doesn't, write **O.K.** on the line.

1. The cat stretched lazily and walked out of the room.
   O.K.

2. I could use the money to buy a new shirt or I could go to the movies.
   I could use the money to buy a new shirt, or I could go to the movies.

3. My sister likes pizza but she doesn't like spaghetti.
   My sister likes pizza, but she doesn't like spaghetti.

4. Mom mixed the batter and poured it into the pan.
   O.K.

5. The teacher passed out the tests and she told us to write our names on them.
   The teacher passed out the tests, and she told us to write our names on them.

6. The car squealed its tires and took off out of the parking lot.
   O.K.

7. The snow fell heavily and we knew the schools would be closed the next day.
   The snow fell heavily, and we knew the schools would be closed the next day.

8. The batter hit the ball and it flew over the fence.
   The batter hit the ball, and it flew over the fence.

Page 271

Punctuation

Directions: Add commas where needed. Put the correct punctuation at the end of each sentence.

1. My friend, Jamie, loves to snowboard.
2. Winter sports such as hockey, skiing and skating are fun.
3. Oh, what a lovely view!
4. The map shows the continents of Asia, Africa, Australia and Antarctica.
5. My mother, a ballet dancer, will perform tonight.
6. What will you do tomorrow?
7. When will the plane arrive at the airport?
8. Jason, do you know what time it is?
9. Friends of ours, the Watsons, are coming for dinner.
10. Margo, look out for that falling rock!
11. The young child sat reading a book.
12. Who wrote this letter?
13. My sister, Jill, is very neat.
14. The trampoline is in our backyard.
15. We will have chicken, peas, rice and salad for dinner.
16. That dog, a Saint Bernard, looks dangerous.

Page 260

Commands, Requests and Exclamations

Directions: Write six sentences for each type listed.

Command

1. _____
2. _____
3. _____
4. _____
5. _____
6. _____

Request

1. _____
2. _____
3. _____
4. _____
5. _____
6. _____

Sentences will vary.

Exclamation

1. _____
2. _____
3. _____
4. _____
5. _____
6. _____

Page 261

Writing: Four Kinds of Sentences

There are four kinds of sentences used in writing. Different punctuation is used for different kinds of sentences.

A **statement** tells something. A period is used after statements.

Examples: I jogged five miles yesterday.
We are going to have a spelling test on Friday.

A **question** asks something. A question mark is used after questions.

Examples: What are you wearing to the dance?
Will it ever stop raining?

An **exclamation** shows strong feeling or excitement. An exclamation mark is used after exclamations.

Examples: Boy, am I tired!
What a beautiful painting!

A **command** tells someone to do something. A period or an exclamation mark is used after a command, depending on how strong it is.

Examples: Please hand me that pen. Don't touch the stove!

Directions: Write the correct punctuation mark at the end of each sentence below. Then write whether the sentence is a statement, question, exclamation or command.

Example: I didn't have time to finish my homework last night. **statement**

1. Why didn't she come shopping with us**?** **question**
2. Somebody call an ambulance **! or .** **command or exclamation**
3. He's been watching TV all morning. **statement**
4. How did you do on the quiz**?** **question**
5. Go sit in the third row **! or .** **command or exclamation**
6. I have to go to the dentist tomorrow. **statement**
7. I've never been so hungry**!** **exclamation**
8. Who tracked mud all over the house**?** **question**
9. That restaurant is too expensive. **or !** **statement or exclamation**

Page 262

Compound Subjects/Compound Predicates

A **compound subject** has two or more nouns or pronouns joined by a conjunction. Compound subjects share the same predicate.

Examples:
Suki and Spot walked to the park in the rain.
Cars, buses and trucks splashed water on them.
He and I were glad we had our umbrella.

A **compound predicate** has two or more verbs joined by a conjunction. Compound predicates share the same subject.

Examples:
Suki **went** in the restroom **and wiped** off her shoes.
Paula **followed** Suki **and waited** for her.

A sentence can have a compound subject and a compound predicate.

Example: **Tina and Maria went** to the mall **and shopped** for an hour.

Directions: Circle the compound subjects. Underline the compound predicates.

1. (Steve and Jerry) went to the store and bought some gum.
2. (Police and firefighters) worked together and put out the fire.
3. (Karen and Marsha) did their homework and checked it twice.
4. In preschool, the (boys and girls) drew pictures and colored them.

Directions: Write compound subjects to go with these predicates.

5. _____ ate peanut butter sandwiches.
6. _____ left early.
7. _____
8. _____
9. _____

Answers will vary.

Directions: Write ___ with these subjects.

10. A scary ___
11. My friend's ___
12. The shadow _____
13. The wind _____
14. The runaway car _____

Page 263

Combining Subjects

Too many short sentences make writing sound choppy. Often, we can combine sentences with different subjects and the same predicate to make one sentence with a compound subject.

Example:
Lisa tried out for the play. Todd tried out for the play.
Compound subject: Lisa and Todd tried out for the play.

When sentences have different subjects and different predicates, we cannot combine them this way. Each subject and predicate must stay together. Two short sentences can be combined with a conjunction.

Examples:
Lisa got a part in the play. Todd will help make scenery.
Lisa got a part in the play, and Todd will help make scenery.

Directions: If a pair of sentences share the same predicate, combine them with compound subjects. If the sentences have different subjects and predicates, combine them using **and**.

1. Rachel read a book about explorers. Eric read the same book about explorers.
   Rachel and Eric read a book about explorers.
2. Rachel really liked the book. Eric agreed with her.
   Rachel really liked the book, and Eric agreed with her.
3. Vicki went to the basketball game last night. Dan went to the basketball game, too.
   Vicki and Dan went to the basketball game last night.
4. Vicki lost her coat. Dan missed his ride home.
   Vicki lost her coat, and Dan missed his ride home.
5. My uncle planted corn in the garden. My mother planted corn in the garden.
   My uncle and my mother planted corn in the garden.
6. Isaac helped with the food drive last week. Amy helped with the food drive, too.
   Isaac and Amy helped with the food drive last week.

Page 264

Combining Predicates

If short sentences have the same subject and different predicates, we can combine them into one sentence with a compound predicate.

Example:
Andy got up late this morning.
He nearly missed the school bus.
Compound predicate: Andy got up late this morning and nearly missed the school bus.

The pronoun **he** takes the place of Andy in the second sentence, so the subjects are the same and can be combined.

When two sentences have different subjects and different predicates, we cannot combine them this way. Two short sentences can be combined with a conjunction.

Examples:
Andy got up late this morning. Cindy woke up early.
Andy got up late this morning, but Cindy woke up early.

Directions: If the pair of sentences share the same subject, combine them with compound predicates. If the sentences have different subjects and predicates, combine them using **and** or **but**.

1. Kyle practiced pitching all winter. Kyle became the pitcher for his team.
   Kyle practiced pitching all winter and became the pitcher for his team.
2. Kisha studied two hours for her history test. Angela watched TV.
   Kisha studied two hours for her history test, but Angela watched TV.
3. Jeff had an earache. He took medicine four times a day.
   Jeff had an earache and took medicine four times a day.
4. Nikki found a new hair style. Melissa didn't like that style.
   Nikki found a new hair style, but Melissa didn't like that style.
5. Kirby buys his lunch every day. Sean brings his lunch from home.
   Kirby buys his lunch everyday, but Sean brings his lunch from home.

Page 265

Writing: Using Commas Correctly

A **comma** tells a reader where to pause when reading a sentence. Use commas when combining two or more *complete* sentences with a joining word.

Examples: We raked the leaves, and we put them into bags.
Brian dressed quickly, but he still missed the school bus.

Do not use commas if you are not combining complete sentences.

Examples: We raked the leaves and put them into bags.
Brian dressed quickly but still missed the school bus.

If either part of the sentence does not have both a subject and a verb, do not use a comma.

Directions: Read each sentence below and decide whether or not it needs a comma. If it does, rewrite the sentence, placing the comma correctly. If it doesn't, write **O.K.** on the line.

1. The cat stretched lazily and walked out of the room.
   O.K.
2. I could use the money to buy a new shirt or I could go to the movies.
   I could use the money to buy a new shirt, or I could go to the movies.
3. My sister likes pizza but she doesn't like spaghetti.
   My sister likes pizza, but she doesn't like spaghetti.
4. Mom mixed the batter and poured it into the pan.
   O.K.
5. The teacher passed out the tests and she told us to write our names on them.
   The teacher passed out the tests, and she told us to write our names on them.
6. The car squealed its tires and took off out of the parking lot.
   O.K.
7. The snow fell heavily and we knew the schools would be closed the next day.
   The snow fell heavily, and we knew the schools would be closed the next day.
8. The batter hit the ball and it flew over the fence.
   The batter hit the ball, and it flew over the fence.

Page 272

Quotation Marks

When a person's exact words are used in a sentence, **quotation marks** (" ") are used to identify those words. Commas are used to set off the quotation from the rest of the sentence. End punctuation is placed inside the final quotation mark.

Examples:
"When are we leaving?" Joe asked.
Marci shouted, "Go, team!"

When a sentence is interrupted by words that are not part of the quotation (he said, she answered, etc.), they are not included in the quotation marks. Note how commas are used in the next example.

Example: "I am sorry," the man announced,
"for my rude behavior."

Directions: Place quotation marks, commas and other punctuation where needed in the sentences below.

1. "Watch out!" yelled Dad.
2. Angela said, "I don't know how you can eat Brussels sprouts, Ted."
3. "Put on your coats," said Mom. "We'll be leaving in 10 minutes."
4. "Did you hear the assignment?" asked Joan.
5. Jim shouted, "This game is driving me up the wall!"
6. After examining our dog, the veterinarian said, "He looks healthy and strong."
7. The toddlers both wailed, "We want ice cream!"
8. The judge announced to the swimmers, "Take your places."
9. Upon receiving the award, the actor said, "I'd like to thank my friends and family."
10. "These are my favorite chips," said Becky.
11. "This test is too hard," moaned the class.
12. When their relay team came in first place, the runners shouted, "Hooray!"
13. "Where shall we go on vacation this year?" Dad asked.
14. As we walked past the machinery, the noise was deafening. "Cover your ears," said Mom.
15. "Fire!" yelled the chef as his pan ignited.
16. "I love basketball," my little brother stated.

Page 273

Capitalization/Punctuation

Directions: Rewrite the paragraphs below, adding punctuation where it is needed. Capitalize the first word of each sentence and all other words that should be capitalized.

most countries have laws that control advertising in norway no ads at all are allowed on radio or TV in the united states ads for alcoholic drinks, except beer and wine, are not permitted on radio or TV england has a law against advertising cigarettes on TV what do you think about these laws should they be even stricter

Most countries have laws that control advertising. In Norway, no ads at all are allowed on radio or TV. In the United States, ads for alcoholic drinks, except beer and wine, are not permitted on radio or TV. England has a law against advertising cigarettes on TV. What do you think about these laws? Should they be even stricter?

my cousin jeff is starting college this fall he wants to be a medical doctor, so he's going to central university the mayor of our town went there mayor stevens told jeff all about the university our town is so small that everyone knows what everyone else is doing is your town like that

My cousin, Jeff, is starting college this fall. He wants to be a medical doctor, so he's going to Central University. The mayor of our town went there. Mayor Stevens told Jeff all about the university. Our town is so small that everyone knows what everyone else is doing. Is your town like that?

my grandparents took a long vacation last year grandma really likes to go to the atlantic ocean and watch the dolphins my grandfather likes to fish in the ocean my aunt went with them last summer they all had a party on the fourth of july

My grandparents took a long vacation last year. Grandma really likes to go to the Atlantic Ocean and watch the dolphins. My grandfather likes to fish in the ocean. My aunt went with them last summer. They all had a party on the Fourth of July.

Page 274

Capitalization

Directions: Write **C** if capital letters are used correctly or **X** if they are used incorrectly.

X 1. Who will win the election for Mayor in November?
C 2. Tom Johnson used to be a police officer.
X 3. He announced on monday that he wants to be mayor.
C 4. My father said he would vote for Tom.
C 5. Mom and my sister Judy haven't decided yet.
C 6. They will vote at our school.
X 7. Every Fall and Spring they put up voting booths there.
C 8. I hope the new mayor will do something about our river.
X 9. That River is full of chemicals.
C 10. I'm glad our water doesn't come from Raven River.
X 11. In late Summer, the river actually stinks.
X 12. Is every river in our State so dirty?
C 13. Scientists check the water every so often.
C 14. Some professors from the college even examined it.
X 15. That is getting to be a very educated River!

Directions: Write sentences that include:

16. A person's title that should be capitalized.

17. The name of a place that should be ~~Answers will vary.~~

18. The name of a time ~~(month, holiday)~~ that should be capitalized.

Page 275

"Who" Clauses

A **clause** is a group of words with a subject and a verb. When the subject of two sentences is the same person or people, the sentences can sometimes be combined with a "who" clause.

Examples:
Mindy likes animals. Mindy feeds the squirrels.
Mindy, **who likes animals**, feeds the squirrels.

A "who" clause is set off from the rest of the sentence with commas.

Directions: Combine the pairs of sentences, using "who" clauses.

1. Teddy was late to school. Teddy was sorry later.
   Teddy, who was late to school, was sorry later.

2. Our principal is retiring. Our principal will be 65 this year.
   Our principal, who will be 65 this year, is retiring.

3. Michael won the contest. Michael will receive an award.
   Michael, who won the contest, will receive an award.

4. Charlene lives next door. Charlene has three cats.
   Charlene, who lives next door, has three cats.

5. Burt drew that picture. Burt takes art lessons.
   Burt, who drew that picture, takes art lessons.

6. Marta was elected class president. Marta gave a speech.
   Marta, who was elected class president, gave a speech.

7. Amy broke her arm. Amy has to wear a cast for 6 weeks.
   Amy, who broke her arm, has to wear a cast for 6 weeks.

8. Dr. Bank fixed my tooth. He said it would feel better soon.
   Dr. Bank, who fixed my tooth, said it would feel better soon.

Page 276

"Which" Clauses

When the subject of two sentences is the same thing or things, the sentences can sometimes be combined with a "which" clause.

Examples:
The guppy was first called "the millions fish." The guppy was later named after Reverend Robert Guppy in 1866.
The guppy, **which was first called "the millions fish,"** was later named after Reverend Robert Guppy in 1866.

A "which" clause is set off from the rest of the sentence with commas.

Directions: Combine the pairs of sentences using "which" clauses.

1. Guppies, which also used to be called rainbow fish, were brought to Germany in 1908.

2. The male guppy, which is about 1 inch long, is smaller than the female.

3. The guppies' colors, which range from red to violet, are brighter in the males.

4. Baby guppies, which hatch from eggs inside the mothers' bodies, are born alive.

5. The young, which are usually born at night, are called "fry."

6. Female guppies, which have 2 to 50 fry at one time, sometimes try to eat their fry!

7. These fish, which have been studied by scientists, actually like dirty water.

8. Wild guppies, which eat mosquito eggs, help control the mosquito population.

Page 277

"Who" and "Which" Clauses

Directions: Combine the pairs of sentences using "who" or "which" clauses.

1. Bullfrogs are rarely found out of the water. They live near ponds and streams.
   Bullfrogs, which are rarely found out of the water, live near ponds and streams.

2. These frogs grow about eight inches long. These frogs can jump three feet.
   These frogs, which grow about 8 inches long, can jump 3 feet.

3. Mark Twain was a famous writer. He wrote a story about a frog-jumping contest.
   Mark Twain, who was a famous writer, wrote a story about a frog-jumping contest.

4. This story took place in California. This story started an annual frog-jumping contest there.
   This story, which took place in California, started an annual frog-jumping contest there.

5. The contest has rules and judges. The contest allows each frog to make three leaps.
   The contest, which has rules and judges, allows each frog to make three leaps.

6. The judges watch carefully. They measure each frog's leap.
   The judges, who watch carefully, measure each frog's leap.

7. Bullfrogs eat many insects. Bullfrogs also eat small snakes.
   Bullfrogs, which eat many insects, also eat small snakes.

8. Scientists study what frogs eat. Scientists know bullfrogs can catch birds.
   Scientists, who study what frogs eat, know bullfrogs can catch birds.

Page 278

"That" Clauses

When the subject of two sentences is the same thing or things, the sentences can sometimes be combined with a "that" clause. We use **that** instead of **which** when the clause is very important in the sentence.

Examples:
The store is near our house. The store was closed.
The store **that is near our house** was closed.

The words "**that is near our house**" are very important in the combined sentence. They tell the reader which store was closed.
A "that" clause is not set off from the rest of the sentence with commas.

Examples:
Pete's store is near our house. Pete's store was closed.
Pete's store, **which is near our house**, was closed.

The words "**which is near our house**" are not important to the meaning of the combined sentence. The words **Pete's store** already told us which store was closed.

Directions: Combine the pairs of sentences using "that" clauses.

1. The dog lives next door. The dog chased me.
   The dog that lives next door chased me.
2. The bus was taking us to the game. The bus had a flat tire.
   The bus that was taking us to the game had a flat tire.
3. The fence is around the school. The fence is painted yellow.
   The fence that is around the school is painted yellow.
4. The notebook had my homework in it. The notebook is lost.
   The notebook that had my homework in it is lost.
5. A letter came today. The letter was from Mary.
   A letter that was from Mary came today.
6. The lamp was fixed yesterday. The lamp doesn't work today.
   The lamp that was fixed yesterday doesn't work today.
7. The lake is by our cabin. The lake is filled with fish.
   The lake that is by our cabin is filled with fish.

Page 279

"That" and "Which" Clauses

Directions: Combine the pairs of sentences using either a "that" or a "which" clause.

1. The TV show was on at 8:00 last night. The TV show was funny.
   The TV show that was on at 8:00 last night was funny.
2. *The Snappy Show* was on at 8:00 last night. *The Snappy Show* was funny.
   The Snappy Show, which was on at 8:00 last night, was funny.
3. The Main Bank is on the corner. The Main Bank is closed today.
   The Main Bank, which is on the corner, is closed today.
4. The bank is on the corner. The bank is closed today.
   The bank that is on the corner is closed today.
5. The bus takes Dad to work. The bus broke down.
   The bus that takes Dad to work broke down.
6. The Broad Street bus takes Dad to work. The Broad Street bus broke down.
   The Broad Street bus, which takes Dad to work, broke down.

Page 280

Combining Sentences

Not every pair of sentences can be combined with "who," "which" or "that" clauses. These sentences can be combined in other ways, either with a conjunction or by renaming the subject.

Examples:
Tim couldn't go to sleep. Todd was sleeping soundly.
Tim couldn't go to sleep, **but** Todd was sleeping soundly.

The zoo keeper fed the baby ape. A crowd gathered to watch.
When the zoo keeper fed the baby ape, a crowd gathered to watch.

Directions: Combine each pair of sentences using "who," "which" or "that" clauses, by using a conjunction or by renaming the subject.

1. The box slipped off the truck. The box was filled with bottles.
   The box that was filled with bottles slipped off the truck.
2. Carolyn is our scout leader. Carolyn taught us a new game.
   Carolyn, who is our scout leader, taught us a new game.
3. The girl is 8 years old. The girl called the emergency number when her grandmother fell.
   The girl, who is 8 years old, called the emergency number when her grandmother fell.
4. The meatloaf is ready to eat. The salad isn't made yet.
   The meatloaf is ready to eat, but the salad isn't made yet.
5. The rain poured down. The rain canceled our picnic.
   The rain poured down and canceled our picnic.
6. The sixth grade class went on a field trip. The school was much quieter.
   When the sixth grade class went on a field trip, the school was much quieter.

Page 281

"Who's" and "Whose"

Who's is a contraction for **who is**.

Whose is a possessive pronoun.

Examples:
Who's going to come?
Whose shirt is this?

To know which word to use, substitute the words "who is." If the sentence makes sense, use **who's**.

Directions: Write the correct word to complete these sentences.

who's	1. Do you know who's/whose invited to the party?
whose	2. I don't even know who's/whose house it will be at.
Whose	3. Who's/Whose towel is on the floor?
Who's	4. Who's/Whose going to drive us?
Whose	5. Who's/Whose ice cream is melting?
whose	6. I'm the person who's/whose gloves are lost.
Who's	7. Who's/Whose in your group?
Whose	8. Who's/Whose group is first?
who's	9. Can you tell who's/whose at the door?
Whose	10. Who's/Whose friend are you?
Who's	11. Who's/Whose cooking tonight?
Whose	12. Who's/Whose cooking do you like best?

Page 282

"Their," "There" and "They're"

Their is a possessive pronoun meaning "belonging to them."

There is an adverb that indicates place.

They're is a contraction for **they are**.

Examples:
Ron and Sue took **their** dog to the park.
They like to go **there** on Sunday afternoon.
They're probably going back next Sunday, too.

Directions: Write the correct words to complete these sentences.

their	1. All the students should bring their/there/they're books to class.
there	2. I've never been to France, but I hope to travel their/there/they're someday.
their	3. We studied how dolphins care for their/there/they're young.
they're	4. My parents are going on vacation next week, and their/there/they're taking my sister.
There	5. Their/There/They're was a lot of food at the party.
their	6. My favorite baseball team lost their/there/they're star pitcher this year.
they're	7. Those peaches look good, but their/there/they're not ripe yet.
there	8. The book is right their/there/they're on the table.

Page 283

"Teach" and "Learn"

Teach is a verb meaning "to explain something." Teach is an irregular verb. Its past tense is **taught**.

Learn is a verb meaning "to gain information."

Examples:
Carrie will **teach** me how to play the piano.
Yesterday she **taught** me "Chopsticks."

I will **learn** a new song every week.
Yesterday I **learned** to play "Chopsticks."

Directions: Write the correct words to complete these sentences.

taught	1. My brother taught/learned me how to ice skate.
learned	2. With his help, I taught/learned in three days.
learn	3. First, I tried to teach/learn skating from a book.
learn	4. I couldn't teach/learn that way.
learn	5. You have to try it before you can really teach/learn how to do it.
teach	6. Now I'm going to teach/learn my cousin.
learned	7. My cousin already taught/learned how to roller skate.
teaching	8. I shouldn't have any trouble teaching/learning her how to ice skate.
taught	9. Who taught/learned you how to skate?
taught	10. My brother taught/learned Mom how to skate, too.
learn	11. My mother took longer to teach/learn it than I did.
teach	12. Who will he teach/learn next?
learn	13. Do you know anyone who wants to teach/learn how to ice skate?
teach	14. My brother will teach/learn you for free.
learn	15. You should teach/learn how to ice skate in the wintertime, though. The ice is a little thin in the summer!

Page 284

"Lie" and "Lay"

Lie is a verb meaning "to rest." Lie is an intransitive verb that doesn't need a direct object.

Lay is a verb meaning "to place or put something down." Lay is a transitive verb that requires a direct object.

Examples:
Lie here for a while. (**Lie** has no direct object; **here** is an adverb.)
Lay the book here. (**Lay** has a direct object: **book**.)

Lie and lay are especially tricky because they are both irregular verbs. Notice the past tense of lie is lay!

Present tense	ing form	Past tense	Past participle
lie	lying	lay	has/have/had lain
lay	laying	laid	has/have/had laid

Examples:
I **lie** here today.
I **lay** here yesterday.
I **was lying** there for three hours.

I **lay** the baby in her bed.
I will be **laying** her down in a minute.
I **laid** her in her bed last night, too.

Directions: Write the correct words to complete these sentences.

1. *lays* Shelly lies/lays a blanket on the grass.
2. *lies* Then she lies/lays down in the sun.
3. *lies* Her dog lies/lays there with her.
4. *laid* Yesterday, Shelly lay/laid in the sun for an hour.
5. *laying* The workers are lying/laying bricks for a house.
6. *laid* Yesterday, they lay/laid a ton of them.
7. *lay* They lie/lay one brick on top of the other.
8. *lay* The bricks just lie/lay in a pile until the workers are ready for them.
9. *lie* At lunchtime, some workers lie/lay down for a nap.
10. *lay* Would you like to lie/lay bricks?
11. *laid* Last year, my uncle lay/laid bricks for his new house.
12. *laid* He was so tired every day that he lay/laid down as soon as he finished.

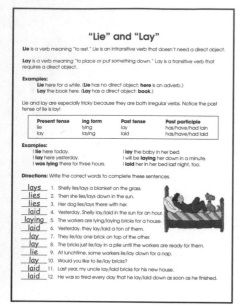

Page 285

"Rise" and "Raise"

Rise is a verb meaning "to get up" or "to go up." Rise is an intransitive verb that doesn't need a direct object.

Raise is a verb meaning "to lift" or "to grow." Raise is a transitive verb that requires a direct object.

Examples:
The curtain **rises**.
The girl **raises** her hand.

Raise is a regular verb. Rise is irregular.

Present tense	Past tense	Past participle
rise	rose	has/have/had risen
raise	raised	has/have/had raised

Examples:
The sun **rose** this morning.
The boy **raised** the window higher.

Directions: Write the correct words to complete these sentences.

1. *rises* This bread dough rises/raises in an hour.
2. *raise* The landlord will rise/raise the rent.
3. *rose* The balloon rose/raised into the sky.
4. *raised* My sister rose/raised the seat on my bike.
5. *raised* The baby rose/raised the spoon to his mouth.
6. *rose* The eagle rose/raised out of sight.
7. *raises* The farmer rises/raises pigs.
8. *raised* The scouts rose/raised the flag.
9. *rose* When the fog rose/raised, we could see better.
10. *rose* The price of ice cream rose/raised again.
11. *raised* The king rose/raised the glass to his lips.
12. *Raise* Rise/Raise the picture on that wall higher.

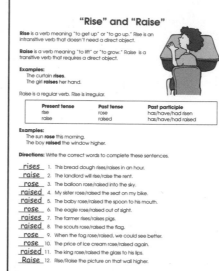

Page 286

"All Right," "All Ready" and "Already"

All right means "well enough" or "very well." Sometimes **all right** is incorrectly spelled. **Alright** is not a word.

Example:
Correct: We'll be all right when the rain stops.
Incorrect: Are you feeling **alright** today?

All ready is an adjective meaning "completely ready."

Already is an adverb meaning "before this time" or "by this time."

Examples:
Are you **all ready** to go?
He was **already** there when I arrived.

Directions: Write the correct words to complete these sentences.

1. *all ready* The children are all ready/already for the picnic.
2. *already* Ted was all ready/already late for the show.
3. *all right* Is your sister going to be all right/alright?
4. *already* I was all ready/already tired before the race began.
5. *already* Joan has all ready/already left for the dance.
6. *all right* Will you be all right/alright by yourself?
7. *all ready* We are all ready/already for our talent show.
8. *already* I all ready/already read that book.
9. *all ready* I want to be all ready/already when they get here.
10. *all right* Dad was sick, but he's all right/alright now.
11. *all ready* The dinner is all ready/already to eat.
12. *already* Cathy all ready/already wrote her report.

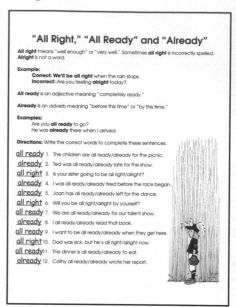

Page 287

"Accept" and "Except"/"Affect" and "Effect"

Accept is a verb meaning "to receive."

Except can be used as a verb or a preposition. As a verb, it means "to leave out." As a preposition, it means "excluding."

Examples:
I will **accept** the invitation to the dinner dance.
No one **except** Robert will receive an award.

Affect is a verb meaning "to impress one's thoughts or feelings."

Effect can be used as a noun or a verb. As a verb, it means "to accomplish." As a noun, it means "the result of an action."

Examples:
Her attitude may **affect** her performance on the test.
He **effected** several changes during his first few months as governor.
The **effects** of the storm will be felt for some time.

Directions: Write the correct words to complete these sentences.

1. *affect* My partner and I will work to affect/effect attitudes toward rainforest renewal.
2. *accepted* He courageously accepted/excepted the challenge of a chess duel.
3. *effect* The affect/effect of the strike by truck drivers was felt nationwide.
4. *effect* The new CEO of the company sought to affect/effect a change in company morale.
5. *except* Everyone accept/except Marlene will attend the game.
6. *accept* My grandmother will never accept/except the fact that she can no longer drive.
7. *Except* Accept/Except for this chewing incident, my puppy has been well-behaved.
8. *affected* The sights of the war affected/effected soldiers for the rest of their lives.
9. *effect* What affect/effect will the drop in the stock market have on the average person?
10. *effect* The affect/effect of the wind was devastating.
11. *affect* How will cheating on a test affect/effect your reputation?
12. *except* I would like to go to the park on any day accept/except Monday.

Page 288

Review

Directions: Use each of these words correctly in a sentence of your own.

1. good _____
2. bad _____
3. who's _____
4. whose _____
5. their _____
6. there _____
7. they're _____
8. teach _____
9. learn _____
10. lie _____
11. lay _____
12. rise _____
13. raise _____
14. all ready _____
15. already _____
16. all right _____
17. accept _____
18. except _____
19. affect _____
20. effect _____

Sentences will vary.

Page 290

Writing: Topic Sentences

The topic sentence in a paragraph usually comes first. Sometimes, however, the topic sentence can come at the end or even in the middle of a paragraph. When looking for the topic sentence, try to find the one that tells the main idea of a paragraph.

Directions: Read the following paragraphs and underline the topic sentence in each.

The maple tree sheds its leaves every year. The oak and elm trees shed their leaves, too. Every autumn, the leaves on these trees begin changing color. Then, as the leaves gradually begin to die, they fall from the trees. <u>Trees that shed their leaves annually are called deciduous trees.</u>

When our family goes skiing, my brother enjoys the thrill of going down the steepest hill as fast as he can. Mom and Dad like to ski because it gets them out of the house and into the fresh air. I enjoy looking at the trees and birds and the sun shining on the snow. <u>There is something about skiing that appeals to everyone in my family.</u> Even the dog came along on our last skiing trip!

If you are outdoors at night and there is traffic around, you should always wear bright clothing so that cars can see you. White is a good color to wear at night. If you are riding a bicycle, be sure it has plenty of reflectors, and if possible, headlamps as well. Be especially careful when crossing the street, because sometimes drivers cannot see you in the glare of their headlights. <u>Being outdoors at night can be dangerous, and it is best to be prepared!</u>

Page 291

Writing: Supporting Sentences

A **paragraph** is a group of sentences that tell about one topic. The **topic sentence** in a paragraph usually comes first and tells the main idea of the paragraph. **Supporting sentences** follow the topic sentence and provide details about the topic.

Directions: Write at least three supporting sentences for each topic sentence below.

Example: Topic Sentence: Carly had an accident on her bike.
  Supporting Sentences: She was on her way to the store to buy some bread. A car came weaving down the road and scared her. She rode her bike off the road so the car wouldn't hit her. Now, her knee is scraped, but she's all right.

1. I've been thinking of ways I could make some more money after school.

2. In my opinion, oats (dogs, fish, etc.) make the best pet.

3. My life _____ later, younger brother, older sister.

4. I'd like to live next door to a (swimming pool, video store, movie theater, etc.).

Answers will vary.

Page 292

Writing: Building Paragraphs

Directions: Read the groups of topic sentences and questions below. On another sheet of paper, write supporting sentences that answer the questions. Use your imagination! Write the supporting sentences in order, and copy them on this page after the topic sentence.

1. On her way home from school, Mariko made a difficult decision.

   Questions: What was Mariko's decision? Why did she decide that? Why was the decision hard to make?

2. Suddenly, Conrad thought of a way to clear up _____

   Questions: What was the confu_____ it? What did he do to clear it up?

3. Bethany used to feel awkward at the school social activities.

   Questions: Why did Bethany feel awkward before? How does she feel now? What happened to change the way she feels?

Answers will vary.

Page 293

Writing: Sequencing

When writing paragraphs, it is important to write events in the correct order. Think about what happens first, next, later and last.

Directions: The following sentences tell about Chandra's day, but they are all mixed up. Read each sentence and number them in the order in which they happened.

  _3_ She arrived at school and went to her locker to get her books.
  _7_ After dinner, she did the dishes, then read a book for a while.
  _8_ Chandra brushed her teeth and put on her pajamas.
  _5_ She rode the bus home, then she fixed herself a snack.
  _2_ She ate breakfast and went out to wait for the bus.
  _1_ Chandra woke up and picked out her clothes for school.
  _4_ She met her friend Sarah on the way to the cafeteria.
  _6_ She worked on homework and watched TV until her mom called her for dinner.

Directions: Write a short paragraph about what you did today. Use words like **first**, **next**, **then**, **later** and **finally** to indicate the order in which you did things.

Paragraphs will vary.

Page 294

Sequencing

Sequencing means to place events in order from beginning to end or first to last.

Example:
To send a letter, you must:
  Get paper, pencil or pen, an envelope and a stamp.
  Write the letter.
  Fold the letter and put it in the envelope.
  Address the envelope correctly.
  Put a stamp on the envelope.
  Put the envelope in the mailbox or take it to the Post Office.

Directions: Write the sequence for making a peanut butter and jelly sandwich.
  Get out bread, peanut butter, jelly and knife.
  Spread jelly on one slice of bread.
  Spread peanut butter on the other slice of bread.
  Put the two pieces of bread together so peanut butter and jelly sides are together.
  Put away knife, peanut butter and jelly.
  Enjoy your sandwich.

Directions: After you finish, try making the sandwich **exactly** the way you wrote the steps. Did you leave out any steps? Which ones?

Does a particular section _____ explanation by adding mi_____

Answers will vary.

Page 295

Author's Purpose

Authors write to fulfill one of three purposes: to **inform**, to **entertain** or to **persuade**.

Authors who write to inform are providing facts for the reader in an informational context.

Examples: Encyclopedia entries and newspaper articles

Authors who write to entertain are hoping to provide enjoyment for the reader.

Examples: Funny stories and comics

Authors who write to persuade are trying to convince the reader to believe as they believe.

Examples: Editorials and opinion essays

Directions: Read each paragraph. Write **inform**, **entertain** or **persuade** on the line to show the author's purpose.

1. The whooping crane is a migratory bird. At one time, this endangered bird was almost extinct. These large white cranes are characterized by red faces and trumpeting calls. Through protection of both the birds and their habitats, the whooping crane is slowly increasing in number.
   inform

2. It is extremely important that all citizens place bird feeders in their yards and keep them full for the winter. Birds that spend the winter in this area are in danger of starving due to lack of food. It is every citizen's responsibility to ensure the survival of the birds.
   persuade

3. Imagine being able to hibernate like a bear each winter! Wouldn't it be great to eat to your heart's content all fall? Then, sometime in late November, inform your teacher that you will not be attending school for the next few months because you'll be resting and living off your fat. Now, that would be the life!
   entertain

4. Bears, woodchucks and chipmunks are not the only animals that hibernate. The queen bumblebee also hibernates in winter. All the other bees die before winter arrives. The queen hibernates under leaves in a small hole. She is cold-blooded and therefore is able to survive slightly frozen.
   inform

Page 296

Author's Purpose

Directions: Write a paragraph of your own for each purpose. The paragraph can be about any topic.

1. to inform

2. to persuade

3. to entertain

Answers will vary.

Directions: Reread your paragraphs. Do they make sense? Check for grammar, spelling and punctuation errors and make corrections where needed.

Page 297

Descriptive Sentences

Descriptive sentences give readers a vivid image and enable them to imagine a scene clearly.

Example:
Nondescriptive sentence: There were grapes in the bowl.
Descriptive sentence: The plump purple grapes in the bowl looked tantalizing.

Directions: Rewrite these sentences using descriptive language.

1. The dog walked in its pen.

2. The turkey was almost done.

3. I became upset when my computer wouldn't work.

4. Jared and Michelle went to the ice-cream par...

5. The telephon...

6. I wrote a...

7. The movie was excellent.

8. Dominique was upset that her friend was ill.

Sentences will vary.

Page 298

Writing: Descriptive Details

A writer creates pictures in a reader's mind by telling him/her how something looks, sounds, feels, smells or tastes. For example, compare **A** and **B** below. Notice how the description in **B** makes you imagine how the heavy door and the cobweb would feel and how the broken glass would look and sound as someone walked on it.

A. I walked into the house.
B. I pushed open the heavy wooden door of the old house. A cobweb brushed my face, and broken glass, sparkling like ice, crushed under my feet.

Directions: Write one or two sentences about each topic below. Add details that will help your reader see, hear, feel, smell or taste what you are describing.

1. Your favorite dinner cooking

2. Old furniture

3. Wind blowing in the trees

4. A t...

5. Wearing wet clothes

6. A strange noise somewhere in the house

Sentences will vary.

Page 299

Writing: Descriptive Details

Directions: For each topic sentence below, write three or four supporting sentences. Include details about how things look, sound, smell, taste or feel. Don't forget to use adjectives, adverbs, similes and metaphors.

Example: After my dog had his bath, I couldn't believe how much better he looked. His fur, which used to be all matted and dirty, was as clean as new snow. He still felt a little damp when I scratched behind his ears. The smell from rolling in our garbage was gone, too. He smelled like apples now because of the shampoo.

1. My little cousin's birthday party was almost over.

2. I always keep my grandpa company while he bak...

3. By th... ...s a mess.

4. Early morning is the best time to go for a bike ride.

Answers will vary.

Page 300

Personal Narratives

A **personal narrative** tells about a person's own experiences.

Directions: Read the example of a personal narrative. Write your answers in complete sentences.

My Worst Year

When I look back on that year, I can hardly believe that one person could have such terrible luck for a whole year. But then again, I should have realized that if things could begin to go wrong in January, it didn't bode well for the rest of the year.

It was the night of January 26. One of my best friends was celebrating her birthday at the local roller-skating rink, and I had been invited. The evening began well enough with pizza and laughs. I admit I have never been a cracker jack roller skater, but I could hold my own. After a few minutes of skating, I decided to exit the rink for a cold soda.

Unfortunately, I did not notice the trailing ribbons of carpet which wrapped around the wheel of my skate, yanking my left leg from under me. My leg was broken. It wasn't just broken in one place but in four places! At the hospital, the doctor set the bone and put a cast on my leg. Three months later, I felt like a new person.

Sadly, the happiness wasn't meant to last. Five short months after the final cast was removed, I fell and broke the same leg again. Not only did it rebreak but it broke in the same four places! We found out later that it hadn't healed correctly. Three months later, it was early December and the end of a year I did not wish to repeat.

1. List the sequence of events in this personal narrative.

   January 26: fell while skating and broke leg in four
   places.
   Three months later: cast removed.
   Five months later: fell and broke leg again in same
   four places.

2. From reading the personal narrative, what do you think were the author's feelings toward the events that occurred?

   Answers will vary.

Page 301

Personal Narratives

A **narrative** is a spoken or written account of an actual event. A **personal narrative** tells about your own experience. It can be written about any event in your life and may be serious or comical.

When writing a personal narrative, remember to use correct sentence structure and punctuation. Include important dates, sights, sounds, smells, tastes and feelings to give your reader a clear picture of the event.

Directions: Write a personal narrative about an event in your life that was funny.

Narratives will vary.

Page 302

Complete the Story

Directions: Read the beginning of this story. Then complete the story with your own ideas.

It was a beautiful summer day in June when my family and I set off on vacation. We were headed for Portsmouth, New Hampshire. There we planned to go on a whale-watching ship and perhaps spy a humpback whale or two. However, there were many miles between our home and Portsmouth.

We camped at many lovely parks along the way to New Hampshire. We stayed in the Adirondack Mountains for a few days and then visited the White Mountains of Vermont before crossing into New Hampshire.

My family enjoys tent camping. My dad says you can't really get a taste of the great outdoors in a pop-up camper or RV. I love sitting by the fire at night, gazing at the stars and listening to the animal noises.

The trip was going well, and everyone was enjoying our vacation. We made it to Portsmouth and were looking forward to the whale-watching adventure. We arrived at the dock a few minutes early. The ocean looked rough, but we had taken seasickness medication. We thought we were prepared for any kind of weather.

Stories will vary.

Page 303

Writing Fiction

Directions: Use descriptive writing to complete each story. Write at least five sentences.

1. It was a cold, wintry morning in January. Snow had fallen steadily for 4 days. I was staring out my bedroom window when I saw the bedraggled dog staggering through the snow.

2. Mindy was home Saturday studying for ... ds were due next Friday, and the test on Mon... needed to do well on the test to ... her best friend, Jenny.

3. Martin works every weekend delivering newspapers. He wakes up at 5:30 A.M. and begins his route at 6:00 A.M. He delivers 150 newspapers on his bike. He enjoys his weekend job because he is working toward a goal.

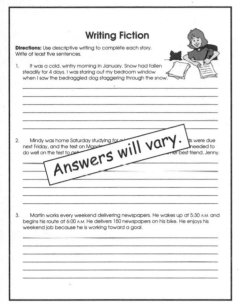

Answers will vary.

Page 304

Writing: Point of View

People often have different opinions about the same thing. This is because each of us has a different "point of view." **Point of view** is the attitude someone has about a particular topic as a result of his or her personal experience or knowledge.

Directions: Read the topic sentence below about the outcome of a basketball game. Then write two short paragraphs, one from the point of view of a player for the Reds and one from the point of view of a player for the Cowboys. Be sure to give each person's opinion of the outcome of the game.

Topic Sentence: In the last second of the basketball game between the Reds and the Cowboys, the Reds scored and won the game.

Terry, a player for the Reds . . .

Chris, a player for the Co... *Paragraphs will vary.*

Directions: Here's a different situation. Read the topic sentence, and then write three short paragraphs from the points of view of Katie, her dad and her brother.

Topic Sentence: Katie's dog had chewed up another one of her father's shoes.

Katie . . .

Katie's father . . .

Katie's brother Mark, w... ...er have a cat . . . *Paragraphs will vary.*

Page 305

Friendly Letters

A **friendly letter** has these parts: return address, date, greeting, body, closing and signature.

Directions: Read this letter. Then label the parts of the letter.

<u>return address</u> → 222 West Middle Street
Boise, Idaho 33444
May 17, 1999 <u>date</u>

Dear Blaine, ← <u>greeting</u>

Hello! I know I haven't written in several weeks, but I've been very busy with school and baseball practice. How have you been? How is the weather in Boston? It is finally getting warm in Boise.

<u>body</u> → As I mentioned, I am playing baseball this year. My team is called the Rockets, and we are really good. We have a terrific coach. We practice two nights a week and play games on the weekends. Are you playing baseball?

I can hardly wait to visit you this summer. I can't believe I'll be flying on an airplane and staying with you and your family for 2 weeks! There is probably a lot to do in Boston. When you write, tell me some ideas you have for the 2 weeks.

<u>closing</u> → Your friend,

<u>signature</u> → Mason

Envelopes should follow this format:

Mason Fitch
222 West Middle Street
Boise, ID 33444

Blaine Morgan
111 E. 9th Street, Apt 22B
Boston, MA 00011

Page 306

Friendly Letters

Directions: Write a friendly letter. Then address the envelope.

Letters should follow format given.

Page 307

Writing: Supporting Your Opinion

Directions: Decide what your opinion is on each topic below. Then write a paragraph supporting your opinion. Begin with a topic sentence that tells the reader what you think. Add details in the next three or four sentences that show why you are right.

Example: Whether kids should listen to music while they do homework

Kids do a better job on their homework if they listen to music. The music makes the time more enjoyable. It also drowns out the sounds of the rest of the family. If things are too quiet while kids do homework, every little sound distracts them.

1. Whether young people should have a choice about going to school, no matter how old they are

2. Whether all parents should give their childre... ...ney for an allowance

3. Whether you should tell someone if you doubt he/she is telling the truth

Paragraphs will vary.

Page 308

Writing From a Prompt: An Opinion Essay

Directions: Write an opinion essay in response to the prompt.

Writing Prompt: Think about rainforests. What is the importance of preserving the rainforests of the world? What problems could arise if there were no longer any rainforest areas? What problems could arise for humans due to the preservation of rainforests? How do rainforests affect you?

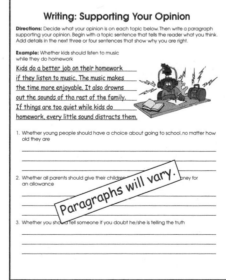

Answers will vary.

Directions: When you finish writing, reread your essay. Use this checklist to help make corrections.

☐ I have used correct spelling, grammar and punctuation.

☐ I have no sentence fragments.

☐ My essay makes sense.

☐ I wrote complete sentences.

☐ I have no run-on sentences.

☐ I answered the prompt.

Page 309

Writing a Summary

A **summary** is a short description of what a selection or book is about.

Directions: Read the following selection and the example summary.

Fads of the 1950s

A fad is a practice or an object that becomes very popular for a period of time. Recent popular fads include yo-yos and Beanie Babies®. In the 1950s, there were many different fads, including coonskin caps, hula hoops and 3-D movies.

Coonskin caps were made popular by the weekly television show about Davy Crockett, which began in December of 1954. Not only did Davy's hat itself become popular but anything with Davy Crockett on it was in hot demand.

Also popular were hula hoops. They were produced by the Wham-O company in 1958. The company had seen similar toys in Australia. Hula hoops were priced at $1.98, and over 30 million hoops were sold within 6 months.

Another fad was the 3-D movie. When television sets began to appear in every American home, the movie industry began to suffer financially. Movie companies rushed to produce 3-D movies, and movie-goers once more flocked to theaters. The first 3-D movie was shown in Los Angeles on November 26, 1952. People loved the special Polaroid® glasses and scenes in the movie that seemed to jump out at them. As with the hula hoop and Davy Crockett, people soon tired of 3-D movies, and they became old news as they were replaced by new fads.

Summary

Over the years, many fads have become popular with the American public. During the 1950s, three popular fads were the hula hoop, Davy Crockett and 3-D movies. Davy Crockett's coonskin cap became a fad with the beginning of the weekly television show. Hula hoops were sold by the millions, and 3-D movies were enjoyed by people everywhere. However, like all fads, interest in these items soon died out.

Page 310

Writing a Summary

Directions: Read the following selection. Using page 309 as a guide, write a summary of the selection.

Man's First Flights

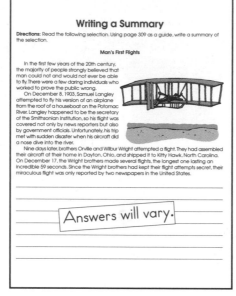

In the first few years of the 20th century, the majority of people strongly believed that man could not and would not ever be able to fly. There were a few daring individuals who worked to prove the public wrong.

On December 8, 1903, Samuel Langley attempted to fly his version of an airplane from the roof of a houseboat on the Potomac River. Langley happened to be the secretary of the Smithsonian Institution, so his flight was covered not only by news reporters but also by government officials. Unfortunately, his trip met with sudden disaster when his aircraft did a nose dive into the river.

Nine days later, brothers Orville and Wilbur Wright attempted a flight. They had assembled their aircraft at their home in Dayton, Ohio, and shipped it to Kitty Hawk, North Carolina. On December 17, the Wright brothers made several flights, the longest one lasting an incredible 59 seconds. Since the Wright brothers had kept their flight attempts secret, their miraculous flight was only reported by two newspapers in the United States.

Answers will vary.

Page 311

Comparing and Contrasting

When writing comparison/contrast essays, it is helpful to write one paragraph which contains all the similarities and another paragraph which contains all the differences.

Directions: Write an essay in response to the prompt.

Writing Prompt: Think of your brother, sister or a friend. What similarities are there between you and this person? What differences are there?

Answers will vary.

Directions: When you finish writing, reread your essay. Use this checklist to help make corrections.

- [ ] My essay makes sense.
- [ ] I listed at least two similarities and two differences.
- [ ] My sentences are correctly written.
- [ ] I used correct spelling, grammar and punctuation.

Page 312

Advantages and Disadvantages

As in the comparison/contrast essay, it is easiest to put all of the advantages in one paragraph and the disadvantages in another paragraph.

Directions: Write an essay in response to the prompt.

Writing Prompt: Think about what a society would be like if all people had the same skin tone, hair color, eye color, height and weight. What would the benefits of living in such a society be? Would there be any disadvantages? What would they be?

Answers will vary.

Directions: When you finish writing, reread your essay. Use this checklist to help make corrections.

- [ ] My essay makes sense.
- [ ] I used correct spelling, grammar and punctuation.
- [ ] I answered the writing prompt.
- [ ] I have varied sentence length.

Page 313

Newswriting

Newswriting is a style of writing used by newspaper reporters and other journalists who write for periodicals. **Periodicals** are newspapers, magazines and newsletters that are published regularly.

Magazine and newspaper writers organize their ideas and their writing around what is called "the five W's and the H" — who, what, when, where, why and how. As they conduct research and interview people for articles, journalists keep these questions in mind.

Directions: Read a newspaper article of your choice. Use the information you read to answer the questions.

Who Who is involved? _____
Who is affected? _____
Who is responsible? _____

What What is the event or subject? _____
What exactly has happen_____

When Whe_____
Whe_____

Where Where_____

Why Why did it happen? _____
Why will readers care? _____

How How did it happen? _____

Answers will vary.

Page 314

Newswriting: Inverted Pyramid Style

Newspaper reporters organize their news stories in what is called the **inverted pyramid** style. The inverted pyramid places the most important facts at the beginning of the story—called the lead (LEED)—and the least important facts at the end.

There are two practical reasons for this approach:

1) If the story must be shortened by an editor, he or she simply cuts paragraphs from the end of the story rather than rewriting the entire story.

2) Because newspapers contain so much information, few people read every word of every newspaper story. Instead, many readers skim headlines and opening paragraphs. The inverted pyramid style of writing enables readers to quickly get the basics of what the story is about without reading the entire story.

Directions: Read the news story. Then answer the questions.

Cleveland—Ohio State University student John Cook is within one 36-hole match of joining some of amateur golf's top performers. The 21-year-old Muirfield Village Golf Club representative will try for his second straight U.S. Amateur championship Sunday against one of his California golf buddies, Mark O'Meara, over the 6,837-yard Canterbury Golf Club course. Starting times are 8 a.m. and 12:30 p.m.

"Winning the U.S. Amateur once is a great thrill," said Cook after Saturday's breezy 5-3 semifinal decision over Alabama's Cecil Ingram III. "But winning the second time is something people don't very often do."

1. Who is the story about? __John Cook__

2. The "dateline" at the beginning of a news article tells where the event happened and where the reporter wrote the story. Where was the story about John Cook written?
__Cleveland__

3. What is Cook trying to accomplish? __win second straight U.S. Amateur Championship__

4. Who did Cook beat on Saturday? __Cecil Ingram III__

5. Which of the above paragraphs could be cut by an editor? __the second one__

Page 315

Writing: Just the Facts

Some forms of writing, such as reports and essays, contain opinions that are supported by the writer. In other kinds of writing, however, it is important to stick to the facts. Newspaper reporters, for example, must use only facts when they write their stories.

Directions: Read the following newspaper story about a fire, and underline the sentences or parts of sentences that are opinions. Then rewrite the story in your own words, giving only the facts.

At around 10:30 p.m. last night, a fire broke out in a house at 413 Wilshire Boulevard. <u>The house is in a very nice neighborhood, surrounded by beautiful trees.</u> The family of four who lives in the house was alerted by smoke alarms, and they all exited the house safely, <u>although they must have been very frightened.</u> Firefighters arrived on the scene at approximately 10:45 p.m., and it took them over 3 hours to extinguish the blaze. <u>The firefighters were very courageous.</u> The cause of the fire has not yet been determined, although faulty electric wiring is suspected. <u>People should have their electric wiring checked regularly.</u> The family is staying with relatives until repairs to their home can be made, <u>and they are probably very anxious to move back into their house.</u>

Paragraphs will vary.

Page 316

Writing: You're the Reporter

Directions: Now, write your own short newspaper story about an interesting event that occurred at your school or in your neighborhood. Find out who and what the story is about, where and when it happened, and why and how it happened. Take some notes, interview some of the people involved and write your story. Give your story a title, and remember to stick to the facts! In the box, draw a picture (or "photo") to go with your story.

Stories will vary.

Pictures will vary.

Page 317

Writing: Personification

Sometimes writers use descriptions like: The fire engine **screamed** as it rushed down the street. The sun **crawled** slowly across the sky. We know that fire engines do not really scream, and the sun does not really crawl. Writers use descriptions like these to make their writing more interesting and vivid. When a writer gives an object or animal human qualities, it is called **personification**.

Directions: For each object below, write a sentence using personification. The first one has been done for you.

1. the barn door
   <u>The old, rusty barn door groaned loudly when I pushed it open.</u>
2. the rain
3. the pickup truck
4. the radiator
5. the leaves
6. the tel...
7. the k...
8. the river

Sentences will vary.

Page 318

Similes

A **simile** is a comparison of two things that have something in common but are really very different. The words **like** and **as** are used in similes.

Examples:
The baby was **as** happy **as** a lark.
She is **like** a ray of sunshine to my tired eyes.

Directions: Choose a word from the box to complete each comparison. The first one has been done for you.

tack	grass	fish	mule	ox	rail	hornet	monkey

1. as stubborn as a ___mule___
2. as strong as an ___ox___
3. swims like a ___fish___
4. as sharp as a ___tack___
5. as thin as a ___rail___
6. as mad as a ___hornet___
7. climbs like a ___monkey___
8. as green as ___grass___

Directions: Use your own words to complete these similes.

9. as _____ as a tack
10. _____ like a bird
11. as hungry as a _____
12. as white as _____
13. as light as a _____
14. as _____ as honey
15. _____ like a snake

Directions:

17. Our new...
18. The cloud...
19. Our new car is...
20. The watermelon tasted _____

Answers will vary.

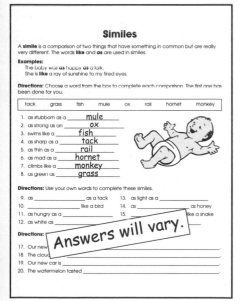

Page 319

Writing: Common Similes

There are many similes that are used often in the English language. For example, "as frightened as a mouse" is a very common simile. Can you think of others?

Directions: Match the first part of each common simile to the second part. The first one has been done for you.

as slippery as	a mule
as smart as	a statue
as sly as	a rock
as still as	a bee
as quick as	an eel
as slow as	a pancake
as busy as	a whip
as cold as	a turtle
as flat as	a fox
as stubborn as	lightning
as hungry as	ice
as hard as	a bear

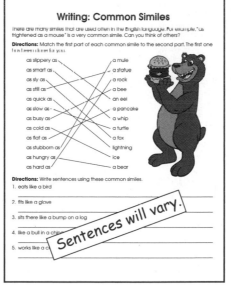

Directions: Write sentences using these common similes.

1. eats like a bird
2. fits like a glove
3. sits there like a bump on a log
4. like a bull in a china...
5. works like a c...

Sentences will vary.

Page 320

Metaphors

A **metaphor** makes a direct comparison between two unlike things. A noun must be used in the comparison. The words **like** and **as** are not used.

Examples:
Correct: The exuberant puppy was a **bundle of energy.**
Incorrect: The dog is **happy.** (**Happy** is an adjective.)

Directions: Circle the two objects being compared.

1. (The old truck) was (a heap of rusty metal.)
2. (The moon) was (a silver dollar in the sky.)
3. (Their vacation) was (a nightmare.)
4. (That wasp) is (a flying menace.)
5. (The prairie) was (a carpet of green.)
6. (The flowers) were (jewels on stems.)
7. This winter, (our pond) is (glass.)
8. (The clouds) were (marshmallows.)

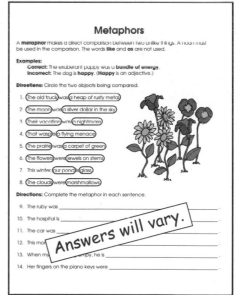

Directions: Complete the metaphor in each sentence.

9. The ruby was _____
10. The hospital is _____
11. The car was _____
12. This mor... _____
13. When my... is lumpy, he is _____
14. Her fingers on the piano keys were _____

Answers will vary.

Page 321

Writing: Similes and Metaphors

Using **similes** and **metaphors** makes writing interesting. They are ways of describing things. **Similes** are comparisons that use **like** or **as**.

Examples: She looked like a frightened mouse.
She looked as frightened as a mouse.

Metaphors are direct comparisons that do not use **like** or **as**.

Example: She was a frightened mouse.

Directions: Rewrite each sentence two different ways to make them more interesting. In the first sentence (a), add at least one adjective and one adverb. In the second sentence (b), compare something in the sentence to something else, using a simile or metaphor.

Example: The baby cried.
a. The sick baby cried softly all night.
b. The baby cried louder and louder, like a storm gaining strength.

1. The stranger arrived.
   a. _____
   b. _____
2. The dog barked.
   a. _____
   b. _____
3. The children danced.
   a. _____
   b. _____
4. The moon ros
   a. _____
   b. _____

Sentences will vary.

Page 322

Writing: Similes and Metaphors in Poetry

Many poems use similes and metaphors to create a more interesting description of what the poem is about.

Directions: Read the following poems and underline any similes or metaphors you see.

Flint

An emerald is <u>as green as grass</u>,
   A ruby <u>red as blood</u>;
A sapphire shines <u>as blue as heaven</u>;
   A flint lies in the mud.

A diamond is <u>a brilliant stone</u>,
   To catch the world's desire;
An opal holds <u>a fiery spark</u>;
   But a flint holds fire.

   —Christina Rossetti

The Night Is a Big Black Cat

The night is <u>a big black cat</u>
The moon is <u>her topaz eye</u>,
The stars are <u>the mice she hunts at night</u>,
In the field of the sultry sky.

   —G. Orr Clark

Directions: Now, write your own poem, using at least one simile and one metaphor.

Poems will vary.

Page 323

Writing: Rhyming Words

Words that share the same vowel sound in their last syllables are **rhyming words**. Rhyming words can have the same number of syllables, like **tent** and **excellent** or **nation** and **conversation**.

Directions: Write words that rhyme with the words below and have the number of syllables shown. The first one has been done for you.

They share the same vowel sound in their last syllables.
spike
hike
like
Mike

1. table _____unable_____ (3)
2. green _____ (3)
3. instead _____ (1)
4. store _____ (2)
5. remember _____ (3)
6. concentration _____
7. stars _____
8. gir
9. neig_____ (2)
10. berry _____ (4)
11. dog _____ (3)
12. bath _____ (1)
13. celebration _____ (4)
14. master _____ (2)
15. baby _____ (2)

Answers will vary.

Page 324

Writing: Poetry

Directions: For the first group of poems below, both lines should rhyme. The first line is given. Complete each poem, using one of the given rhyming words, or use one of your own. Make sure to add the correct punctuation.

Example: mile / pile / dial   Kevin James has a certain style.
To get his way, he'd walk a mile.

ape / grape / cape   Mindy Lou got a very bad scrape!
_____

hide / fried / cried   Sometimes you _____

Directions: Complete ... poems, using one of the given words, or use one of your own. Each poem sh... have four lines. The second and fourth lines should rhyme.

Example: cape / tape / grape   Kenny skidded on his bike.
And got himself all **scraped**.
Now his bike has a flat tire,
And his whole leg is **taped**.

I / cry / my   I put some water in a bucket
And then threw in some **dye**.
_____

file / dial / Nile   Kelly got her hair cut,
But I don't like the **style**.
_____

ride / hide / cried   When B... ...e race,
It really h... ...ide.
_____

Poems will vary.

Page 325

Haiku

Haiku is a form of unrhymed Japanese poetry. Haiku have three lines. The first line has five syllables, the second line has seven syllables and the third line has five syllables.

Example:

The Fall
Leaves fall from the trees.
Do they want to leave their home?
They float on the breeze.

Directions: Write a haiku about nature. Write the title on the first line. Then illustrate your haiku.

Nature _____

Poems should follow format.

Page 326

Lantern

Lantern is another type of five-line Japanese poetry. It takes the shape of a Japanese lantern. Each line must contain the following number of syllables.

Line 1: 1 syllable
Line 2: 2 syllables
Line 3: 3 syllables
Line 4: 4 syllables
Line 5: 1 syllable

Example: Cats—
Stealthy
wild creatures
want to be your
pet.

Directions: Write and illustrate your own lantern.

Poems should follow format.

Page 327

Alliterative Poetry

Alliteration is the repetition of a consonant sound in a group of words.

Example: Barney Bear bounced a ball.

Alliterative story poems can be fun to read and write. Any of several rhyming patterns can be used. Possibilities include:
Every two lines rhyme.
Every other line rhymes.
The first line rhymes with the last line and the two middle lines rhyme with each other.
All four lines rhyme.

Example:
Thomas Tuttle tries to dine,
On turkey, tea and treats so fine.
Thomas eats tomatoes and tortellini,
He devours tuna and tettrazini.

When tempting tidbits fill the table,
Thomas tastes as much as he is able,
He stuffs himself from top to toes,
Where he puts it, goodness knows!

Directions: Write an alliterative story poem using any rhyming pattern listed above. Your poem should be at least four lines long.

Poems will vary.

Page 328

How to Write a Book Report

Writing a book report should not be a chore. Instead, consider it an opportunity to share the good news about a book you have enjoyed. Simply writing, "I really liked this book. You will, too!" is not enough. You need to explain what makes the book worth reading.

Like other essays, book reports have three parts. An essay is a short report that presents the personal views of the writer. The three parts of an essay (and a book report) are introduction, body and conclusion.

The **introduction** to a book report should be a full paragraph that will capture the interest of your readers. The **body** paragraphs contain the main substance of your report. Include a brief overview of the plot of your book, along with supporting details that make it interesting. In the **conclusion**, summarize the central ideas of your report. Sum up why you would or would not recommend it to others.

Directions: Answer these questions about writing book reports.

1. Which of these introductory sentences is more interesting?

☑ Richie, a 12-year-old runaway, cries himself to sleep every night in the bowling alley where he lives.

☐ Many children run away from home, and this book is about one of them, a boy named Richie.

2. In a report on a fiction book about runaways, where would these sentences go?

"Richie's mother is dead. He and his father don't get along."

☑ introduction
☐ conclusion

3. In the same report, where would these sentences go?

"Author Clark Howard has written a sad and exciting book about runaways that shows how terrible the life of a runaway can be. I strongly recommend the book to people of all ages."

☐ body
☑ conclusion

Page 329

Book Report: A Book I Devoured

Directions: Follow the writing prompts to write a short book report on a book you truly enjoyed.

Recently, I read a book I could not put down.

Its title is _____

One reason I "devoured" this book was _____

If I could be one of the characters, I'd be _____ because _____

My fa[vorite] ...

Answers will vary.

Page 330

Book Report: Comparing Two Books

Directions: Follow the writing prompts to write a short book report comparing two books on the same subject.

Two books I recently read on the same subject

are _____

by _____

and _____

by _____

I liked _____ better because _____

Answers will vary.

The be...

Even though I did not like it as well, one good thing I can say about the other book is _____

Page 331

Reference Sources: Languages, Social Studies

Reference sources are books and other materials which provide facts and information. Dictionaries, encyclopedias and nonfiction books are reference books. Magazine and newspaper articles, the Internet and computer CD's are also reference sources.

There are many other kinds of reference sources on specific topics. Some of these are listed below by the topics covered.

Language:
1. *The American Heritage Dictionary*
2. *The Dictionary of Contemporary Slang* by Jonathan Green
3. *The Misspeller's Dictionary* by Peter and Craig Norback
4. *Dictionary of Foreign Terms* by C. O. Mawson
5. *Webster's Dictionary of Synonyms*

Social Studies:
1. *The Black American Reference Book* by Mabel M. Smythe
2. *The Encyclopedia of Drug Abuse* by Robert O'Brien and Sidney Cohen
3. *Women's Rights Almanac* by Nancy Gager
4. *Encyclopedia of Psychology* by Raymond J. Corsini
5. *Webster's New Geographical Dictionary*

Directions: Answer the questions.

1. Which book would be the best source for finding the meaning of the Spanish term, *que pasa*?

Dictionary of Foreign Terms

2. Which book would be the best source of information on Martin Luther King, Jr.?

The Black American Reference Book

3. Where would you find information on cocaine use in the U.S.?

The Encyclopedia of Drug Abuse

4. Which book would have information on equal employment opportunities for women?

Women's Rights Almanac

5. Where would you look for a list of terms that mean the same as **incredible**?

Webster's Dictionary of Synonyms

Page 332

Reference Sources: General, Science and Technology

These reference sources are listed by the topics covered.

General:
1. *Books in Print*
2. *International Who's Who*
3. *World Book Encyclopedia* (on computer CD)
4. *Rand McNally Contemporary World Atlas*
5. *Statistical Abstract of the United States*

Science and Technology:
1. *A Field Guide to Rocks and Minerals* by Frederick H. Pough
2. *Grzimek's Animal Life Encyclopedia*
3. *Living Plants of the World* by Lorus and Margery Milne
4. *Scientific American Library Guide to the Universe* (on computer CD)
5. *Your Vital Statistics: The Ultimate Book About the Average Human Being* by Gyles Brandreth

Directions: Answer the questions.

1. Which reference source would you check to find a map of Poland?

Rand McNally Contemporary World Atlas

2. Which source would you consult to find the most recent statistics on the number of single parents in the United States?

Statistical Abstract of the United States

3. Where would you find the most complete information on the Milky Way and other galaxies?

Scientific American Library Guide to the Universe

4. Where would you find the most complete information about a rock crystal called quartz?

A Field Guide to Rocks and Minerals

5. Where would you find the most complete information on the chancellor of Germany?

International Who's Who

Grade 5 - Comprehensive Curriculum

Page 333

Using the Library Catalog

Directions: Read about library catalogs. Use this information to answer the questions on the next page.

A **library catalog** lists on separate index cards, or in a computer file, all the books, videos, CD's, etc. in the library's collection. There are three ways to find a particular book: by title, by author or by subject.

Library catalogs that are on cards provide three different cards for each book—one for each of the ways the book is filed. Computerized library catalogs also list books in the same three ways. Usually, you simply type the title, author or subject in the appropriate box on the screen. A list of books by that author, title or subject will appear on the screen.

In both card and computerized catalogs, authors are filed alphabetically by last name.

Information on cards in a card catalog is arranged somewhat the same as information on a computerized catalog screen.

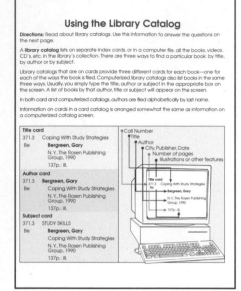

Title card
371.3 Coping With Study Strategies
Be   **Bergreen, Gary**
        N. Y., The Rosen Publishing
        Group, 1990
        137p.: ill.

Author card
371.3 **Bergreen, Gary**
Be   Coping With Study Strategies
        N. Y., The Rosen Publishing
        Group, 1990
        137p.: ill.

Subject card
371.3 STUDY SKILLS
Be   **Bergreen, Gary**
        Coping With Study Strategies
        N. Y., The Rosen Publishing
        Group, 1990
        137p.: ill.

Call Number
Title
Author
City, Publisher, Date
Number of pages
Illustrations or other features

Page 334

Using the Library Catalog

The **call number** for a book is printed on its spine and also appears in the library catalog. Nonfiction books are shelved in order by call number.

Directions: Use what you learned about library catalogs to answer these questions.

1. What should you type into a library's computerized catalog for a listing of all the books the library has on birds? __birds__

2. What should you type into the library's computerized catalog for a list of all the books by Louisa May Alcott? __Louisa May Alcott__

3. What should you type into the library's computerized catalog to see if the library owns a book called *Birds of North America*? __*Birds of North America*__

4. According to the card catalog card shown on the previous page, what company published the book *Coping With Study Strategies*? __The Rosen Publishing Group__

5. Under what subject is *Coping With Study Strategies* listed? __study skills__

6. What is the call number for *Coping With Study Strategies*? __371.3 Be__

7. What are three ways to find a book in the library? __by title, author and subject__

8. How are authors' names listed in library catalogs? __alphabetically by last name__

9. Besides the call number, title and author, what are three other types of information given for a book in a library catalog?
__city, publisher, date__
__number of pages__
__illustrations or other features__

Page 335

Library Research

Directions: Read about doing research in a library. Then answer the questions.

Step 1: Look in a general encyclopedia, such as *Encyclopedia Americana* or *World Book*, for background information on your topic. Use the index volume to locate the main article and all related articles. Look at the suggested cross-references that direct you to other sources. Also, check for a bibliography at the end of the article for clues to other sources. A **bibliography** lists all the books and magazines used to write the article.

Step 2: Use a special encyclopedia for more specific information or for definitions of special terms. The *Encyclopedia of Education*, *International Encyclopedia of the Social Sciences* and the *Encyclopedia of Bioethics* are examples of special encyclopedias.

Step 3: Look for a general book on your topic using the subject headings in the library catalog. Be sure to note the copyright date (date published) on all books you select. For current topics such as medical research or computers, you will want to use only the most recently published and up-to-date sources.

Step 4: Use *Facts on File* to pinpoint specific facts or statistics related to your topic. *Facts on File* is a weekly summary of national and international news.

Step 5: An index helps you locate magazine articles on your topic. To find the most current information, try the *Reader's Guide to Periodical Literature*. The *Guide* lists articles by subject published during a particular month, the magazines containing the articles and the date and page numbers of the articles.

1. Name two general encyclopedias. __*Encyclopedia Americana*, *World Book*__

2. Name three special encyclopedias. __*Encyclopedia of Education*, *International Encyclopedia of the Social Sciences*, *Encyclopedia of Bioethics*__

3. Which reference book contains a weekly summary of national and international news? __*Facts on File*__

Page 336

Library Research

Directions: Read the remaining steps for doing library research. Then answer the questions.

Step 6: Newspaper indexes will direct you to newspaper articles related to your topic. See *The New York Times Index* for national and international coverage of a topic or event. If you are researching a local subject or event, ask the librarian if indexes for the local newspapers are available.

Step 7: Ask the librarian if the library keeps "clip files" of articles on particular topics. Clip files contain articles librarians have cut out and saved in folders. Consulting a clip file can sometimes save time because the librarian has already done the research and filed it together in one place!

Step 8: If your research topic is a person—for example, President Bill Clinton—a good source is *Current Biography*. This reference contains long articles about people in the news. Another source is *Biography Index*, which will direct you to articles in magazines and newspapers.

Step 9: If you need to locate statistics—for example, how many students play a certain school sport—check the *World Almanac and Book of Facts* or *Statistical Abstract of the United States*. The *Abstract* contains government statistics on education, politics and many other subjects.

Step 10: For detailed instructions about writing your paper, check one of these references: *Elements of Style* by Strunk and White or *A Manual for Writers of Term Papers, Theses, and Dissertations* by Kate Turabian.

1. What index should you consult if you're researching an article about water pollution in your town? __a local newspaper index__

2. What is a "clip file"? __folders of articles cut out and saved by librarians__

3. What are two sources of information on people in the news?
__*Current Biography*__
__*Biography Index*__

Page 337

Using the *Reader's Guide to Periodical Literature*

Here is an example of a *Reader's Guide to Periodical Literature* entry for an article in *Discover* magazine. An explanation of terms follows the entry.

Science
  Science experiments for young people
  M. Watson, il *Discover* 11:33-7 Ja '90

Science is the topic under which the article (one of many) is listed.
Science experiments for young people is the title of the article.
M. Watson is the author of the article.
il means the article is illustrated.
Discover is the magazine where you will find the article.
11:33-7 means the article is in volume 11 on pages 33 to 37.
Ja '90 means the article was in the January 1990 issue of the magazine.

Directions: Circle the correct answers.

1. An **O 18, 1998** listing in the *Reader's Guide* means:
   The article can be ordered on October 18, 1998.
   (The article was published on October 18, 1998.)
   The article was written on October 18, 1998.

2. An **il** listing in an article about birds means:
   (The article contains pictures of birds.)
   The article is about ill birds.
   The author's last name is il.

3. How many pages are contained in a listing that reads 12:32-41?
   Eight
   Forty-one
   (Ten)

Page 338

Fiction, Nonfiction and Biographies

Fiction books are stories that are not based on facts or real events. They are based on the imagination of the author.
Examples: picture books and novels

Nonfiction books are about facts or events that actually occurred.
Examples: reference books and history books

Biographies are written about a person's life. They are based on true events. Biographies have been written about Presidents and First Ladies, as well as other people.

Directions: Use your library to answer the following questions.

1. What are the titles and authors of three fiction books? _____

2. What are the titles and authors of three nonfiction _____

3. What _____ books you listed? _____

Answers will vary.

Directions: Use the library catalog to locate two biographies of each of the people listed. Write the titles, authors and call numbers.

4. Abraham Lincoln _____

5. George Washington Carver _____

6. John F. Kennedy _____

7. Princess Diana _____

8. Pocahontas _____

Page 339

Book Search: Fiction

Have you ever been on a scavenger hunt? Usually, when you go on a scavenger hunt, you need to find unusual items on a list. This scavenger hunt will take place at your library. Instead of finding unusual items, you will need to find books.

Directions: Find these books at your library. They will be in alphabetical order by the author's last name in the picture book section of the children's department. Then answer the questions.

Author: Margaret Wise Brown   **Title:** *Goodnight Moon*

1. Where is the cow jumping over the moon? __in the picture__
2. What is the old lady whispering? __"Hush."__
3. How many kittens are in the story? __3__

Author: Audrey Wood   **Title:** *Napping House*

4. In the beginning, what is everyone in the house doing? __napping__
5. What kind of flea is in this story? __a wakeful flea__
6. What breaks at the end of the story? __the bed__

Author: Audrey Wood   **Title:** *Heckedy Peg*

7. Who is Heckedy Peg? __a witch__

8. What did Heckedy Peg lose? __her leg__

9. What two things does the mother tell her children not to do?
__Not to let strangers in and not to touch fire__

Page 340

Book Search: Nonfiction

Directions: Look in your library catalog to find the types of nonfiction books listed. Then go to the shelf in the nonfiction section and locate the books. Write the information requested for each book.

A book about gorillas

Title: _____
Author: _____
Call number: _____
First sentence in book: _____

A book about the solar system

Title: _____
Author: _____
Call _____
Last se_____

A book ab_____

Title: _____
Author: _____
Call number: _____
Color of book's cover: _____

A book about flowers

Title: _____
Author: _____
Call Number: _____
Name of a flower pictured in book: _____

Answers will vary.

Page 341

Book Search: Biographies

Biographies may be located in the 920 section in your library or may be filed by call number according to subject.

Directions: Use the library catalog and the actual books to answer these questions.

1. How many books can you find about Elizabeth Blackwell? _____
2. What is the title of one of the books? _____
3. How many books can you find about Kareem Abdul-Jabar? _____
4. What are the titles, authors and call numbers of three books about George Washington?

_____
_____
_____

5. What are th_____
Mar_____

6. What are the titles, authors and call numbers of three books about Eleanor Roosevelt?

_____
_____
_____

7. What are the titles, authors and call numbers of three books about Marie Curie?

_____
_____
_____

Answers will vary.

Page 342

Reports: Choosing a Topic

Directions: Read about how to write a report. Then answer the questions.

A report is a written paper based on the writer's research. It is logically organized and, if it is a good report, presents information in an interesting way. Reports can focus on many different topics. A social studies report may provide information about a city or state. A science report may explain why the oceans are polluted.

If possible, choose a topic you're interested in. Sometimes a teacher assigns a general topic to the whole class, such as the solar system. This is a very broad topic, so you must first narrow it to a smaller topic about which you can write an interesting four- or five-page report. For example, your report could be on "The Sun, the Center of the Solar System" or "Jupiter, the Jumbo Planet."

A narrower topic gives your paper a better focus. Be careful not to make your topic too narrow, because then you may not be able to find much information about it for your report.

The inverted pyramid on the right shows how to narrow your topic from the general, at the top of the pyramid, to the specific, at the bottom.

The solar system

Planets in the solar system

Jupiter, the jumbo planet

Directions: Select a topic for a paper you will write. You may choose one of these topics or select one of your own. Then answer the questions.

American wars   Games   Presidents   States
Famous American women   Solar system   Sports heroes   Ecology

1. What is a report? __A report is a written paper based on the__
__writer's research.__

2. Which general topic did you choose? __Answers will vary.__

3. What specific topic will you write about? _____

Page 343

Reports: Doing Research

Directions: Review the information on pages 335 and 336 about doing library research. Then read about how to do research for a report and answer the questions.

Before starting your report, locate the most likely places to find relevant information for your research. Ask the librarian for help if necessary. A good report will be based on at least three or four sources, so it's important to find references that provide varied information.

Is the topic a standard one, such as a report on the skeletal system? A general encyclopedia, such as *World Book*, is a good place to begin your research. Remember to use the encyclopedia's index to find related entries. For related entries on the skeletal system, you could check the index for entries on bones, health and the musculo-skeletal system. The index entry will show which encyclopedia number and pages to read to find information related to each entry topic.

Does your report require current statistics and/or facts? *Facts on File* and *Editorial Research Reports* are two sources for statistics. Ask the librarian to direct you to more specialized reference sources, such as *The People's Almanac* or *The New Grove Dictionary of Music and Musicians* which are related specifically to your topic.

For current magazine articles, see the *Reader's Guide to Periodical Literature*, which lists the names and page numbers of magazine articles related to a variety of topics. If you need geographical information about a country, check an atlas such as the *Rand McNally Contemporary World Atlas*.

1. How many reference sources should you consult before writing your report? __3-4__
2. What are two references that provide statistics and facts? __Facts on File,__
__Editorial Research Reports__
3. Where will you find a listing of magazine articles? __Reader's Guide__
__to Periodical Literature__
4. Where should you look for geographical information? __Rand McNally__
__Contemporary World Atlas__
5. If you're stumped or don't know where to begin, who can help? __the__
__librarian__

Page 344

Reports: Taking Notes

Directions: Read about taking notes for your report. Use the "index card" below to write a sample note from one of your reference sources.

When gathering information for a report, it is necessary to take notes. You'll need to take notes when you read encyclopedia entries, books and magazine or newspaper articles related to your topic.

Before you begin gathering information for a report, organize your thoughts around the who, what, when, where, why and how questions of your topic. This organized approach will help direct you to the references that best answer these questions. It will also help you select and write in your notes only useful information.

There are different ways of taking notes. Some people use notebook paper. If you write on notebook paper, put a heading on each page. Write only notes related to each heading on specific pages. Otherwise, your notes will be disorganized, and it will be difficult to begin writing your paper.

Many people prefer to put their notes on index cards. Index cards can be easily sorted and organized when you begin writing your report and are helpful when preparing an outline. If you use index cards for your notes, put one fact on each card.

Take several notes from each reference source you use. Having too many notes is better than not having enough information when you start to write your report.

Answers will vary.

Grade 5 - Comprehensive Curriculum

Page 345

Encyclopedia Skills: Taking Notes

A **biography** is a written report of a person's life. It is based on facts and actual events. To prepare to write a biographical essay, you could look up information about the person in an encyclopedia.

Directions: Select one of the people listed below. Read about that person in an encyclopedia. Take notes to prepare for writing a biographical essay. Then use your notes to answer the questions.

Babe Ruth
Mikhail Baryshnikov
Golda Meir
Dolly Madison
Pearl S. Buck

Billie Jean King
Willie Mays
Woodrow Wilson
Charles Darwin
Marie Curie

My Notes:

1. Where and when was he/she born? _____

2. If deceased, when did the person die? _____

3. When and why did he/she first become famous? _____

4. What are some _____

Answers will vary.

Page 346

Reports: Making an Outline

An outline will help you organize your ideas before you begin writing your report.

Title
I. First Main Idea
  A. A supporting idea or fact
  B. Another supporting idea or fact
    1. An example or related fact
    2. An example or related fact
II. Second Main Idea
  A. A supporting idea or fact
  B. Another supporting idea or fact
III. Third Main Idea
  A. A supporting idea or fact
  B. Another supporting idea or fact

Directions: Use information from your notes to write an outline for your report. Follow the above format, but expand your outline to include as many main ideas, facts and examples as necessary.

Outlines will vary.

Page 347

Reports: Writing the Paper

Directions: Read more about writing a report. Then write your report.

Before you begin, be certain you clearly understand what is expected. How long should your report be? Must it be typed? Can it be written in pen? Should it be double-spaced?

Begin the first draft of your report with a general introduction of your topic. In the introduction, briefly mention the main points you will write about. One paragraph is usually enough to introduce your paper.

Next, comes the body of your report. Start a new paragraph for each main point. Include information that supports that point. If you are writing a long report, you may need to write a new paragraph for each supporting idea and/or each example. Follow your outline to be certain you cover all points. Depending on the number of words required to cover your topic, the body of the report will be anywhere from three or four paragraphs to several pages long.

In one or two concluding paragraphs, briefly summarize the main points you wrote about in the body of your report and state any conclusions you have drawn as a result of your research.

Once you finish the first draft, you will need to edit and rewrite your report to make it read smoothly and correct errors. You may need to rewrite your report more than once to make it the best it can be.

If possible, put the report aside for a day or two before you rewrite it so you can look at it with fresh eyes and a clear mind. Professional writers often write several drafts, so don't be discouraged about rewrites! Rewriting and editing are the keys to good writing—keys that every writer, no matter how old or experienced, relies on.

Directions: Circle the words in the puzzle related to writing a report.

```
K K N K T O P I C D T B
L D O R T T O D P T D O
I N T R O D U C T I O N
E N E R G D E E O O O N
D W S R G E Y C P C X R
S A T E A T T E I E Y O
R W A Q U B W P C D G F
L I C O N C L U S I O N
O U T L I N E D U T T E D
R E S E A R C H R E S E
```

topic
facts
outline
introduction
body
conclusion
notes
research
edit

Page 348

Review

1. Why should you narrow your topic when writing a report?
  ☑ So you can include specific, relevant information.
  ☐ So you can write a short paper.
  ☐ So you can use only one reference book.

2. Which of the following is not a reference book?
  ☐ Facts on File
  ☐ Rand McNally Contemporary World Atlas
  ☑ Flowers For Cosmo
  ☐ World Book Encyclopedia

3. Writing an outline for your report will help you
  ☐ narrow your topic.
  ☐ gather many notes.
  ☑ get organized and follow a plan.
  ☐ broaden your topic.

4. Which of the following is not a part of a finished report?
  ☐ Introduction
  ☐ Conclusion
  ☐ Body
  ☑ Outline

5. When taking notes, index cards will help you
  ☐ check spelling, grammar and punctuation.
  ☑ organize your writing later.
  ☐ find things quickly on the shelves.
  ☐ transfer facts to your notebook.

Page 349

Editing

To **edit** means to revise and correct written work. Learning how to edit your work will help you become a better writer. First, you should write a rough draft of your paper, then edit it to make it better. Remember these things when writing your rough draft:
▶ **Do not overcrowd your page.** Leave space between every line and at the sides of your pages to make notes and changes.
▶ **Write so you can read it.** Don't be sloppy just because you're only writing a rough draft.
▶ **Number your pages.** This will help you keep everything in order.
▶ **Write on only one side of the page.** This gives you plenty of space if you want to make changes or add information between paragraphs.
▶ **Use the same size notebook paper for all drafts.** If all pages are the same size, you're less likely to lose any.

Before turning in your report or paper, ask yourself these questions:
▶ **Have I followed my outline?**
▶ **Have I told the who, what, when, where, why and how?**
▶ **Have I provided too much information?** (Good writers are concise. Don't repeat yourself after you have made a point.)
▶ **Do I still have unanswered questions?** (If you have questions, you can bet your readers will also. Add the missing information.)

It is always a good idea to let a day or so pass before rereading your paper and making final corrections. That way you will see what you actually wrote, instead of what you **think** you wrote.

When you edit your work, look for:
▶ **Correct grammar.**
▶ **Correct spelling.** Use the dictionary if you are not 100 percent sure.
▶ **Correct punctuation.**
▶ **Complete sentences.** Each should contain a complete thought.

Directions: Answer these questions about editing by writing T for true or F for false.

T 1. When you are editing, you should look for correct grammar and spelling.
F 2. Editors do not look for complete sentences.
F 3. Editors do not have to read each word of a story.
F 4. It is best to use both sides of a sheet of paper when writing the rough draft of your report.
T 5. It does not matter how neat your first draft is.
T 6. Editors make sure that sentences are punctuated correctly.

Page 350

Editing

Editors and proofreaders use certain marks to note the changes that need to be made. In addition to circling spelling errors and fixing capitalization mistakes, editors and proofreaders also use the following marks to indicate other mistakes that need to be corrected.

the	Delete.	∧	Insert a comma.
c͝nt	Remove the space.	∨	Insert an apostrophe.
In͜this	Insert a space.	∨∨	Insert quotation marks.
is	Insert a word.	⊙	Insert a period.

Directions: Use editing marks to correct the errors in these sentences. Then write the sentences correctly on the lines.

1. Mr. Ramsey was a man who liked to do nothing⊙
  Mr. Ramsey was a man who liked to do nothing.

2. Lili,a young hawaiian girl, liked to swim in the sea.
  Lili, a young Hawaiian girl, liked to swim in the sea.

3. Youngsters who play baseball always have a favorite player.
  Youngsters who play baseball always have a favorite player.

4. Too many people said,That movie was terrible.
  Too many people said, "That movie was terrible."

5. I didn't want to go to the movie with sally⊙
  I didn't want to go to the movie with Sally.

6. Prince charles always wants to play polo⊙
  Prince Charles always wants to play polo.

7. The little boy's name was albert leonard longfellow⊙
  The little boy's name was Albert Leonard Longfellow.

Page 351

Editing

Directions: Use editing marks to show the changes that need to be made in the following sentences.

1. billy bob branstool was was the biggest bully at our school.
2. mr. Smith told my mother that I was not a good student.
3. I heard my mom say, "give your mother a kiss."
4. david and justin liked reading about dinosaurs, especially tyrannosaurus rex.
5. milton said to to mabel "maybe we can play tomorrow."
6. lisa and Phil knew the answers to the questions, but they would not raise their hands.
7. too many people were going to see the movie, so we decided to go get pizza instead.
8. tillie's aunt teresa was coming to visit for the month of may.
9. we lived in a small town called sophia, north carolina, for 20 days before we decided to move away.
10. little people do not always live under bridges, but sometimes little fish do.
11. I was reading the book called, haunting at midnight.
12. kevin and I decided that we would be detective bob and detective joe.
13. there were thirteen questions on the test. kevin missed all but the first one.
14. thirty of us were going on a fieldtrip, when suddenly the teacher told the bus driver to turn around.

Page 352

Editing

noits	Flip the words around; transpose.
wantut	Flip letters around; transpose.
¶That was when Peter began talking.	Indent the paragraph or start a new paragraph.
with you The movie we went to see was good.	Move text down to line below.
There were no people there. ⌐ Jason thought we should go.	Move text up to line above.

Directions: Use editing marks to edit this story.

The Fallen Log

There was once a log on the floor of a very damp and eerie forest. two men came upon the log and sat down for a rest. these two men, leroy and larry, did not know that someone could hear every word they said. "I'm so tired," moaned larry, as he began unlacing his heavy hiking boots. "and my feet hurt, too."

"Quit complaining, friend," he said. "We've got miles to walk before we'll find the cave with the hidden treasure. besides, if you think you're tired," at look feet my. with that, he kicked off his tennis shoe and discovered a very red big toe. "I think I won't be able to go any farther."

"Sh h h, already!" the two men heard a voice. "enough about feet, enough!" Larry and Leroy began looking around them. they couldn't see anyone, though. "I'm in here," the voice said hoarsely.

Page 353

Editing

Directions: Use editing marks to edit the continuing story of Larry and Leroy.

Larry and Leroy

larry and leroy jumped up from the log as soon as they realized that they were sitting on something that had a voice. "Hey, that was fast," said the voice.

"How did you figure out where I was?"

By this time larry and leroy felt a little silly. They certainly didn't want to talk to a log. they looked at each other and then back at the log again. together they turned around and started walking down the path that had brought them to this point in the forest. "Hey, where are you going?" the voice called.

"Well, I I I don't know," Larry replied, wondering if he should be answering a log. "Who are you?"

"I'm a tiny elf who has been lost in this tree for years," said the voice.

"Sure you are." replied larr. With that, he and troy began running for their lives.

Page 354

Editing

Directions: Draw a line from the editing mark on the left to its meaning on the right.

caplmain — Close up a word

The two boys came to class. The girls, though. — Insert an apostrophe

¶This is the best pie ever. — insert a comma

the — Delete a word

copy editor — Transpose words

We went zoo to the. — Transpose letters

There were two of us in the house. — Insert a space

Once upon a time, there were — Capitalize

leonardo da vinci — Move text down to line below

Thomas was the best. — Change letter to lower-case

The two girls came to class. The two boys never came back until the principal left. — Start a new paragraph

Now I will end the story. — Move text up to line above

My mother was the best lady I know — Insert a period

This is my mothers hat. — Insert a word

Page 355

Review

Directions: Use editing marks to edit the story. Also watch for and change:
Important details that may have been left out.
Places where the wording could be livelier.
Information that is not related to the story.

Answers may vary.

My friend Annie and I decided to go windsurfing one day. We gathered up our equipment—our windsurfing boards and sails—and headed down to the lake. The air was a cool day, so annie and I didn't wear our bathing suits. we were just in cut-off shorts and t-shirts.

It took us a few minutes to get our windsails put together. This was the first time Annie and I had ever did this alone. Usually, our big brothers helped us. They had to be in school, though, and and annie and I don't so we decided to try the sport alone.

Annie's smile was ok. But I was glad the sun was shining brightly. it made it feel warmer like it was warming outside that it really was. "Are you sure we should do this?" said annie, just as I was pulling my windsurf board down to the water. "It will be fine," I assured her. I had candy in my mouth.

I put my toe in the lake.

"Wow is it cold!" I yelled back to Annie. She pulled her windsurf board down beside mine. Hers was orange, blue and yellow. Mine was just purple and green. I finally got in the water with my board. Annie was right beside me. We got onto our boards, and finally, both of us were standing up. But our windsails wouldn't move. Then Annie and I realized there was no wind that day!

Page 356

Proofreading

Proofreading or "proofing" means to carefully look over what has been written, checking for spelling, grammar, punctuation and other errors. At a newspaper it is the job of a copyeditor. All good writers carefully proofread and correct their own work before turning it in to a copyeditor—or a teacher.

Here are three common proofreading marks:

Correct spelling   dog

Replace with lower-case letter

Replace with upper-case letter

Directions: Carefully read the following paragraphs. Use proofreading marks to mark errors in the second paragraph. Correct all errors. The first sentence has been done for you.

alarm
A six-alarm fire at 2121 windsor Terrace on the northeast side awoke apartment residents at 3 A.M. yesterday morning.
Eleven   building
Elven people were in the building. No one was hurt in the
blaze
blaze, which caused $200,000 of property damage.

Property
Property manager Jim smith credits a perfectly functioning smoke alarm
alarm
sprinkler
system for waking residents so they could get out safely. A sprinkler system
was   place   panic   Everyone
were also in plase. "There was No panick." Smith said proudly. "Everyone was calm and Orderly."

Page 357

Proofreading

Directions: Proofread the news article. Mark and correct the 20 errors in capitalization and spelling.

Be Wise When Buying a Car

Each year, about five percent of the U.S. ~~populaton~~ population buys a new car. ~~acording~~ according to J.D. Link and Associates, a New York-based auto industry ~~reserch~~ research company.

"A new car is the second most ~~expensve~~ expensive purchase most people ~~Ever~~ ever make." says Link. "~~it's~~ It's amazing how ~~litle reserch~~ little research people do before they enter the car showroom."

Link says ~~reserch~~ research is the most ~~importent~~ important ~~Ihing~~ thing a new car buyer can do to ~~perfect~~ protect himself or herself. That way, he or she ~~wil~~ will get the ~~bset~~ best car at the best price.

"~~the~~ The salesman is not trying to get ~~You~~ you the best deal." says Link. "~~he's~~ He's trying to get himself the best deal. ~~Bee~~ Be smart! Read up on new cars in magazines like Car and Driver and ~~motortrend~~ before you talk to a ~~salesman!~~ salesman."

NEW MODELS

Page 358

Editing: Check Your Proofreading Skills

Directions: Read about the things you should remember when you are revising your writing. Then follow the instructions to revise the paper below.

After you have finished writing your rough draft, you should reread it later to determine what changes you need to make to ensure it's the best possible paper you are capable of writing.

Check yourself by asking the following questions:
Does my paper stick to the topic?
Have I left out any important details?
Can I make the writing more lively?
Have I made errors in spelling, punctuation or capitalization?
Is there any information that should be left out?

Directions: Revise the following story by making changes to correct spelling, punctuation and capitalization; add details; and cross out words or sentences that do not stick to the topic. *Answers may vary.*

Hunting for Treasure

¶No one really believes me when I tell them that I'm a ~~treasue~~ treasure hunter. But, really, ¶I am. It isn't just any treasure that I like to hunt, though. I like treasures related to coins. Usually, when I go treasure ~~huntng~~ hunting ¶go alone. ~~I always wear my blue coate.~~

¶One day my good friend Jesse wanted to come with me. ¶Why would you want to do that?" I said. "Because I like coins, too," he replied. What Jesse did not know was that the ¢oins that i dig ~~to find~~ are not the coins that just anyone collects. The coins i like are special. They are coins that have been buried in dirt for years!

Page 359

Ancient Egypt

Have you ever wished you could visit Egypt for a first-hand look at the pyramids and ancient mummies? For most people, learning about Egypt is the closest they will come to visiting these ancient sites.

Directions: Test your knowledge about Egypt by writing as many of the answers as you can.

1. Write a paragraph describing what you already know about Egypt.
   <u>Answers will vary.</u>

2. Name at least two famous Egyptian kings or queens. <u>Sample answers: King Tut, Queen Nefertiti</u>

3. What was the purpose of a pyramid? <u>Sample answers: to bury Egyptian kings in; to worship the gods</u>

4. What was the purpose of mummification? <u>to preserve bodies after death</u>

5. What major river runs through Egypt? <u>the Nile</u>

Page 360

Taking Notes: Egyptian Mummies

Taking notes is the process of writing important points to remember, such as taking notes from material prepared by your teacher or from what is discussed in class or from an article you read. Taking notes is useful when preparing for a test or when writing a report. When taking notes, follow these steps:

1. Read the article carefully.
2. Select one or two important points from each paragraph.
3. Write your notes in your own words.
4. Reread your notes to be sure you understand what you have written.
5. Abbreviate words to save time.

Directions: Read about Egyptian mummies. Select one or two important points from each paragraph. Write your notes in your own words.

After the Egyptians discovered that bodies buried in the hot, dry sand of the desert became mummified, they began searching for ways to improve the mummification...

Sample notes: Sample answers:

Paragraph 1 <u>Bodies buried in hot dry sand became mummified. Natron is vital for embalming.</u>

Paragraph 2 <u>Natron is a salt that is found when water from an oasis evaporates, leaving behind salts that were in it.</u>

Paragraph 3 <u>The body was soaked in natron for up to 40 days, causing it to shrink and the skin to become leathery. Natron was used for thousands of years.</u>

Page 361

Outlining

Outlining is a way to organize information before you write an essay or informational paragraph. Outlining helps you understand the information you read.

This sample form will help you get started. When outlining, you can add more main points, more smaller points and/or more examples.

    Title
    I. First Main Idea
       A. A smaller idea
          1. An example
          2. An example
       B. Another smaller idea
    II. Second Main Idea
       A. A smaller idea
       B. Another smaller idea
          1. An example
          2. An example
    III. Third Main Idea
       A. A smaller idea
       B. A smaller idea

Directions: Read about building pyramids. Then complete the outline on the next page.

The process of building pyramids began as a way to honor a king or queen. Since the Egyptians believed in an afterlife, they thought it only fitting for their kings and queens to have elaborate burial tombs filled with treasures to enjoy in the afterlife. Thus, the idea of the pyramid was born.

At first pyramids were not built as they are known today. In the early stages of the Egyptian dynasty, kings were entombed in a *mastaba*. Mastabas were tombs made of mud-dried bricks. They formed a rectangular tomb with angled sides and a flat roof.

Later, as the Egyptian kingdom became more powerful, kings felt they needed grander tombs. The step pyramid was developed. These pyramids were made of stone rather than mud and were much taller. A large mastaba was built on the ground. Then, four more mastabas (each smaller than the previous) were stacked on top.

Finally, the pyramids took the shape that is familiar today. They were constructed with a flat bottom and four slanting sides which ascended to a final point. One of the tallest is over 400 feet high. These pyramids were also built of stone and were finished with an exterior of white limestone.

Page 362

Outlining: Egyptian Pyramids

Directions: Complete the outline. Then answer the question.

<u>Egyptian Pyramids</u>
(title)

I. Mastabas
   A. <u>made of mud-dried bricks</u>
   B. <u>rectangular tomb</u>
   C. <u>angled sides and a flat roof</u>

II. Step pyramids
   A. <u>made of stone</u>
   B. <u>much taller than a mastaba</u>
   C. <u>large mastaba with four smaller mastabas stacked on top</u>

III. Pyramids
   A. <u>flat bottom and four slanting sides ascending to a final point</u>
   B. <u>tallest is over 400 feet high</u>
   C. <u>built of stone and finished with white limestone exterior</u>

What do you find is the most interesting aspect about the pyramids of ancient Egypt? Why?
<u>Answers will vary.</u>

Page 363

Summarizing

A **summary** includes the main points from an article, book or speech.

Example:

Tomb robbing was an important business in ancient Egypt. Often entire families participated in the plunder of tombs. These robbers may have been laborers, officials, tomb architects or guards, but they all probably had one thing in common. They were involved in the building or designing of the tomb or they wouldn't have had the knowledge necessary to successfully rob the burial sites. Not only did tomb robbing ensure a rich life for the robbers but it also enabled them to be buried with many riches themselves.

Summary:

Tomb robbing occurred in ancient Egypt. The robbers stole riches to use in their present lives or in their burials. Tomb robbers usually had some part in the building or design of the tomb. This allowed them to find the burial rooms where the treasures were stored.

Directions: Read about life in ancient Egypt. Then write a three- to five-sentence summary.

 Egyptologists have learned much from the pyramids and mummies of ancient Egypt from the items left by grave robbers.

Women of ancient Egypt wore makeup to enhance their features. Dark colored minerals called *kohl* were used as eyeliner and eye shadow. Men also wore eyeliner. Women used another mineral called *ocher* on their cheeks and lips to redden them. Henna, a plant which produces an orange dye, tinted the fingernails, the palms of their hands and the soles of their feet.

Perfume was also important in ancient Egypt. Small cones made of wax were worn on top of the head. These cones contained perfume oils. The sun slowly melted the wax, and the perfume would scent the hair, head and shoulders.

Sample answer:

We have learned much from the pyramids and mummies. Women wore makeup made out of the minerals kohl and ocher and a plant called henna. Men wore eyeliner, too. Perfume made out of wax was also important to the ancient Egyptians.

Page 364

Summarizing: King Tut

Directions: Read about King Tut. Then write a five- to seven-sentence summary.

King Tutankhamen (TO-TAN-KO-MEN) became king of Egypt when he was only nine years old. Known today as "King Tut," he died in 1355 B.C. when he was 18. Because King Tut died so young, not much is known about what he did while he was king.

After his death, Tut's body was "mummified" and buried in a pyramid in the Valley of the Kings in Egypt. Many other kings of ancient Egypt were buried there also.

In 1922, King Tut became famous when an Englishman named Howard Carter discovered and explored his tomb. The king's mummy, wearing a gold mask decorated with precious stones, was found intact. Amazingly, all King Tut's riches were still in his tomb. His was the only one in the Valley of the Kings that had not been discovered and robbed.

The King's tomb contained four rooms. One contained his mummy. The other rooms were filled with beautiful furniture, including King Tut's throne. Also found in Tut's tomb were more than 3,000 objects, like clothes, jewelry, wine, food—and a trumpet that could still be played. Obviously, King Tut planned to live royally in the next world!

Sample answers:

King Tut ruled Egypt from age 9 to 18. Because he died so young, not much is known about his life. He was buried in the Valley of the Kings. His tomb was discovered by Howard Carter. All of King Tut's riches were still inside. There were more than 3,000 objects found in the tomb, including his mummy and his throne.

Page 366

Place Value

The place value of a digit or numeral is shown by where it is in the number. In the number 1,234, 1 has the place value of thousands, 2 is hundreds, 3 is tens and 4 is ones.

Example: 1,250,000,000

Read: One billion, two hundred fifty million

Write: 1,250,000,000

Billions	Millions	Thousands	Ones
h t o	h t o	h t o	h t o
1,	2 5 0,	0 0 0,	0 0 0

Directions: Read the words. Then write the numbers.

twenty million, three hundred four thousand ... 20,304,000

five thousand, four hundred twenty-three ... 5,423

one hundred fifty billion, eight million,
one thousand, five hundred ... 150,008,001,500

sixty billion, seven hundred million,
one hundred thousand, three hundred twelve ... 60,700,100,312

four hundred million, fifteen thousand,
seven hundred one ... 400,015,701

six hundred ninety-nine million, four thousand,
nine hundred forty-two ... 699,004,942

Here's a game to play with a partner.

Write a ten-digit number using each digit, 0 to 9, only once. Do not show the number to your partner. Give clues like: "There is a five in the hundreds place." The clues can be given in any order. See if your partner can write the same number you have written.

Page 367

Place Value

Directions: Draw a line to connect each number to its correct written form.

1. 791,000 — Three hundred fifty thousand
2. 350,000 — Seventeen million, five hundred thousand
3. 17,500,000 — Seven hundred ninety-one thousand
4. 3,500,000 — Seventy thousand, nine hundred ten
5. 70,910 — Three million, five hundred thousand
6. 35,500,000 — Seventeen billion, five hundred thousand
7. 17,000,500,000 — Thirty-five million, five hundred thousand

Directions: Look carefully at this number: 2,071,463,548. Write the numeral for each of the following places.

8. **6** ten thousands

9. **1** millions

10. **5** hundreds

11. **2** billions

12. **4** hundred thousands

13. **7** ten millions

14. **3** one thousands

15. **0** hundred millions

2,342

Page 368

Addition

Addition is "putting together" two or more numbers to find the sum.

Directions: Add. Fill the backpacks with the right answers.

38 +92 = 130	71 +48 = 119	43 +62 = 105	56 +14 = 70	87 +13 = 100
24 +39 = 63	16 +67 = 82	83 +47 = 130	35 +80 = 115	17 +64 = 81
95 +25 = 120	54 +19 = 73	61 +77 = 138	42 +89 = 131	37 +97 = 134
62 +39 = 101	18 +43 = 61	27 +94 = 121	11 +89 = 100	48 +58 = 106

Page 369

Addition

Teachers of an Earth Science class planned to take 60 students on an overnight hiking and camping experience. After planning the menu, they went to the grocery store for supplies.

Breakfast	Lunch	Dinner	Snacks
bacon	hot dogs/buns	pasta	crackers
eggs	apples	sauce	marshmallows
bread	chips	garlic bread	chocolate bars
cereal	juice	salad	cocoa mix
juice	granola bars	cookies	
$34.50	$ 52.15	$ 47.25	$ 23.40

Directions: Answer the questions. Write the total amount spent on food for the trip.

What information do you need to answer the question? the total for each meal and snacks added together

What is the total? $157.30

Directions: Add.

462 +574 = 1,036	918 +359 = 1,277	527 +582 = 1,109	386 +745 = 1,131	295 +764 = 1,059
397 +448 = 845	524 +725 = 1,249	906 +337 = 1,243	750 +643 = 1,393	891 +419 = 1,310
1,568 +2,341 = 3,909	3,214 +2,896 = 6,110	5,147 +4,285 = 9,432	7,259 +2,451 = 9,710	9,317 +3,583 = 12,900

Grade 5 - Comprehensive Curriculum

Page 370

Addition

Directions: Add.

1. Tourists travel to national parks to see the many animals which live there. Park Rangers estimate 384 buffalo, 282 grizzly bears and 426 deer are in the park. What is the total number of buffalo, bears and deer estimated in the park?
   1,092 buffalo, bears and deer
2. Last August, 2,248 visitors drove motor homes into the campgrounds for overnight camping. 647 set up campsites with tents. How many campsites were there altogether in August?
   2,895 campsites
3. During a 3-week camping trip, Tom and his family hiked 42 miles, took a 126-mile long canoeing trip and drove their car 853 miles. How many miles did they travel in all?
   1,021 miles
4. Old Faithful is a geyser which spouts water high into the air. 10,000 gallons of water burst into the air regularly. Two other geysers spout 2,400 gallons of water during each eruption. What is the amount of water thrust into the air during one cycle?
   14,800 gallons
5. Yellowstone National Park covers approximately 2,221,772 acres of land. Close by, the Grand Tetons cover approximately 310,350 acres. How many acres of land are there in these two parks?
   2,532,122 acres
6. Hiking trails cover 486 miles, motor routes around the north rim total 376 miles, and another 322 miles of road allow visitors to follow a loop around the southern part of the park. How many miles of trails and roadways are there?
   1,184 miles

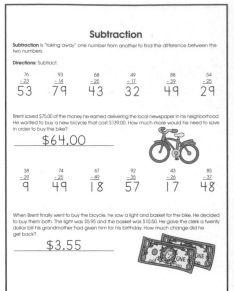

Page 371

Addition

Bob the butcher is popular with the dogs in town. He was making a delivery this morning when he noticed he was being followed by two dogs. Bob tried to climb a ladder to escape from the dogs. Solve the following addition problems and shade in the answers on the ladder. If all the numbers are shaded when the problems have been solved, Bob made it up the ladder. Some answers may not be on the ladder.

1. 986,145 621,332 + 200,008 1, 807,485	2. 1,873,402 925,666 + 4,689 2,803,757	3. 506,328 886,510 + 342,225 1,735,063
4. 43,015 2,811,604 + 987,053 3,841,672	5. 18,443 300,604 + 999,999 1,319,046	6. 8,075 14,608 + 33,914 56,597
7. 9,162 7,804 + 755,122 772,088	8. 88,714 213,653 + 5,441,298 5,743,665	9. 3,244,662 1,986,114 + 521,387 5,752,163
10. 4,581 22,983 + 5,618,775 5,646,339	11. 818,623 926 + 3,260,004 4,079,553	12. 80,436 9,159 + 3,028,761 3,118,356

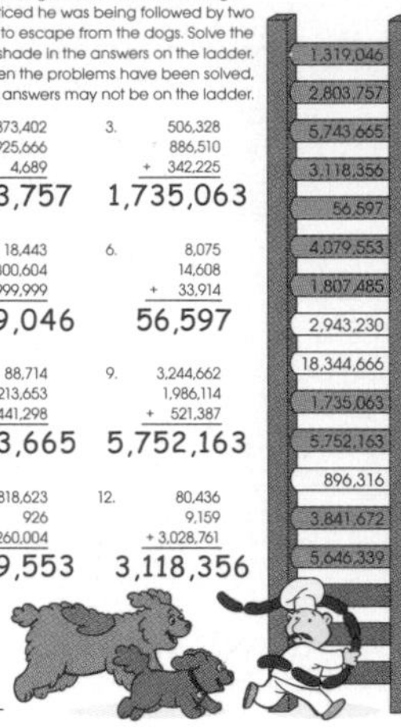
1,319,046
2,803,757
5,743,665
3,118,356
56,597
4,079,553
1,807,485
2,943,230
18,344,666
1,735,063
5,752,163
896,316
3,841,672
5,646,339

Does Bob make it? no

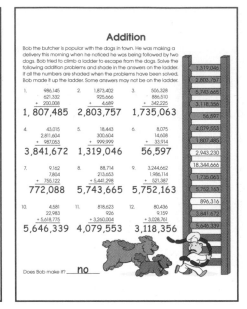

Page 372

Subtraction

Subtraction is "taking away" one number from another to find the difference between the two numbers.

Directions: Subtract.

76 – 23 53	93 – 14 79	68 – 25 43	49 – 17 32	88 – 39 49	54 – 25 29

Brent saved $75.00 of the money he earned delivering the local newspaper in his neighborhood. He wanted to buy a new bicycle that cost $139.00. How much more would he need to save in order to buy the bike?

$64.00

38 – 29 9	74 – 25 49	67 – 49 18	92 – 35 57	43 – 26 17	85 – 37 48

When Brent finally went to buy the bicycle, he saw a light and basket for the bike. He decided to buy them both. The light was $5.95 and the basket was $10.50. He gave the clerk a twenty dollar bill his grandmother had given him for his birthday. How much change did he get back?

$3.55

ONE
ONE

Page 373

Subtraction

When working with larger numbers, it is important to keep the numbers lined up according to place value.

Subtract.

398 – 149 249	543 – 287 256	491 – 311 180	
786 – 597 189	1,825 – 495 1,330	4,172 – 2,785 1,387	
8,391 – 5,492 2,899	63,852 – 34,765 29,087	24,107 –19,350 4,757	52,900 – 43,081 9,819

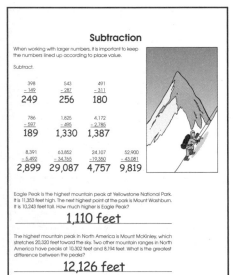

Eagle Peak is the highest mountain peak at Yellowstone National Park. It is 11,353 feet high. The next highest point at the park is Mount Washburn. It is 10,243 feet tall. How much higher is Eagle Peak?

1,110 feet

The highest mountain peak in North America is Mount McKinley, which stretches 20,320 feet toward the sky. Two other mountain ranges in North America have peaks at 10,302 feet and 8,194 feet. What is the greatest difference between the peaks?

12,126 feet

Page 374

Checking Subtraction

You can check your subtraction by using addition.

Example: 34,436 – 12,264 = 22,172 Check: 22,172 + 12,264 = 34,436

Directions: Subtract. Then check your answers by adding.

15,326 – 11,532 3,794	Check: 3,794 +11,532 15,326	28,615 – 25,329 3,286	Check: 3,286 +25,329 28,615
96,521 – 47,378 49,143	Check: 49,143 +47,378 96,521	46,496 – 35,877 10,619	Check: 10,619 +35,877 46,496
77,911 – 63,783 14,128	Check: 14,128 +63,783 77,911	156,901 –112,732 44,169	Check: 44,169 +112,732 156,901
395,638 –187,569 208,069	Check: 208,069 +187,569 395,638	67,002 – 53,195 13,807	Check: 13,807 +53,195 67,002
16,075 –15,896 179	Check: 179 +15,896 16,075	39,678 –19,769 19,909	Check: 19,909 +19,769 39,678
84,654 – 49,997 34,657	Check: 34,657 +49,997 84,654	12,335 –10,697 1,638	Check: 1,638 +10,697 12,335

During the summer, 158,941 people visited Yellowstone National Park. During the fall, there were 52,397 visitors. How many more visitors went to the park during the summer than the fall?

106, 544 visitors

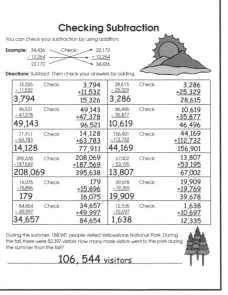

Page 375

Addition and Subtraction

Directions: Check the answers. Write **T** if the answer is true and **F** if it is false.

Example: 48,973 – 35,856 = 13,118 Check: F 35,856 + 13,118 = 48,974

18,264 + 17,893 36,157	Check: T	36,157 -17,893 18,264	458,342 – 297,652 160,680	Check: F	160,680 +297,652 458,332
39,854 + 52,713 92,577	Check: F	92,577 -52,713 39,864	631,928 – 457,615 174,313	Check: T	174,313 +457,615 631,928
14,389 + 93,587 107,976	Check: T	107,976 - 93,587 14,389	554,974 – 376,585 178,389	Check: T	178,389 +376,585 554,974
87,321 – 62,348 24,973	Check: T	24,973 +62,348 87,321	109,568 + 97,373 206,941	Check: T	206,941 - 97,373 109,568

Directions: Read the story problem. Write the equation and check the answer.

A camper hikes 53,741 feet out into the wilderness. On his return trip he takes a shortcut, walking 36,752 feet back to his cabin. The shortcut saves him 16,998 feet of hiking. True or (False?)

53,741 – 36,752 = 16,989 16,989 + 36,752 = 53,741

Page 376

Addition and Subtraction

Directions: Add or subtract to find the answers.

Eastland School hosted a field day. Students could sign up for a variety of events. 175 students signed up for individual races. Twenty two-person teams competed in the mile relay and 36 kids took part in the high jump. How many students participated in the activities?
251 students

Westmore School brought 42 students and 7 adults to the field day event. Northern School brought 84 students and 15 adults. There was a total of 300 students and 45 adults at the event. How many were from other schools?
174 students   23 adults

The Booster Club sponsored a concession stand during the day. Last year, they made $1,000 at the same event. This year they hoped to earn at least $1,250. They actually raised $1,842. How much more did they make than they had anticipated?
$592.00

Each school was awarded a trophy for participating in the field day's activities. The Booster Club planned to purchase three plaques as awards, but they only wanted to spend $150. The first place trophy they selected was $68. The second place award was $59. How much would they be able to spend on the third place award if they stay within their budgeted amount?
$23.00

The Booster Club decided to spend $1,000 to purchase several items for the school with the money they had earned. Study the list of items suggested and decide which combination of items they could purchase.

A. Swing set $425   **A+B+D**
B. Sliding board $263   **B+C+D**
C. Scoreboard $515   **A+C**
D. Team uniforms $180

Page 377

Rounding

Rounding a number means to express it to the nearest ten, hundred, thousand and so on. When rounding a number to the nearest ten, if the number has five or more ones, round up. Round down if the number has four or fewer ones.

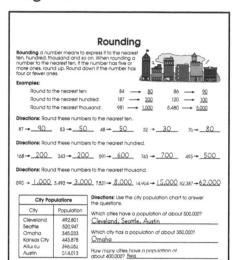

Examples:

Round to the nearest ten: 84 → **80**   86 → **90**
Round to the nearest hundred: 187 → **200**   120 → **100**
Round to the nearest thousand: 981 → **1,000**   5,480 → **5,000**

Directions: Round these numbers to the nearest ten.

87 → **90**   53 → **50**   48 → **50**   32 → **30**   76 → **80**

Directions: Round these numbers to the nearest hundred.

168 → **200**   243 → **200**   591 → **600**   743 → **700**   493 → **500**

Directions: Round these numbers to the nearest thousand.

895 → **1,000**   3,492 → **3,000**   7,521 → **8,000**   14,904 → **15,000**   62,387 → **62,000**

City Populations	
City	Population
Cleveland	492,801
Seattle	520,947
Omaha	345,033
Kansas City	443,878
Atlanta	396,052
Austin	514,013

Directions: Use the city population chart to answer the questions.

Which cities have a population of about 500,000?
Cleveland, Seattle, Austin

Which city has a population of about 350,000?
Omaha

How many cities have a population of about 400,000? **two**

Which ones? **Kansas City and Atlanta**

Page 378

Estimating

To **Estimate** means to give an approximate rather than an exact answer. Rounding each number first makes it easy to estimate an answer.

Example:

$$93 + 48 \rightarrow 90 + 50 = 140$$
$$321 + 597 \rightarrow 300 + 600 = 900$$
$$1,859 - 997 \rightarrow 2,000 - 1,000 = 1,000$$

Directions: Estimate the sums and differences by rounding the numbers first.

68 +34 → 70 +30 = **100**	12 +98 → 10 +100 = **110**	89 +23 → 90 +20 = **110**
638 -395 → 600 -400 = **200**	281 - 69 → 300 -100 = **200**	271 -126 → 300 -100 = **200**
1,532 - 998 → 2,000 -1,000 = **1,000**	8,312 -4,789 → 8,000 -5,000 = **3,000**	6,341 +9,286 → 6,000 +9,000 = **15,000**

Bonnie has $50 to purchase tennis shoes, a tennis racquet and tennis balls. Does she have enough money?

yes

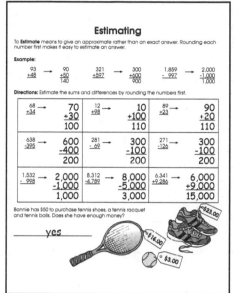

$23.00
$16.00
$3.00

Page 379

Rounding and Estimating

Rounding numbers and estimating answers is an easy way of finding the approximate answer without writing out the problem or using a calculator.

Directions: Circle the correct answer.

Round to the nearest ten:

73 → **(70)** / 80   48 → 40 / **(50)**   65 → 60 / **(70)**
85 → **(80)** / 90   92 → **(90)** / 100   37 → 30 / **(40)**

Round to the nearest hundred:

139 → **(100)** / 200   782 → 700 / **(800)**   390 → 300 / **(400)**
640 → **(600)** / 700   525 → **(500)** / 600   457 → 400 / **(500)**

Round to the nearest thousand:

1,375 → **(1,000)** / 2,000   21,800 → **21,000** / **(22,000)**   36,240 → **(36,000)** / 37,000

Sam wanted to buy a new computer. He knew he only had about $1,200 to spend. Which of the following ones could he afford to buy?

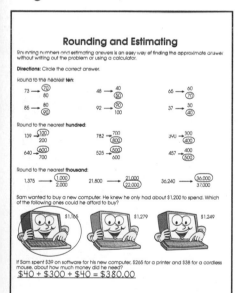

$1,165 $1,279 $1,249

If Sam spent $39 on software for his new computer, $265 for a printer and $38 for a cordless mouse, about how much money did he need?
$40 + $300 + $40 = $380.00

Page 380

Prime Numbers

Example: 3 is a prime number 3 + 1 = 3 and 3 + 3 = 1
Any other divisor will result in a mixed number or fraction.

An easy way to test a number to see if it is prime is to divide by 2 and 3. If the number can be divided by 2 or 3 without a remainder, it is not a prime number. (Exceptions, 2 and 3.)

Example:

11 cannot be divided evenly by 2 or 3. It can only be divided by 1 and 11. It is a prime number.

Directions: Write the first 15 prime numbers. Test by dividing by 2 and by 3.

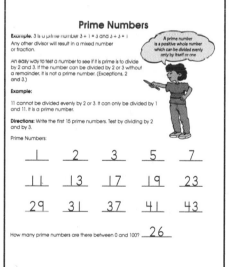

A prime number is a positive whole number which can be divided evenly only by itself or one

Prime Numbers:

1   2   3   5   7

11   13   17   19   23

29   31   37   41   43

How many prime numbers are there between 0 and 100? **26**

Page 381

Prime Numbers

Directions: Circle the prime numbers.

(71)	**(3)**	82	20	**(43)**	69
128	**(97)**	**(23)**	111	75	51
(13)	44	**(137)**	68	171	**(83)**
(61)	21	77	**(101)**	34	16
(2)	39	92	**(17)**	52	**(29)**
(19)	156	63	99	27	147
121	25	88	12	87	55
57	**(7)**	**(139)**	91	9	**(37)**
(67)	183	**(5)**	**(59)**	**(11)**	95

Grade 5 - Comprehensive Curriculum

Page 382

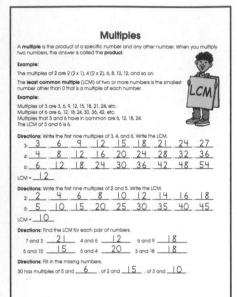

Multiples

A **multiple** is the product of a specific number and any other number. When you multiply two numbers, the answer is called the **product**.

Example:

The multiples of 2 are 2 (2 x 1), 4 (2 x 2), 6, 8, 10, 12, and so on.

The **least common multiple (LCM)** of two or more numbers is the smallest number other than 0 that is a multiple of each number.

Example:

Multiples of 3 are 3, 6, 9, 12, 15, 18, 21, 24, etc.
Multiples of 6 are 6, 12, 18, 24, 30, 36, 42, etc.
Multiples that 3 and 6 have in common are 6, 12, 18, 24.
The LCM of 3 and 6 is 6.

Directions: Write the first nine multiples of 3, 4, and 6. Write the LCM.

3: 3   6   9   12   15   18   21   24   27
4: 4   8   12   16   20   24   28   32   36
6: 6   12   18   24   30   36   42   48   54

LCM = 12

Directions: Write the first nine multiples of 2 and 5. Write the LCM.

2: 2   4   6   8   10   12   14   16   18
5: 5   10   15   20   25   30   35   40   45

LCM = 10

Directions: Find the LCM for each pair of numbers.

7 and 3 21   4 and 6 12   6 and 9 18
5 and 15 15   5 and 4 20   3 and 18 18

Directions: Fill in the missing numbers.

30 has multiples of 5 and 6 , of 2 and 15 , of 3 and 10 .

Page 383

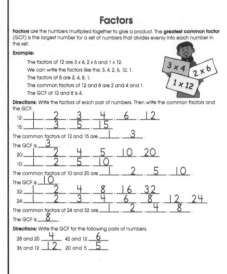

Factors

Factors are the numbers multiplied together to give a product. The **greatest common factor (GCF)** is the largest number for a set of numbers that divides evenly into each number in the set.

Example:

The factors of 12 are 3 x 4, 2 x 6 and 1 x 12.
We can write the factors like this: 3, 4, 2, 6, 12, 1.
The factors of 8 are 2, 4, 8, 1.
The common factors of 12 and 8 are 2 and 4 and 1.
The GCF of 12 and 8 is 4.

Directions: Write the factors of each pair of numbers. Then write the common factors and the GCF.

12: 1   2   3   6   12
15: 1   3   5   15

The common factors of 12 and 15 are 1 , 3 .
The GCF is 3 .

20: 1   2   4   5   10   20
10: 1   2   5   10

The common factors of 10 and 20 are 1 , 2 , 5 , 10 .
The GCF is 10 .

32: 1   2   4   8   16   32
24: 1   2   3   4   6   8   12   24

The common factors of 24 and 32 are 1 , 2 , 4 , 8 .
The GCF is 8 .

Directions: Write the GCF for the following pairs of numbers.

28 and 20 4   42 and 12 6
36 and 12 12   20 and 5 5

Page 384

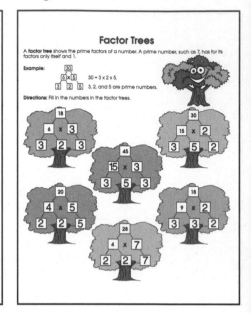

Factor Trees

A **factor tree** shows the prime factors of a number. A prime number, such as 7, has for its factors only itself and 1.

Example:

30 = 3 x 2 x 5.
3, 2, and 5 are prime numbers.

Directions: Fill in the numbers in the factor trees.

Page 385

Factor Trees

Directions: Fill in the numbers in the factor trees. The first one has been done for you.

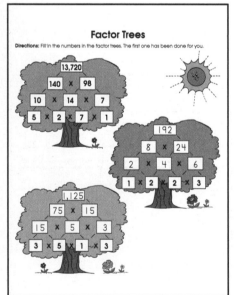

Page 386

Greatest Common Factor

Directions: Write the greatest common factor for each set of numbers.

10 and 35 5
2 and 10 2
42 and 63 21
16 and 40 8
25 and 55 5
12 and 20 4
14 and 28 14
8 and 20 4
6 and 27 3
15 and 35 5
18 and 48 6

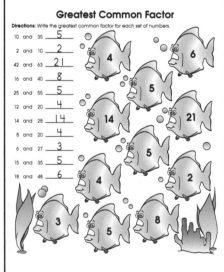

Page 387

Least Common Multiple

Directions: Write the least common multiple for each pair of numbers.

12 and 7 84
2 and 4 4
22 and 4 44
6 and 10 30
3 and 7 21
6 and 8 24
5 and 10 10
8 and 12 24
9 and 15 45
7 and 5 35
3 and 8 24
9 and 4 36

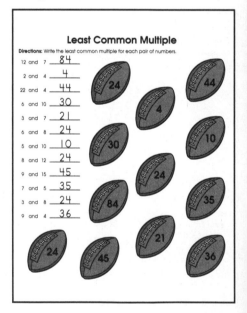

Page 388

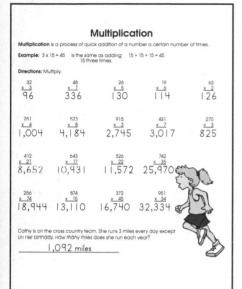

Multiplication

Multiplication is a process of quick addition of a number a certain number of times.

Example: 3 x 15 = 45 is the same as adding 15 + 15 + 15 = 45
15 three times.

Directions: Multiply.

32 x 3 = 96	48 x 7 = 336	26 x 5 = 130	19 x 6 = 114	63 x 2 = 126
251 x 4 = 1,004	523 x 8 = 4,184	915 x 3 = 2,745	431 x 7 = 3,017	275 x 3 = 825
412 x 21 = 8,652	643 x 17 = 10,931	526 x 22 = 11,572	742 x 35 = 25,970	
256 x 74 = 18,944	874 x 15 = 13,110	372 x 45 = 16,740	951 x 34 = 32,334	

Cathy is on the cross country team. She runs 3 miles every day except on her birthday. How many miles does she run each year?

1,092 miles

Page 389

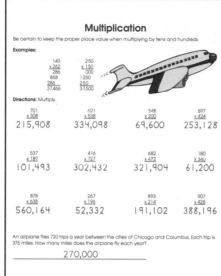

Multiplication

Be certain to keep the proper place value when multiplying by tens and hundreds.

Examples:

```
  143        250
x 262      x 150
  286        000
  858       1250
 286         250
37,466     37,500
```

Directions: Multiply.

701 x 308 = 215,908	621 x 538 = 334,098	348 x 200 = 69,600	507 x 424 = 253,128
537 x 189 = 101,493	416 x 727 = 302,432	682 x 472 = 321,904	180 x 340 = 61,200
878 x 638 = 560,164	267 x 196 = 52,332	893 x 214 = 191,102	907 x 428 = 388,196

An airplane flies 720 trips a year between the cities of Chicago and Columbus. Each trip is 375 miles. How many miles does the airplane fly each year?

270,000

Page 390

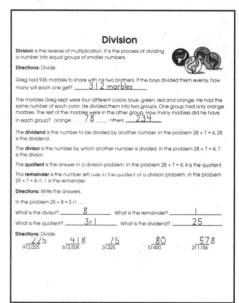

Division

Division is the reverse of multiplication. It is the process of dividing a number into equal groups of smaller numbers.

Directions: Divide.

Greg had 936 marbles to share with his two brothers. If the boys divided them evenly, how many will each one get? 312 marbles

The marbles Greg kept were four different colors: blue, green, red and orange. He had the same number of each color. He divided them into two groups. One group had only orange marbles. The rest of the marbles were in the other group. How many marbles did he have in each group? orange 78   others 234

The **dividend** is the number to be divided by another number. In the problem 28 ÷ 7 = 4, 28 is the dividend.

The **divisor** is the number by which another number is divided. In the problem 28 ÷ 7 = 4, 7 is the divisor.

The **quotient** is the answer in a division problem. In the problem 28 ÷ 7 = 4, 4 is the quotient.

The **remainder** is the number left over in the quotient of a division problem. In the problem 29 ÷ 7 = 4 r1, 1 is the remainder.

Directions: Write the answers.

In the problem 25 ÷ 8 = 3 r1 . . .

What is the divisor? 8   What is the remainder? 1

What is the quotient? 3 r1   What is the dividend? 25

Directions: Divide.

| 225 9⟌2,025 | 418 6⟌2,508 | 75 3⟌225 | 80 5⟌400 | 578 2⟌1,156 |

Page 391

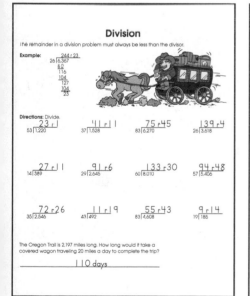

Division

The remainder in a division problem must always be less than the divisor.

Example:
```
      244 r 23
26⟌6,367
    52
    116
    104
    127
    104
     23
```

Directions: Divide.

23 r1 53⟌1,220	41 r11 37⟌1,528	75 r45 83⟌6,270	139 r4 26⟌3,618
27 r11 14⟌389	91 r6 29⟌2,645	133 r30 60⟌8,010	94 r48 57⟌5,406
72 r26 35⟌2,546	11 r19 43⟌492	55 r43 83⟌4,608	9 r14 19⟌185

The Oregon Trail is 2,197 miles long. How long would it take a covered wagon traveling 20 miles a day to complete the trip?

110 days

Page 392

Checking Division

Answers in division problems can be checked by multiplying.

Example:
```
      481 r 17
33⟌15,890      Check:    481
   132               x  33
   269               1443
   264              1443
    50              15,873
    33             +   17
    17              15,890
```
Add the remainder

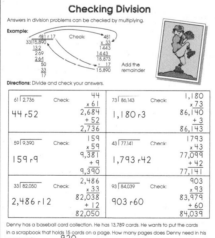

Directions: Divide and check your answers.

61⟌2,736 44 r52	Check: 44 x 61 = 2,684 + 52 = 2,736	73⟌86,143 1,180 r3	Check: 1,180 x 73 = 86,140 + 3 = 86,143
59⟌9,390 159 r9	Check: 159 x 59 = 9,381 + 9 = 9,390	43⟌77,141 1,793 r42	Check: 1793 x 43 = 77,099 + 42 = 77,141
33⟌82,050 2,486 r12	Check: 2,486 x 33 = 82,038 + 12 = 82,050	93⟌84,039 903 r60	Check: 903 x 93 = 83,979 + 60 = 84,039

Denny has a baseball card collection. He has 13,789 cards. He wants to put the cards in a scrapbook that holds 15 cards on a page. How many pages does Denny need in his scrapbook? 920

Page 393

Multiplication and Division

Directions: Multiply or divide to find the answers.

Brianne's summer job is mowing lawns for three of her neighbors. Each lawn takes about 1 hour to mow and needs to be done once every week. At the end of the summer, she will have earned a total of $630. She collected the same amount of money from each job. How much did each neighbor pay for her summer lawn service? $210

If the mowing season lasts for 14 weeks, how much will Brianne earn for each job each week? $15

If she had worked for two more weeks, how much would she have earned? $720

Brianne agreed to shovel snow from the driveways and sidewalks for the same three neighbors. They agreed to pay her the same rate. However, it only snowed seven times that winter. How much did she earn shoveling snow? $315

What was her total income for both jobs? $945

Directions: Multiply or divide.

| 623 12⟌7,476 | 940 23⟌21,620 | 815 40⟌32,600 |

32 x 45 = 1,440   28 x 15 = 420   73 x 14 = 1,022   92 x 30 = 2,760

Grade 5 - Comprehensive Curriculum

Page 394

Adding and Subtracting Like Fractions

A **fraction** is a number that names part of a whole. Examples of fractions are $\frac{1}{2}$ and $\frac{1}{4}$. **Like fractions** have the same **denominator**, or bottom number. Examples of like fractions are $\frac{1}{2}$ and $\frac{3}{2}$.

To add or subtract fractions, the denominators must be the same. Add or subtract only the **numerators**, the numbers above the line in fractions.

Example:

numerators
denominators
$\frac{5}{8} - \frac{1}{8} = \frac{4}{8}$

Directions: Add or subtract these fractions.

$\frac{6}{12} - \frac{3}{12} = \frac{3}{12}$	$\frac{4}{9} + \frac{1}{9} = \frac{5}{9}$	$\frac{1}{3} + \frac{1}{3} = \frac{2}{3}$	$\frac{5}{11} + \frac{4}{11} = \frac{9}{11}$
$\frac{3}{5} - \frac{1}{5} = \frac{2}{5}$	$\frac{5}{6} - \frac{2}{6} = \frac{3}{6}$	$\frac{3}{4} - \frac{2}{4} = \frac{1}{4}$	$\frac{5}{10} + \frac{3}{10} = \frac{8}{10}$
$\frac{3}{8} + \frac{2}{8} = \frac{5}{8}$	$\frac{1}{7} + \frac{4}{7} = \frac{5}{7}$	$\frac{2}{20} + \frac{15}{20} = \frac{17}{20}$	$\frac{11}{15} - \frac{9}{15} = \frac{2}{15}$

Directions: Color the part of each pizza that equals the given fraction.

$\frac{2}{4}$ + $\frac{1}{4}$ = $\frac{3}{4}$

Page 395

Adding and Subtracting Unlike Fractions

Unlike fractions have different denominators. Examples of unlike fractions are $\frac{1}{4}$ and $\frac{2}{5}$. To add or subtract fractions, the denominators must be the same.

Example:

Step 1: Make the denominators the same by finding the least common denominator. The LCD of a pair of fractions is the same as the least common multiple (LCM) of their denominators.

$\frac{1}{3} + \frac{1}{4} =$ Multiples of 3 are 3, 6, 9, **12**, 15.
Multiples of 4 are 4, 8, **12**, 16.
LCM (and LCD) = 12

Step 2: Multiply by a number that will give the LCD. The numerator and denominator must be multiplied by the same number.

A. $\frac{1}{3} \times \frac{4}{4} = \frac{4}{12}$ B. $\frac{1}{4} \times \frac{3}{3} = \frac{3}{12}$

Step 3: Add the fractions.

$\frac{1}{3} + \frac{1}{4} = \frac{4}{12} + \frac{3}{12} = \frac{7}{12}$

Directions: Follow the above steps to add or subtract unlike fractions. Write the LCM.

$\frac{2}{4} + \frac{3}{8} = \frac{7}{8}$ LCM __8__	$\frac{3}{6} + \frac{1}{3} = \frac{5}{6}$ LCM __6__	$\frac{5}{4} - \frac{1}{5} = \frac{11}{20}$ LCM __20__
$\frac{2}{3} + \frac{2}{9} = \frac{8}{9}$ LCM __9__	$\frac{4}{7} - \frac{2}{14} = \frac{6}{14}$ LCM __14__	$\frac{7}{12} - \frac{2}{4} = \frac{1}{12}$ LCM __12__

The basketball team ordered two pizzas. They left $\frac{1}{3}$ of one and $\frac{1}{4}$ of the other. How much pizza was left? $\frac{7}{12}$

Page 396

Reducing Fractions

A fraction is in lowest terms when the GCF of both the numerator and denominator is 1. These fractions are in lowest possible terms: $\frac{2}{3}$, $\frac{4}{5}$, and $\frac{99}{100}$.

Example: Write $\frac{4}{8}$ in lowest terms.

Step 1: Write the factors of 4 and 8.
Factors of 4 are **4**, 2, 1.
Factors of 8 are 1, 8, 2, **4**.
Step 2: Find the GCF: 4.
Step 3: Divide both the numerator and denominator by 4.

$\frac{4}{8} \div \frac{4}{4} = \frac{1}{2}$

Directions: Write each fraction in lowest terms.

$\frac{6}{8} = \frac{3}{4}$ lowest terms $\frac{9}{12} = \frac{3}{4}$ lowest terms

factors of 6: 6, 1, 2, 3   factors of 9: __1__ __3__ __9__   __3__ GCF

factors of 8: 8, 1, 2, 4   factors of 12: __1__ __2__ __3__ __4__ __6__ __12__ __4__ GCF

$\frac{2}{6} = \frac{1}{3}$	$\frac{10}{15} = \frac{2}{3}$	$\frac{8}{32} = \frac{1}{4}$	$\frac{4}{10} = \frac{2}{5}$
$\frac{12}{18} = \frac{2}{3}$	$\frac{6}{8} = \frac{3}{4}$	$\frac{4}{6} = \frac{2}{3}$	$\frac{3}{9} = \frac{1}{3}$

Directions: Color the pizzas to show that $\frac{4}{6}$ in lowest terms is $\frac{2}{3}$.

Page 397

Improper Fractions

An **improper fraction** has a numerator that is greater than its denominator. An example of an improper fraction is $\frac{7}{4}$. An improper fraction should be reduced to its lowest terms.

Example: $\frac{5}{4}$ is an improper fraction because its numerator is greater than its denominator.

Step 1: Divide the numerator by the denominator: $5 \div 4 = 1$, r1
Step 2: Write the remainder as a fraction: $\frac{1}{4}$

$\frac{5}{4} = 1\frac{1}{4}$ $1\frac{1}{4}$ is a mixed number—a whole number and a fraction.

Directions: Follow the steps above to change the improper fractions to mixed numbers.

$\frac{9}{8} = 1\frac{1}{8}$	$\frac{11}{5} = 2\frac{1}{5}$	$\frac{5}{3} = 1\frac{2}{3}$	$\frac{7}{6} = 1\frac{1}{6}$	$\frac{8}{7} = 1\frac{1}{7}$	$\frac{4}{3} = 1\frac{1}{3}$
$\frac{21}{4} = 4\frac{1}{5}$	$\frac{9}{4} = 2\frac{1}{4}$	$\frac{3}{2} = 1\frac{1}{2}$	$\frac{9}{6} = 1\frac{1}{2}$	$\frac{25}{4} = 6\frac{1}{4}$	$\frac{8}{3} = 2\frac{2}{3}$

Sara had 29 duplicate stamps in her stamp collection. She decided to give them to four of her friends. If she gave each of them the same number of stamps, how many duplicates will she have left? __1__

Name the improper fraction in this problem. $\frac{29}{4}$

What step must you do next to solve the problem? __change to a mixed number__

Write your answer as a mixed number. __$7\frac{1}{4}$__

How many stamps could she give each of her friends? __7__

Page 398

Mixed Numbers

A **mixed number** is a whole number and a fraction together. An example of a mixed number is $2\frac{3}{4}$. A mixed number can be changed to an improper fraction.

Example: $2\frac{3}{4}$

Step 1: Multiply the denominator by the whole number: $4 \times 2 = 8$
Step 2: Add the numerator: $8 + 3 = 11$
Step 3: Write the sum over the denominator: $\frac{11}{4}$

Mixed Numbers

Directions: Follow the steps above to change the mixed numbers to improper fractions.

$3\frac{2}{3} = \frac{11}{3}$	$6\frac{1}{5} = \frac{31}{5}$	$4\frac{7}{8} = \frac{39}{8}$	$2\frac{1}{2} = \frac{5}{2}$
$1\frac{4}{5} = \frac{9}{5}$	$5\frac{3}{4} = \frac{23}{4}$	$7\frac{1}{8} = \frac{57}{8}$	$9\frac{1}{9} = \frac{82}{9}$
$8\frac{1}{2} = \frac{17}{2}$	$7\frac{1}{6} = \frac{43}{6}$	$5\frac{3}{5} = \frac{28}{5}$	$9\frac{3}{8} = \frac{75}{8}$
$12\frac{1}{5} = \frac{61}{5}$	$25\frac{1}{2} = \frac{51}{2}$	$10\frac{2}{3} = \frac{32}{3}$	$14\frac{3}{8} = \frac{115}{8}$

Page 399

Adding Mixed Numbers

To add mixed numbers, first find the least common denominator.

Always reduce the answer to lowest terms.

Example:

$5\frac{1}{4} \longrightarrow 5\frac{3}{12}$
$+ 6\frac{1}{3} \longrightarrow + 6\frac{4}{12}$
$11\frac{7}{12}$

Directions: Add. Reduce the answers to lowest terms.

$8\frac{1}{2}$ $+ 7\frac{1}{4}$ $15\frac{3}{4}$	$5\frac{1}{4}$ $+ 2\frac{3}{8}$ $7\frac{5}{8}$	$9\frac{3}{10}$ $+ 7\frac{1}{5}$ $16\frac{1}{2}$	$8\frac{1}{3}$ $+ 6\frac{7}{10}$ $14\frac{9}{10}$
$4\frac{4}{5}$ $+ 3\frac{3}{10}$ $8\frac{1}{10}$	$3\frac{1}{2}$ $+ 7\frac{1}{4}$ $10\frac{3}{4}$	$4\frac{1}{2}$ $+ 1\frac{1}{3}$ $5\frac{5}{6}$	$6\frac{1}{2}$ $+ 3\frac{1}{3}$ $9\frac{5}{6}$
$5\frac{1}{3}$ $+ 2\frac{1}{3}$ $7\frac{2}{3}$	$6\frac{1}{3}$ $+ 2\frac{2}{5}$ $8\frac{11}{15}$	$2\frac{2}{7}$ $+ 4\frac{1}{14}$ $6\frac{5}{14}$	$3\frac{1}{2}$ $+ 3\frac{1}{4}$ $6\frac{3}{4}$

The boys picked $3\frac{1}{2}$ baskets of apples. The girls picked $5\frac{1}{2}$ baskets. How many baskets of apples did the boys and girls pick in all? __9__

Page 400

Subtracting Mixed Numbers

To subtract mixed numbers, first find the least common denominator. Reduce the answer to its lowest terms.

Directions: Subtract. Reduce to lowest terms.

Example:

$$6\frac{5}{8} \rightarrow 6\frac{10}{16}$$
$$-3\frac{4}{16} \rightarrow -3\frac{4}{16}$$
$$3\frac{6}{16} = 3\frac{3}{8}$$

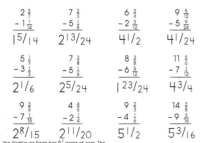

$2\frac{3}{7}$ $-1\frac{1}{14}$ $1\frac{5}{14}$	$7\frac{2}{3}$ $-5\frac{1}{8}$ $2\frac{13}{24}$	$6\frac{3}{4}$ $-2\frac{3}{12}$ $4\frac{1}{2}$	$9\frac{5}{12}$ $-5\frac{9}{24}$ $4\frac{1}{24}$
$5\frac{1}{2}$ $-3\frac{1}{3}$ $2\frac{1}{6}$	$7\frac{3}{8}$ $-5\frac{1}{6}$ $2\frac{5}{24}$	$8\frac{1}{3}$ $-6\frac{5}{12}$ $1\frac{23}{24}$	$11\frac{5}{6}$ $-7\frac{1}{12}$ $4\frac{3}{4}$
$9\frac{3}{5}$ $-7\frac{1}{15}$ $2\frac{8}{15}$	$4\frac{4}{5}$ $-2\frac{1}{4}$ $2\frac{11}{20}$	$9\frac{2}{3}$ $-4\frac{1}{6}$ $5\frac{1}{2}$	$14\frac{3}{8}$ $-9\frac{3}{16}$ $5\frac{3}{16}$

The Rodriguez Farm has $9\frac{1}{2}$ acres of corn. The Johnson Farm has $7\frac{1}{3}$ acres of corn. How many more acres of corn does the Rodriguez Farm have? __$2\frac{1}{6}$__

Page 401

Comparing Fractions

Directions: Use the symbol > (greater than), < (less than) or = (equal to) to show the relationship between each pair of fractions.

$\frac{1}{2}$ __>__ $\frac{1}{3}$ $\frac{2}{5}$ __<__ $\frac{3}{7}$ $\frac{3}{8}$ __<__ $\frac{2}{4}$

$\frac{3}{4}$ __=__ $\frac{6}{8}$ $\frac{2}{5}$ __<__ $\frac{4}{5}$ $\frac{3}{9}$ __=__ $\frac{1}{3}$

$\frac{3}{12}$ __=__ $\frac{1}{4}$ $\frac{2}{14}$ __=__ $\frac{1}{7}$ $\frac{5}{15}$ __<__ $\frac{2}{3}$

If Kelly gave $\frac{1}{3}$ of a pizza to Holly and $\frac{1}{5}$ to Diane, how much did she have left? __$7/15$__

Holly decided to share $\frac{1}{2}$ of her share of the pizza with Deb. How much did each of them actually get? __$1/6$__

Page 402

Ordering Fractions

When putting fractions in order from smallest to largest or largest to smallest, it helps to find a common denominator first.

Example:

$\frac{1}{3}$, $\frac{1}{2}$ changed to $\frac{2}{6}$, $\frac{3}{6}$

Directions: Put the following fractions in order from least to largest value.

				Least			Largest
$\frac{1}{2}$	$\frac{2}{7}$	$\frac{4}{5}$	$\frac{1}{3}$	$2/7$	$1/3$	$1/2$	$4/5$
$\frac{3}{12}$	$\frac{3}{6}$	$\frac{1}{3}$	$\frac{3}{4}$	$3/12$	$1/3$	$3/6$	$3/4$
$\frac{2}{5}$	$\frac{4}{15}$	$\frac{3}{5}$	$\frac{5}{15}$	$4/15$	$5/15$	$2/5$	$3/5$
$3\frac{4}{5}$	$3\frac{2}{5}$	$3\frac{2}{5}$	$3\frac{1}{5}$	$9/5$	$3\,1/5$	$3\,2/5$	$3\,4/5$
$9\frac{1}{3}$	$9\frac{2}{3}$	$9\frac{9}{12}$	$8\frac{2}{3}$	$8\,2/3$	$9\,1/3$	$9\,2/3$	$9\,9/12$
$5\frac{8}{12}$	$5\frac{5}{12}$	$5\frac{4}{24}$	$5\frac{3}{6}$	$5\,4/24$	$5\,5/12$	$5\,3/6$	$5\,8/12$
$4\frac{3}{5}$	$5\frac{7}{15}$	$6\frac{2}{5}$	$5\frac{1}{5}$	$4\,3/5$	$5\,1/5$	$5\,7/15$	$6\,2/5$

Four dogs were selected as finalists at a dog show. They were judged in four separate categories. One received a perfect score in each area. The dog with a score closest to four is the winner. Their scores are listed below. Which dog won the contest? __Dog A__

Dog A $\left(3\frac{4}{5}\right)$ Dog B $3\frac{2}{3}$ Dog C $3\frac{5}{12}$ Dog D $3\frac{9}{12}$

Page 403

Multiplying Fractions

To multiply fractions, follow these steps:

$\frac{1}{2} \times \frac{3}{4} =$ **Step 1:** Multiply the numerators. $1 \times 3 = 3$
           Step 2: Multiply the denominators. $2 \times 4 = 8$

When multiplying a fraction by a whole number, first change the whole number to a fraction.

Example:

$\frac{1}{2} \times 8 = \frac{1}{2} \times \frac{8}{1} = \frac{8}{2} = 4$ reduced to lowest terms

Directions: Multiply. Reduce your answers to lowest terms.

$\frac{3}{4} \times \frac{1}{6} = \frac{1}{8}$	$\frac{1}{2} \times \frac{5}{8} = \frac{5}{16}$	$\frac{2}{3} \times \frac{1}{6} = \frac{1}{9}$	$\frac{2}{3} \times \frac{1}{2} = \frac{1}{3}$
$\frac{5}{6} \times 4 = 3\frac{1}{3}$	$\frac{3}{8} \times \frac{1}{16} = \frac{3}{128}$	$\frac{1}{5} \times 5 = 1$	$\frac{7}{8} \times \frac{3}{4} = \frac{21}{32}$
$\frac{7}{11} \times \frac{1}{3} = \frac{7}{33}$	$\frac{2}{3} \times \frac{9}{4} = \frac{1}{2}$	$\frac{1}{3} \times \frac{1}{3} \times \frac{1}{3} = \frac{1}{27}$	$\frac{1}{4} \times \frac{1}{4} \times \frac{1}{2} = \frac{1}{64}$

Jennifer has 10 pets. Two-fifths of the pets are cats, one-half are fish and one-tenth are dogs. How many of each pet does she have?

Cats = 4
Fish = 5
Dogs = 1

Page 404

Multiplying Mixed Numbers

Multiply mixed numbers by first changing them to improper fractions. Always reduce your answers to lowest terms.

Example:

$2\frac{1}{3} \times 1\frac{1}{8} = \frac{7}{3} \times \frac{9}{8} = \frac{60}{24} = 2\frac{12}{24} = 2\frac{5}{8}$

Directions: Multiply. Reduce to lowest terms.

$4\frac{1}{4} \times 2\frac{1}{5} = 9\frac{7}{20}$	$1\frac{1}{3} \times 3\frac{1}{4} = 4\frac{1}{3}$	$1\frac{1}{9} \times 3\frac{3}{5} = 4$
$1\frac{6}{7} \times 4\frac{1}{2} = 8\frac{5}{14}$	$2\frac{3}{4} \times 2\frac{3}{5} = 7\frac{3}{20}$	$4\frac{2}{3} \times 3\frac{1}{7} = 14\frac{2}{3}$
$6\frac{2}{5} \times 2\frac{1}{8} = 13\frac{3}{5}$	$3\frac{1}{7} \times 4\frac{5}{8} = 14\frac{15}{28}$	$7\frac{3}{8} \times 2\frac{1}{9} = 15\frac{41}{72}$

Sunnyside Farm has two barns with 25 stalls in each barn. Cows use $\frac{3}{5}$ of the stalls, and horses use the rest.

How many stalls are for cows? __30__

How many are for horses? __20__

(Hint: First, find how many total stalls are in the two barns.)

Page 405

Dividing Fractions

To divide fractions, follow these steps:

$\frac{3}{4} \div \frac{1}{4} =$

Step 1: "Invert" the divisor. That means to turn it upside down.

$\frac{3}{4} \div \frac{4}{1} =$

Step 2: Multiply the two fractions:

$\frac{3}{4} \times \frac{4}{1} = \frac{12}{4}$

Step 3: Reduce the fraction to lowest terms by dividing the denominator into the numerator.

$12 \div 4 = 3$
$\frac{3}{4} \div \frac{1}{4} = 3$

Directions: Follow the above steps to divide fractions.

$\frac{1}{4} \div \frac{1}{5} = 1\frac{1}{4}$	$\frac{1}{3} \div \frac{1}{12} = 4$	$\frac{3}{4} \div \frac{1}{3} = 2\frac{1}{4}$
$\frac{5}{12} \div \frac{1}{3} = 1\frac{1}{4}$	$\frac{3}{4} \div \frac{1}{6} = 4\frac{1}{2}$	$\frac{2}{9} \div \frac{2}{3} = \frac{1}{3}$
$\frac{3}{7} \div \frac{1}{4} = 1\frac{5}{7}$	$\frac{3}{2} \div \frac{4}{1} = 1$	$\frac{1}{4} \div \frac{1}{3} = \frac{3}{16}$
$\frac{4}{5} \div \frac{1}{3} = 2\frac{2}{5}$	$\frac{3}{4} \div \frac{1}{2} = 1$	$\frac{5}{12} \div \frac{6}{8} = \frac{5}{9}$

Grade 5 - Comprehensive Curriculum

Page 406

Dividing Whole Numbers by Fractions

Follow these steps to divide a whole number by a fraction:

$8 \div \frac{1}{4} =$

Step 1: Write the whole number as a fraction:

$\frac{8}{1} \div \frac{1}{4} =$

Step 2: Invert the divisor.

$\frac{8}{1} \div \frac{4}{1} =$

Step 3: Multiply the two fractions:

$\frac{8}{1} \times \frac{4}{1} = \frac{32}{1}$

Step 4: Reduce the fraction to lowest terms by dividing the denominator into the numerator: $32 \div 1 = 32$

Directions: Follow the above steps to divide a whole number by a fraction.

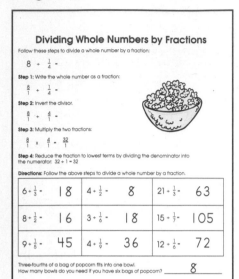

$6 \div \frac{1}{3} =$ **18**	$4 \div \frac{1}{2} =$ **8**	$21 \div \frac{1}{3} =$ **63**
$8 \div \frac{1}{2} =$ **16**	$3 \div \frac{1}{6} =$ **18**	$15 \div \frac{1}{7} =$ **105**
$9 \div \frac{1}{5} =$ **45**	$4 \div \frac{1}{9} =$ **36**	$12 \div \frac{1}{6} =$ **72**

Three-fourths of a bag of popcorn fits into one bowl.
How many bowls do you need if you have six bags of popcorn? **8**

Page 407

Decimals

A **decimal** is a number with one or more places to the right of a decimal point.

Examples: 6.5 and 2.25

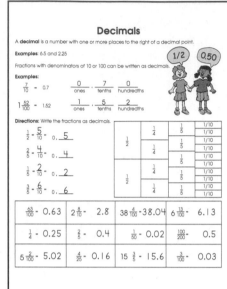

Fractions with denominators of 10 or 100 can be written as decimals.

Examples:

$\frac{7}{10} = 0.7$ | 0 . 7 0
ones . tenths . hundredths

$1\frac{52}{100} = 1.52$ | 1 . 5 2
ones . tenths . hundredths

Directions: Write the fractions as decimals.

$\frac{1}{2} = \frac{5}{10} = 0.\underline{5}$

$\frac{2}{5} = \frac{4}{10} = 0.\underline{4}$

$\frac{1}{5} = \frac{2}{10} = 0.\underline{2}$

$\frac{3}{5} = \frac{6}{10} = 0.\underline{6}$

	$\frac{1}{4}$	$\frac{1}{10}$ 1/10
$\frac{1}{2}$	$\frac{1}{4}$	$\frac{1}{5}$ 1/10
	$\frac{1}{4}$	$\frac{1}{5}$ 1/10
$\frac{1}{2}$	$\frac{1}{4}$	$\frac{1}{5}$ 1/10
	$\frac{1}{4}$	$\frac{1}{5}$ 1/10

$\frac{63}{100} =$ 0.63	$2\frac{8}{10} =$ 2.8	$38\frac{4}{100} =$ 38.04	$6\frac{13}{100} =$ 6.13
$\frac{1}{4} =$ 0.25	$\frac{2}{5} =$ 0.4	$\frac{1}{50} =$ 0.02	$\frac{100}{200} =$ 0.5
$5\frac{2}{100} =$ 5.02	$\frac{4}{25} =$ 0.16	$15\frac{3}{5} =$ 15.6	$\frac{3}{100} =$ 0.03

Page 408

Decimals and Fractions

Directions: Write the letter of the fraction that is equal to the decimal.

0.25 = **G**
0.5 = **L**
0.7 = **O**
0.8 = **N**
0.37 = **J**
0.2 = **K**
0.65 = **C**
0.75 = **B**
0.6 = **D**
0.12 = **E**
0.33 = **A**
0.95 = **F**
0.24 = **M**
0.3 = **I**
0.4 = **H**

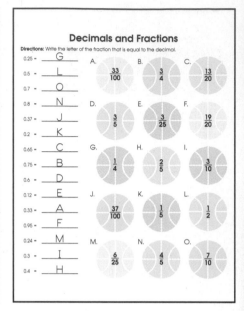

A. $\frac{33}{100}$ B. $\frac{3}{4}$ C. $\frac{13}{20}$

D. $\frac{3}{5}$ E. $\frac{3}{25}$ F. $\frac{19}{20}$

G. $\frac{1}{4}$ H. $\frac{2}{5}$ I. $\frac{3}{10}$

J. $\frac{37}{100}$ K. $\frac{1}{5}$ L. $\frac{1}{2}$

M. $\frac{6}{25}$ N. $\frac{4}{5}$ O. $\frac{7}{10}$

Page 409

Adding and Subtracting Decimals

Add and subtract with decimals the same way you do with whole numbers. Keep the decimal points lined up so that you work with hundredths, then tenths, then ones, and so on.

Directions: Add or subtract. Remember to keep the decimal point in the proper place.

0.5 +0.8 **1.3**	0.35 +0.25 **0.60**	47.5 -32.7 **14.8**	85.7 -9.8 **75.9**
13.90 +4.23 **18.13**	9.53 -8.16 **1.37**	72.8 -63.9 **8.9**	6.43 +4.58 **11.01**
638.07 -19.34 **618.73**	811.060 +78.430 **889.490**	521.09 -148.75 **372.34**	
916.635 +172.136 **1,088.771**	287.768 -63.951 **223.817**	467.05 -398.19 **68.86**	

Sean ran a 1-mile race in 5.58 minutes. Carlos ran it in 6.38 minutes. How much less time did Sean need?

0.8 minutes

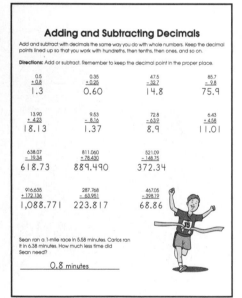

Page 410

Multiplying Decimals

Multiply with decimals the same way you do with whole numbers. The decimal point moves in multiplication. Count the number of decimal places in the problem and use the same number of decimal places in your answer.

Example:

3.5
x 1.5
175
35
5.25

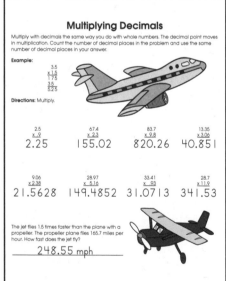

Directions: Multiply.

2.5 x.9 **2.25**	67.4 x 2.3 **155.02**	83.7 x 9.8 **820.26**	13.35 x 3.05 **40.851**
9.06 x 2.38 **21.5628**	28.97 x 5.16 **149.4852**	33.41 x .93 **31.0713**	28.7 x 11.9 **341.53**

The jet flies 1.5 times faster than the plane with a propeller. The propeller plane flies 165.7 miles per hour. How fast does the jet fly?

248.55 mph

Page 411

Dividing With Decimals

When the dividend has a decimal, place the decimal point for the answer directly above the decimal point in the dividend. The first one has been done for you.

$3\overline{)37.5}$ **12.5**
-3
07
-6
15
-15

8.6 $4\overline{)34.4}$	**15.8** $2\overline{)31.6}$	**43.8** $3\overline{)131.4}$	
37.5 $5\overline{)187.5}$	**25.9** $7\overline{)181.3}$	**56.8** $6\overline{)340.8}$	**32.7** $9\overline{)294.3}$
45.2 $3\overline{)135.6}$	**52.9** $5\overline{)264.5}$	**67.3** $2\overline{)134.6}$	**94.3** $8\overline{)754.4}$
7.05 $5\overline{)35.25}$	**11.35** $7\overline{)79.45}$	**3.19** $9\overline{)28.71}$	**5.54** $36\overline{)199.44}$

Page 412

Dividing Decimals by Decimals

When the divisor has a decimal point you must eliminate it before dividing. You can do this by moving the decimal point to the right to create a whole number. You must also move the decimal point the same number of spaces to the right in the dividend.

Sometimes you need to add zeros to do this.

Example:

$0.25\overline{)85.50}$ changes to $25\overline{)8550}$

$$\begin{array}{r} 342 \\ 25\overline{)8550} \\ -75 \\ \hline 105 \\ -100 \\ \hline 50 \\ -50 \\ \hline 0 \end{array}$$

Directions: Divide.

$0.3\overline{)27.9} = 93$

$0.6\overline{)42.6} = 71$

$0.9\overline{)81.9} = 91$

$0.7\overline{)83.3} = 119$

$0.4\overline{)23.2} = 58$

$0.7\overline{)56.7} = 81$

$1.2\overline{)10.8} = 9$

$2.2\overline{)138.6} = 63$

$12.6\overline{)5,670} = 450$

$4.7\overline{)564} = 120$

$8.6\overline{)842.8} = 98$

$3.7\overline{)2,009.1} = 543$

$5.9\overline{)1,917.5} = 325$

$4.3\overline{)1,376} = 320$

$2.9\overline{)922.2} = 318$

$2.7\overline{)5613.3} = 2079$

Page 413

Geometry

Geometry is the branch of mathematics that has to do with points, lines and shapes.

Directions: Use the Glossary on pages 446–455 if you need help. Write the word from the box that is described below.

| triangle | square | cube | angle |
| line | ray | segment | rectangle |

a collection of points on a straight path that goes on and on in opposite directions — **line**

a figure with three sides and three corners — **triangle**

a figure with four equal sides and four corners — **square**

part of a line that has one end point and goes on and on in one direction — **ray**

part of a line having two end points — **segment**

a space figure with six square faces — **cube**

two rays with a common end point — **angle**

a figure with four corners and four sides — **rectangle**

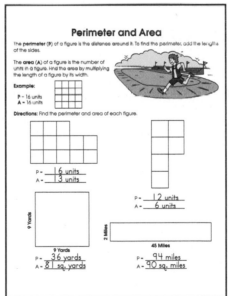

Page 414

Geometry

Review the definitions on the previous page before completing the problems below.

Directions: Identify the labeled section of each of the following diagrams.

AB = **segment**

ABC = **angle**

AB = **segment**

CD = **line**

AC = **ray**

AB = **segment**

EBC = **angle**

BC = **ray**

Page 415

Similar, Congruent and Symmetrical Figures

Similar figures have the same shape but have varying sizes.

Figures that are **congruent** have identical shapes but different orientations. That means they face in different directions.

Symmetrical figures can be divided equally into two identical parts.

Directions: Cross out the shape that does not belong in each group. Label the two remaining shapes as similar, congruent or symmetrical.

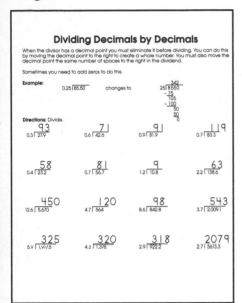

congruent ___ congruent

congruent congruent ___

similar similar ___

symmetrical ___ symmetrical

Page 416

Perimeter and Area

The **perimeter (P)** of a figure is the distance around it. To find the perimeter, add the lengths of the sides.

The **area (A)** of a figure is the number of units in a figure. Find the area by multiplying the length of a figure by its width.

Example:

P = 16 units
A = 16 units

Directions: Find the perimeter and area of each figure.

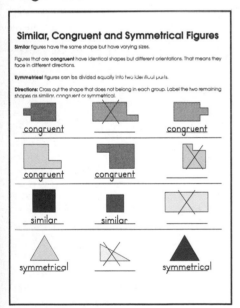

P = 16 units
A = 13 units

P = 12 units
A = 6 units

P = 36 yards
A = 81 sq. yards

P = 94 miles
A = 90 sq. miles

Page 417

Volume

The formula for finding the volume of a box is length times width times height (**L x W x H**). The answer is given in cubic units.

Directions: Solve the problems.

Example:
Height 8 ft.
Length 8 ft.
Width 8 ft. L x W x H = volume
8' x 8' x 8' = 512 cubic ft. or 512 ft.³

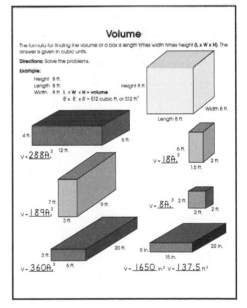

V = 288 ft.³

V = 18 ft.³

V = 189 ft.³

V = 8 ft.³

V = 360 ft.³

V = 1650 in.³

V = 137.5 ft.³

Page 418

Perimeter and Area

Directions: Use the formulas for finding perimeter and area to solve these problems.

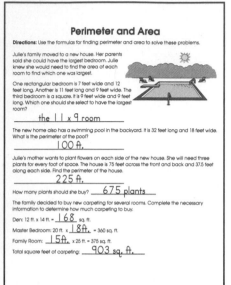

Julie's family moved to a new house. Her parents said she could have the largest bedroom. Julie knew she would need to find the area of each room to find which one was largest.

One rectangular bedroom is 7 feet wide and 12 feet long. Another is 11 feet long and 9 feet wide. The third bedroom is a square. It is 9 feet wide and 9 feet long. Which one should she select to have the largest room?

the 11 x 9 room

The new home also has a swimming pool in the backyard. It is 32 feet long and 18 feet wide. What is the perimeter of the pool?

100 ft.

Julie's mother wants to plant flowers on each side of the new house. She will need three plants for every foot of space. The house is 75 feet across the front and back and 37.5 feet along each side. Find the perimeter of the house.

225 ft.

How many plants should she buy? 675 plants

The family decided to buy new carpeting for several rooms. Complete the necessary information to determine how much carpeting to buy.

Den: 12 ft. x 14 ft. = 168 sq. ft.

Master Bedroom: 20 ft. x 18ft. = 360 sq. ft.

Family Room: 15ft. x 25 ft. = 375 sq. ft.

Total square feet of carpeting: 903 sq. ft.

Page 419

Perimeter, Area and Volume

Directions: Find the perimeter and area.

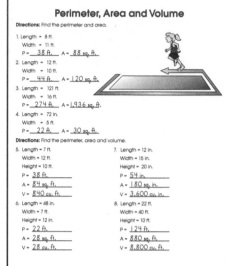

1. Length = 8 ft.
   Width = 11 ft.
   P = 38 ft.   A = 88 sq. ft.
2. Length = 12 ft.
   Width = 10 ft.
   P = 44 ft.   A = 120 sq. ft.
3. Length = 121 ft.
   Width = 16 ft.
   P = 274 ft.   A = 1,936 sq. ft.
4. Length = 72 ft.
   Width = 5 ft.
   P = 22 ft.   A = 30 sq. ft.

Directions: Find the perimeter, area and volume.

5. Length = 7 ft.
   Width = 12 ft.
   Height = 12 ft.
   P = 38 ft.
   A = 84 sq. ft.
   V = 840 cu. ft.

6. Length = 48 in.
   Width = 40 in.
   Height = 12 in.
   P = 22 ft.
   A = 28 sq. ft.
   V = 28 cu. ft.

7. Length = 12 in.
   Width = 15 in.
   Height = 20 in.
   P = 54 in.
   A = 180 sq. in.
   V = 3,600 cu. in.

8. Length = 22 ft.
   Width = 40 ft.
   Height = 10 ft.
   P = 124 ft.
   A = 880 sq. ft.
   V = 8,800 cu. ft.

Page 420

Circumference

Circumference is the distance around a circle. The **diameter** is a line segment that passes through the center of a circle and has both end points on the circle.

To find the circumference of any circle, multiply 3.14 times the diameter. The number 3.14 represents **pi** (pronounced *pie*) and is often written by this Greek symbol, π.

The formula for circumference is C = π × d

C = circumference
d = diameter
π = 3.14

Example:

Circle A
d = 2 in.
C = 3.14 x 2 in.
C = 6.28 in.

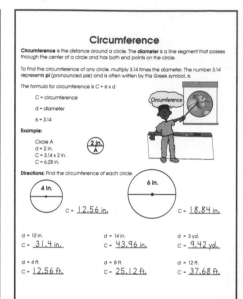

Directions: Find the circumference of each circle.

4 in.   C = 12.56 in.

6 in.   C = 18.84 in.

d = 10 in.   d = 14 in.   d = 3 yd.
C = 31.4 in.   C = 43.96 in.   C = 9.42 yd.

d = 4 ft.   d = 8 in.   d = 12 ft.
C = 12.56 ft.   C = 25.12 ft.   C = 37.68 ft.

Page 421

Circumference

The **radius** of a circle is the distance from the center of the circle to its outside edge. The diameter equals two times the radius.

Find the circumference by multiplying π (3.14) times the diameter or by multiplying π (3.14) times 2r (2 times the radius).

C = π × d or C = π × 2r

Directions: Write the missing radius, diameter or circumference.

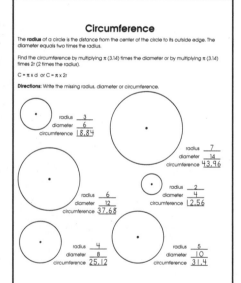

radius 3
diameter 6
circumference 18.84

radius 7
diameter 14
circumference 43.96

radius 6
diameter 12
circumference 37.68

radius 2
diameter 4
circumference 12.56

radius 4
diameter 8
circumference 25.12

radius 5
diameter 10
circumference 31.4

Page 422

Diameter, Radius and Circumference

C = π × d or C = π × 2r

Directions: Write the missing radius, diameter or circumference.

Katie was asked to draw a circle on the playground for a game during recess. If the radius of the circle needed to be 14 inches, how long is the diameter? 28 in.

What is the circumference? 87.92 in.

A friend told her that more kids could play the game if they enlarged the circle. She had a friend help her. They made the diameter of the circle 45 inches long.

What is the radius? 22.5 in.

What is the circumference? 141.3 in.

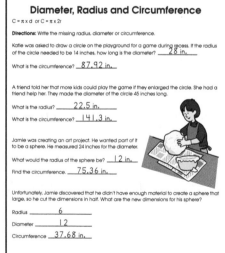

Jamie was creating an art project. He wanted part of it to be a sphere. He measured 24 inches for the diameter.

What would the radius of the sphere be? 12 in.

Find the circumference. 75.36 in.

Unfortunately, Jamie discovered that he didn't have enough material to create a sphere that large, so he cut the dimensions in half. What are the new dimensions for his sphere?

Radius 6

Diameter 12

Circumference 37.68 in.

Page 423

Triangle Angles

A **triangle** is a figure with three corners and three sides. Every triangle contains three angles. The sum of the angles is always 180°, regardless of the size or shape of the triangle.

If you know two of the angles, you can add them together, then subtract the total from 180 to find the number of degrees in the third angle.

Directions: Find the number of degrees in the third angle of each triangle.

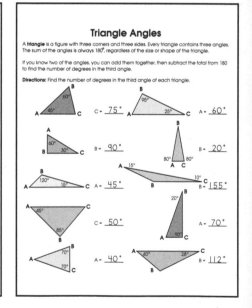

C = 75°   A = 60°

B = 90°   B = 20°

A = 45°   B = 155°

C = 50°   A = 70°

A = 40°   B = 112°

Page 424

Area of a Triangle

The area of a triangle is found by multiplying $\frac{1}{2}$ times the base times the height.
$A = \frac{1}{2} \times b \times h$

Example:

$\overline{CD}$ is the height.   4 in.
$\overline{AB}$ is the base.   8 in.
Area $= \frac{1}{2} \times 4 \times 8 = \frac{32}{2} = 16$ sq. in.

Directions: Find the area of each triangle.

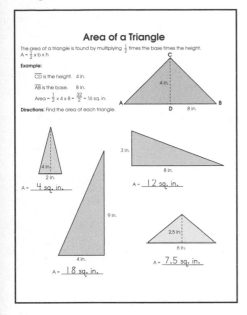

A = __4 sq. in.__

A = __12 sq. in.__

A = __18 sq. in.__

A = __7.5 sq. in.__

Page 425

Space Figures

Space figures are figures whose points are in more than one plane. Cubes and cylinders are space figures.

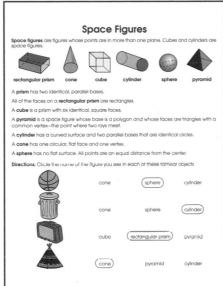

rectangular prism   cone   cube   cylinder   sphere   pyramid

A **prism** has two identical, parallel bases.
All of the faces on a **rectangular prism** are rectangles.
A **cube** is a prism with six identical, square faces.
A **pyramid** is a space figure whose base is a polygon and whose faces are triangles with a common vertex—the point where two rays meet.
A **cylinder** has a curved surface and two parallel bases that are identical circles.
A **cone** has one circular, flat face and one vertex.
A **sphere** has no flat surface. All points are an equal distance from the center.

Directions: Circle the name of the figure you see in each of these familiar objects

cone   (sphere)   cylinder

cone   sphere   (cylinder)

cube   (rectangular prism)   pyramid

(cone)   pyramid   cylinder

Page 426

Length

Inches, feet, yards and **miles** are used to measure length in the United States.

12 inches = 1 foot (ft.)
3 feet = 1 yard (yd.)
36 inches = 1 yard
1,760 yards = 1 mile (mi.)

Directions: Circle the best unit to measure each object. The first one has been done for you.

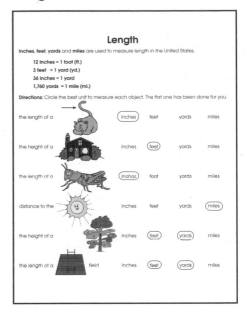

the length of a ➝   (inches)   feet   yards   miles

the height of a   inches   (feet)   yards   miles

the length of a   (inches)   feet   yards   miles

distance to the   inches   feet   yards   (miles)

the height of a   inches   (feet)   (yards)   miles

the length of a   field   inches   (feet)   (yards)   miles

Page 427

Length

Directions: Use a ruler to find the shortest paths. Round your measurement to the nearest quarter inch. Then convert to yards using the scale.

Scale: 1 inch = 100 yards

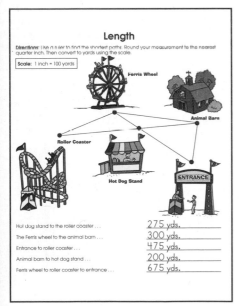

Hot dog stand to the roller coaster . . .   __275 yds.__
The Ferris wheel to the animal barn . . .   __300 yds.__
Entrance to roller coaster . . .   __475 yds.__
Animal barn to hot dog stand . . .   __200 yds.__
Ferris wheel to roller coaster to entrance . . .   __675 yds.__

Page 428

Length: Metric

Millimeters, centimeters, meters and **kilometers** are used to measure length in the metric system.

1 meter = 39.37 inches
1 kilometer = about $\frac{6}{8}$ mile
10 millimeters = 1 centimeter (cm)
100 centimeters = 1 meter (m)
1,000 meters = 1 kilometer (km)

Directions: Circle the best unit to measure each object. The first one has been done for you.

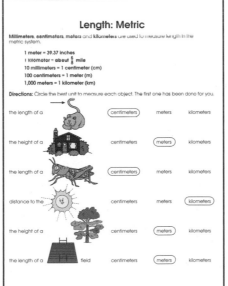

the length of a ➝   (centimeters)   meters   kilometers

the height of a   centimeters   (meters)   kilometers

the length of a   (centimeters)   meters   kilometers

distance to the   centimeters   meters   (kilometers)

the height of a   centimeters   (meters)   kilometers

the length of a   field   centimeters   (meters)   kilometers

Page 429

Weight

Ounces, pounds and **tons** are used to measure weight in the United States.

16 ounces = 1 pound (lb.)
2,000 pounds = 1 ton (tn.)

Directions: Circle the most reasonable estimate for the weight of each object. The first one has been done for you.

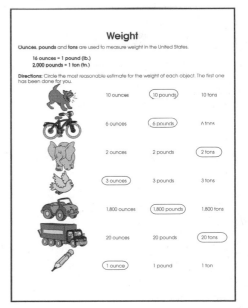

10 ounces   (10 pounds)   10 tons

6 ounces   (6 pounds)   6 tons

2 ounces   2 pounds   (2 tons)

(3 ounces)   3 pounds   3 tons

1,800 ounces   (1,800 pounds)   1,800 tons

20 ounces   20 pounds   (20 tons)

(1 ounce)   1 pound   1 ton

Page 430

Weight: Metric

Grams and **kilograms** are units of weight in the metric system. A paper clip weighs about 1 gram. A kitten weighs about 1 kilogram.

1 kilogram (kg) = about 2.2 pounds
1,000 grams (g) = 1 kilogram

Directions: Circle the best unit to weigh each object.

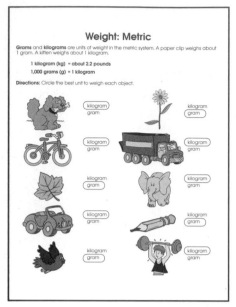

Page 431

Capacity

The **fluid ounce, cup, pint, quart** and **gallon** are used to measure capacity in the United States.

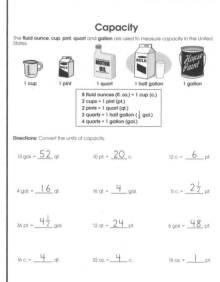

1 cup   1 pint   1 quart   1 half gallon   1 gallon

8 fluid ounces (fl. oz.) = 1 cup (c.)
2 cups = 1 pint (pt.)
2 pints = 1 quart (qt.)
2 quarts = 1 half gallon ($\frac{1}{2}$ gal.)
4 quarts = 1 gallon (gal.)

Directions: Convert the units of capacity.

13 gal. = 52 qt.   10 pt. = 20 c.   12 c. = 6 pt.

4 gal. = 16 qt.   16 qt. = 4 gal.   5 c. = $2\frac{1}{2}$ pt.

36 pt. = $4\frac{1}{2}$ gal.   12 qt. = 24 pt.   6 gal. = 48 pt.

16 c. = 4 qt.   32 oz. = 4 c.   16 oz. = 1 pt.

Page 432

Capacity: Metric

Milliliters and liters are units of capacity in the metric system. A can of soda contains about 350 milliliters of liquid. A large plastic bottle contains 1 liter of liquid. A liter is about a quart.

1,000 milliliters (mL) = 1 liter (L)

Directions: Circle the best unit to measure each liquid.

Page 433

Comparing Measurements

Directions: Use the symbols greater than (>), less than (<) or equal to (=) to complete each statement.

10 inches	>	10 centimeters
40 feet	<	120 yards
25 grams	<	25 kilograms
16 quarts	=	4 gallons
2 liters	>	2 milliliters
16 yards	>	6 meters
3 miles	>	3 kilometers
20 centimeters	<	20 meters
85 kilograms	>	8 grams
2 liters	<	1 gallon

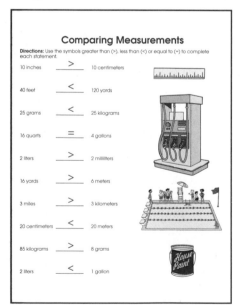

Page 434

Temperature: Fahrenheit

Degrees Fahrenheit (°F) is a unit for measuring temperature.

Directions: Write the temperature in degrees Fahrenheit (°F).
Example:

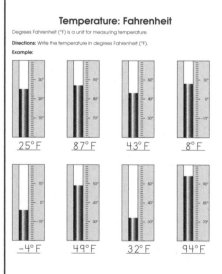

25°F   87°F   43°F   8°F

-4°F   49°F   32°F   94°F

Page 435

Temperature: Celsius

Degrees Celsius (°C) is a unit for measuring temperature in the metric system.

Directions: Write the temperature in degrees Celsius (°C).
Example:

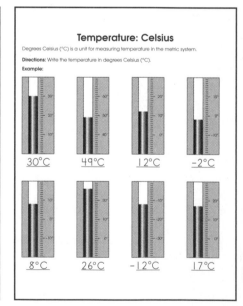

30°C   49°C   12°C   -2°C

8°C   26°C   -12°C   17°C

Page 436

Review

Directions: Write the best unit to measure each item: inch, foot, yard, mile, ounce, pound, ton, fluid ounce, cup, pint, quart or gallon.

distance from New York to Chicago	miles
weight of a goldfish	ounces
height of a building	feet
water in a large fish tank	gallons
glass of milk	ounces
weight of a whale	tons
length of a pencil	inches
distance from first base to second base	feet
distance traveled by a space shuttle	miles
length of a soccer field	yards
amount of paint needed to cover a house	gallons
material needed to make a dress	yards

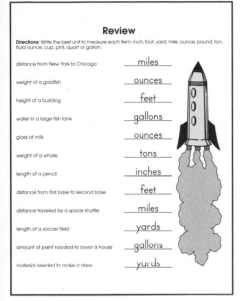

Page 437

Ratio

A **ratio** is a comparison of two quantities.

Ratios can be written three ways: 2 to 3 or 2 : 3 or $\frac{2}{3}$. Each ratio is read: two to three.

Example:

The ratio of triangles to circles is 2 to 3.
The ratio of circles to triangles is 3 to 2.

Directions: Write the ratio that compares these items.

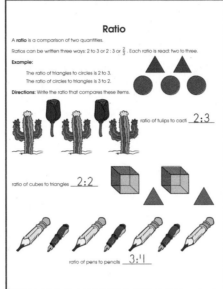

ratio of tulips to cacti   **2:3**

ratio of cubes to triangles   **2:2**

ratio of pens to pencils   **3:4**

Page 438

Percent

Percent is a ratio meaning "per hundred." It is written with a % sign. 20% means 20 percent or 20 per hundred.

Example:

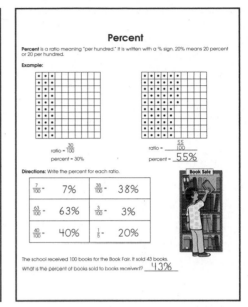

ratio = $\frac{30}{100}$
percent = 30%

ratio = $\frac{55}{100}$
percent = **55%**

Directions: Write the percent for each ratio.

$\frac{7}{100}$ =	7%	$\frac{38}{100}$	38%
$\frac{63}{100}$ =	63%	$\frac{3}{100}$	3%
$\frac{40}{100}$ =	40%	$\frac{1}{5}$	20%

The school received 100 books for the Book Fair. It sold 43 books.
What is the percent of books sold to books received?   **43%**

Page 439

Probability

Probability is the ratio of favorable outcomes to possible outcomes of an experiment.

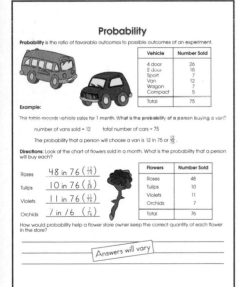

Vehicle	Number Sold
4 door	26
2 door	10
Sport	7
Van	12
Wagon	7
Compact	5
Total	**75**

Example:

This table records vehicle sales for 1 month. What is the probability of a person buying a van?

number of vans sold = 12   total number of cars = 75

The probability that a person will choose a van is 12 in 75 or $\frac{12}{75}$.

Directions: Look at the chart of flowers sold in a month. What is the probability that a person will buy each?

Roses	48 in 76 $\left(\frac{12}{19}\right)$	
Tulips	10 in 76 $\left(\frac{5}{38}\right)$	
Violets	11 in 76 $\left(\frac{11}{76}\right)$	
Orchids	7 in 76 $\left(\frac{7}{76}\right)$	

Flowers	Number Sold
Roses	48
Tulips	10
Violets	11
Orchids	7
Total	**76**

How would probability help a flower store owner keep the correct quantity of each flower in the store?

Answers will vary

Page 440

Using Calculators to Find Percent

A **calculator** is a machine that rapidly does addition, subtraction, multiplication, division and other mathematical functions.

Example:

Carlos got 7 hits in 20 "at bats."

$\frac{7}{20} = \frac{35}{100} = 35\%$

To use a calculator:

Step 1: Press 7.
Step 2: Press the ÷ symbol.
Step 3: Press 20.
Step 4: Press the = symbol.
Step 5: 0.35 appears.
          0.35 = 35%.

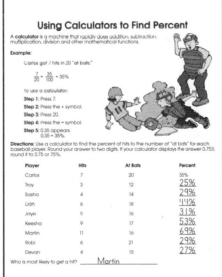

Directions: Use a calculator to find the percent of hits to the number of "at bats" for each baseball player. Round your answer to two digits. If your calculator displays the answer 0.753, round it to 0.75 or 75%.

Player	Hits	At Bats	Percent
Carlos	7	20	35%
Troy	3	12	25%
Sasha	4	14	29%
Lian	8	18	44%
Jaye	5	16	31%
Keesha	9	17	53%
Martin	11	16	69%
Robi	6	21	29%
Devan	4	15	27%

Who is most likely to get a hit?   **Martin**

Page 441

Finding Percents

Find percent by dividing the number you have by the number possible.

Example:

15 out of 20 possible: $\frac{0.75}{20\overline{)16.00}} = 75\%$
                         $\underline{-140}$
                         100
                         $\underline{100}$

Annie has been keeping track of the scores she earned on each spelling test during the grading period.

Directions: Find out each percentage grade she earned. The first one has been done for you.

Week	Number Correct	Total Number of Words	Score in Percent
1	14	(out of) 20	70%
2	16	20	80%
3	18	20	90%
4	12	15	80%
5	16	16	100%
6	17	18	94%
Review Test	51	60	85%

If Susan scored 5% higher than Annie on the review test, how many words did she get right?   **54**

Carrie scored 10% lower than Susan on the review test. How many words did she spell correctly?   **48**

Of the 24 students in Annie's class, 25% had the same score as Annie. Only 10% had a higher score. What percent had a lower score?   **65%**

Is that answer possible?   **no**   65% of 24 is 15.6

Why?   **cannot have a percent of a person**

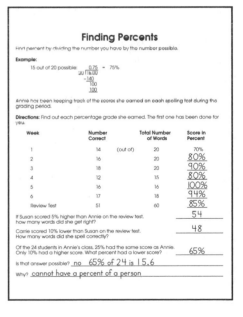

Page 442

Locating Points on a Grid

To locate points on a grid, read the first coordinate and follow it to the second coordinate.

Example: C, 3

Directions: Maya is new in town. Help her learn the way around her new neighborhood. Place the following locations on the grid below.

Grocery	C, 10
Home	B, 2
School	A, 12
Playground	B, 13
Library	D, 6
Bank	G, 1
Post Office	E, 7
Ice-Cream Shop	D, 3

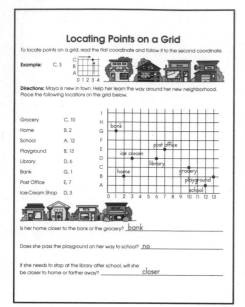

Is her home closer to the bank or the grocery? **bank**

Does she pass the playground on her way to school? **no**

If she needs to stop at the library after school, will she be closer to home or farther away? **closer**

Page 443

Graphs

A **graph** is a drawing that shows information about changes in numbers.

Directions: Use the graph to answer the questions.

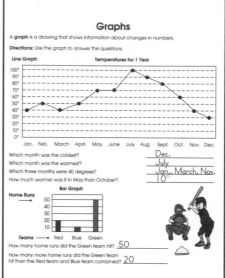

Line Graph — Temperatures for 1 Year

Which month was the coldest? **Dec.**
Which month was the warmest? **July**
Which three months were 40 degrees? **Jan., March, Nov.**
How much warmer was it in May than October? **10°**

Bar Graph — Home Runs

How many home runs did the Green team hit? **50**
How many more home runs did the Green team hit than the Red team and Blue team combined? **20**

Page 444

Graphs

Directions: Read each graph and follow the directions.

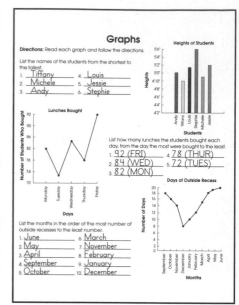

List the names of the students from the shortest to the tallest.
1. **Tiffany**   4. **Louis**
2. **Michele**   5. **Jessie**
3. **Andy**   6. **Stephie**

Lunches Bought

List how many lunches the students bought each day, from the day the most were bought to the least.
1. **92 (FRI)**   4. **78 (THUR)**
2. **84 (WED)**   5. **72 (TUES)**
3. **82 (MON)**

Days of Outside Recess

List the months in the order of the most number of outside recesses to the least number.
1. **June**   6. **March**
2. **May**   7. **November**
3. **April**   8. **February**
4. **September**   9. **January**
5. **October**   10. **December**

Page 445

Graphs

Directions: Complete the graph using the information in the table.

Student	Books read in February
Sue	20
Joe	8
Peter	12
Cindy	16
Dean	15
Carol	8

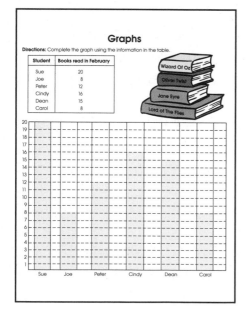

ADJECTIVES AND ADVERBS

Choose a page or two from a book your child is reading. Go through the pages with your child and underline all the adjectives and adverbs. Then ask him/her to rewrite the paragraph, replacing all the adjectives and adverbs with synonyms and/or antonyms.

BASIC MATH OPERATIONS

Addition, subtraction, multiplication and division are the four basic math functions we use every day. Play counting games, including skip counting by threes, fours, etc. While tossing a ball back and forth, alternate turns counting by a given number. The person catching the ball says the next consecutive number in the sequence.

Make up word problems with addition, subtraction, multiplication and division at odd moments when you are with your child, such as while traveling in the car, waiting at the doctor's office or doing the dishes together. Use the situation to add relevance to the word problems. Include your child's name or friends' names in the problems. Examples: 1) It is 375 miles to Grandma's house. We have traveled 217 miles. How much farther do we need to drive? 2) It Is 375 miles to Grandma's house. We will take a break about half-way there. After how many miles will we take a break?

Each day, post a math question on the refrigerator, and award a point to each family member who answers it correctly. Present a reward to the person who answers the most questions accurately during the week.

CAPITALIZATION

Help your child develop listening skills while playing a capitalization game. Have your child listen carefully while you say a sentence. Ask him/her to tell you which word or words need to be capitalized and why.

CHAPTER BOOKS

Invite your child to write a different ending or a new chapter to a story. If your child can logically build on previous plot events, you will know that he/she has grasped the main ideas of the story.

Your child is now reading "chapter books." These books usually have very few pictures. Check your child's comprehension by having him/her draw pictures representing the action or problem for each chapter. Before starting each new chapter, ask your child to predict what will happen.

FACT OR OPINION?

Many advertisements are confusing or misleading. Your child should be aware that not everything in an ad may be factual. Cut out ads from magazines and newspapers or listen to ads on the radio or television. Help your child sort through the information. Ask him/her to point out the parts that are facts and those that are opinions.

For a period of about 5 minutes, have your child keep a record of sentences he/she hears friends or family members saying. Then have your child review the list of sentences and decide which ones are facts, which ones are opinions and which ones are neither facts nor opinions. Have him/her explain the reasons for the classification.

FRACTIONS

Let your child cut sandwiches into fractional parts other than one-half or one-quarter. Ask him/her to cut a pizza into equal parts. Calculate the fraction of the pizza each member of the family can eat.

HOMOPHONE CHALLENGE

Homophones are words that are pronounced the same but are spelled differently and have different meanings, such as "to," "two" and "too." Challenge your child to a contest to see who can write the most homophones.

KITCHEN MATH

Baking and cooking are great opportunities for using math skills like measurement, multiplication and fractions. Have your child help double or triple a recipe and calculate the ingredients needed.

If your child invents a new recipe, encourage him/her to write down both the ingredient list and the steps to follow in making the dish. Be sure to share the recipe with family members and friends.

On your shelves or at the grocery, ask your child to find items labeled in standard or metric units. At home, work together to change a recipe to metric measures.

MEASUREMENT

A tape measure is a great learning tool. Let your child measure and compare the size of various objects. Challenge him/her to find two unlike objects with the same perimeter.

MONEY

Involve your child in math activities dealing with money. Ask him/her to estimate prices on a shopping list, calculate change, double check a bill at a restaurant and calculate tips.

Have your child determine how he/she spends his/her money. When your child receives a money gift or allowance, ask him/her to figure the percent spent on savings, gifts and items purchased.

NEWSPAPER ACTIVITIES

Newspapers may be the most convenient and versatile learning tools you have around your house. Encourage your child to read parts of the newspaper every day. You can help by asking your child to check some information for you. Questions like these will encourage your child to read the newspaper: "What is tomorrow's weather forecast?" or "What's on TV at 7 tonight?" or "Who won the baseball game last night?"

Cut out articles of interest to your child—ones about neighborhood events, people you know or items relating to school or special hobbies and favorite sports. Some children will find newspaper reading less intimidating and more appealing when they read only one article a day.

Read news articles with your child. Help him/her find the "who, what, when, where, why and how" answers to the stories. Each week, help your child write one news article about something that has happened in his or her life. Ask other family members to write short articles, too. Combine the articles and make a family newspaper once a month. Send the articles to family and friends when you write or send cards.

Ask your child, "If a news article were about something that happened to you today, what should the headline say?" Encourage your child to think up short, snappy headlines to summarize an event.

OPINIONS

Write a thought-provoking question on a piece of paper and post in on the refrigerator early in the day for all family members to read and think about. At dinner or in the evening, use that topic for a family discussion. Encourage your child to give reasons for his/her opinions.

You might pose a question about a fad or fashion, a current TV series or a computer game. Let your child and other family members take turns writing the question of the day.

Use the time you spend taking a walk or riding in the car with your child to discuss the pros and cons of your "question of the day." Encourage your child to look at both sides of an issue to see other viewpoints.

PARTS OF SPEECH

Copy sentences from a book, newspaper or magazine article. Ask your child to read the sentences aloud. Then have him/her identify the part of speech of each word. If he/she has trouble, suggest consulting a dictionary. Most dictionaries list the part of speech for each word.

Help your child practice recognizing parts of speech as you travel. Point out billboards and ask your child to name the part of speech for each word in the advertisements.

PERCENTS

Help your child collect family data on time usage, such as time spent sleeping, driving to work or in school. Ask him/her to create a graph showing time usage or to calculate the percent of a day or week spent doing various tasks.

POSSESSIVE ADJECTIVES AND APOSTROPHES

Write a story that contains several phrases with possessive adjectives, such as Mom's keys or Joshua's backpack, and leave out all the apostrophes. Have your child go through the paragraph and insert apostrophes where needed.

PRACTICAL MATH

If you are planning any project involving measurement and materials, such as planting a garden, building a doghouse, buying new carpeting or painting a room, involve your child in the process by letting him/her help measure and calculate expenses. Create a supply list together. Use ads to find prices and calculate the total cost. Explore alternate ways to complete the project at a lower cost.

PREFIXES, SUFFIXES AND ROOT WORDS

Write a list of common root words, prefixes and suffixes. Write the root words on squares of colored construction paper, the prefixes on squares of another color and the suffixes on squares of a third color. Help your child mix and match the squares, seeing how many different word combinations he/she can make. Ask your child for the meaning of each new word created.

PROOFREADING

Help your child proofread letters and reports he/she writes. Proofreading consists of checking for grammatical errors and correcting spelling, punctuation and capitalization errors. Make the corrections together until your child is able to handle proofreading on his or her own. Even when you write using a word processing program, material needs to be read and checked. Spell checkers are helpful but cannot find and correct all types of errors.

Have your child help you with your own writing, whether it is a short report or memo for work or a letter to a friend. Ask your child to use his/her proofreading skills to check for errors before you write the final draft. Your child can even proofread your e-mail before you send it.

Choose a paragraph from a book your child is reading. Rewrite the paragraph, leaving out all punctuation and capitalization. Ask your child to proofread the paragraph, putting in correct punctuation and capitalization without looking back at the book. He/she can check the book when finished.

READING LABELS

Reading and understanding labels is a skill everyone needs. As you shop, let your child read labels to compare ingredients and other nutritional information. Reading labels will help your child become a better consumer and may encourage him/her to eat more healthful foods.

Stress the importance of reading labels and following directions, particularly on medications or products that may be hazardous.

RECALLING DETAILS

As you read with your child, encourage him/her to picture what is happening. Forming a mental picture will help your child recall the story using the "mind's eye," as well as the ear. Then ask him/her to retell the story, noting details from the beginning, middle and end.

SEQUENCING

Cut out an article from a newspaper or magazine. Cut the article into separate paragraphs. Ask your child to arrange the paragraphs in the correct order. (Keep in mind that the final story may not be in the exact order as the original but may still make sense.) Discuss with your child why he/she chose that particular sequence and why it makes sense to him/her.

SPELLING

Have your child keep a spelling log in which he/she writes previously misspelled words. Ask your child to write each word several times and also use it in a sentence.

Together with your child, review the writing exercises he/she has done in this book, looking for spelling errors. Then have your child correct any misspelled words, using a dictionary, if necessary. As an alternative, write short paragraphs or sentences that contain minor spelling and punctuation errors. Invite your child to find the mistakes and have him/her rewrite the sentences correctly.

SUMMARIZING AND COMPARING

Visit the library and borrow two copies of a book so both you and your child can read and discuss the book together. After each chapter, ask your child to summarize story events. Discuss what you both liked and disliked about the book, the characters and the plot. Encourage your child to compare and contrast the book with another he/she has read.

SYNONYMS AND ANTONYMS

Play a synonym/antonym game when you and your child are together for an extended time, perhaps on a walk or a long car ride. Say a word and ask your child to name a synonym or antonym for that word. If your child is correct, ask him/her to take a turn in thinking of a word.

USING REFERENCE SOURCES

If your child has a question about a topic in a newspaper or magazine article, use various reference sources to find the answer. If you don't have the references you need at home, go to the library with your child and help him/her find the answer.

Help your child do research on the Internet, a source of up-to-the-minute information on a variety of topics. Be sure to teach your child "Internet safety" and closely monitor his/her use of the Internet.

Select a topic of the month for you and your child to research. Prepare a report together. Select one of the topics below or one of your own.

> The history of a sport
>
> A specific 10-year period of American history
>
> The Constitution or Declaration of Independence
>
> The development of computers
>
> Virtual reality

Follow the steps of the Writing Process as you prepare the report together.

1. Gather information from reference sources.
2. Take notes listing the main points. Summarize what you have read, and write an outline.
3. Write a research paper based on the information found.
4. Edit your work. Make corrections and rewrite if necessary.

A good dictionary, along with a thesaurus and set of encyclopedias (or encyclopedia on CD), is a valuable resource. When you and your child come across a word you don't know, look it up together. Check the pronunciation. Use the word in a sentence.

WORD GAMES

Word games such as crossword puzzles and word scrambles will expand your child's vocabulary and develop spelling skills. You can find word games and puzzles in the newspaper or in puzzle books at the library or the bookstore.

WRITING EXPERIENCES

Help your child write friendly letters to relatives and friends. Saying "thank you" in writing is a good habit for your child to learn. Thank you notes can be sent for gifts and for thoughtful actions like an invitation from a friend's parents for dinner or an overnight visit.

Read several movie reviews with your child. Then rent a movie of your child's choice, and invite him/her to write a movie review. You may want to write one yourself. Then compare the two and discuss why you felt differently/ similarly about the movie.

Show your child that writing is important. Make sure he/she sees you and other family members writing frequently. Invite your child to help you write grocery lists, letters to relatives and friends, holiday cards and notes to other family members. Let your child see you proofreading and correcting your own writing.

An anthology is a collection of short stories, poems, essays, etc., by one author. As your child completes a writing project or special artwork, save it in a three-ring binder. Date each item. When the binder if full, pack it away and start another. Save the full binders until your child is older. Gift wrap a binder and give it to your child as a unique present for a special occasion.

Encourage your child to keep a personal journal. You might suggest writing topics, but your child should understand that the journal is his or her outlet for thoughts and feelings. Make it clear that you will not check or correct the journal and that you will not read it unless he/she chooses to show it to you. Encourage your child to write every day about anything he/she wishes. Suggested topics might include a trip to the store, favorite TV show episode, going to the park, favorite things to do with friends or favorite foods.

If you have access to the Internet, have your child write to someone using e-mail. Whether on a computer or with paper and pen, the format of a letter is the same. Stress correct grammar, spelling, punctuation and sentence structure.

WRITING POETRY

Help your child use metaphors, similes and alliteration to create poetry.

Encourage your child to illustrate his/her poems for greater visual effect or write his/her best poems with glittery pens on fancy paper. Or enter your child's original poetry on the computer and print it out, perhaps with a fancy border from a card-making program. Frame and hang them in your home for all to enjoy.

Read favorite poems to your child to give him/her a better appreciation for this type of writing. Then write a "tandem poem" with your child. Either you or your child can start by writing a single line or stanza, then give the poem to the other to continue. Switch back and forth until the poem is complete. You may want to decide on a length before beginning the poem. You can carry out this exercise over the course of several days. When the poem is finished, ask your child to illustrate it and display it prominently in your home. Help your child brainstorm topics to write about in a poem. You may want to use one of the following suggestions: All About Me, What If?, A Strange Dream, What I Smelled, The Perfect Day, The One That Got Away, If Wishes Came True or What I Saw.

NOTES